THERE ARE MANY QUESTIONS, that have continually emerged over the years—questions that have never fully been answered—questions that have been asked, discussed, deliberated and evaluated about Joseph Smith and The Mormon Church.

WHY ARE THE MORMONS considered to be a "peculiar,"exceptional, distinctive, unique people? What makes them so different from others?

WHY WAS THE NAME, JOSEPH SMITH, known for both good and evil among all nations, kindreds, tongues and people?"

THIS BOOK IS WRITTEN for the express purpose of your drawing your own conclusions as to whether Joseph Smith was really . . .

An Imposter—

A Pretender—

A Deceiver—

Or A Prophet of God?

WAS HE THE MAN called by God for our times, to show us the way, to help open the floodgates to peace, happiness, success in our righteous desires, and the building of the most important organization on the face of the earth—"THE FAMILY?"

WAS HE THE MAN?

IT'S NOW UP TO YOU TO—

DECIDE FOR YOURSELF—

The Unauthorized Biography of Joseph Smith, Mormon Prophet

The Unauthorized Biography of Joseph Smith, Mormon Prophet

Norman Rothman

Published by:

THE NORMAN ROTHMAN FOUNDATION, Inc.
Salt Lake City, Utah U.S.A.

1997

International Standard Book Number: 1-56-236-982-2

Library of Congress Catalog Card Number: 97-91903

Printed in the United States of America

Dedicated To:

The most remarkable, precious woman, and scribe in the world,
the girl of my dreams—Sadie Annette.

And To:

The greatest children and grandchildren in the world . . .
The Nitta Family
The Leazenby Family
The Rothman Family
and daughter, Leah Rothman

This book is also dedicated to all men and women who are prayerfully and anxiously seeking a better life here on earth—only attainable through truth and a personal relationship with the greatest team ever—**God the Eternal Father, His Son Jesus Christ, the Messiah and Savior of the world, and the Holy Ghost.**

Acknowledgments

In order to bring to the reader the truth about Joseph Smith and The Church of Jesus Christ of Latter-day Saints (The Mormons) I've had the opportunity over the past two years, by and through the power of the Holy Spirit, along with my own writing, to conduct research from over thirty-five various publications which belong to some very special people and organizations that are contained herein. For the use of some of their significant information, I give my humble thanks and love.

Francis M. Gibbons, *Joseph Smith, Martyr, Prophet of God*
Bruce R. McConkie, *Mormon Doctrine*
Leonard J. Arrington and David Bitton, *The Mormon Experience, a History of the Latter-day Saints*
Alma P. Burton, *Discourses of the Prophet Joseph Smith*
Duane S. Crowther, *The Prophecies of Joseph Smith*
Lucy Mack Smith, *History of Joseph Smith by His Mother*
William E. Berrett, *The Restored Church*
J. Christopher Conkling, *A Joseph Smith Chronology*
Emma Marr Peterson, *The Story of Our Church*
Truman G. Madsen, *Joseph Smith, the Prophet*
Susan Evans McCloud, *Joseph Smith, A Photo Biography*
George E. Clark, *Why I Believe: 54 Evidences of the Divine Mission of the Prophet Joseph Smith*
Scot F. and Maurine Proctor, *Witness of the Light*
Joseph Smith, Jr., *The Journal of Joseph*
Buddy Youngreen, *Reflections of Emma*
Franklin L. West, *Discovering the Old Testament*
Dr. Irving H. Cohen, *Jews of the Torah*
LeGrand Richards, *Israel! Do You Know?*
N.B. Lundwall, *The Fate of the Persecutors of the Prophet Joseph Smith*
E. Cecil McGavin, *The Family of Joseph Smith*
LDS, Church Education System, *Church History In The Fulness Of Times*
B. H. Roberts, *Comprehensive History of the Church*
The Holy Bible, Authorized King James Version
The Holy Scriptures, according to the Masoretic Text by the Jewish Publication Society of America
The Book of Mormon, Another Testament of Jesus Christ
The Doctrine and Covenants, containing Revelations given to Joseph Smith,

the Prophet, with some additions by his successors in the
Presidency of The Church of Jesus Christ of Latter-day Saints
Pearl of Great Price

In addition, there are several people, who have contributed mightily to the success of this project, with their time, effort, funding, prayers and blessings, that have made this project so worthwhile and able to be completed. Their names are herein listed with my personal thanks, gratitude, and love.

Larry and Alice Beebe; Dee Jay Bawden; Bishop Douglas D. Neuenswander; Howard and Doris Bethers; Paul and Lilly Jespersen; Ray Beckham; Lysle and Patricia Cahoon; Joanne Mudry; Dorothea Nelson; Robert and Mary Christensen; Kathy Joy Lott; Beverley Sorenson; Kevin and J'Lynne Hatch; Ruby Hasler; Michael and Susan Murano; Ray and Helen Barton; Charles and Jeanne Beam; Thomas and Norman Johnson; Eldon and Mary Alice Brinley; Clint Patterson; Ruth Ellen Rands; Harry and Bonita Cross; Lisa Hubbard; Barbara Lee; Norinne Callister; Helene Holt; Don and Judy Bowman; David and Darelyn Peterson; Guy and Tineka Patterson; Richard Winwood.

Table of Contents

"Joseph Lived Great, and he Died Great in the Eyes of
God and his People"

Joseph Smith lived only thirty-eight and one half years
Brigham Young was Miraculously Transfigured by the—
Power of the Holy Spirit, before the Eyes of the People
Although it was President Young who was Speaking—
it was Truly the Voice of Joseph Smith
The Spirit and Mantle of Joseph was upon Brigham
Brigham Young was Chosen Unanimously as
The President of the Quorum of the Twelve Apostles
Brigham Young renamed Nauvoo "The City of Joseph"—
a name approved by the Saints
Leaving Nauvoo was an "Act of Faith" for the Saints
The First of the Saints Left Nauvoo in early 1846
Brigham Young was Called by God the Father
to be the Prophet, Seer and Revelator in 1847
Brigham Young Lead the Saints West
to a New, Fulfilling Life and Religious Freedom . . .

Foreword

Where Did We Come From?

Why Are We Here?

And Where Are We Going?

Every person who is born to this earth will someday die. Is dying therefore final or is there something beyond?

Our Earth Life is but a test period, and we do not cease living when our bodies are placed in the ground.

There is life after death, and we do live on . . . not, as some believe, in a reincarnated state, but advancing to another world as physical as this one, that God has prepared for us. Every person on earth, be they good or otherwise, is guaranteed to live again.

The Resurrection is a gift from the Savior and Redeemer to all mankind. We also lived before. When we lived with God and Jesus Christ in the pre-earth life, we were spirit children of a loving Heavenly Father. We were there to learn and grow spiritually, as well as prepare ourselves for earth life. How we progress or whether we progressed was our own choice. No matter what we learned or didn't learn, we were destined to come to earth to be tested.

Then the time came for us individually to accept earth life as the next leg of the spiritual journey which could eventually lead us back to the presence of God. We *will* live again.

Those who desire to progress spiritually, and to be reunited with their families for eternity, can have this blessing called **"Eternal Life."**

There is a catch though; one must learn to accept the truths of God and live them. Proclaiming that one believes in God and the Messiah is certainly a sign of faith, but that alone is not enough to make it.

Keeping all the Lord's commandments is the only way to achieve "Eternal Life," and to be reunited with one's family (if that is our desire) . . . **"For Time and All Eternity.**

Why I Had to Write this Book

It's time for all the world to know the real Joseph Smith, how he lived as a Prophet of God and how he died as a martyr. It's time to separate the truths from the myths. And why do I, **Norman Rothman—a Jew** who has converted to **Mormonism**—presume to play a role in this drama? Not because of any offical assignment, or because I presume to have any unusual credibility, but because of **my love** for the **Gospel of Jesus Christ.** There are no words to adequately describe the thrill, the exhilaration, the joy and excitement, the happiness and satisfaction, the pleasure and peace of mind, of the greatest day of my life—the day I was baptized a member of The Church of Jesus Christ of Latter-day Saints (Mormon). I was thirty-seven years old, and had spent much time, emotion, energy, and prayer searching for the truth and true Church. When I read the 531 pages of the Book of Mormon (which is a second witness to the world that Jesus is the Christ), it was with an eye single to either gaining a solid conviction that the contents were true, or that the whole thing was a hoax. I tore apart the Book of Mormon, piece by piece to find the gimmick, to find misinformation, to find a lack of continuity, or to find the unbelievable. **When I put it all back together again, everything fit,** everything fell into place. I could find no negatives and I felt a personal emotional release. I knew that a giant-size burden had been lifted and I was thrilled and excited right out of my head. I knew that the Book of Mormon was the word of God, and God knew that I knew it through the power of the Holy Spirit who touched my heart and soul.

Then I began researching the life and teachings of the Prophet Joseph Smith who translated the Book of Mormon and brought it to life. **The greatest message of our time is that the account given by Joseph Smith is the absolute truth.** Beginning with his **First Vision,** there was once more direct revelation from the heavens. **The God of Abraham, Isaac, and Jacob,** had raised up Joseph Smith Jr. to be His Prophet. In later visions and revelations, Joseph received further instructions and commandments regarding the work God had prepared for him to do.

In order for anyone to understand, to believe and accept these truths, one must have a fertile, open mind and heart and the desire to know the truth. **All truth comes from God**. If anyone seeks the truth through God and the Holy Spirit, the truth will be revealed to that person. **I can personally testify** that I know the story of Joseph Smith's life and his calling as a Prophet of God in the latter days is true. I have received personal confirmation of this from God—as can anyone who is seeking the truth. I found the truth in the Restored Church of Jesus Christ. I came to know for the first time, the real, the living Jesus Christ, the Messiah of the world for all people. I proved to myself that the Book of Mormon is a second witness that Jesus is the Christ, and that Joseph Smith was and is a Prophet of God, chosen to restore the true Church in this last dispensation.

There is so much evidence of these things. One of these is the fact that Joseph Smith **translated the Book of Mormon from the gold plates** (metal plates) in less than ninety working days without the advantage of any formal high school or college education. In addition, there were eleven witnesses who saw the plates, eight of whom actually handled them. Then there are archaeologists and anthropologists, primarily non-Mormon, who provide extensive evidence that the Book of Mormon is true through their findings—artifacts and the remains of vast civilizations and highly-developed cultures which once thrived and, that were concentrated most heavily in Southern Mexico, Central America, and the Western section of South America.

When I joined The Church of Jesus Christ of Latter-day Saints, it was a great joy for me to acquire an understanding in regard to where I came from, why I was here on earth, and where I could be going. I learned that my total trust should lie in God, the source of all truth, and that error is of man because man primarily depends upon himself and other people without requesting assistance from God. I learned that there is only one way to acquire happiness, peace of mind, success, and most importantly, eternal life—only through love and obedience to God's commandments. The more I studied, the more I realized that everything fits, ie., the Old Testament succeeded by the New Testament, the Book of Mormon, the Doctrine and Covenants (revelation given to Joseph Smith and other Latter-day Prophets) and the Pearl of Great Price (revelations, translations, and narrations of the Prophet Joseph Smith). The continuity is unmistakable, each volume of scripture supporting the other, from the First Dispensation of Time, beginning with Adam, to the present. I had finally found my answers to the truth. No one taught me, no one pressured me, no one sold me on the Church: I found out for myself. I knew for myself, since I received personal revelation from God through the Holy Spirit, that it was all true. And so can any earnest seeker of truth.

Through study and prayer and through learning from the Bible and Book of Mormon prophets, I finally came to understand the purpose of prophets in God's plan, yesterday, today, and forever. There have been Prophets on the earth from the very beginning, but there have been many misunderstandings as to their calling and purpose. **What is a Prophet of God?** A Prophet is one who foretells events; who under the spirit of inspiration, predicts the future. However, there are other qualifications just as essential as that of revealing things to come. **The Savior said—that John the Baptist "*was a burning and a shining light*"** (John 5: 35). In fact, He said: *"there is not a greater prophet than John the Baptist"* (Luke 7: 28). Yet John was not called to predict future events, except to prepare the way for the mission of the Messiah—which was even then close at hand. Therefore, in addition to prophesying the future, **a Prophet** is one who has the inspiration of the Holy Spirit, one who can testify from revelation that Jesus Christ is the Son of God. He is one who is faithful in that knowledge, and who magnifies the authority placed upon him.

The work of a Hebrew Prophet was to act as God's messenger and make known God's will. He taught men about God's character, showing the full meaning of His dealings with Israel in the past. It was therefore part of the prophetic office to preserve and edit the records of the nation's history; such historical books as Joshua, Judges, 1st and 2nd Kings were known by the Jews as the former Prophets.

It was also the Prophet's duty to denounce sin and foretell its punishment and to correct, so far as he could, both public and private wrongs. He was to be, above all, a preacher of righteousness. When the people had fallen away from a true faith in Jehovah (who is in reality—the Messiah), the prophets of the Old Testament tried to restore that faith and remove false views about the character of God and the nature of the divine calling. In certain cases, prophets predicted future events. e.g., there are the very important prophecies announcing the coming of the Messiah's kingdom; but as a rule, a Prophet was a ***"forth-teller"*** more than a "fore-teller."

The Old Testament Prophets acted as authorized spokesmen for the Lord. They taught the true nature of God and declared God's will with respect to men and their conduct. Generally, these men, called of God, served as official record keepers. They promoted faithfulness and obedience among the people and foretold the consequences of men's acceptance or rejection of God's will. They were leaders in the government of the Lord's work. **The record gives ample testimony that all prophets were called by God. None of them were self-appointed.**

I am a witness that Joseph Smith was called by God as His chosen Prophet to unite all mankind under the Restored Gospel and Church of Jesus Christ. I have carefully researched the facts, and have become convinced by the Spirit that Joseph Smith was chosen by God and Jesus Christ as the Prophet in this, the Seventh and last Dispensation, the Dispensation of the Fulness of Times, in advance of the Second Coming of the Messiah and Savior, Jesus Christ.

Adam was the Prophet to open the First Dispensation, and Joseph Smith was the Prophet who opened the Seventh Dispensation. What is a dispensation? A dispensation of the Gospel is a period of time in which the Lord has at least one authorized servant on the earth who bears the Holy Priesthood and keys, and who has a divine commission to spread the Gospel to the people of the earth. A dispensation is a period of time when the Lord reveals His will to prepare mankind for their spiritual growth. Dispensation after dispensation has led to this Seventh and last Dispensation which has the purpose of preparing mankind for the Second Coming of the Lord Jesus Christ. Every previous dispensation, due to man's disobedience to God's commandments, culminated in an apostasy (a falling away from the true principles of God). Because of a loving Father in Heaven who doesn't give up on us, and through His Prophets, there was the—**Restoration**—which gave all mankind an opportunity to get their lives in order, become obedient to God's commandments, and ultimately gain eternal life.

The keys (rights to preside) and powers exercised by the Lord's Prophets in each of these ancient dispensations, have been conferred upon men in this final dispensation, which is called the Dispensation of the Fulness of Times. In *"the fulness of times,"* the Lord says: *"I will gather together in one all things, both which are in heaven, and which are on earth"* (Ephesians 1: 10, Doctrine and Covenants 27: 13).

This is the truly remarkable story of a most dedicated man, called as a Prophet of God, ***not*** to be worshiped as a God, ***not*** to be worshiped as Jesus Christ, but as a **mouthpiece and messenger for God,** carrying out the wishes of His Father in Heaven, regardless of the consquences to his own life which he subsequently gave up through his martyrdom.

As it is written, as it is said . . . ***"Joseph Smith, the Prophet and Seer of the Lord, has done more, save Jesus only; for the salvation of men in this world, than any other man that ever lived in it"*** (Doctrine & Covenants 135: 3, written by Elder John Taylor).

I testify that Joseph Smith was the first Prophet of the Seventh and last Dispensation which is the Dispensation of the Fulness of Times—the gathering of all previous dispensations. No doubt, you will decide for yourself after you read this book whether Joseph Smith Jr. was an imposter or a Prophet of God. Joseph Smith was not the inventor of a new American religion, one of thousands of subculture religions on the earth. I also testify that he was the man chosen by God in the pre-earth life to come in these latter days as a chosen Prophet, mouthpiece, and messenger of God—**not to be worshiped by man, but to teach man to worship God.**

As a side issue, I've been told by those in the know, that I'm breaking all the rules of acceptable writing and editing. Nevertheless, I testify, I've done what the Lord has asked me to do through personal revelation, that is—to tell all and tell it truthfully.

Now let's focus on the early days of Mormonism—the opening chapter of this last dispensation.

Introduction

When I began writing this book about Joseph Smith and The Church of Jesus Christ of Latter-day Saints, (the Mormons) after researching over thirty-five publications on the subject matter, the one word that stood out in my mind was **Persecution**. That's what the lives of the Mormons were all about in the early days of the Church. From 1820 until the Latter-day Saints entered the Salt Lake Valley in 1847, history records that they were the most persecuted people in this country.

Since we are speaking about persecution, we should also consider the Jewish people and what they experienced during World War II through the infamous ***Holocaust***. Why did six million Jews have to be annihilated by an obvious madman named Adolph Hitler in one of the most heinous, deplorable, unconscionable crimes ever perpetrated on any people.

Certainly I'm not overlooking the death of millions of soldiers and civilians caught up in the devastation caused by wars, but the *Holocaust* was the very worst. Having been born a Jew, I have greater sympathies for the Jews, but it was a blight on all mankind. It was the ultimate of—"man's inhumanity to man"—in the history of the world. It was pure hatred, prejudice and bigotry, just as the Mormons experienced in the United States and why?

Interestingly enough, all that the Jewish people ever wanted was to worship God according to the dictates of their own hearts, and to live in peace and harmony with the world. They, too, wanted religious freedom, peace, joy and happiness, and most importantly, their families. How truly important the family is to the Jew. In addition, Jewish people never push their religious beliefs on anyone, and generally take offense to anyone trying to proselyte them. Judaism is for the Jews; they just want to be left alone, at least most of them. They say very candidly: "Born a Jew, Die a Jew." Isn't that the same case with some other religions? Similarly, the Mormons have always had their doors open to share their beliefs with others, but never pushing their religion on anyone.

Nevertheless, from the beginning of the Restored Church of Jesus Christ, the Messiah's True Church, persecution was an ongoing way of life for the Mormons. There isn't a part of Mormon history that was devoid of persecution.

Today we live in a free land, freer than any country on the face of the earth, a country dedicated from its inception to religious freedom and the rights of the individual as guaranteed in the United States Constitution. But has there been true freedom of religion for all Americans? When we review the history of the United States, hatred, narrow-mindedness, prejudice, and bigotry have pervaded our country from day one. Because of this, there never was any lasting period of peace in the lives of the early Mormons—or for many other groups. The Mormons were driven from place to place by angry mobs. They built up the land, established communities of peace, education, and religious freedom, but time after time were forced to leave their homes. Persecution came in all forms including trumped up charges against Church leaders which often led to unjust imprisonment. During the short term of his almost thirty-nine years on earth, Joseph Smith was jailed approximately forty-seven times, but never convicted.

The question has been asked time and time again: "If this was the true Church of Jesus Christ, why did the Lord allow the people to suffer such persecutions?" Some of the problems resulted from apostasy within the Church. The faithful remained true, but the Church was purged of the weak and rebellious who often joined with the most bitter non-Mormons to persecute the Saints. Other facts also contributed to the persecutions.

Thoughout history those who have attempted to radically change the society in which they lived have always faced persecution, and often violent death. The only exceptions are those who have, through force and violence, seized control of government, and by a reign of terror, crushed all opposition.

Joseph Smith was primarily a peaceful man, winning his way through love and not through fear. His doctrines were revolutionary, but I have gained a personal witness that they weren't Joseph's doctrines; they came from God Almighty. **Joseph Smith was not building a kingdom unto himself for his own personal aggrandizement.** He was chosen of God as God's Prophet, and was following the counsel, direction, and guidance from a loving Heavenly Father and Jesus Christ—to build the foundation of the kingdom of God on the earth. However, the social order he was creating was a radical departure from that to be found anywhere in America. The clash of the new doctrines he taught, with those of established society, subsequently led to his death.

Three specific features of the Mormon Society aroused continual opposition and persecution:

First: The Uniqueness and Oneness of the Saints

It was apparent in the Ohio and Missouri settlements and later in Illinois, that the Saints acted as a unit—economically, politically, and socially—to the exclusion of others. The uniqueness of the Saints was demonstrated in their social and religious life and their general neighborliness. But they tended to work, play, and inter-marry only with other Mormons. The nicknames of—**Mormons**; **Latter-day Saints** or **LDS**—are given to members of **The Church of Jesus Christ of Latter-day Saints,** their religion centered on the **Messiah, Jesus Christ.** They accomplished amazing things in short periods of time because cooperation, rather than ruthless competition is the core of the Mormon economic life. Cries of "communism" the first in the modern world, were frequent. The very success of the Mormon society drew the attention of its neighbors and aroused fears.

The oneness of the Saints was especially felt at the polls. As opposition against the Saints grew, this oneness became a thorn in the flesh of some candidates who hoped to gain the Mormon's vote, while retaining the vote of the non-Mormon—a position that became more and more impossible as the opposition to the Saints increased. By 1843, the politicians had sided with the majority against the Saints in order to save their own political careers. It soon became difficult—and later impossible for the Saints to support the candidates of either political party, and they eventually formed their own "Reform Party."

Second: The Proselyting Activites of Missionaries

The Saints did not sit quietly by their hearthsides satisfied with their own peculiar beliefs. They had a mission to perform in carrying the message of the Restored Church and Gospel to their neighbors and to the whole world. So strong was the desire and the feeling of duty in this matter that many were willing to sacrifice all their earthly possessions, if necessary to further the cause. Missionary activity to the family, friends, and neighbors of the Saints began long before the official organization of the Church and continued wherever they settled in their search for religious freedom—Kirtland, Ohio, Independence and Far West, Missouri and finally Nauvoo, Illinois. Early missionaries found success in Canada and the missionary program also increased abroad. Thousands of converts were eventually harvested from the shores of England. The successful proselyting of the Mormons resulted in the active opposition of Christian Ministers who were losing their congregations. This was a powerful factor in every persecution.

Third: Differences in Religious Beliefs

The religious beliefs of the Saints clashed with those of other people. Mormonism became feared because of the aggressive nature of its religious teachings. Mormonism was not a passive religion. The very assertion of the Saints that they possessed the Gospel in its fulness, while all other denominations only had a part of the truth, raised much opposition.

Published in March 1842, The Articles of Faith has become one of the most important statements of inspiration, history, and doctrine for the Church. The Articles of Faith were written primarily for non-Mormons, and were never intended to be a complete summary of Gospel principles and practices. They do, however, provide a clear statement about the unique beliefs of the Latter-day Saints. Each article is a **positive statement** of the differences between Mormonism and the sectarian beliefs of other denominations.

THE ARTICLES OF FAITH

OF THE CHURCH OF JESUS CHRIST
OF LATTER-DAY SAINTS

We believe in God, the Eternal Father, and in His Son, Jesus Christ, and in the Holy Ghost.

2 **We believe** that men will be punished for their own sins, and not for Adam's transgression.

3 **We believe** that through the Atonement of Christ, all mankind may be saved, by obedience to the laws and ordinances of the Gospel.

4 **We believe** that the first principles and ordinances of the Gospel are: first, Faith in the Lord Jesus Christ; second, Repentance; third, Baptism by immersion for the remission of sins; fourth, Laying on of hands for the gift of the Holy Ghost.

5 **We believe** that a man must be called of God, by prophecy, and by the laying on of hands, by those who are in authority to preach the Gospel and administer in the ordinances thereof.

6 **We believe** in the same organization that existed in the Primitive Church, namely, apostles, prophets, pastors, teachers, evangelists, and so forth.

7 **We believe** in the gift of tongues, prophecy, revelation, visions, healing, interpretation of tongues, and so forth.

8 **We believe** the Bible to be the word of God as far as it is translated correctly; we also believe the Book of Mormon to be the word of God.

9 **We believe** all that God has revealed, all that He does now reveal, and we believe that He will yet reveal many great and important things pertaining to the Kingdom of God.

10 **We believe** in the literal gathering of Israel and in the restoration of the Ten Tribes; that Zion (the New Jerusalem) will be built upon the American continent; that Christ will reign personally upon the earth; and, that the earth will be renewed and receive its paradisiacal glory.

11 **We claim** the privilege of worshiping Almighty God according to the dictates of our own conscience, and allow all men the same privilege, let them worship how, where, or what they may.

12 **We believe** in being subject to kings, presidents, rulers, and magistrates in obeying, honoring, and sustaining the law.

13 **We believe** in being honest, true, chaste, benevolent, virtuous, and in doing good to all men; indeed, we may say that we follow the admonition of Paul—We believe all things, we hope all things, we have endured many things, and hope to be able to endure all things. If there is anything virtuous, lovely, or of good report or praiseworthy, we seek after these things.

JOSEPH SMITH

All other doctrines that raised opposition however were lackluster in contrast with the doctrine of plural marriage. As I have conversed with hundreds of people around the country who know literally nothing about—The Church of Jesus Christ of Latter-day Saints—nicknamed the Mormons, the one thing they have all heard is that Mormons practice polygamy. Of course, nothing is said that the practice of polygamy was discontinued in 1890 by commandment. In this book you will get the "straight talk" on Mormons and polygamy as I see it, and not a lot of meaningless or foolish rhetoric. Because of all the lies and misinformation bandied about to influence people for the negative, it is vitally important that you know that I have prayed mightily, researched thoroughly, and prayed as if my life depended upon how I treated this subject. At the appropriate point in this book I will explain it more thoroughly, but because misinformation has made it such a bugaboo to so many people, it is my desire to summarize in this introduction how polygamy and plural marriage came about.

Soon after the organization of the Church, Joseph Smith inquired of the Lord why the Old Testament Prophets practiced polygamy and was informed by revelation that it was in response to commandments from God. He asked if such a commandment would be given in his own dispensation and received a revelation with a solid Yes! He learned that he would be told when it was the right time and for the approved purpose. It is important to note that both polygamy and plural marriage were given by revelation and commandment to the Prophet Joseph in 1831. Nevertheless, Joseph did not begin the practice himself until 1841 **by commandment from the Lord.** The practice of polygamy and plural marriage was begun in the Church in general on July 12, 1843, but was never practiced by more than two to three percent of the male Priesthood as approved. The practice of polygamy and plural marriage was discontinued by commandment from God to President Wilford Woodruff, who issued the **Manifesto (proclamation)** to the Church and the world in 1890. Its practice has never been reinstated in this dispensation.

A COMMANDMENT FROM GOD

Joseph taught that families are eternal. Part of the New and Everlasting Covenant was the practice of plural marriage—a man having more than one wife when and only when—commanded by the Lord. Even when this principle was first revealed to Joseph in 1831, he felt strongly that its practice would cost him his life. During the summer of 1840, an angel from God visited the Prophet and told him the time had come, and commanded him to obey the law or perish. Thus, after ten years of painful reflection and anguish, Joseph took the fateful step that he knew would lead inescapably to his death as he took his first plural wife. This step was not taken hastily or recklessly, nor was it taken in ignorance of the consequences. He was intelligent enough and wise enough to know that while a large segment of the public might tolerate adultery and fornication—part of the human conduct for so long—they would be incensed at the thought of a man having more than one wife. He knew also how genuine, careful, and considerate a man would have to be in entering into this relationship—knowing he would be denounced by enemies who would attribute his actions to a carnal mind. It was for these reasons, and others equally compelling, that he procrastinated teaching of this highly charged and emotional commandment and revelation from the Lord. Even when he knew the time was soon coming when he and some of the other Church leaders would be called upon to practice it, Joseph still hesitated teaching about it. The whole Anglo-Saxon training of the Church was opposed to plural marriage, although it had never been forbidden at the time by any State or Federal Constitution.

Even after settling in Nauvoo, when the Prophet said he was commanded of the Lord to put the Law of Plural Marriage into practice, he hesitated to teach the revelation to any but his closest confidants. Since many in the Church, some in positions of high leadership, were ignorant of the revelation, there were occasional fierce and downright honest denials by influential members of the Church that they were involved in this doctrine in any way. Thus, some members, when they first learned of Joseph's support and practice of this doctrine, denounced him as a fallen prophet.

No greater mistake could be made than to suppose that Joseph Smith, Brigham Young, or any of the Church leaders hailed the doctrine of plural marriage with delight or introduced it through lustful desires. **Brigham Young** later said, "If any man had asked me what was my choice when Joseph Smith revealed [plurality of wives], provided that it would not diminish my glory, I would have said, 'Let me have but one wife' . . . I was not desirous of shrinking from any duty, nor to failing in the least to do as I was commanded, but it was the first time in my life that I had desired the grave, and I could hardly get over it for a long time." **John Taylor,** who became the third president of the Church adds: "I had always entertained strict ideas of virtue, and I felt as a married man that this was to me, outside of *this* principle, an appalling thing to do. The idea of going and asking a woman to be married to me when I already had a wife! It was a thing calculated to stir up feelings from the innermost depths of the human soul. I had always entertained the strictest of chastity . . . With the feeling I had entertained, nothing but a knowledge of God, and the revelations of God, and the truth of them could have induced me to embrace such a principle as this."

To **Heber C. Kimball** the commandment of the Prophet that Heber take another wife was an unusually severe trial. This commandment was kept from Heber's wife Vilate for a time.

His wife noticed that Heber was greatly perplexed. She claimed that in answer to her prayer, concerning what it was that was causing her husband such concern, she received a vision of the eternal world. Just what she witnessed is not known, but in any event, thereafter she became a staunch supporter of the doctrine of plural marriage.

If the doctrine caused such a struggle on the part of the most devoted and dependable men of the Church, is it little wonder that large numbers would not receive it. Keeping the revelation under wraps for some time prevented a wholesale apostasy from the Church.

When the doctrine was publicly announced, there was greater opposition to the Church as well as increased mob violence. However, the leaders of the Church soon became aware of some of the reasons for the Lord's command. During the period between 1835 and 1843, and for a number of years after the arrival of the Saints in Utah—as long as converts made up the mass of Church membership—more women than men were joining the Church. **The greatest number of new converts to the Church—the majority of them women—came from England, and they came by the thousands.** They loved the new Church and the Gospel of Jesus Christ. As the persecution of the Saints continued, they were driven from state to state, from one city to another. It became more and more apparent that hardships to the single convert women were taking their toll. It was difficult for them to keep body and soul together. How could these women take care of themselves without funds? Certainly they didn't have funds to return to England, nor did they want to. **America was their home, and the Church became their spiritual home, and Joseph was their Prophet.**

The Gospel taught that the primary purpose of existence is to develop our human personality to its greatest capacity for happiness, and that the greatest development for all mankind would be accomplished if every man and every woman, mentally and physically fit for marriage, would enter into the marriage relationship and become parents. When the sexes are approximately equal in number, a system of monogamous marriage, one man to one woman, normally prevails. Such a law was given by the Lord to the Nephites in the Book of Mormon. The Saints, however, were as isolated a people as if they had been on an island of the sea and there were not enough men to go around. Marriage outside the Church was discouraged. In addition to suffering for want of protection and support, these women, should they remain single, would also be deprived of the growth and development that comes only through the experience of marriage and children.

Therefore, following the direct commandment from God, in council meetings with the leaders of the Church, men in the Church who were worthy Priesthood holders and had the finances to care for these convert women were directed to enter into plural marriage. The Priesthood holder would care for the needs of the convert women and welcome them into their already established families.

While **The Principle of Plural Marriage** solved some of their problems, it escalated others. The initial concealment, which surrounded the introduction of the practice, led to outrageous misrepresentations and charges of adultery—a potent factor in creating great resentment against the Prophet. None of the other teachings of the Church clashed so directly with the social order of the day or aroused such bitterness. It was a primary factor in the apostasy of several of the most influential leaders in the Church, which eventually resulted in a conspiracy against Joseph Smith.

On Sunday, March 24, 1844, the Prophet spoke at the temple about the conspiracy, having just learned of it from an informant. He revealed who some of his enemies were. Confident that the majority of the Saints would oppose the principle of plural marriage, they planned to bring up the subject at the business session of the April Conference. They were also prepared to argue that Joseph Smith was a fallen prophet because few if any revelations had been published and circulated among Church members in the previous months. In an effort to thwart the conspirators—the Prophet testified—at the beginning of the conference, **that he was not a fallen prophet,** and he had never felt nearer to God than at that time, and that he would show the people before the conference closed that **God was with him** (Wilford Woodruff Journal, 6 April 1844). The next day, at the April 1844 Conference of the Church, the Prophet Joseph Smith preached his greatest sermon ever delivered by mortal man. Speaking before 20,000 Saints, while moved upon by the **Holy Ghost,** he delivered the funeral sermon of Elder King Follett, (which had been given on March 10, 1844), in which he revealed the nature and kind of being that God is and told how man as a joint-heir with Christ—may become like the Father (*Teachings,* pp. 342-362). This sermon became known as the King Follett Discourse. On that occasion, the faithful witnessed the majesty of their Prophet.

Leaders of the conspiracy were exposed in the *Times and Seasons* and were excommunicated from the Church. Thwarted in their plans, the dissenters decided to publish an opposition newspaper. The first and only issue of their paper, which was called the *Nauvoo Expositor,* appeared on June 7, 1844.

Throughout the paper, they accused Joseph Smith of teaching vicious principles, practicing whoredoms, advocating so-called spiritual wifery, grasping for political power, preaching that there were many gods, speaking blasphemously of God, and promoting an inquisition.

The City Council met in long session on Saturday, June eighth, and again the following Monday. Using the famous English jurist William Blackstone as their legal authority, and having examined various municipal codes, the council ruled that the newspaper was a public nuisance in that it slandered individuals in the city. Moreover, they reasoned that if nothing were done to stop the libelous paper, the anti-Mormons would be aroused to mob action.

Joseph Smith, as Mayor, ordered the City Marshall, John Greene, to destroy the press, scatter the type, and burn any remaining newspapers. The order was carried out within hours. The City Council acted legally to abate a public nuisance, although the legal opinion of the time allowed only the destruction of the published issues of the offending paper. The demolition of the press was a violation of property rights (Dallin H. Oaks, *Utah Law Review,* winter 1965-pp. 890-01).

After the destruction of the press, the publishers rushed to Carthage and obtained a warrant against the Nauvoo City Council on charges of riot for the action. On June thirteenth and fourteenth, Joseph Smith and the other council members were released following a habeas corpus hearing before the Nauvoo Municipal Court. This further aroused the public. Illinois had experienced twenty similar destructions of printing presses over the previous two decades with little reaction; still the enemies of The Church proclaimed the *Nauvoo Expositor* incident a violation of freedom of the press.

These actions prompted citizens' groups in Hancock County to call for the removal of the Saints from Illinois. Thomas Sharp vehemently expressed the feelings of many of the enemies of The Church when he editorialized in the *Warsaw Signal:* "War and extermination is inevitable! Citizens Arise, one and all!!! Can you stand by, and suffer such infernal devils to rob men of their property and rights, without avenging them. We have no time for comment, every man will make his own. Let it be made with powder and ball!!!" (*Warsaw Signal*, 12 June, 1844). Was this the beginning of the end?

At this point, **let us turn back the clock to Joseph Smith's beginnings,** his life and times and the Restoration of The Church of Jesus Christ of Latter-day Saints.

If you **persist**, and don't **resist**, and do **insist** on the truth—if you hang in there, you'll get the whole story, step by step, and then you'll be able to **decide for yourself the answer to the question:** Was Joseph Smith an imposter, a pretender, a deceiver, or a Prophet of God?

Chapter 1

The Beginning of Joseph Smith's Unique Life

Heritage and Legacy of the Smith Family

Introducing the Young Joseph Smith

Families can be forever—they will never go out of style! They are here to stay no matter how hard Satan works to destroy them—***Families are Forever.***

The story of Joseph's family history of heartache and heartbreak, happiness and joy, wonderfully and uniquely blended. It's a story of trials, temptations, separations, sorrows and conflicts . . . mixed with love, dedication, and companionship.

Because of the unusual, extraordinary and glorious life of the Prophet Joseph Smith Jr. many curious readers share there is an eager interest to know about his entire family whose lives were closely interwoven with the exciting and moving drama of the **Restoration of the Gospel of Jesus Christ in these latter days.**

Remarkable events in the life of the Prophet Joseph that shone brightly as beacons along the rugged and bumpy road of his life and service to God . . . **the First Vision**, the loyal and loving devotion of his parents, brothers and sisters, the visitation of various heavenly messengers, the bringing forth of precious ancient scriptures as well as the building of temples, cities, and communities. There was his remarkable wife Emma, and his special children, added to the precious new revelations, his loyal friends, and of course, his bitter enemies. And one must never forget the growth of the Church, and the gathering of the Saints as well as the unyielding and willful persecutions which finally led to the sealing of Joseph's testimony with his blood. His life gave off giant beams of light to inspire the honest in heart to greater heights of courage, humility, service, and faith.

Like Lehi of old from the Book of Mormon scriptures, the Prophet's grandfather Asael had some children with hard, unyielding hearts and other children with open, receptive hearts, loyal to the mission of the Restoration. Of his descendants, numbering in the thousands, many of Asael Smith's family have been active members and leaders in the Church, while numerous others have never accepted the Restored Church of Jesus Christ.

* * *

As mentioned in the Preface—when we lived with God and Jesus Christ in the pre-earth life, we were individual spirit children of a loving Heavenly Father. We were there to learn and grow spiritually, as well as prepare ourselves for earth life. How we progressed or whether we progressed was strictly—between God and you—or between God and I, no one else can speak or learn for us. We were on our own, doing our own thing. No matter what we learned or didn't learn, we were destined to come to earth to be tested.

Then the time came for us individually to accept earth as our next home, as the next leg of our spiritual journey which could eventually lead us back to the presence of God if we had been proven worthy. In addition, and most important to our progress, before leaving the pre-earth world, as I see it, we were individually assigned to an earth family. We probably didn't have a choice in this case, since God knew where He wanted us to be for our best interests and results. Why? Because He loves us and wants us to succeed. Although we were assigned families, we still had our free agency to decide how we wanted to live our lives in that family setting. Again, it was part of the test. Earth life is our test, and an earthly family would be our greatest test. How we fit into an earthly family might be our greatest challenge because *Families are Forever.* Our family relationships might not be all that was hoped for, but we were counseled by God to give earth life our very best effort, if we wanted eventually, to live with God for all eternity.

* * *

Most assuredly, we are all affected socially and culturally, being influenced by our own surroundings. We are generally encouraged, taught, prepared, cherished and loved by our families and friends, and we certainly respond to our environment.

Joseph Smith grew up on the family farm, and was almost exclusively under his family's influence. The things he learned at home were the most important legacy of his New England heritage. His parents emphasized hard work, patriotism, and personal religion. Joseph learned, listened well, and acquired much from his heritage. During his formative years Joseph Smith began to incorporate and demonstrate qualities that would help him fulfill his foreordained mission.

An examination of Joseph Smith's ancestry shows that his family possessed important and significant traits that were perpetuated in him. He developed strong family bonds, learned to work hard, to think for himself, to serve others, and to love liberty. He recalled: *"Love of liberty was diffused into my soul by my grandfathers while they dangled me on their knees"* (*History of the Church,* 5: 498).

Although not always affiliated with a church, generations of his ancestors made every effort to live by correct religious principles, and some anticipated that an important spiritual leader would be raised up among their posterity.

The Prophet's paternal grandfather, Asael Smith, was the great-grandson of Robert Smith, who arrived in Boston, Massachusetts in 1638 as a twelve-year-old immigrant from London, England. Robert, a tailor by trade, eventually purchased a good-sized farm located partly in Boxford and Topsfield Townships, Massachusetts. His descendants' settlement of this farm began an era by the Smith line through several generations, which resulted in their being called "the Topsfield Smiths" (John Henry Evans, *Joseph Smith: an American Prophet* SLC, Deseret Book, 1966, p. 24).

Robert Smith married March French, and after a brief stay in nearby Rowley, settled in Topsfield, Massachusetts. They became the parents of ten children. When Robert died in 1693, he left an estate valued at 189 English

Pounds, a fairly substantial sum for that period of time. Samuel Smith, a son of Robert and Mary, was born in 1666. He was listed on town and county records as a *"gentleman"* and apparently held a public office. He married Rebecca Curtis, and they had nine children.

Samuel and Rebecca's first son was born in 1714. Samuel Jr. was a distinguished community leader and a promoter of the American War of Independence. According to his obituary: "He was a sincere friend to the liberties of his country, and a strenuous advocate for the doctrines of Christianity" (*Salem Gazette*, 22 Nov. 1785 cited in Richard Lloyd Anderson, *Joseph Smith's New England Heritage,* SLC, Deseret Book, 1971, pp. 89, 91). Samuel Jr., married Priscilla Gould, a descendant of the founder of Topsfield. Priscilla died after bearing five children, and Samuel married her cousin, also named Priscilla who bore no children but reared those of Samuel's first wife including Joseph Smith's grandfather, Asael, born in 1744.

Samuel, Asael's father as has been mentioned—was a deeply religious man. Of him it was written that: "He subscribed to the Christian conviction that by 'the mighty power of God' he would stand again at 'the general resurrection.' A deeply religious man who took his Congregational covenant seriously, he was active in public worship. His five children were all baptized in the Topfield Church, including youngest Asael, four days after birth" (Richard Lloyd Anderson, *Joseph Smith's New England Heritage,* SLC, Deseret Book, 1971, p. 90).

Asael seems to have followed the example of his father in almost every detail, combining the business of farming with public service. Like his father, Asael was also interested in religion and apparently had become affiliated with the established religion in New England, the Congregationalists. Nevertheless, he eventually became skeptical and distrustful of organized religion. To his thinking, the teachings of established churches did not conform nor harmonize with scripture and common sense.

At the age of twenty-three, Asael married Mary Duty of Rowley, Massachusetts. At great sacrifice to himself and his family, Asael moved from Derry Field, New Hampshire, back to Topsfield where he worked for five years to liquidate the debts of his father, who had been unable to meet his obligations.

The Smiths remained in Topsfield until 1791 when Asael, Mary, and their eleven children moved briefly to Ipswich, Massachusetts, and then on to Tunbridge, Vermont, in quest of undeveloped land. At Tunbridge, Asael continued his community service, and during his thirty years there held nearly every elective office.

Asael's philosophy agreed with that of the Universalists, who believed in Jesus Christ as a God of love who would save all His children. Like all Universalists, Asael was more comfortable with a God who was truly interested in saving—rather than in destroying mankind. He believed that life continued after death.

In a special communication to his family, Asael wrote: "The soul is immortal . . . Do all to God in a serious manner. When you think of Him, speak of Him, pray to Him, or in any way make your addresses to His great majesty, be in good earnest."

Asael Smith also predicted that: "God was going to raise up some branch of his family to be a great benefit to mankind" (George A. Smith, "Memoirs of George A. Smith," p. 2, cited in Anderson, *Joseph Smith's New En-*

gland Heritage, p. 112; see also *History of the Church,* 2: 443). Many years later when his son Joseph Smith Sr. gave him a recently published Book of Mormon, he was vitally interested. George A. Smith recorded: "My grandfather Asael fully believed in the Book of Mormon, which he read nearly through" (Smith, "*Memoirs*," p. 2, cited in Anderson, *Joseph Smith's New England Heritage*, pp.112-13). Asael died in the fall of 1830, confident that his grandson Joseph was the long-anticipated Prophet, and that he had proclaimed a new religious era.

Mary Duty Smith outlived her husband Asael by six years. In 1836, Mary made a very difficult and strenuous journey of 500 miles to join her descendants, who by then had moved to Kirtland, Ohio. The next day after her arrival at the home of the Prophet, she was welcomed with an overwhelming display of kindness and affection. Her children, grandchildren, and great-grandchildren, who were now residents of Kirtland, and two of her sons who arrived with her, all came together to enjoy with her a social family meeting. And a happy one it was—a festive time in which her cheerfulness and good spirits greatly added to the general joy and happiness of the occasion. Just imagine for a moment this aged matron surrounded by her four sons, Joseph, Asael, Silas, and John, as well as several of her grandsons who were upwards of six feet in height, and with a score of her great-grandchildren of various sizes intermixed.

Like her husband, Asael, Mary accepted the testimony of her grandson Joseph. In making the pilgrimage to Kirtland in her old age, she told her daughter-in-law, Lucy Mack Smith: "I am going to have your Joseph Jr. baptize me, and my Joseph Sr., bless me." Four of her sons, Joseph, Asael Jr., Silas, and John, also accepted the testimony of the Prophet and were baptized into the Church. All four died in full fellowship in the Church after having rendered significant service. The chief holdout from Mormonism among the children of Asael and Mary Duty Smith was their eldest son, Jesse, who adamantly refused to place any credence in the claim of the Prophet or his followers. Jesse stood alone among his family in open dissent. He had his free agency, and certainly it was his personal decision to make. Both of his parents and his four living brothers accepted the Prophet's testimony, a most singular fact considering the Prophet's youth and lack of schooling and the position the Smith family held toward independent thought. The meeting between the grandmother and her Prophet descendant and his brother was most touching; Joseph the Prophet blessed her and said she was the most honored woman on earth" (Edward W. Tullidge, *History of Salt Lake City,* Star Printing Co., 1886, p. 157). She completely accepted the testimony of her grandson, and fully intended to be baptized. Unfortunately, her age and her health prevented this. She died May 27, 1836, just ten days after she arrived in Kirtland.

When Asael Smith, grandfather of the Prophet Joseph, named his second son, Joseph, he had no way of knowing that thousands of years before **Joseph of Egypt** had prophesied that a great prophet should be raised up from his descendants and be named after him, and that the prophet's father would also be named **Joseph**: "*And thus prophesied Joseph, saying: Behold, that seer will the Lord bless; and they that seek to destroy him shall be confounded; for this promise, which I have obtained of the Lord, of the fruit of my loins, shall be fulfilled. Behold, I am sure of the fulfilling* *of this promise: And his name shall be called after me; and it shall be after the name of his father. And he shall be like unto me; for the things, which the Lord shall bring forth by his hand, by the power of the Lord shall bring my people unto salvation"* (2 Nephi 3: 14-15—Book of Mormon).

The Prophet's ancestral roots on his mother's side extended into Scotland. His great-great-grandfather, John Mack, came from Iverness, Scotland, and arrived in Boston Harbor in about 1669, when he was sixteen years old. At age thirty-eight, John Mack married Sarah Bagley. They lived successively in Salisbury, Massachusetts; Concord, Massachusetts; and Lyme,Connecticut. The eighth of their twelve children was Ebenezer Mack who became the pastor of the Second Congregational Church in Lyme. Ebenezer married Hannah Huntley and to them were born five children including Solomon Mack who was born in 1732. They prospered for a time on the Mack estate, but prosperity was short-lived. Through various misfortunes, they lost their property. As a result at the ripe old age of four, Solomon was "bound out to" (pledged to) a farmer in the neighborhood with whom he remained as an indentured servant (apprentice) for seventeen years. This period of indenture was an extremely trying one. In his old age, Solomon recalled these years: "I was treated by my master as his property and not as a fellow mortal. He taught me to work and was very careful that I should have little or no rest . . . he never taught me to read or spoke to me at all on the subject of religion" (Richard Lloyd Anderson, *Joseph Smith's New England Heritage,* LDS, Deseret Book, 1971, p. 34).

For most of the remainder of his life, Solomon searched for the haven he never found as a youth. Having fulfilled his term of indenture, Solomon enlisted in the army and saw extensive service during the French and Indian War. In succeeding years, Solomon was a merchant, land developer, shipmaster, mill operator, and farmer. Though he expended considerable time and effort, fortune did not favor him, and he was tormented with accidents, hardships, and financial reverses.

This zealous adventurer did experience some good fortune in 1759. After a brief acquaintance, he married Lydia Gates, a trained and accomplished school teacher and eldest child of the respected and successful Congregationalists deacon, Daniel Gates. Lydia had been a practicing Congregationalist from her early youth. Although Solomon and Lydia came from contrasting backgrounds, theirs was an enduring marriage. Lydia took charge of both the secular and religious educations of their eight sons and daughters. She probably taught her husband to read and write along with their children. Solomon believed that Lydia not only exhibited "the polish of education, but she also possessed that inestimable jewel which in a wife and mother of a family is truly a pearl of great price, namely a pious and devotional character" (Lucy Mack Smith, Manuscript of Biography, *Sketches of Joseph Smith,* cited in Anderson, *Joseph Smith's New England Heritage,* p. 27).

Soon after their marriage, Solomon purchased 1,600 acres of wilderness land in Northern New York. A leg injury prevented him from clearing the land as the contract stipulated, and he lost the property. In 1761, Solomon and Lydia settled with their two young sons in Marlow, New Hampshire. They remained there for ten years and had four more children. In 1771, the Macks moved to Gilsum, New Hampshire, where two additional children were born. Lucy, the youngest, would become the mother of the Prophet Joseph Smith.

During the American Revolution, Solomon enlisted in an artillery company but soon took sick and was sent home to recover. He might have been safer with his unit, because in rapid succession, Solomon was crushed by a tree, bruised on a waterwheel, and knocked unconscious by a falling tree limb. The last accident was particularly severe, and thereafter he was subject to periods of unconsciousness or "fits" as he called them (See Mack, *A Narrative Life of Solomon Mack,* pp. 11,12,17).

But Solomon Mack could never forego adventure for long. With his teenage sons, Jason and Stephen, Solomon signed on as a sailor on an American privateer. After four years and calamities which included a hurricane, a shipwreck, and illness, they returned empty-handed to find Lydia and the children homeless, swindled out of their property. "I did not care whether I lived or died," he wrote concerning this period of his life (Mack, *A Narrative Life of Solomon Mack,* p. 17). This despondency was only temporary because through hard work, Solomon was able to provide for his family again.

Solomon Mack had not been outwardly religious, though he was a God-fearing and good-hearted man. He showed little inclination toward scripture reading or church-going, but in 1810, rheumatism forced him to reassess his values. "After this, he said, I determined to follow phantoms no longer, but devote the rest of my life to the service of God and my family" (Lucy Mack Smith, *History of Joseph Smith by His Mother,* edited Preston Nibley, SLC, Bookcraft, 1958, pp. 7-8).

That winter he read the Bible and prayed earnestly; eventually he found peace of soul and mind. Until his death in 1820, Solomon spent much of his time telling others of his conversion and admonishing them to serve the Lord. He wrote an autobiography with the hope that others would not become enamored with material gain as he had. He enthusiastically shared his conviction with his grandchildren, among whom was young Joseph Smith Jr. Solomon died just three weeks before his eighty-eighth birthday, several months after his grandson's remarkable vision of the Father and the Son of which he was probably unaware.

During the years of Solomon's mishaps and adventures, his wife, Lydia Gates, provided stability and direction for their children. All the children, especially Lucy, the youngest daughter, reflected her influence. Lucy gave credit to her mother "for all the religious instructions as well as most of the educational privileges which I had ever received" (Lucy Mack Smith, *Biography Sketches*, p. 68, cited in Anderson, *Joseph Smith's New England Heritage,* p. 29).

Lucy, though intelligent, assertive and reared in religious surroundings, did not experience significant spiritual excitement until she was nineteen years old. She questioned whether life had meaning, and soon concluded she needed to revise her gloomy attitude. To avoid being labeled worldly, she decided to join a church, but was frustrated at the rival claims made by various clergymen. Her question: "How can I decide in such a case as this, seeing that they all are unlike the Church of Christ, as it existed in former days?" (Lucy Mack Smith, *History of Joseph Smith by His Mother,* p. 31).

Lucy did not find a satisfying answer to her spiritual dilemma. Recognizing that existing churches could not fulfill her needs, she temporarily put aside her desire for a church, and gradually her anxiety was dispelled. In less than two years, she met and married Joseph Smith Sr.—little did Lucy realize that from that union would come—a Prophet-son who would give comfort, assurance, truth, and direction from God to all who, like herself, were seeking to find The Church of Jesus Christ.

AND NOW, LET'S TALK ABOUT THE PARENTS OF THE PROPHET JOSEPH SMITH

Lucy Mack met Joseph Smith Sr., while visiting her brother Stephen Mack at Tunbridge, Vermont. Joseph was twenty-five and Lucy was nineteen. He was over six feet tall and powerfully built, like his father, Asael. After their marriage on January 24, 1796, they settled on one of the family farms in Tunbridge. They spent six years there living in very comfortable circumstances. It was in Tunbridge that their eldest son, Alvin, was born in 1798, and their second son, Hyrum, was born in 1800.

Joseph became attracted to the little town of Randolph, where he was getting involved in a commercial venture. They rented out their Tunbridge farm and moved to Randolph in 1802 to proceed with the business opportunity.

In Randolph, Lucy became ill. A physician diagnosed her condition as tuberculosis, the illness her older sisters, Lovisa and Lovina, had died from. Hearing that doctors said she would die, **Lucy pleaded with the Lord to spare her life** so that she might bring comfort to her children and husband.

Lucy wrote: "I made a solemn covenant with God that if He would let me live, I would endeavor to serve him according to the best of my abilities. Shortly after this, I heard a voice say to me: 'Seek, and ye shall find; knock, and it shall be opened unto you. Let your heart be comforted; ye believe in God, believe also in me.'" Lucy was still in a spiritual dilemma because her earlier search for spiritual truth led her no place, and she had temporarily given up. Now she made a covenant with the Lord which she wanted to and had to fulfill. These are her words: "As soon as I was able, I made all diligence in endeavoring to find someone who was capable of instructing me more perfectly in the way of life and salvation . . . I went from place to place for the purpose of getting information and finding, if it were possible, some harmonious spirit who could enter into my feelings, and thus be able to strengthen and assist me in carrying out my resolutions . . . I said in my heart that there was not then upon earth the religion which I sought. I therefore determined to examine my Bible—taking Jesus and His disciples for my guide, to endeavor to obtain from God that which man could neither give nor take away . . . At length, I considered it my duty to be baptized, and finding a minister who was willing to baptize me, and leave me free in regard to joining any religious denomination, I stepped forward and yielded obedience to this ordinance" (Lucy Mack Smith, *History of Joseph Smith by His Mother,* pp. 34-36).

While Lucy was preoccupied with religion and salvation, her husband was embarking on an ill-fated economic venture. Joseph invested all his funds in an enterprise to export crystallized ginseng root to China. Ginseng root grew wild in Vermont and was highly valued in China because of its supposed ability to heal and to enhance life. Prior to this venture, Joseph had experienced a series of financial setbacks, but nevertheless, invested heavily in the herb. Unfortunately, a combination of his lack of business insight and the dishonesty of an agent with whom he entrusted a large shipment of the product, ended in a complete business failure. Not only did he lose all he had invested in the venture, he also had to liquidate his interest in the farm and use Lucy's dowry to satisfy his debtors. Therefore, at age thirty-one, Joseph was out of debt, but penniless with a wife and two young sons to support.

Joseph Sr. and Lucy moved to Royalton, Vermont, for a few months and then on to Sharon in Windsor County. There Joseph rented Solomon Mack's farm. He farmed in the summer and taught school in the winter, and was eventually able to reestablish his financial stability. While in Sharon, Joseph and Lucy had their third son, Joseph Jr., who was born December 23, 1805. Naming him thus fulfilled a prophecy of Joseph in Egypt who had predicted that a "choice seer" would be raised up among his descendants. One way this seer could be identified was that he would receive the name of **the Ancient Patriarch Joseph**, which would also be his father's name (See 2 Nephi 3: 14-15).

Joseph was a tenant farmer; therefore, between 1805 and 1816, the family lived successively at Tunbridge, Vermont; Royalton, Vermont; Lebanon, New Hampshire; and Norwich, Vermont. Meanwhile, the family continued to grow. Samuel Harrison was born in Tunbridge in 1808; Ephraim and William in Royalton in 1810 and 1811 respectively; Catherine in Lebanon in 1812; and Don Carlos in Norwich in 1816.

After three successive crop failures at Norwich because of untimely frosts, Joseph Sr. decided to look for a more moderate climate. While Lucy remained in Norwich with the children, he went to Palmyra, New York, in the summer of 1816, and made preparations for them to join him there. Within two years, the hard-working family had saved enough for a down payment on the farm where, in the spring of 1820, **Joseph Jr. was to experience the first of an amazing series of spiritual experiences** that preceded the Restoration of the Gospel of Jesus Christ and the subsequent organization of The Church of Jesus Christ of Latter-day Saints.

From outward appearances, there was little to distinguish the Smith family from hundreds of others of that day. They had lived an unsubstantial, drifting life as they tried to earn a living from the soil. The unpredictable weather created special hazards and introduced into their lives an element of uncertainty that seemed to permeate everything they did. But along with this uncertainty in their outward lives, there existed within them **faith in a Supreme Being,** which proved itself in the form of prayer, Bible reading, and regular attendance at religious gatherings, including high-powered and frequent camp meetings.

While Joseph Sr. and Lucy demonstrated most of the qualities that symbolized so many of their contemporaries, theirs had a special dimension and significance. This probably resulted, in large part, from the influence and example of their parents, whose unusual spiritual qualities have already been mentioned. Yet family influence alone cannot explain the depth and scope of the religious sense found in these parents of the young man who was soon to become the **Prophet of the Restoration.**

While we are left to surmise how Lucy communicated to her children the assurance she had about the existence of God and the manner in which He informs His earthly children, there is no doubt concerning the key role she played in the conversion of her husband. Lucy records that during the time they resided at Tunbridge, Joseph Sr. accompanied her to Methodist meetings "in order to oblige [please] me." When Jesse Smith, her husband's oldest brother [who was always "bitterly opposed to every form of religion"], learned about this, he raised such strong objections that Joseph "thought it best to desist." Significantly, Lucy did not respond openly to this challenge. Instead, she followed a procedure that later became a way of life for her Prophet-son. "I retired to a grove not far distant," she wrote: "where I prayed to the Lord in behalf of my husband, that the true Gospel might be presented to him and that his heart might be softened so as to receive it, or, he might become more religiously inclined."

That night, **Lucy had a vivid dream** in which she saw two beautiful trees standing by a stream in an open meadow. One was encircled by a bright belt with the appearance of gold. It moved and swayed gently in the breeze, conveying "the idea of joy and gratitude." The other "stood erect and fixed as a pillar of marble," and regardless of how strong the wind blew, "not a leaf was stirred, not a bough was bent; but obstinately stiff it stood." According to the interpretation of this dream given to Lucy, these two trees represented her husband Joseph and his brother Jesse; "that the stubborn and unyielding tree was like Jesse; that the other, more pliant and flexible, was like Joseph, my husband; that the breath of heaven, which passed over them, was the pure and undefiled Gospel of the Son of God, which Gospel Jesse would always resist, but which Joseph, when he was more advanced in life, would hear and receive with his whole heart and rejoice therein; and unto him would be added intelligence, happiness, glory, and everlasting life."

How accurately the substance of this dream was fulfilled is made clear from the subsequent lives of these brothers. Jesse adamantly set his mind against all religion, and to the end derided the Prophet and his message. On the other hand, Joseph Sr. became convinced of the reality and power of God, and when the message of the Restoration was delivered to him by his son, he readily accepted it and affiliated himself with the Church, becoming its first Patriarch.

For this purpose, however, the most meaningful thing about Lucy's dream and its fulfillment is that she appears to have been the catalyst in her husband's conversion. The depth and sincerity of that conversion is proved by his later life, during which he showed an unalterable allegiance to the religious principles he had accepted. In no instance, however, are they more dramatically portrayed than in the special series of dreams and visions that he himself experienced. These began in about 1811, several years after Lucy's remarkable dream and at a time when the young Prophet was only six years of age. The first of these dreams occurred near the time when Lucy's father, Solomon Mack, experienced his near-miraculous conversion, and was proceeded by a marked change in Joseph's attitude toward religion. Of this change, Lucy commented: "About this time, my husband's mind became much excited upon the subject of religion; yet he would not subscribe to any particular system of faith, but contended for the ancient order, as established by our Lord and Savior Jesus Christ and His Apostles."

It was in this state of high mental excitement that **Joseph Sr. had his first dream**

or night vision, which he related in detail to Lucy the next morning. In it he saw himself as a traveler in a land of utter barrenness accompanied only by an oracular "attendant spirit" who declared that the desolation he saw was likened to the world devoid of true religion. The spirit also told him that further along in the journey he would see a box, the contents of which would make him wise. Finding the box, he opened it and was beginning to eat its contents when a horde of beasts, horned cattle, and roaring animals "rose up on every side in the most threatening manner possible, tearing the earth, tossing their horns, and bellowing most terrifically." So endangered was he in the dream that Joseph was compelled to drop the box and flee. "Yet," he said: "in the midst of all this I was perfectly happy, though I awoke trembling." Although Joseph's Sr. **second dream** varied from the first in significant detail, the substance of it was essentially the same. Again he saw himself as a traveler, first in a place of desolation, and then in a pleasant valley where he sampled the delicious fruit from a beautiful tree. He summoned his family to share the fruit, when they were intimidated and derided by a host of "finely dressed" people who occupied a spacious building across the valley. In the **third dream**, Joseph, lame from traveling a long distance on foot, found himself in a beautiful garden in which were twelve wooden images seated in two rows of six facing each other. As he walked down the separating aisle, each in turn arose and, bowing, paid obeisance to him, after which he was "entirely healed" of his lameness.

There then followed **two dreams** of which we have no record. Of them Lucy merely said: "I cannot remember them distinctly enough to rehearse them in full." In the **sixth dream** (but only the fourth that was recorded), Joseph was debarred from entering a large meetinghouse because a porter informed him he had arrived too late. Anguished by this rebuff and finding that "his flesh was perishing," he implored: "Oh, Lord God, I beseech thee, in the name of Jesus Christ, to forgive my sins." He then commenced to mend and was admitted to the building.

The **seventh and final dream** occurred in 1819, only a short while before the Prophet was visited by the Father and the Son. It culminated an eight-year period of spiritual preparation and enlightenment for the man who not only stands at the head of the Prophet's own family, but who was honorerd as the first Patriarch of the Restored Church. Its symbolic significance seems to justify repeating it in full: "I dreamed, said he, that a man with a peddler's budget on his back, came in and thus addressed me: 'Sir, will you trade with me today? I have now called upon you seven times. I have traded with you each time, and have always found you strictly honest in all your dealings. Your measures are always heaped and your weights over-balanced; and I have now come to tell you that **this is the last time** I shall ever call on you, and that there is but one thing which you lack in order to secure your salvation.' As I earnestly desired to know what it was I still lacked, I requested him to write the same upon paper. He said he would do so. I then sprang to get some paper, but in my excitement, I awoke."

Joseph Smith Sr. was given this series of dreams which opened his spiritual awareness. Through the dreams, he understood that there was still something very important missing in his life. **It is interesting that his final dream came shortly before his young son, Joseph Jr. received his vision of the Father**

and Son. Joseph Sr. began to prepare himself for the Lord's will to be done in his life. Building upon this foundation, the Prophet's parents matured and developed the spirituality they would need to face the challenges and pressures of the years ahead.

It is important at this point, to enlarge upon the experiences of the Smith family in those early years; to give us a better understanding of how powerful and potent the family unit is, then and now. A good family relationship will always have its ups and downs, because challenges are vital to the spiritual growth of a family. If we want happiness and joy in our lives, we have to work at it. Nothing good comes easily. Nevertheless, it is important in God's eyes that we strive to **build positive family relationships**, through love and togetherness because—*Families can be Forever.*

During the twenty-three year period from 1798 to 1821, Lucy Mack Smith gave birth to ten children, only one of whom—Ephraim, who was born in 1810—died in infancy. The burdens of carrying the children during pregnancy and of washing, diapering, feeding, nursing, teaching, and comforting them would, alone, have been overwhelming. Add to these burdens the frequent moving from one location to another, the lack of modern household appliances, and Lucy's activities in producing and selling oil-cloth paintings to alleviate the family's tight financial conditon and it is hardly surprising that Lucy failed to keep a detailed record of her children during their formative years. Had she known in advance the dramatic role her son Joseph was to play, she most certainly would have kept more detailed records. As it is, we have only the most sketchy account of those early years, gathered from Lucy's recollections, recorded years later—indirect references made by the Prophet and others, concerning conclusions drawn from the facts known about the Smith family and the circumstances in which they lived.

The Prophet's birth on December 23, 1805, heralded the official beginning of winter on Vermont's wooded, rolling hills. Sheltered in a protected hollow on the partially developed farm of Solomon Mack was a plain but comfortable cabin occupied by Joseph Sr. and Lucy Mack Smith and their young brood. The appearance of the winter season two days before had marked the beginning of lengthened days, anticipating both the season of heavy snow immediately ahead and the greenness of the spring that did lie beyond. With the onset of winter, Joseph Sr. had suspended farming activities except for the ever-present chores of feeding and milking the cows and caring for other barnyard animals. Seven-year-old Alvin and five-year-old Hyrum were hardly old enough to shoulder much of this load, although they were pressed into service to help feed the animals and chickens and do other light chores. Lucy's days were fully occupied with the numerous household duties facing any farmer's wife, amplified by the added tasks of caring for a newborn infant and a two-year-old toddler, Sophronia. Although extremely busy, with the never-ending chores. Lucy lived with an inner peace and serenity resulting from the dramatic experience three years earlier in Randolph when **the Lord had spoken to her in the agony of her soul** and promised she would be permitted to live and be a comfort to her husband and children.

During the winter season, Joseph Sr. was occupied teaching school for children from surrounding farms. This assignment is vital to an understanding of the influences that shaped the character of the growing Prophet. From his earliest days, he was exposed to an atmostphere of study, questioning, and discussion. A favorite book in the small Smith family library was the Holy Bible, which was read and discussed regularly. The religious direction of the Prophet's parents which added to the dramatic spiritual evidence they had already experienced made certain that their study of the Bible went hand in hand with the practical application of its guidelines through prayer and the manifestations of love, humility, and reverence.

The basic point of view already well-established in the mind of young Joseph was reinforced by frequent contact with his grandparents who lived nearby. They lost no opportunity to share with their beloved grandchildren the one overriding interest and concern in their lives—their conviction of the reality and power of God and of the need to pray to Him often for guidance and direction to help keep His commandments. Although Joseph Sr. and Lucy moved frequently during those early years, their basic environment remained unchanged. Always visible were the essential elements of frontier farm life, the endless chores and struggles, the relative isolation, the long, uninterrupted evenings which invited conversation and family solidarity, and the reassuring miracle of nature's cycle from seed to plant to fruit.

One of the few recorded instances of young Joseph's early years occurred when he was nine years of age, when the family was residing at Lebanon, New Hampshire. It was there that Catherine was born, bringing to seven the number of living Smith children, who ranged in age from fifteen to one. An epidemic of typhus fever ravaged the area. In turn, each of the Smith children took ill, and over a period of several months, they infected and reinfected each other. Sophronia, then ten years old, was the most seriously afflicted, and was attended by a physician for eighty-nine days and was kept under constant medication. On the ninetieth day, the doctor despaired of her life and informed the distraught parents there was nothing else he could do for her. Being pushed to the extreme of their own resources, the couple turned to the only other source of help about which they knew. "In this moment of distraction," Lucy recorded: "my husband and myself clasped our hands, fell upon our knees by the bedside, and poured out our grief to God in prayer and supplication, beseeching him to spare our child yet a little longer." An improbable, scene ensued when the anguished mother took the ten-year-old into her arms as if she were an infant and commenced to pace the floor. Someone present counseled with Lucy for what appeared to be wholly irrational conduct, saying: "You are certainly crazy. Your child is dead." Undeterred, the mother continued to walk the floor until at length the child sobbed, looked up into the mother's face, and commenced to breathe quietly and freely. With a combined sense of relief and self-vindication, Lucy observed: "From this time forward, Sophronia continued mending, until she entirely recovered" (Lucy Mack Smith, *History of Joseph Smith by His Mother,* pp. 52-53). The typhoid fever that came into West Lebanon and "raged tremendously," was part of an epidemic that swept the upper Connecticut valley leaving some 6,000 people dead.

Young Joseph was an observant nine-year-old who was witness to this dramatic event involving his older sister and playmate. We are left to venture a guess at the impact this experience had upon his attitude toward prayer and faith in God.

Joseph Jr.'s siege of typhus fever appeared to be quite mild and lasted only about two weeks. The aftermath, however, produced one of the most traumatic and terrifying experiences of a life destined to be filled with torment and adversity. It started with severe pain in his shoulder so intense that it caused him to scream involuntarily. The doctor diagnosed the ailment as a sprain, and treated it accordingly with a remedy called "bone linament." After two weeks of excruciating pain, accompanied by Joseph's protests that he had not suffered any injury, the doctor conducted a more searching examination, which disclosed the presence of a "fever sore." When this was lanced by the doctor, a full quart of matter was discharged. No sooner had the pain subsided in Joseph's shoulder than it "shot like lightning" into his leg. Almost immediately the leg began to swell and became exceedingly painful. For two weeks he received almost constant nursing care from his mother and other members of the family, especially twelve-year-old Hyrum. During a good part of this time, Hyrum sat beside Joseph, who had been placed on a low bed to clear the way for his proper care, and pressed the afflicted leg between his hands to help alleviate the pain. Nothing, unfortunately, gave the boy relief. When, after three weeks, there was no improvement in his condition, the doctor was again summoned. The only remedy he could prescribe was to lance the boy's leg. Accordingly, a six-inch incision was opened up between the knee and the ankle, which seemed to afford some welcome but only temporary relief. When, within a short time, the pain returned with even greater intensity, the doctor was called again. The wound was reopened and deepened to the bone, providing some relief. Soon, however, the leg commenced to swell again and the pain became almost unbearable. At this juncture, several doctors were called in for consultation. They recommended that the boy's leg be amputated. So persistent and anguished were the protests of the family, especially Lucy, that the doctors were persuaded to follow an intermediate course. They would instead remove the infected portion of the bone.

One can imagine the fears, the apprehension, and the anxieties that tore away at young Joseph and his family as they faced the prospect of such an operation without the benefit of hospital facilities or anesthetics. The doctors offered the only antidote they had for the excruciating pain that was sure to follow—a cord to bind his arms to prevent him from thrashing about during the ordeal, and a drink of wine to deaden his senses. Joseph declined both. Instead, he asked that his father hold him in his arms during the operation. He also insisted that his mother leave the room. These sparse preparations having been made, the surgeons commenced their work. Holes were bored into the bone on either side of the infected part; then, using pincers or forceps, the doctors tore away the diseased bone, piece by piece. So intense was the pain when the first piece of bone was torn away, that Joseph screamed. This brought his mother running into the room. She was promptly ushered out, but was soon drawn into the room again by another terrifying scream from Joseph. Lucy penned this vivid picture of the scene: "Oh, my God! What a spectacle for a mother's eye! The wound torn open, the blood still gushing from it, and the bed literally covered with blood. Joseph was pale as a corpse, and large drops of sweat were rolling down his face, whilst upon every feature was depicted the utmost agony" (Lucy Mack Smith, *History of Joseph Smith by His Mother,* p. 58). After this intrusion, Lucy was taken from the room and restrained from reentering until the operation had been completed and the room tidied up.

This terrible ordeal marked the turning point in Joseph's recovery. His body began to mend, and with it came a release from the tensions and anxieties that had accompanied his illness. To help speed his recovery, he was sent to visit Uncle Jesse at Salem where, it was hoped, the sea air and change of scenery would provide a needed tonic. Lucy reported that: "in this he was not disappointed."

It is interesting to picture this frail, young convalescent, whose prophetic character had not yet begun to emerge, in the home of his opinionated, agnostic uncle. Jesse's subsequent rejection of Joseph's revelations were in all probability or likelihood influenced in part by his recollection of Joseph as a dependent, almost helpless boy.

Joseph Jr. carried the physical and emotional scars of his traumatic experience for the remainder of his life. Nevertheless, he suffered no serious impairment as a result. In fact, the experience taught him several valuable lessons. From the intense pain came an increased appreciation of the daily blessing of health. Face to face with death, he learned that the duration of life is, at best, tenuous and uncertain. He learned that man's knowledge and skill are severely limited, and that beyond the scope of man's ability, lies the infinite field of God's knowledge and power. Finally, he became conscious as never before of the great love and concern of his family for him—especially that of his parents and his brother Hyrum. A few years later these three were to accept, without doubt or qualification, the amazing manifestations of their son and younger brother, who, at this point, seemed so vulnerable.

Relating back to 1813, when the family moved to Norwich, Vermont, Joseph Jr. probably attended a common, or grammar, school for a brief period. He also received religious instruction and education in his home and likely engaged in the outdoor activities and games of his day. He was tall, athletic, and energetic, but was also thoughtful, reflective and even-tempered. His mother said that Joseph "seemed much less inclined to the reading of books than any of the rest of our children, but far more given to meditation and deep study" (Lucy Mack Smith, *History of Joseph Smith by His Mother,* p. 83).

That year farming in New England was hard hit. Four killing frosts struck between June sixth and August thirtieth, which destroyed all but the hardiest of crops. Unaware of the cause, but nevertheless discouraged by successive crop failures, hundreds of people left New England—among them the Smiths of Norwich, Vermont. During the decade of 1810 to 1820, there was a major exodus from Vermont. More than sixty Vermont towns experienced population losses (Larry C. Porter, "A Study of the Origins of The Church of Jesus Christ of Latter-day Saints in the States of New York and Pennsylvania, 1816-1831," Ph.D. diss., BYU, 1971, p. 30). **Most Vermonters who left, headed westward**—aroused by newspaper advertisements of available lands in New York, Pennsylvania, and Ohio, lands that were said to be "well-timbered, well-watered, easily accessible and undeniably fertile—all to be had on long-term payments for only two or three dollars an acre" (Lewis D. Stilwell, Migration from Vermont,

1776-1860, cited in Proceedings of the Vermont Historical Society, Montpelier, Vt.: Vermont Historical Society 1937, p. 135).

Responding to this newspaper ad, in 1816, Joseph Smith Sr. hastily set out for Palmyra, Ontario County, New York, in the company of a Mr. Howard. Before departing, he called on his creditors and debtors to settle existing accounts, but some of them neglected to bring their accounts to that settlement. Apparently, their claims against him were satisfied either by payment of cash or by the transfer of claims Joseph Sr. had against his debtors. Believing that all accounts were settled, he proceeded to Palmyra and purchased land. He then sent a communication to Lucy instructing her to stow their belongings on a wagon and prepare to move. Joseph arranged with Calab Howard, cousin of the Mr. Howard who had traveled with him to Palmyra, to drive the team and bring his family to New York. Before Lucy Smith left to join her husband, however, additional creditors appeared and presented their uncanceled accounts for payment. Lucy described this event: "I concluded it would be more to our advantage to pay their unjust claims than to hazard a lawsuit. Therefore, by making a considerable effort, I raised the required sum which was 150 dollars, and liquidated the demand." When well-meaning neighbors proposed to ease the burden by raising money through subscription, Lucy refused. "The idea of receiving assistance in such a way as this was indeed very repulsive to my feelings" (Lucy Mack Smith, *History of Joseph Smith by His Mother,* p. 61).

Accounts being settled, Lucy and her eight children, ranging in age from the infant, Don Carlos, to seventeen-year-old Alvin, set out for New York with Calab Howard. In South Royalton, Lucy's mother, Lydia, was injured by an overturning wagon. When Lydia was taken to her son's home in Tunbridge, mother and daughter tearfully exchanged good-byes. The aged Lydia admonished her daughter: "I beseech you to continue faithful in the service of God to the end of your days, that I may have the pleasure of embracing you in another and fairer world above" (Lucy Mack Smith, *History of Joseph Smith by His Mother,* p. 62). Lydia died two years later in Royalton of the injuries she had received at that time.

As the Smith family continued their journey, it became apparent to Lucy that: "Mr Howard, our teamster, was an unprincipled and unfeeling 'good-for-nothing'" (Lucy Mack Smith, *History of Joseph Smith by His Mother,* p. 62). Howard spent the money that Joseph Sr. paid him to bring the Smith family to New York was in drinking and gambling at inns along the way. Joseph Jr., at the time a boy of ten, later remembered that even though he had not yet fully recovered from his leg operation, Howard made him walk *"in my weak state through the snow 40 miles per day for several days, during which time I suffered the most excruciating weariness and pain"* (Manuscript, *History of the Church,* cited in Dean C. Jessee, ed., *The Personal Writings of Joseph Smith,* SLC, Deseret Book, 1984, p. 666; spelling standardized).

At Utica, New York, several miles from their destination, Howard unloaded the Smith's belongings and was about to leave with their team when Lucy confronted him: "Sir, I now forbid you touching the team, or driving it one step further." The determined Lucy then reloaded the wagon and drove the team the rest of the way to Palmyra. She arrived with only two cents, but was: "happy in once more having the society of my husband, and in throwing myself and children upon the care and affection of a tender companion and father" (Lucy Mack Smith, *History of Joseph Smith by His Mother,* p. 63).

The Smith family's physical resources were never again as depleted as they were when Lucy and the children arrived in Palmyra. She only had part of the family's personal belongings, the remainder having been disposed of to satisfy the creditors' claims. Neither did Joseph Sr. have any funds. He had, however, made arrangements for temporary housing in Palmyra, where the family resided for about two years. Then they moved to Manchester, where he contracted to purchase one hundred acres of virgin wooded land as a farm site.

During the first year after they moved to Manchester, the father and his sons cleared thirty acres and constructed a log house. They were able to make the first of two installment payments on the land, chiefly from the proceeds of Lucy's sale of painted oilcloth coverings. By this means they were also able to complete the furnishing of their home. As the due date of the second installment approached, it became necessary for Alvin, their oldest son, to hire out in order to obtain the necessary cash. Thus, through hard work and cooperative effort, the family was able to restore its financial stability within a few short years.

During this period, young Joseph advanced into his teens. His leg was now fully healed. He was able to run errands and perform light manual labor in assisting his father and two older brothers in clearing the land and building the log home. Nothing yet appeared in his character or outward demeanor, behavior, or conduct that marked him as being destined for any unusual role or achievement in life. He was an obedient, cheerful boy, inclined to be gregarious (talkative, communicative, demonstrative, unreserved and unrestrained) yet thoughtful, introspective and somewhat subjective. Yet there was something about him that could evoke deep and sometimes destructive and hateful feelings in certain people. We have already observed their antagonistic feelings toward young Joseph. It is also reported that near the end of the family's trip from Vermont, the son of another family that was traveling with them struck Joseph, who was on crutches at the time, and left him alongside the road. Joseph was picked up and brought into Palmyra by another traveler. Three years after the Smiths arrived in Palmyra, another incident occurred that demonstrated that someone else had a bitter, if not murderous, attitude toward Joseph. One evening, as he returned from an errand, someone fired a gun at him as he neared the cabin. Terrified and badly shaken, he leaped through the door to safety. His family attempted to find the would-be assassin but were unable to do so in the gathering dusk. The next morning, however, they found his tracks and the place where he had lain beneath a wagon. They also found one of their animals dead from gunshot wounds. Nothing ever came to light about the identity of the assailant or his motives.

DID NEW ENGLAND HAVE ANY GREAT INFLUENCE ON JOSEPH SMITH?

The Smiths were but one of many New England families whose names are linked to the Restoration. Brigham Young, Joseph's successor; Heber C. Kimball, faithful Apostle; and numerous other Church leaders had New England roots. Among their ancestors were men and women who sailed on the Mayflower or served in the American Revolution (See

Gustive O. Larson, "New England Leadership in the Rise and Progress of the Church," *Improvement Era,* Aug. 1968, p.81). These industrious and independent people, who carved homes and societies out of the New England wilderness, were remarkable. They were patriotic, socially responsible, and religious. **Joseph Smith had no need to apologize for his comparatively humble origins—his was an enduring moral legacy.**

Many of the principles of Puritanism that shaped and molded Joseph's environment, complemented the revealed principles and doctrines he would later receive as a Prophet. When Joseph learned by revelation that: *"Thou shalt not be idle"* (Doctrine & Covenants 42: 42), this demonstrated the suitability of the prudent and resourceful New England life. Later the Lord told him to seek learning out of the best books *"even by study and also by faith"* (Doctrine & Covenants 88: 118), it reaffirmed the Puritan emphasis on education. When Joseph later proclaimed the concept of an ideal, divinely guided society, he embraced a principle with which Puritan New England could readily identify.

Nevertheless, Joseph Smith was not bound by his New England heritage. More than any environmental influence, it was God who shaped his ideas. In his lifetime, he introduced Gospel doctrines and ordinances that directly opposed his Puritan background. His concept of a personal and caring God opposed the Calvinistic idea of a stern God of justice. Revelations declaring the Godhead to be three separate and distinct personages directly contradicted traditional Calvinistic Trinitarian theology.

Certainly, it is part of Latter-day Saint theology that the Lord knew and prepared Joseph Smith in a previous domain of existence to assume his central role in restoring God's Church upon the earth. Joseph spoke of his foreordination when he said: *"Every man who has a calling to minister to the inhabitants of the world, was ordained to that very purpose in the Grand Council of heaven before this world was. I suppose that I was ordained to this very office in that Grand Council."*

It was Brigham Young who said of Joseph Smith: "It was decreed in the counsels of eternity, long before the foundations of the earth were laid, that he should be the man, in the last dispensation of this world, to bring forth the word of God to the people, and receive the fulness of the keys and power of the Priesthood of the Son of God. The Lord had his eye upon him, and upon his father, and upon his father's father, and upon their progenitors clear back to Abraham, and from Abraham to the flood, from the flood to Enoch, and from Enoch to Adam. He has watched that family and that blood as it has circulated from its foundation to the birth of that man. He was foreordained in eternity to preside over this last dispensation" (*Journal of Discourses,* 7: 289-90).

However traumatic the worldly pressures may have been in Joseph's early life, they were mild forerunners of the storm of abuse and vilification, defamation, slander, smear campaigns and persecutions, soon to break into his life. Unknown to Joseph, events had merged to prepare for one of the most dramatic and unusual spiritual experiences of the nineteenth century, or, in fact, of almost any preceding century.

Joseph Smith's First Prayer

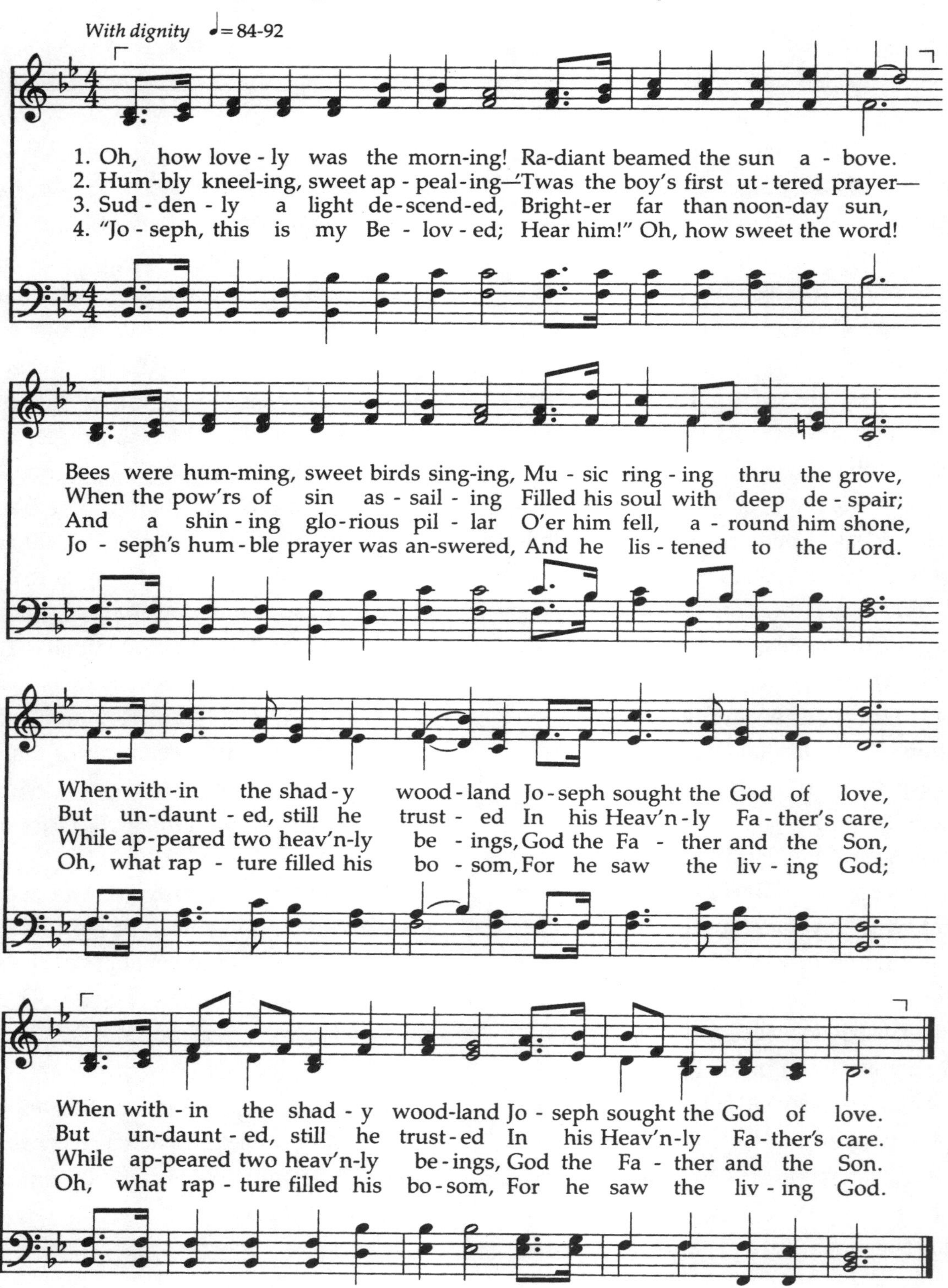
With dignity ♩= 84-92
1. Oh, how love - ly was the morn-ing! Ra-diant beamed the sun a - bove.
2. Hum-bly kneel-ing, sweet ap - peal-ing—'Twas the boy's first ut - tered prayer—
3. Sud - den - ly a light de-scend-ed, Bright-er far than noon-day sun,
4. "Jo - seph, this is my Be - lov - ed; Hear him!" Oh, how sweet the word!
Bees were hum-ming, sweet birds sing-ing, Mu - sic ring - ing thru the grove,
When the pow'rs of sin as - sail - ing Filled his soul with deep de - spair;
And a shin - ing glo-rious pil - lar O'er him fell, a - round him shone,
Jo - seph's hum - ble prayer was an-swered, And he lis - tened to the Lord.
When with - in the shad - y wood - land Jo - seph sought the God of love,
But un-daunt - ed, still he trust - ed In his Heav'n-ly Fa - ther's care,
While ap-peared two heav'n-ly be - ings, God the Fa - ther and the Son,
Oh, what rap - ture filled his bo - som, For he saw the liv - ing God;
When with - in the shad - y wood-land Jo - seph sought the God of love.
But un-daunt - ed, still he trust-ed In his Heav'n-ly Fa - ther's care.
While ap-peared two heav'n-ly be - ings, God the Fa - ther and the Son.
Oh, what rap - ture filled his bo - som, For he saw the liv - ing God.

Text: George Manwaring, 1854-1889
Music: Sylvanus Billings Pond, 1792-1871; adapted by A.C. Smyth, 1840-1909

Joseph Smith—History 1:14-20, 25
James 1:5

Chapter 2

Did God and Jesus Christ appear in Person to the Young Joseph Smith?

Did a First Vision Actually Happen or was it a figment of Joseph's imagination?

What's all this Nonsense about a man seeing God and Jesus Christ?

No man has ever seen or can see God and Jesus Christ—Is that true?

We **Mormons believe** that when we lived in the pre-mortal, pre-earth life with God the Father, as His spirit children, we were learning and preparing for our upcoming earth life. It would be the second leg of our spiritual and physical journey, an essential part of our quest to ultimately return to live with God one day. In that sphere we were being prepared for our earth mission, tests, assignments and activities. We were informed there—that based upon our valiance, service, and worthiness in the pre-earth existence, we'd be called upon to accept certain commissions on earth from God and Jesus Christ, in accordance with our free agency.

In that pre-mortal sphere there were noble and great spirits who wore the full armor of God. *Joseph Smith Jr.* was among them . . . a valiant warrior for God's plan in the pre-earth life, who would be foreordained to come to earth as a leader of men and a Prophet of God, chosen for the Seventh and last Dispensation of the Fulness of Times. His valiance and worthiness placed him in a unique and special category of men, called by God to serve in the latter days.

* * *

Why do we shrink from discussing religion . . . yours, mine and others? Why is the discussion of religion such a no-no? We seem to discuss everything else under the sun; then why not religion, as long as we're tolerant of one another? I've heard it said all of my life, if you want to keep a friend, then don't discuss religion or politics. Why? If we consider ourselves to be such an open-minded, sophisticated society being able to discuss any subject within reason, then why not religion? What are we afraid of? Do we fear the unknown, if we learn about others' beliefs? I'll always remember that when I was growing up as a Jewish kid in New York City, I was told in no uncertain terms, that as a Jew, I was only to worship from the Old Testament—the Jewish Scriptures. That was the word from the Rabbi, and one doesn't argue with a Rabbi. That was the old days. **I've also heard it said that the discussion of religion was too personal. Too personal, nonsense.** The more educated we become, the more understanding and tolerant we become. Are we so caught up in our ancestral background—in the religious intolerance of the past—that our minds are closed to anything new—anything that can spiritually uplift us to a higher plane of spirituality—to bring us closer to God? And who said that because one learns, and increases their education they are being proselyted to another form of religious worship? Hopefully, I've made my point about being open-minded, tolerant, understanding and kind to one another "that says it all."

* * *

The unique and dramatic events about to take place in the life of young Joseph Smith would eventually have an infinite effect upon the religious world. They had actually begun in the Prophet's infancy and early youth when he was exposed to the spiritual qualities and experiences of his parents and grandparents. He had his mother's testimony of how the Lord had heard her prayers and spared her life and his father's review of the unusual dreams and visions he had experienced over a period of several years. He also had his grandfather Mack's almost miraculous conversion in his old age grandfather Smith's solemn instructions to his descendants to be earnest in all matters pertaining to God, and his grandmothers' sincere, abiding faith in Deity. All these combined had produced in young Joseph an attitude of absolute faith in the existence and power of God.

At this time, Joseph's opportunities for schooling were extremely limited. He attributed this to "indigent circumstances," the poverty of his family. *"We were deprived of the benefit of an education. Suffice it to say, I was merely instructed in reading, writing, and the ground rules of arithmetic which constituted my whole literary acquirement"* (*History of Joseph Smith By Himself,* p. 1; Jessee, *Personal Writings of Joseph Smith,* p. 4).

As more and more Americans crossed the Catskill and Adirondack Mountains to settle in the Finger Lakes area of Western New York, they tended to lose contact with the churches they had attended. These "unchurched" settlers worried religious leaders of the main denominations, principally the Baptists, Methodists, and Presbyterians who established proselyting programs for their disadvantaged brothers in the West.

The Methodists and Baptists were particularly zealous in their efforts to bring religion to those without its benefits. The Methodists hired circuit riders—traveling ministers who rode horseback from town to town throughout a given area, or circuit, ministering to the religious needs of the people. The farming communities used the farmer-preacher method where a local man earned his living by farming but occupied a nearby pulpit on the Sabbath. These efforts were supported by the enthusiasm of the "Second Great Awakening" which was then sweeping the United States.

Nearly all churches in upstate New York conducted revivals—evangelistic gatherings designed to awaken the religiously inactive. Revivals were often in the form of camp meetings held on the edge of a grove of trees or in a small clearing in the forest. Those who participated often traveled many miles over dusty or rut-filled roads to pitch their tents or park their wagons on the outskirts of the encampment. Camp meetings very often lasted several days with some sessions lasting nearly all day and into the night. Ministers rotated, but it was not uncommon to find two or three ministers warning and counseling their listeners simultaneously (See Milton V. Backman Jr., *Joseph Smith's First Vision*, 2nd ed. SLC, Bookcraft, 1980, pp. 72-74).

So passionate and enthusiastic was the religious zeal in Western New York in the early 1800s that the area became known as the "Burned-Over District." Because the Finger Lakes area was set figuratively ablaze with evangelistic fire, it is not surprising that young Joseph Smith and his family were caught up in the excitement.

Revivals had as their main objective the awakening or reinforcement of religious sentiment and commitment. Had this been the only purpose, it is doubtful that the revival of 1819-20 around Palmyra would have had any significant effect on Joseph other than to confirm his faith in God. However, the existence of a variety of religious denominations in the vicinity brought into the revival an air of contention and controversy. These different religious groups had a two-fold purpose—one, turn people to God and two, turn the people to their particular religion. Differences in concept and aggressive efforts to attract converts to one sect or another transformed the revival into a free-for-all—a stormy, sometimes bitter contest. Within a radius of eight miles of the Smith farm were thirteen different religious congregations including Quaker, Baptists, Presbyterians, and Methodists. Several members of the Smith family, including Lucy, were proselyted to the Presbyterian faith. According to his own account, Joseph *"became somewhat partial to the Methodist sect"* (*History of the Church,* 1: 3). This interest in Methodism was inspired in large part by a local Methodist minister, the Reverend Lane. "Much good instruction was always drawn from his discourse on the scriptures . . . and Joseph Smith's mind became awakened."

Joseph was also confused by the bitterness and hypocrisy he witnessed among ministers and fellow Christians. He said: *"My intimate acquaintance with those of different denominations led me to marvel exceedingly, for I discovered that they did not adorn their profession by a holy walk and Godly conversation agreeable to what I found contained in that sacred depository* [The Holy Scriptures]. *This was a grief to my soul"* (*History of Joseph Smith By Himself,"* p. 2; Jessee, *Personal Writings of Joseph Smith,* p. 5). When the converts joined first one church and then another, he saw that the: *"seemingly good feelings of both the priests and the converts were more pretended than real; for a scene of great confusion and bad feeling ensued—priest contending against priest, and convert against convert; so that all good feelings one for another, if they ever had any, were entirely lost in a strife of words and a contest about opinions"* (Joseph Smith—History, 1: 6).

One can only imagine the impact such conditions had on Joseph's youthful, searching mind. The very men he thought could point the way to God: *"understood the same passages of scripture so differently as to destroy all confidence in settling the question by an appeal to the Bible."* Joseph explained: *"In the midst of this war of words and tumult of opinions, I often said to myself: What is to be done? Who of all these parties are right; or, are they all wrong together? If any one of them be right, which is it, and how shall I know it?"* (Joseph Smith—History 1: 12, 10).

Joseph Smith came from a religious family. His mother, a sister, and two brothers had joined the Presbyterian faith, but their sermons did not satisfy him. Nevertheless, his parents had instructed him in the Christian religion from childhood. One of the existing churches must be right, he reasoned, but which one was it? In his search for the true church, Joseph did not intend to start his own church, nor did he think that the truth was not on the earth at the time. He simply did not know where to find the truth. Since he was trained to believe in the scriptures, he would turn there for his support and answers.

In the early part of 1820, the Reverend Lane preached the most effective sermon of his career, the results of which, to a great extent, are evident even today. On that occasion, he addressed himself to the subject: *"What church shall I join?"* He took as his text, the familiar instruction found in James: ***"If any of you lack wisdom, let him ask of God, that giveth to all men liberally, and upbraideth not; and it shall be given him"*** (James 1: 5). In his audience that day was young Joseph Smith, who had been caught up in the spirit of the revival, and who, to say the least, was bewildered by the conflicting doctrines taught as the ministers competed for converts. The Prophet later recorded his deep feelings of confusion at the time: *"So great was the confusion and strife among the different denominations, that it was impossible for a person young as I was, and so unacquainted with men and things, to come to any certain conclusion who was right and who was wrong. My mind at times was greatly excited, the cry and tumult* [uproar] *were so great and incessant* [continuous]*"* (*History of the Church,* 1: 3-4).

Like many other frontier families, the Smiths owned a Bible. Seeds planted by "goodly parents," were nurtured by the Holy Spirit. How many days and nights had he pondered, searched, and prayed for light and truth he does not say. Nor does he tell us whether he confided his secret feelings and desires to his family. His years of preparation and his time, effort, and meditation were to be rewarded.

As he did so often in his home, he opened the Bible to the passage in James 1: 5 and began to ponder its meaning. This passage had a profound impact on Joseph: *"Never did any passage of scripture come with more power to the heart of man than this did at this time to mine. It seemed to enter with great force into every feeling of my heart. I reflected on it again and again, knowing that if any person needed wisdom from God, I did; for how to act I did not know, and unless I could get more wisdom than I then had, I would never know"* (Joseph Smith—History 1: 12). The Bible did not tell Joseph which church was true, but it told him that prayer could help solve his problem and Joseph had never before faced a crisis of this intensity, he reflected on this idea: *"At length I came to the conclusion that I must either remain in darkness and confusion, or else I must do as James directs that is, ask of God."*

So it was that in his fifteenth year of age, Joseph felt that he had found a solution to his problem through the scripture James chapter one verse five. In the midst of his turmoil, the simple instruction in James was a beacon to Joseph, showing him the way out of the darkness that overwhelmed him.

On this occasion, so intense were his feelings and so desirous was he of obtaining an answer to the bewildering problem he faced, that he decided to find a place of seclusion where, following the instruction of James, he could appeal to God for counsel and direction.

It was the morning of a beautiful, clear day, early in the spring of 1820. Near the Smith farm was a beautiful grove of trees that afforded the privacy and solitude so necessary for the purpose he had in mind. Joseph later confided that as he entered the grove, there remained no doubt that God would hear and answer his prayer. The extraordinary examples of his parents and grandparents in receiving answers to their prayers had convinced him that God was a reality—a kind, gracious, loving and sympathetic Father. The instruction found in James had also convinced him that God would give him guidance and direction if not solutions. For the first time, Joseph was really putting his faith to the test.

As he entered the grove that special spring morning, he headed for the location that would afford him the most "splendid isolation." Having looked around and finding himself alone, Joseph knelt down and began to offer up the desires of his heart to God. Never before had he attempted to pray vocally and alone. He had scarcely done so, when immediately he was seized upon by some evil power of such force and intensity that it entirely overcame him as to bind his tongue so that he could not speak. The sun had been shining, and it was a beautiful clear spring day. **And yet, thick darkness gathered around him,** and it seemed for a time as if he were doomed to sudden destruction. But rallying his strength, he continued to call upon God with all the fervor of his soul. He knew that the evil power was not imaginary, but was the real and terrifying influence of a being from the unseen world. Not since the Resurrection of Jesus Christ had there been such a threat to the devil's kingdom. Little wonder, then, that Satan was present that morning doing all he could to destroy Joseph Smith and the future of The Church of Jesus Christ. That influence had such incredible power which Joseph had never experienced before. Nevertheless, exerting all his power to call upon God, at the very moment when he was ready to sink into despair, when he was about to give up hope and abandon himself to destruction—just at that moment of great alarm, **Joseph saw a pillar of light** exactly over his head, above the brightness of the sun, which descended gradually until it fell upon him. As soon as the light appeared, he was free from the evil enemy which held him bound, and the darkness was dispelled by the bright light from heaven.

When the pillar of light rested upon him, **he saw two Personages,** whose brightness and glory defy all description, standing above him in the air. One of them spoke unto him, calling him by name and said, pointing to the other: ***"This is My Beloved Son, Hear Him!"*** God the Father and His Son Jesus Christ appeared together to the fourteen-year-old Joseph Smith. As soon as Joseph was able to regain his composure, he asked Jesus Christ which church he should join? He was directed to join none of them because all their creeds were an "abomination" in the sight of God. The Lord said that the professors of those creeds were *"corrupt,"* because they were teaching for doctrine *"the commandments of men, having a form of godliness but denying the power thereof."* Also He said that their

"The First Vision," by Dee Jay Bawden. Used by Permissi

leaders *"draw near to me with their lips, but their hearts are far from me."* Again, He forbid Joseph to join any of the churches and promised him *"that the fulness of the Gospel should at some future time be made known unto him."*

Joseph was also told "many other things" that he was instructed not to divulge. We do know that Joseph's vision of Jesus Christ in the presence of the Holy Eternal Father, is the first known recorded instance when these two members of the Godhead appeared together to Joseph face to face.

The appearance in the grove of God the Eternal Father and His Son Jesus Christ to Joseph Smith would set Joseph apart from his contemporaries forever after.

Nevertheless, was Joseph Smith the only other human to see God and/or His Son, Jesus Christ? Not if you believe in the Holy Bible.

The word **"theophany"** is used to describe a vision of Deity. The Bible confirms that theophanies are real. At Penial, Jacob rejoiced, saying: *"for I have seen God face to face, and my life is preserved"* (Genesis 32: 30). With Moses, God spoke *"face to face, as a man speaketh unto his friend"* (Exodus 33: 11 see also Numbers 12: 8). And Isaiah wrote: *"mine eyes have seen the King, the Lord of hosts"* (Isaiah 6: 5).

Many other scriptures document the fact that men have seen God and/or Jesus Christ here on earth . . .

Old and New Testaments

Genesis 1: 28—God spoke to Adam & Eve in the Garden of Eden.
Genesis 5: 24—*"Enoch walked with God"*
Exodus 3: 6—*"Moses was afraid to look upon God."*
Exodus 19: 11—*"The Lord will come down in the sight of all the people upon mount Sinai."*
Exodus 24: 9-10—*"Then went up Moses, and Aaron, Nadab, and Abihu and seventy of the elders of Israel: And they saw the God of Israel."*
1 Kings 11: 9—*"his heart was turned from the Lord God of Israel which had appeared unto him twice"* (Solomon).
Revelation 1: 17—*"And when I saw him, I fell at his feet as dead. And he laid his right hand upon me"* (Preface to chapter says: John sees the Risen Lord).
Revelation 22: 4—*"And they shall see his face: and his name shall be in their foreheads."*

Book of Mormon Scriptures

2 Nephi 11: 3—*"And my brother, Jacob also has seen him as I have seen him"* (Nephi).
2 Nephi 2: 4—*"Thou has beheld in thy youth his glory"* (Lehi speaking to his son Jacob).
Alma 19: 13—*"For as sure as thou livest, behold, I have seen my Redeemer"* (Lamoni).
Ether 3: 13—*"behold the Lord showed himself unto him . . . therefore ye are brought back into my presence; therefore I show myself unto you"* (Christ appears to Brother of Jared).
Mormon 1: 15—*"And I, being fifteen years of age and being somewhat of a sober mind, therefore I was visited of the Lord, and tasted and knew of the goodness of Jesus"* (Mormon).
3 Nephi 11: 7—*"Behold my Beloved Son, in whom I am well pleased."*
3 Nephi 11: 8—*"They saw a Man descending out of heaven"*
3 Nephi 11: 15—*"and did see with their eyes and did feel with their hands and did know of*

a surety and did bear record,that it was he, of whom it was written by the prophets should come."

3 Nephi 11-27—These Chapters all tell of the appearance of Jesus Christ to Nephite people after His Resurrection in A.D. 34.

This appearance led to the Indians legend of the Great White Father.

Doctrine and Covenants Scriptures

SECTIONS:

35: 21—*"hear my voice, and shall see me"* (Joseph Smith and Sidney Rigdon).

50: 45—*"And the day cometh that you shall hear my voice, and see me, and know that I am"* (Joseph Smith).

76: 23—*"For we saw him even on the right hand of God"*

76: 117—*"To whom he grants this privilege of seeing and knowing for themselves"* (Joseph Smith and Sidney Rigdon).

110: 2—*We saw the Lord standing upon the pulpit"*

130: 3—*"The appearing of the Father and the Son . . . is a personal appearance"*

Pearl of Great Price Scriptures

Moses 1: 2—*"And he saw God face to face,"*

Moses 1: 11—*"eyes have beheld God . . . my spiritual eyes,"*

Moses 6: 39—*"fear came on all them . . . for he walked with God"*

Abraham 3: 11—*"I Abraham talked with the Lord face to face"*

Joseph Smith—History 1: 17—*"I saw two Personages whose brightness and glory defy all description"*

Jesus the Christ, (James E. Talmadge) Adam, Enoch, Noah, Abraham, and Moses saw God.

In addition to these references documenting the appearance of Deity there are many scriptures promising such appearances in the future . . .

Old and New Testaments

Job 19: 26—*" in my flesh shall I see God"*

Acts 7: 56—*"Behold I see the heavens opened, and the Son of man standing on the right hand of God"* (Stephen).

Hebrews 12: 14—*"Follow peace with all men and holiness without which no man shall see the Lord"* (Preface to chapter says—to see God, follow peace and holiness—Paul).

1 John 3: 2—*"when he shall appear, we shall be like him; for we shall see him as he is"* (John).

Doctrine and Covenants

SECTIONS:

84: 23—*"sanctify his people that they may behold the face of God"*

97: 16—*"pure in heart . . . shall see God"*

93: 1—*"shall see my face and know that I am"*

It was God, the Eternal Father, and His Beloved Son, Jesus Christ who had been crucified in Jerusalem, who appeared to the young boy Joseph. They had answered his humble prayer. Now he knew that he must not join any of the contending churches, but that the Lord would bring to earth again His own true Church.

When the light had departed, Joseph was naturally weary from the power of his spiritual experience; when he came to himself again, he was lying on his back, looking up into heaven. He soon recovered in some degree in order to return to his home.

Joseph was profoundly affected by the heavenly vision. In addition to being given the answer to his question about which church was right, he was told that his sins were forgiven, and that the fulness of the Gospel should at some future time be made known unto him. The effects of this experience influenced the Prophet throughout his life. In later years, he remembered its impact vividly: *"My soul was filled with love and for many days I could rejoice with great joy, and the Lord was with me."*

As with Moses, Abraham, and Enoch, Joseph had been filled with a spirit which made it possible for him to endure the presence of God. The young man that left the grove that day was hardly the same young man who entered it. His life thereafter was absolutely changed. He had sure knowledge of the reality and attributes of God not possessed by any other mortal. Joseph had been given those insights into the nature and purpose of God based upon the experiences of his own eyes and ears.

Orson Pratt later explained: "One minute of instruction from personages clothed with the glory of God, coming down from the eternal worlds, is worth more than all the volumes that were written by uninspired men." Joseph also had keen insights into the design and purposes of God in respect to the reestablishment of the true church and the leading role he was to play in that great drama.

When Joseph entered his home that day, he leaned against the fireplace. His mother, noting his pale color, asked what the matter was. Joseph replied: *"I am well enough off . . . I have learned for myself that Presbyterianism is not true"* (Joseph Smith—History 1: 20).

Then Joseph related his remarkable vision to his parents and brothers and sisters, since he had always conferred with them honestly on all things, they believed him. His mother simply stated that Joseph had always been a truthful boy.

Scholars have commented that Joseph Smith's account of the First Vision is the only surviving record of both the Father and the Son appearing and speaking to man. Elder James E. Faust, a modern Apostle and now a member of the First Presidency of The Church of Jesus Christ of Latter-day Saints said: "it is possibly the most singular event to occur on the earth since the Resurrection." Certainly, it is the basis for all the work Joseph Smith did. A later Prophet, Spencer W. Kimball, expressed it most powerfully: "Nothing short of this total vision to Joseph could have served the purposes to clear away the mists [darkness] of centuries. Merely an impression, a hidden voice, a dream could have dispelled the old vagaries [uncertainties] and misconceptions. The God of these worlds and the Son of God, the Redeemer, our Savior, in person, attended this boy. He saw the living God. He saw the living Christ. Of all the great events of the century, none compared with the First Vision of Joseph Smith."

It is important to hear some of the personal testimony of Joseph Smith: *"However, it was nevertheless a fact that I had beheld a vision, I have thought since, that I felt much like Paul, when he made his defense before King Agrippa, and related the account of the vision he had when he saw a light and heard a voice; but still there were but a few who believed him; some said he was dishonest, others said he was mad; and he was ridi-*

culed and reviled. But all this did not destroy the reality of his vision. He had seen a vision, he knew he had, and all the persecution under heaven could not make it otherwise; and though they should persecute him unto death, yet he knew, and would know to his latest breath, that he had both seen a light and heard a voice speaking unto him, and all the world could not make him think or believe otherwise.

So it was with me. I had actually seen a light, and in the midst of that light, I saw two Personages, and they did in reality speak to me; and though I was hated and persecuted for saying that I had seen a vision, yet it was true; and while they were persecuting me, reviling me, and speaking all manner of evil against me falsely for so saying, I was led to say in my heart: Why persecute me for telling the truth? I have actually seen a vision; and who am I that I can understand God, or why does the world think to make me deny what I have actually seen? For I had seen a vision; I knew it, and I knew that God knew it, and I could not deny it, neither dared I do it; at least I knew that by so doing I would offend God, and come under condemnation" (Joseph Smith—History 1: 24-25).

On the great problem that had previously confused him, Joseph Smith's mind was now settled. He joined none of the existing churches that had sought his interest. More importantly, he had learned that the promise of James in the New Testament was true: One who lacked wisdom might ask of God, and receive, and not be upbraided (rebuked).

HOW OFTEN DO WE ASK OF GOD FOR GUIDANCE AND DIRECTION?

You're probably wondering why Joseph visited so many churches in search of the right church. Was the right church not to be found at that time? Why didn't he follow his mother and a few of the Smith children and join the Presbyterian Church?

Most Christian people believe all churches that preach about Jesus Christ are good, true and right, never questioning their churches teachings. In most cases they are taught and believe that they can be saved, (resurrected) which is their understanding of exaltation. This is only partially true because their belief is based upon limited knowledge. Most church members follow the teachings of their spiritual leaders who teach from the Holy Bible mixed with their own personal interpretations.

When Jesus Christ was on this earth, He gave us a set of rules (commandments) to live by, teaching us that earth life was our big test. If we did well enough, (notwithstanding we wouldn't find out until judgment day), we could return to live with God and Jesus Christ in Their kingdom. Our families are an important part of that test and plan. They too, have to be tested and judged before we can be reunited with them as a family. Again, most Christians believe that as long as they believe in Jesus Christ, they are saved. Nevertheless, **faith without works is dead.**

Jesus Christ and the Twelve Apostles left man with the pure teachings of the Gospel of Jesus Christ. Then man began changing the pure teachings to their own way of thinking, and to their own devices. Of course, the leaders of those people thought their ideas were better, more acceptable and appropriate than those of Jesus Christ. Man began making radical changes in the true Gospel of Jesus Christ with their own set of religious rules. And so the world entered the period of time called the "Dark Ages."

* * *

Even though we're rarely as hateful to one another in these days as in past times, we still live in a state of confusion . . . even greater confusion when it comes to God the Father and Jesus Christ with the direction They want us to follow for our Salvation and Exaltation. We mustn't forget—man will always have his free agency, because that power to choose is a *gift* from God.

And so, we recognize that numerous Christian denominations are generally following their Bible and the personal interpretations made from their Bible by their church leaders, in addition to all the manmade rules passed down from generation to generation. We also find many charismatic religious leaders in this day, being very bright, articulate and highly intellectual, having developed their own special collection of preferred scriptures to back up their personalized religious beliefs and convictions.

Different churches have different degrees of truth about God and Jesus Christ. Since researching all that has been presented to me, in addition to fasting, prayer and personal revelation, I have found that there that there is only one Church on the face of the earth, not better than any other church, but the Church with all of the revealed truth—that being: **The Church of Jesus Christ of Latter-day Saints.**

There is a very important scripture in the New Testament in the Book of Ephesians, chapter four, verse five: *"One Lord, one faith, one baptism,"*—not ten, not a 100, and certainly not 1,000—just one true church with all the revealed truth. This is the Church Joseph was searching for and did subsequently find, the one he was chosen by God and Jesus Christ in these latter days to restore and lead.

Since the Lord has blessed us with free agency, we have the right and privilege to believe or not believe as we so choose. That's what the war in heaven was fought over. God's plan of free agency is ours through Jesus Christ; therefore, we're held responsible by the Lord for the decisions we make. There's no free ride to God's kingdom.

* * *

Most people take for granted their religious beliefs as part of the birth process. Their belief's passed down from one generation to another are often accepted without question. How many times throughout my life have I heard: "Born a Jew, Die a Jew," or "Born a Catholic, Die a Catholic." People in general, seem to be settled in their ways unless something unique, or catastrophic happens to upset their usual routine, and increase their interest in exploring further or finding new truths to help live a better, more spiritual, more productive life.

When people talk about belief in Jesus Christ and being saved, they are generally not aware or understand that **"saved" means being "Resurrected"** which is promised to every human being who ever lived or will live upon this earth, through the Atonement of Jesus Christ.

As for "Exaltation," people have to earn this blessing by passing the all-important earth test, that of being obedient to the God's commandments. It never cease to amaze me that many of us in our society believe that confessing one's sins fairly regularly, let's us "off the hook" with God, and that nothing else is required for forgiveness. It's true that God does forgive our sins, if true repentance is sincere and a pledge is made not to repeat the sin again. More times than not, and being human those of us who sin usually repeat the sin. Nevertheless, God will not give up on us because He loves us, and will help us overcome our weaknesses, if we but try harder. This isn't a game we're playing with the Lord because if we think so, we're the big losers. He's seriously serious about helping us to become worthy enough to return to His presence one day. For those of us who don't take the Lord at His word, will *all* be in for a rude awakening. When we go before the Lord on Judgment Day—surely everyone will, He will read from the Book of Life, how well we did or didn't do during their earth life and where we will go from that point.

With the Second Coming of the Lord just around the corner, we need to get our lives in order for ourselves as well as for the Lord. We will *all* be judged. No one is exempt from reporting on how we handled our earth experiences. It's important to recognize that faith *with* works is what we need to accomplish our spiritual goals.

When we lived in the pre-earth life with God the Father and Jesus Christ, there was no such thing as different religions. We were all spirit children of a loving Heavenly Father. Then we came to earth and were given a body of flesh and bones, to live and be tested, to raise families if possible.

When we leave this earth existence, we will go to a place—be it called Paradise or the Spirit Prison, whichever we're assigned. There will be no separate denominations in that sphere. There—we are all brothers and sisters under one God the Father, and Jesus Christ, the Messiah, the Savior and Redeemer of the world.

Chapter 3

Who was that Special Messenger sent from God? "Moroni"—was His Name.

The Gold Plates—a Sacred Record

Satan's Plan—Destroy Joseph Smith and the Plates

When Joseph Smith, then but a boy in his fifteenth year, en tered that sacred grove to seek an answer to his spiritual question: *"which of all the religious sects was right,"* he carried with him the unpredictable doctrines of the day as to the personality of God. He thought that God was a three-in-one Spirit that filled the immensity of space, intangible, uncreated, immaterial, without body, parts, or passions, concepts universally taught in Christianity at the time.

"The Father has a body of flesh and bones as tangible as man's; the Son also; but the Holy Ghost has not a body of flesh and bones, but is a personage of Spirit. Were it not so, the Holy Ghost could not dwell in us" (Doctrine & Covenants 130: 22).

When Joseph returned from the grove, he had a sure knowledge of the true characteristics of God and Jesus Christ—for his eyes had seen them; and the Holy Ghost (whose power he had felt on that sacred occasion) had borne record to his soul that the Father and the Son were two glorified Personages in the express image of each other—two separate and distinct Personages always individual, but one in purpose, one in-spirit.

The First Vision was the core event in the rise of the kingdom of God on the earth in the last days. Joseph Smith, although only an uneducated youth, learned profound truths in that vision that have become the foundation of the faith of the Latter-day Saints. He had actually seen and spoken with God the Father and the Son, Jesus Christ. Therefore, he learned that the promise in James chapter one verse five is true. God *will* answer sincere prayer of inquiry and not chastise. To Joseph, God became an approachable reality, a vital source of truth and a loving Heavenly Father. Joseph Smith's belief in the reality of God was no longer a matter of faith; it was based upon personal experience. He was qualified, as was the Apostle Peter, to be a witness chosen by God and commanded to preach and testify of Jesus Christ (Acts 10: 39-43). He could also testify that the Father and the Son were separate and distinct glorious beings in whose literal image man is made.

Joseph Smith now also knew of the reality of Satan, a being who possessed tremendous power, who was a foe determined to destroy the work of God. Satan failed in the Sacred Grove, but the conflict had just begun. Joseph would fight many battles with this adversary to righteousness before his work on earth was done. Additionally, the Lord's answer to Joseph's question about which church was true was a sweeping indictment of Nineteenth-Century Christianity, for no church then on earth had divine approval. The Savior taught Joseph that the existing churches: *"teach for doctrines the commandments of men"* (Joseph Smith—History 1: 19).

If this inexperienced boy had been trying to perpetrate a spiritual fraud by inventing some great spiritual experience, he could never have invented a story that would strike so irreconcilably at the heart of all Christian creeds. In an attempt to deceive, he might have said that an angel appeared or that some other miraculous event transpired. Never would it have occurred to him to rock the whole religious foundation of the Christian world with such a startling claim as the one he did make. But, miracle of miracles, all those willing to attain greater spiritual enlightenment in Joseph's day as well as ours have discovered that Joseph's new revelation about God's personality is the same truth to which all the prophets bear record.

Life for Joseph Smith was never the same once he told the story of his vision. For one thing, that remarkable experience left an unforgettable, lasting impression upon his sensitive nature. The knowledge he had received placed him in a unique position, yet his manner of living did not immediately change. His daily life was not greatly different from that of any other ordinary farm boy of his day, except he was often referred to as a dreamer, and became the "whipping boy" of the unbelievers, scoffers, and doubters.

The belief and acceptance with which Joseph's family received the account of his vision was totally different from the rude and unbelieving reception given outside the Smith family circle. Especially shocking to young Joseph was the manner in which his experience was rejected, defiled and belittled by the very man who had urged him to seek God for an answer to the question: *"Which church shall I join?"* It was only natural that Joseph went looking for Reverend Lane to tell him of the wonderful news, and to confide in him the miraculous results that occurred when Joseph had followed the direction given in the minister's sermon. Instead of commending the young man for his faith and rejoicing with him in the amazing results of his prayer, the minister scoffed at his story. Joseph said: *"he treated my communication not only lightly, but with great contempt, saying, it was all of the devil, that there were no such things as visions or revelation in these days; that all such things had ceased with the apostles, and that there would never be any more of them"* (Joseph Smith—History 1: 21).

Under normal circumstances, one would surmise that the boy's story might have been ignored or that an effort might have been made to change his thinking had the Reverend Lane and others believed that he was either deluded or was deliberately telling a lie. Certainly, this would not have been the first time in which they were confronted with a person who told an unimaginable or hard-to-believe story. But for some reason, they seemed to go out of their way to attack and ridicule this young man. Joseph did not react in the same manner to those who turned against him. *"My soul was filled with love,"* he recorded: *"and for many days I could rejoice with great joy and the Lord was with me."* As he thought about their reactions, he was bewildered and troubled: As Joseph said: *"It caused me serious reflection then, and often has since, how very strange it was that an obscure boy, of a little over fourteen years of age, and one, too, who was doomed to the necessity of obtaining a scanty maintenance by his daily labor, should be thought a character of sufficient importance to attract the attention of the great ones of the most popular sects of the day, and in a manner to create in them a spirit of the most bitter persecution and reviling"* (Joseph Smith—History 1: 23). And this is Joseph's own interpretation of these events: *"It seems as though the adversary was aware, at a very early period of my life, that I was destined to become a disturber and a troublemaker of his kingdom; else why should the powers of darkness combine against me? Why the opposition and persecution that arose against me, almost in my infancy?"* (*History of the Church,* 1: 6).

While it is true that the boy who left the grove that spring morning in 1820 was never quite the same thereafter, it is equally true that he was just a fourteen-year-old youngster, and had much seasoning and maturing ahead of him. One cannot expect that a single spiritual experience would have suddenly transformed Joseph into a state of perfection.

Even Jesus Christ the Only Begotten Son, learned obedience and qualified for His great mission *"by the things which he suffered"* (Hebrews 5: 8).

So it was that after the profound experience Joseph had in the grove with God the Father and Jesus Christ, he continued to fill his normal role in the family of Joseph and Lucy Mack Smith. He still performed the menial but necessary tasks of a farm boy, sometimes in the employ of neighboring farmers. Joseph considered himself to be both imperfect and vulnerable with many things to learn before he would be qualified to fill the special mission to which he had been called. He was still subject to the physical, emotional, and mental pressures of that day to which all young men were subject. Those who knew him (those of his own age) describe him as a strong, active boy of cheerful disposition, who enjoyed wrestling and other sports.

Still, this was one of the most difficult periods in Joseph's life. He had been specially favored of the Lord with an experience the likes of which had not been known *for centuries*, (not since the Garden of Eden) one that had marked him as a person destined for a special and significant work. Yet, he had neither the means nor ability to lift himself out of obscurity and the difficult circumstances in which he then lived. What was even worse, he found that the more he related his remarkable experience outside the Smith family circle, the more bitter criticism, and even persecution was leveled at him.

Many years later, when he recorded the events of that trying period, he wrote about his frustration, his disappointment, resentment and isolation. He complained that he was: *"persecuted by those who ought to have been my friends, and to have treated me kindly, and if they supposed me to be deluded, to have endeavored in a proper and affectionate manner to have reclaimed me."*

Therefore, feeling abandoned and rejected and lacking the experience and maturity that would have enabled him to ignore these rejections or to turn them to his advantage, Joseph committed minor indiscretions that caused him great remorse, and ultimately led him again to seek guidance from the Lord. He wrote: *"I was left to all kinds of temptations; and mingling with all kinds of society. I frequently fell into many foolish errors, and displaying the weakness of youth, and the foibles* [imperfections] *of human nature; which, I was sorry to say, led me into divers temptations, offensive in the sight of God"* (*History of the Church,* 1: 9). To reject any implication that he had committed any especially shameful or wicked sins, he hastened to add: *"In making this confession, no one need to suppose I'm guilty of any great or malignant* [harmful] *sins. A disposition to commit such was never in my nature"* (*History of the Church,* 1: 9). He then went on to define his transgression as a spirit of "levity," (fun-loving) which caused him, on occasion, to be associated with "jovial, festive company," not consistent with that character which ought to be maintained by one who was called of God as he had been. In his own mind, Joseph had been convicted of hypocrisy because of the differences between his conduct and the profound nature and implication of the heavenly vision he had beheld. In an attempt to rid himself of these feelings of unworthiness and also to learn his status before God, Joseph therefore decided to make a second attempt to directly appeal for God's special blessing.

In 1822, Joseph had begun helping his older brother, Alvin, build a new frame house for the family. By September of 1823, it was two stories high, but without a roof. The family continued to live in their small log house, where late in the evening on Sunday, 21 September 1823, seventeen-year-old Joseph had retired for the night. Three and one-half years had elapsed since Joseph's vision in the grove at Palmyra. His second experience also came by obedience to the spiritual law of prayer. Often, Joseph had wondered why the heavens remained silent for so long—why the Lord had not made clear His purpose in regard to him. Now, on the evening of the 21st of September 1823, Joseph came to the realization that the reason for that silence was within himself.

The Savior, while living in the flesh upon the earth, had instructed His followers: *"Ask, and it shall be given you; seek, and ye shall find; knock, and it shall be opened unto you: For everyone that asketh, receiveth; and he that seeketh, findeth; and to him that knocketh it shall be opened"* (Matthew 7: 7-8). For three and one-half years, he had failed to properly knock at the door of God. He had done so once and the promise had not failed; he would do it again.

Concerned about his standing before the Lord, Joseph earnestly prayed for forgiveness of his sins. He was confident that he would again receive a divine manifestation. As he was in the act of appealing to God through prayer for forgiveness of his *"sins and follies"* and to learn his *"state and standing before Him,"* **he saw a light appear in his room,** which continued to increase until it was *"lighter than at noonday."* **Then a personage appeared at his bedside *"standing in the air, for his feet did not touch the floor"*** (Joseph Smith—History 1: 29-30). The messenger who stood at his bedside was in partial fulfillment of the great prophecy of John the Apostle: *"And I saw another angel fly in the midst of heaven, having the everlasting gospel to preach unto them that dwell on the earth, and to every nation, and kindred, and tongue, and people, Saying with a loud voice, Fear God, and give glory to him; for the hour of his judgment is come: and worship him that made* *heaven, and earth, and the sea, and the fountains of waters"* (Revelation 14: 6-7).

Earlier, when the Father and the Son appeared to him, Joseph made no attempt to describe Their appearance. But after this second manifestation he took the time to paint a word picture of this new visitor. Joseph said: ***"He had on a loose robe of the most exquisite whiteness.*** *It was a whiteness beyond anything earthly he had ever seen; nor do I believe that anything earthly could be made to appear so exceedingly white and brilliant. His hands were naked, and his arms also, a little above the wrists; so also were his feet naked, as were his legs, a little above the ankles. His head and neck were also bare"* (Joseph Smith—History 1: 31).

Not only was his robe exceedingly white, but his whole person was glorious beyond description, and his countenance truly like lighting. The room was intensely lit, but not so bright as immediately around his person. When Joseph first looked upon him, he was afraid, but the fear soon left him.

He called Joseph by name, said that he was a messenger sent from the presence of God, and introduced himself as **Moroni,** a prophet who had lived on the American continent. As holder of the keys of the *"stick of Ephraim"* (Doctrine & Covenants 27: 5), **Moroni came at the appointed hour to reveal the existence of a record written on gold plates** which had lain hidden in the ground for fourteen centuries. The record was *"an account of the former inhabitants of this continent. He also said that the fulness of the everlasting Gospel was contained in it, as delivered by the Savior to the ancient inhabitants"* (Joseph Smith—History 1: 34). Joseph was to translate the record and publish it. God had this and other works for Joseph to do, and because of this, his name should be had for good and evil among all nations, kindreds and tongues, meaning that both good and evil would be spoken of him among all people.

Moroni recited several passages from the Bible quoting prophets such as Malachi, Isaiah, Joel, and Peter concerning the preparations to be made in the last days for the Millennial (1,000 year) reign of Jesus Christ. **This began the instruction and direction of Joseph Smith by Moroni.** Moroni explained to Joseph about the book written on gold plates that contained: *"the fulness of the everlasting Gospel"* and that deposited with the book was a Urim and Thummim—two stones in silver bows fastened to a breastplate. Joseph was informed that the possession and use of these were what qualified a man to be a "seer" in ancient times, and they had been prepared for the purpose of translating the inscriptions on the gold plates.

Additionally, Moroni imparted to Joseph the knowledge that the concluding scenes of the earth's drama were near at hand, that they would be accompanied by disastrous events and preceded by the Restoration of the Priesthood and the true Church, and that this Restoration would produce a marvelous change in the attitudes and conduct of men. Joseph learned that men's hearts could be and would be turned toward their departed families, and that there would be demonstrated among the living, a marvelous outpouring of the Spirit, with dreams and visions and other spiritual signs that would become widely known among both the old and the young. **Joseph received additional instructions concerning the care of the plates and when they would ultimately be delivered into Joseph's possession.** There was opened to his understanding a vision of the precise place the plates were then deposited. He was directed that when he obtained the plates, he was to show them to no one except when commanded. This ended the interview. The light in the room commenced to gather around the visitor and a passageway opened up into heaven through which Moroni ascended until he disappeared from view, and the room was again left dark except just around him.

As Joseph lay reflecting upon the singularity of his experience, his room again was filled with light and the heavenly personage reappeared, repeating exactly what he had said during the first visit, except that he also described the fearful judgments that were soon to be carried out upon the earth and its inhabitants, accompanied by *"famine, sword, and pestilence."* Following his ascension after the second visit, the messenger appeared still a third time and recounted the entire instruction again without variation, except that he cautioned Joseph against any selfish motive or intention when he obtained the plates.

So important was Moroni's message and the need to impress it on the mind of the young Prophet, that the substance of Moroni's three visits *bear repeating*. **During the first visit, Joseph saw in a vision the location of the plates.** They were buried in a hillside about three miles from his home. In the second visit, Joseph was told of judgments which were coming upon the earth. At the end of the third visit, Moroni warned Joseph that Satan would try to tempt him to get the plates for their temporal value because of his family's poverty. Moroni directed the seventeen-year-old Joseph that he was to have only one purpose for obtaining the plates, and that was to glorify God. Only one motive should influence him, and that was to build God's kingdom. **Through subsequent events, the Prophet learned why Moroni had given such warnings and directions.** Joseph's visits with Moroni occupied most of the night. At the end of Moroni's third visit he heard a rooster crow. Indeed, a new day of spiritual light was about to dawn. Isaiah spoke of this day as a time when a *"marvelous work and a wonder"* would come forth (Isaiah 29: 14).

That morning, Joseph went to work as usual with his father and brothers in the field. Lack of sleep and having been in the presence of a glorified, resurrected being most of the night had weakened him so that he had trouble working. Noticing his son's condition and thinking he was ill, Joseph's father told him to go back to the house. On the way home, Joseph collapsed. The next thing he knew, there was someone calling him by name. As he became aware of his surroundings, to his surprise, **Moroni again stood before him.** Moroni then repeated the same message he had given to Joseph the night before, and further commanded him to inform his father of the vision and commandments he had received. Obedient to that command, Joseph returned to the field and told his father everything. Without hesitation, Joseph Sr. assured his son that it was from God and instructed him to do as he had been commanded.

The absolute confidence Joseph Sr. expressed in his seventeen-year-old son could likely be traced back to his own spiritual experiences as well as the oft-repeated prediction of his own father, Asael Smith, to the effect that a great Prophet would be born in his line. Whatever the reason, Joseph Smith Sr. did not ever question his son's truthfulness. He accepteded Joseph Jr.'s leadership and direction in many things as if his son were his elder. This tendency to defer to young Joseph was evidenced also by his mother, older brothers, and sister. Their submissiveness and respect, void of any hint of inferiority or jealousy, was founded on a recognition that their son and brother was an agent through whom the Almighty had seen fit to reveal His will.

Joseph left his father in the field and went to the place where the messenger had told him the plates were deposited. Because of the distinctiveness of the vision which he had concerning it, he knew the place the instant that he arrived. **Near the top of the hill, Joseph found a large stone,** "thick and rounding in the middle on the upper side, and thinner towards the edges." It was the lid of a stone box. Eagerly, he removed the earth so that he could get a lever under the edge. **One can imagine his excitement** as he opened the box. There, having lain hidden for centuries, were the plates (a book of gold leaves bound together with three rings), the Urim and Thummim, the breastplate and the two stones set in silver bows just as Moroni had explained. The box in which they were laid had been formed by stones laid together in some kind of cement. In the bottom of the box were laid two stones crossways of the box, and on these stones lay the plates and the other things with them (Joseph Smith—History 1: 50-52).

While in mortality, Moroni had prophesied that the plates could not be used for temporal gain because of the commandment of God, but would one day be of *"great worth"* to future generations in bringing them to a knowledge of God (Mormon 8: 14-15).

As Joseph approached the Hill Cumorah, he had thoughts about the poverty of his family and the possibility that the plates or the popularity of the translation would produce enough wealth to *"raise him above a level with the common earthly fortunes of his fellow men, and relieve his family from want."* (Oliver Cowdery, *Messenger and Advocate,* July 1835). When he reached down for the plates, he received a shock like that produced by electricity, that rendered his arm powerless. Twice more he tried with the same result—only each time the shock seemed harder than before. In frustration he cried out: *"Why can I not secure this book?"* Moroni appeared and told him it was because he had not kept the commandments but had yielded to the temptations of Satan to acquire the plates for riches instead of having his eye single to the glory of God as he had been commanded (Oliver Cowdery, *Messenger and Advocate,* Oct. 1835, p. 198).

In a state of repentance, Joseph humbly sought the Lord in prayer and was filled with the Spirit. A vision was opened to him, and the *"glory of the Lord shone round about and rested upon him . . . He beheld the prince of darkness . . . The heavenly messenger Moroni said: 'All this is shown, the good and the evil, the holy and impure, the glory of God and the power of darkness, that you may know hereafter the two powers and never be influenced or overcome by that wicked one. You now see why you could not secure this record; that the commandment was strict, and that if ever these most sacred things are obtained, they must be by prayer and faithfulness in obeying the Lord. They are not deposited here for the sake of accumulating gain and wealth for the glory of this world: they were sealed by the prayer of faith, and because of the knowledge which they contain, they are of no worth among the children of men, only for their knowledge."* Moroni concluded by warning Joseph that he would not be allowed to obtain the plates *"until he had learned to keep the commandments of God—not only till he was willing but able to do it."*

"The following evening when the family was altogether, Joseph made known to them all that he had communicated to his father in the field and also of his finding the record, as well as what passed between him and the messenger while he was at the place where the plates were deposited" (Lucy Mack Smith, *History of Joseph Smith by His Mother,* p. 81).

One must prepare and be prepared in order to do the work of God. Mere willingness is not enough. The angel (messenger) made this perfectly clear to Joseph. **That he must spend four years in preparation**—years of vigorous study, of living the commandments of God, of receiving instruction from this glorious personage who would meet him annually at the same location. *"Accordingly,"* said the Prophet, *"as I had been commanded, I went at the end of each year, and at each time, I found the same messenger there, and received instruction and intelligence from him at each of our interviews, respecting what the Lord was going to do, and how, and in what manner His kingdom was to be conducted in the last days"* (*History of the Church,* 1: 16).

When Joseph first climbed this peculiar rising ground, it was to him a mere hill, one of many in the vicinity; but his return was from "Cumorah," a sacred shrine, which held the secrets of a once-great people, and the glorious message of Christ to all the world.

Because sharing the experience of his First Vision in 1820 with some of his trusted friends outside the family circle had brought a storm of opposition, disapproval, and abuse, he did not reveal Moroni's visits to anyone outside his immediate family. He made a strong appeal to them that they were not to tell others. He was concerned that an untimely exposure and disclosure of what had happened and what was to come in the not-too-distant future, would seriously delay, if not frustrate and hinder, his mission.

Joseph had great confidence in his family, however, and felt free to tell them in detail what had happened. In the evening of the day when he was visited by Moroni in the field, he related to them the marvelous events of the preceding twenty-four hours. His mother, Lucy, kept an account of the family council where Joseph related these sacred events: "We were all seated, and Joseph began telling us of the great and glorious things which God had revealed to him; but before proceeding, he first counseled us not to discuss those things that he was about to spell out to us, out of the family unit. Since most of the world was so wicked, sinful and naughty, that when they came to a knowledge of these things, they would try to take our lives; and that when we would obtain the plates, our names would be cast out as evil and ungodly by all the people. Therefore, it is necessary and important to restrict and suppress these things as much as possible, until the time will come for them to go forth to all the world.

"After giving us this charge, he proceeded to relate further matters concerning the work which he was appointed to do, and we received from him" (Lucy Mack Smith, *History of Joseph Smith by His Mother,* p. 82).

Later, as further instructions were given, the young Prophet shared them with his family insofar as he was permitted to do so. Lucy wrote: "I presume our family presented an aspect as singular as any that ever lived upon the face of the earth, all seated in a circle—father, mother, sons and daughters—and giving the most profound attention to a boy, almost eighteen-years-of-age, who had never read the Bible through in his life . . .

"During our evening conversations, Joseph would, on occasion, give us some of the most amusing narratives that could be imagined. He would describe the ancient inhabitants of this continent, their dress, mode of traveling, and the animals upon which they rode; their cities, their buildings, with every particular; their mode of warfare; and also their religious worship. This he would do with much ease, seemingly, as if he had spent his whole life among them" (Lucy Mack Smith, *History of Joseph Smith by His Mother,* pp. 82-83).

Joseph, at his young age, had vast knowledge of past and future events and the unseen world, which was attributable to his sensitive, spiritual nature. At the time of Moroni's first visits, such a clear vision of the Hill Cumorah was opened in the Prophet's mind that he instantly recognized the place when he later walked to it. Subsequent events proved that this visionary gift applied to things past, present, and future.

* * *

Throughout this book, we've spoken often about **visions** and what they mean to us, and so, let's clearly define the word.

Through supernatural means, **by the power of the Holy Ghost,** devout, faithful, God-loving people are permitted to have visions and to see within the veil. They are enabled to see spiritual personages and to view scenes hidden from ordinary sight. These visions are gifts of the Spirit (Seventh Article of Faith).

They come by faith and vanish when faith dies (1 Samuel 3: 1; Isaiah 29: 9-14). Therefore, they stand as an evidence of the divinity of the Lord's work in any age. If the Lord is giving visions and revelations to a people, such a group constitutes the people of God. If visions and revelations are not being received by any church or people, then that group is not the Lord's people. By this test, the identity of the true Church is known (Moroni 7: 30-38).

Actual personages from the unseen world frequently appear to mortals in visions. In the First Vision, the Prophet beheld and conversed with the Father and the Son (Joseph Smith—History 1: 15-20).

"The Lord came unto Abram in a vision," promised him seed (Genesis 15: 1), and made covenant with him (Genesis 17: 2). Similarly: *"God spake unto Israel in the visions of the night,"* authorizing him *"to go down into Egypt"* (Genesis 46: 1-4). Saul, later Paul the Apostle, saw the risen Lord in vision (Acts 9: 1-9; 26: 12-19), even as the weeping women at the empty tomb saw *"a vision of angels"* saying their Lord had risen from the dead (Luke 24: 1-23). Moses and Elias personally appeared on the Mount of Transfiguration where they were seen by Peter, James, and John in vision (Matthew 17: 1-9).

Power is given to the Lord's prophets to see and converse with heavenly beings in vision, though such divine personages are not, at the time, in the immediate and personal presence of the one receiving the vision. Being *"overcome with the Spirit,"* Lehi for instance, *"was carried away in a vision, even that he saw the heavens open, and he thought he saw God sitting upon his throne, surrounded with numberless concourses of angels in the attitude of singing and praising their God"* (1 Nephi 1: 8). Joseph Smith and Sidney Rigdon *"beheld the glory of the Son, on the right hand of the Father, and received of his fulness; And saw the holy angels, and them who are sanctified before his throne, worshiping God, and the Lamb, who worship him forever and ever"* (Doctrine & Covenants 76: 20-21).

Stephen saw saying: *"Behold I see the heavens opened, and the Son of man standing on the right hand of God"* (Acts 7: 51-56). In his glorious vision of the celestial world, given January 21, 1836, the Prophet also saw *"the blazing throne of God, whereon was seated the Father and the Son"* (*Teachings of the Prophet Joseph Smith,* p. 107).

By visions, the Lord reveals past, present, and future events. Nephi saw in vision the destruction of Jerusalem after he and his people had left that wicked city (2 Nephi 1: 4). Moroni opened to the view of the Prophet the hiding place of the plates in Cumorah (Joseph Smith—History 1: 42). Daniel foresaw the great gathering at Adam-ondi-Ahman (Daniel 7: 9-14), and Ezekiel saw the resurrection of the house of Israel (Ezekiel 37: 1-10). The kingdoms of glory in the eternal worlds were opened to the view of the Prophet (Doctrine & Covenants 76).

Images, figures, and symbolical representations are often portrayed in visions as means of conveying gospel truths. Visions serve the Lord's purposes in preparing men for salvation. By them, knowledge is revealed, conversions are made, the Gospel message is spread abroad, the Church organization is perfected, and righteousness is increased in the hearts of men. And visions are to increase and abound in the last days, for the Lord has promised to pour out His *"spirit upon all flesh,"* so that *"old men shall dream dreams,"* and *"young men shall see visions"* (Joel 2: 28-32).

And what about dreams? An inspired dream is a vision given to a person while he sleeps. *"Behold, I have dreamed a dream; or, in other words I have seen a vision,"* Lehi said (1 Nephi 8: 2). All inspired dreams are visions, but all visions are not dreams. Visions are received in hours of wakefulness or of sleep and in some cases when the recipient has passed into a trance; it is only when the vision occurs during sleep that it is termed a dream (Isaiah 29: 7; Daniel 2: 7; 1 Nephi 1: 16; Alma 30: 28).

As with other visions, inspired dreams foretell future events; (Genesis 37: 5; 40: 5; 8; 41: 15), the Lord appears to men in dreams; (Genesis 28: 10-22; 31: 24; 1 Kings 35; 1 Nephi 2: 1-2; 3: 2), angels appear and minister to faithful persons in their dreams; (Genesis 31: 11; Matthew 1: 20; 2: 13, 19), prophetic warnings are given by this means; (Ether 9: 3) and symbolic representations portrayed in dreams teach marvelous truths (1 Nephi 8; 9; 10; 15: 21). Inspired dreams are the fruits of faith; they are not given to apostate people (1 Samuel 28: 6, 15).

How does God communicate with us (and He certainly does, *if* we seek Him). There are two ways. The first is that God speaks to the world—to all His children—through His prophets only—by way of visions, revelations, and dreams. The second is we are given the opportunity to receive personal revelations, dreams, and visions for our own lives only, and for no one else. But how do we know whether the personal revelations, visions, and dreams come from God and Jesus Christ, or from Satan? It's easy to be fooled and misled because Satan is the great deceiver. And yet, through prayer, fasting, and obedience to the commandments of God, and the chances are we cannot be fooled, we can know we are going in the right direction. We just have to get our priorities straight, and we'll become winners.

Satan is not a dummy. He knows all

about God, but does not know the mind and will of God, and he is not stronger than God. He lived with us and God in the pre-earth life as a Son of the Morning (Lucifer). He fought bitterly against God's plan of free agency. He wanted everything and everyone controlled, and he greatly desired to take the glory for himself and not give it to God. For this reason, he and his followers who believed in his way (one-third of all spirit children) joined with Satan and were cast out from the presence of God. Satan and his followers came to earth without bodies, and that's what makes them so dangerous, because spirits cannot be seen. Satan has great knowledge, but has not the power of God. And Satan's plan is to get us off God's track which leads to salvation, resurrection, and exaltation. Satan *cannot* force us to do anything, he cannot read our thoughts either, but he has the power of suggestion, the power to plant seeds of destruction in our lives, through fears and nightmares, if we allow him. We must always remember that Satan is the great deceiver, but God is Almighty, all powerful, Jesus Christ is the great Deliverer, and the great Redeemer.

* * *

It was Joseph's visionary qualities and his ability to communicate with beings from the unseen world that distinguished him from all others in his day. By this process, he acquired the knowledge that empowered him to fulfill his prophetic role. Especially during the years 1823 to 1827, he was instructed through revelation by divine beings,and prepared for the day when the sacred record would be delivered to him.

Joseph's unique gifts did not relieve him of the pressures of work nor the pressures of daily cares. Therefore, while he was often lifted to great spiritual heights, he was constantly confronted with the hard realities of life.

A prophet, all things being considered, is a human being like any one of us. He must eat and sleep—he must seek warmth and shelter—which also means he is subject to long hours of physical labor. He is subject to the same laws, exposed to the same pains, and governed by the same passions. His fitness to be an instrument in God's hands is not a gift from the Eternal, but a result of his growth from within.

Between Moroni's first appearance, and the time Joseph received the plates, several significant events occurred. In November 1823, tragedy struck the Smith home. Alvin, Joseph's oldest brother, became ill; Father Smith was unable to find their family physician. The doctor who finally came, administered calomel (mercurous chloride), a laxative, which at the time was used as a remedy for many ailments. Unfortunately, the medicine settled in Alvin's stomach, creating great suffering. He died after four days of illness on November 19, 1823. When his death seemed imminent, Alvin asked that each of his brothers and sisters be brought to his bedside. Since he was then a mature man of twenty-five, he seemed to them more of a second father than an elder brother, and he acted toward them like a father, giving each fatherly instruction. He asked Hyrum to finish the house he, Alvin, had started. The eldest daughter, Sophronia, was called upon to care for her parents. Alvin was a faithful and serious young man, and Joseph idolized him. Joseph saw in him a simple, open-hearted person who lived an upright life. Alvin loved Joseph too, and was greatly interested in the sacred record. He counseled Joseph: "I want you to be a good boy, and do everything that lies in your power to obtain the record. Be faithful in receiving instruction, and in keeping every commandment that is given you" (Lucy Mack Smith, *History of Joseph Smith by His Mother,* p. 87). Alvin gave the other children specific instructions except for the baby, Lucy, who clung to Alvin, calling out, "Amby, Amby," her infant version of her brother's name. After kissing her, Alvin requested that she be taken away, for he feared that his breath offended her. This final scene having been acted out, Alvin declared, "I can now breathe out my life as calmly as a clock," and according to his mother, "immediately closed his eyes in death" (Lucy Mack Smith, *History of Joseph Smith by His Mother,* pp. 86-88).

Judging from their frequent references to him after his death, Alvin had a powerful influence on all of his family, and his death represented the greatest tragedy that had come into their lives. His mother characterized him as "a youth of singular goodness of disposition" (Ibid.).

The following year, on September 22, 1824, Joseph again visited the location of the buried plates. He believed that he would be permitted to take the plates until the time of translation because he had been faithful in keeping the commandments of God. But as he handled the plates, his thoughts turned to worldly concerns, and he set the plates down to look in the box for something of monetary value to help his struggling family. He was severely reprimanded by the angel (messenger), and he returned empty-handed. Joseph Sr. and Lucy became concerned that Joseph might fail in his solemn purposes. They increased their perseverance in prayer and appeal to God that Joseph might be more fully instructed in his duty, his obligation, and his responsibility to God, and be preserved from all deceptions and schemes as perpetrated by Satan, the great deceiver.

Joseph always proved to be a willing student. Lucy reminds us that during his first visit to the Hill Cumorah, "the angel [messenger] showed him, by contrast, the difference between good and evil—the consequences of both obedience and disobedience—in such a striking manner," Lucy explained: "that the impression was always vivid in his memory until the very end of his days; not long prior to his death, he remarked that ever afterwards, he was willing to keep the commandments of God."

Following Alvin's death, the Smiths experienced more economic difficulties. Joseph and his brothers hired out by the day at whatever work was available. **Treasure hunting or "money-digging" as it was then called, was a craze in the United States at that time.** In October 1825, Josiah Stowell, from South Bainbridge, New York, a farmer, a lumber mill owner, and deacon in the Presbyterian Church, came to ask Joseph to help him in such a venture. Stowell had relatives in Palmyra and probably heard of Joseph from them. Stowell was looking for a legendary lost silver mine thought to have been opened by Spaniards in Northern Pennsylvania. Stowell was one of many men of character and substance in his day who were convinced that treasures were buried in various places in America and who spent money and effort searching for them. Stowell had heard that Joseph was able to discern invisible things and desired his assistance in the project. The Prophet was reluctant, but Stowell was persistent, and since Joseph's family was in need, he and his father together with other neighbors agreed to go. It was a decision that would have great importance to Joseph's life and the future of the Church.

Joseph and his associates boarded with Isaac Hale in Harmony Township in Pennsylvania. The village of Harmony was several miles away where a bend of the Susquehanna River dips into Northern Pennsylvania not far from the supposed mine site. Isaac Hale and his wife, Elizabeth, had nine children. **Their third daughter, Emma,** was a beautiful young woman with dark hair, luminous hazel eyes, and a graceful, quiet manner. She was a careful housekeeper and an excellent cook. She also had a beautiful singing voice and a quick, intelligent mind. Joseph became very attracted to her. Joseph later confided to his parent: *"She would be my choice in preference to any other woman I have ever seen."* She was also attracted to him, although she was Joseph's senior by a year and a half. The budding romance, however, was frowned upon by Emma's father who disliked money-digging and rejected Joseph's lack of education. Hale's daughter was a schoolteacher, and he wanted better for her.

Meanwhile, the search for the silver mine was unproductive. After nearly a month's work, Joseph was able to persuade Josiah Stowell that his efforts were in vain, and the pursuit of the mine in Harmony was abandoned.

At that time, in New England and Western New York, such activities were not frowned upon, as they came to be later. Years later, Joseph candidly acknowledged his participation in the venture, but pointed out that it was insignificant (*History of the Church,* 3: 29). However from that time on Joseph's enemies used what they called his "money-dig" project to attack his character, to question his motives, and to cast doubt upon the authority of the Church he was about to organize.

While working in the border areas of New York and Pennsylvania, Joseph made another contact in addition to the Hales that became important to him and the early Church in New York. Joseph Knight Sr., a friend of Josiah Stowell, was a humble farmer and miller who lived in Colesville, Broome County, New York. Joseph Smith also worked for him for a time, and in the process developed close friendships with him and his sons, Joseph Jr. and Newel. They accepted the testimony of the young Prophet as he recounted his sacred experiences to them.

While working for Josiah Stowell and Joseph Knight Sr., and visiting his own family in Manchester, Joseph continued to court Emma Hale. **Because of her father's strong opposition to the marriage, Joseph and Emma eloped.** They were married by a Justice of the Peace, Squire Tarbill, in South Bainbridge, New York, on January 18, 1827. Immediately after the marriage, **Joseph moved his new bride to the Smith family home in Manchester** where he spent the next summer with his father. Emma was well received by Joseph's family, and a close relationship developed between Emma and Lucy Mack Smith. It was a year of quiet happiness for the two young people. It proved to be the calm before the storm the prelude to years of persecution.

In spite of the fact that Joseph had been charged "a disorderly person, also, an imposter" in the Bainbridge area, (because of his claims of seeing a vision), he had been acquitted from the foolish charge, and he left many friends behind him. These friends were older, successful men who had seen into the heart of the young man and were willing to support him; among these were Joseph Knight, Martin Harris, and Peter Whitmer. They would later come forward to help and work with the

"Joseph Smith Receiving the Gold Plates," by Kenneth Riley, © The Church of Jesus Christ of Latter-day Saints, Used by Permission

young Prophet.

There was little known of Joseph's visits with Moroni between 1824 and 1827, but sometime before the fall of 1827, Joseph returned home one evening later than usual. His family was concerned, but he told them he had been delayed because he had just received a severe chastisement from Moroni. He said that as he passed by the Hill Cumorah: *"The angel met me and said that I had not been engaged enough in the work of the Lord; that the time had come for the record to be brought forth; and that I must be up and doing, and set myself about the things which God had commanded me to do"* (Lucy Mack Smith, *History of Joseph Smith by His Mother,* pp. 100-101).

There was much that must have transpired in Joseph's four years of preparation. He passed through his teen years largely unspotted by the dogma of men. He enjoyed the emotional support of his family, and he took on the responsibilities associated with marriage. Angels prepared him to translate a divinely inspired record and taught him the necessity of self-discipline and obedience. He was undeniably anxious to begin translating the plates and record of the inhabitants of this land. At this time, Joseph Knight and Josiah Stowell were in Manchester visiting with the Smith family. This might have been in anticipation of Joseph's receiving the plates.

Long before sunrise on September 22, 1827, Joseph and his wife, Emma, hitched Joseph Knight's horse to Josiah Stowell's spring wagon and drove the three miles to the Hill Cumorah. Leaving Emma at the base, Joseph climbed the hill for his final interview with Moroni. Moroni gave him the plates, the Urim and Thummim, and the breastplate. He also gave Joseph a specific warning and promise concerning his responsibilities. Joseph was now responsible for these sacred objects, and if he was careless or negligent and lost them, he would be cut off. On the other hand, if he used all his efforts to preserve them until Moroni returned for them, he was assured that they would be protected (Joseph Smith—History 1: 59).

For the fifth time, Joseph knelt before the stone receptacle in which the ancient records had lain hidden for fourteen centuries—but now that receptacle was empty. The sacred treasure was in his arms and he heard the angel beside him say: "Now you have got the record in your own hands, and you are but a man. Therefore, you will have to be watchful and faithful to your trust, or you will be overpowered by wicked men. For they will lay every plan and scheme that is possible to get it away from you, and if you do not take heed, they will succeed. While it was in my hands, I could keep it, and no man had power to take it away. But now I give it up to you. Beware and look well to your ways, and you shall have power to retain it, until the time for it to be translated" (Lucy Mack Smith, *History of Joseph Smith by His Mother*).

The angel Moroni left him, and the young Prophet was alone on the hillside, surrounded by forests and scattered settlements. From that elevation, he could see evidences of a civilization which was spreading over the great American continent. He held in his hands the records of another group of people who long, before had witnessed their civilization cover the land for centuries and then pass away.

The importance of the record, the seriousness of his calling, the realization of his own weaknesses and of the trials which awaited him, must have humbled him greatly as he made his way down from the hill which had housed the plates for 1,400 years.

If his mind did foresee, for a time, that remarkable past, the feel of the plates beneath his outer coat must have brought him into a sharp reality of the present. And there was his wife, Emma, at the foot of the hill, awaiting his return, and the beginning of the greatest adventure of their lives.

When Joseph and Emma returned to the Smith home in Manchester, they were without the gold plates. Joseph had carefully hidden the plates in a hollow log near his home. Joseph did not take anyone, not even his wife, into his confidence concerning the plates or their hiding place. His reason was clear—the Prophet's friends were not the only ones who eagerly anticipated his receiving the plates. Others in the community had heard that Joseph was about to bring home valuable metal plates. Some of them also had been involved in searching for the silver mine and now felt that they should have a share in any treasure. Joseph soon learned why Moroni had strictly charged him to protect the plates.

As the news spread that Joseph had in his possession a book with gold leaves, all kinds of violence and strategies erupted to steal it from him. The major motive prompting these attempts was probably greed. Joseph left us little in writing concerning it. Joseph said: *"As soon as the news of this discovery was made known, false reports, misrepresentations, and slander flew as on the wings of the wind in every direction; the house was frequently besieged by mobs and evil designing persons. Several times, I was shot at, and very narrowly escaped, and every trick, every device and every ruse was used to get the plates away from me"* (Account of the Wentworth letter. Footnote, p. 9).

During the following months, **the records found many curious hiding places**—an excavation beneath the Smith hearthstone, the loft of a workshop, a barrel of beans, etc. All efforts to get them from Joseph met with failure. (The details of these experiences, the successive hiding places of the plates, and the various attempts of the mob to obtain them are found only in one church account, Lucy Smith's, *History of the Prophet Joseph Smith.*)

In a very short period, much of our writings become dim and faded. In a few hundred years time, if it is not otherwise destroyed, this book in your hands will have utterly decayed, despite any attempts to preserve it. The record in Joseph's keeping had lain buried in the earth for fourteen hundred years, yet the characters were plain and decipherable. What type of record was this? What materials had the writers used that could withstand the elements for so long? The best answer is the written statement of the Prophet: *"These records were engraven on plates which had the appearance of gold; each plate was six inches wide, and eight inches long, and not quite so thick as common tin. They were filled with engraving, in Egyptian characters, and bound together in a volume as the leaves of a book, with three rings running through the holes. The volume was something near six inches in thickness, a part of which was sealed. The characters on the unsealed part were small, and beautifully engraved. The whole book exhibited many marks of antiquity* [age] *in its construction, and much skill in the art of engraving. Along with the records, was found a curious instrument which the ancients called 'Urim and Thummim,' which consisted of two transparent stones set in the rim of a bow fastened to a breastplate. Through the medium of the*

Urim and Thummim, Joseph translated the record by the gift and power of God" (A reprint of the letter in *History of the Church*, 4: 537).

The secret of the preservation of the record lay in the fact that ordinary writing materials were not used. There was no ink to fade—the letters had been cut or engraved in thin leaves of a gold alloy which would not corrode or alter in appearance with the passing of time.

It is impossible at this time to accurately estimate the weight of such a set of gold leaves or plates. Neither the Prophet nor those witnesses who were privileged to handle the plates left written testimony as to the weight of the volume.

The major part of the record was written in the language which is called "reformed Egyptian." Perhaps the nearest known language is the ancient Phoenician which likewise developed from the Egyptian. Hieroglyphic symbols were used rather than the common written language of the people, which was akin to Hebrew.

During this period in Joseph's life, he was constantly in danger, so he decided to take Emma back to Harmony where he hoped to begin the translation in peace. Before they left, **Martin Harris, a prominent citizen of Palmyra** who would later play a great role in the Restoration, stepped forward and offered help. He was a prosperous farmer and businessman who had met the Smiths when they first settled in Palmyra and had hired various family members to work for him over the years. Joseph had received an invitation to the home of his father-in-law, Isaac Hale in Harmony, Pennsylvania. Desiring a place where he could find the necessary peace and quiet for his work, he accepted the invitation. Martin Harris provided funds so that Joseph and Emma could pay off their debts and also gave them fifty dollars for their trip. With the plates hidden in a barrel of beans in the back of the wagon, they drove out of town on a wintry day in December of 1827.

Following a brief stay with the Hales in Harmony, Pennsylvania the couple purchased a house from Emma's eldest brother, Jesse. It was a small two-story home on a thirteen-acre farm bordering the Susquehanna River. For the first time in weeks, Joseph was able to work in relative peace. Between December 1827, and February 1828, he copied many of the characters from the plates and translated some of them by using the Urim and Thummim. In the early stages of the work, Joseph spent a good deal of time and effort becoming familiar with the language of the plates and learning how to translate.

According to previous arrangements, Martin Harris visited Joseph in Harmony sometime in February of 1828. By then, **the Lord had prepared Martin to assist Joseph** in his mission. According to his own testimony, Martin was instructed by the Lord in 1818 not to join any church until the words of Isaiah were fulfilled. "*And the vision of all is become unto you as the words of a book that is sealed, which men deliver to one that is learned, saying, Read this, I pray thee: and he saith, I cannot; for it is sealed: And the book is delivered to him that is not learned, saying, Read this, I pray thee: and he saith, I am not learned"* (Isaiah 29: 11-12).

Sometime later, it was revealed to Martin that the Lord had a work for him to do. In 1827, several manifestations convinced Martin Harris that Joseph Smith was a Prophet, and that he should assist Joseph in bringing the plates, (to be known as the Book of Mormon) to this generation. Therefore, Martin went to Harmony to obtain a copy of some of the characters from the plates to show several noted linguists of the time. He was hoping to gather evidence to help convince an unbelieving world of the authenticity of the record.

Martin visited at least three men who had reputations as able linguists. In Albany, New York, he spoke with Luther Bradish, a diplomat, statesman, world traveler, and student of languages. In New York City, he met with Dr. Samuel Mitchell, Vice President of Rutgers Medical College. He also visited a man who knew four languages including Hebrew and Babylonia—**Professor Charles Anthon of Columbia College in New York City**. **Anthon who was among the leading classical scholars of his day,** was probably the most qualified of Martin's contacts to judge the characters on the document. At the time of Martin Harris's visit, Charles Anthon was adjunct professor of Greek and Latin. He knew French, German, Greek, and Latin, and was familiar, if books in his library are evidence, with the latest discoveries pertaining to the Egyptian language including the early work of Champollion ("Charles Anthon and the Egyptian Language," *Improvement Era,* October 1960, pp. 708-10).

According to Martin Harris, Professor Anthon examined the characters and their translation, and willingly gave him a certificate stating to the citizens of Palmyra that the writings were authentic. Anthon further told Martin that the characters resembled Egyptian, Chaldean, Assyrian, and Arabic, **and expressed his opinion that the translation was correct.** Martin put the certificate in his pocket, and was about to leave when Anthon called him back and asked how Joseph Smith found the gold plates in the hill. Martin explained that an angel of God revealed the location to Joseph, whereupon Charles Anthon asked for the certificate, which Martin gave to him. He took it and tore it to pieces, saying, "that there was no such thing now as ministering of angels, and that if I [Martin] would bring the plates to him, he would translate them." I informed him: "that part of the plates were sealed, and that I was forbidden to bring them." He replied: "I cannot read a sealed book" (*History of the Church,* 1: 20). This statement we Mormons believe fulfilled the prophecy of Isaiah (Isaiah 29: 11-12).

Martin Harris's trip was significant for several reasons. First, it showed that scholars had an interest in the characters and were willing to give them serious consideration as long as an angel was not part of their story. Second, it was, in view of Martin and Joseph, the direct fulfillment of prophecy relative to the Book of Mormon. Third, it was a demonstration that translating the record would require the assistance of God; intellect alone was insufficient (Isaiah 29: 11-12; 2 Nephi 27: 15-20). Finally, it built up Martin's own faith. He returned to his home near Palmyra, New York, confident that he had evidence to convince his neighbors of Joseph Smith's work. Now ready to wholeheartedly commit himself and his means to the bringing forth of the Book of Mormon, he arranged his personal affairs so that he could be away from home for some time.

Martin could not foresee the obstacles that awaited him in Palmyra. His wife, Lucy, was angry that he had gone to the East without her. She was concerned that the Smiths were trying to swindle Martin, and she resented the time he spent with Joseph and away from her. Her bitterness was more evident when Martin returned. She was the kind of person who demanded positive proof, so that when Martin prepared to leave for Pennsylvania again, she insisted on accompanying him. He agreed to take her along for a few days. In Harmony, her first priority was to see the plates. **Imagine the nerve, the arrogance and boldness of this woman,** who was a complete stranger to Joseph, coming into his home and practically taking over. She virtually ransacked the house. In consequence, Joseph was forced to hide the plates outside. Lucy thought she had found where they were buried outside, but when she crouched down to look, she was frightened away by a large black snake. Angered and upset by failing to find the plates, she told anyone and everyone who would listen that her husband had been duped by a "grand imposter." After two weeks, Martin took her home. Despite her attempts to discourage him, he returned to Harmony. In Martin's absence, his wife Lucy continued her criticism in Palmyra (Lucy Mack Smith, *History of Joseph Smith by His Mother,* pp. 119-23).

When Martin arrived back in Pennsylvania on April 12, 1828, he and Joseph began working on the translation until June 14, 1828, although there were frequent interruptions.

The upset caused by Lucy Harris during her two-week visit to Harmony was almost negligible compared to the traumatic upheaval she would cause a few months later. In the interim, Martin moved to Harmony to work full time as the Prophet's scribe, returning at intervals to Palmyra to oversee his farming and business interests and to attempt to calm his troubled wife. His failure to accomplish this is confirmed by the outbreak of hardship and torment she was soon to bring around the Prophet and by the fact that Martin divorced her a few years later.

Joseph Smith and his scribe presented an interesting study in persons and personalities as they proceeded with the translation. Seated on one side of a curtain that divided a small room was the young, handsome, intense Prophet, with the interpreters at hand and the sacred plates spread before him. On the other side of the curtain, the middle-aged, plain looking farmer sat at a solid wooden table on which were arranged pen and ink and a supply of white manuscript paper. Using the interpreters and all his powers of concentration, the Prophet understood the sense of the inscriptions on the plates and then dictated them in English to Martin, who wrote them in longhand. Martin would then read back what he had written, and when the Prophet was satisfied that the transcription was correct, he would move on.

No attempt was made to punctuate the transcript, and the Prophet did not edit it once he had received confirmation that it was correct. At the beginning of a new day of translating, the Prophet would merely begin where he had left off the night before, and with the help of his scribe, would repeat the process.

From April to June 1828, Martin filled up 116 pages of manuscript. His constant attention to the work and his daily exposure to the spiritual influences surrounding the Prophet increased his confidence in what he was doing. During his visits home, however, Lucy would raise additional questions and plant new seeds of doubt. She continued to press Martin for more convincing, objective evidence that Joseph had the plates and that his claims of divine assistance were true. Martin was anxious to satisfy his nagging, ill-tempered wife, and wanted something tangible to point to as evidence of the truthfulness of the Prophet's claim. **Martin, in turn, pleaded to Joseph for the privilege of taking the manuscript home. He assured the Prophet that it would be safe in his possession,** and that it would be a great help in relieving the constant pressure being exerted by his wife and others.

Through the Urim and Thummim, Joseph inquired of the Lord. The answer was no. Martin, not satisfied, persisted until Joseph again asked the Lord; still the answer was no. Martin's pleas and petitions continued. The Prophet felt great anguish about granting this request, especially since he had been told twice through the Urim and Thummim that he should not turn over the 116 page manuscript to Martin. Nevertheless, in spite of the Prophet's great anxiety about allowing the manuscript out of his hands and sight, he looked to Martin for continued assistance in translating the record and for financial backing in publishing it. Therefore, Joseph felt justified in asking the Lord for permission to let Martin borrow the manuscript. **Finally, the Lord granted a conditional permission.** Martin agreed in writing to show the manuscript to only four or five people, including his wife; his brother, Preserved Harris; his father; his mother; and Lucy's sister, Mrs. Polly Cobb. Martin then left for Palmyra with the only copy of the manuscript.

Shortly after Martin's departure, Emma Smith bore a son, Alvin, who died the day he was born. Emma nearly died herself, and for two weeks Joseph was constantly at her bedside. When she improved, his attention returned to the manuscript. By this time, Martin had been gone for three weeks, and they had heard nothing from him. Martin had not been totally irresponsible. He had spent time with his wife, taken care of his business in Palmyra, and served on a jury.

Emma encouraged Joseph to catch the stage to Palmyra and check on the matter. After traveling from Harmony to the Palmyra area and walking the last twenty miles during the night, Joseph finally arrived at his parents' home in Manchester. He immediately sent for Martin. When Martin didn't show up promptly, Joseph knew that something was wrong. When Martin finally arrived, his head was hung low and he was despondent and sorrowful. Mr. Harris pressed his hands upon his temples, and cried out in a tone of deep anguish: "Oh, I have lost my soul! I have lost my soul." Joseph, who had not expressed his fears till now, arose from a table, and asked Martin: ***"Did you lose the manuscript?*** *Have you broken your oath, and brought down condemnation upon my head as well as your own?"* **Martin replied: "Yes; it is gone, and I know not where."**

Joseph felt condemned, and feared the retribution from the Lord. He said: *"I should have been satisfied with the first answer which I received from the Lord; for He told me that it was not safe to let the writing go out of my possession. It is I,"* said Joseph, *"who has tempted the wrath of God. All is lost! All is lost!"*

"The next morning," Joseph wrote, he set out for home. *"We parted with heavy hearts for it now appeared that all which we had so fondly anticipated, and which had been the source of so much secret gratification had in a moment fled, and fled forever"* (Lucy Mack Smith, *History of Joseph Smith by His Mother,* pp. 128-29).

Upon returning to Harmony without the 116 pages of manuscript, Joseph immediately began to pray for the Lord to forgive him for acting contrary to His will.

Moroni appeared to Joseph and required him to return the plates and the Urim and Thummim, but promised that he could receive them back if he were humble and repentant. Some time later, he received a revelation which chastised him for negligence and for setting *"at naught the counsels of God,"* but also comforted him that he was still chosen to perform the work of translation if he repented (Doctrine & Covenants 3: 4-10).

Joseph did repent and again received the plates and the Urim and Thummim, along with a promise that the Lord would send a scribe to assist him in the translation. There was a special message: *"The angel seemed pleased with me . . . and he told me that the Lord loved me for my faithfulness and humility"* (Lucy Mack Smith, *History of Joseph Smith by His Mother,* p. 135).

Above everything else, Joseph desired only to do what the Lord wished him to do. Now that the sacred instruments were in his hands again, he used them to inquire of the Lord what His desires were. Further into Doctrine & Covenants, Section three, the Lord informed the young Prophet that the schemes of wicked men could not destroy the work of the Lord. He said: *" remember, that it is not the work of God that is frustrated, but the work of man."*

The Lord again chastised the Prophet for the loss of the manuscript and told him once more that unless he was careful, he would fail and would not be allowed to carry on the work. But comforting the young man again, the Lord said: *"God is merciful; therefore repent of that which thou hast done which is contrary to the commandment which I gave you, and thou art still chosen, and art again called to the work."*

Then the Lord informed him that when he gave the manuscript into Martin's hands, he allowed the sacred writings to fall into the hands of wicked men who would try to prove the Book of Mormon false. The scheme of these evil men, as explained by the Lord, was that they now had the original translation of the first 116 pages of the manuscript. They thought that if they kept it, the Prophet would have to translate it over again. They thought he either would not do it the same way twice or, if he did, they would change the original writings which Martin had allowed to fall into their hands. In this way, they would say that Joseph was a false prophet, and try to prove it with the original writings.

The manuscript had fallen into evil hands who wanted to prove the work a fraud. Nevertheless, it is remarkable to know that the material in the lost 116 pages were actually included in other sections of the plates. While preparing the plates in the abridgment, Mormon included two versions of this information. In this way, none of the important history was lost. **The lost portion—was not redone**—since it was evident to Joseph that his enemies could alter the original and publicly belittle and demean him.

Having both the Urim and Thummim and the gold plates taken from him for a few days had further humble the Prophet and allow him to see how dependent he was upon the Lord. During this time, Joseph was greatly worried for fear he would not be thought worthy to continue. When they were restored to him again, the Lord said: *"Now behold, I say unto you, that because you delivered up those writings which you had power given unto you to translate by means of the Urim and Thummim, into the hands of a wicked man, you have lost them. And you also lost your gift at the same time, and your mind became darkened. Nevertheless, it is now restored unto you again; therefore see that you are faithful and continue on unto the finishing of the remainder of the work of translation as you have begun"* (Doctrine & Covenants 10: 1-3). The Lord explained that He had a way of protecting Joseph and the sacred work from these evil men, and He did; and God's way is the only true way.

The period of five and one-half years between September 1823 and April 1829 were important in Joseph Smith's preparation for translating the Book of Mormon, and leading the Restored Church in the Dispensation of the Fulness of Times. He was now twenty-three years old. He was tall and strong. He worked on the farm, in the fields, and at odd jobs. Although he had had little formal schooling, Joseph had a hungry and curious mind. He liked to discover things for himself, and to seek and find answers from the scriptures (Joseph Smith—History 1: 11-12). This thirst for knowledge, especially spiritual knowledge, never left him.

In June of 1843, **Joseph told the Saints: *"I am a rough stone. The sound of the hammer and chisel was never heard on me until the Lord took me in hand"*** (*History of the Church,* 5: 423). Courage, optimism, and faith were hallmarks of his personality. He had shown great courage at an early age when he endured the painful leg operation referred to in and later, when he faced hostile neighbors who were trying to get the plates from him. Despite his poverty and lack of formal education, he was optimistic about himself and life. Reprimanded by the Lord and corrected by Moroni, he was always submissive, repentant, and energetic. He faced despair when the 116 pages were lost, but from that experience he learned obedience, and was later able to say: *"I made this my rule: When the Lord commands, do it"* (*History of the Church,* 2: 170). He also learned valuable lessons about controlling his motives and purposes, and was therefore, able to keep his *"eye single to the glory of God"* (Doctrine & Covenants 4: 5), and channel his energies and thoughts toward building the kingdom.

By this time, Joseph had gained considerable experiences with various means of revelation. He had communed with God and His Son and with angelic messengers. He had seen visions, felt the promptings of the Spirit, and grown in skill in using the Urim and Thummim. We should not conclude that revelation came easy to him, for another lesson he learned during this time was the price of faith, diligence, persistence, worthiness, and obedience—all of which he had to pay in order to receive communication from God.

Chapter 4

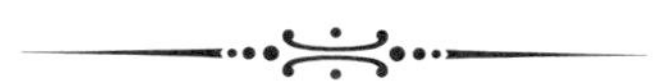

The Coming Forth of the "Book Of Mormon— Another Testament of Jesus Christ"

The Book of Mormon is the Word of God, a Second Witness to the World that Jesus is the Christ—(Messiah)

The Bible (Tribe of Judah)— *Book of Mormon* (Tribe Of Joseph)— *are Companion Scriptures*

The Restoration of the Holy Priesthood of God

The ten months following the time when Joseph first received the plates from the angel Moroni were filled with frustration and failure. He had very little to show for his burdensome labors. From the standpoint of his future work, nevertheless, this period was vitally productive. It taught the Prophet humility and the need for constant diligence. It gave him vital training in measuring the character and design of men. And most importantly, it dramatically brought the realization that he was directly responsible for the work and was accountable to God should he fail to perform. What had happened previously (losing the 116 pages) could have produced an urgent sense of anxiety and concern and the need to hurry to make up for the lost time and to please the Lord. Such feelings, could have produced more misjudgement and greater confusion, but were effectively dissipated by this meaningful statement in the revelation: ***"Do not run faster or labor more than you have strength and means provided, to enable you to translate; but be diligent unto the end"*** (Doctrine & Covenants 10: 4). With this warning in mind, Joseph settled into a more quiet, relaxed routine.

For the next nine months, Joseph fulfilled his domestic role as husband and head of the household. He worked in the fields, cared for his animals, and gave comfort to Emma, who was still grieving the loss of her first child. The farm on which they lived was small, so it is likely that they received some assistance from Emma's parents or from their many friends at Colesville or Bainbridge who were interested in the Prophet's work.

As time permitted, Joseph translated from the plates of Nephi, using Emma as his scribe. Joseph worked slowly and deliberately in the full confidence that the Lord, in His own time, would provide those necessary people to help him finish the work.

During this long, painful, and agonizing interval, two events of special significance occurred. In February 1829, Joseph received a visit from his father, who came to check up on the Prophet's health and the progress of the work. It was a constant source of strength to Joseph that those who knew him best, trusted him the most. His father had never doubted his story and had always stood ready, willing, and hopefully able, to give assistance when and where needed. While visiting with his father, the Prophet informed him (insofar as the restrictions placed upon him by the angel would permit) of the details of his past activities, his pressures and struggles, and his plans for the future. As father and son conferred and **prayed together**, young Joseph, moved upon by the spirit of prophecy, received a special revelation for his father. Now recognized as the fourth Section of the Doctrine & Covenants, this short, seven-verse revelation began with a startling prediction that foreshadowed the completion of the work of translating the ancient record, and of establishing a formal church. Joseph Sr. was told: *"Now behold, a marvelous work is about to come forth among the children of men. Therefore, O ye that embark in the service of God, see that ye serve him with all your heart, might, mind, and strength, that ye may stand blameless before God at the last day."* Then followed brief instruction about the credentials of those to be called to service. The revelation ended with this instruction, which seems to be the key to all that the Prophet did: *"Ask, and ye shall receive; knock, and it shall be opened unto you"* (Doctrine & Covenants 4: 1-2, 7).

About a month later, Martin Harris came to see the Prophet in Harmony. This meeting revived many unpleasant memories. It had been Martin Harris's persistence that had resulted in the loss of the Prophet's early work, in the separation of the Prophet from his heavenly sources of information, and in the subsequent nine months of nonproductivity insofar as his divine calling was concerned. Martin was a curious man, which often got him into trouble, yet he was truly interested in the work Joseph was doing. So he asked the Prophet to approach the Lord once more in his behalf. Also Martin began to ask permission to see the plates. Since Joseph had been told not to show the plates to anyone, the fact that Martin was now begging to see them was another test for Joseph. Would he show his friend the plates, or would he keep them hidden as the Lord had told him? Joseph had learned his lesson in the loss of the manuscript and would do nothing without the complete approval of the Lord from now on. When Martin continued asking to see the plates, possibly because of an insight into the role Martin was yet to play in the publication of the Book of Mormon or out of sympathy for the harassment Martin had suffered at the hands of his wife, Joseph prayed about Martin's request. He consequently received his fourth formal revelation, now known as the fifth Section of the Doctrine and Covenants. The first verse discloses how little Martin had learned or profited from his close association with Joseph and from his recent traumatic experience in losing the manuscript: *"BEHOLD, I say unto you, that as my servant Martin Harris has desired a witness at my hand, that you, my servant Joseph Smith, Jun., have got the plates of which you have testified and borne record that you have received of me;"* Martin was told that at an appropriate time, **three special witnesses** would be shown the plates, and that he would be one of them if he would *"humble himself in mighty prayer and faith, in the sincerity of his heart"* (Doctrine & Covenants 5: 1, 24). The Lord, knowing how Martin had begged to see the plates, now instructed the Prophet to tell Martin not to trouble him any more about this matter.

This revelation also contained hints about **the establishment of the Church** sometime in the near future. But Joseph was told: *"you must wait yet a little while, for ye are not yet ordained—"* (Doctrine & Covenants 5: 17).

Of great importance to Joseph, as he looked forward to continuing the work of translation and to the equally important work that lay beyond was the following: *"Stop, and stand still until I command thee, and I will provide a means whereby thou mayest accomplish the thing which I have commanded thee"* (Doctrine & Covenants 5: 34).

These words brought comforting assurance that at the proper time, the Lord would raise up those whom the Prophet would need to help complete his important work. In fact, events were unfolding at that exact time that would bring to the Prophet's aid the man who was to be the chief scribe of the Book of Mormon and the second Elder of the Church.

ENTER—OLIVER COWDERY INTO JOSEPH SMITH'S LIFE

In the early pioneer days of Western New York, there were small country schools for the children of the communities, and as a rule, the school teachers came from other cities to take charge of these schools.

Several months before, Oliver Cowdery from Virginia, had contracted to teach school in Palmyra. He had not been in the vicinity very long before he began to hear rumors about the controversial young man, Joseph Smith, who claimed to have an ancient record that had been given to him by an angel (messenger), and that he was then in the process of translating the record from golden plates.

Since some of the younger Smith children were among Oliver's pupils, he soon after went to board with Joseph Sr. and Lucy Smith in partial satisfaction for the tuition of the children. There he learned more about the Prophet's spiritual experiences and about his charge to translate the sacred plates. Almost intuitively, Oliver was drawn to the Prophet, although he had not as yet met him. As if he were destined to do so, he exerted every effort to meet the young Prophet, and if possible, to assist him.

Oliver had a great desire to know firsthand about Joseph and his work, and decided to travel to visit with the Prophet. Before going, he talked it over with his friend David Whitmer who lived in the nearby community of Fayette, Seneca County, New York. Mr. Whitmer was also curious about Joseph's work, and desired to know more about it. Oliver told David he was going to visit Joseph; Mr. Whitmer asked him to write back telling what his impressions were of Joseph and his work. This Oliver promised to do. The friendship with the Whitmer family later had significant impact on the coming forth of the Book of Mormon and the establishment of the Church. Oliver said: "If there is a work for me to do in this thing, I am determined to attend to it" (Lucy Mack Smith, *History of Joseph Smith by His Mother,* p.139).

In company with the Prophet's brother, Samuel, Oliver traveled to Harmony following the school term in the spring. It was the first week of April 1829, as they traveled over roads that were "almost impassable, particularly in the middle of the day, because of the alternate raining, freezing, and thawing" (Ibid, p. 141). En route, Oliver stopped in Fayette to see his friend, David Whitmer, to whom he promised that he would "report his findings . . . concerning Joseph having the plates" (B. H. Roberts, *Comprehensive History of the Church,* 1: 120).

Little did these two young men realize that they would soon be caught up in a drama that would be the focal point of their entire lives. Not only would they learn for themselves that the Prophet had the plates, but they would learn that fact from an angel of the Lord.

It was Sunday, the fifth of April, 1829 when Oliver reached the Prophet's home in Pennsylvania. Joseph had never seen Oliver before, but Joseph recognized him as the assistant that the Lord had promised. Oliver told him that he had lived in the home of the Prophet's parents, they had told him about the sacred records, and Oliver said: "that he had come to find out about them for himself."

They sat down together until late in the evening, while Joseph told Oliver of his mission. The two young men immediately became close friends, then Oliver volunteered to become the scribe for the Prophet—to write down the translation as Joseph would dictate it. The next day they attended to some business and on Tuesday, April 7, 1829, they began the work of translation—in earnest. The same procedure was followed as when Martin Harris served as the scribe. Joseph would be seated on one side of a curtain dividing the room, and would give the translation to Oliver, who would record then proofread the words, line by line. Any editing in the substance of the text occurred at the time of this proofreading. Referring to this period, Oliver wrote, "These were the days never to be forgotten to sit under the sound of a voice, dictated by the inspiration of heaven, awakened the utmost gratitude of this bosom. Day after day, I continued uninterrupted to write from his mouth, as he translated with the Urim and Thummim, or as the Nephites would have said, 'Interpreters,' the history or record called—the **Book of Mormon**" (B. H. Roberts, *Comprehensive History of the Church,* 1: 122).

The Lord gave a revelation to Joseph for Oliver. In it, He told the new scribe: (Oliver) *"A GREAT and marvelous work is about to come forth,"* and He said: *" Behold thou art Oliver, and I have spoken unto thee because of thy desires; therefore treasure up these words in thy heart. Be faithful and diligent in keeping the commandments of God."* He was told that if he would be faithful all of his life, the riches of heaven would be his, and if he desired a further witness that the work was true, he should remember the prayer that Oliver had offered one night, when the Lord said to Oliver: *"Did I not speak peace to your mind concerning the matter? What greater witness can you have than from God?"* (Doctrine & Covenants 6: 1, 20, 23). No one but the Lord and Oliver knew of Oliver's prayer; consequently Oliver was sure that the revelation came from the Lord, and that the work which Joseph was doing was true. He hadn't told Joseph about this prayer until after—the revelation had been received.

In this same revelation, the Lord commanded Oliver to carry on the work with the Prophet and assist him to translate the records. Oliver accepted the commandment and worked fervently and earnestly.

By the time Oliver came to write for him, the Prophet had had the plates and the

Urim and Thummim in his possession for over eighteen months. Now, with a willing, alert scribe, who by the standards of the day and locality was fairly well educated, he was prepared to move rapidly. During April and May of 1829, **they worked steadily without interruption.** They often discussed questions or points of interest raised by the translation. Whenever they were unable to reach agreement or understanding, they turned to the divine source of knowledge. The Prophet recorded one such occasion when a difference of opinion arose between them as to whether the Apostle John died or continued to live as a translated being. At length, they agreed to settle it by the Urim and Thummin. In response, Joseph received what is now Section seven of the Doctrine & Covenants, which told him that John was to continue in mortality in order that he might *"minister for those who shall be heirs of salvation who dwell on the earth"* (Doctrine & Covenants 7: 6).

From the events that were soon to take place, Oliver developed a false notion of his role in the work. Not only did he conclude that he was without question Joseph's equal, but he apparently thought he was Joseph's superior. Therein lay the seeds of Oliver's future disaffection from the Prophet and from the Church. As will be seen shortly, however, the disaffection was based upon personal conflict and misunderstanding and not upon any question of the divinity of the work.

Oliver soon desired to have the power to translate as well as to serve as a scribe. He was tested as a translator by the Lord and failed, but Oliver did continue on to the end of the work as a faithful scribe.

Translation was not, apart from anything else, a mechanical process. Success in doing it required a delicate balancing of the mental and spiritual. Oliver seems to have failed because he did not apply himself mentally to the assignment; however, no amount of mental effort would have brought success without the proper spiritual harmony. David Whitmer, who was very close to the Prophet during the latter phase of the translation, has left us with an insight into the spiritual discipline the work demanded: "At times when Joseph would attempt to translate, he would look into a holder in which the stone was placed, [to exclude the light], he found he was spiritually blind and could not translate. He told us that his mind dwelt too much on earthly things, and various causes would make him incapable of proceeding with the translation. When in this condition, **he would go out and pray**, and when he became sufficiently humble before God, he could then proceed with the translation. Now we see how very strict the Lord is, and how He requires the heart of a man to be just right in His sight before he can receive revelation from Him" (B. H. Roberts, *Comprehensive History of the Church,* 1: 130, 131).

In the same frame of mind, David Whitmer wrote on another occasion: "He, Joseph, was a religious and straightforward man. He had to be; for he was unschooled and needed constant guidance. He had to trust in God. He could not translate unless he was humble and possessed the right feelings toward everyone. To illustrate so you can see: One morning, when he was getting ready to continue the translation, something went wrong about the house, and he was put out about it. Something that Emma, his wife, had done. Oliver and I went upstairs, and Joseph came up soon after to continue the translation, but he could not do anything. He could not translate a single syllable. He went downstairs, out into the orchard, and **made supplication to the**

Lord; was gone about an hour—came back to the house, and asked Emma's forgiveness, and then came upstairs where we were, and then the translation went on all right. He could do nothing save he was humble and faithful" (B. H. Roberts, *Comprehensive History of the Church,* 1: 131).

Joseph and Oliver worked diligently on the translation throughout April. With Oliver's help, Joseph proceeded faster than ever before. During the next three months, Joseph and Oliver completed the amazing task of translating approximately 500 printed pages. This was a glorious period in their lives. Oliver wrote: "day after day I continued, uninterrupted, to write from his mouth, as he translated, with the Urim and Thummim . . . the history, or record, called 'The Book of Mormon'" (*Latter-day Saints Messenger and Advocate,* Oct. p.14).

The Book of Mormon was written in less than ninety working days with those few scribes the Lord sent to Joseph Smith—an amazing spiritual feat. About this time, an old friend, Joseph Knight Sr., came from Colesville, New York, a distance of about thirty miles, with provisions, including potatoes, mackerel, and several bushels of grain. He also brought lined paper and money to purchase more. Knight's visit was important in keeping the work moving along because Joseph and Oliver, being in dire need, had been looking for employment. Had they been forced to work for their daily needs even temporarily, the translation would have been delayed. Therefore, they were deeply grateful for the timely assistance which they considered a gift from heaven.

As Joseph and Oliver worked on the Book of Mormon records, they found several references to **baptism by immersion for the remission of sins.** Both young men wondered what this meant. They had not learned anything like it in the churches of the world. They decided to pray to God for enlightenment. **It was the fifteenth day of May, 1829,** when Joseph and Oliver went into the woods near Joseph's home in harmony, on the banks of the Susquehanna River, and knelt in prayer. Before they began to pray, they recalled once again the writings on the gold plates relating to baptism: *"And again the Lord called others, and said unto them likewise; and he gave unto them power to baptize. And he said unto them: On this wise shall ye baptize; and there shall be no disputations among you. Verily I say unto you, that whoso repenteth of his sins through your words and desireth to be baptized in my name, on this wise shall ye baptized them—Behold, ye shall go down and stand in the water, and in my name ye shall baptize them. And now behold, these are the words which ye shall say, calling them by name, saying: 'Having the authority given me of Jesus Christ, I baptize you in the name of the Father, and of the Son, and of the Holy Ghost, Amen.' And then shall ye immerse them in the water, and come again out of the water"* (Book of Mormon, 3 Nephi 11: 22-26; see 2 Nephi 31: 5).

As they began their prayer, a messenger of the Lord descended in a cloud of light and stood before them. The messenger told the young men that he was **John the Baptist of the New Testament,** and that he had come under the direction of Peter, James, and John, the three chief Apostles of the Lord during his earthly ministry in ancient times, who held **the keys of the Holy Priesthood.** John said that he had come to confer upon Joseph and Oliver **the Priesthood of Aaron,** which is the authority to administer in the temporal affairs of the Gospel. He said that shortly thereafter, **the Holy**

"The Restoration of the Aaronic Priesthood," by Del Parson, © The Church of Jesus Christ of Latter-day Saints, Used by Permission

Melchizedek Priesthood would be restored, as well. John said that when this should happen, Joseph was to be called the first Elder of the Church and Oliver was to be the second Elder.

John the Baptist, it will be remembered, baptized Jesus Christ in the River Jordan, and was later killed by the wicked King Herod. He came to Joseph and Oliver—as a resurrected personage, placed his hands upon the heads of Joseph and Oliver, and ordained them to the Aaronic Priesthood by saying the following: *"UPON you my fellow servants, in the name of Messiah I confer the Priesthood of Aaron, which holds the keys of the ministering of angels, and of the gospel of repentance, and of baptism by immersion for the remission of sins; and this shall never be taken again from the earth, until the sons of Levi do offer again an offering unto the Lord in righteousness*" (Doctrine & Covenants 13: 1). John told them that this Priesthood was the power to baptize with water, but that it did not include the power to lay on hands for the **Gift of the Holy Ghost**, which source would be given as part of the Holy Melchizedek Priesthood that was soon to be restored.

The messenger told them that they must be baptized in the water now that they held the Priesthood. He gave them directions as to how to do so, saying: that Joseph should first baptize Oliver, and then Oliver should baptize Joseph. They went to the nearby river, and there they baptized each other, as John had told them to do. When both were baptized according to John's instruction, they ordained each other to the Aaronic Priesthood, Joseph first ordaining Oliver and then Oliver ordaining Joseph.

As recorded in Joseph's journal: *"Immediately, on coming out of the water, after we had been baptized, we experienced great and glorious blessings from our Heavenly Father. No sooner had I baptized Oliver Cowdery, than the Holy Ghost fell upon him, and he stood up and prophesied many things which should shortly come to pass. And, again as soon as I had been baptized by him, I also had the spirit of prophesy, when standing up. I prophesied concerning the rise of this church, and many other things connected with the church, and this generation of the children for men. We were filled with the Holy Ghost, and rejoiced in the God of salvation"* (*History of the Church,* 1: 42). What joy must have been theirs when the Lord poured out His Spirit upon them! The power to act in God's name was restored and conferred upon them.

Oliver, the new scribe, was thrilled beyond words. He wrote about it later and said: "What a joy. What wonder. What amazement. Our eyes beheld, our ears heard. His voice, though mild, pierced to the center and his words, 'I am thy fellow servant,' dispelled every fear. We listened, we gazed, we admired. 'Twas the voice of a messenger from glory, twas a message from the Most High,' and as heard, we rejoiced, while his love enkindled upon our souls, and we were rapt in the vision of the Almighty. Where was room for doubt? Nowhere. Uncertainty had fled, doubt had sunk no more to rise, while fiction and deception had fled forever.'"

Oliver wrote much more about this great event, but from what he had been given, it is plain to see that if Oliver had had doubts before—they were gone now. He knew the word was true, and he knew that a messenger from heaven had appeared to him and had placed his hands upon his head, ordaining him to the Priesthood. It was one of the most glorious experiences of latter days.

As Joseph and Oliver continued their work of translation at Joseph's home in Pennsylvania, word began spreading around the village concerning their activities. Enemies lied about them to stir up bitterness and hatred among the people and they were threatened with bodily harm from one mob. Other mobs came forward against them, some led by ministers of other churches. Emma Smith's family, headed by her father, Isaac Hale, had become very friendly to her prophet husbands' work, and did much to help him at this time. They protected Joseph and Oliver from their enemies and contributed other acts of kindness. They were very much opposed to mob violence and did all they could to prevent evil men from injuring Joseph and Oliver.

The spirit of the special work they were doing for the Lord rested upon the two young men, even though mobs threatened them. They began to teach the Restored Gospel, as far as they understood it, to their friends and acquaintances. They taught from the Bible, showing what the Lord planned to do in the latter days. This effort brought about the first formal conversion in the person of Samuel H. Smith, the Prophet's younger brother, who was visiting from Palmyra at the time. Samuel's relationship to the Prophet and his acceptance of the account of the early visions did not automatically guarantee his acceptance of the need for baptism. Joseph and Oliver taught him many of the truths of the Gospel, as they understood them, under the inspiration of the Lord. Samuel was not easily persuaded by what he heard, having the Smith family qualities of independent thought and prayerfulness. He went into the woods by himself and knelt in prayer, asking God for wisdom that he might know the truth. He obtained personal revelation for himself, which convinced him of the truthfulness of the Gospel. On the twenty-fifth day of May, 1829, the same month Joseph and Oliver were baptized and ordained, Oliver baptized Samuel, who returned to his father's house, glorifying and praising God for the privilege which had come to him.

A good friend, Joseph Knight Sr., made the thirty-mile trip from his home to the Hale's several times with food and supplies for Joseph and Oliver. By this time, the opposition had become so open and intense that Joseph and Oliver's work was being impeded. It was at this juncture that David Whitmer and his family entered the picture. Oliver had been writing to his friend, David Whitmer, about the progress of the translation. **As people around Harmony continued their harassment,** both Joseph and Oliver wrote to David to ask for assistance. The Prophet had become acquainted with the father, Peter Whitmer, and some of his family, shortly after he started the translation. In the beginning of the month of June, David Whitmer, in answer to the request of Joseph and Oliver, left his family's farm in Fayette, Seneca County, New York, and traveled to Harmony. David arrived at Joseph's home in a large wagon drawn by two horses. He had come to move Joseph and Oliver to his father's place in Fayette. They would be provided with free room and board by his father, Peter Whitmer, until the work of the translation had been completed and the copyright secured. Not only did the Whitmer family provide room and board, but the Whitmer sons, especially John, also aided the Prophet in the translation by alternating with Oliver as scribe.

Once Joseph and Oliver were settled in their new home, they proceeded again with the work and made steady progress. The projected time for publication of the book was rapidly approaching, but the Prophet did not intend to place the only copy of the manuscript in the hands of the printer. Therefore, while John (or one of the other Whitmer boys) acted as a scribe to the Prophet, Oliver prepared a second copy of the manuscript. They were impressed with the interest shown in their work by the Whitmer family and some neighbors. Joseph and Oliver were so excited about their work and the profound nature of the teachings in the record, that they spent whatever spare time they had explaining these teachings to the people in the neighborhood. **Unlike the bitterness and enmity** (hatred) **they experienced in Palmyra and Harmony,** the people of Seneca County were friendly and very interested in the work. In fact, the Prophet made mention that many homes were open to them to conduct meetings with friends for the purpose of instruction and explanation. As a result, several persons were converted and baptized in June of 1829, approximately nine months before the Church was organized. The Prophet also recorded that his brother, Hyrum, David Whitmer, and Peter Whitmer Jr. were baptized in Seneca Lake.

The work of translation and the readying of the second copy of the manuscript moved forward at an accelerated pace. During the concluding period of the translation of the record, Joseph read about what had been predicted earlier in the translation, and what had been clearly stated in a revelation directed to Martin Harris in March of 1829. It was predicted that three special witnesses were to be provided by the Lord, whom He would allow to see the plates from which the Book of Mormon was translated. These witnesses should bear record of the same. That witness is found recorded in the Book of Mormon. These special three, seeing the plates "by the power of God" would establish the truth of the Prophet's declarations and stand "as a testimony against the world at the last day."

Almost immediately after they had made this discovery, Oliver Cowdery, David Whitmer, and Martin Harris, who had traveled from Palmyra to see about the progress of the translation, asked Joseph to inquire of the Lord if they might not obtain of Him the privilege to be these three special witnesses. After much persistence by the three, Joseph made the inquiry of the Lord, and it was revealed that Oliver, David, and Martin should be the special witnesses, having the blessing of seeing the ancient record and the responsibility of testifying to the world of what they and seen. But while Martin Harris looked forward to the event with excitement and anticipation, he was still troubled by the doubts and uncertainties that had clouded his relationship with the Prophet from the very beginning.

Shortly after the revelation identifying the three witnesses, Joseph's parents arrived at the Whitmer farm. They knew from a report sent to them by the Prophet that the work of translation was nearing completion. They also learned from their sons, Hyrum and Samuel, of the restoration of the Priesthood and about the baptisms that had been performed. Expressing that very same interest in their son and his work that they had shown from the time of his first glorious manifestation nine years earlier, these faithful parents came to give encouragement and support and to share in the feelings of joy and jubilation that they knew would accompany the completion of so great a task.

The viewing of the plates by the three witnesses occurred the day after Joseph's parents arrived. On that June day in 1829, the three received their evidence. The usual morning service was held at the Whitmer residence—scripture reading, singing, and prayers. The

Whitmer family, the Prophet and his wife, and Oliver Cowdery were present along with the Prophet's father, mother, and Martin Harris. As soon as Joseph arose from his knees, he approached Martin Harris (as related by the Prophet's mother, Lucy Smith) and said: *"Martin Harris, you have got to humble yourself before your God this day, that you may obtain a forgiveness for your sins. If you do, it is the will of God that you should look upon the plates in company with Oliver Cowdery and David Whitmer."* Due to earlier transgression of Martin Harris, betraying the trust of the Prophet in allowing the 116 pages of the manuscript to be lost or stolen, there certainly was a necessity for the strong counsel which the Prophet gave Martin Harris that morning.

The Prophet and the three witnesses went into the nearby woods close to the Whitmer home. In broad daylight they knelt in impassioned and humble prayer, Joseph praying first, followed by the others in succession, **asking Almighty God to grant them the opportunity to see the plates.** There was no response. They followed the same procedure a second time, and again, nothing happened. After the second failure, Martin Harris suggested that he withdraw from the group, since he felt that it was he who stood in their way of receiving revelation. With Joseph's approval, he left the circle and went further into the woods alone.

After his departure, Joseph, Oliver, and David knelt once again in prayer, and within a few minutes, it happened. They beheld a light of overwhelming brightness. A heavenly messenger stood before them above them in the air. He was holding the plates in his hands, and deliberately turned them leaf by leaf before their eyes, so that they would see the engravings thereon. Then they heard a voice from heaven saying: *"These plates have been revealed by the power of God, and they have been translated by the power of God, and the translation of them which you have seen is correct, and I command you to bear record of what you now see and hear"* (Bruce R. McConkie, *Mormon Doctrine,* SLC, Bookcraft, 1966, p.842).

As soon as Oliver and David had experienced this divine occurrence, Joseph went in search of Martin, whom he found nearby, engaged in sincere prayer. At Martin's request, Joseph joined him, and soon the same vision was opened to his view. In an ecstatic outburst, the prophet's doubting friend declared: "tis enough; tis enough; mine eyes have beheld; mine eyes have beheld." Then jumping to his feet, Martin shouted: "Hosanna," blessing God. And, according to the Prophet, he *"otherwise rejoiced exceedingly."*

Having obtained these glorious manifestations through the mercy of God, it now remained for these three individuals to fulfill the commandment which they had received, to bear record of these things. The heavy emotional burden lifted from Joseph's shoulders through the events of this day is beyond calculation. Until then, the matter of testifying to the divinity of the work in which he was engaged depended upon him alone. For almost two years, he had been forbidden by Moroni to show the plates to anyone and the most elaborate precautions had been taken to conceal them from the sight of others. In the minds of those who questioned the Prophet's truthfulness, these preventive measures were a scheme invented to cover up an unscrupulous hoax. Unable to retaliate, Joseph endured these insults in silence. To one so affected with the importance of honor and integrity, this was a heavy and awful burden for Joseph to bear. But *now* he had witnesses to help carry that load—witnesses who could corroborate his story. **Joseph was truly overjoyed that others had seen the plates and knew of their existence.** He was pleased that others now had the responsibility of bearing testimony with him concerning the records.

The four young men returned to the Whitmer home between three and four o'clock in the afternoon. Joseph sat down by the side of his father and mother and said: *"Father, Mother, you do not know how happy I am? The Lord has now caused the plates to be shown to three more besides myself. They have seen a heavenly messenger who has testified to them, and they will bear witness to the truth of what I have said, for now they know for themselves that I do not go about to deceive people."* Based upon their unique experience, the three witnesses wrote the following signed declaration which has appeared in every edition of the Book of Mormon:

The Testimony of Three Witnesses

"BE IT KNOWN unto all nations, kindreds, tongues and people unto whom this work shall come: That we, through the grace of God the Father, and our Lord Jesus Christ, have seen the plates which contain the record, which is a record of the people of Nephi, and also of the Lamanites, their brethren, and also of the people of Jared, who came from the tower of which hath been spoken. And we also know that they have been translated by the gift and power of God, for his voice hath declared it unto us; wherefore we know of a surety that the work is true. And we also testify that we have seen the engravings which are upon the plates; and they have been shown unto us by the power of God, and not of man. And we declare with words of soberness, that an angel of God came down from heaven, and he brought and laid before our eyes, that we beheld and saw the plates and the engravings thereon; and we know that it is by the grace of God the Father, and our Lord Jesus Christ, that we beheld and bear record that these things are true. And it is marvelous in our eyes. Nevertheless, the voice of the Lord commanded us that we should bear record of it; wherefore, to be obedient unto the commandments of God, we bear testimony of these things. And we know that if we are faithful in Christ, we shall rid our garments of the blood of all men, and be found spotless before the judgment seat of Christ, and shall dwell with him eternally in the heavens. And the honor be to the Father, and to the Son, and to the Holy Ghost, which is one God. Amen."

Oliver Cowdery
David Whitmer
Martin Harris

Soon after these things transpired**, eight other witnesses** saw the plates near the Smith residence at Manchester. It was on the occasion of the Prophet Joseph's coming to Manchester from Fayette accompanied by several of the Whitmers and Hiram Page, to make the arrangements for getting the Book of Mormon printed.

After arriving at the Smith's residence, Joseph Smith Sr., Hyrum Smith, and Samuel Smith joined Joseph's company from Fayette, and together they went into an area of the woods where members of the Smith family were accustomed to holding secret prayer. The gathering took place only a day or two after the three witnesses had been shown the record by the heavenly messenger. Their experience, however, was without the miraculous element. They gathered around Joseph as he showed them the record. It was broad daylight, and each handled the strange volume with complete liberty. They were allowed to leaf through the unsealed portion and closely examine the engravings. There was no appearance of heavenly beings. It was a simple matter-of-fact exhibition of the plates by the Prophet to his friends. Their testimony on the matter follows. It also appears in all editions of the Book of Mormon.

The Testimony of Eight Witnesses

"BE IT KNOWN unto all nations, kindreds, tongues and people, unto whom this work shall come: That Joseph Smith, Jun., the translator of this work, has shown unto us the plates of which hath been spoken, which have the appearance of gold; and as many of the leaves as the said Smith had translated, we did handle with our own hands; and we also saw the engravings thereon, all of which had the appearance of ancient work, and of curious workmanship. And this we bear record with words of soberness, that the said Smith has shown unto us, for we have seen and hefted, and know of a surety, that the said Smith has got the plates of which we have spoken. And we give our names unto the world, to witness unto the world that which we have seen. And we lie not, God bearing witness of it."

Christian Whitmer
Hiram Page
Jacob Whitmer
Joseph Smith, Sen.
Peter Whitmer, Jun.
Hyrum Smith
John Whitmer
Samuel H. Smith

Scores of writings deal with the statement of these two sets of witnesses. For more than a century, various explanations have been offered in an attempt to account for their testimonies on some basis other than the one the witnesses reported to be the case. In the last analysis, all of the circumstances—the fact that both experiences took place in broad daylight, that there were two widely-different types of experiences, that all concerned were mature men of proven judgment—these facts, together with the future acts and affirmations of these parties, all point to the conclusion that the situation in each case was as stated. There was no collusion, no trickery, no underhanded dealing and no juggling. In each case, it was a sober, factual experience that no one who shared in the phenomenon would ever forget.

All of the original three witnesses (Oliver Cowdery, David Whitmer, and Martin Harris) later left the Church. Two of them took a strong position in opposition to Joseph. Martin Harris and Oliver Cowdery—returned to the Church after years of disaffection, but even when they were on the outside of the Church, they boldly informed the world of the truthfulness of their testimonies published over their names in the Book of Mormon—even more meaningful in light of that fact is their disaffection. **This was up to the time of their deaths *not one* of them ever denied their testimonies concerning the Book of Mormon.**

David Whitmer never returned to the Church, but repeatedly took the same stand as his associates had taken. Shortly before his death, he published a pamphlet denying statements made in the Encyclopedia Americana and the Encyclopedia Britannica to the effect that the witnesses had disclaimed their testimony. **Nothing could be further from the truth.**

Of the eight witnesses, three left the

"The Restoration of the Melchizedek Priesthood," by Kenneth Riley, © The Church of Jesus Christ of Latter-day Saints, Used by Permission

Church, but *not one* of them ever so much as hinted a denial of his testimony—all the more convincing when we realize that once disaffected with the Church, they had no reason whatsoever to stick to their original story— **except that it was true**.

In the month of June, 1829, with several unsolved matters coming to a head, Joseph and Oliver continued with the translation, although they took time to answer numerous inquiries about the Gospel. In addition, they were becoming anxious to have the promise fulfilled that was given by John the Baptist, the messenger who conferred the Aaronic Priesthood upon them. He said that if they continued faithful, they would also receive the Holy Melchizedek Priesthood, which holds the authority of the laying on of hands for the **Gift of the Holy Ghost.** As they were engaged in humble prayer in a private room of the Whitmer house, the word of the Lord came to them. **They received instructions concerning ordinations and procedures for organizing the Church.** In conjunction with this, Joseph also received revelation that Oliver Cowdery and David Whitmer were called to help determine who the Twelve Apostles should be.

Shortly thereafter, toward the end of June, 1829, as Joseph and Oliver continued seeking knowledge from the Lord through solemn and intense prayer regarding the higher authority which had been promised them, their petition brought about another remarkable occurrence. It took place in the wilderness between Harmony, Pennsylvania, and Colesville, New York, on the banks of the Susquehanna River. **The three ancient Apostles—Peter, James, and John—appeared to them as resurrected beings and conferred upon Joseph and Oliver the keys of the Holy Melchizedek Priesthood.** Through this apostleship, they were authorized to become **special witnesses of the Messiah**, to organize the Church, to administer in spiritual things, to ordain each other Elders, and to call and ordain others to the same office. This was the **same authority that Peter, James, and John received anciently from the Messiah.** With this ordination, there was restored to the earth the same authority to act in God's name that had been enjoyed in the primitive church. It was not until both of these Priesthoods were restored to earth, that Joseph was authorized to organize—The Church and to speak and act in the name of God.

The story of the restoration of the Priesthood is one of the most significant stories of all time. The Priesthood once again assumed the importance, the greatness, and the prominence it had in the days of the Apostles. It is a power so real and vital as to be cherished above wealth, position, or fame.

From the time of the First Vision in the grove at Palmyra, Joseph had looked forward to the day when a definite organization of those who believed in the latter-day Restoration of the Gospel could be effected. He had the needed authority and nucleus of individuals eligible for membership. In answer to further prayers, the Lord revealed other matters concerning the organization and declared the exact day when the Church should come into being: April 6, 1830. These various revelations were grouped together and published in a book called: Doctrine and Covenants. During the months between June of 1829, and April 6, 1830, other baptisms were performed, and the Restoration of the Gospel was being discussed in meetings that were held in the homes of friends.

Although the translation was completed about July 1, 1829, and the plates had been returned once more to the custody of Moroni, the heavenly messenger, the Prophet's difficulties were far from being over. The publication of the book presented many problems; Joseph Smith was without funds, and so great was the feeling against the unseen book, that publishers hesitated to undertake that task. Martin Harris, the first scribe to the Prophet and one of the three witnesses who had originally committed himself to arrange for the funds to publish the book, now came to the rescue. Martin persuaded a reluctant printer, Egbert B. Grandin of Palmyra, who also was publisher of the *Wayne Sentinel*, to print 5,000 copies of the Book of Mormon at a price of $3,000. Martin mortgaged his farm to Grandin, agreeing that if he did not pay the full amount within eighteen months, Grandin could sell the farm. The contract was signed on August 25, 1829, and arrangements were made to start printing. While in Palmyra, the Prophet also obtained a copyright for the book, which would give legal protection against persons stealing or reprinting any part of it.

Extreme precaution was taken by Joseph to protect the publication. The Prophet had instructed Oliver to make a second copy of the translation, and only the copy was entrusted to the printer, a few pages at a time. The Prophet kept the original manuscript under guard day and night, as protection from the enemies who were trying to steal it. As Oliver Cowdery would go to and from the printer with portions of the translation, he was always accompanied by a guard. Notwithstanding these precautions, a garbled account of the Book of Mormon story nearly reached publication before the Book of Mormon itself. An ex-Justice of the Peace, Esquire Cole, obtained the use of E. B. Grandin's printing press during the evenings and on Sundays for the publication of his new weekly periodical called: *"Dogberry Paper on Winter Hill."* One Sunday morning, Hyrum Smith and Oliver Cowdery found him stealing parts of the Book of Mormon record, and preparing a mutilated account of the sacred record, with many vulgarisms added. He was warned to stop, but he didn't. Joseph was sent for, and went up during the week from Harmony. By firmly asserting his rights under the U.S. copyright laws and by threatening to prosecute those who infringed them, Cole was persuaded to abandon his plans to publish portions of the Book of Mormon in his papers.

As this difficulty passed, another arose. **The people of Palmyra and vicinity** held a mass meeting and passed a resolution pledging themselves not to purchase the Book of Mormon when it was published and to use their influence to prevent others from purchasing it. This action caused Mr. Grandin to suspend printing. Again the Prophet was sent for and again he made the trip from Harmony to Palmyra, alleviating Mr. Grandin's fears by giving renewed assurances that the amount agreed upon for printing the 5,000 books would be paid. The work proceeded and at last was completed, notwithstanding all the difficulties it had encountered. **The printing of the Book of Mormon began in August of 1829, and was completed by March 26, 1830. It was a great day when the Book of Mormon came off the press ready to be shared with all the world—a great work brought to a successful conclusion.**

* * *

Since we've spoken about the Book of Mormon frequently, it's time to explain its contents: Like the Bible, the Book of Mormon was written by prophets of God. It is sacred scripture that was written anciently, and has been revealed once again in modern times. The Book of Mormon contains the fulness of the Gospel of Jesus Christ, the Messiah, and is an abridged account of God's dealings with the ancient inhabitants of the American Continent from: 2247 B.C. to 421 A.D. It represents three migrations from the Eastern Hemisphere. The original records that were compiled and abridged to form the Book of Mormon were written on metallic plates by prophets of ancient times who were commanded to keep records of God's dealings with them and their people. These records preserved a true knowledge of God, of the mission and ministry of His Son, the Messiah Jesus Christ, and the teachings necessary to salvation. Incidental to these Gospel truths, much information was also preserved relative to the history and the social, economic, cultural, educational, governmental, and other conditions that existed among Book of Mormon people.

Why is the Book of Mormon so important to the world? (In the section on "Why I Had To Write This Book" I have borne my testimony. I choose now to have it impressed upon your mind once again.) The answer to this question—was something that I had to find out for myself. I read those 522 pages of scripture with an eye single to either gaining a solid conviction that the contents were true, or that the whole thing was a hoax. I literally tore apart the Book of Mormon, piece by piece, trying to find the gimmick, to find misinformation, to find a lack of continuity, or to find the unbelievable. When I put it back together again, everything fit, everything fell into place. I could find no negatives and I felt a personal, emotional release. I knew that a giant-size burden had been lifted, and I was thrilled and excited right out of my head. I began to feel as I did that first Sunday in July 1963, after my first visit to a Mormon Church.

I know that the Book of Mormon is the word of God, and God knows that I know it through the power of the Holy Ghost, who touched my heart and soul. This special personage of the Godhead has a Spirit Body in the form and likeness of man. He can only be in one place at a time, and yet His influence can be experienced every place at the same time (Bruce R. McConkie, *Mormon Doctrine,* SLC, Bookcraft, 1966, p. 359). Generally when Jewish people hear the words, 'Holy Spirit' or 'Holy Ghost,' they become turned off because they've been taught that their only relationship is to be strictly with God. In the Old Testament, there are scriptures that talk about the Holy Spirit, and the profound effect He had on peoples' lives. I personally felt His guidance and direction, helping me to know the truth. I didn't know for certain what I was feeling, nor did I fully understand who or what He was at the time. Subsequently, I learned that the Holy Spirit is able to dwell within us as a Comforter, as a Companion, and as the Spirit of Truth. He is a Revelator, a Spirit of the Lord, and Messenger of God the Father and His Son. His companionship is the greatest gift that mortals can enjoy, as long as they obey God's commandments.

The Book of Mormon is true scripture, and the Spirit informed me of that as I sought light and truth. I had received personal revelation from God through the power of the Holy Spirit and I could never deny my testimony, once I had finally received it. What is it that can make that Book of Mormon so important in our lives? Answer: **It's a second witness, a second confirmation to the world that Jesus is the Christ, the Messiah, the Son of the living God.** The Book of Mormon has never been proclaimed as a replacement of the Bible or scripture unto itself, but it is a companion to the Old and New Testaments.

The Book of Mormon is the word of God, and I found that through reading it, not just as literature like a book—but by reading a few pages each day—and then praying about it—I gained a deeper appreciation and understanding of the truths that God has revealed in the Bible.

In that sacred record, Moroni had engraved the following promise to those who read the Book of Mormon, an infallible test of it's divinity which may be applied by all— ***"And when ye shall receive these things, I would exhort you that ye would ask God, the Eternal Father, in the name of Christ, if these things are not true; and if ye shall ask with a sincere heart, with real intent, having faith in Christ, he will manifest the truth of it unto you, by the power of the Holy Ghost. And by the power of the Holy Ghost ye may know the truth of all things"*** (Moroni 10: 4, 5). Applying this test, I received my personal confirmation of the truth of the Book of Mormon.

* * *

It seems that we mortals have a tendency to fight against those things that are good for us. We're a stubborn people, and we don't want to be told what to do with our lives. We've been given our free agency from God, and in many instances, with this freedom of choice, we make poor, sometimes disastrous decisions for our lives. If we could only open our minds and our hearts, and allow the truth to enter through the power of God! And then again, if we don't like what we see and hear, and say no, why deny others their rights and privileges? Why should anyone be persecuted for their beliefs as long as they don't infringe upon the rights, privileges or beliefs of others? There's no denying the fact that at times, we are our own worst enemy, and continue to fool ourselves. Nevertheless, we should know for a certainty **all truth comes from one direction only—from God.**

* * *

During the latter part of the fourth century A.D., Mormon, a Prophet-General, and record keeper, made a compilation and abridgement of the records of the people of Lehi, a Jewish prophet who led a colony of his family and friends from Jerusalem to their American promised land in 600 B.C.—the Book of Mormon is a recounting of actual events, beginning about 600 years before the birth of the Messiah. In the ancient City of Jerusalem, then the home of God's chosen people and His prophets. **One of these prophets, whose name was Lehi,** preached of the unrighteousness of the people calling them to repentance and warning them of the impending destruction of Jerusalem. When his message was rejected, the Lord commanded Lehi to take his family and a small group of people and leave Jerusalem. **They were also required to take with them a set of brass plates which contained a scriptural history of God's dealings** with men from the beginning down to that day. This was the record of the Jews, a record of many prophecies, the law, the five books of Moses, and other writings of the prophets. Traveling in the wilderness for some time near the Red Sea, Lehi and his family camped for an extended period on the Southern shores of Arabia. There the Lord commanded them to build a ship, and the small colony began the eventful voyage which carried them across the Pacific Ocean to a promised land on the shores of South America.

In this new world they began to cultivate the earth and were abundantly blessed.

Here they found all kinds of ore: gold, silver, and copper. One of Lehi's sons, Nephi, shaped thin sheets or plates from these metals, on which to engrave a record of his people. They had brought with them from the old world a knowledge of both Jewish and Egyptian culture, and the records were engraved in reformed Egyptian characters.

When Lehi died, Nephi, also a prophet, was called by God to succeed his father as the religious leader of his people. However, because of jealousy and unrighteousness, his older brothers, rebelled against him. Nephi took his family and his followers, called **Nephites**, and traveled to another part of the land to settle. The leader of the rebellious group was named Laman, and his people became known as the **Lamanites**. Both colonies grew and prospered; over the years they developed into two great civilizations.

The value of the brass plates to the Nephites cannot be overemphasized. By means of the plates brought from Jerusalem, they were able to preserve the language, most of the civilization, and religious knowledge for the people from whom they came. From prophet to prophet and generation to generation, the brass plates were handed down and preserved by the Nephites. At some future day, the Lord had promised to bring forth undimmed by time and retaining their original brightness, the scriptural accounts recorded on them to *"go forward unto every nation, kindred, tongue and people."* Throughout Nephi's life, he continued to instruct the people in the ways of righteousness. As did the Old Testament prophets, he taught the Law of Moses, but also prophesied the coming of the Messiah. **Following the death of Nephi, other prophets were called, and continued to receive the word of the Lord to teach the people.** They also continued to engrave on metal plates their teachings, prophecies, experiences, and histories of their people. The records were passed down from one prophet to the next.

One of these prophets was a Nephite king named Benjamin, who lived about 124 B.C. He taught many things of the Messiah who was yet to come—about His life, His death, and His Resurrection. As the prophets in both hemispheres foretold, **the Son of God was born among the Jews, and was crucified to atone for the sins of mankind.**

In the new world, signs were given to the people in evidence of the fulfillment of these momentous events that were taking place halfway around the globe. Soon after the Messiah's ascension into heaven from the Mount of Olives in Jerusalem, following the Resurrection, the Book of Mormon prophets recorded that a voice was heard in the heavens. *"and it was said unto them: 'Behold my Beloved Son, in whom I am well pleased, in whom I have glorified my name—hear ye him.' . . . and behold, they saw a Man descending out of heaven; and he was clothed in a white robe; and he came down and stood in the midst of them . . . And it came to pass that he stretched forth his hand and spake to the people, saying: 'Behold, I am Jesus Christ, whom the prophets testified shall come into the world'"* (3 Nephi 11: 7-10). **The resurrected Lord had come to visit some of His other sheep! This was the fulfillment of the prophesy made as stated in the New Testament (John 10: 16), saying: *"other sheep I which are not of this fold: them also I must bring, and they shall hear my voice; and there shall be one fold, and one shepherd."***

The Messiah spent many days among them, healing the sick, blessing little children, introducing the sacrament, and teaching the glorious truths of the Gospel, as He had done during His ministry in Palestine. Here, too, He ordained Twelve Disciples and conferred the authority upon them to carry on His work. So profound was the influence of the Messiah upon the inhabitants of ancient America, that following His visits, they lived in peace and righteousness for nearly 200 years! But gradually, they began to grow wicked and fight among themselves. Throughout the next two centuries of their history, the Lamanite and the Nephite nations warred against one another continually.

These conflicts climaxed in a great battle, centered in the Eastern part of North America. About this time, a great Nephite Prophet and historian named Mormon gathered the records of his people and abridged them into a single volume that he called the Plates of Mormon. It is from this prophet that the Book of Mormon received its name. Mormon was killed in battle, but his son, Moroni, lived to witness the complete annihilation of his people by the Nephites. He alone remained, sole survivor of a once great nation, the last living prophet of the ancient American continent. After adding some writings of his own to the plates of Mormon, **Moroni buried them in a hill as directed by the Lord,** in Western New York State, that they would be preserved until the Lord was ready to bring them forth in the latter days

Following the extermination of the Nephite civilization, the Lamanites continued to inhabit the Western Hemisphere. Their posterity, with some supplementary groups, constituted the many aboriginal tribes, now known as the American Indians, that were found by European discoverers of the new world. Generally not a record keeping people, and for the most part nomadic, their culture deteriorated. They lived in cities already built. They built less magnificent structures of their own, often upon the ruins of earlier cities, or more often, abandoned sedentary life altogether to follow game trails in the wilderness. It is generally agreed that even the great Incan and Aztec civilizations had declined from the level achieved by their Nephite predecessors. **Today, throughout the Americas and concentrated most heavily in Southern Mexico, Central America, and the Western section of South America,** are found the remains for the vast civilizations and highly-developed cultures which once thrived there. Until only a few decades ago, relatively little was known about these civilizations, apart from the Book of Mormon history. When the record was first published, there was considerable skepticism by some concerning many of its claims. As **archeologists and anthropologists** began to explore these areas, the Book of Mormon claims, fantastic as some once thought them to be, were soon substantiated with concrete physical evidence. Buildings, fortifications, great highways, entire cities, and thousands of artifacts have now been discovered and can be visited on location or viewed in museums. The vast number of discoveries and extensive research of recent years—verify the Book of Mormon story—over and over again.

And what about the truth of metal plates being used anciently to keep records? In the 1,000s of years of recorded history in the world, ancient peoples have used various means of preserving their writings. Some have engraved their messages upon rock, such as the Rosetta Stone. Others marked up clay tablets which then were sun-baked. Writings have been found upon wood, cloth, leather and bark. Patterns have been woven into fabrics in some instances. Probably one of the

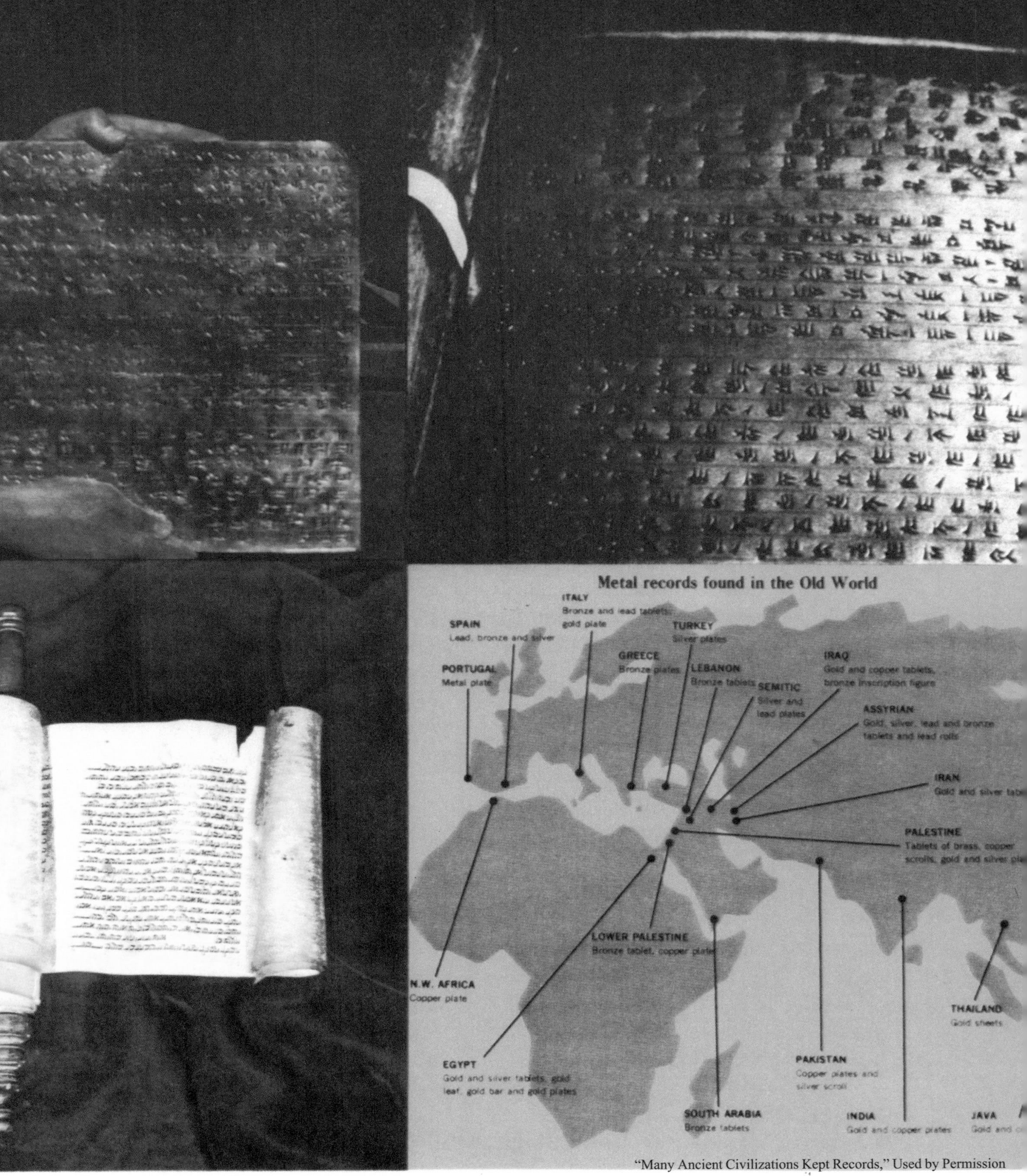

"Many Ancient Civilizations Kept Records," Used by Permission

Many Ancient Civilizations Kept Records

Museums throughout the world contain numerous examples of ancient records. Many of them permanently inscribed upon metal plates have been discovered and translated.

best known methods of preserving records anciently had been through the use of papyrus. For many years, it was not known that ancient records were kept upon plates of metal. **However in recent times, archeologists have discovered scores of instances where such metallic plates were kept. Some were engraved upon beautiful gold and silver. Others were made upon copper, bronze, and lead.** The metals used for these records were beaten into thin plates of various sizes. Sometimes alloys were used which made the metal very hard and durable. The most recent of ancient metal engravings discovery was the Dead Sea Scrolls, part of which consisted of two copper scrolls rolled up together. The text was inscribed so deeply upon them that it stood out in relief on the back. **One of the most important discoveries of ancient metal records, was the gold and silver plates of the Emperor Darius of Persia (518 B.C.),** found sealed in a box of stone and bearing a text in three languages. Sargon, king of Assyria (722 B.C.), repeats over and over in his "Annals," that he kept his records on plates of gold, silver, bronze, and lead. Such plates have been found in many parts of the world, including America and the Orient.

While reading the Book of Mormon, I was continually seeking additional information and evidence about the relationship between the Bible and the Book of Mormon. I found my answers in the Old Testament, verifying what I had already found. One of the greatest of God's purposes in the latter days is to—gather the Twelve Tribes of Israel. Ezekiel was a favored prophet of the Lord, who lived some 600 years B.C., at about the same time Lehi was commanded to leave Jerusalem. Through him, the Lord revealed that two records were to be kept. **As Ezekiel spoke of the gatherings of the tribes, he wrote particularly of the Jews and the descendants of Joseph (Ephraim and Manasseh).** Before the tribes come together, their records will be joined, eventually to become one in the hand of the Lord's servants. Ezekiel spoke of their records in his thirty-seventh chapter, as he foretold the gathering of Israel in the last days. He speaks of two "sticks," and allows these "sticks" to represent the nations of Judah and Joseph (Ephraim) which will be united eventually. There will also be **"two records—one for Judah, and one for Joseph."** Because some ancient records were kept on parchment or other material, and rolled on sticks, they were referred to as—sticks. *"Moreover, thou son of man, take thee one stick, and write upon it, For Judah, and for the children of Israel his companions: then take another stick , and write upon it, For Joseph, the stick of Ephraim, and for all the house of Israel his companions: And join them one to another into one stick; and they shall become one in thine hand"* (Ezekiel 37: 16-17).

The *Stick of Judah*—is the Bible and the *Stick of Joseph* (Ephraim)—is the Book of Mormon. Much of the Old Testament, as well as the New Testament, is largely the record of God's dealings with the Jews and fulfillment of the blessings promised Judah and his posterity—the Stick of Judah. From the Book of Mormon, we learn that Lehi was the descendant of Joseph. The Book of Mormon—the Stick of Joseph is the story of his people, and records the fulfillment of blessings promised his posterity. The records support and compliment each other. They both contain the word of God, and they have become as one. **The Bible and the Book of Mormon are companions,** the Book of Mormon is a second witness another testament that Jesus is the Christ, the Messiah and Savior of the world. These great truths were opened to me because my mind and my heart were receptive and fertile, and not closed by family traditions, past environment, or worldly prejudices and pressures. Those many weeks I spent in constant study and prayer, seeking knowledge and information to help me know God's counsel and direction for me, finally came to fruition. I gained the testimony that the Book of Mormon was authentic, genuine, and irrefutable. It was equally apparent that the other background material and studies about Jesus Christ, Joseph Smith, the apostasy, and the Restoration of the true Church, were also true. **Everything tied together, the physical and spiritual; it all fit**.

The majority of the early converts to Mormonism came into the Church because they read and gained a witness of the truthfulness of the Book of Mormon. Thousands gave their lives for their beliefs. Since its first publication, the book has affected the lives of men and women in many lands who have testified of this. The sufferings they have endured and the works they have accomplished have become perhaps the strongest of all testimonies for the reality of the gold plates and their translation into the Book of Mormon to become in this lifetime, another witness of Christ.

And again, the great and conclusive evidence of the divinity of the Book of Mormon is the testimony of the Spirit to the honest truth seeker. Moroni, the angel and messenger from God promised: ***"And when ye shall receive these things, I would exhort you that ye would ask God, the Eternal Father, in the name of Christ, if these things are not true; and if ye shall ask with a sincere heart, with real intent, having faith in Christ, he will manifest the truth of it unto you, by the power of the Holy Ghost"*** (Moroni 10:4).

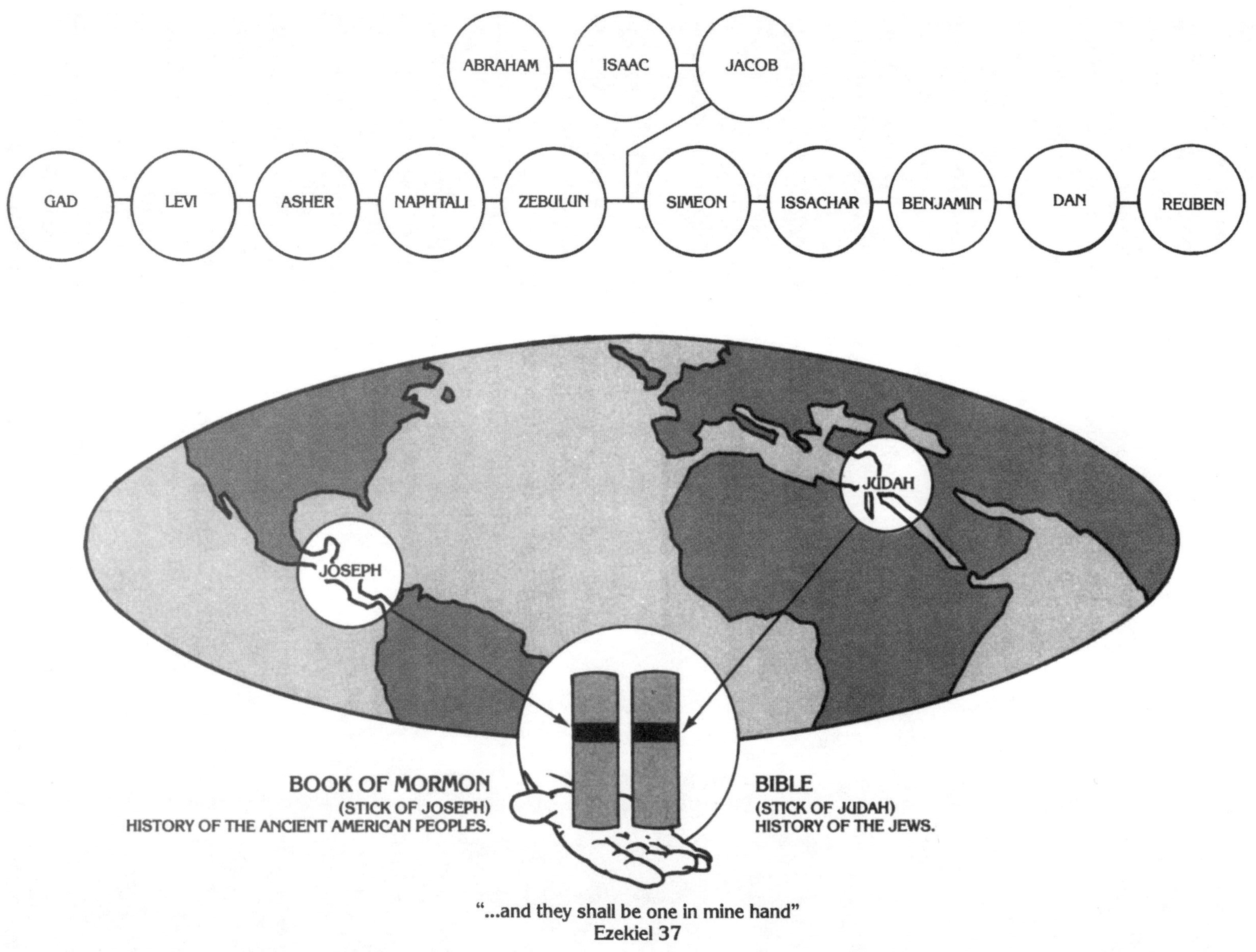

"The Bible and The Book of Mormon"
Used by Permission

Chapter 5

The Church of Jesus Christ is Organized

The First Miracle

Significant Revelations Given to the Newborn Church

Joseph Smith Receives a Revelation for his wife Emma

Importance of the Sacrament

The Church Continues to Grow Rapidly

The Book of Mormon became a Religious Bombshell

***A Mission to the American Indians—
Joseph Smith Called: "The Paleface Prophet"***

Ten years had passed since Joseph Smith had gone into the grove to inquire of the Lord which of the churches was right and which he should join. Ten years of prayer, training, instruction under the hands of heavenly messengers, of study and of inspiration had passed since he had learned from Jesus Christ, the Messiah Himself, that he should join none of them. The Priesthood had been restored, the keys to the Holy Apostleship had been returned, and the authority to officiate in the Messiah's name had been given. In accordance with revelation, Joseph was instructed that the time had come to organize the true Church.

Since April sixth had been identified as the anniversary of the Messiah's birth, it was also designated by revelation to be the day on which the Church should be organized. On Tuesday, April 6, 1830, The Church of Jesus Christ, was officially organized at the home of Peter Whitmer Sr., in Fayette, New York, with about thirty people present. Articles of Incorporation of The Church of Jesus Christ had been previously drawn up in conformity to the laws of the State of New York concerning religious organizations. As a part of the proceedings of the first meeting, the papers were signed by the first six baptized in this dispensation. These were in order of their baptism: Oliver Cowdery, Joseph Smith Jr., Samuel H. Smith, Hyrum Smith, David Whitmer, and Peter Whitmer Jr. They became the first legal members of the Church. The young Prophet was twenty-four years of age, and the others ranged in age from twenty-one to thirty.

Approximately twenty of those in attendance had come from Colesville, a distance of about 100 miles, to participate in the events of this sacred occasion. The meeting was opened with solemn prayer. According to previous commandment, the Prophet Joseph called upon the brethren present to indicate their willingness to accept him and Oliver Cowdery as their teachers and spiritual advisors in the things of the kingdom of God. If they were willing, they would proceed to organize the Church according to the commandments of the Lord. To this they consented by unanimous vote. Members of the group who had been baptized previously were all rebaptized on the day of the organization. Joseph then ordained Oliver an Elder in The Church of Jesus Christ; after which Oliver ordained Joseph an Elder of said church. They next administered the Sacrament of the Lord's Supper and passed it to those present as stated by Joseph: *"We took the bread, blessed it, and brake it with them: also wine, blessed it, and drank it with them."* The prayers they used had been received through revelation—as recorded in Doctrine and Covenants Section twenty, verses seventy-five to seventy-nine.

After this, they laid their hands upon the heads of each individual member of the Church present, that they might receive the **Gift of the Holy Ghost** and be confirmed members of The Church of Jesus Christ. There was a special spirit present that touched each person's heart, all in attendance praised the Lord and felt wonderfully joyful. During the meeting, Joseph received another revelation directing him: *"BEHOLD, there shall be a record kept among you; and in it thou shalt be called a seer, a translator, a prophet, an apostle of Jesus Christ, an elder of the church, through the will of God the Father and the grace of your Lord Jesus Christ"* (Doctrine & Covenants 21: 1).

In this manner the will of God was set forth in relation to the organization of the Church. But nothing was to be effective except by consent and vote of the people. For the Lord said: *"all things shall be done by common consent in the Church and by prayer and faith"* (Doctrine & Covenants 26: 2). Further, *"No person is to be ordained to any office in the Church, where there is a regularly organized branch of the same, without the vote of that Church"* (Doctrine & Covenants 20: 65). **Therefore, the members were taught that God would give counsel and use persuasion in guiding the Church, but never use compulsion**. The Lord expects His officers in the Church to stand on high moral ground and follow the same principle. Therefore, from the beginning, He applied **the principle of common consent** in His dealings with the Saints, reflecting the basic teaching that the eternal spirits of mankind are free agents.

This concept found frequent expression in the Prophet's dealings with his brethren. Later, while wrongfully imprisoned in a Missouri jail, Joseph wrote a lengthy letter that included this meaningful restatement of that principle: *"No power or influence can or ought to be maintained by virtue of the priesthood, only by persuasion, by long-suffering, by gentleness and meekness, and by love un-*

feigned; By kindness and pure knowledge, which shall greatly enlarge the soul without hypocrisy, and without guile" (Doctrine & Covenants 121: 41-42). Earlier in the same letter, he deplored the tendency of men to attempt to impose their will upon others: *"We have learned by sad experience that it is the nature and disposition of almost all men, as soon as they get a little authority, as they suppose, they will immediately begin to exercise unrighteous dominion"* (Doctrine & Covenants 121: 39). On another occasion, when he was asked how he was able to maintain such effective control over his followers, he answered: ***"I teach them correct principles, and they govern themselves."*** Still, the Lord instructed members of the infant Church to receive Joseph's word *"as if from my own mouth, in all patience and faith"* (Doctrine & Covenants 21: 5).

Directed by the Spirit of the Lord, Joseph and Oliver ordained some of the other brethren to different offices of the Priesthood that unforgettable day. After a happy time spent in witnessing and feeling the power and blessings of the Holy Ghost, they were dismissed from the meeting with the pleasing knowledge that they now had been acknowledged of God as members of The Church of Jesus Christ. They knew they were organized in accordance with the commandments and revelations given by God to them in these last days, as well as according to the order of the Church as recorded in the New Testament (*History of the Church,* 1: 79). Joseph also took the opportunity to teach the Saints and bear his own testimony.

Several persons who had attended the meeting, became convinced of the truth when they saw and felt the working of the Spirit of the Lord during the meeting, and desired baptism. **Among those who asked for baptism soon after the organization of the Church, were Lucy and Joseph Smith Sr., (Joseph's parents)** Martin Harris, and Orrin Porter Rockwell. It was a time of joy and happiness in the life of the Prophet, who exclaimed: *"Praise to my God! That I lived to see my father baptized into the true Church of Jesus Christ!"* (Lucy Mack Smith, *History of Joseph Smith by His Mother,* p.168).

The new organization was designated by revelation as The Church of Jesus Christ, to which the phrase "Latter-day Saints" was later added. **This is worthy of note—the Church was not named for Joseph Smith or for any man.** Nor was it named for any characteristic of government or function, as had been the case with many other religious societies. It was: The Church of Jesus Christ, restored to earth in "the latter days," and was so designated.

Again, the manner in which the officers of the Church are selected is a matter of interest. Joseph Smith had been divinely chosen to lead the work, but his position as leader was subject to the consent of the members. Ever since that first meeting on April 6, 1830, the members of the Church have convened periodically to "sustain" or vote by common consent, all those chosen to direct the affairs of the Church. **No man presides without the consent of the membership.**

On April 11, 1830, the Sunday following the organization of the Church, Oliver Cowdery delivered the Church's first public sermon in the ministry of the Church, at the Peter Whitmer Sr., home in Fayette, New York—in the very same room in which the Church was formed a week earlier. Many people attended, and on that same day, six people were baptized. A week later, on Sunday April eighteenth, along with seven others, Peter Whitmer Sr. asked for baptism. They went to as Seneca Lake, as those who were baptized a week earlier had done; there Oliver performed the ordinance.

One might have expected that at this first meeting the Prophet would have been the principal speaker. Surely he was the best qualified because of his insight into spiritual things. The Prophet requested that Oliver Cowdery deliver that first public sermon. He was content to provide Oliver with a platform for growth in leadership ability, something the infant Church sorely needed at that time. This fact revealed a facet of Joseph's leadership that, without question, contributed to the rapid growth of the Church in the years that followed. He never felt prompted to do everything himself; on the contrary, he called on others to have them develop themselves in leadership roles.

During this time, Joseph also received a revelation answering the question in regard to the necessity of being baptized again when an individual had previously been baptized in another church. The answer was: *"Wherefore, although a man should be baptized an hundred times it availeth him nothing, for you cannot enter in at the straight gate by the law of Moses, neither by your dead works"* (Doctrine & Covenants 22: 2). The Lord affirmed that proper authority was essential to perform a valid baptism. That authority had been lost and was restored to earth at this time by John the Baptist.

During this same month of April, the Prophet Joseph went to visit the little town of Colesville, not far from Fayette, to spend some time with friends. He stayed with the Joseph Knight family. Mr. Knight had helped the Prophet and Oliver by providing for their material needs on several occasions while the Prophet and Oliver were translating the Book of Mormon. They went the extra mile; they were truly lifesavers. The Knights belonged to the Universalist Church, and they enjoyed talking about the Gospel.

Aside from the social aspects of the visit, Joseph wanted to proselyte his friends and former neighbors. Meetings were set up in homes in the area, at which Joseph taught the principles of the Restored Gospel, discussed the scriptures, including the Book of Mormon (which was by then printed and available), and reviewed several spiritual experiences he had enjoyed over the years. The impact of these meetings was electrifying. Many were converted and baptized, and later organized into the Colesville Branch. Members of this group maintained their identity as the Colesville Branch even after they moved on from the small community from which they took their name. Almost two years later, after they had migrated to distant Missouri, the Prophet made this entry in his journal while visiting the Saints in Kaw township, just a few miles west of Independence, Missouri: *"I visited the brethren . . . and I received a welcome only known by brethren and sisters united as one in the same faith, and by the same baptism, and supported by the same Lord. The Colesville branch, in particular, rejoiced as the ancient Saints did with Paul"* (*History of the Church,* 1: 269).

The reference to Paul, of course, related to the joy the ancient apostle had in associating with those whom he had been instrumental in converting. But unlike Paul, Joseph spent most of his ministry in the main areas of great concentration, giving administrative direction to the growing and developing affairs of the Church. And so while he was the "main man" in converting many people during his short ministry, and while he was second to none in the influence he exerted on the Church and its membership, Colesville seems to have been the single example in which he was responsible for the conversion of a large group of people.

It isn't difficult to understand why the Prophet's appearance in Colesville created such an uproar. A few years earlier, when Joseph came there as a laborer for Josiah Stowell, there had been talk about his having received an unusual spiritual manifestation. Later on, the curiosity and interest increased when word spread that he had returned with the gold plates and was in the process of translating them. When the word spread that he and one of his scribes had been visited by resurrected beings (messengers), the neighborhood erupted into unreasoning and uncontrolled opposition, hostility, and abuse, resulting in Joseph's immediate exit from Colesville to Fayette, where he was able to complete the work of translation in an atmosphere of peace. Now, almost a year later, he had returned, but not in failure as his critics had predicted. He had brought with him concrete evidence of success in the form of bound copies of the Book of Mormon, which not only contained the witness of eleven mature men, attesting to the divine nature of the book, but also the startling promise that **anyone who read the book with an open mind and a prayerful heart could learn of its truthfulness by heavenly means.**

One of the regular attenders at the numerous home meetings held in and near Colesville was Newel Knight, a son of the Prophet's longtime friend and supporter, Joseph Knight. In a private conversation with Newel, Joseph emphasized the role of prayer in gaining a personal conviction of the reality of the power of God. Somewhat convinced of the truthfulness of these statements, Newel agreed reluctantly to attempt to offer a public, vocal prayer at one of the home meetings. When the time came, however, he became frightened and embarrassed, and despite the persuasive challenge and encouragement of the Prophet and others, he decided not to participate. The next morning he went into the woods where he tried to pray, but failed because he felt guilty for refusing to pray publicly. He began to feel uneasy and even ill, and returned home where his wife became alarmed at his appearance. By this time, his inner torment, pain, and misery had produced in his outward appearance an ugly, frightening image, and he seemed to be unable to control his movements. His body began to gyrate and to be tossed around his apartment. The noise and commotion attracted the attention of some neighbors who came running to learn the cause. They were taken aback by what they saw; they found themselves powerless to either control the erratic, violent movement of Newel's body or to calm the agonizing terror of his mind. In the midst of all this, Newel pleaded for his wife to send for Joseph Smith. This is the Prophet's account of what happened after he arrived: *"I succeeded in getting hold of him by the hand, when almost immediately he spoke to me, and with great earnestness, requested me to cast the devil out of him, saying that he knew he was in him, and that he also knew that I could cast him out."*

Acting on Newel's faith as well as his own, Joseph replied: *"if you know that I can it shall be done; and then almost unconsciously I rebuked the devil, and commanded him in the name of Jesus Christ to depart from him; when immediately Newel spoke out and said that he saw the devil leave him and vanish . . . from his sight.* ***This was the first***

miracle which was done in the Church, *or by any member of it; and it was done not by man, nor by the power of man, but it was done by God, and by the power of Godliness; therefore, let the honor and the praise, the dominion and the glory, be ascribed to the Father, Son, and the Holy Spirit, for ever and ever. Amen"* (*History of the Church,* 1: 82-83).

The Prophet then continued with his narration: *"This scene was now entirely changed, for as soon as the devil had departed from our friend, his countenance became natural, his distortions of the body ceased, and almost immediately, the Spirit of the Lord descended upon him, and the visions of eternity were open to his view. So soon as consciousness returned, his bodily weakness was such that we were obliged to lay him upon his bed, and wait upon him for some time"* (*History of the Church,* 1: 83).

This happening was witnessed by a number of neighbors who began to study the Gospel, and most of them joined the Church. Because of what they had seen for themselves, they were convinced beyond a shadow of doubt of the reality and power of both God and Satan and of the authority of Joseph to speak and act in the name of God.

Though this represented the first miracle performed in the newly organized Church, to Joseph it was but another in the seemingly endless chain of spiritual experiences he had enjoyed during the previous decade. Newel Knight continued to study, then during the last week of May 1830, he visited the Prophet and the other Saints at Fayette, and was baptized by David Whitmer.

News of the Newel Knight miracle spread rapidly throughout the area. Its effect upon the public depended upon their individual state of mind. Those who truly believed in a supreme being and in the reality of the unseen world were anxious to see and hear the Prophet. The independent testimony of those who had witnessed the event, caused the believer to investigate Joseph's claims in a candid and sincere way, it was from this group that converts came. However, among Joseph's enemies and slanderers, and among disbelievers in the community, word of the incident was greeted with contempt and ridicule. Some of them were content solely to criticize and cast aspersions on the Prophet; others were more destructive and seemed determined to do him bodily harm. In the forefront of this group were several prominent ministers, who lost no opportunity to provoke others against the Prophet whether in their own pulpits or in private conversation.

THE FIRST GENERAL CONFERENCE OF THE CHURCH IS HELD

When Joseph returned to Fayette, he found that the publication of the Book of Mormon had created much excitement and interest. Many were converted and became members of the Church. Naturally there was the usual opposition, but it lacked the accent on violence and harmfulness that had been evident at Colesville.

By June 1830, the numbers of Joseph's followers had increased to the point that it was thought necessary to hold a conference to give them motivation and direction. Thus began a practice that has become one of the distinguishing features of the Church. On June ninth, about thirty members were in attendance along with some friends and investigators. They were barely able to crowd into Peter Whitmer's home, the place where the

Church had been organized a meager two months before. As was true with the meetings at Colesville, this conference was charged with an almost electric atmosphere that was heightened by the presence of Newel Knight. The business of the conference, which included the confirmation of those who had been baptized and the conferring of the Priesthood upon a number of the brethren, was followed by a period of guidance and direction, advice, and instruction. Many were blessed with the power of the Holy Spirit in this conference. This ecstatic event filled Joseph's followers with an almost unlimited devotion, eagerness, and enthusiasm, and an unshakable testimony of the divine nature of the work of the Lord.

After the conference was over, eleven more people joined the Church, including Joseph Smith's brothers, William and Don Carlos and his sister, Katherine. They were baptized by David Whitmer in Seneca Lake.

Soon after this first conference, Joseph returned to Colesville to continue with his proselyting activities and to get his personal affairs in order. The reception he received was something he had not fully expected. Not only were his followers, happy and excited at his return; their enthusiasm and personal conviction had also had its effect on many others who were anxious for baptism or to learn more about the doctrines he taught.

In addition to the increase of interest and devotion on the part of the Prophet's followers there came to the front a destructive spirit of hostility, confrontation, and opposition from his enemies—and he had many due to his calling from God. Those against him were not content to attempt to expose the Church on theological grounds; they resorted to physical violence.

Along with Joseph on this Colesville trip was his wife, Emma, Oliver Cowdery, John Whitmer, and David Whitmer. The brethren planned to baptize those who desired baptism, just before the meeting on Sunday. On Saturday afternoon, June twenty-sixth, the brethren dammed a stream in order to make a pond suitable for baptisms. That night, a good-sized mob of unwieldy, people, incited by leaders of some area churches who feared losing members of their own congregations to the Prophet Joseph, demolished the dam. Although they could not perform baptisms that Sunday, the Saints did gather together in a meeting where Oliver Cowdery preached and others present bore their testimonies to the truthfulness of—the Book of Mormon.

Some of the men who had destroyed the dam in the creek also attended this meeting. They did not cause any trouble until after the meeting was over, when they began to argue with the friends of the Prophet, trying to get them to forsake him and his teachings.

A Presbyterian preacher named the Reverend Mr. Shearer came for this purpose. Miss Emily Coburn, a sister of the wife of Newel Knight was a member of Mr. Shearer's congregation. When he saw her there, he seized her by the arm and tried to force her to leave the meeting and go home to her father. She refused to leave. He tried to physically pull her down the road, but her sister ran to her assistance, helping her get away from Mr. Shearer. Nevertheless, Mr. Shearer was determined to prevent her from attending any more of Joseph's meetings. He spoke to her father, but to no avail. All his efforts were in vain, and a short time later Emily was baptized into The Church of Jesus Christ.

Early the next day, Monday morning, June twenty-eighth, the brethren repaired the dam and held the baptismal service. Thirteen people were baptized, including Emma Smith. Her baptism brought great joy to the Prophet. Joseph Knight and his son, Joseph Jr., were also in the group baptized.

As soon as the Saints were completing the service, some of the local mob came near. Not wishing to cause trouble, the Saints left the creek and headed for Joseph Knight's house. Soon after, about fifty of the mob surrounded the house, shouting and threatening to injure the Prophet and his friends. Joseph was concerned; he felt that for the safety of the Knight family he and his wife and some others should leave. The mob did not give up and continued to follow them. It was the plan of the Prophet to hold a meeting that same Monday evening to confirm those who had been baptized that morning. He decided not to allow the mob to frighten him away; and so he prepared to hold the meeting.

Just as he was ready to begin, a police officer came in and arrested the Prophet on the grounds that he was upsetting the community with his teachings of the Book of Mormon. He was taken to South Bainbridge in Chenango County for trial as a disorderly person. Mobs tried to intercept Joseph and the constable, but the officer succeeded in protecting the Prophet.

The officer told the Prophet that he was certain that those who signed the complaint merely wanted to get the Prophet out of the house where they could harm him. He said that the vicious neighbors were planning to attack both of them. The officer told Joseph that he would protect him. As he and the Prophet got into the officer's wagon, the mob tried to surround them, but the officer lashed the horse and drove quickly out of their reach.

While the horse was running at top speed, one of the wheels came off their wagon, and they were forced to stop. The mob was close behind, and Joseph became concerned that they might catch him. Nevertheless, they found the wheel and quickly put it back on, leaving the mob behind at a goodly distance.

They drove to the town of South Bainbridge in a neighboring county and took a room in a hotel for the night. The officer told Joseph to sleep in the bed. He himself slept on the floor with his gun at his side and his feet against the door so that he would wake up if anyone tried to come in, but no one disturbed them during the night.

The next day Joseph was taken into court, where a trial was held. His enemies tried to prove that he was a dishonest man. They brought in Josiah Stowell, from whom Joseph bought a horse, and Jonathan Thompson, from whom Joseph had bought a cow. They tried to make both men say that Joseph had obtained the animals dishonestly, but both men said that: "Joseph paid for the animals." Then Mr. Stowell's two daughters were called in. They had both kept company with Joseph a few times. The enemies of the Prophet tried to get the girls to say he had been unkind to them. They both said: "Joseph was a fine young man." When the judge of the court saw that the Prophet's accusers could not prove a thing against him, he let Joseph go.

When Joseph was about to leave the courtroom, another officer came in with a new complaint signed by Joseph's enemies. Again he had to stand trial, and again his enemies tried to prove false claims against him, but could not. Joseph's lawyers showed that Joseph was not a lawbreaker, but a good citizen. The policeman who had arrested him now came forward and apologized to him. He told Joseph that if the court freed him again, the mob would tar and feather him. He offered to take Joseph to safety. After the judge closed the court, saying that Joseph was innocent, the officers took the Prophet out of the building by a back door and helped him escape from the mob. He went to his wife's sister's house where Emma was waiting for him. Soon they proceeded to their home in Harmony.

A few days later, Joseph Smith returned to Colesville with Oliver Cowdery to confirm those who had been baptized. They had scarcely arrived when a mob began to gather at the Knight home. The mob shouted their reckless rage and frustration. They shoved the Prophet, and pushed him down. They shouted threats against him, sometimes in vulgar and profane language. Joseph and Oliver thought it best to leave without even taking time to rest. They barely escaped the mob that pursued them throughout the night. Joseph said: *"Thus we were persecuted on account of our religious faith—in a country the Constitution of which guarantees to every man the indefeasible* [permanent] *right to worship God according to the dictates of his own conscience—and by men, too, who were professors* [ministers] *of religion, and who were not backward to maintain the right of religious liberty for themselves, though they could thus wantonly* [wrongfully] *deny it to us"* (*History of the Church,* 1: 97).

In the meantime, the Saints in Colesville were praying for the return of Joseph and Oliver, which happened in early August and involved a miracle. Since hostile feelings persisted, Joseph and Hyrum Smith and John and David Whitmer **prayed mightily** before their journey to Colesville. As Newel Knight declared: *"Their prayers were not in vain. A little distance from my house, they encountered a large company of men at work upon the public road, amongst whom were some of our most bitter enemies who looked earnest at the brethren, but not knowing them, the brethren passed unmolested"* (*Newel Knight's Journal,* LDS Church Historical Department, Salt Lake City, p. 11). The confirmations at Colesville finally took place, along with the partaking of the Sacrament—a joyful breather between troubles and challenges.

A remarkable feature of the Prophet's character and leadership ability became apparent during the hectic summer of 1830. Although heavily preoccupied in avoiding the mobs and in providing the daily necessities of life for himself and Emma, he received several significant revelations. In June, he received part of what is now known as the Book of Moses in the Pearl of Great Price scriptures, which is the record of a revelation given to Moses at a time when he saw God face-to-face on *"an exceedingly high mountain"* (Mount Sinai). This revelation announced that God had created: *"worlds without number,"* and that the chief work and glory of God was *"to bring to pass the immortality and eternal life of man."*

Several other revelations were received in July, telling Joseph to be patient in his afflictions, and instructing him to continue in prayer and in writing those things which would be given him by the Comforter, (Holy Ghost) and teaching all scriptures to the Church. He was also counseled to let his time be devoted to the studying of the scriptures, to preaching and to performing his labors on his land, such as was required, until after he would hold the next conference, in Fayette in September, at which time he would receive further instructions (Doctrine & Covenants 26: 1).

In July, Joseph received a revelation for his wife, Emma. The Lord gave Emma Smith, an important work to do. It is always pleasing to the Lord when his Saints sing sacred hymns in their meetings, but the hymns for his new Church must be carefully chosen.

The Lord spoke to Emma through the Prophet Joseph, with these words: *"HEARKEN unto the voice of the Lord your God, while I speak unto you Emma Smith, my daughter; for verily I say unto you, all those who receive my gospel are sons and daughters in my kingdom. A revelation I give unto you concerning my will; and if thou art faithful and walk in paths of virtue before me, I will preserve thy life, and thou shalt receive an inheritance in Zion. Behold thy sins are forgiven thee, and thou art an elect lady, whom I have called*" (Doctrine & Covenants 25: 1-3).

As the Lord continued His revelation to Emma through Joseph, He told her that one of her great missions in life was to be a comfort to her husband, saying that when he was troubled by his enemies, she should console him with comforting words in a spirit of meekness. He told her that when Oliver Cowdery was not present, she should act as a scribe for Joseph in making a record of what he did. He promised her that she should be greatly blessed as she had the opportunity to explain the Gospel to others, and write for the good of the Church.

As the revelation continued, when God explained the work He had in mind for her regarding the hymns to be sung by the Saints, He said to her: *"And it shall be given thee also, to make a selection of sacred hymns, as it shall be given thee, which is pleasing unto me, to be had in my church."* **She was directed to compile the first hymnbook for the Church.**

At this early date, just a few months after the Church had been organized, there were no Latter-day Saint composers producing **Latter-day Saints hymns. But selections were made from the best hymns of other churches.** The hymns which had words in keeping with the true Gospel were selected and sung by the Latter-day Saints. As the Church grew, there were some great poets and hymn-writers among the converts who wrote many beautiful new hymns.

In this revelation to Emma Smith, and because of the insight of the Lord into Emma's personality, Emma was told: *"Murmur not because of the things which thou has not seen, for they are withheld from thee and from the world, which is wisdom in me in a time to come."* She was also warned to *"beware of pride"* and assured that she need not fear about how Joseph would support her. The conclusion from this revelation is that Emma was being warned against becoming a prideful, fearful, murmuring woman, and later events confirmed the reasoning for that warning. Such a warning must be tempered by the recognition, that in this same revelation, as had been stated previously, Emma was referred to as an *"elect lady"* whom the Lord called to further His work on the earth (Doctrine & Covenants, Section 25).

During the summer of 1830, the Prophet received several other revelations covering a wide range of subjects. Once again, there were words of caution to Joseph Smith and Oliver Cowdery to let their time *"be devoted to the studying of the scriptures, and to the preaching,"* as well as the restatement of the law of common consent as a governing principle of the Church (Doctrine & Covenants 26).

In addition, instruction were given authorizing the use of water instead of wine in administering the Sacrament and there was a

"Emma Smith," ©The Church of Jesus Christ of Latter-day Saints, Used by Permission

reaffirmation of the Priesthood which had been conferred on Joseph and Oliver by John the Baptist and by Peter, James, and John (Doctrine & Covenants 27).

When the Church was organized on April 6,1830, the Lord gave many teachings to the Saints concerning the work. **Among other things, instructions were given about the Sacrament of the Lord's Supper.** The Lord gave the prayers to be offered in this sacred ordinance.

For many years, it had been the custom for the Christian churches to use wine in the Sacrament. When Jesus first gave the Sacrament while He lived on earth, He used wine. After He had blessed it, He passed it among His disciples and told them to drink of the cup of wine in remembrance of His blood which was shed for the sins of all men.

In those days in Palestine, juice from the grapes was the main drink of the people. They had no way of keeping their water supply pure. Many grapes were grown in the Holy Land, and the juice people drank, much as we drink water, they called "wine."

The Prophet believed that wine was to be used in the Latter-days for the Sacrament but wine today is an alcoholic beverage, and alcohol is bad for the human body. The Lord told us this in the *Word of Wisdom* (Doctrine & Covenants 89; and 27: 2).

One day, as the Prophet was going to buy wine for use in the Sacrament, an angel stopped him, and he was given this revelation: *"LISTEN to the voice of Jesus Christ your Lord and your God, and your Redeemer, whose word is quick and powerful. For behold, it mattereth not what ye shall eat or what ye shall drink when ye partake of the sacrament, if it so be that ye do it with an eye single to my glory—remembering unto the Father my body was laid down for you, and my blood which was shed for the remission of your sins. Wherefore, a commandment I give unto you, that you shall not purchase wine, neither strong drink of your enemies. Wherefore you shall partake of none except it is made new among you; yea, in this my Father's kingdom which shall be built up on the earth"* (Doctrine & Covenants 27: 1-4).

Since fresh grapes could not always be obtained, the leaders of the Church decided to use water instead of wine or grape juice. This was in accordance with the revelation which said that it did not matter what we used, as long as no wine was purchased, because the wine we have today is intoxicating.

While these and other events were taking place in the growth of the infant Church during the summer of 1830, missionary work was also underway in other parts of New York State. People began sharing the Gospel with family, friends, and neighbors even before the Church was organized. More than one ambitious missionary had been told through revelation: *"Behold, the field is white already to harvest; therefore, whoso desireth to reap, let him thrust in his sickle with his might, and reap while the day lasts, that he may treasure up for his soul everlasting salvation in the kingdom of God"* (Doctrine & Covenants 6: 3; 4: 4; 11: 3; 12: 3; 14: 3).

In April of 1830, ten years after the experience of Joseph Smith in the grove, the religious frontier was startled by the appearance of a strange book. The title on the cover was the Book of Mormon, but everywhere people spoke of it as the *Golden Bible*, 5,000 copies found their way from Palmyra, New York, into nearly every hamlet and settlement of the frontier. It was a religious bombshell which threatened to shake the very foundation of the religious creeds. In the ten years following the First Vision of 1820, the name of Joseph Smith was scarcely known outside a few small villages. Brigham Young, living only forty miles away, and later to become Joseph's trusted lieutenant, had not as yet heard of him. Within a year after the Book of Mormon appeared, his name was known for good or evil along the entire frontier as far North as Canada, as far South as New Orleans, and a 1,000 miles to the West at the trading post of Independence, Missouri. The *Golden Bible* was a lively topic of conversation. Newspapers took a sudden interest in the "Prophet of Palmyra" as he was named. More often than not, the work was bitterly denounced in those days of religious bigotry.

The Book of Mormon met with great resistance from those in the Christian world who believed that the Book of Revelation completed the Bible and that Revelation chapter twenty-two verse eighteen and nineteen referred to the whole Bible: *"If any man shall add unto these things, God shall add unto him the plagues that are written in this book; And if any man shall take away from the words of the book of this prophecy, God shall take away his part out of the book of life, and out of the holy city, and from the things which are written in this book."* Because of this scripture, many believed that God has spoken and completed His teachings and prophecies, that there is nothing beyond what is stated in the Book of Revelation, that Prophets and revelations have ceased for all time. However, those verses could only have been referring to the Book of Revelation itself because there was no Bible as such when they were written. The Book of Revelation was made part of the Bible and placed as the last book of the Bible much later in history—by man, not God. Deuteronomy chapter four verse two says something similar: *"Ye shall not add unto the word which I command you, neither shall ye diminish ought from it, that ye may keep the commandments of the Lord your God which I command you."* We would have to discard all but the first five books of the Bible if we were to take that literally, but it, too, referred to the words of that current revelation. **The Book of Mormon boldly declared that the Lord reveals His words consistently to all people of faith through prophets** that He calls in every dispensation of time.

GREAT EXCITMENT GENERATED BY THE BOOK OF MORMON

The printing of the Book of Mormon created increased interest in Joseph Smith and Mormonism. Rumors spread like wildfire about the "gold book" being printed in Palmyra. One man who heard the rumors was Thomas B. Marsh of Boston, who later became the first president of the Quorum of the Twelve Apostles. His curiosity led him to Grandin's print shop where he met Martin Harris, who gave him proof sheets for the first sixteen printed pages of the Book of Mormon and then accompanied him to the Smith home in Manchester. Oliver Cowdery spent two days telling him about Joseph Smith and the Restoration. Thomas returned to Massachusetts and taught his family about the new work. When he heard that the Church had been organized, he moved his family to Palmyra. In September 1830, he was baptized and called on a mission (Doctrine & Covenants 31).

Samuel H. Smith, the Prophet's younger brother, was ordained an Elder at the first conference of the Church on June 9,

1830, **and was the first missionary of the Church** to go into the field. Samuel was soon taking summer trips into neighboring countries, alone or with his parents, to sell the Book of Mormon. He was often discouraged because his efforts were for the most part, rejected. He did, however, leave one copy of the Book of Mormon with a Reverend John P. Greene, who although not interested in reading it himself, said he would ask his congregation whether they would like to buy a copy. Three weeks later, Samuel went again to see Reverend Greene, but he had not returned from his circuit tour. His wife, Rhoda, said that the book had not sold, but she had read the book and liked it. Samuel left the book with her, and later her husband read it and was converted.

Phineas Young, a brother of Rhoda Young Greene, had purchased a copy of the Book of Mormon from Samuel earlier in April 1830 when he met Samuel returning from Lima, New York, where he had been preaching. **He gave the Book of Mormon to Brigham Young,** who gave it to his sister, Fanny Young Murray, the mother-in-law of Heber C. Kimball. After intense study, these men and their families were baptized into the Church. Brigham Young spent two years in study and comparison before he was baptized in April of 1832.

It was evident that Samuel Smith's early missionary labors resulted in some of the most influential converts of the early Church. He was a dedicated missionary who labored in New York, New England, Ohio, and Missouri, converting scores of people and organizing several branches of the Church. Joseph Smith Sr. also thrust his sickle into "ripe fields" that first summer. With his fourteen-year-old son, Don Carlos, he preached to his father's family in St. Lawrence County, and his message was received with joy. Asael's son John, brother to Joseph Sr. accepted the Gospel, as did John's son, George A. Smith, who later became one of the Twelve Apostles. Thus, three generations were united in the faith of the Restoration.

Twenty-three-year-old Parley P. Pratt was another New York convert that summer. Parley had settled in the wilderness of Northeastern Ohio, and there he joined a group of restorationists (disciples or Campbellites) under Sidney Rigdon's leadership. In the summer of 1830, as Parley journeyed by canal through New York to visit relatives, the Spirit prompted him to send his wife, Thankful, on ahead so he could stop to preach his religious ideas near Palmyra at the Village of Newark. A Baptist deacon told him about the Book of Mormon and let him read it. With eagerness he read the title page and the testimony of the witnesses and began to read the text. He recounted the following: "I read all day; eating was a burden, I had no desire for food; sleep was a burden when the night came, for I preferred reading to sleep. As I read, the Spirit of the Lord was upon me, and I knew and comprehended that the book was true, as plainly and manifestly as a man comprehends and knows that he exists. My joy was now full, as it were, and I rejoiced sufficiently to more than pay me for all sorrows, sacrifices and toils of my life. I soon determined to see the young man who had been the instrument of its discovery and translation.

"I accordingly visited the Village of Palmyra, and inquired for the residence of Mr. Joseph Smith. I found it some two or three miles from the village. As I approached the house at the close of the day, I overtook a man who was driving some cows—it was Hyrum Smith. I informed him of the interest I felt in the Book of Mormon, and of my desire to learn more about it. He welcomed me to his house. We conversed most of the night, during which I unfolded to him much of my experience in my search after truth, and my success so far; together with that which I felt was lacking, viz. a commissioned Priesthood, or apostleship to minister in the ordinances of God" (Pratt, *Autobiography of Parley P. Pratt,* SLC, Deseret Book, 1985, pp. 20-22).

Hyrum continued to teach Parley and they soon journeyed to Fayette to meet the Whitmers and other members of the growing branch of the Church. Parley was baptized and ordained an Elder by Oliver Cowdery in September 1830. Invested with authority, Parley traveled to his boyhood home in Columbia County, New York, where he addressed large audiences each day, but only his brother Orson accepted the message. Orson was baptized on his nineteenth birthday and left within two weeks to meet the Prophet Joseph Smith in Fayette.

Meanwhile in Harmony, Joseph Smith, assisted by John Whitmer, began to arrange and copy the revelations Joseph had received. While absorbed in this project, Joseph received a letter from Oliver Cowdery that grieved him. Oliver said that he had discovered the following error of language in one of the revelations: *"and truly manifest by their works that they have received of the Spirit of Christ unto the remission of their sins"* (Doctrine & Covenants 20: 37). Believing that his position as the second Elder in the Church authorized him to do so, Oliver wrote to Joseph. Joseph reported: "The . . . quotation, he said, was erroneous, and added: 'I command you in the name of God to erase those words, that no priestcraft be amongst us!'

"I immediately wrote him in reply, in which I asked him by what authority he took upon him to command me to alter or erase, to add to or diminish from, a revelation or commandment from Almighty God?'"

Joseph was to be confronted with a series of dissensions within the Church which he had to control. Satan never let down, and was continuing with his efforts to destroy the Church. Sensing that this embryonic rebellion among some of his closest and most trusted associates could, unless checked, greatly hinder and delay the work, Joseph immediately went to Fayette to confront Oliver and the Whitmers. After extensive debate and discussion Joseph commented: *"Christian Whitmer at length became convinced that the sentence was reasonable and according to Scripture; and finally, with his assistance, I* [Joseph] *succeeded in bringing, not only the Whitmer family, but also Oliver Cowdery to acknowledge that they had been in error, and that the sentence in dispute was in accordance with the rest of the commandments* (*History of the Church,* 1: 105).

This comparatively insignificant event reveals a vital aspect of the Prophet's leadership and of the relationship between him and his followers; he led not by the exercise of authority or coercion, but rather by reasoning and discussion. It seems to me, both then and now, there always seem to be too many Chiefs but never enough Indians.

In the summer of 1830, there was a final rift between the Prophet and his father-in-law, Isaac Hale. Except for short intervals, Joseph and Emma had made their home in Harmony since December 1827, either under the same roof with the Hales or on a small adjoining farm. It was here, or in the vicinity, that most of the translation of the Book of Mormon was accomplished and that Joseph suffered the pain of losing the 116 page manuscript which had been dictated to Martin Harris. Here too, John the Baptist and later Peter, James, and John appeared to restore the Aaronic and Melchizedek Priesthoods; many of the early significant revelations were received. The first branch of the Church was organized, and the first miracle of the Church was performed there. Isaac Hale had observed or had been involved in all of these events. Yet from the beginning, he held onto the low opinion he had formed of Joseph when the Prophet eloped with his favorite child, Emma.

From time to time, Isaac had appeared to heal the breach with the Prophet and had given him necessary support and protection. In fact, during the earlier part of the summer of 1830, he even appeared to be genuinely interested in Joseph's work, especially the publication of the Book of Mormon and the organization of the Church. Later in the summer though, Isaac's mind was again poisoned against the Prophet. About this time a Methodist minister convinced Isaac Hale of many lies and farfetched stories in regard to his son-in-law. As a result, life became unbearable for Joseph and his family in Harmony and the Prophet decided to distance himself from his in-laws. Joseph made preparations to permanently move to Fayette where he had been invited to live with Peter Whitmer Sr. again. In late August, Newel K. Knight took his team and wagon to Harmony to move Joseph and his family from the area, never to return except for short visits.

As the Prophet left Harmony, he was very aware of having reached a focal point in his life. Now that the Book of Mormon had been published, the Church had been organized, and thriving congregations were being established by enthusiastic and able disciples, he realized that he must enlarge the scope and dimension of his activities and change his base of operations. For the time being though, he decided to take up residence at Fayette.

In Fayette, Joseph encountered another serious problem regarding revelation. Hiram Page, one of the eight witnesses and a brother-in-law to the Whitmers, was in the possession of a stone through which he claimed he received revelation about the building of Zion and the order of the Church. Joseph insisted that these claims *"were entirely at variance with the order of God's house, as laid down in the New Testament, as well as in our late revelations"* (*History of the Church,* 1: 110). Since a conference was scheduled for September twenty-sixth, the Prophet decided not to do more than talk with the brethren about the subject until the conference met. Many people, especially Oliver Cowdery and the Whitmers, believed in the claim of Hiram Page. Once again the adversary (Satan) was turning the heads of the people in the direction of Joseph, attempting to destroy the work of the Lord and His Prophet.

The Prophet turned to the Lord in prayer and received a revelation directed to Oliver Cowdery in which he was charged not to command Joseph Smith, the leader of the Church. **The Lord made it clear that only the President of the Church had the right to receive revelations for the Church as a whole** (Doctrine & Covenants 28: 2). He was also told that the location of the City of Zion had not yet been revealed, but would be in due time (v. 9). Furthermore, Oliver was instructed to go to Hiram Page and convince him that the stone and the purported revelations came from Satan (v. 11). At the scheduled September Conference, Hiram Page's stone was discussed; those present, including Hiram, renounced it and the "revelations" received through it as false. The conference also voted and sustained that Joseph Smith was to "receive and write revelations and commandments for this Church" (Doctrine & Covenants 28). The conference lasted three days. Joseph testified that *"much of the power of God manifested amongst us; the Holy Ghost came upon us, and filled us with joy unspeakable; and peace, and faith, and hope, and charity abounded in our midst"* (*History of the Church,* 1: 115). From this conference and several key revelations received in connection with it, there emerged three vital concepts that were to consume much of the time and energies of the Prophet and the Church during the following decade. These were the concepts of "gathering, proselyting among the Indians and others, and the establishment of the City of Zion."

In reviewing some of the events of the past several months, progress for the infant Church began to look more positive: *"On Sunday, April 11,1830, Oliver Cowdery preached the first public discourse that was delivered by any of our number"* (*History of the Church,* 1: 81). In those few simple words, Joseph Smith relates the beginning of a missionary movement which has made Mormonism the most dynamic religion in the world. At the close of his discourse, Oliver baptized six new members into the Church. About a week later, he baptized seven more. The beautiful Seneca Lake was again his baptismal font.

In reality, the first conversions came through the Prophet Joseph—he might be called the first missionary of the Church. But his missionary efforts had previously not been directed to the converting of the public nor the bringing of members into an organization. Rather his conversations and informal talks in the homes of his friends had been for the purpose of satisfying their curiosity and arousing their faith in his experiences—their faith *had* been aroused. His father and mother, his brothers and sisters, his wife, his neighbors, Martin Harris and Josiah Stowell, the schoolteacher Oliver Cowdery, the family of Whitmers, and the Knights—all who came to know him felt the truth of his simple testimony and were ready to follow his leadership.

Through the missionary efforts of its members and the influence of the Book of Mormon, the Church grew rapidly. By the first conference, held on June 9, 1830, there were some ninety people in attendance, about thirty of them already members (*History of the Church,* 1: 84). At the September Conference, held on the twenty-sixth day of the month, the number had more than doubled. When a conference was held on January 1, 1831, in Fayette, New York, the New York Saints numbered seventy, with several hundred new members in Ohio. By the time of the first annual conference in April 1831, the number of members in Ohio alone numbered over a 1,000, (B. H. Roberts, *Comprehensive History of the Church,* 1: 250). At the June conference held in Kirtland, Ohio, 2,000 Saints were in attendance.

The growth was nothing short of extraordinary. There were three important reasons for this rapid expansion. First: the missionary spirit which came upon the members of the Church; second: the effect of the Book of Mormon; third: the preparation which had been going on for some time in the minds of people along the frontier for just such a dynamic religion. The step into Mormonism was a short one indeed for great numbers of people who were already dissatisfied with their old creeds.

In the days of Jesus Christ, the missionary zeal came to His Apostles at the feast of Pentecost, following the Resurrection of the

Master, on which occasion the Holy Ghost came upon them. Under the influence of the Holy Ghost, the Twelve Apostles became greatly accepted and Christianity spread like a wildfire over the Mediterranean world. So, too, in this "Latter-day Church of Jesus Christ," missionary zeal followed the reception of the Holy Ghost by the laying on of hands.

A new spirit seems to have possessed Joseph Smith and Oliver Cowdery after they received the Priesthood and the Holy Ghost on the banks of the Susquehanna. One cannot read the story of their respective lives without being made aware of it. A new energy and power seems to have possessed them. It was as if they had suddenly increased in stature. A newborn desire to carry their message to the world and to effect an organization for that purpose gave direction to their energies. This was true with all who were baptized into the Church, and received the same rights to the influence of the Holy Ghost.

Many such as Samuel H. Smith, the Prophet's younger brother followed in the work. The Lord announced to those who might have the urge to proselyte: *"Behold, the field is white already to harvest; therefore, whoso desireth to reap; let him thrust in his sickle with his might, and reap while the day lasts, that he may treasure up for his soul everlasting salvation in the kingdom of God"* (Doctrine & Covenants 6: 3).

THE TEACHING OF THE AMERICAN INDIANS REFERRED TO AS—THE LAMANITES

Since early 1830, the Latter-day Saints have acknowledged the American Indian as a remnant of the House of Israel, to whom great promises had been extended. **Referring to these people as "Lamanites,"** a Book of Mormon prophet declared: *"at some period of time, they will be brought to believe in his word, and to know of the incorrectness of the traditions of their fathers; and many of them will be saved"* (Alma 9: 17). The 1830 Saints believed these promises and had been moved since the early days of the Church to bring to pass their fulfillment. The Church was barely six months old when Oliver Cowdery was called by revelation to go to the Lamanites and preach the Gospel (Doctrine & Covenants 28: 8). Subsequently, Peter Whitmer Jr., Ziba Peterson, and Parley P. Pratt were called to assist him (Doctrine & Covenants 30: 5; 32: 1-3). The Lord said that His power would accompany these brethren on this special mission. The destination of the missionaries was *"the border by the Lamanites"* (Doctrine & Covenants 28: 9). This phrase was understood to refer to the line between Missouri and the Indian territory to the West. For more than twenty years, many Americans had stirred up a great controversy for the removal of the Indians from the Eastern States to a permanent Indian Frontier in the Western plains. As a result of this controversy, less than four months before the call of the missionaries, President Andrew Jackson signed into law the "Indian Removal Act." The Shawnee and Delaware Indians from Ohio anticipated these developments, and made the move on their own as early as 1828-29. Both tribes settled near the Kansas River, just west of the Missouri border.

Following the second conference of the Church, preparations for the missionary journey began in earnest. Emma Smith and several other sisters made arrangements to furnish the missionaries with necessary clothing. Even though Emma was not well, she spent many hours sewing suitable clothing for each missionary. The Saints in the Fayette, New York, area, generously furnished food, and Martin Harris supplied copies of the Book of Mormon for distribution. Before departing, the missionaries bound themselves in writing to give "heed unto all the words and advice" of Oliver Cowdery. They pledged to proclaim the "Fulness of the Gospel" to their Brethren, the Lamanites (Letter dated, 17 Oct.1830, in *Ohio Star*, 8 Dec. 1831, p. 1). On Oct.18, 1830, they began 1,500 mile westward trek.

The missionaries visited a friendly tribe of Seneca Indians on the Cattaraugus Reservation near Buffalo, New York, where they briefly interrupted their trip long enough to introduce the Book of Mormon as a record of their forgotten ancestors. "We were kindly received, and much interest was manifested by them on hearing this news," Parley reported (Pratt, *Autobiography of Parley P. Pratt,* SLC, Deseret Book, 1985, p. 35). Leaving two copies of the book, the missionaries journeyed onward. So far as it is known, these were the first American Indians to hear the message of the Restoration in this dispensation.

When the Elders arrived in Northeastern Ohio, they reached an area popularly known as the Western Reserve because in colonial times it was allotted to Connecticut as a "Western Reserve." Parley P. Pratt was familiar with this country, having lived at Amherst, fifty miles west of Kirtland, for about four years before his conversion to the Church. Parley had studied under Sidney Rigdon, a prominent minister in the area who presided over a group of "Seekers" (people seeking a return to New Testament Christianity). At one time, Sidney merged his interest with those of another "Seeker," Alexander Campbell, and helped found a church called the Disciples of Christ, also known as Campbellites. But Rigdon disagreed with Campbell on certain doctrinal practices, and formed his own group, the Reformed Baptist Society. Because of his former close associations with Rigdon, Elder Pratt convinced his companions to visit Sidney in Mentor, Ohio, where he testified to his former teacher that the revelation had occurred, including the restoration of divine authority. Oliver Cowdery, an eyewitness to the restoration of the Priesthood, bore firsthand testimony of that event.

Although Sidney Rigdon treated the missionaries cordially and with respect, his was no instantaneous conversion. He told the Elders: "I will read your book, and see what claims it has upon my faith." The Elders then asked to present their message in Rigdon's church. The consent was given, "the appointment was accordingly published, and a large and respectable congregation was assembled." At the end of the meeting, Rigdon, with commendable open-mindedness, told his listeners that the message they had just heard "was of an extraordinary character, and certainly demanded their most serious consideration." He reminded the congregation of the Apostle Paul's advice to: *"Prove all things; hold fast to that which is good"* (1 Thessalonians 5: 21, *History of the Church,* 1: 124).

Meanwhile, the Elders were not idle. Less than five miles from Rigdon's home in Mentor was the village of Kirkland, where many members of Sidney's congregation lived. The missionaries preached from house to house, likewise receiving respectful attention. Soon some of the residents were convinced that no one among them possessed the divine authority necessary to administer Gospel ordinances and that they had not been authoritatively baptized themselves. After much study and prayer, many people, including Sidney Rigdon, his wife, and Frederick G. Williams, requested baptism at the hands of the missionaries. Both Sidney Rigdon and Frederick G. Williams later became members of the First Presidency of the Church.

News of the teachings of the missionaries spread rapidly. Parley reported, "The people thronged us night and day, insomuch that we had no time for rest and retirement. Meetings were convened in different neighborhoods, and multitudes came together soliciting our attendance; While thousands flocked about us daily; some to be taught, some for curiosity, some to obey the Gospel, and some to dispute or resist it" (Pratt, *Autobiography of Parley P. Pratt,* pp.35-36). Within three weeks of the missionaries' arrival, 127 persons were baptized. Prominent among the number were Edward Partridge, W. W. Phelps, Newel K. Whitney, Isaac Morley, Levi Hancock, Lyman Wight, and John Murdock, well-known residents of the area who were destined to play an important role in future Church affairs.

Shortly after the missionaries left Kirtland, Sidney Rigdon and a close personal friend and associate, Edward Partridge, decided to go to New York, "to inquire further" into the origins of the restored Gospel that had just been introduced to them.

Arriving at Manchester, New York, in December 1830, Sidney and Edward learned that Joseph was living with the Whitmers in Fayette Township, about twenty miles away. They spoke to several neighbors about the Smith family, and found that their reputation had been impeccable until Joseph had made known his discovery of the Book of Mormon. They also noted the excellent order and workings of the family farm. Edward and Sidney found the Prophet at his parent's place in Waterloo, where Edward asked Joseph Smith to baptize him. Four days later, Edward was ordained an Elder by Sidney Rigdon, his friend and traveling companion.

THE MISSIONARY EFFORT TO THE WESTERN INDIANS CONTINUES

After resting from their long journey from New York State to Ohio and having organized their new converts into a branch of the Church, the missionaries to the Indians prepared to continue their trip West. Mr. Williams expressed a desire to join them, and they permitted him to come.

The missionaries had not forgotten their charge to teach the Gospel to Native Americans. At Sandusky, Ohio, they stopped for several days among the Wyandot Indians. Parley wrote: "They rejoiced in the tidings, bid us God speed, and desired us to write to them in relation to our success among the tribes further west" (Pratt, *Autobiography of Parley P. Pratt,* p. 39).

It was winter when the valiant, courageous missionaries left Sandusky for Cincinnati, and they walked all the way. The winter of 1830-1831 is known in the midwest annals as the winter of the deep snow. The latter part of December 1830 was "bitter cold, a blinding, swirling blur of snow, and leaden, lowering skies, combined to make this storm a thing to paralyze that prairie country. It seems to have continued for days, at full strength and force—a wonder, at first, then a terror, a benumbing horror as it became a menace to the life of men and animals" (Eleanor Atkinson, *Winter of the Deep Snow,* 1909, p. 49). In Cincinnati, Ohio, five days before Christmas, the Elders boarded a steamboat bound for St.

Louis. Ice floes, however choked the Ohio River, forcing them to disembark in Cairo, Illinois, and continue on foot. About twenty miles from St. Louis, a howling storm of rain and snow forced a week's delay and left them in snow nearly three feet deep in some places.

Slowly they pressed westward, pushing through the knee-deep snow for whole days without shelter or a fire, "the bleak northwest wind always blowing in our faces with a sharpness which would almost take the skin off," wrote Parley. The cold was so intense that it did not melt, even at midday on the south side of houses, for nearly six weeks. For 300 miles, they carried their clothes, books, and food in knapsacks on their backs. All they had to eat was frozen cornbread and raw pork. Parley said the bread was "so frozen that we could not bite or penetrate any part of it but the outside crust." For a month and a half, they endured fatigue and suffering as they traveled from Kirtland to Independence. On January 13, 1831, the missionaries arrived in Independence, Missouri, the extreme Western frontier of the United States (Pratt, *Autobiography of Parley P. Pratt,* p. 40).

Nearing their destination, the missionaries took up residence in the home of Colonel Robert Patterson on the western boundary of Missouri, while waiting for the weather to moderate. About February first, Peter Whitmer and Ziba Peterson set up a tailor shop in Independence to earn needed funds while Oliver Cowdery, Parley Pratt, and Frederick Williams entered the Indian lands to preach and introduce the Book of Mormon.

The missionaries found a willing listener in William Anderson, the aged chief of the Delawares, son of a Scandinavian father and an Indian mother. The Chief had been unwilling to listen to other Christians, but he was finally persuaded to hear the missionaries. With about forty tribal leaders comfortably seated in the Chief's lodge, Oliver Cowdery was invited to speak. He quickly gained their confidence as he recounted the long and difficult trip from the East to bring news of the Book of Mormon to them. He acknowledged the Indians' present plight: once they were many, now they were few; at one time their possessions were great, now they are few. Skillfully, he wove the Book of Mormon story into his narrative: "Thousands of moons ago, when the red men's forefathers dwelt in peace and possessed this whole land, the Great Spirit talked with them, and revealed His law and His will, and much knowledge to their wise men and prophets." Oliver told them that this, their history, and prophesies of the "things that should befall their children in the latter days" were written in a book. He promised them if they would receive and follow this book, their **"Great Father"** would make them prosperous again and return them to their former greatness. He explained that he and his companions had come to bring them copies of the book, which held the key to their future success. Chief Anderson expressed his gratitude for the white mans'—kindness: "It makes us glad in here [placing his hand on his heart]. It is now winter, we are new settlers in this place; the snow is deep, our cattle and horses are dying, our wigwams are poor; we have much to do in the spring—to build houses, and fence and make farms; but we will build a council house, and meet together, and you shall read to us and teach us more concerning the book of our fathers and the will of the Great Spirit."

The Elders "continued for several days to instruct the old chief and many of his tribe." Their hosts' desire to learn more about the Book of Mormon grew each day, and

"Joseph Smith Preaching to the Indians
by William Armitage

the Elders, finding several people who could read, distributed copies among them, and the readers helped to spread the word (Pratt, *Autobiography of Parley P. Pratt,* pp. 42-44).

Government Indian agents were in control of the area, and unfortunately the missionaries had not obtained the required permit to enter Indian lands and teach the Gospel. The local Indian agent informed them that they were in violation of the law and ordered them to desist until they had secured permission from General William Clark, Superintendent of Indian Affairs in St. Louis (General William Clark, *Kansas State History,* Soc. roll 2, vol. 6, p. 113-114). Parley P. Pratt stated, however, that when news of the missionaries' success reached the frontier settlement of Missouri, it "stirred up the jealousy and envy of the Indian agents and sectarian missionaries to that degree, that we were soon ordered out of the Indian country as disturbers of the peace; and even threatened with the military in case of noncompliance" (Pratt, *Autobiography of Parley P. Pratt,* p. 44).

In a letter dated February 14, 1831, Oliver Cowdery wrote to General Clark explaining that he represented a religious society centered in New York State, and wished to establish "schools for the instruction of Indian children, and also teaching their Elders the Christian religion." This they would do, he said, "without intruding or interfering with any missionary now established" (Letter from Oliver Cowdery to General William Clark).

It is not known if Clark ever responded to their request or granted permission, but the missionaries settled in Independence, and preached the Gospel to those interested settlers in that community.

Meanwhile, Parley P. Pratt was selected to return to the East and report the mission, and to obtain more copies of the Book of Mormon. After he left the Independence area, the other missionaries' interest in the Indians had increased. They also learned about the existence of the Navashoes [doubtless the Navajo Indians], a large, industrious tribe living about three hundred miles west of Santa Fe (*History of the Church,* 1: 182). Nevertheless, circumstances forced the missionaries to discontinue any further attempt to take the Gospel to any other Indian tribes. **Joseph's fame among the Indian tribes had been growing. They called him the: "Paleface Prophet"** and understood the sufferings his people had endured. Joseph was invited to visit an Indian village across the river. As he spoke, the Indian agent interpreted his word. But the interpreter was a deceitful man who wished to stir up the natives against the Mormons. He said that the "paleface" was going to gather an army to destroy the "redmen's" families and homes. As Joseph listened to the translation, the spirit of discernment came over him. He pushed the agent aside and begun speaking in the language of his listeners correcting the false information the interpreter had given him. The Indians saw this miracle as wrought by the hand of the "Great Spirit" and accepted Joseph with loyalty and respect.

In the summer of 1841, Indian Chief Keokuk brought a hundred chiefs and braves of the Sac and Fox tribes to visit the Prophet in Nauvoo. He listened to Joseph attentively with solemn respect, believing him to be a "great and good man" who, like his own people, was a "true son of the Great Spirit." Joseph always enjoyed teaching them the history of their forefathers as taught in the Book of Mormon. He was the one Prophet who could hold out promise to their people, which no one else could.

In terms of conversions and immediate impact, the mission was most successful among the white settlers in the Western Reserve. Many people who would have a significant effect on the growing Church were drawn into the Gospel network in Ohio. Within a few short months there were more members in Ohio than in New York. Therefore, when conditions in New York required a move, **Ohio was designated by the Lord as the gathering place and headquarters of the Church.** In another sense, the mission demonstrated the motivating power of the Book of Mormon as a means of conversion and the strength conversion brought. This unique book of scripture was the means of redirecting the course of many lives.

Although the "Lamanite mission" was not very successful in proselyting Native Americans, it did have a significant impact on the subsequent history of the Church. It not only introduced the Gospel for the first time to this remnant of the House of Israel, but it created an awareness of how important these people were in the eyes of the Lord.

The "Lamanite mission" also paved the way for future revelation respecting the land of Zion, although it was not so recognized immediately. The precise location of the center of Zion should be *"on the borders by the Lamanites"* (Doctrine & Covenants 28: 9).

Five mighty, valiant, and courageous members of the Church walked 1,500 miles across mid-America, and could now bear witness from their unique experience that this was a goodly land. What special spirit prompted the new converts to The Church of Jesus Christ to leave their homes, their friends, and their comforts, in order to carry the Gospel message to others? If we take into account what prompted the ancient apostle Paul to embrace the land and sea, endure sacrifice, beatings, shipwrecks, prisons, and even walk cheerfully to his death in order that men might hear the message of Jesus—if we can answer why Jesus Himself took that certain road to the cross when he knew so clearly what lay ahead, then we can further understand the spirit of the missionaries in the early days of the Mormon Church. To them, their sacrifices and suffering was nothing compared to the priceless joy which they testified to having received. In each situation, the individual bears witness to a happiness in the work, a new-found joy in the service of humanity and God, which becomes an irresistible driving force. **There were barriers and obstacles to overcome,** and they did overcome them; there were barriers and pitfalls thrown in for good measure, but they, were avoided. Men and woman everywhere were caught up in the excitement of the times, and it did permeated every fiber of their beings.

The discontented in religion felt the pressure and severed the few remaining ties with their old creeds, for this new religion did breathe power and attain results. It had voiced a challenge to the world and was making good its promise.

Prayer had once again become a vital force, and many who had previously prayed with doubts and misgiving, now received the needed bolstering which brought them the Spirit of God. Men prayed for a testimony concerning Joseph Smith's message, and their prayers were answered. Men read the Book of Mormon with prayer in their hearts that they might know of its truth, and the Lord remembered His promise. Men are always lifted by the faith of their associates. Confidence inspires confidence. When the Savior and Messiah walked the earth, His presence , His voice, and His touch dispelled fear and doubt, and the sick arose from their beds of affliction and the blind opened their eyes. His apostles finally acquired that same faith and confidence, and rejoiced in the power they possessed. And so, in this Seventh and Last Dispensation of the Fulness of Times, Christ had revealed Himself and a tangible book had appeared. The confidence and faith of Joseph Smith had opened the heavens, and prayers were being answered. Many were caught up in the same faith that motivated the ancient Apostles and having been firmly established with the powers and authority of the Priesthood, went forth to instill faith in others.

The fire and enthusiasm of the movement made insignificant all other motives in life. The desire for gain or power seemed to disappear for most people. In the giving of service to others, self was forgotten, and a new social brotherhood began—a true kingdom of God.

The principle that he who "loseth his life" in the service of others "shall find it" is still the fundamental principle of Mormon missionary activity at home or abroad. It cools off when service cools off, and bursts brightly into a new flame when service is resumed. In the early Mormon community, it permeated everything and enriched all that it touched. The spirit of service and of brotherhood entered into home and community life and brought dreams of a new Zion—a place of brotherly happiness and service to one another where there should be no rich and no poor—where greed and selfishness should be banished forever. It sounds like Paradise and a Utopian society, and it can be any time *when*—a people choose to follow the teachings and commandments of Jesus Christ, the Savior, the Messiah, the Redeemer of all mankind, and of all the world.

Chapter 6

1831-1833
The Ohio—Missouri Years

Gathering to Ohio

Continued Revelation

The Kirtland Period

Other Miraculous Healings

Hatred Exploded into violent action against Joseph Smith

"Prophecy on the Civil War"—
and the "Olive Leaf"—a Revelation of Peace

A revelation was given to the Prophet Joseph in late December of 1830 that the Church should assemble together in Ohio (Doctrine & Covenants 37: 3). This was the first, explicit and unconditional direction given to the Saints to gather together in one place.

The main purpose of the gathering was to concentrate the power and influence of the Church into a single locality. This would ease the problems of supervision and give the members a sense of unity and strength that could never be achieved if they were to remain scattered. It would also bring most of the membership under the direct influence of Joseph Smith for their best interests. The remarkably successful proselyting efforts had brought into the Church a distinct and diverse, highly independent assortment of persons whose primary commitment was their inner self-conviction and firm belief that Joseph's story about the Book of Mormon and the restoration of the Priesthood was true. They had yet to learn the full meaning, substance, and scope of that story. This learning could best be accomplished by direct association with the teacher.

On New Year's Day 1831, the Prophet and his associates in Fayette completed preparations for the third general conference of the Church, which had been scheduled to consider the move of the Saints to Ohio.

On January 2, 1831, the Saints from various branches throughout the New York area met in the home of Peter Whitmer Sr. After transacting some Church business, Joseph Smith prayed to the Lord about the move to Ohio and received in the presence of the congregation, a revelation that became Doctrine and Covenants Section thirty-eight. It promised the Saints *"greater riches, even a land of promise, a land flowing with milk and honey, upon which there shall be no curse when the Lord cometh; And I will give it unto you for the land of your inheritance, if you seek it with all your hearts"* (Doctrine & Covenants 38: 18-19). **The precise location of Zion, however, was not revealed.** For the present, the Saints were to go to Ohio, where the Lord promised to reveal to them His *"law,"* endow them with power, and give further instructions pertaining to the growth of the Church (Doctrine & Covenants 38: 32-33).

Certainly, not everyone at the conference was in harmony with this revelation. A few people claimed that Joseph Smith invented the revelation to deceive the people and enrich himself. John Whitmer wrote in his history that this claim arose because the hearts of the Saints "were not right in the sight of the Lord, for they wanted to serve both God and man." In addition, some people were reluctant to leave farms and comfortable circumstances for the uncertainties of the Western Reserve in Ohio. There was the prospect that many would lose money; some might even be unable to sell their property (Doctrine & Covenants 38: 37). Most of the New York Saints, nevertheless, adapted themselves to the commandment and made preparations to leave.

Following the conference, Joseph Smith and Sidney Rigdon went to Colesville to strengthen the members of the Colesville Branch and to preach for the last time to non-member in the area. Threats on their lives prevented them from extending their proselyting efforts. Upon their return to Fayette, the Prophet sent John Whitmer to Ohio with copies of several of the revelations to comfort and strengthen the Saints. In addition, John Whitmer was assigned to be the presiding Elder until the arrival of the Prophet. By the time he arrived in Kirtland, the membership of the Church in Geauga and Cuyahoga Counties in Ohio had grown to about 300, more than twice the number reported only two months earlier. Since the departure of the missionaries to the Lamanites (Native Americans), proselyting in the area had continued unrestricted. One of the most successful missionaries was the former restorationist preacher, John Murdock. Between November 1830 and March 1831, he baptized over seventy settlers living in Cuyahoga County (Journal of John Murdock, Nov. 1830 - July 1859). Other missionaries fared equally well in their labors in Ohio.

The move to Ohio was productive, beneficial, and desirable to the young Church. By leaving New York, the Saints hoped to leave behind religious persecution, particularly in the Colesville area. In addition, there were more Church members in Ohio than anywhere else, and gathering in one place enabled everyone to receive instruction from the Prophet, thus maintaining doctrinal and organizational uniformity. Ohio's available waterways also provided a gateway to the rest of the country for missionary work. But most importantly, the move to Ohio was a step closer to *"the borders by the Lamanites,"* where Zion would be established (Doctrine & Covenants 28: 9). In Ohio, many principles relating to the building of Zion could be fulfilled and very benefical.

Joseph Smith was eager to meet with the Saints in Ohio, and John Whitmer wrote the Prophet urging him to come quickly. Joseph inquired of the Lord's will and was told to leave immediately, but the expectation of moving seemed grim and disheartening to Emma. She had moved seven times in the first four years of marriage, was just recovering from a month-long illness, and was six months pregnant. The 300 mile trip to Ohio in the dead of winter would be rough and rugged at best. Joseph Knight graciously provided a sleigh to make the traveling less strenuous for her. At the end of January, 1831, Joseph and Emma Smith, Sidney Rigdon, and Edward Partridge set out for Kirtland.

Around the first of February, the sleigh pulled up in front of Newel K. Whitney's store in Kirtland. The Prophet greeted him with the words: *"Newel K. Whitney! Thou art the man!... You've prayed me here, now what do you want of me?"* Joseph explained to the amazed merchant that back in New York, he had seen Newel in a vision praying for him to come to Kirtland (*History of the Church,* 1: 146). When Newel had sufficiently recovered from the shock of this unorthodox greeting, the Whitneys invited Joseph and Emma Smith to live with them temporarily. During the next several weeks, the Smiths received every kindness and attention which could be expected, especially from Mrs. Whitney.

Between the end of January and the middle of May, 1831, most of the New York Saints sold their possessions, packed their most precious material goods, and migrated to Kirtland and the adjacent areas. Joseph Smith and a few others went early and were followed by three separate companies—Colesville Saints, members from Fayette and surrounding locations in Seneca County, and those from Palmyra-Manchester. A few others came later in the year.

The Colesville Branch was the first group to leave. They arrived in Buffalo, New York, on May first, to find that bitter lake winds had blown ice into the Buffalo harbor, which delayed them for eleven dreary days. They finally arrived in Fairport, Ohio, on May fourteenth. Over 200 people went to Ohio, some by sleigh and stagecoach, but most by canal barges to Buffalo, and then by steamboats and schooners on Lake Erie.

Meanwhile, Church members in the Fayette vicinity also prepared for the journey. With her older sons and husband having gone ahead, Lucy Smith, a natural leader in her own right, organized a party of about fifty people, (twenty adults and thirty children) to occupy a barge on the Cayuga and Seneca Canal. Another group of about thirty, organized by Thomas B. Marsh, took passage on an accompanying barge, and together the two boats traveled to Buffalo.

During the trip, Lucy "called the brethren and sisters together, and reminded them that they were traveling by the commandment of the Lord, as much as Father Lehi was in the Book of Mormon, when he left Jerusalem; and, if faithful, they had the same reasons to expect the blessings of God" (Lucy Mack Smith, *History of Joseph Smith by His Mother*, SLC, Bookcraft 1958, p. 196). Although they suffered from hunger because some had brought insufficient food, they nevertheless sang and prayed as they journeyed, and left a favorable impression on the captain. Lucy took charge of the situation and prevented greater suffering.

When they arrived in Buffalo, they met the ice-bound Colesville Saints. After several anxious, fearsome, and apprehensive days in Buffalo, a number of the children had become sick, and many of the group were hungry and discouraged. They took deck passage on a boat, put their things on board, and secured temporary shelter for the women and children until early the next morning. When they were back on board the boat, Lucy persuaded the murmuring, complaining group to ask the Lord to break the twenty-foot clogs of ice that jammed the harbor. She later wrote: "A noise was heard, like bursting thunder. The captain cried out: 'Every man to his post.' The ice parted, leaving barely a passage for the boat, and was so narrow, that as the boat passed through, the buckets of the waterwheel were torn off with a crash . . .We had barely passed through the avenue when the ice closed together again." The Colesville group followed a few days later (Lucy Mack Smith, *History of Joseph Smith by His Mother,* pp. 200-205).

As these New York Latter-day Saints were arriving in Ohio, a third party of about fifty people left Palmyra, New York, under the direction of Martin Harris. With their arrival in Ohio, the first phase of the westward movement of the Saints ended. In contrast to many Americans who migrated westward at the same time seeking free or inexpensive land, adventure, or escape from creditors, these humble people moved in response to a commandment of God.

The toil and trouble through which the Saints would pass was repeated time and time again by other groups of migrating Saints. Most of them had arrived in Kirtland in about the same disorganized, disheveled condition: tired, hungry and very concerned about their living conditions, with no homes, little food or money and few prospects initially of getting any. Most of them had to rely upon the kindness and hospitality of the local members until they were able to reestablish themselves on farms, in businesses or trades. This imposed an enormously heavy burden upon the local members. It was in these dire circumstances that a Bishop would be called by the Prophet through revelation and the common consent of the members, whose chief duty was to see that the needy would be cared for.

During the three months Joseph Smith was in Kirtland, before the Saints from New York began to arrive, Joseph Smith faced several challenges arising from the rapid growth of the Church there. The first problem was the demonstration of bizarre actions of some of the young people. They claimed they saw visions, and would sometimes run into the fields, get on stumps of trees and preach as though they were surrounded by a congregation. Yet all the while they were so completely preoccupied in visions as to be unmistakably ignorant of all that was passing around them. This seems to have been another evidence of Satan's desire to destroy the Church.

Only a few members behaved in this manner, however. "The more substantial minded looked upon it with astonishment, and were suspicious that it was from an evil source" (John Corrill, *Brief History of the Church*, p. 13). Distressed by what they saw, Joseph felt that these excesses were *"calculated to bring disgrace upon the Church of God; to cause the Spirit of God to be withdrawn; and to uproot and destroy those glorious principles which had been developed for the salvation of the human family"* (*Times and Seasons,* 1 Apr. 1842, p. 747). *"With a little caution and some wisdom"* and the guidance of several revelations, Joseph succeeded in overcoming these problems.

Still, in late February 1831, some individuals continued to claim they had received revelations. This was not a new problem; Hiram Page had done the same thing in Fayette the previous Fall (Doctrine & Covenants 28). One of these so-called "revelators" was a professed prophetess named Hubble, who claimed she should be allowed to become a teacher in the Church. According to John Whitmer, she "appeared to be very sanctimonious and deceived some who were not able to detect her in her hypocrisy." Many saw through her false claims, however, and "her follies and abominations were made manifest." The Prophet inquired of the Lord about her intrigue and scheming. In a revelation directed to the Elders of the Church, the Lord declared: *"that there is none other appointed unto you to receive commandments and revelations until he* [Joseph Smith] *be taken, if he abide in me"* (Doctrine & Covenants 43: 3). So-called revelations through others for the guidance of the whole Church, rather than the individual, were not of God (Doctrine & Covenants 43: 4-6).

Shortly thereafter, Joseph received another revelation that called the Elders to go forth by twos in all directions to preach the Gospel (Doctrine & Covenants 42: 6-7; 44: 1-3). Soon, many Elders were seen going into villages and towns throughout Ohio. For example, John Corrill recounted that he and Solomon Hancock "went to New London, about one hundred miles from Kirtland, where we built up a church (branch) of thirty-six members in about three weeks time, though we were bitterly opposed by other preachers" (John Corrill, *History of the Church,* p. 13). That spring, the Church in Ohio increased by several hundred converts.

The growing Church did not go unnoticed in Northern Ohio. Joseph Smith wrote that in the spring of 1831, *"many false reports, lies, and foolish stories, were published in the newspapers, and circulated in every direction, to prevent people from investigating the work, or embracing the faith"* (*History of the Church,* 1: 158). For example, a devastating earthquake struck near Peking, China, which a young Mormon girl had predicted six weeks earlier. This event convinced Simonds Ryder, a well-known Campbellite preacher, who had been confused over Mormonism for some time, to join the Church. His conversion caused quite an uproar in the area, and the earthquake *"was burlesqued in some papers as "'Mormonism' in China. But to the joy of the Saints, who had to struggle against everything that prejudice and wickedness could invent,'"* (*History of the Church,* 1: 158), the Prophet received a revelation that identified numerous signs that will precede the Second Coming of the Lord. In it, the Saints were commanded to *"stand in holy places"* and take *"the Holy Spirit for their guide,"* and they were promised that they would be rewarded for this with the establishment of the *"New Jerusalem"* (Doctrine & Covenants 45: 32, 57, 66).

Also in the spring of 1831, a Methodist preacher named Ezra Booth brought some friends to Kirtland, including a well-to-do farmer named John Johnson and his wife, Elsa, from Hiram, Ohio. Elsa's arm was partially paralyzed from rheumatism and she could not raise it above her head. As they talked with the Prophet, one of the visitors asked if there was anyone on earth who had the power to cure Elsa's arm. When the conversation turned to another subject, Joseph went up to Mrs. Johnson, took her by the hand, and with calm assurance said: *"Woman, in the name of the Lord Jesus Christ, I command thee to be whole."* As Joseph went from the room, leaving everyone astonished and speechless, she raised her arm. The next day, she hung out her wash without any pain for the first time in over six years. Ezra Booth and some members of the Johnson family joined the Church as a result of the healing. The miracle also attracted wide acclaim throughout Northern Ohio (*History of the Church,* 1: 215-16).

That same spring, Parley P. Pratt returned to Kirtland with a report on the mission to the Lamanites, and was delighted to see the tremendous growth of the Church. He was especially happy that Joseph had moved to Ohio. Parley was soon called to go on a mission to a religious group called the "Shakers" in Northern Ohio.

The Shakers (United Society of Believers in Christ's Second Coming), originated in England, and came to America in 1774 because of persecution. They derived their name from their manner of worship, which involved singing, dancing, and clapping hands to music, but their dress and manner were similar to those of the Quakers, so they were sometimes called the Shaking Quakers. The Shaking Quakers were led by Ann Lee (she was credited as being its founder) from 1754 to 1784. She had claimed to be the Messiah returned to earth in female form. She taught that men and women were equals, and that there should be no marriage among the believers. Leman Copley, a former Shaker, had converted to Mormonism, but still believed that the Shakers were correct in many of their doctrines, so he asked Joseph for guidance on the matter (*History of the Church,* 1: 167). The revelation Joseph Smith received repudiated the Shaker doctrines of celibacy, abstaining from meat, and God appearing in the form of a woman. Sidney Rigdon, Parley P. Pratt, and Leman Copley were also called to take the Gospel to the Shakers (Doctrine & Covenants 49). The trio visited a settlement of Shakers near Cleveland, Ohio, but according to Parley, "they utterly refused to hear or obey the Gospel" (Pratt, *Autobiography of Parley P. Pratt,* 1985, p. 47).

Through determined and resourceful missionaries **the word spread that God had spoken and was speaking again through a living prophet.** As they learned of the commandment to gather in Ohio, the converts flocked to Kirtland. Almost invariably, the first request of each one was to see the Prophet. Many were content merely to gaze upon him; others were desirous to hear him speak or to teach the scriptures, while others, more bold and aggressive, sought personal direction from the Lord through the Prophet as to their course of action. Some few were disappointed when they met Joseph because his appearance and demeanor did not correspond with their preconceived notions of how a Prophet should look and act. These few were surprised to find him engaged in the normal pursuits that occupied a good part of the time of any man on the frontier: sawing or splitting logs, tending farm animals, cultivating the land, or performing necessary chores around the house. Nor were these few prepared for the Prophet's sunny disposition, good natured wit, his easy and friendly way with acquaintances, or his fun-loving desire for sports activities or harmless practical jokes. However, those who faulted the Prophet for these qualities, did not detract from his stature or influence, but simply revealed their own narrow views and understanding of the role of a Prophet.

Before Mormonism had reached the Kirtland vicinity, a group of Campbellites or Disciples had begun the experiment of holding all property in common and living as one large family. Practically the entire group had embraced the new faith after the visit of Parley P.

Pratt and his companions on their way to the Lamanite Mission; they continued their social experiment until the arrival of Joseph Smith. If they expected his approval of the order, they were disappointed . He praised them for their brotherly spirit, but soon persuaded them to give up on the venture because it was not a model of God's law for His people. The Saints were anxious to know what the law of God was in this matter, and were ready, willing, and eager to live it, so **Joseph inquired of the Lord through prayer.** He was desirous to know the Lord's will concerning the economic salvation of the Saints, many of whom were impoverished, particularly those who had left their homes and belongings in New York.

The Prophet Joseph realized the need to establish a more perfect system to meet the growing economic needs of the Church. Revenue was required to finance various Church undertakings, such as publishing revelations and missionary tracts. The Prophet was without a home for his family; when he joined the Church Sidney Rigdon lost his ministerial home and the economic support he had previously received from his Campbellite congregation. Money, goods, and property were needed to help the poor and to assist immigrants who were sacrificing much to gather to Ohio. On February 4, 1831, the Prophet received a revelation from the Lord calling for Edward Partridge to serve as the first Bishop of the Church, with instructions for him to devote his full time to this calling (Doctrine & Covenants 41: 9).

Five days later, another important revelation was received, embracing the law of the Church. It gave Bishop Partridge further instruction on his responsibilities and outlined the new economic system (Doctrine & Covenants 42).

LAW OF CONSECRATION

One of the underlying principles of this new economic system was that the earth and everything on it belonged to the Lord, and man was a steward (Psalm 24: 1; Doctrine & Covenants 104: 13-14). Under the **Law of Consecration,** members of the Church were asked to consecrate, or deed, all their property, both real and personal, to the Bishop of the Church. He would then grant an *"inheritance,"* or stewardship, to each individual from the properties received. The size of the stewardship depended on the circumstances, wants, and needs of the family, as determined jointly by the Bishop and the prospective steward (Doctrine & Covenants 42: 32-33; 51: 3). The family then administered its stewardship to the best of their ability. If they were industrious and successful, then at the year's end, they would have a net gain called a surplus. Any surplus remaining beyond the wants and needs of the family, was turned over to the storehouse to be used by the Bishop to *"administer to the poor and needy"* (Doctrine & Covenants 42: 34). **The Law of Consecration was designed to bring about relative economic equality and eliminate greed and poverty.** This was a system designed to prevent the rise of class distinction, to abolish hoarding, selfishness, and those elements which, in a modern community, would be inclined to prevent a spirit of Christian brotherhood. Products and services were to be bought and sold as usual, and he that was idle should not eat the bread nor wear the garment of the laborer (Doctrine & Covenants 42: 42). The Law of Consecration was first followed in settling those Saints who were arriving from the Eastern States in the two settlements of Kirtland and Thompson. Not all of the members of the Church in either place participated in the plan, and experiments in both locations came to an early end, but the principles of stewardship and brotherhood continued.

The spirit of community fellowship and cooperation which reached its finest expression in the Law of Consecration, set the Latter-day Saints apart socially and economically from their neighbors. It struck deep at the roots of the American economic system and served notice upon the profit incentive as a basis of human activity. This spirit of concern for the mutual good of all bound the Mormon people closer and closer together in the various communities. The fact that the practice of the Law of Consecration was short-lived must not be construed as meaning that the spirit of brotherhood disappeared. The spirit was to grow stronger with the years until Mormons came to be known as a "peculiar people." It was the lack of maturity of the young people of the Church and the newness of the movement which brought about the failure to live a law which they desired, but didn't have sufficient maturity to live. Nevertheless, the spirit of brotherhood continued and found demonstration and meaning in community projects and missionary activity.

The fact that the Mormons were motivated and energized by **a different concept of community life—a concept that stressed cooperation above competition**—aroused much suspicion. Persecution increased as nonmembers witnessed the number in the Church double and redouble with amazing rapidity. Ministers of other religions became alarmed as they witnessed their own flocks declining, as converts by the score moved away to Mormon settlements or set up new Mormon communities in the same locality. Often, the ministers became embittered and active in stirring up negative feelings against the new religion and helped create much persecution.

The settlements of the Saints in Ohio were considered by Joseph Smith as temporary. The permanent settlement was to be farther to the West, in a place unknown at that time. In a revelation received at Kirtland in May 1831, the following was declared: *"I consecrate unto them this land for a little season, until I, the Lord, shall provide for them otherwise, and command them to go hence; And the hour and the day is not given unto them, wherefore let them act upon this land as for years, and this shall turn unto them for their good"* (Doctrine & Covenants 51: 16-17).

THE WORK OF THE LORD CONTINUES

In the February revelation calling Edward Partridge to be Bishop, the Lord directed Joseph and Sidney to resume the translation of the scriptures. One of the projects undertaken by Joseph Smith before moving to Kirtland, Ohio, was a revision of the English Bible. He certainly did not discredit the King James' translation, but he knew that some errors and omissions in that record had led to numerous difficulties among the Christian religions. (This fact has since been generally recognized.) He had received his first understanding of this from the angel Moroni, who, on his initial visit in 1823, had quoted scripture to Joseph Smith, with the text altered somewhat from the language of the Bible.

Because the Book of Mormon had prophesied that many of the *"parts which are plain and precious; . . . have they taken away"* from the Bible which would be removed by evil men (1 Nephi 13: 26), the Prophet had been toiling over the Bible, translating verses that needed clarification. Joseph considered this translation and revision an important part of his calling, and he received many revelations concerning doctrines that had been lost.

Upon his arrival in Ohio, Joseph continued with this labor, working as time permitted. Though he was never able to complete it before his life was taken, the changes he made indicate some interesting interpretations of parts of the scripture. However, since the work was never finished, the Church has accepted the King James translation as its standard English text of the Bible, referring to those passages of Joseph's translated version that were published for clarificaton.

We have seen how Joseph Smith and the Church developed in responce to various questions and problems that arose. He did seek the Lord for guidance, and testified to the world that he received it. Most of the revelations which have since regulated the Church were received during the Ohio-Missouri period.

Soon after settling in Kirtland, Emma Smith went into labor. She had not yet recovered from her illness and the strenuous, stressful mid-winter journey from New York. On April thirtieth, she delivered twins; but they only lived for three hours. She and Joseph had now lost all three children born to them. Coincidentally, twins were born on May first, to Julia Murdock, who died following their birth. Elder John Murdock was leaving on a mission about this time, and gladly consented when Joseph asked if he and Emma could adopt the children. Emma's grief was eased, and she willingly took the infants—a girl named Julia and a boy named Joseph—to raise as her own.

The fourth general conference of the Church was held in a schoolhouse just outside Kirtland on Friday, June 3, 1831 with approximately 2,000 persons in attendance. Gathered together where they could feel each other's dedication and enthusiasm, many of the Saints began to see for the first time the strength and potential of the Church they had embraced. As Joseph looked out over this vast congregation, he too marveled at the phenomenal growth and success of the Church since its organization just fourteen months before on April 6, 1830. At this conference, several men were ordained to the office of High Priest, the first in the Church and in this dispensation. On this special occasion, there sat before Joseph about 2,000 members of the Church, most of whom had been uprooted from their homes, and who were prepared to do whatever else was required of them. Even as the conference met, many missionaries were out proselyting others into the Church.

Remarkable experiences had taken place on an almost daily basis in the early days of Kirtland. Parley P. Pratt was personally touched by one such experience, and he left his account of the miraculous healing of a member:

"About this time, a young lady, by the name of Chloe Smith, being a member of the Church, was lying very low with a lingering fever. . . Many of the Church had visited and prayed with her, but all to no effect; she seemed at the point of death, but would not consent to have a physician. This greatly enraged her relatives, who had cast her out because she belonged to the Church, and who, together with many of the people of the neighborhood, were greatly stirred up to anger, saying 'these wicked deceivers will let her lie and die without a physician because of their superstitions; and if they do, we will prosecute them for so doing.' Now, these were daily watching for her last breath, with many threats.

"Under these circumstances, the Prophet Joseph and myself, with several other Elders, called to see her . . . We did kneel down and prayed vocally all around, each in turn; after which President Smith arose, went to the bedside, took her by the hand, and said unto her with a loud voice: 'in the name of Jesus Christ, arise and walk!' She immediately arose, was dressed by a woman in attendance, then she walked to a chair before the fire, and was seated and joined in singing a hymn. The house was thronged with people in a few minutes, and the young lady arose and shook hands with each as they came in; and from that minute, she was perfectly restored to health'" (*Pratt, Autobiography of Parley P. Pratt,* pp. 66-67).

Thus ended the first critical months of gathering the New York Saints to Ohio, and establishing the headquarters of the Church there. While members experienced several encounters with evil spirits, they also received valuable instructions and saw the power of God overcome the power of the evil one. Joseph Smith and Sidney Rigdon resumed work on the inspired translation of the Bible. The eternal principles of the Law of Consecration were revealed, and further foundations were laid for the great latter-day missionary work for the growth of the Lord's Church.

The day following the June 1831 conference in Kirtland, a revelation directed Joseph Smith and other Church leaders to go to Missouri where the land of their inheritance would be revealed—**Zion**. In addition, thirteen pairs of missionaries were called to travel two by two, each pair taking a different route to Missouri, to preach and teach along the way (Doctrine & Covenants 52: 3-8; 22-23; 56: 5-7). There was a great deal of excitement in and around Kirtland the following two weeks as the leaders and the Elders made preparations to leave. After all, the Lord gave them a promise: *"if ye are faithful ye shall assemble yourselves together to rejoice upon the land of Missouri, which is the land of your inheritance, which is now the land of your enemies. But, behold, I, the Lord, will hasten the city* [the New Jerusalem] *in its time, and will crown the faithful with joy and with rejoicing"* (Doctrine & Covenants 52: 42-43).

Because of the physical and emotional strain of the trip, Emma was to remain in Kirtland with the Newel K. Whitneys. Joseph left in her possession his valuable papers, including the manuscript of the revision of the Bible on which he had been working intermittently for several months.

In the interim prior to his departure, the Prophet received several other revelations which came in response to specific inquiries from individual groups as to their duty or conduct. Therefore, A. S. Gilbert was directed to accompany the Prophet and Sidney Rigdon to Missouri and Newel Knight was told to lead the Colesville Branch to Missouri in search of a new place to settle. William W. Phelps was also instructed to go to Missouri to assist Oliver Cowdery in the selection, writing and printing of books for schools in the Church and finally, the missionaries were informed of their directions—all were to meet in Missouri.

Their preparations all completed, the Prophet and his party left Kirtland on June 19, 1831. Their first stop was Cincinnati, which they reached by means of wagons, canal boats, and stages. While waiting for a steamer to take the party to Louisville, Kentucky, the Prophet had an interview with the Reverend Walter Scott, one of the founders of the Campbellite or Newlight church, with which both Sidney Rigdon and Parley P. Pratt had been affiliated prior to their conversion to The Church of Jesus Christ. Many had followed these and other Campbellite leaders into the new Church. The infectious enthusiasm of these converts, coupled with a positive, active (not pushy) and spiritually exciting missionary program for their families and friends, certainly caused the leaders of other churches great concern. These two factors created an unsettling possibility that the flow of membership from one church to the other would not only continue, but would grow in size and intensity. Thus the meeting with Reverend Scott was understandably tense. He rejected the account of the spiritual experiences of the Prophet and his followers. In recording the interview in his journal, Joseph later observed: *"he manifested one of the bitterest spirits against the doctrine of the New Testament* [that "these signs shall follow them that believe" as recorded in Mark the 16th chapter,] *that I ever witnessed among men"* (*History of the Church,* 1: 188).

Eleven years of ridicule and opposition for his religious beliefs had seasoned the Prophet to accept rejection as almost a matter of course. As always, he did not allow the rejection to alter his course because he knew his direction, neither did he find it necessary to explain himself nor embarrass or degrade his critics. With this attitude, one can see; why Joseph exerted such a strong, spiritual influence upon his followers. Not only did he present himself as a Prophet; he acted like a Prophet. His followers found no uncertainty or confusion in him; no tendency to explain, argue, or rationalize. He asserted his strong convictions with positive finality without being opinionated or "stuffy." Yet it was precisely this quality of positiveness that, while attracting and impressing his followers, offended, and alienate, antagonized, and embittered his contenders.

A ZION PEOPLE

To the Prophet Joseph Smith, the word Zion had two meanings: *"The pure in heart,"* and, *"the place where the pure in heart dwell together in righteousness."* It is quite evident that a successful *"Zion community"* is impossible without a *"Zion people."*

It was approximately 1,000 miles from Kirtland, Ohio, to Independence, Missouri. It was a tremendous journey in that day, yet leaders of the Church were to travel back and forth many times without complaint and with no thought of material reward. And over that great distance, thousands of covered wagons were to carry Mormon men, women and children to the New Zion during the succeeding years. One such company, the group of Saints from Colesville, who had stopped for a few months at Thompson, Ohio, arrived in Jackson County, Missouri two weeks in advance of the Prophet and his party. They were led by Newel Knight. This group, about sixty strong, planned on settling in Kaw township, about twelve miles west of Independence.

The journey from Cincinnati to Louisville, and from Louisville to St. Louis, gave Joseph an opportunity to momentarily relax on a river steamer. The leisurely, comfortable ride on the river gave him time for reflection on the past. It also permitted him to give prayerful contemplation and examination to his future course.

Accompanied by four of his associates, the Prophet covered the last leg of the journey from St. Louis to Independence on foot. This enabled him to observe the scenery and to assess the spirit and attitudes of the inhabitants. He was impressed by the openness of the country, and by the *"beautiful rolling prairies,"* which, he recorded, *"lie spread out like a sea of meadows . . . decorated with a growth of flowers so gorgeous and grand as to exceed description."* He also made mention that unlike the heavily forested lands in the Eastern United States, timber here was to be found *"only along the water courses."* He was positively affected by the richness of the soil and the abundance of wild game (*History of the Church,* 1: 197). He could envision this rich, bountiful land inhabited by Latter-day Saints whose thrift, industry, and dedication to Christian principles would make of it a literal Zion, a place of beauty where the pure in heart would dwell and which would be a fit dwelling place for the Savior at His Second Coming.

These thoughts were quickly jolted and shaken when the Prophet caught sight of the scruffy character of the people who occupied the land. In one of the most scathing denunciations he ever was known to offer, he said of the people who then occupied Missouri: *"how natural it was to observe the degradation, leanness of intellect, ferocity* [inhumanity, violence] *and jealousy of a people that were nearly a century behind the times, and to feel for those who roamed about without the benefit of civilization, refinement or religion"* (*History of the Church,* 1: 189).

In simple terms, Independence in 1831, was a small frontier town, the outfitting place for trappers and hunters and a rendezvous for many rough characters of the West. It had a brick courthouse, two or three general stores, and some twenty log houses. The settlers provided a sharp contrast to the New England people, now searching for a new Zion in that land. The old settlers were generally unschooled, ignorant of the ways of civilization, and unskilled in the arts of the newcomers.

Within a few days after the Prophet's party had arrived in Independence, he received a revelation that answered the dual questions that had been uppermost in the minds of his followers for many months. Where was the ultimate place of gathering to be, where was the temple to be built? The revelation specified *"the land of Missouri"* as *"the land which I have appointed and consecrated for the gathering of the Saints."* Furthermore, Independence was designated *"the center place,"* and the site where the temple was to be constructed (Doctrine & Covenants 57: 1-3). This revelation also warned the Saints to purchase as much land as their resources would permit, and that Bishop Edward Partridge was appointed to remain in Independence to divide unto the Saints their inheritance; Sidney Gilbert, a young merchant, was appointed to remain as agent of the Church to purchase lands for the Saints. William W. Phelps was appointed printer of the Church with Oliver Cowdery to assist him. They were to establish a printing shop.

The great difference between the magnitude and prominence of the Zion to be, and the disorganized, slovenly, and neglected frontier village that Joseph's followers now saw before them, caused some to have doubts and anxieties. Therefore, the Prophet did seek for and received a revelation that elaborated upon the future of the land and City of Zion and the role of those who were to participate in establishing them. The revelation first cautioned the Saints not to be impatient about the fulfillment of the great promises concerning the City of Zion and the temple: *"Ye cannot behold with your natural eyes,* it said, *the design of your God concerning those things which shall come hereafter, and the glory which shall follow after much tribulation. For after much tribulation come the blessings"* (Doctrine & Covenants 58: 3-4). There followed an explanation of the reasons for the difficult and strenuous trip to Missouri and the designation of the ultimate place of gathering that some considered to be premature: *"I have sent you—that you might be obedient, and that your hearts might be prepared to bear testimony of the things which are to come; And also, that you might be honored in laying the foundation, and in bearing record of the land upon which the Zion of God shall stand"* (Doctrine & Covenants 58: 6-7). Reemphasis was given to the need for those who had been specifically appointed to settle in the land, as well as encouragement to those who might *"desire it through the prayer of faith."* All others, nevertheless, were given meaningful direction: *"And now, verily, I say concerning the residue of the elders of my church, the time has not yet come, for many years, for them to receive their inheritance in this land . . ."* (Doctrine & Covenants 58: 44).

The obvious effect of this revelation was to minimize the short-range importance of Missouri in the eyes of the Saints. While they realized that Independence would ultimately be the center of Church power and influence, most also knew that this condition would not exist "for many years" and only "after much tribulation." Even those who realized that there would be a delay in the ultimate gathering, mistakenly believed that it would occur during their lifetimes.

On August 2, 1831, Joseph helped the Colesville Branch *"to lay the first log, for a house, as a foundation of Zion in Kaw township, twelve miles west of Independence."* Symbolically, this *"log was carried and placed by twelve men in honor of the twelve tribes of Israel."* Sidney Rigdon then consecrated and dedicated the land of Zion *"for the gathering of the Saints"* (*History of the Church,* 1: 196). The following day, August third, the Prophet, in the presence of six of his brethren, dedicated the temple site.

With the dedication of the temple site and the dedication and consecration of the land of Zion, the Prophet had completed the necessary and vital work that had brought him to the land of Missouri. He was now ready to return to Kirtland and began making preparations. He gave final instructions to those who were remaining in Missouri and directed the plans of those who were returning to Kirtland. In a revelation received shortly before their departure, the returning brethren were instructed to go *"two by two and to preach the word . . . among the congregations of the wicked"* (Doctrine & Covenants 60: 8).

On August 9, 1831, the Prophet and ten Elders set out from the Independence landing in canoes. They paddled downstream for three days, pulling to shore only to rest, to eat, and to sleep. They experienced much disturbance because of the small size of their canoes, which were bounced about like bubbles on the angry river. On the third night out of Independence, while they were camped at McIlwaine's Bend, William W. Phelps—as the Prophet Joseph wrote: *"in open vision by daylight, saw the destroyer in his most horrible power, ride upon the face of the waters;"* the Prophet continued that *"others heard the noise, but saw not the vision"* (*History of the Church,* 1: 203). The following morning, the Prophet received a revelation which warned about the great dangers lurking upon the waters, and which instructed the Saints coming to Zion to avoid the waterways except for the placid canals.

Shortly after his return to Kirtland, the Prophet received two additional revelations that further enlarged upon the present and future status of the land of Zion in Missouri: the Church was to acquire land there—by purchase; a few were directed to go to the land of Zion to settle; and the general body of the Church was counseled to hold off any thought of moving there until some future time. These revelations and those received by the Prophet while he was in Missouri, potently convinced his followers of the subordinate role Missouri was to play in the development of the Church within the immediate future. At the same time, they were made to understand the ultimate, prevailing role of that special land.

In Kirtland, Joseph found a strong undercurrent of opposition, fault-finding, and apostasy at work. These problems were further complicated by a difficult personal family problem. Since their arrival in Kirtland in January 1831, Joseph and Emma had lived as guests in the home of Newel K. Whitney, the Kirtland merchant. While they had been made to feel welcome, the Whitney home was not very large, and the crowded conditions created strains upon both families—heavily increased when Joseph and Emma adopted the Murdock twins. Therefore, the Prophet began looking for other housing accommodations for his family. The pressing and overwhelming duties that rested upon him as the Prophet and head of the Church made it impossible for him to devote personal time to building a home or to earning money with which to buy one. Therefore, he had to look to the members of the Church or to the Church itself to satisfy this need. His problem was solved when John Johnson of nearby Hiram offered him the use of a bungalow located on the large and thriving Johnson farm.

In Hiram, the Prophet found the privacy, seclusion, retreat, and leisure necessary to enable him to continue with the assignment of revising the Bible. Sidney Rigdon, who was living nearby, served as his scribe. Through the months of October and November 1831, they devoted themselves almost exclusively to this work, taking time out a number of conferences held in the area to give instruction and inspiration to the Saints. The most important one was held on November first, at Hiram, where a decision was made to compile and publish 10,000 copies of the commandments and revelations received by the Prophet since the beginning of his ministry.

During the course of the conference, he received a revelation that was adopted as the Preface of the **"Book of Commandments,"** and that is now identified as the first Section of the **Doctrine and Covenants**. This revelation was directed not only to the members of the Church, but also to nonmembers throughout the world. Its tone was bold and authoritative: *"the voice of warning,* it said, *shall be unto all people, by the mouths of my disciples, whom I have chosen in these last days. And they shall go forth and none shall stay them, for I the Lord have commanded them. Behold, this is mine authority, and the authority of my servants, and my preface unto the book of my commandments, which I have given them to publish unto you, O inhabitants of the earth"* (Doctrine & Covenants 1: 4-6).

Herein lies the key to the vigorous, potent, and all-powerful spirit of preaching the Gospel which has distinguished Mormonism from the beginning. The Mormons consider themselves to be the only religion on earth empowered by God to perform the saving ordinances (though they believe the opportunity to accept those saving ordinances will be offered to all mankind either here or hereafter) and to speak and act authoritatively in His name. **While acknowledging that there are elements of truth in all churches,** and that God is no respecter of persons and is willing to hear and bless the non-Mormons as well as the Mormons, the Saints maintain that theirs is the "strait and narrow way" through which any truth seeker must pass in his search for the ultimate good or happiness. It was because of this that the Mormon missionaries were ambitious and excited to proselyte among Protestants and Catholics as well as among non-Christians. In fact, they preferred and gave greater emphasis to proselyting among other Christian religions because they found that familiarity with the basic beliefs of Christianity made them more likely candidates for conversion to Mormonism. The phenomenal success the missionaries had among some Protestant religions produced a violent reaction that was to cause great trouble and upset for the Saints in years to come.

At this same conference, Oliver Cowdery was appointed to take charge of the final arranging, proofreading, and publication of the Book of Commandments. The printing would be done on the Church Press, which was to be set up in Missouri, under the direction of W. W. Phelps. For nearly two weeks after the conference, the Prophet carefully reviewed the revelations with Oliver, who then left with John Whitmer for Missouri.

At the conclusion of the conference, some of the Prophet's followers became involved in a discussion about the method in which revelations from the Lord are received. A few of the brethren made negative comments about the language and style of the revelations. They had their doubts as to whether the revelations the Prophet had received for the Church actually represented the mind and will of the Lord or were merely an expression of runaway thoughts that came into Joseph's mind. Therefore, the Lord in a revelation challenged the critics to select the *"least"* of the commandments, and to have the wisest man among them try to write a better one (Doctrine & Covenants 67: 4-9). William E. McLellin, a school teacher and recent convert, hastily accepted the challenge. The Prophet said that McLellin: *"as the wisest man, in his own estimation, having more learning than sense, endeavored to write a commandment like unto one of the least of the Lord's, but failed; it was an awful responsibility to write in the name of the Lord."* This experience renewed the brethren's faith in the revelations, and they agreed *"to bear testimony of their truth to all the world"* (*History of the Church* 1: 226). Subsequently, **the Prophet wrote that the revelations were *"the foundation of the Church in these last days"*** (*History of the Church,* 1: 235). Further conference sessions completed the details in preparation to the publication of the Book of Commandments. On November 3, 1831, an "Appendix" (later renamed Doctrine & Covenants 133) was added to the revelations. Another session on November eighth counseled Joseph Smith, under the direction of the Holy Ghost, to correct the errors he discovered in the written copy of the revelations. On November twelfth, the Lord called John Whitmer, the Church historian and recorder, to accompany Oliver Cowdery who had been commanded to carry the manuscripts to Missouri for printing (Doctrine & Covenants 69). Another revelation given that day called six brethren *"to be stewards over the revelations and commandments"* (Doctrine & Covenants 70: 3). The group became known as the "Literary Firm"

(*History of the Church,* 2: 482-83).

The Prophet's relatively brief stay at Hiram turned out to be one of the most productive, fruitful, and prolific periods from a literary viewpoint, of any in his career. Thirteen revelations were received there. A good part of his work on the revision of the Bible was performed at Hiram at the same time. For this reason, the Johnson bungalow later became known as the "revelation house." Among the several revelations received there was one regarded by many as the most significant and meaningful he ever received. Joseph's journal contains this explanation of the conditions under which it was received:

"From sundry revelations which had been received, it was apparent that many important points, touching the salvation of man, had been taken from the Bible, or lost before it was compiled. It appeared self-evident from the truths that were left, that if God rewarded every one according to the deeds done in the body, the term 'Heaven,' as intended for the Saints' eternal home, must include more kingdoms than one. Accordingly, on the 16th of February 1832, while translating the St. John Gospel, myself [Joseph] *and Sidney Rigdon saw the following vision"* (*History of the Church,* 1: 245).

This revelation is recorded in Doctrine & Covenants Section seventy-six (119 verses), elaborating in great detail **the status of men and women in the life after death.** It confirmed the fulness and completeness of the Resurrection: that all who have lived, those who are now living, and those who are yet to live, will be resurrected with tangible bodies of flesh and bone, and that upon resurrection, they will be assigned to that degree of afterlife which their lives on earth have merited. It specified that there are three degrees of glory likened unto the sun, the moon, and the stars, called the: **Celestial**, **Terrestrial**, and **Telestial** degrees. It also specified degrees of afterlife not considered to be degrees of glory. Those who hope to attain the highest degree, are expected to live according to the strictest standard of conduct, and be baptized into The Church of Jesus Christ of Latter-day Saints, to receive the **Gift of the Holy Ghost**, and by faith and continuing repentance from improper conduct, **to strive to perfect their lives through the Atoning Blood of Jesus Christ.**

This revelation, probably more than any other received by the Prophet, released the Church from any real charge of bigotry, fanaticism, or over-ambition in its proselyting efforts. The message was clear, sound, and reasonable. God, who is no respecter of persons, has provided for the resurrection of *all* through the Atoning Sacrifice of the Messiah and Savior, and by that same means, has made it possible for the sinful man to be reconciled to God's perfection through obedience to the principles Jesus taught. Therefore, salvation is dependent not only upon the great vicarious sacrifice fulfilled by the Savior (offering His life for the sins of all mankind) but also the diligent effort of each individual, remembering that resurrection is a free gift from God to all mankind. The message this revelation provided the Elders, as they proselyted among other Christian sects, was that of a better way of life. In essence they said: "Bring all that is good and true with you from your present religion and follow us to a higher ground."

Depending upon the importance of salvation in one's life, the Lord has offered three directions to reach our desired goal:

The first one is classified as: Unconditional or general salvation, that which comes by grace alone without obedience to gospel law, consists in the mere fact of being resurrected. In this sense, salvation is synonymous with immortality; it is the inseparable connection of body and spirit so that the resurrected personage lives forever.

The second classification is called: Conditional or individual salvation, that which comes by grace coupled with gospel obedience, consists in receiving an inheritance in the Celestial kingdom of God. This kind of salvation follows faith, repentance, baptism, receipt of the Holy Ghost, and continued righteousness to the end of one's mortal probation (Doctrine & Covenants 20: 29; 2 Nephi 9: 23-24).

Finally: Salvation in its true and full meaning is synonymous with exaltation or eternal life and consists in gaining an inheritance in the highest of the three heavens within the Celestial kingdom. With few exceptions, this is the salvation of which the scriputes speak. It is the salvation of which the Saints seek. It is of this which the Lord says: ***"there is no gift greater than the gift of salvation"*** (Doctrine & Covenants 6: 13; Bruce R. McConkie, *Mormon Doctrine*, SLC, Bookcraft, 1966, pp. 669-670).

An unfortunate side effect of the concepts taught by this revelation was that they gave a small handful of the members an unjustified feeling of superiority. Because the Church was considered to be the gateway into the Celestial Kingdom, this small special interests group felt that membership in the Church gave them some special status, leading to an unfortunate arrogant and patronizing feeling toward nonmembers. Negative reaction and attitude against this feeling on the part of outsiders, produced much of the friction and unrest that existed between the Church and others in those early days.

The reaction of the Prophet toward this revelation is significant. *"Nothing could be more pleasing to the Saints,* Joseph wrote, *upon the order of the Kingdom of the Lord, than the light which burst upon the world through the foregoing vision. Every law, every commandment, every promise, every truth, and every point touching the destiny of man, from Genesis to Revelation, where the purity of the scriptures remains unspotted and undefiled by the foolishness and stupidity of men, go to show the perfection of the theory* [of different degrees of glory in the future life] *and witnesses the fact that the document is a transcript from the records of the eternal world. The greatness and prominence of the ideas; the purity of the language; the period for action; the continued duration for completion, in order that the heirs of salvation may confess the Lord and bow the knee; the rewards for faithfulness, and the punishments for sins, are so much beyond the narrow-mindedness of men, that every honest man is prompted to exclaim: 'It came from God.'"*

One of the most important occasions in early Church history, took place on February 16, 1832 in Kirtland. A magnificent vision was given to Joseph Smith and Sidney Rigdon in which some of the most important truths of the Gospel were revealed. These two men were permitted to look into the heavens and see God, the Eternal Father, with Jesus Christ, the Messiah and Savior on His right hand. In telling of this, he said: *"this is the testimony, last of all, which we give of him: That he lives! For we saw him, even on the right hand of God; and we heard the voice bearing record that he is the Only Begotten of the Father—That by him, and through him, and of him, the worlds are and were created, and the inhabitants thereof are begotten sons* *and daughters unto God"* (Doctrine & Covenants 76: 22-24).

Secondly, they were permitted to see Satan, whose other names are Lucifer and the Devil. They saw that *before* he rebelled, Lucifer was an angel in the presence of God, and that he had great power. But because of his selfishness, he had the desire and passion to have the power and glory of God. This rebellion took place in our pre-existent life, while we were all yet living with our Heavenly Father, before our earth was created (Revelation 12: 7; Doctrine & Covenants 76: 28).

Joseph and Sidney were permitted to see that as Lucifer rebelled against God, in his thirst for power he led away with him one-third of the hosts of heaven. A war in heaven occured; Michael, the Archangel, who later became known as Adam, the first man on the earth, led the righteous spirits in their fight against Satan and his army, and cast them out of heaven. They came down to the earth as the devil and his followers. They are spirit personages without bodies, and they are using their deceptive spirits to attempt to destroy all mankind (Revelation 12: 9). The host of heaven—those who remained loyal to God and Jesus Christ—wept in grief at the rebellion of Lucifer.

Then Joseph and Sidney were permitted to see the way we will live after death and the resurrection. In this vision, they saw those Saints who would live the Gospel all their lives and go to the Celestial Kingdom, where they will enjoy the presence of God.

Joseph and Sidney also saw that those who are not worthy of Celestial Glory, but who are the "*honorable men of the earth*," will be assigned a lesser kingdom, known as the Terrestrial Glory.

There is a third place for those not worthy to enter the Celestial or Terrestrial Glories. Their place is called the Telestial Kingdom. And a fourth place with no glory at all. Where Satan and his followers and the extremely wicked and sinful men on this earth will be sent in the next world (see 1 Cor.15: 40-41; 2 Cor. 12: 2; Revelation 12: 4; 17: 8).

To help men on earth better understand the differences between these glories (kingdoms), He compared them to the brightness of the sun, the moon, and the stars. The Celestial Glory is brighter than the Terrestrial Glory as the sun is brighter than the moon; and the Terrestrial is brighter than the Telestial as the moon is brighter than the stars. It is also shown that within the Telestial Glory, there are many differences, as the stars differ in glory. Other churches teach that in the next life, there are only two places, heaven and hell; but this new doctrine shows that everyone will be judged in the next world according to his works in this life.

TWO MAIN CENTERS OF CHURCH ACTIVITY

The Church had two main centers of activity and influence at the time of this revelation. It is essential to keep in mind that the Mormon settlements in Kirtland, Ohio, and Independence Missouri were developing concurrently as important centers of Church activity for a number of years. These centers were a 1,000 miles apart, with the country between them, to a great extent, unsettled. Communication and travel was very slow and difficult, making the Prophet's mission of directing the Church a hard one.

By the summer of 1832, nearly all of the New York members of the Church had migrated to Jackson County, Missouri. Some had stopped briefly in Ohio, while others had made the 1,500 mile journey directly to the New Zion.

The converts of the Church in Ohio were content to remain in the Kirtland area. The Prophet, in fact, urged the members to remain and concentrate their efforts on building a temple to the Lord in order to earn the blessings that God had promised them in that land.

With the announcement of the location for the New Zion and its dedication as a gathering place for the Saints, the Prophet devoted most of his time to the building up of the Church in Kirtland. Kirtland offered a more convenient center for directing the affairs of the Saints everywhere, and for directing missionary activity in Canada and the Eastern States. In addition, God had given the Prophet Joseph specific commandments which required him to remain in Kirtland until they were fulfilled.

Of the two communities, Independence offered the better opportunity for putting into effect God's complete law of consecration and for establishing a city which would serve as a model for all future centers of Zion. The practice of the Law of Consecration, which began in Kirtland, was given up there and in Thompson when the Colesville Saints moved as a body to Missouri. Joseph made no attempt to re-establish the practice of the Law of Consecration in Ohio. He nevertheless insisted that all who moved to the New Zion in Missouri, must be willing to uphold that law, and they were required to enter into a covenant with God that they would do so.

While the greater Law of Consecration was not continued in Kirtland, there did developed a very special community spirit of cooperation among the Saints. These associations had a tendency to separate them from nonmembers, and brought upon them the envy, jealousy, and hatred of many apostates. The Church demanded high standards of its members, resulting in the apostasy or falling away of those who were lukewarm in the faith, or had joined the Church for ulterior motives. These apostates did much to trigger false accusations, hostility, and antagonism against the Latter-day Saints. More often than not, the opposition from various classes of people against the Church expressed itself in open mob action.

The spirit of apostasy and conflict that had been agonizing in Ohio, finally came to a head in the spring of 1832, and produced the first and only act of open violence against the Prophet of the Church in Ohio. Several weeks before the unfortunate, disastrous experience took place, the Prophet saw threatening signs of its coming. The number of embittered former members were growing. They included three of the sons of the Prophet's host, John Johnson. The Prophet's enemies and mudslingers outside the Church rallied around this small center of apostates, joining in their blind hatred of him and feeding on false stories and disparaging, ugly remarks.

So loud, so persistent and demanding had the opposition become, that by March, Joseph began using fictitious names in the revelations he received (Doctrine & Covenants 78). This approach prevented enemies from within and outside the Church from knowing which members received special instructions.

The hatred exploded into violent actions on a spring evening in March 1832. Joseph had been dozing while tending one of the twins who had been sick with the measles. Emma was in the bedroom with the healthier twin, and was trying to get some much needed sleep. The first sign of danger was a light tapping on a windowpane. Shortly thereafter, the front door burst open and within seconds, the room was filled with a horde of angry, shoving men, who grabbed the Prophet and carried him outside. As they did so, he managed to free one of his legs and violently kicked one of the mobbers. The infuriated mob overpowered him and swore they would kill him unless he submitted to them. This threat quieted him. The man whom the Prophet had kicked, shoved a blood-covered hand into Joseph's face, (with that one shove) bruising, mauling, and roughing Joseph. Another choked him so violently that he momentarily lost consciousness. On reviving, he saw Sidney Rigdon stretched out on the ground, and thinking him dead, pleaded for his own life. He was told to call on God for help, as the mob intended to show no mercy.

At that moment, the mob seemed uncertain as to what they should do. While some of the mob held him, others stood nearby discussing their next move. Finally, Joseph was stripped naked except for his shirt collar, and his body was scratched all over by a man who fell upon him like a wild animal. Then he was tarred and feathered, beaten senseless, and left for dead.

When he revived, he crawled back to the house where several of his friends and neighbors who had been aroused by the turmoil and fury of the confrontation, had gathered. The sight of his tar-covered body caused Emma to think that Joseph had been fatally injured, and she fainted. He was given a blanket to cover his nakedness, and friends and family spent most of the night scraping the tar and feathers from his beaten body—a process very painful to Joseph.

The attack took place on a Saturday night. The next day, Joseph spoke at Sabbath Day services despite his bruised appearance. In the audience were several of the mobbers, including the leaders, who were amazed and flabbergasted at his recuperative powers and daring.

On Monday, Joseph visited Sidney Rigdon at his home, where he found his scribe badly lacerated and delirious from the mob beating. When Sidney saw the Prophet, he demanded his razor so he could kill him; when his wife left the room, he demanded his razor again so he could kill her. His mind was temporarily deranged because the mobbers had dragged him from his home by the heels, permitting his head to bump over the steps and rocky ground. Older and less resilient than Joseph, Sidney carried the emotional and physical scars of his ordeal through the remainder of his life.

Joseph was not discouraged or turned from his course by this act of violence, although it brought great sorrow into his home. One of the twins, already weakened by the measles, contracted a cold while being exposed to the cold night air during the mobbing, and died shortly thereafter. The death and burial of a fourth baby, added to the trauma produced by the beating inflicted upon her husband, caused Emma Smith to become sorrow-stricken, heart broken, and disconsolate. She, too, was permanently affected by this tragedy, and thereafter was filled with terror and anxiety when thoughts of that horrifying, dreadful night came to mind. It is important to recognize all Emma went through from these and other countless tragedies, adversities, and sacrifices she was called upon to endure for the sake of her husband.

Any expectation by the mobbers that their use of violence would prevent, discourage, or slow down the Prophet in his work, absolutely failed to recognize the depth of his belief in the truth and importance of what he was doing. It was the same kind of error in judgement that caused those responsible for his martyrdom to believe that Joseph's death would eliminate his influence and result in the demise of the Church he had established. In point of fact, this mobbing served to fuel Joseph's energies and determination. It also revealed the extent of the bitterness and hatred his teachings had aroused and made him more wary and cautious in his future associations and dealings with those both in and out of the Church.

Previous to the outbreak of violence, the Prophet was planning another trip to Missouri. Reports of dissension and disputes within the Church and conflicts with Gentiles had given him much concern, and he was anxious to be there to help resolve any difficulties. He was also interested in accelerating and advancing the completion of the Church-owned press in Independence and the publication of the Book of Commandments. The recent mobbing changed his previous schedule; he made immediate plans to leave for Independence.

Joseph was only twenty-six years old as he made plans for his second trip to Missouri. He would be facing decisions of great magnitude and complexity affecting the physical, emotional, and spiritual well-being and the very lives of hundreds of Saints who looked to him for guidance and direction. He had no experience or training in the past to qualify him to solve the difficult and pressing problems of finance, economics, and organization that now confronted him and his followers. In the past, his practical experience had been limited to farming and working as a hired hand. Add to that of course, the phenomenal spiritual experiences he had enjoyed and the mental discipline he had acquired from his work in translating the Book of Mormon, in revising the scriptures, and in dictating the revelations he had received, from God the Father and Jesus Christ. Nevertheless, all this scarcely qualified him for the arduous task of directing the business affairs of a rapidly growing Church and of counseling its members about their most intimate personal problems.

It was a strong trait of the Prophet Joseph's character that he demonstrated no uncertainty about involving himself in activities about which he knew very little when the need was apparent. His approach was to see the need, to decide to satisfy it, and then to organize and arrange the necessary means to achieve the end. There is a similarity to the character of one of the main figures in the Book of Mormon. Nephi, commanded by his father to obtain a valuable historical record from a wealthy and powerful prince, (Laban) accepted the task without question and without knowledge of the means of accomplishment, declaring: *"I will go and do the things which the Lord hath commanded, for I know that the Lord giveth no commandment unto the children of men, save he shall prepare a way for them that they may accomplish the thing which he commandeth them"* (1 Nephi 3: 7).

As Joseph prepared himself for his second trip to Missouri, he reviewed in his mind all that had taken place on his first go-round. **Two important events required Joseph Smith's attention in Missouri**—the dedication of the land as a gathering place for the Saints, and the dedication of the temple site. Both events were presided over by the Prophet Joseph Smith. Remembering again: At a special service on August 2, 1831, twelve men, (in honor of the Twelve Tribes of Israel), laid the first log *"as a foundation of Zion in Kaw township, twelve miles west of Independence"* (*History of the Church,* 1: 196). Sidney Rigdon consecrated and dedicated the land unto the

Lord. The dedication of the temple site in Independence took place the next day; again the services were simple but inspiring. Following the reading of Psalm eighty-seven, which extols the glory and majesty of Zion, a single stone, marking the southeast corner, was laid in place. Joseph Smith then dedicated the temple site with a dedicatory prayer.

A NEW LIFESTYLE AND A NEW ENVIRONMENT

Settling in a frontier land was a new experience for most of the Saints who had arrived from the East. Timber needed to be cut; ferries, bridges, mills, and dams had to be built; homes, outbuildings, and fences had to be constructed. Remembering the fall of 1831, Newel Knight wrote: "**We were not accustomed to a frontier life,** so things around us seemed new and strange and the work we had to do was certainly different to that which had been done in the East." Yet, they took hold with cheerful hearts, and a determination to do their best; with all diligence, they went to work to secure food and prepare for the coming winter.

Parley P. Pratt commended the industry and optimism of a group of the Missouri Saints: "They had arrived late in the summer, and cut some hay for their cattle, sowed a little grain, and prepared some ground for cultivation, and were engaged during the fall and winter in building log cabins, etc. **The winter was cold, and for some time, about ten families lived in one log cabin, which was open and unfinished,** while the frozen ground served as a floor. Their food consisted of beef and a little bread made of corn. This was, without doubt, an inconvenient way of living. Nevertheless, it was for the Gospel's sake, and all were very cheerful and happy. There was a spirit of peace and union, of love and good will, manifested in this little Church in the wilderness, the memory of which will be ever dear to my heart. Plainly, it was not what Zion was, but what it could become that buoyed up the Saints and lifted sagging spirits" (Pratt, Autobiography of Parley P. Pratt p. 56).

Gradually, funds began arriving from the Saints in the East. With these funds, Bishop Edward Partridge was able to purchase more land and superintend the establishment of a storehouse to receive and distribute the benefits and assistance from the Saints.

Church leaders in Missouri began a printing enterprise as they had been commanded. (Doctrine & Covenants 58: 37) W. W. Phelps, who was called to be the printer and newspaper editor in Zion (Doctrine & Covenants 57: 11-12), prepared to publish the Church's first periodical, a monthly newspaper, *The Evening and Morning Star*.

During the spring and summer of 1832, 300 to 400 more Saints arrived in Missouri, where they received their inheritances from the Bishop and began developing the land. There was great intensity of their efforts and industry. It was a strange sight to see four or five yoke of oxen turning up the rich soil. Fencing and other improvements went on in rapid succession. Cabins were built and prepared for families as quickly as time, money, and labor could accomplish the work; and their homes in this new country presented a prosperous appearance, almost equal to Paradise itself. There was peace, joy, and happiness, and no labor was spared in the cultivation of flowers and shrubbery, the choicest selection.

Although land was plentiful, skilled craftsmen and builders were scarce. The majority of residents in Zion were farmers and common laborers. What was needed were wheelwrights blacksmiths, brick masons, and carpenters. A revelation, specifying the need to send for workmen *"of all kinds unto this land, to labor for the saints of God"* did not bring swift response (Doctrine & Covenants 58: 54). Levi Hancock, a carpenter and resident of Zion, had more work than he could handle. His first project was the building of a combined home and printing office for W. W. Phelps. On May 29, 1832, a conference was held in the newly completed printing office for the purpose of dedicating the facility.

In June 1832, Elder Phelps began publishing *The Evening and Morning Star*. Over the next year, the *Star* published numerous revelations given to Joseph Smith that later were included in the Doctrine and Covenants. Since it was the only newspaper in the county, and since it printed both national and international news, it was read by non-Mormons as well as by members of the Church; but the paper performed its greatest service for the Saints. Considerable attention was devoted in every issue to urging members to faithfulness in performing religious and family duties. In the first edition, W. W. Phelps urged the Saints: "The disciples should lose no time in preparing schools for their children, that they may be taught as is pleasing unto the Lord, and brought up in the way of holiness. Those appointed to select and prepare books for the use of schools, will attend to that subject, as soon as more weighty matters are finished. But the parents and guardians in the Church of Jesus Christ need not wait—it is all important that children, to become good, should be taught so" ("Common Schools," *The Evening and Morning Star*, June 1832). In the fall of 1832, a school, known as the Colesville School, was started near a large spring in Kaw township; Parley P. Pratt was the first teacher. Later that same year, a second school was opened in Independence in a log schoolhouse erected for that purpose near the temple lot (*Journal of History*, July 1922).

Proper observance of the Lord's Day received special emphasis in the *Star*. One of the first revelations received by Joseph Smith in Zion admonished the Saints to *"go to the house of prayer and offer up thy sacraments upon my holy day . . . and to pay thy devotions unto the Most High"* (Doctrine & Covenants 59: 9-10).

Setting Sunday apart from other days and acknowledging it as a holy day was not the custom of the other residents of Jackson County. Reinforcing the message of this revelation, the *Star* offered this advice to the Saints: "Observe the Sabbath Day to keep it holy. The Lord is not well pleased with a disciple that does anything on that holy day that should be done on a laboring day. Nor should a disciple go to a meeting one Sabbath here, and another there; let all that can, be strict to attend their meeting in their own place. Neither should the children be allowed to slip off and play, rather than meet where they may be trained up in the way they should go to be saved. We are the children of God, and let us not put off His law. When a Saint works on the Sabbath Day, the world can reply: "So do we." When the Saints travel to do business on the Sabbath Day, the world can reply: "So do we." When the Saints go from one meeting to another to see and be seen, the world can reply: "So do we." When the children of the Saints play on the Sabbath, the world can reply: "So do ours." Brethren, watch, that you may enter into the Lord's sacred rest" ("The Saints in the Land of Zion, and Abroad," *The Evening and the Morning Star, Oct.* 1832, p. 5).

The subject of the gathering received the most attention in the pages of the *Star,* and many articles were printed dealing with the matter. In July, Elder Phelps reminded the migrating Saints that they were to bring authorization from the Bishop in Ohio (Newel K. Whitney) or from three Elders. They were also advised not to proceed to Zion without being told by one of the Bishops that preparations had been made for them. Failure to recognize this caution, he warned, could produce affliction and cause confusion. In addition, by being hasty and forcing the sale of property, unreasonable sacrifices would be made. Although this was a day of sacrifice and tithing, yet to make wasteful and unreasonable sacrifices is not well pleasing in the sight of the Lord. Later, Saints traveling to Zion were counseled to keep God's commandments "in every point" and set such a good example, that others would "be constrained to say: They act like the children of God" (*The Evening and the Morning Star,* Dec. 1832, p.5).

By November 1832, there were 810 Saints in Missouri. Up to this point, Zion was able to absorb its immigrants, and the Saints were pleased with the results. Editorials in the *Star* reflected their optimism; future prospects for Zion appeared bright and promising.

The Lord instructed the Prophet Joseph to return a second time to Missouri. Some of the Jackson County Saints were becoming jealous because Joseph Smith lived in Ohio rather than on the frontier. The Lord explained that Joseph should go to Missouri and counsel with the Saints because Satan was seeking to use the situation to *"turn their hearts away"* (Doctrine & Covenants 78: 10). Another reason for visiting Missouri was to coordinate the operation of the Church's storehouses in Kirtland and Independence. In March 1832, Joseph received a revelation, the language of which is vital to an understanding of what transpired in Independence at that time: *"For verily I say unto you, the time has come, and is now at hand; and behold, and lo, it must needs be that there be an organization of my people, in regulating and establishing the affairs of the storehouse for the poor of my people, both in this place and in the land of Zion—For a permanent and everlasting establishment and order unto my church, to advance the cause, which ye have espoused,* [embraced] *to the salvation of man, and to the glory of your Father who is in heaven; That you may be equal in the bonds of heavenly things, yea, and earthly things also, for the obtaining of heavenly things . . . For if you will that I give unto you a place in the celestial world, you must prepare yourselves by doing the things which I have commanded you and required of you"* (Doctrine & Covenants 78: 3, 4, 5, 7).

The profits of the Independence store were to assist the migrating Saints. One of the items of business in Missouri was to unite the two firms and consolidate the economic activities of the Church. The revelation also established what came to be known as a Central Board of Control "to manage the affairs of the poor, and all things pertaining to the Bishopric both in the land of Zion and in the land of Kirtland." The effect of this organizational change was to divest Bishop Partridge of the absolute control he had exerted over welfare matters in the land of Zion; it also increased the prominence in Zion of Oliver Cowdery and Martin Harris, two of the scribes and witnesses to the Book of Mormon.

Jointly, with the creation of the Central Board of Control, the Prophet and his associates brought into existence a single firm to control the business activities of the Church in Zion and in Kirtland. Each branch of the firm was to operate under a separate name: in Zion, as Gilbert, Whitney and Company, and in Kirtland, as Newel K. Whitney and Company (B. H. Roberts, *Comprehensive History of the Church,* 1: 285).

The stay in Missouri was short but productive. On April twenty-sixth, a "general council" sustained Joseph as President of the High Priesthood, as he had been ordained at a similar conference at Amherst, Ohio, on January 25, 1832. In the afternoon session, Joseph was instructed in a revelation (Doctrine & Covenants 82: 20), to combine the economic orders in Kirtland and in Independence into the **United Order,** so they could *"be independent of every incumbrance beneath the celestial kingdom, by bonds and covenants of mutual friendship, and mutual love"* (*History of the Church,* 1: 269). Other major business transacted by the general council related to the Church press. Because of lack of funds and supplies, the number of copies printed in the first edition of the Book of Commandments was reduced from 10,000 to 3,000 copies. Also, W. W. Phelps was directed to correct and publish the selection of hymns that had been collected by Emma Smith.

In the establishment of the periodical, the Prophet recognized the power of the written word and the need for an official organ through which the Saints could be given consistent instructions, and by which the aims and doctrines of the Church could be correctly represented to the world. The power and effectiveness of the *Star* was confirmed only a year after the publication of its first issue when enemies of the Church, angered by a misinterpretation of an article that appeared in it, burned the print shop and scattered the type.

On the return trip to Kirtland, the Prophet reflected with some pleasure upon the sound accomplishments of his few weeks in Independence. His position of unquestioned leadership in the Church in Zion had been reaffirmed. The organization to care for the needs of the poor who were flocking to Zion had been expanded and strengthened. A commercial arm of the Church had been established, and arrangements had been made to print the Book of Commandments and a hymnbook and to begin the publication of an official periodical of the Church.

Of greater significance than all of these achievements, was the fact that the primary responsibility for carrying them out had been trusted to well-qualified associates. Joseph was never one to become involved in the complicated details of the ventures he set in motion. He was inclined to delegate extensively to others while retaining ultimate authority. He was the organizer and motivator, the final mediator of what was or was not to be done. To a degree, everyone in the Church became instruments through whom his will and designs were executed. Yet, in all this there was no sense of blind submission to his authority and leadership, nor was there a tendency on his part to aggrandize (glorify) himself. Each member seemed to have the desire to excel in the performance of his own stewardship, exercising a high degree of independence and imagination.

The essentially key to the motivation, however, was the recognition by the Prophet and his followers that the earthly organization of the Church was, in fact—governed and directed from beyond the veil—that its actual head is Jesus Christ, whose name it bears. **The Prophet Joseph, therefore, was merely regarded as an agent of the Savior;** just as the members are agents of the Savior, nevertheless, the nature of their respective duties and authority differed. The members of the Church saw themselves during that period of time and now, collectively as "the body of Christ," with each one fulfilling a vital and indispensable role. This "body" was made up of many interdependent parts, the loss of any one of which would greatly impair the efficient and healthful functioning of the whole.

A LETTER OF REFLECTIONS TO EMMA

Joseph Smith, Newel K. Whitney, and Sidney Rigdon left for home by stagecoach early in May. Near the town of Greenville, Indiana, the horses were frightened, broke and ran. Bishop Whitney jumped from the coach, but his coat tangled and his foot got caught in one of the wheels, breaking his leg in several places. Joseph and Sidney leaped from the stagecoach unhurt. The Prophet remained with Bishop Whitney a month in Greenville to nurse and care for him while Sidney traveled on to Kirtland with the news. During this time, Joseph often enjoyed the solitude of walking in the woods. He wrote to Emma that he visited a grove outside of town nearly every day to pray and meditate: *"I have called to mind all the past moments of my life, and am left to mourn and shed tears of sorrow for my folly in suffering the adversary of my soul to have so much power over me as he has had in times past, but God is merciful and has forgiven my sins"* (Letter, Joseph Smith to Emma Smith, 6 June 1832—Per. Dean C. Jessee, *The Personal Writings of Joseph Smith,* SLC, p. 238).

After dinner one day, Joseph became deathly ill. In his own words: *"I walked directly to the door and commenced vomiting most profusely . . . so great were the muscular contortions of my system, that my jaw in a few moments was dislocated. This I succeeded in replacing with my own hands and made my way to Brother Whitney* [who was on the bed], *as speedily as possible; he laid his hands on me and administered to me in the name of the Lord, and I was healed in an instant, although the effect of the poison was so powerful, as to cause much of the hair on my head to become loosened from my head. Thanks be to my Heavenly Father for His interference in my behalf at this critical moment, in the name of Jesus Christ. Amen"* (*History of the Church,* 1: 271).

The combination of spiritual devotion, sincerity, and simple faith that characterize the Prophet, are clearly evident in this brief account. It is interesting to note that when faced with a grave crisis involving a question of life or death, he turned instinctively to God for assistance. Nor was it adequate for him to simply call upon God in his own behalf. Instead, he went to his ailing companion "as speedily as possible" to seek a blessing at his hands. It was significant also that his companion knew immediately what was expected of him, and without any hesitancy or coaching, proceeded to bless the Prophet with power and authority "in the name of the Lord." It is one thing to express faith and confidence in God and to teach the principles He has given to men in the scriptures—It is quite another thing to speak and to act in His name as an authorized agent, exercising Godly power. This is exactly what Newel K. Whitney did, believing full well that God, through Priesthood delegation, had endowed and blessed him with that power.

When the Prophet arrived back in Kirtland, he recognized that the bitter spirit of hostility and persecution that produced the mobbing at Hiram had greatly diffused. Briefly, all was quiet on the Kirtland front. This made it possible for him to continue on with his assignment to revise the Holy Bible. While working with a variety of scribes, but more often with Sidney Rigdon, the Prophet stayed with this exacting and demanding assignment for most of the summer.

A HARVEST OF POSITIVE AND NEGATIVE LEADERSHIP

As the fall of the year approached, some of the missionaries, who had been sent to proselyte in the Eastern United States, began returning to Kirtland, and they then began to *"present the histories of their several stewardships in the Lord's vineyard"* (*History of the Church,* 1: 286).

Overall, it certainly was an uplifting experience to hear of the extraordinary degree of success in their labors. **Many branches of the Church had been organized,** and the new converts seemed instilled with a great desire to share the message with others, and ultimately, to gather with the Saints either in Kirtland or Independence. The gathering of new converts at this time was one of the most fruitful of any comparable period in terms of the impact the converts had upon the history of the Church. This harvest included **Brigham Young,** who later became a member of the First Quorum of Twelve Apostles and the second President and Prophet of The Church of Jesus Christ, succeeding the Prophet Joseph Smith. Others in that special harvest—George A. Smith, Heber C. Kimball, and Joseph Young—would eventually assume positions of importance in the Church. They would overshadow some of the earlier convert leaders, including Sidney Rigdon, Oliver Cowdery, and David Whitmer, who for the moment were in the forefront but gradually faded into the background or apostatized. The failings and falling of these early leaders demonstrated the unstable, disloyal, and unfaithful nature of many men, a fact with which the Prophet was to become intimately acquainted as he saw first one and then another of his most trusted aides turn away from him in times of great stress or difficulty. What happened to their testimonies of the Restored Gospel and Church of Jesus Christ? Several years later, while he was imprisoned in the **Liberty Jail** he wrote: *"Behold, there are many called, but few are chosen. And why are they not chosen? Because their hearts are set so much upon the things of this world, and aspire to the honors of men, that they do not learn this one lesson—That the rights of the priesthood are inseparably connected with the powers of heaven, and that the powers of heaven cannot be controlled nor handled only upon the principles of righteousness."* Further, he reflected: *"We have learned by sad experience that it is the nature and disposition of almost all men, as soon as they get a little authority, as they suppose, they will immediately begin to exercise unrighteous dominion. Hence, many are called, but few are chosen"* (Doctrine & Covenants 121: 34-36; 39-40).

In September, 1832, the Prophet received an important revelation that expanded on the role and function of the Aaronic and Melchizedek Priesthoods. To him who receives both of these priesthoods and magnifies his callings therein, the revelation holds out this awesome prospect: *"all that my Father hath shall be given unto him"* (Doctrine & Covenants 84: 38). Stated in simple theological terms, this means that those who satisfy these standards will become joint heirs with Christ, to share fully with Him all that the Father has. This concept, added to the fast growing storehouse of new doctrines taught by the Prophet, provided fresh encouragement for the Saints in their active search for perfection.

Also in the early fall of 1832, the Prophet, accompanied by Bishop Newel K. Whitney, made a hasty trip to Albany, New York City, and Boston, to transact loans in accordance with the decision reached at the general council in Independence. Not only was this trip successful in acquiring funds for the Church's religious and temporal activities, but it also expanded the degree of the Prophet's vision and understanding. This was his first trip to the financial and cultural centers of the United States and it was somewhat overwhelming. Nevertheless, in his thought-provoking letter to his dear Emma from New York City, he explained all that he had seen and was exposed to, but he elaborated upon God and His relationship with man. Joseph was neither aloof nor stuffy, but he knew where the worldly man was heading. He said: *"I prefer reading and praying and holding communion with the Holy Spirit, and writing to you Emma than walking the streets and beholding the distractions of men."*

The Prophet's tender references to Emma and Julia, the surviving twin, take on new meaning when it is known that at the time Emma was in the last stages of pregnancy. Just before the Prophet returned from his trip, she gave birth to their fourth child, Joseph Smith III. After the grief of losing three children at birth, along with the male twin who died following the mobbing at Hiram, young Joseph III came as a great joy to his parents. At the same time, his arrival inflicted greater burdens on them, especially Emma, who now had two babies to care for, and who was almost camping out until Joseph could arrange for suitable and permanent housing for his family. Within a short period of time, he was able to find a house for them.

He was so caught up with the pressures and responsibilities of giving direction to the fast-growing Church and of counseling his brethren about the numerous challenges facing them, that he seemed to have little time for his own personal affairs. Nevertheless, this preoccupation should not be construed as meaning a lack of concern or love for his family. **His intimate and sensitive letters to Emma when he was away from home, are the greatest indication of his love and devotion for his family.**

During the latter part of 1832, the Prophet received many discouraging reports from Missouri. Lack of experience in administering the affairs of the Church, lack of means, and the rapid inflow of new converts caused the Missouri leaders difficulties in allocating stewardship and making provision for all. On November 27, 1832, Joseph wrote to Bishop W. W. Phelps in Independence, unburdening himself of strong feelings he had about the situation there. Since the letter states that some of the views expressed in it had been given to him *"by a vision from heaven,"* a portion of it was later adopted as part of the Doctrine and Covenants, and things began to improve for a reasonable period of time.

As the year 1832 came to a close, the Prophet received two unique and contrasting revelations within a period of three days. The first one, received on Christmas Day, was a bleak and ominous prediction about a destructive, catastrophic, and bloody war that was to agonize the United States, and that would terminate in the *"death and misery* *of many souls"* (Doctrine & Covenants 87: 1).

The second revelation, received on December twenty-seventh, was designated by the Prophet as the *"Olive Leaf."* Joseph pointed out that this revelation was *"the Lord's message of peace to us"* (Preface, Doctrine & Covenants 88). The multifaceted quality of the Prophet's mind is shown clearly by his study of these revelations dealing with war and peace.

In all probability, the first revelation was prompted by a political crisis that originated in the United States in 1832 as a result of the protective tariff law passed by Congress in 1828. Additional import duties imposed under the law in 1832, caused a violent reaction among the residents of the rural Southern States who had little industry, and who were almost exclusively dependent upon the import of manufactured goods to sustain their economy. In the forefront of the bitter opposition to this action was the State of South Carolina, whose state convention declared the additional duties unconstitutional, and stated that any attempt to enforce them would be resisted by arms or by secession from the Union. Reports of this crisis filled the press of the day, and the subject was a favorite topic of conversation during the Prophet's trip to New York in October.

While meditating upon this grave crisis on Christmas Day in 1832, Joseph received one of the most startling and specific revelations of his mission: *"I prophesy in the name of the Lord God, that the commencement of the difficulties which will cause much bloodshed previous to the coming of the Son of Man will be in South Carolina. It may probably arise through the slave question. This a voice declared to me, while I was praying earnestly on the subject, December 25th, 1832"* (Doctrine & Covenants 130: 12-13). The Prophet was greatly worried over the increasing bad feelings between the Northern and Southern States. The Southern States permitted slavery, and all the plantations were manned by Negro (African American) workers who were not allowed to have their personal freedom. These poor slaves were sometimes beaten by cruel masters. They were forced to work hard and long, and many of them were sold like cattle. Families were broken up when children or father and mother were sold to other slave owners at a public auction.

This situation and many others troubled the Prophet, and he prayed to the Lord. **In answer to his prayers, Joseph received this great prophecy concerning the wars that would come upon the world—remarkably because it foretold the Civil War nearly thirty years before it broke out.**

The revelation began with these words: *"VERILY, thus saith the Lord, concerning the wars that will shortly come to pass, beginning at the rebellion of South Carolina, which will eventually terminate in the death and misery of many souls."* This revelation revealed that a great war would begin in "*South Carolina,"* and that thereafter, "*war will be poured out upon all nations"* (Doctrine & Covenants 87: 1-2).

The revelation continued: *"For behold, the Southern States shall be divided against the Northern States, and the Southern States will call upon other nations, even the nation of Great Britain, as it is called, and they shall also call upon other nations in order to defend themselves against other nations; and then war shall be poured out upon all nations"* (Doctrine & Covenants 87: 3).

The missionaries of the Church who were counseled to call everyone to repentance, took handwritten copies of this revelation with them as they preached to the people. One of their duties was to tell them that the Lord had raised up a new Prophet on the earth, named Joseph Smith, who at that time lived in Kirtland, Ohio. To prove that Joseph had received revelations from the Lord, they showed the prophecy on war to the people. Some believed, but many did not.

The missionaries in England printed the revelation in the *Millennial Star,* a Church publication, in the year 1851, ten years *before* the Civil War broke out.

In the year 1860, Elder George Q. Cannon was in Omaha with other missionaries who were on their way to England. They held a special meeting in Omaha when Abraham Lincoln was running for the Presidency of the United States. The feelings of the people ran high and were greatly aroused because of the troubles between the north and the south. The brethren's sermons about the prophecy on war greatly interested the people, and after the meeting many came up to see the book containing the prophecy and marveled that it could have been given so long before. They could now see that war was near.

The Civil War began with the first shots being fired at Fort Sumter, South Carolina, on April 12, 1861, and the Southern States did call on Great Britain for assistance. **That war occurred some ten years after the revelation was published, and twenty-eight years and four months after the Prophet first received the revelation** (Doctrine & Covenants 87: 3-6).

In World War I, Britain had to call on other nations for help, as the revelation says and in that war—a world war—nearly all the nations of the earth were affected.

THE MESSAGE OF PEACE

When the *"Olive Leaf"* revelation was received two days later, there was no suggestion of the somber, mournful spirit that seemed to occupy the Prophet's thinking on Christmas Day. Now, instead of focusing upon the terror of war and the catastrophic events the world will face before the end of this dispensation, his mind was turned toward eternal things and great philosophical concepts of intelligence and knowledge. The revelation confirmed the eternal nature of the soul and the universality of the Resurrection. It also affirmed the influence and supervision of law in the universe, the infinity of space and God's creations, and the indestructibility of matter. It acknowledged the influence of God throughout the universe by means of His Holy Spirit, thus distinguishing between God the person, and the influence and power of God. Most importantly, perhaps, the revelation dwelt upon the gradations which would exist in the hereafter and the conditions to be met by those who aspired to the highest of those grades, the Celestial Kingdom. Those who hoped to attain that kingdom were admonished to seek learning *"out of the best books."* They were told to cease from all *"light speeches, laughter, lustful desires, pride, light-mindedness, and wicked doings."* They were admonished to love one another and to share. Finally, they were enjoined: *"Cease to be idle; cease to be unclean; cease to find fault one with another; cease to sleep longer than is needful; retire to thy bed early, that ye may not be weary; arise early, that your bodies and your minds may be invigorated. And above all things, clothe yourselves with the bond of charity, as with a mantle, which is the bond of perfectness and peace. Pray always, that ye may not faint, until I come"* (Doctrine & Covenants 88: 118, 124-126).

For the next several months, the Prophet

again spent most of his time on the inspired translation of the Bible. Joseph Smith's inspired translation of the Bible was one of the crucial developments of his work as a Prophet, and has had a profound influence on the Church. Joseph's knowledge about the principles of the Gospel and God's work with his ancient prophets and people, increased immensely through this project. He considered it an important branch of his calling, and labored diligently at it. When he and Sidney Rigdon were at home in Ohio, this was their major preoccupation. The frequency with which the "translation" is referred to in the revelations and historical documents of the period, underscores the importance of this project. The Prophet first began this work in New York in 1830. When he arrived in Ohio in February 1831, he continued his work in the Old Testament with the help of his scribe, Sidney Rigdon. But early in March, Joseph was commanded to work on the translation of the New Testament (see Doctrine & Covenants 45: 60-61). During the next two years, Joseph and Sidney continued their work on both the Old and New Testaments. They optimistically and happily declared their work finished on July 2, 1833: *"We this day finished the translating of the Scriptures, for which we returned gratitude to our Heavenly Father"* (*History of the Church,* 1: 368).

In addition to the **great legacy** left to the Church in the Joseph Smith Translation (JST) itself, numerous revelations now recorded in the **Doctrine and Covenants,** came to the Prophet while he worked on the inspired translation. The study of the Bible stimulated him to inquire of the Lord about significant doctrinal and organizational matters.

The destruction of the press in Zion a few months later, and the hectic, pressured and persecuted condition of Joseph Smith's life thereafter, prevented him from publishing an approved, verified version of this work during his lifetime.

* * *

It is important to discuss the inspired translation of the Bible as assigned by the Lord to the Prophet Joseph Smith, and the Bible itself, for all to be edified.

That segment of the writing of inspired men in the old world which, in the providence of the Almighty, has been handed down from age to age until modern times,—is known as the Bible. These writings in their original form were perfect scripture; they were *"the mind and will of the Lord,"* His voice to His chosen people, and to all who would hear it (Doctrine & Covenants 68: 4). However they have not come down to us in their perfect form—a fact known in the Church and by all reputable scholars. Only a few among certain denominations of Christendom close their eyes to this reality and profess to believe in what they call verbal revelation, that is, that every word and syllable in some version or other of the Bible, is the exact word spoken by Deity.

"I believe the Bible as it read, when it came from the pen of the original writers," the Prophet said. Also he said: *"Ignorant translators, careless transcribers, or designing and corrupt priests, have committed many errors"* (*Teachings of the Prophet Joseph Smith,* p. 327). Nephi, a Prophet from the Book of Mormon times, recorded that the Bible, in its original form, contained "the plainness of the gospel of the Lord." After it had passed through the hands of *"a great and abominable church, which is the most abominable above all other churches,"* however, he saw that many *"plain and precious"* things were deleted, in consequence of which error and falsehood poured into the various churches (see 1

Nephi 13).

Nevertheless, with it all, the Bible is a book of books. It has enlightened and influenced the Christian world generally as no other book has ever done. When such measure of truth as was preserved in its pages became known to the people generally it was instrumental in bringing to pass a revival and of laying the foundation for the Restoration of the Gospel. When the Bible is read under the guidance of the Spirit and in harmony with the many latter-day revelations, which interpret and make plain its more mysterious parts, it becomes one of the most priceless volumes known to man. *"He who reads it often, will like it best, and he who is acquainted with it, will know the hand of the Lord wherever he can see it,"* the Prophet taught (*Teachings of the Prophet Joseph Smith*, p. 56).

In its present form, the Bible is divided into the Old and New Testaments, and has a total of sixty-six books within its covers. These books contain doctrinal, historical, prophetic, and poetic materials of profound worth. Members of The Church of Jesus Christ are commanded to teach the principles of the Gospel *"which are in the Bible"* (Doctrine & Covenants 42: 12).

One of the great fallacies of modern Christendom is the unfounded assumption that the Bible contains *all* of the inspired teachings now existent among men. Anticipating that Satan would darken the minds of men in this way, and knowing that other scripture would come forth in the last days, the Prophet Nephi prophesied that unbelieving Christians would reject new revelation with a cry: *"A Bible! A Bible! We have got a Bible, and there cannot be any more Bible"* (2 Nephi 29: 3).

And then Nephi recorded this answering—Proclamation from the Lord: *"Thou fool, that shall say: A Bible, we have got a Bible, and we need no more Bible. Have ye obtained a Bible save it were by the Jews? Know ye not that there are more nations than one? Know ye not that I, the Lord your God, have created all men, and that I remember those who are upon the isles of the sea; and that I rule in the heavens above, and in the earth beneath; and I bring forth my word unto the children of men, yea, even upon all the nations of the earth? Wherefore, murmur ye, because that ye shall receive more of my words?"* (2 Nephi 29: 6-8).

Various versions of the Bible have found common usage among numbers of the earth's inhabitants from time to time. Nevertheless, **the King James Version is considered the greatest of the completed English translations.** Scholars universally acclaim it as containing as forceful, direct, and majestic prose as has ever been produced in the English language. Joseph Smith read, respected, reverenced, and taught the King James Version *"as far is it is translated correctly"* (Eighth Article of Faith). Whenever he found Biblical quotations in the Book of Mormon (having been copied from the brass plates and preserved by the Nephite Prophets), he rendered them into English in the exact language of the King James Version, except in instances in which the language of that version did not convey accurately the original thought. It was the King James Version that the Prophet worked on when he corrected portions of the Bible by and through the spirit of revelation, always preserving the existing language unless a content change was necessary. The King James Version has been and remains the official version of—The Church of Jesus Christ of Latter-day Saints. This official usage, most assuredly, will not be changed until such time, as the Lord directs that the needed corrections in the Inspired Version be completed (J. Reuben Clark, Jr., *Why the King James Version?* pp. 1-441).

Several English versions that have come forth since the King James Version, and particularly the Revised Standard Version, have been translated by individuals and groups, who have questioned the divinity of Jesus Christ and His mission. As a consequence, there are passages in many of these versions which have been so altered as to leave in question our Lord's Divine Sonship and other basic doctrines of the Gospel.

Only under the direction of the Lord by revelation did the Prophet Joseph begin the revision of the Bible, we know this—because man had changed the original meaning of God's words to us, His children.

* * *

The rapid growth of the Restored Church of Jesus Christ required a substantial expansion of its organization, under the direction of the Lord and His chosen Prophet. With the expansion came the pressure of selecting able leadership. **Although the Gospel and the Church are true, all people have weaknesses and hangups.** The early leaders used their skills to the best of their abilities, both spiritually and temporally, even though at times they made serious errors of judgement in serving the Lord. **The Gospel is true—but people are imperfect.**

In early 1833, the Prophet's thoughts turned to a serious problem that had developed once again within the ranks in Missouri. Correspondence from some of the leadership there, especially W. W. Phelps and Sidney Gilbert, disclosed a spirit of despair and defection that greatly troubled Joseph. If the leaders in Zion were reacting in this way, then what about the attitudes developing among the lay members? Unhesitatingly determined to head off even the most minute, small-scale rebellion among the brethren, the Prophet wrote a blunt letter to Phelps, telling him to change his ways: *"Our hearts are greatly sorrowful,"* he wrote: *"at the spirit which is conveyed both in your letter and that of Brother Gilbert's, the very spirit which is wasting the strength of Zion like a plague; and if it is not detected and driven from you, it will prepare Zion for the threatened judgments of God . . . Brother, suffer us to speak plainly, for God has respect to the feelings of His Saints, and He will not suffer them to be enticed with freedom from punishment. Also tell Brother Gilbert that God hates belittling and low disparaging remarks; but He rejoices in an honest heart, and who knows better who is guilty than He does. We send him this warning voice, and let him fear greatly for himself, lest a worse thing overtake him."*

As a follow-up, the Prophet added this word of warning: *"It is vain to try to hide a bad spirit from the eyes of them who are spiritual, for it will show itself in speaking and in writing, as well as in all our other conduct. It is also needless to make great pretensions when the heart is not right; the Lord will expose it to the view of His faithful Saints."*

As if it were not enough to bring Brother Phelps to a recognition of his failings, the Prophet concluded with this criticism: *"We wish you to render the* Star [The Evening and Morning Star] *newspaper, as interesting as possible, by setting forth the rise, progress, and faith of the Church, as well as the doctrine; for if you do not render it more interesting than at present, it will fall, and the Church will suffer a great loss thereby"* (*History of the Church,* 1: 317).

In order to add strength to this stinging

rebuke, the Prophet caused to have written on the same day, a letter to "the Bishop, his Council and the Inhabitants of Zion" representing the decision of a conference of twelve High Priests held in Kirtland, which reemphasized and elaborated on what the letter to Brother Phelps had said: *"Brother Gilbert's letter of December 10th, has been received and read attentively, and the low, dark, and blind insinuations, which were in it, were not received by us as from the fountain of light, though his claims and pretensions to holiness were great . . . We are aware that Brother Gilbert is doing much, and has a multitude of business on hand; but let him eliminate his practices of the past, and do his business in the spirit of the Lord, and then the Lord will bless him, otherwise the frown of the Lord will remain upon him."* The letter continued: *"Brother Phelps' letter of December 15th, is also received and carefully read, and it betrays a lightness of spirit that ill becomes a man placed in the important and responsible station that he was placed in"* (*History of the Church,* 1: 319).

The last paragraph of this same letter noted in passing that the *"School of the Prophets will begin, if it's the Lord's will, sometime in January 1833."* This signaled a commitment and undertaking that hardly had a parallel in modern religious history. As the name suggests, the school represented a unique and deliberate effort on the part of its members to cultivate and develop their spiritual powers. This was done through study and a practical application of the principles of spirituality. This training and preparation, commenced by the Prophet, has continued among the leadership of the Church to this present day, although the format of the meetings has changed over the years, and the name of the school has not always been used.

To expand on the foregoing, it is important to recognize the importance of knowledge in the Church. The desire of Joseph Smith for knowledge concerning the problems confronting the Church during this period, sent him, time and time again, to his knees in prayer for divine help; this was consequently the greatest period for revelation in Church history. The Prophet's fervor and eagerness to learn spread like wildfire through the Church.

Chapter 7

1833-1834

The Formation of a School of the Prophets in Kirtland

Word of Wisdom—a Health Code Revealed

Saints Ousted from Jackson County

Zion's Camp Organized to Help the Missouri Saints

Zion's Camp Returns

In December, 1832, Joseph organized at Kirtland, the "School of the Prophets." The upper story of Newel K. Whitney's store was first used for this purpose. Although the objective of the school was to prepare the membership of the Church to carry the message of the Restored Gospel to all the world, the subjects taught and discussed were as broad as human interests.

In a revelation received by the Prophet Joseph Smith, December 27, 1832, and addressed to the brethren assembled to attend the School of the Prophets, which actually began in late January, 1833, it is so stated:

"And I give unto you a commandment, that ye shall teach one another the doctrine of the kingdom; Teach ye diligently and my grace shall attend you, that you may be instructed more perfectly in theory, in principle, in doctrine, in the law of the gospel, in all things that pertain unto the kingdom of God, that are expedient for you to understand; Of things both in heaven and in the earth; things which have been, things which are, things which must shortly come to pass; things which are at home, things which are abroad; the wars and the perplexities [dilemmas] *of the nations, and the judgments which are on the land; and a knowledge also of countries, and of kingdoms—"* (Doctrine & Covenants 88: 77-79). As we have quoted in Chapter six—in Section eighty-eight it reads: *"yea, seek ye out of the best books, words of wisdom; seek learning even by study, and also by faith"* (Ibid., Sec. 88: 118). This revelation has become the charter for learning given by God to the Church. It is a commandment to learn, which is further strengthened by the words of the rev-

elation: *"Cease to be idle; cease to be unclean; cease to find fault one with another; cease to sleep longer than is needful; retire to thy bed early, that ye may not be weary; arise early, that your bodies and minds may be invigorated"* (Ibid., Sec. 88: 124).

"The School of the Prophets" was the first organized school for adult education in America. Its sessions were held chiefly in the evenings and were attended by all the male leaders of the Church in and around Kirtland. A School for Elders had been conducted in Missouri, but would hardly be recognized under the formal name "school."

Among the many fine and choice expressions of Joseph Smith upon the subject of learning, first expressed to the School of the Prophets, are the following:

"You cannot be saved in ignorance."
"A man can be saved no faster than he gains knowledge."
"The Glory of God is Intelligence."

In these pointed sentences, the Prophet epitomizes—summarizes concisely—the law of the Church on the importance of learning. The influence of this law has done much to shape the educational policies of the Church for well over a century and a half.

Those participating in the School of the Prophets were required to fully keep the commandments of God. The members of the school were received into fellowship only after participating in prayer, the Sacrament, and the ordinance of the washing of feet. The school was to be *"a sanctuary, a tabernacle of the Holy Spirit"* for their edification (Doctrine & Covenants 88: 137-141). These meetings provided the setting for many remarkable spiritual experiences and in-depth discussions of Gospel principles.

During the winter of 1833, the School of the Prophets frequently held their meetings in the upstairs room above the Whitney store. **As was the custom of the time, many of the brethren would light up their pipes, smoke, and chew tobacco, then spit it on the floor.** As Brigham Young recalled: Joseph Smith became very concerned at having to instruct the school, having to discuss the affairs of the Church and important spiritual matters "in a cloud of tobacco smoke," and Emma complaining at having to clean up the smelly room after the brethren had left.

THE WORD OF WISDOM

In his early years of leading the Church, **Joseph read in several national newspapers that smoking and alcohol were bad for the health of the individual.** He had never taken the matter to the Lord before, but he needed to know the Lord's will in this matter. Not wanting to create any hassle amongst the brethren, he decided to take the matter directly to the Lord.

In response to his prayer on February 27, 1833, the Lord gave the Prophet Joseph Smith the revelation known as the **Word of Wisdom.** It is called Section eighty-nine in the Doctrine and Covenants. In this revelation, the Lord forbade the use of tobacco among His people and told Joseph that it was not good for man. There was a proper use for tobacco, he explained, but that use was for bruises and sick cattle.

In this same revelation, the Lord also forbade His people to use alcoholic drinks. Alcohol was for the washing of the body, and not for drinking. The Lord also explained that hot drinks were bad, and should not be used. The brethren of that day had been using hot drinks—tea and coffee.

Proper diet and nutrition was a concern during the early years of the Church. A nearby Shaker colony adhered to an unusually stringent dietary code forbidding the eating of meat. In March 1831, the Lord told Joseph that this Shaker doctrine was not ordained of God because *"the beasts of the field and the fowls of the air, and that which cometh of the earth, is ordained for the use of man for food and for raiment"* (Doctrine & Covenants 49: 19).

The Lord explained in this revelation, that grain is the *"staff of life,"* and that both men and animals should use it as an important part of their diet. But He said: *"wheat for man, corn for the ox, oats for the horse, and rye for the fowls and for swine . . . Barley,* He said, *"for all useful animals."* He also taught that meat is for the food of man, but that it is to be eaten sparingly, and only in times of cold weather and famine.

The Word of Wisdom was intended for all members of the Church, even for the weakest of all Saints. The Lord gave a great promise to all who would observe it, for He said: *" all saints who remember to keep and do these sayings, walking in obedience to the commandments, shall receive health in their navel, and marrow in their bones; And shall find wisdom and great treasures of knowledge, even hidden treasures; And shall run and not be weary, and shall walk and not faint. And I, the Lord, give unto them a promise, that the destroying angel shall pass by them, as the children of Israel, and not slay them"* (Doctrine & Covenants 89: 18-20).

The Word of Wisdom constitutes an all-inclusive code of health, revealing another meaningful step in expanding the influence of the Church into every phase of the lives of its members. When the Word of Wisdom was first revealed, it was not a commandment. Nevertheless, since the mid-1850s, it has become a commandment. Its object was to help produce a community of near-perfect "Celestial" beings, since the health of the body has a direct, if not a controlling, effect upon the health and vitality of the spirit.

What began as a sound code of health, not given by way of "commandment" or "compulsion," later took on a new and different role. In the United States where alcohol and tobacco are used extensively, the abstainer—non-user—was marked as being different or peculiar, especially when it was learned that his abstinence—non-use—was based upon a revelation from God. Therefore, the Word of Wisdom easily identifies members of the Church and sets them apart from the rest of the world. Within the Church, it also became a means of recognizing those who were wholeheartedly committed to its principles. Subsequently, it produced a powerful adherent force among the Latter-day Saints not unlike that produced among the Orthodox Jews as a result of their stricter, more comprehensive dietary laws. More to the point, however, it helped to produce in time, a society of people noted for long lives, general good health, confident optimism, and the ability to endure hardship and persecution.

There were two significant events that occurred in the life of the Prophet during the first half of 1833 that were to have a vital, lasting effect on the Church. The first was the receipt of the revelation known as the Word of Wisdom; the second was the organization of the highest governing body of the Church, the First Presidency.

FORMING THE FIRST PRESIDENCY

The roles of the President of the Church, and later the First Presidency, were defined in the early Kirtland years. At the meeting where the Church was organized, Joseph Smith was called by revelation *"a seer, a translator, a prophet, and apostle of Jesus Christ, and an elder of the church"* (Doctrine & Covenants 21: 1), and the Lord specified once more that he was the only one authorized to receive revelations for the whole Church (see Doctrine & Covenants 28: 1-6). At the June third to the sixth, 1831 conference, several brothers were ordained to the office of High Priest for the first time. Subsequently, on January 25, 1832, at a conference in Amherst, Ohio, Joseph was ordained as "President of the High Priesthood" (*History of the Church,* 1: 267).

For nearly two years, Joseph presided over the Church without counselors. Early in March, 1832, he was authorized to appoint counselors for the first time. On March eighth, Joseph selected Jesse Gause and Sidney Rigdon from among the recently ordained High Priests. On March fifteenth, a revelation announced that this Presidency held the *"keys of the kingdom"* (Doctrine & Covenants 81: 2). Jesse Gause fell away from the Church in 1832, and so the First Presidency, the highest governing body of the Church were organized on March 18, 1833, and by revelation, Frederick G. Williams was called as the new counselor.

And then followed a general direction to the First Presidency and a description of the scope and purpose of their ministry: *"And now verily I say unto you, I give unto you a commandment that you continue in the ministry and presidency. And when you have finished the translation of the prophets, you shall from thenceforth preside over the affairs of the church and the school; And from time to time, as shall be manifested by the Comforter, receive revelations to unfold the mysteries of the kingdom; And set in order the churches, and study and learn, and become acquainted with the good books, and with languages, tongues, and people. And this shall be your business and mission in all your lives, to preside in council, and set in order, all the affairs of this church and kingdom"* (Doctrine & Covenants 90: 12-16).

The make-up of the First Presidency reveals clearly the down-to-earth, positive nature of Joseph's leadership and of the organization he headed. New concepts and changes were prescribed by the Lord meet the needs of the moment. Like a vibrant, living entity, the Church acquired new capacities and capabilities as it grew toward maturity. With the addition of two able men to help shoulder the ever-increasing burden of Church administration, Joseph was freed, to some degree, to devote himself to the higher aspects of the work: to regulate and set in order all the affairs of the Church, to counsel, and to broaden the measure of his understanding.

The formation of the First Presidency also brought to an earlier conclusion, an unfortunate situation that had begun some time before. Oliver Cowdery and David Whitmer, who were involved in the complex network of Missouri events, saw in this change a further decline in their position and influence. These early confidants and close friends of the Prophet, who had shared some of his most sacred, precious, and important experiences, now felt banished—not only by the great distance that separated Kirtland and Independence, but also by what they considered to be an organizational rift between them and their leader. As they enlarged on these and other imagined rebuffs, they became more and more out of harmony with the Prophet and other church leaders.

Had a conspiracy of some kind existed between the Prophet and these associates, as some critics would like to believe, a major scandal would likely have ensued. With their rejection from the now formalized governing body of the Church, these men, had they been conspirators, would have seen the fruits of the conspiracy, whether it be money, power, or notoriety, slipping away from them. In that event, it would have been logical for them to have exposed the Prophet and attempted to force the leadership of the Church from him, or to have deserted the Church and set up a rival organization. Neither of these alternatives happened. Instead, they continued their membership, for the time being at least, and nursed their hurt feelings at having been excluded.

THE RIGHTS AND PRIVILEGES OF THE CONSTITUTION

In 1833, the Lord also helped to shape the Latter-day-Saints' political perception, especially regarding the nature of the Constitution of the United States. Two principles were fundamental. **The Constitution was an inspired document, written *"by the hands of wise men . . . raised up unto this very purpose"*** (Doctrine & Covenants 101: 80). It also had global application. The Lord explained that constitutional law, which guarantees rights and freedoms, *"belongs to all mankind, and is justifiable before me"* (Doctrine & Covenants 98: 5). He reaffirmed that it was established to maintain the *"rights and protection of all flesh, according to just and holy principles; That every man may act in doctrine and principle . . . according to the moral agency which I have given unto him, that every man may be accountable for his own sins in the day of judgement"* (Doctrine & Covenants 101: 77-78). Joseph Smith best expressed the Saints' attitudes toward the Constitution when he said, it is *"a glorious standard; it is founded in the wisdom of God. It is a heavenly banner . . . It is like a great tree, under whose branches, men from every clime can be shielded from the burning rays of the sun"* (*History of the Church,* 3: 304).

Not long after the First Presidency was organized, the first apostate of any influence—appeared on the scene in the person of "Doctor" Philastus Hurlburt. He gained his title from being one who turned against the Restored Gospel and Church of Jesus Christ. This man, who later proved to be a vengeful, vindictive person to the Church, was not a medical doctor but being the seventh son in his father's family, and according to "the old folk-lore superstition that the seventh son would possess supernatural qualities that would make him a physician." He had a diversified career before joining the Mormons, having been previously excluded from the Methodist Church for immoralities. He was described by one of his contemporaries as being "a man of fine physique, very pompous, good looking, and ambitious, with some energy, though of poor education" (*History of the Church,* 1: 355).

He was ordained an Elder on March 18, 1833, the same day on which Sidney Rigdon and Frederick G. Williams were set apart as counselors in the First Presidency, and was excommunicated on June 3, 1833, for "unChristian conduct with the females sex," while on a mission to the East (*History of the Church,* 1: 354). After a rehearing on June twenty-first, he was forgiven and reinstated "because of the liberal confession which he made" (*History of the Church,* 1: 354). In any case just two days later, he was again cut off from the Church because of additional verified testimony brought against him.

Hurlburt, enraged by the acts of discipline imposed upon him by the Church, immediately decided to take revenge against those who had humiliated and offended him. He decided that the most effective way to get back at the Church was to deliver a crippling blow against its leader, Joseph Smith. And so Hurlburt began his insidious, underhanded campaign to gather information which he hoped would destroy the reputation of the Prophet, and to denounce and condemn his motives. What Hurlburt lacked in truthfulness, honesty, and integrity, he compensated for in diligence and single mindedness. He began interviewing former acquaintances of the Prophet and his family in various areas where they had lived. If he could not find those who had been personally acquainted with the Smiths, he was satisfied to find those who had heard about them, and concentrated strictly upon their enemies and those who would defame. There were about a 100 who signed so-called affidavits to support his notion that the Prophet was a fraud, imposter, pretender, deceiver. These affidavits, which all appear to have a common authorship, deal almost exclusively with hearsay, and are filled with unsound and speculative conclusions.

It was during his anxious hustling to seek out the critics of the Prophet that Hurlburt heard rumors that the Book of Mormon was a plagiarism (literary piracy) of what has since been known as the **Spaulding manuscript.** According to these rumors, the Prophet had come into the possession of an old manuscript, written by a man named Solomon Spaulding, which reportedly contained an account of the origin of the American Indians and the migration of their ancestors to the American continent many centuries ago. The rumors alleged that Joseph had altered the manuscript in minor details, had invented the story of the Angel Moroni, and had either conspired with the eleven witnesses or deceived them. Hurlburt eagerly embarked on a search for the Spaulding manuscript, even going to the expense of taking a trip to Massachusetts to question Spaulding's widow. He was directed by her to Eastern New York, where he eventually found the manuscript in the attic of an old farmhouse among some papers in 1844. One of the Prophet's most severe critics mentioned Hurlburt's grave disappointment in finding the Spaulding theory without foundation. "Now, to his bitter embarrassment, he found that the long chase had been in vain; for while the romance did concern the ancestors of the Indians, its resemblance to the Book of Mormon ended there. None of the names, found in one, could be identified in the other; the many battles which each described, showed not the slightest similarity with those of the other, and Spaulding's prose style totally differed from the style of the Mormon Bible."

Although the so-called Spaulding theory failed miserably, almost before it had taken root, it has nevertheless been presented again and again over the years by enemies or critics of the Prophet who anxiously grasp at any straw that offers to explain away Joseph's claim of divine influence in the translation of the Book of Mormon.

Mentioning again—the Hurlburt affidavits were later made available to Eber D. Howe, a local editor, who included them in his book *Mormonism Unveiled,* along with a packet of critical letters written by Ezra Booth

(Bruce R. McConkie, *Mormon Doctrine*, SLC, Bookcraft, 1966 p. 749). Most of the slanderous and derogatory books written since that time about the Church or Joseph Smith, have been based upon these affidavits and the other anti-Mormon materials gathered by Howe. Most authors and media people, whose object is to attack the Prophet or the Church, have accepted these materials at face value and have used them uncritically and as authoritative. It is both curious and strange that able and competent people, who in most other situations are objective and fair, would place credence in a man like Philastus Hurlburt, an admitted adulterer, who was excommunicated from two religious denominations for unchristian like conduct, in preference to thousands of moral and credible men and women who testify that Joseph Smith was a great Prophet whose moral and ethical standards rank among the highest of any known today . . . Crazy, isn't it?

The case of Philastus Hurlburt demonstrated a facet of the newly restored Church, that came into prominence, importance, and greatness at that time—namely, the use of priesthood sanctions, along with a good-size portion of love, to enforce discipline among its members. At that time, the Church had been in existence for approximately three years. The numerous converts being brought into the fold represented an almost unbelievable variety of beliefs and practices. **The Prophet and his associates were faced with the gigantic assignment of molding the membership into a society** that was homogenous, uniform, consistent, and uncomplicated in its acceptance and observance of fundamental principles. To those who had braved the ridicule and rejection of family and friends to join the unpopular religion, there was nothing more to be feared than to have their fellowship with the Church severed. Nevertheless, when the leaders of the Church found a person in violation of basic tenets or beliefs, who stubbornly refused to repent and follow the rules, they were not at all reluctant to cut that person off by means of excommunication or disfellowshipment.

* * *

It is vitally important to know, unlike that in other religious denominations, excommunication does not mean a permanent separation from The Church of Jesus Christ. When a person breaks minor rules, he might be disfellowshipped for a brief period of time, in order to "get their act together." Those who break major rules are excommunicated to give them the needed time to overcome their faults and weaknesses and get their lives in order. There is a rebuilding period—mostly in rebuilding their relationship with Jesus Christ. Members and leaders in the Church are to be there with their love and support, fellowshipping that person back into the Church. Discipline combined with love makes an effective team to help restore excommunicated members to peace and happiness once more.

* * *

The work of the Lord was progressing very nicely in the Kirtland, Ohio area during the winter months of 1832 and 1833. Many Latter-day Saints who had been newly converted by the missionaries, gathered to that place. The Prophet Joseph Smith continued to receive additional revelations from the Lord, and the people seemed happier, more relaxed and content.

It was made known to the Prophet that there were two important assignments that had to be carried out in Kirtland. First, a Stake of Zion must be organized, and second, and most important, a temple was to be built in that city.

And what is a stake? The stake we are referring to is not a piece of wood like a tent peg and it is not a piece of meat that you eat (like a steak). From the early days of the Church, "stake" was the name given to the Church organizational unit, (under the leadership of the First Presidency), that was to oversee, guide and direct the activities of the smaller congregational units called branches. In certain other religions, a stake would be called a diocese. As the Church continued to grow and progress in numbers, small branches expanded into the larger unit called ward congregations, still under the stake leadership. Nevertheless, at this period in the Church, there were only smaller congregations (branches) spread out over the Kirtland area, and they needed the guidance and direction of the First Presidency and especially the Prophet Joseph Smith. The First Stake of Zion was organized in Kirtland on February 17, 1834.

KIRTLAND TEMPLE CONSTRUCTION BEGINS

It was now the time for the building of the first temple to be located in Kirtland, Ohio. For about three years, the time and energies of the Kirtland Saints were devoted to the building of the First Temple of this dispensation. This endeavor began in December, 1832, when the Lord commanded them to: *"establish a house, even a house of prayer, a house of fasting, a house of faith, a house of learning, a house of glory, a house of order, a house of God"* (Doctrine & Covenants 88: 119). About five months later, the Lord chastised the Church for their delay and warned them to move forward with the building of the Temple (Doctrine & Covenants 95). The Saints then faithfully devoted themselves to the charge. The Prophet, on one occasion, asked a conference of High Priests how the temple should be built? Some favored building it of logs; others preferred a frame structure. *"'Shall we brethren,' said he, 'build a house for our God, of logs? No, I have a better plan than that. I have a plan of the house of the Lord, given by himself; and you will soon see by this, the difference between our calculations and his idea of things.'"* (Lucy Mack Smith, *History of Joseph Smith by His Mother,* SLC, Bookcraft, 1958, p. 230). Truman O. Angell, one of the construction supervisors, testified that the Lord's promise to show the Prophet the building's design was literally fulfilled. He said that when the First Presidency knelt in prayer, "the Building appeared within viewing distance." Later, while speaking in the completed temple, Frederick G. Williams said that the hall in which they met coincided in every detail with the vision given to them (*Autobiography of Truman O. Angell,* LDS Historical Dept., SLC).

The temple's exterior looked like a typical New England meetinghouse, but its interior was unique. The Lord had specified that the building should include two large rooms, one above the other, each measuring fifty-five by sixty-five feet. The lower hall was to be the chapel, for praying, preaching, and administering the Sacrament. The upper hall was for educational purposes (see Doctrine & Covenants 95: 8, 13-17). Construction on the temple began June 6, 1833. In response to the Lord's warning, a committee was directed to procure materials for the work. A stone quarry was located about two miles south of the building site, and a wagonload of stone was immediately quarried. Hyrum Smith and Reynolds Cahoon started digging a trench for the foundation. But the Saints were so destitute, an early member recalled: "that there was not a scraper and hardly a plow that could be obtained among the Saints." Nevertheless, "unity, harmony and charity abounded to strengthen" them to fulfill the commandment of God to build the temple (*History of the Church,* 1: 349). On July 23, 1833, the cornerstones were laid "after the order of the Holy Priesthood" (*History of the Church,* 1: 400).

Almost all able-bodied men who were not away on missions worked on the temple. Joseph Smith served as foreman in the quarry. On Saturdays, men brought teams and wagons and hauled enough quarried rock to the site to keep the masons busy during the coming week. Under Emma Smith's direction, the women "made stockings, pantaloons and jackets" for the temple workmen. Heber C. Kimball recalled: "Our wives were all the time knitting, spinning and sewing; . . . they were just as busy as any of us" (Heber C. Kimball, *Journal of Discourses,* 10: 165).

The work on the temple was not without difficulty. Mobs threatened to destroy the temple, and those who worked on it by day, guarded it at night. Night after night for weeks, Heber C. Kimball said: "we were not permitted to take off our clothes, and were obliged to lay with our fire locks in our arms" (*History of the Church,* 2: 2). With the Church in constant financial distress during this period, the Saints in the United States and Canada were invited to make contributions, and many did so at great personal sacrifice. Vienna Jacques was one of the first to donate, giving much of her material resources. John Tanner loaned money to pay for the temple site, and then sold his 2,200 acre farm in New York in order to give 3,000 dollars to buy supplies. He continued to give until he had given almost all he owned.

Zion's Camp, to be discussed shortly, interrupted the work during the summer of 1834, since few workmen were available and funds were diverted to aid the distressed Missouri Saints. When the brethren returned from Zion's Camp, work progressed more rapidly. That fall, Joseph Smith wrote: *"Great exertions were made to expedite the work of the Lord's house, and notwithstanding, it was commenced almost with nothing, as to means, yet the way opened as we proceeded, and the Saints rejoiced"* (*History of the Church,* 2: 167). The walls were about four feet high in the fall of 1834, but rose quickly during the winter months. By November 1835, the exterior plastering commenced; crushed glassware was mixed with the stucco to make the walls glisten. Under Brigham Young's direction, the interior was finished during February of 1836. The sisters put the finishing touches on the temple by making the curtains and carpets.

Those who dedicated their lives to the building of the temple were to be rewarded by the Lord with great spiritual and emotional experiences in the temple between January 21, 1836, and the day of dedication, March 27, 1836. This subject will be expanded upon when we reach that time in the events of the Church.

One of the most critical problems that arose out of the Independence, Missouri incident, was the purposeful destruction of the Church Press by local residents. The Prophet was keenly aware of the need for the Church to have a public voice, heightened by his witness of the almost miraculous results that had followed the publication of the Book of Mormon. Accordingly, and without hesitation, he began making arrangements to acquire another press. On September 11, 1833, a council was convened in Kirtland, that established the need for a new press which was to publish a periodical called *The Latter-day Saints Messenger and Advocate.* Shortly thereafter, representatives were sent East to purchase the press and other necessary equipment.

While recognizing that the Prophet had considerable ability as an administrator, his real talent was as a teacher and motivator. He was never more content than when he was describing and defining the principles of the Gospel and bearing personal witness of the reality and power of God.

In the fall of 1833, Joseph Smith, Sidney Rigdon, and Freeman Nickerson, who was a recent convert to the Church, went to Upper Canada at the urging of Brother Nickerson, who convinced the brethren that his sons who lived there would be receptive to the Gospel. The journey was historic. While it was not the first time that missionaries had been in Canada (brief excursions had been made in 1830, 1832 and 1833), Joseph's visit gave the work there considerable spark. The Prophet developed such a love for the Canadians that he visited them again in 1837, and saw to it that missionary work there continued throughout his life.

In Mount Pleasant, Joseph Smith and Sidney Rigdon baptized twelve people, including the sons of Elder Nickerson and their families, who became the nucleus of the branch there. Lydia Bailey was one of those in the Eleazer Freeman Nickerson household in Mount Pleasant who responded to the Gospel with all of her heart. She was raised in Massachusetts and New York, and at the age of sixteen, married Calvin Bailey. Because he drank, her life with him was most unhappy. After three years of marriage, he abandoned her, her daughter, and the child she was expecting. Her son died at birth, and less than a year later, her daughter also died. At age twenty, Lydia went to Canada with Nickersons to recover her emotional health. There she met Joseph Smith, and he told her: *"You shall yet be a savior to your father's house."* Lydia later moved to Kirtland, where she met and married Newel Knight, a widower. Many years later in Utah, Lydia did the temple ordinance work for 700 of her kindred dead in the St. George Temple, thereby fulfilling the Prophet Joseph's prophecy.

The Upper Canadian Mission was one of the fourteen missions undertaken by Joseph Smith during the Kirtland era. He left Ohio at least once each year between 1831 and 1838, to labor as a full-time missionary, while still serving as the President of the Church and Prophet of God.

The calling of Patriarch to the Church eliminated one of Joseph Smith's responsibilities. Frequently, individuals wanted him personally to ask the Lord for a revelation for them, but as the Church grew, this became impractical if not impossible. On December 18, 1833, while giving blessings to his family, **the Prophet was inspired to call and ordain his father as the First Patriarch to the Church**. From that time until his death in 1840, Joseph Smith Sr. traveled among the many branches, holding special blessing meetings where he gave many faithful Saints their patriarchal blessings. In addition to providing revelation to individuals, the patriarchal blessings also identified the person's lineage in the house of Israel.

A GROWING MISSIONARY PROGRAM

Kirtland, as the headquarters of the Church, was also the center, hub, and focal point of missionary work during the 1830s period. It was near the main routes of transportation and contained the largest concentration of Church membership. Kirtland was the point of departure for missions to Canada, the Northeast, the Mid-Atlantic States, the Midwest, and the South. The State of Ohio itself had an overwhelming number of missionaries who crossed the state on their way to or from other fields of labor. Frequently, those unable to go on longer missions or those home during the winter months visited local communities.

Generally, missionaries proselyted among their relatives or in the communities they had migrated from. Missions ranged in length from a few days to a year or more, although most were fairly short. Normally, there was a rhythmic pattern as missionaries went out for a few weeks or months to preach, returned to Kirtland for rest and recuperation, and then went out again on another mission. Often, as was the case with Orson Pratt, Orson Hyde, Erastus Snow, Brigham Young, and others, this pattern was repeated many times during the first decade of their lives in the Church.

Before the organization of the Quorum of the Twelve and the First Quorum of the Seventy in 1835, the direction of missionary work rested with the local Priesthood quorums, the High Council, or the Presidency of the Church. Some effort was made to improve the training of the missionaries. The School of the Prophets and the School of Elders played a key role in this training. In the School of Elders, Joseph Smith and Sidney Rigdon presented lectures on faith, and the missionaries were encouraged to memorize them so they could teach the precepts of the Gospel logically and systematically. A revelation commanded the brethren to study geography, geology, history, prophecy, culture, war, and language—all: *"That ye may be prepared in all things, when I shall send you again, to magnify the calling whereunto I have called you, and the mission with which I have commissioned you"* (Doctrine & Covenants 88: 80).

Although going from door to door was a common practice, missionaries often found their best success in small groups in the homes of the receptive. Many missionaries preferred public meetings. They used any available space where they could preach, such as a barn, school, church, home, or courthouse. They spoke about prophecy, the Book of Mormon, the signs of the times, spiritual gifts, the Apostasy, and the Restoration, but the missionaries were cautioned to avoid the mysteries of the Gospel in their teaching. Ordinarily, an Elder preached and then gave "liberty" to anyone who desired to respond to his message. This technique put the local clergy on the spot because silence on their part would be interpreted as consent or defeat. Therefore, it frequently generated discussions or debates on the Gospel. At the close of the meetings, the missionary companion encouraged the congregation to accept baptism.

Missionaries often encountered rejection, hostility, or indifference. Their disappointment was particularly painful when a disbeliever was a member of the missionary's family. In 1832, Orson Hyde visited his relatives in New York and New Hampshire to teach them the Gospel. His brother, Asahel, remained unmoved by the Gospel message, and Orson recorded that they separated "with hearts full of grief." Three months later, he tried with his sister and her husband, but they too rejected his message. He wrote: "We took our things and left them, and tears for all eyes freely ran . . . but it was like piercing my heart;

and all I can say is 'The Will of the Lord Be Done.'"

The clergy were particularly vehement and sometimes unrestrained and candid in their opposition to the missionaries. In 1835, a Baptist deacon passed a pop-gun and ammunition through a window to a friend while listening to a missionary sermon by Elder George A. Smith. Elder Smith wrote that the man shot "wads of tow [short broken fiber from flax that is used for yarn] at me all the time I was preaching. He was an excellent shot with the pop-gun, and most of the wads hit me in the face. I caught several of them in my hands. Many of the audience were tickled, but some of them paid good attention. I finished my discourse without noticing the insult."

Despite the harassment, these early missionaries, inspired by faith and their testimonies, were remarkably successful. They remained unwavering in spite of constant opposition, heckling, and criticism, and the work prospered and set a pattern of continuous and fast-paced growth. Had not the Lord declared: *"the field was white already to harvest?"* (Doctrine & Covenants 4: 4).

Letters from outlying branches, published in Church periodicals, *Evening and Morning Star* and *The Latter-day Saints Messenger and Advocate,* frequently pleaded for more missionaries. These publications also communicated instructions, decisions of authorities, information about developments throughout the Church, and explanations of Gospel doctrines.

Most conferences and meetings, both in Kirtland and in the outlying branches, were devoted to missionary matters. The charge to take the Restored Gospel to the whole earth, received great recognition, impact, and acceptance in the Kirtland headquarters of the Church. The Church of Jesus Christ of Latter-day Saints fully believed itself to be the missionary arm of the Lord, which made **every member of the Church a missionary.**

As the Church was growing and prospering in Ohio, serious problems were rapidly developing in Zion between the Saints and their Jackson County, Missouri neighbors.

The Prophet Joseph Smith requested of the Lord: *"When will Zion be built up in her glory, and where will thy temple stand?"* The Lord's reply, given on July 20, 1831, was simple and direct: *"this land, which is the land of Missouri . . . is the land which I have appointed and consecrated for the gathering of the saints . . . Behold, the place which is now called Independence is the center place; and a spot for the temple is lying westward, upon a lot which is not far from the courthouse"* (Doctrine & Covenants 57: 1, 3). Joseph Smith and the gathering Saints were elated that at last the exact location of the promised City of Zion was revealed to them. Little did they know that within two years the Saints would be driven from their homes in Western Missouri. Although the Church members were unaware of the persecutions that were before them, the Lord had told them that the glory of Zion would come only *"after much tribulation"* (Doctrine & Covenants 58: 4).

The year of 1833 was one of *many* trials and tribulations for the Saints in Jackson County, Missouri. It seemed as though there was nothing the Saints could do to make their neighbors happy. Irreconcilable differences, hostility, and conflicts developed over several issues, causing some of the local residents to take decisive and crucial action against the members of the Church. The conflict began during the summer of 1833, and by November, organized mobs, without mercy, drove the Saints from their homes and across the Missouri River under the worst possible conditions.

By the end of 1832, there were over 800 Saints gathered into five branches in Jackson County. New members were arriving almost every week to establish their homes. Seven High Priests were appointed by the Prophet to preside over the affairs of the rapidly expanding Church in Zion. These brethren called other Elders to preside over individual branches.

Some members tried to avoid and deceive the Church leaders in Missouri by ignoring their authority to preside, therefore making it troublesome to set some of the branches in order. Others "sought to obtain their inheritances in some other way than according to the laws of consecration and stewardship" (B.H. Roberts, *Missouri Persecutions,* SLC, p. 61). Elder Phelps wrote a letter to Joseph Smith in Kirtland about the predicament, and received a quick response containing revealed instructions. The Lord warned those who had or would evade the revealed laws, that they were not worthy to *"have their names enrolled with the people of God . . . written in the book of the law of God"* (Doctrine & Covenants 85: 3, 5).

Other difficulties occurred in Zion at the same time. Petty jealousies, envy, greed, lightmindedness, unbelief, and general neglect in keeping the commandments of God, came to the attention of the Prophet. Some people in Zion even charged Joseph Smith with "seeking after monarchial power and authority," and said that he was purposely putting off settling in Zion (*History of the Church,* 1: 318-19).

The Prophet wrote back in the Spirit of Peace, and sent a copy of the *"Olive Leaf"* in Doctrine and Covenants eighty-eight: *"Though our brethren in Zion indulge in feelings toward us, which are not according to the requirements of the new covenant, yet, we have the satisfaction of knowing that the Lord approves of us, and has accepted us, and established his name in Kirtland for the salvation, of the nations; . . . if Zion will not purify herself . . . He will seek another people . . . Repent, repent, is the voice of God to Zion"* (*History of the Church,* 1: 316).

At the same time, a council in Kirtland appointed Hyrum Smith and Orson Hyde to write a letter of reproof to the Church in Missouri. The letter was a stern warning to "repent, repent, or Zion must suffer, for the scourge and judgement must come upon her." It went on to plead with the Saints to read and obey the scriptures and humble themselves before God. "They have not come up to Zion to sit down in idleness, neglecting the things of God, but they are to be diligent and faithful in obeying the new covenant" (*History of the Church,* 1: 320).

Following the receipt of the *Olive Leaf* revelation—the Lord's message of peace—a council of High Priests met on February 26, 1833, and called for a special day of prayer, confession, and repentance in each of the branches. Elders Cowdery, Corrill, and Phelps also wrote to the authorities in Kirtland in behalf of the Saints in Zion, expressing their desire to keep the commandments in the future (*History of the Church,* 1: 327). The Lord was pleased with this new spirit and revealed to the Prophet that *"the angels rejoice"* over the Saints in Missouri (Doctrine & Covenants 90: 34).

The migration of new Saints to Missouri in the spring and early summer of 1833 exceeded that of the previous season. Parley P. Pratt remembered that as new arrivals purchase land, built homes, and cultivated the land, "peace and plenty had crowned their labors, and the wilderness became a fruitful field, and the solitary place began to bud and blossom as a rose." The Saints assembled each Sunday with the other members of their branches to worship. Peace and harmony prevailed among them during these early days in June. Parley said: "there has seldom, if ever, been a happier people upon the earth than the Latter-day Saints now were" (Pratt, *Autobiography of Parley P. Pratt,* SLC, Deseret Book, 1985, p. 75).

During the summer, a school for the Elders was organized in Zion that was modeled after the School of the Prophets in Kirtland. Parley P. Pratt was called to preside and to teach the class of about sixty Elders, who met in shady groves. Elder Pratt fondly remembered: "Here is where great blessings were poured out and many great and marvelous things were manifested and taught. The Lord gave me great wisdom, and enabled me to teach and edify the Elders." Meanwhile, W. W. Phelps continued to prepare the Book of Commandments for publication, and he also edited the *Evening and Morning Star,* which appeared monthly.

Late in June 1833, the Prophet sent a plat (plan) for the building up of the City of Zion and its accompanying temple to the Saints in Missouri. The city was designed for 15,000 to 20,000 people, and was to be a one-mile square development with ten-acre blocks divided into half-acre lots, one house per lot. A complex of twenty-four temples were to be built and used as houses of worship. At that time, the Prophet had not been made aware by revelation from the Lord that temples were subsequently to be used for more sacred ordinances for the living as well as for the dead. The schools were to be located on two central city blocks. Lands on the north and south of the city were to be used for barns, stables, and farms. The farmer, as well as the merchant and mechanic, was to live in the city to enjoy all the social, cultural, and educational advantages to be offered (*History of the Church,* 1: 357-58). Unfortunately, mob interference prevented the fulfillment of this plan, although many of its basic ideas were later used by the Latter-day Saints in Northern Missouri, Nauvoo, Illinois, and in hundreds of other settlements in the West. It was pretty obvious that the local residents were very unhappy when they heard of the plans of the Prophet Joseph, not realizing that the building up of Zion could have been good for all who lived in that community.

The happy and favorable circumstances of the Saints in Jackson County ended suddenly in July of 1833. The original inhabitants of the area became increasingly suspicious as the number of Church members in Jackson County grew rapidly. Many people feared that they would soon be outnumbered by the new religiously-motivated pioneers from the East. The old settlers came from a completely different background than the incoming Latter-day Saints, and it was natural that cultural, political, religious, and economic differences would arise.

The Jackson County's residents were a rough-and-ready group who had come from the mountainous regions of several Southern States to the western edge of the United States to find freedom from social limitations and restrictions. Most of the old settlers were uneducated and lacked the cultural taste that was more common in New England and the East. Many of them indulged in profanity, (lots of swearing and cursing), Sabbath-breaking, horse-racing, cock-fights, idleness, drunkenness, gambling, and violence were common. Following his first visit to Jackson County, the Prophet Joseph Smith reflected on: *"how natural it was to observe the degradation, leanness of intellect, ferocity, and jealousy of a people that were nearly a century behind the times, and to feel for those who roamed about without the benefit of civilization, refinement, or religion"* (*History of the Church,* 1: 189).

The old settlers observed the growing body of Saints as a political threat, even though members of the Church did not run for office or vote as a bloc during their short stay in Jackson County. By July 1833, the Mormon population in the county numbered almost 1,200 with more arriving each month. Some members foolishly boasted that thousands more were coming to live in the county. "By simple arithmetic, a few hundred additional Mormons could have captured political control from those who had previously controlled and established the city and county."

More disturbing to the old settlers than almost anything else was the belief of the Latter-day Saints that Missouri was their promised land. This concept, in addition to the confident, often-described expectation that the Saints would one day possess the land of Jackson County to the exclusion of all others, created a sense of anxiety and concern for the old settlers. When these ideas were first mentioned, the Missourians either ignored them or passed them off as the fantasies of a deluded but harmless people. But when the ranks of Mormons began to increase, and when the native settlers discovered that the Saints were intelligent and industrious, were in dead earnest about their religion, and were directed by inspired and courageous leaders, they became fearful and began to seek ways to combat these infringements on their security. There was no way around it; the local citizens would continue to be apprehensive of a religious devotion and zeal that predicted that all "gentiles" (non-Mormons) would be cut off when the millennial kingdom was established in Jackson County.

Throughout Mormon history, the clergy of other churches played an important role in the persecutions of the Latter-day Saints. This is not hearsay or conversation, but an undeniable fact. At this point in time, Protestant ministers intensely resented the Mormon intrusion into the county. Latter-day Saints were labeled fanatics and villains, and were denounced as gullible and ignorant because they believed in the frequently-experienced miracles, prophecy, healings, and other spiritual experiences. Jealousy and fear of losing some of their flocks added to the antagonism of the ministers. For example, the Reverend Finis Ewing of the Cumberland Presbyterian Church asserted: "The 'Mormons' are the common enemies of mankind and ought to be destroyed.'" A reverend of the Missionary Society (sent to Christianize the American Indians) went "from house to house, seeking to destroy the Church by spreading slanderous falsehoods, to incite the people to acts of violence against the Saints" (Roberts, *Missouri Persecutions,* pp. 73-74).

Both the Santa Fe and Oregon trails began in Independence, Missouri. Here fur traders, pioneers, and adventurers of all types were outfitted for the trek West. When Mormon merchants and tradesmen successfully took over a portion of the profitable Santa Fe Trail trade previously controlled by the Missourians, some of the old settlers feared that the Church members were determined to take over their lands and businesses as well. The Saints "did not purchase goods from the local merchants, as they had no money, but traded among themselves at the Church storehouse." Some of the old settlers attempted to sell their property to the Mormons and then they began moving away, which meant fewer and fewer customers in the stores. The remaining settlers feared financial ruin.

To further complicate matters, in the spring of 1833, the Missouri River flooded, destroyed the landing at Independence, and shifted the channel of the river away from the community. A new town with a better landing, Westport, was established farther upstream, and the business in Independence declined. Entrepreneurs in Independence blamed the Mormons for this situation. Anticipating what the future might bring, some of the old settlers again offered to sell out to the Saints. Several members of the Church wanted to buy the farms and possessions, but didn't have enough capital to do so. This irritated the Missourians no end, and soon they were spreading additional tales of how poverty-stricken the Mormons were.

Many of the Missouri frontiersmen feared and hated the Indians. Their hostility and opposition increased in the 1830s as the government began to resettle Eastern tribes on lands just west of Independence. After the 1832 Black Hawk War, citizens of Western Missouri petitioned Congress to establish a line of military posts for their protection. The first Mormon missionaries came into this tense and combative environment declaring the word of God and the prophetic destiny of the native Americans. The old settlers were afraid that the Saints would use the Indians to help them conquer the area for their New Jerusalem. In addition, matters became further complicated by the ongoing pressures of the Protestant ministers who were jealous of the Latter-day Saints proselyting efforts among the Indians.

Especially prominent in his efforts to arouse feelings of hatred against the Saints in Independence was a Reverend Pixley. Of him, Newel Knight said: "he was not content in just slandering and down grading the Saints to the people of Jackson County, but also wrote to several Eastern newspapers, telling horrible lies about them, with the obvious intention of arousing a spirit of hatred." His comments were bitter, his speeches inflammatory; and he appeared to have an influence among the people to carry them with him in his vicious designs. Nor did he confine his actions to the white settlers, but tried to stir up the Indians against us, and use every means in his power to accomplish his purposes. The public mind became so excited against the Mormons that on July twentieth, a meeting was called and largely attended by not only the negative masses of the county, but also the men holding official positions (*History of the Church,* 1: 372).

The Reverend Pixley wrote a pamphlet entitled: "Beware of False Prophets." The lead article in the July 1833 issue of the Church the *Evening and Morning Star* newspaper presented the same title, and attempted to clarify some of the distortions and untruths in the minister's pamphlet, but it was considered by non-Mormons to be an attack on *their* churches.

A second article, appearing in that July issue of the *Star*, produced an even more violent reaction among the Gentile community and **the conflict and struggle between the Saints and the old settlers came to a head over the slavery issue**. The title: "Free People of Color" was intended to warn the Saints for their own safety against encouraging free blacks to migrate to Missouri. Nevertheless, in the prejudiced minds of enemies of the Church, it was interpreted to have an opposite meaning.

Slaveholders in the area were especially disturbed by reports that the Mormons were openly encouraging free blacks to enter the state in violation of Missouri Law. Control of their slaves was difficult even under the most favorable circumstances, and they could envision endless trouble in the morale of their slaves if free blacks were admitted into the community. Once the false rumors were circulated that the Mormons were attacking the very foundation of their slave economy, the idea spread like wildfire among the old settlers.

Missouri had come into the Union as a slave state under the famous Compromise of 1820. Slaveholding was limited, but the old settlers valued their right to hold slaves and they despised abolitionism. Some of the Saints brought abolitionist sentiments from the North and East, and the possibility of a black rebellion was a fear throughout the South at this time. In 1831, Nat Turner's slave uprising in Virginia had resulted in the death of over seventy whites and 100 slaves. An irrational and unsound fear of revolts swept over the slave states. Taking everything into consideration, Missourians were highly aroused early in 1832 by rumors that the Saints were trying to persuade slaves to disobey their masters or run away.

During the summer of 1833, the many differences between the Saints and the old settlers combined to set the stage for violence. A mob atmosphere had been developing since April, 1833; in early July, hundreds of people, including prominent citizens, signed: **"The Manifesto of the Mob" sometimes referred to as "The Secret Constitution," denouncing the Mormons** and calling for a meeting on July twentieth. "The Manifesto of the Mob" accused the Mormons of tampering with slaves, encouraging rebellion, and inviting free Negroes and mulattoes to join the Church and immigrate to Missouri. It declared the intent of the signers to remove the Mormons "peaceably if we can, forcibly if we must" (*History of the Church,* 1: 374).

Additionally, **the Church and its members were accused of blasphemy because of their belief in modern revelation** as well as their teachings that Jackson County was the land of promise, and the place where the City of Zion, the New Jerusalem and the great temple of the Saints would be built.

On Saturday, July twentieth, 400 or 500 disgruntled citizens met at the Independence courthouse. They chose officers and selected a committee to draft a document, defining and summarizing their demands of the Mormons. The officers and committee members were some of the leading citizens of Jackson County: "In the main, they were the county officers—the County Judge, the Constables, Clerks of the Court and Justices of the Peace" (Roberts, *Missouri Persecutions,* p. 87). The Lieutenant Governor of Missouri, Lilburn W. Boggs, a resident and large landholder in the county, also attended the meeting and encouraged the anti-Mormon activity.

The "Secret Constitution" was read at the meeting, and the committee drafted the bitter ultimatum that no Latter-day Saints would be allowed to move to or settle in Jackson County, and those that were already there must pledge to leave within a reasonable time. The Church newspaper was also to cease publication. A committee of twelve was appointed to present these demands to the Saints. The brethren, startled and upset by the request and realizing that they should not abandon Zion, requested three months to consider the proposal and to consult with Church leaders in Ohio. This was denied them. They then asked for at least ten days, but the committee allowed them only fifteen minutes, and returned to the meeting at the courthouse.

The men attending the meeting rapidly turned into a mob that decided to destroy the printing office and the press. They surrounded the printing office and residence of W. W. Phelps, threw the furniture into the street and garden, broke the press and hauled it away, scattered the type, and destroyed nearly all the printed work, including most of the unbound sheets of the **Book of Commandments**. They soon leveled the two-story printing office. The mob decided to destroy the goods of the Gilbert and Whitney Store next. Only when Sidney Gilbert promised that he would pack up the goods in three days were they persuaded not to take physical action. With loud profanities, the mob then searched for the leading Elders of the Restored Church of Jesus Christ. Men, women, and children ran in all directions to avoid the mob. The mob took Bishop Edward Partridge from his home bodily, and dragged him to the public square. Charles Allen, a twenty-seven-year-old convert from Pennsylvania, was also taken by force to the public square. The mob demanded that they renounce the Book of Mormon or leave the county. The two men refused to do either, so the mob prepared the tar and feathers. Bishop Partridge calmly declared that he was willing to suffer for the sake of Christ as the Saints had done in former ages. The two bore the cruel indignity of tarring and feathering with so much resignation, submission, and meekness, that the crowd, which had been shouting vile oaths and obscenities, dispersed in silence (Roberts, *Missouri Persecutions,* pp. 84-86).

A small number of copies of the Book of Commandments, which contained revelations received by the Prophet Joseph Smith, were providentially preserved. Two sisters, Mary Elizabeth and Caroline Rollins, ages fourteen and twelve, watched the mob throw the large, unbound sheets out onto the ground outside the printing office. Determined to save some of the copies, the girls grabbed as many sheets as they could carry in their arms and ran behind the building. The mobbers shouted at them to stop, but the girls escaped through a gap in a wooden fence and ran into a cornfield. For a long time, they heard the men searching for them as they lay quietly on the ground.

When the mobbers left, Mary and Caroline found Sister Phelps and her family hidden in an old stable. Sister Phelps took charge of the sheets, and later on, the few preserved copies were bound. Each of the girls subsequently received a copy of the Book of Commandments, which they prized for the rest of their lives.

Twenty-year-old John Taylor (not the future President of the Church), risked his life by reaching between the logs of the print shop to retrieve a few sheets, and he also miraculously escaped from the mob as they tried to stone him ("Tales of Mobs," Gerry Avant, *Church News,* Dec. 30, 1984, p. 6).

The mob appeared again on July twenty-third with rifles, pistols, whips, and clubs. They searched for the Church leaders, cursing and profaning as they went. They set fire to haystacks and grain fields, and destroyed several homes, barns, and businesses. The mob eventually confronted six leaders of the Church who, seeing the property and lives of the Saints in jeopardy, offered their lives as a ransom. Their names—Edward Partridge, Isaac Morley, John Corrill, John Whitmer, W. W. Phelps, and Sidney Gilbert—are held in honorable remembrance by the Church.

Rejecting this offer, **the mob leaders**

threatened that every man, woman, and child would be whipped unless they consented to leave the county—the leaders by January 1, 1834, and the members themselves by April first. John Corrill and Sidney Gilbert were allowed to remain as agents to sell the property of the Saints. Corrill wrote that the members of the Church up to this time, "had not so much as lifted a finger, even in their own defense, so tenacious and persevering were they for the precepts of the Gospel—turn the other cheek."

After the agreement was signed, Oliver Cowdery was sent to Ohio to confer with Church authorities on the plight of the Saints in Missouri. A council in Kirtland met on August twenty-first, and sent Elders Orson Hyde and John Gould to Jackson County as special messengers. They instructed the Saints not to dispose of their lands or property, nor to move from the county unless they had specifically signed the agreement to do so. This message did not arrive in Western Missouri until September twenty-eighth.

Meanwhile a few Church members attempted to settle in Van Buren County, but the citizens there also drew up an agreement to drive the Mormons out, so they returned again to their former homes. Throughout the summer, the mobs broke into the Mormon homes daily and continued their violence to the Jackson County inhabitants, even though they had agreed to refrain from harassing and persecuting the Saints.

In August, 1833, **the *Western Monitor*, a newspaper in Fayette, Missouri, ran a series of articles censuring the mob action in Jackson County** and suggesting that the Latter-day Saints seek redress from state authorities for the wrongs they had suffered. Regarding this matter, Church leaders prepared a written petition detailing their grievances and denying the false accusations of the old settlers of Jackson County: "Influenced by the precepts of our beloved Savior, when we have been smitten on the one cheek, we have turned the other also; . . . we have borne the above outrages without murmuring; but we cannot patiently bear them any longer; according to the laws of God and man, we have borne enough" (*History of the Church,* 1: 414-15).

In early October, W. W. Phelps and the Church representative from Ohio, Orson Hyde, went to Jefferson City, the state capitol, and presented the petition to Governor Daniel Dunklin. They asked him to raise troops to defend them in their rights, to give them permission to sue for damaged and lost property, and to bring the mob element to justice.

After a few days of consultation with the Attorney-General, the governor replied that he felt force would not be necessary to carry out the laws. He advised the Church representatives to seek redress and protection under the laws through petitioning the circuit judge and justices of the peace in Jackson County. If this effort failed, he promised to use other means to enforce the law (*History of the Church,* 1: 423-24).

His advice proved ineffective. Samuel D. Lucas, the County Judge for Jackson County and two of the Justices of the Peace in the county, were among those who were trying to drive the Mormons out. Nevertheless, following the Governor's instructions, Church leaders engaged the services of four prominent lawyers in Clay County. These lawyers became friends of the Saints and defended them against their oppressors throughout the rest of the decade in Missouri. Two of them, Alexander Doniphan and David Atchison, attained State and National prominence between 1845 and

1865.

In addition to seeking legal redress, Church leaders ended their policy of passive resistance, and counseled the members to arm themselves for the defense of their families and homes. A delegation was sent to Clay County to purchase powder and lead, and the Church officials announced on October 20, 1833, their intent to defend themselves against any physical attack.

When the old settlers saw that the Saints intended to defend themselves, they renewed their acts of violence and circulated rumors about the blasphemy of the Mormons' doctrines and their supposed intentions to take possession of Jackson County by force. Within a week, the mood of the county was at a fevered pitch. On the night of Thursday, October thirty-first, a mob of about fifty horsemen attacked the Whitmer Settlement on the Big Blue River, west of Independence. They unroofed thirteen houses and nearly whipped to death several men, including Hiram Page, who was one of the eight witnesses of the Book of Mormon. This plundering, pillaging, looting, and rape of the communities continued for the next two nights in Independence, in Blue township, in Kaw township, and again in the Whitmer Settlement. **Men were severely beaten, and women and children were raped and terrorized.** When Church leaders were unable to obtain a warrant against the raiders, the Elders posted guards at each of their settlements to defend themselves.

Certainly, not all of the citizens of Jackson County were against the Saints. Some of those who were friendly toward the members of the Church had no sympathy with the rioters or with the lawlessness of the mobs. Unfortunately, little was done by these sympathizers to prevent the violence inflicted upon the religious newcomers—they were afraid for their own skins, and their position in the community.

Monday, November fourth, became known as the "bloody day" of the hostility and conflict. Several Missourians captured a Mormon ferry on the Big Blue River, and soon thirty or forty armed men from each side confronted each other in the corn fields. The mob fired first, wounding Philo Dibble in the stomach, but he was miraculously healed through a Priesthood blessing by Newel Knight. Unfortunately, Andrew Barber was mortally wounded. The Mormons returned their fire, and killed two Missourians and a few horses. The same day, several Church leaders had been arrested in Independence and brought to trial. As their trial progressed in the courthouse, some unfounded news of the battle had reached the town, accusing the Mormons of entering the house of a citizen and shooting his son. This enraged the crowd, and they threatened to kill the prisoners. The prisoners, however, were quickly taken to the jail and locked up for their safety.

Throughout the night, citizens were collecting arms and ammunition in preparation for a general massacre of the Saints the next day. Rumors also had circulated that the Mormons were going to call upon the Indians to fight with them. Meanwhile, the jailed prisoners, hearing of these preparations, informed the sheriff that they intended to leave the county and would urge all other Church members to do the same.

At the urging and insistence of Lt. Governor Boggs, a unit of the state militia, under the command of the acknowledged anti-Mormon Colonel Thomas Pitcher, was called in to drive the Mormons out of the county. Meanwhile, Lyman Wight, hearing of the imprisonment of Church leaders, gathered about 200 armed brethren and marched toward the jail. About a mile outside of Independence, they learned that the militia had been called in. Boggs negotiated an agreement that both camps would give up their arms and that the Saints would leave the county within ten days. The Saints surrendered their weapons with the understanding that the weapons would be returned once the Saints had moved to Clay County. Unfortunately, the militia retained the surrendered arms, and the Saints never saw them again. As usual, the anti-Mormon Lt. Governor Boggs, never lived up to his commitment.

True to their pledge, as soon as they were released, the prisoners and other Latter-day Saints made plans for a quick departure across the Missouri River. A number of ravaging marauders rode through the countryside the next three days harassing the Mormon settlers, including a group of about 130 women and children who had been left alone while their men hunted for wagons. At least two women died while the Saints were making a quick exit from the county.

Both shores of the Missouri near the ferry were lined with refugees. Some families were fortunate enough to escape with their household goods, but many of them lost everything. Parley P. Pratt wrote: "When night again closed upon us, the cottonwood bottom had much the appearance of a camp meeting. Hundreds of people were seen in every direction, some in tents and some in the open air around their fires, while the rain descended in torrents. Husbands were inquiring for their wives, wives for their husbands; parents for children, and children for parents. The scene was indescribable, and I am sure, would have melted the hearts of any people on the earth, except our blind oppressors" (Pratt, *Autobiography Parley P. Pratt,* p. 82).

The mob in Jackson County continued tormenting and preying upon the few remaining members of the Church until all of them were driven out of the county. Lyman Wight reported: "I saw one hundred and ninety women and children driven thirty miles across the prairie, with three decrepit, aging old men, in their company, in the month of November, the ground thinly crusted with sleet; and I could easily follow on their trail by the *blood that flowed from their lacerated feet* on the stubble of the burnt prairie!" (*History of the Church,* 3: 439). Early in the spring of 1834, the Missourians learned of the approach of Mormons from Ohio, and burned the remainder of the houses belonging to the Saints in an attempt to discourage the return and resettlement of the exiled, ostracized Mormons.

Most of the exiled Saints found temporary quarters in Clay County, although a few did seek refuge in other nearby counties. The citizens of Liberty, the county seat of Clay County, charitably offered shelter, work, and provisions. The refugees moved into abandoned slave cabins, built crude huts, pitched tents, and lived on a meager subsistence until the arrival of spring. Some men found work splitting rails, building houses, and grubbing brush. Several of the women worked in the households of well-to-do farmers, while others taught school. In the spring, some were able to rent land and plant crops. Although most of the citizens of Clay County were friendly, they considered the settlement of the Saints in their midst as only temporary. Hostile elements in Jackson County named these sympathizers "Jack-Mormons," a term applied in the nineteenth century to friendly non-Mormons.

In the interim, Joseph Smith closely followed the events in Western Missouri

from his base in Kirtland. Having heard of the July persecutions, he wrote to the Church in Zion: *"Brethren, if I were with you, I should take an active part in your sufferings, and although nature shrinks, yet my spirit would not let me forsake you unto death, God helping me"* (Dean C. Jessee, *The Personal Writings of Joseph Smith,* SLC, 1984, p. 283). In October 1833, the Lord revealed to Joseph that: *"Zion shall be redeemed, although she is chastened for a little season . . . let your hearts be comforted; for all things shall work together for good to them that walk uprightly, and to the sanctification of the church"* (Doctrine & Covenants 100: 13,15).

Elders Hyde and Gould, emissaries from Kirtland to Missouri, returned to Ohio on November twenty-fifth with *"the melancholy intelligence of the mob in Jackson County persecuting the brethren"* (*History of the Church,* 1: 446). This deeply distressed the Prophet. He wrote: *"I cannot learn from any communication by the Spirit to me, that Zion has forfeited her claim to a celestial crown, notwithstanding the Lord has caused her to be thus afflicted . . . I know that Zion, in the due time of the Lord, will be redeemed; but how many will be the days of her purification, tribulation, and affliction, the Lord has kept hid from my eyes; and when I inquire concerning this subject, the voice of the Lord is: Be still, and know that I am God! All those who suffer for my name, shall reign with me, and he that layeth down his life for my sake shall find it again"* (*History of the Church,* 1: 453-54).

A few days later, the Lord explained that the Saints in Missouri suffered affliction *"in consequence of their transgressions; . . . there were jarrings, and contentions, and envyings, and strifes, and lustful and covetous desires among them; therefore by these things, they polluted their inheritances"* (Doctrine & Covenants 101: 2, 6).

The Saints in Missouri wondered whether they should establish permanent or temporary settlements in Clay County, since there was little hope of returning to their homes in Jackson County. At a conference held on January 1, 1834, they decided to send two Elders to Kirtland to counsel with the Prophet and arrange for relief for the Missouri Saints. Lyman Wight and Parley P. Pratt volunteered. Unfortunately, they lacked the means to make the trip. Parley wrote: "I was at this time, entirely destitute of proper clothing for the journey; and I had neither horse, saddle, bridle, money nor provisions to take with me; or to leave with my wife, who lay sick and helpless most of the time" (Pratt, *Autobiography Parley P. Pratt,* p. 87). These noble brethren were outfitted with the aid of other faithful members. They proceeded by horseback as rapidly as possible, but inclement weather delayed their arrival until the early spring.

While awaiting counsel and instruction from their Prophet, Church leaders in Missouri sought reparations from the State of Missouri. A court of inquiry was held in Liberty in December, and called for the arrest of Colonel Thomas Pitcher of the state militia. It soon became evident, nonetheless, that public opinion in Jackson County was so strongly against the Saints that criminal prosecution was virtually impossible. Church leaders decided to abandon the struggle and trial. Governor Dunklin ordered the arms of the Church members to be returned, but his order was defied.

The Saints continually reminded the Missouri state authorities of the persecution and destruction of their homes, lands, and crops. At the same time, they petitioned

Andrew Jackson, President of the United States, on their grievances, and enclosed with their petition, the reply of Governor Dunklin on their petition to him. The governor claimed that the law did not authorize him to keep a military force in Jackson County to protect the Mormons after they were returned to their homes. The Saints asked the President to restore them to their homes and possessions and to ensure their protection. Unfortunately, this request came during one of the great debates in American history over the question of the sovereign rights of states. The general feeling in America was that the Federal Government had no authority to intervene in a state's internal affairs, such as those occurring in Jackson County, unless the governor declared a state of insurrection. In May 1834, the federal government denied the Saints' petition, arguing that the offenses listed were violations of state, not Federal law. Meanwhile, Governor Dunklin also hesitated to take action. Lawyers for the Church argued the Saints' case before the state legislature, but that body also refused to help.

The July 1833 to July 1834 period—was the time of the "refiner's fire" for the Latter-day Saints in Western Missouri. Members of the Church throughout the United States were deeply, emotionally, and profoundly disappointed that the land of Zion had to be abandoned. Their only recourse was to wait patiently upon the Lord for deliverance and direction, and hope that that day would not be too far in the future.

JOSEPH'S INCREASING CHALLENGES

It was the growth of a nation, and the growth of the Lord's Restored Church that had Joseph Smith in a constant state of spiritual, emotional and physical action and activity. His brilliant, keen, and resourceful mind was rarely resting, always vigorous and dynamic. He moved with remarkable, exceptional and lighting speed on subjects as urgent and grave as the threatened destruction of a humble, God-loving, God-fearing people in the American frontier to those as simple and commonplace as fixing a leak on his own roof. When his mind was concentrating on a particular subject, he would focus his full attention and energies upon it. He would tenaciously and diligently stick to that subject until its possibilities had been exhausted. Then he would move to another subject, project, program, whatever, on which he would expend the same kind of unyielding, persevering devotion.

He faced the year 1834 with some feelings of internal / external frustration and stress. It was apparent though, from a long-range vantage point, that he and the Church had taken giant strides in accomplishing the Lord's work. The Saints were established in two major centers, thin and few in numbers, but growing. The missionaries of the Church continued to proselyte ambitiously, with great enthusiasm and success. Most of the converts were genuinely committed to the principles of the Gospel, including the one of gathering, and were loyal followers of the Prophet. As a result, his influence and power was increased almost daily as converts continued to pour into the Kirtland area. Work on the temple was being pushed, a new press had been established, and the sleepy little town of Kirtland had fully come to life and was bustling with activity. Considering all this, Joseph could not help but rejoice, especially in view of the exciting prospects ahead. After all, the achievements of the Church to this time, were but a minor prelude to what was anticipated in the future. Joseph and his followers confidently believed that theirs was to be the enviable task of hopefully creating a perfect society, suitable for a home of the Savior.

Nevertheless, a close-up view of the Church gave the Prophet some real cause for concern. The most immediate pressing problem was the sad plight of the Saints in Missouri. Until now, he had attempted to resolve the complicated difficulties through letters or personal couriers. This proved to be ineffective. The time it took to travel from city to city made the counsel in his letters inapplicable to the constantly changing conditions. What the Saints faced in Missouri was like a war, and the Prophet knew it wasn't feasible to help the Missouri Saints long distance. Therefore, he began thinking about leading a force of Saints to Missouri to help their embattled brothers and sisters in Jackson County. The law enforcement machinery in that state was in the hands of admitted enemies of the Church, and any thought that the Saints could obtain justice was wishful thinking.

Throughout the course of the winter of 1833-1834, the Saints still hoped and prayed that Governor Daniel Dunklin would assist them in regaining their homes in Jackson County. On December 16, 1833, however, Joseph Smith received a revelation that raised significant possibilities. The Lord recommended various means by which the Saints were to settle the Missouri dispute, but warned that if all peaceful and corrective methods failed, they might have to occupy their rightful lands by force (see Doctrine & Covenants 101). As events unfolded, the Lord instructed the brethren in Kirtland to raise an army and go to Missouri.

The Missouri crisis was only one of a number of grave concerns facing Joseph Smith at the beginning of 1834. Equally serious was an internal eruption in the Church at Kirtland, brought on by the rebellion of some of the members. With an aggressive, enthusiastic proselyting campaign such as the one conducted by the Church, it was only natural that converts of every imaginable disposition would be brought into the fold, including many complainers and troublemakers.

As has previously been noted—during January, the Prophet met with other leaders in Kirtland to draft a procedure to govern the Church's High Council in handling cases of Church discipline. One of the cases brought before the council—one that would have far-reaching effects on the Prophet and the Church—was that of Philastus Hurlburt, who, after his excommunication, redoubled his efforts to embarrass and destroy Joseph Smith and the Church through questionable affidavits and theories on the origin of the Book of Mormon.

It is revealing to see how the Prophet's character was disclosed by the way he reacted to the great pressures exerted upon him during this period. Violent attacks upon his people, dissensions within the Church, and threats upon his life by aggressive and determined apostates did not produce feelings of bitterness, fear, or retaliation, as might be expected. Rather, they produced in him increased feelings of humility and reliance upon the Lord. One is struck, in reading his journal entries of this period, by the frequency with which he implored the Lord for help and guidance in all aspects of his temporal and physical responsibilities, ranging from pleas for protection for the Saints, to economic affairs and concerns for his family and personal associates.

ZION'S CAMP

BECOMES A REALITY

On February 24, 1834, Joseph's previous idea to lead a force of Saints to aid the Missouri brethren crystallized in his mind. On that date, he received a revelation which contained this key statement: *"Behold, I say unto you, the redemption of Zion must needs come by power; Therefore, I will raise up unto my people, a man who shall lead them like as Moses led the children of Israel. For ye are the children of Israel, and of the seed of Abraham, and ye must needs be led out of bondage by power, and with a stretched—out arm. And as your fathers were led at the first, even so shall the redemption of Zion"* (Doctrine & Covenants 103: 15-18).

The revelation added some specific instructions about the procedure to be followed in preparing for this undertaking. Joseph was directed to assemble the necessary manpower: *" say unto the strength of my house, my young men and the middle aged—Gather yourselves together unto the land of Zion, upon the land which I have bought with money that has been consecrated unto me"* (Doctrine & Covenants 103: 22).

After an arduous, difficult journey, Parley P. Pratt, and Lyman Wight arrived in Kirtland from Missouri on February 22, 1834. The High Council in Kirtland, which had been organized less than a week (Doctrine & Covenants 102, Section heading), assembled in the Joseph Smith home to hear their report and consider the Missouri brethren's request for help. At the conclusion of the meeting, Joseph Smith announced that he was going to Zion to help redeem it. He asked for a vote of the High Council to sanction his decision. He was supported unanimously. The Prophet then asked for volunteers to go with him. Thirty to forty of the men present volunteered, and Joseph was selected to be the *"commander-in-chief of the armies of Israel"* (*History of the Church,* 2: 39).

The same day, Joseph Smith received a revelation concerning the recruitment and size of the army. Eight men, including the Prophet, were called to help gather young and middle-aged members for Zion's Camp, and to raise money to help the oppressed members in Missouri.

The revelation was very specific about the size of the army to be taken to Missouri. Along with the Prophet, among the eight men called, which included Parley P. Pratt and Lyman Wight, they were directed to recruit: *"companies to go up unto the land of Zion, by tens, or by twenties, or by fifties, or by an hundred, until they have obtained to the number of five hundred of the strength of my house . . . if you cannot obtain five hundred, seek diligently that peradventure you may obtain three hundred. And if you cannot obtain three hundred, seek diligently that peradventure ye may obtain one hundred. But verily I say unto you, a commandment I give unto you, that ye shall not go up into the land of Zion, until you have obtained a hundred of the strength of my house, to go up with you unto the land of Zion"* (Doctrine & Covenants 103: 30, 32-34).

Armed with these instructions, **the Prophet and his associates spread out in different directions to find manpower, weapons, money, and supplies for the expedition,** which came to be known as "Zion's Camp." Beginning in late February, these eight missionaries traveling two by two, visited the branches of the Church throughout the Eastern United States, gathering contributions of all types and recruiting for Zion's Camp. With Parley P. Pratt as his companion, Joseph went into Western New York, speaking along the way, and informing the brethren what had happened to the members of the Church in Zion, and communicating to them *"the prophecies and revelations concerning the order to gathering to Zion, and the means of her redemption"* (*History of the Church,* 2: 42).

While the importance of this mission was to mobilize volunteers for the march of Zion, every opportunity was taken also to preach the Gospel to nonmembers. At a small town named Freedom, the Prophet and Parley P. Pratt preached "to an overflowing house." There was such great interest shown that they stayed over an extra day to hold another meeting. As a result of this proselyting effort, a young Methodist by the name of Herman T. Hyde was baptized. The cumulative effect of this single conversion is shown from the following account written later on by Parley P. Pratt: " his parents were Presbyterians, and his mother, on account of the strength of her traditions, thought that we were wrong, and told me afterwards that she would much rather have followed him to an earthly grave than to have seen him baptized. Soon afterwards, however she, her husband, and the rest of the family, with some thirty or forty others, were all baptized and organized into a branch of the Church—called the Freedom Branch—from which core the light spread and souls were gathered into the fold in all the regions round about. Thus mightily grew the word of God, or the seed sown by that extraordinary personage, Joseph Smith, the Prophet and Seer of the nineteenth century" (Pratt, *Autobiography of Parley P. Pratt,* pp. 109-10).

On March seventeenth, a conference was held at Avon, Livingston County, New York, with a number of Priesthood holders in attendance. There the goals to raise money and to recruit men for Zion's Camp were discussed and assignments were made. Two fund-raising groups were appointed to work in assigned areas, and it was also decided that the Prophet, with Sidney Rigdon and Lyman Wight, would return to Kirtland, preaching and soliciting funds on the way. *"Arrived home in Kirtland on the 28th of March,"* Joseph recorded in his journal: *"finding my family all well. The Lord be praised for this blessing!"* (*History of the Church,* 2: 45).

As the Prophet reviewed the recruitment numbers from the Eastern United States, he was greatly disappointed. In April, he strongly suggested that the brethren in the East volunteer to go to Missouri with Zion's Camp, or lose the chance to *"better themselves by obtaining so goodly a land, . . . and stand against that wicked mob.*

"If this Church, which is essaying to be the Church of Christ will not help us, when they can do it without sacrifice, . . . God shall take away their talent, and give it to those who have no talent, and shall prevent them from ever obtaining a place of refuge, or an inheritance upon the land of Zion" (*History of the Church,* 2: 48).

Nevertheless, few in the East volunteered for the camp. One who did was a recent convert at the time, twenty-seven-year-old—Wilford Woodruff of Connecticut. Wilford was impressed with Parley P. Pratt's impassioned appeal for volunteers, but he was hesitant to go because of his business affairs. Wilford Woodruff recorded in his journal: "I told Brother Parley our circumstances. He told me it was my duty to try to prepare myself and go up to Zion. And accordingly, I used every exertion to settle my accounts, arrange my affairs, and prepare myself to join my brethren to go to Missouri" (*Wilford Woodruff Journal,* April 11,1834, LDS Historical Department). By April twenty-fifth, Wilford was living at Joseph Smith's home in Kirtland, helping to prepare others for the camp.

On April twenty-first, Hyrum Smith and Lyman Wight went northwest from Kirtland to seek out more recruits. They were to lead those who joined them to meet Joseph's company at the Salt River in Eastern Missouri. They visited branches of the Church in Northern Ohio, Michigan, and Illinois, and eventually recruited more than twenty volunteers, over half of them from Pontiac, Michigan. Hosea Stout, who later played key roles in the Church, had not yet become a member in 1834 when Hyrum and Lyman went to his hometown in Michigan. Hosea later wrote: "The effect of their preaching was powerful on me, and when I considered that they were going up to Zion to fight for their lost inheritances, under the special directions of God, it was all that I could do to refrain from going."

Recruiting efforts in Kirtland were less disappointing. Many able-bodied Priesthood holders in that community volunteered to march to Zion. Thirty-two-year-old Brigham Young stepped forward and tried to convince his older brother Joseph to go, too. Joseph Smith informed the two brothers: *"Brother Brigham and brother Joseph, if you will go with me in the camp to Missouri, and keep my counsel, I promise you, in the name of the Almighty, that I will lead you there and back again, and not a hair of your heads shall be harmed."* Hearing this, Joseph Young agreed to participate, and the three men clasped hands in confirmation of this promise (History of Brigham Young, *Millennial Star, 18* July 1863, p. 455).

Many of the men in Zion's Camp left families with little or no money and no source of income. To help prevent undue hardships, members of the Church planted gardens so that the women and children could harvest corn and other crops during the army's absence. The volunteers also gathered supplies and teams for their journey, as well as clothing, bedding, food, and arms for the Saints in Missouri. A few Elders, including Oliver Cowdery and Sidney Rigdon, were left behind to supervise the ongoing construction of the temple, and to direct the other affairs of the Church in Kirtland.

On May first, the day chosen to begin the 1,000 mile march, only twenty people were ready to go. Joseph Smith sent them fifty miles south to New Portage, where they were to wait for the others to join them. By Sunday, May fourth, over eighty volunteers assembled in Kirtland. Nearly all of them were young men. Some were fearful of what lay ahead. Heber C. Kimball said: "I took leave of my wife and children and friends, not knowing whether I would see them again in the flesh." That day, the Prophet spoke to the Kirtland Saints before departing. George A. Smith wrote: "He impressed upon them the necessity of being humble, exercising faith and patience and living in obedience to the commands of the Almighty. He bore testimony of the truth of the work which God had revealed through him, and promised the brethren that if they all would live as they should, before the Lord, keeping his commandments, they should all safely return" (*Memories of George Albert Smith,* May 4, 1834, LDS Historical Department p.13).

The next day, Joseph Smith assumed his role as Commander-in-Chief of the army. The eighty men joined the twenty brethren in New Portage late Tuesday evening, May 6, 1834. There the Prophet organized the camp.

He divided it into companies of tens and fifties and instructed each group to elect a captain who was to assign each man his responsibilities. One recruit, Joseph Holbrook, reported that the camp was organized "according to the ancient order of Israel." The men also consolidated their money into a general fund, which was managed by Frederick G. Williams, second counselor in the First Presidency, who was appointed paymaster. The average age of the recruits was twenty-nine, the age of their leader, Joseph Smith. George A. Smith, cousin of the Prophet, was the youngest at age sixteen, and Samuel Baker was the oldest at seventy-nine.

On May eighth, the army of Israel resumed its long march West. Throughout its journey, the camp was gradually strengthened with additional volunteers, arms, supplies, and money. Officers continued to recruit help from Latter-day Saints living in Ohio, Indiana, and Illinois. By the time Zion's Camp crossed the Mississippi River into Missouri, it numbered 185 people. On June eighth, at the Salt River in Missouri where Joseph Smith had arranged to meet Hyrum Smith's company, **the army reached its maximum numerical strength: 207 men, 11 women, 11 children, and 25 baggage wagons.**

The comfort and well-being of the groups within Zion's Camp depended on the foresight and resourcefulness of their immediate leaders, not Joseph Smith. Consequently, groups headed by men of the caliber of Brigham Young were well cared for. Others did not fare so well, and when something went wrong within the group, the tendency of several in the camp was to blame the Prophet rather than the immediate leaders—a sign of weaknesses of character.

In many respects, the daily routine of Zion's Camp was similar to that of other armies. Most able-bodied men walked beside the heavily loaded wagons along the muddy and dusty trails. Many of them carried knapsacks and held guns. It was not unusual for them to march thirty-five miles a day, despite blistered feet, stifling heat, heavy rains, high humidity, hunger, and thirst. Armed guards were posted around the camp at night. The trumpeter, using an old, battered French horn, called the brethren to prayer night and morning. The call sounded just before bedtime, when in their respective tents, the men presented their *"thank-offerings with prayer and supplication."* And it sounded again the next morning, usually at four a.m., when *"every man was again on his knees before the Lord, imploring His blessing for the day"* (*History of the Church,* 1: 65). In addition, each company gathered for prayer, then went to work at their respective assignments. Some members of the company gathered firewood, others carried water, cooked breakfast, and took down tents. Wagon wheels had to be greased and horses fed and groomed before being hitched up for the day's journey.

Feeding the camp was one of the most persistent problems. The meager provisions with which the travelers began their journey were certainly insufficient to last them the entire trip, so that the commissaries were kept very busy hunting for food as they spread out in front and to the sides of the route of the march. These men also doubled as recruiters who encouraged able-bodied Saints along the way to join the march in order to bring relief to the besieged members in Missouri. For this reason the size of the camp was enlarged from time to time as it moved slowly toward its destination.

The aggressive open effort that the

Prophet and his associates made to enlist men and gather money and supplies for Zion's Camp generated countless rumors about its objectives. There was constant speculation that Joseph had designs of building a personal empire. His enemies claimed that he looked upon himself as a modern Mahomet, inclined to force and coerce all who he met into his beliefs and way of life. In the eyes of some of his acknowledged enemies, Zion's Camp represented a bold attempt to advance his ambition of dominance by force. Beginning with this false premise, it is understandable why opposition to the camp became so extreme and bitter. This, in turn, intensified the concern for the safety of the camp and produced unusual countermeasures to disguise its identity and purpose. Accordingly, the men were very secretive and reluctant to reveal their destination or the purpose of their journey to those who inquired.

On a number of occasions, Joseph Smith taught those in the camp to conserve natural resources and to avoid killing. One afternoon, while preparing to pitch his tent, Joseph and others discovered three rattlesnakes. As the men prepared to kill them, the Prophet said: *"Let them alone—don't hurt them! How will the serpent ever lose his venom, while the servants of God possess the same disposition, and continue to make war upon it? Men must become harmless, before the brute creation."* The snakes were carefully carried across a creek on sticks and released. Joseph instructed the camp to refrain from killing any animal unless it was necessary to avoid starvation (*History of the Church,* 2: 71-72).

Unlike most armies, Zion's Camp placed great emphasis upon spirituality. Besides company prayers, the men were counselled to pray privately morning and evening. On Sundays the camp rested, held meetings, and partook of the Sacrament. They were often privileged to hear the Prophet teach the doctrines of the kingdom. Those in the camp had faith that the Lord was accompanying them. The Prophet recalled: *"God was with us, and His angels went before us, and the faith of our little band was unwavering. We know that angels were our companions, for we saw them"* (*History of the Church,* 2: 73).

On June 2, 1834, the army crossed the Illinois River at Phillips Ferry. The Prophet and a few others walked along the bluffs and found huge mounds with human bones scattered about, and what appeared to be the remains of three ancient altars. While digging in one of these mounds, they discovered a large human skeleton with a stone arrowhead between its ribs. As the brethren left the hill, the Prophet inquired of the Lord and learned in an open vision that the remains were those of a man named Zelph, a former Lamanite warrior-chieftain who was killed *"during the last great struggle of the Lamanites and Nephites"*—names of the people from the Book of Mormon scriptures (*History of the Church,* 2: 80).

This account is mindful of instances in the early days of Joseph's prophetic career while he was translating the Book of Mormon. So intimate and detailed was his knowledge of the early American Indian culture that he was able to discuss conditions, events, and personalities as if—he had lived among the people for years. With the Prophet Joseph, the veil between this life, the past, the future, and the unseen world of spirits was so thin that he moved easily and almost at will from one realm to the other. In doing so, he reported to his astonished followers what he saw and felt. These incidents happened so often, and the reported results had proven to be so precise and undeviating that Joseph's followers automatically looked to him for an explanation of any event they did not fully understand.

While most of the members of Zion's Camp were young, virile, and conditioned to the rigors of farm life, they were not prepared for the physical endurance such a march would require. Added to the physical pressures were anxieties about what they might run into in the form of illness or attack from their enemies, and the concern about what lay ahead at the end of the trail. It is little wonder then, that there were provocations along the way. Considering the circumstances, the inexperience of the marchers, the fatigue they suffered, the scarcity and poor quality of their food, and their inferior equipment, the miracle is that the men fared as well as they did. Those who would try to discredit and belittle the Prophet are anxious to dwell on the negative aspects of the march and to apply an unrealistic standard of performance—one that might be expected of a well-provisioned, well-equipped, disciplined and experienced military force. It is fortunate that the camp included among it members an able and precise diarist, Wilford Woodruff who wrote: "We pitched our tents at night and had prayers night and morning. The Prophet gave us our instructions every day. We were nearly all young men, brought together from all parts of the country, and were therefore strangers to each other. We soon became acquainted, and had a happy time in each others association. It was a great school for us, to be led by a Prophet of God, a 1,000 miles through cities, towns, villages, and through the wilderness" (M.F. Cowley, *Wilford Woodruff,* SLC, Bookcraft, 1964, p. 40).

The Lord also blessed the camp to travel safely through sometimes threatening circumstances. Members of the camp generally tried to conceal their identity and objectives as they marched. Occasionally, the army appeared larger or smaller than it actually was to those who tried to determine its strength. Near Dayton, Ohio, a dozen men entered the camp and concluded there were 600 soldiers. As the camp crossed the Illinois River, the ferryman thought there were 500 in the company. When they faced opposition at Indianapolis, Joseph assured the brethren that they would pass through the city without anyone being aware of their doing so. He divided them into small groups which dispersed and took different routes through the community undetected.

Potential enemies notwithstanding, quarreling and contention within the camp became its most annoying and disturbing problem. The Prophet's small army of Saints were not long on the trail before a spirit of griping, complaining, and faultfinding showed its ugly head among some of its members. **There is no good condition that cannot be made bad and no bad condition that cannot be made worse by the sour and disagreeable attitude of those affected with this spirit.** A number of men feared possible dangers, some complained about serious changes in their lifestyle, and a few questioned the decisions of their leaders. For forty-five days they marched together, and the inevitable personality clashes were intensified by the harsh conditions they encountered. Reflecting back—those who were discontent often blamed Joseph Smith for their anguish and discomfort.

A standout complainer, Sylvester Smith (no relation to the Prophet), a sharp-tongued group captain, often led the dissention. He complained that the food was disastrous, preparations for the journey were inadequate, and that Joseph's watchdog kept him awake at night. On the evening of May seventeenth, Joseph was called upon to settle another dispute among some of the brethren. The Prophet Joseph said that he found: *"a rebellious spirit in Sylvester Smith, and to some extent in others, I* [Joseph] *told them that they would meet with misfortunes, difficulties and hindrances, and said, 'and you will know it before you leave this place,' exhorting them to humble themselves before the Lord and become united, that they might not be scourged"* (*History of the Church,* 2: 68). The following day, the prophecy was fulfilled: nearly every horse was sick or lame. The Prophet promised that if they would humble themselves and overcome their discord, their animals would be immediately restored to health. By noon, the horses were nimble and alert once again, with the exception of Sylvester Smith's mount, which soon died.

Contention showed its ugly face once again when Sylvester Smith threatened to kill Joseph's dog. On June third, a frustrated Joseph Smith stood on a wagon wheel, scolding the men for their lack of humility, their murmuring and fault-finding: *"I said the Lord had revealed to me that a scourge would come upon the camp in consequence of the fractions* [disobedience] *and unruly spirits that appeared among them, and they should die like sheep with the rot; still, if they would repent and humble themselves before the Lord, the scourge, in a great measure, might be turned away; but, as the Lord lives, the members of this camp will suffer for giving way to their unruly temper"* (*History of the Church,* 2: 80). This sad prophecy would be fulfilled within a few weeks.

The anti-Mormons in Jackson County learned of the advancing army in June when the postmaster in Chagrin, Ohio, wrote to his counterpart in Independence: "The Mormons in this region are organizing an army to restore Zion, that is to take it by force of arms." Believing that a Mormon invasion was forthcoming, Jackson County troops began to drill, and sentries were posted at all ferries along the Missouri River. In a vengeful spirit, hoping by chance to discourage the return of the Saints, mobbers burned 150 homes belonging to the Mormons who lived in the county. Members of Zion's Camp suspected that spies from Missouri had followed them for hundreds of miles. One night, a Missourian went into camp and swore that he knew their destination was Jackson County, and that they would never cross the Mississippi River alive.

About the same time, Church leaders in Clay County continued to petition Governor Daniel Dunklin for assurance that he would support the Saints in returning to their homes, regaining their property, and living in peace in Jackson County. The Governor admitted that the Saints had been wronged by being driven from their homes, and he attempted to have the arms returned that were taken from the Saints when they were expelled from Jackson County the previous November. In addition, he recognized that an armed force sent by the state would be necessary to restore the Mormons to their lands and protect them while the courts decided the legal issues involved.

Once Zion's Camp was in Missouri, Joseph Smith sent Elders Orson Hyde and Parley P. Pratt to Jefferson City, the State Capitol, to ascertain whether Governor Dunklin was still willing to honor his promise to reinstate and restore the Saints in Jackson County with the assistance of the state militia. The interview was a bitter disappointment. Dunklin claimed that calling out the militia would probably plunge the state into open war. He advised the brethren that they could avoid bloodshed by surrendering their rights, selling their lands, and settling elsewhere. This approach was unacceptable to the Church. The governor then advised an appeal to the courts, but the brethren felt that the governor knew this was not practical—officers of the court were among the anti-Mormons in the county, so it was like referring them to a band of thieves to sue for the recovery of stolen property (Pratt, *Autobiography Parley P. Pratt,* SLC, Deseret Book, 1985, p. 94). Parley was also convinced that the governor was a coward, and was morally obliged to resign for failing to live up to the obligations of his office.

Elders Pratt and Hyde rejoined the approaching Zion's Camp. Their report dashed any hopes that the Missouri Saints would be allowed to return to their homes peacefully. The brethren also realized that the anti-Mormons were waiting to destroy all Mormons who attempted to settle in Jackson County. The Prophet called upon God to witness the justice of the Saints' cause, the sincerity of their vows, and the injustice of the Missouri government's words and action. Angered and frustrated by the governor's decision, Zion's Camp resumed marching.

In the meantime, Judge John J. Ryland of Clay County, arranged a meeting for June sixteenth, at the courthouse in Liberty. A committee of citizens from Jackson County and representatives of the Saints in Clay County were to meet in an effort to resolve the dispute. A large, unruly, hostile crowd gathered at the meeting. The non-Mormons proposed to purchase within thirty days all property owned by the Saints in Jackson County at prices determined by three disinterested negotiators, or to have the Mormons do likewise and buy all *their* property within the same period. This proposal was unreasonable and unrealistic. The Saints did not have enough funds to purchase even a fraction of the land owned by the non-Mormons, and they could not sell their land in Zion because they had been commanded by the Lord to purchase and settle it. These facts, of course, were all known by the anti-Mormons. Tempers flared as Jackson County representative Samuel Owens swore that the Missourians would fight for every inch of ground rather than let the Saints return.

Joseph recorded: *"A Baptist Priest . . . said: 'The Mormons have lived long enough in Clay County; and they must either clear out, or be cleared out.' Mr. Turnham, the moderator of the meeting, answered in a masterly manner; saying. 'Let us be republicans; let us honor our country, and not disgrace it like Jackson county. For God's sake, don't disfranchise or drive away the Mormons. They are better citizens than many of the old inhabitants'"* (*History of the Church,* 2: 97-98).

The Mormon committee prepared a statement stipulating that the Saints would not initiate hostilities, and they promised to respond to the Jackson County proposition within a week. Soon thereafter, the Saints prepared a counterproposal recommending that a neutral committee determine the value of the property of those in Jackson County who refused to live with the Latter-day Saints, and that the Saints buy that property within a year. Moreover, the Saints promised to stay out of Jackson County until full payment was made. Unfortunately, these negotiations proved useless and futile.

By June eighteenth, Zion's Camp arrived within a mile of Richmond, the county seat of Ray County. As the army encamped, the Prophet had a premonition of danger. He went into the woods and prayed for safety, and he was assured that the Lord would protect them. He had the camp roused in the early morning hours, and they left without prayers or breakfast. As they marched through Richmond, a black slave woman, who was agitated and troubled, told Luke Johnson, "There is a company of men lying in wait here, who are scheming and plotting to kill you this morning as you pass through." Fortunately, they met no opposition or confrontation, although they were able to make only nine miles that day, because they were slowed down by broken wagon wheels.

Instead of reaching their intended destination of Liberty, they camped just outside Clay County on a hill between seven small streams or branches of the Little Fishing and Big Fishing rivers. When Joseph learned that mobs in the area were preparing to attack, he knelt and prayed again for divine protection. Joseph's fears were confirmed when five armed Missourians rode into camp, cursing, and swore that the Mormons would "see hell before morning." They boasted that nearly 200 men had joined forces from Ray, Lafayette, Clay, and Jackson Counties, and were then preparing to cross the Missouri River at Williams Ferry and completely destroy the Mormons (*History of the Church,* 2: 102-3). Sounds of gunfire were heard, and some of the men wanted to fight, but the Prophet promised that the Lord would protect them. He declared: *"Stand still and see the salvation of God."*

Within a few short minutes after the Missourians had left, a small black cloud appeared in the clear western sky. It moved eastward, unrolling like a scroll, filling the heavens with darkness. As the first ferry loaded with mobbers crossed the Missouri River to the south, a sudden squall made it nearly impossible for the boat to return to pick up another load. The storm was so intense that Zion's Camp abandoned their tents and found shelter in an old Baptist meetinghouse nearby. When Joseph Smith came in, he cried aloud: *"Boys, there is some meaning to this. God is in the storm"* (*History of the Church,* 2: 104). It was virtually impossible for anyone to sleep, so the group sang hymns and rested on the rough benches. One camp member recorded that "during this time, the whole covering of the wide horizon was in one complete blaze with terrifying claps of thunder."

Not too far away, the besieged mobbers were searching for any refuge they could find to be safe from the storm. This furious storm broke branches from trees and destroyed crops. It soaked and made the mobbers' ammunition useless; it frightened and scattered their horses and raised the level of the Fishing River, preventing them from attacking Zion's Camp. The Prophet recalled: *"it seemed as if the mandate of vengeance had gone forth from the God of battles, to protect His servants from the destruction of their enemies"* (*History of the Church,* 2: 105).

Two days later, on June twenty-first, Colonel John Sconce and two associates of the Ray County militia rode into Zion's Camp to learn of the Mormons intentions: "I see that there is an Almighty power that protects this people," Sconce admitted (*History of the Church,* 2: 106). The Prophet explained that the only purpose of Zion's Camp was to help their brethren be reinstated and returned to their lands, and that their intent was not to injure anyone. He said: *"The evil reports circulated about us were false, and planned by our enemies to procure our destruction."* Sconce and his companions were so affected by the stories of the unjust trials and suffering of the Saints, that they promised to use their influence to offset feelings against the Mormons.

The next day, June twenty-second, Joseph received a revelation communicating the Lord's dissatisfaction with the members of the Church for their disobedience and selfishness: They *"do not impart of their substance, as becometh saints, to the poor and afflicted among them; And are not united according to the union required by the law of the celestial kingdom"* (Doctrine & Covenants 105: 3-4).

This chastisement was directed specifically to members of the branches who were slow in sharing themselves and their means for the cause of Zion (vv. 7-8). The Saints had to learn their duty and gain more experience before Zion could be redeemed (vv. 9-10). Thus the Lord said: *"It is expedient in me that mine elders should wait for a little season, for the redemption of Zion"* (v. 13). He promised the obedient that they would receive an endowment from on high if they continued faithful (vv. 11-12). If Zion's Camp did not succeed in its military objective, it did succeed in serving the purposes of the Lord. Speaking of the men in the camp He said: *"I have heard their prayers, and will accept their offerings; and it is expedient in me that they should be brought thus far for a trial of their faith"* (v. 19).

For a few of the Saints, the Lord's command not to do battle was the *final* trial of their faith. Disappointed and angry, they apostatized. **As a result of their rebellion, the Prophet again warned the camp that the Lord would send a devastating scourge upon them** as a consequence of their unrighteous complaints. The day before the revelation was given, two men contracted **cholera**. Three days later, several more were struck with the dreaded, deadly disease, which was carried in contaminated water. The epidemic spread, causing severe diarrhea, vomiting, and cramps. Before it ended, about sixty-eight people, including Joseph Smith, were stricken by the disease, and fourteen members of the camp died, one of whom was a women named Betsy Parrish. On July second, Joseph Smith told the camp that: *"if they would humble themselves before the Lord, and covenant to keep His commandments, and obey my counsel, the plague should be stayed from that hour, and there should not be another case of cholera among them. The brethren covenanted to that effect with uplifted hands, and the plague was stayed"* (*History of the Church,* 2: 120).

On June twenty-fifth, **during the height of the cholera attack,** Joseph Smith divided Zion's Camp into several small groups to demonstrate the Saints' peaceful intent to the Missourians. Ten days later, formal written discharges were prepared for each faithful member of the camp. Lyman Wight reported, that the Prophet: "said that he was now willing to return home, that he was fully satisfied that he had done the will of God, and that the Lord had accepted our sacrifice and offering, even as he had accepted Abraham's when he offered his son Isaac; and in his benediction, asked the Heavenly Father to bless us with eternal life and salvation."

The camp dispersed after being released by the Prophet. Some people remained in Missouri in accordance with the Fishing River revelation, (see Doctrine & Covenants 105: 20), and some returned to the mission field, but most of them returned to their families in the East. On the same day, July third, the Prophet organized a Presidency and High Council in Missouri to help Bishop Edward Partridge administer the affairs of the Church in that area. Joseph Smith discouraged the Missouri Saints from holding church meetings in an attempt to lessen the fears of the local citizens.

Life in Clay County was easier for the Saints throughout the remainder of 1834 and during 1835. This period of time was comparatively free from persecution, and the Saints enjoyed some much needed prosperity. Most of the non-Mormons in Clay County were generally cordial. The spirit of good will, nevertheless, began to change when the Saints continued to migrate to Missouri in anticipation of returning to Jackson County and when some members of the Church bought property in Clay County. Unfortunately, a few of the members had not learned from the persecutions of Jackson County, and they provoked the old settlers with talk that their lands would eventually belong to the Saints. As a whole, the members failed to observe the Lord's counsel: *"Talk not of judgements, neither boast of faith nor of mighty works, but carefully gather together, as much in one region as can be, consistently with the feelings of the people; And behold, I will give unto you favor and grace in their eyes, that you may rest in peace and safety"* (Doctrine & Covenants 105: 24-25).

Joseph Smith and several other leaders of Zion's Camp had worried about reports that Joseph Smith had been killed in Missouri, arrived back in Kirtland in early August to the relief of the Saints in Kirtland. Later in the month, a High Council heard complaints of Sylvester Smith and others who were still bitter over Zion's Camp. Ten men who had participated in Zion's Camp, disputed the charges of Sylvester Smith and testified that Joseph Smith was not guilty of improper conduct. After reviewing the evidence, Sylvester admitted that he was in error and had behaved improperly. Of great importance is a clear definition between the Prophet as an individual, and the Prophet's work. Joseph was looked upon fundamentally as a channel through which the Lord did His work and made His will known, so the work far surpassed the man. To the true disciple, nothing the man might do would ever lessen or overshadow the enormity of the work he produced.

Joseph was not a man to nurse a grudge. Though he could and did speak out boldly and with authority, sometimes harshly, against those who opposed or injured him, he was inclined and eager to forgive and forget once an enemy showed signs of repenting, moderating, and changing. Only a few months after the members of Zion's Camp returned to Kirtland, Sylvester was called and ordained as one of the Seven President's of the First Quorum of Seventy.

Zion's Camp failed to help the Missouri Saints regain their lands and was marred by some dissension, apostasy, and unfavorable publicity, **but a number of positive results came from the journey.** By volunteering, the members demonstrated their faith in the Lord and His Prophet and their earnest desire to comply with latter-day revelation. They showed their concern for the exiled Saints in Missouri by their willingness to lay down their lives, if necessary, to assist them.

The rugged journey served as a test to determine who was worthy to serve in positions of leadership and trust and to receive a special spiritual blessing in the Kirtland Temple. The Prophet later explained: *"God did not want you to fight. He could not organize His kingdom with twelve men to open the Gospel door to the nations of the earth, and with seventy men under their direction to follow in their tracks, unless He took them from a body of men who offered their lives, and who had made as great a sacrifice as did*

Abraham" (*History of the Church,* 2: 182). In February 1835, the Quorum of the Twelve Apostles and the First Quorum of the Seventy were organized. Nine of the original Apostles, all Seven Presidents of the Seventy's quorum, and all sixty-three other members of that quorum had served in the army of Israel that marched to Western Missouri in 1834.

As Joseph reviewed once again the conditions in Missouri in light of revelation, he was struck with the realization that the time for the "redemption" of the land of Zion lay in the distant future. Plans for the building up the Center Stake of Zion and erecting the beautiful temple would have to be shelved for the time being. For the present, the brethren would have to be content to pursue a delaying action designed to retain a foothold in Missouri, while salvaging everything possible from the Jackson County expulsion. In order to strengthen the local brethren and provide more direct control of their affairs, the Prophet organized the Missouri Saints, (as has been stated earlier) in the same manner that the Saints in Kirtland had been organized with a Presidency of three and a High Council of twelve. David Whitmer was appointed "President of the Church [in that area] of Zion" with W. W. Phelps and John Whitmer as assistants. The Prophet later recorded the instructions given to the leaders in Zion on this historic occasion: *"After singing and prayer, I gave the Council such instructions in relation to their high calling, as would enable them to proceed to minister in their office agreeable to the pattern heretofore given; read the revelation on the subject; and told them that if I should now be taken away, I had accomplished the great work the Lord had laid before me, and that which I had desired of the Lord; and that I had done my duty in organizing the High Council, through which the will of the Lord might be made known on all important occasions,· in the building up of Zion, and establishing truth in the earth"* (*History of the Church,* 2: 124). The Prophet Joseph did all within his power to strengthen the Saints in Zion against the terrible ordeal that still faced them there.

The most beneficial aspect of Zion's Camp was the experience in discipline and sacrifice provided to its members. Those who endured the fatigue and uncertainties of the trip were never quite the same again thereafter. The fact that they had responded willingly and had survived under the most trying conditions gave them a sense of self-confidence and resiliency which would sustain them in facing the many future trials and difficulties that lay ahead.

Zion's Camp tempered, polished, and spiritually refined many of the Lord's servants. The observant, the attentive, the watchful and the dedicated received invaluable practical training and spiritual experience that served them well in later struggles for the Church. The hardships and challenges experienced over its 1,000 miles provided invaluable training for Brigham Young, Heber C. Kimball, and others who led the exiled Saints from Missouri to Illinois, and from Nauvoo across the plains to the Rocky Mountains. When a skeptic asked what he had gained from his journey, Brigham Young promptly replied: "I would not exchange the knowledge I have received this season for the whole of Geauga County" (*Journal of Discourses*, 2: 10). Though he didn't know it then, Zion's Camp was Brigham Young's training for the great exodus westward that he was to lead a few years later. The problems of supply, organization, and discipline he observed in the camp were to appear again in the westward trek, except on a magnified scale. Instead of the responsibility of leading 200 healthy young men through an area with well-defined and heavily traveled roads and waterways to a predetermined place, he would lead thousands of men, women, and children of all ages, healthy and ill alike, through an uncharted and unknown desert country toward a destination, a place for religious freedom, which at the outset, was uncertain. And probably, without ever consciously intending to do so, Brigham marked with care and attention every detail of Joseph's mode and means of operation against the time when he would have a similar responsibility in an entirely different setting.

After his return, the Prophet Joseph's life settled into a comfortable routine for a short season. It was a welcome change to enjoy the love and companionship of his family and to give direction to the local affairs of the Church. The most pressing matter of the moment was the construction of the temple. While a building committee had the chief responsibility for carrying this project forward, Joseph was an active participant in practically all phases of the work. He recorded under the date of September 1, 1834: *"I continued to preside over the Church, and in forwarding the building of the house of the Lord in Kirtland. I acted as foreman in the Temple stone quarry, and when other duties would permit, labored with my own hands"* (*History of the Church,* 2: 161).

Chapter 8

1834-1836

School of the Elders opened in Kirtland

Those Unusual Days in Kirtland

Covenant of "a Tenth"

Quorum of the Twelve Apostles— and Quorum of the Seventy are Called

Publication of New Scripture: Doctrine and Covenants / Papyrus Scrolls

Kirtland Temple Completed and Dedicated

These were exciting, unique, and special times in Kirtland. A small, lazy town was growing into an active community of people who enjoyed and helped each other. Of course, there were lots of ups-and-downs for the Latter-day Saints, but for the most part they did what they were to do—stay close to God and family.

In October 1834, the Church launched the first publication of *The Latter-day Saints Messenger and Advocate* periodical in Kirtland under Joseph's leadership. The earlier church newspaper published in Missouri was called the *Evening and Morning Star*. It was decided that another name would be more suitable for the Kirtland area. Since the name of the Church had lately been known as The Church of the Latter-day Saints, and since it was destined, at least for a season, to bear the disfavor and stigma of this world, it was no more than just that, a paper circulating the doctrines believed by the same, and advocating its character and rights, should be entitled: *The Latter-day Saints Messenger and Advocate* (*History of the Church,* 2: 167).

The relatively subdued voice of the new Church-sponsored publication was hardly a match for the loud, unceasing, and usually inaccurate anti-Mormon press, which would on an almost daily basis touch off a stream of half-truths or outright concocted lies against this resilient and high-spirited, ever-growing young religion. To a large extent, this campaign of defamation, mudslinging, and abuse was instigated and promoted by sectarian clergymen who were alarmed by the heavy inroads on their membership being made by the energetic proselyting of the Mormons.

At about this time, Joseph made preparations to teach the Elders in a special school. He prepared and delivered a series of *Lectures on Theology,* which were later published in the Doctrine and Covenants under the title *Lectures on Faith.* These were more than a simple doctrinal discourse on an important subject. They were intended to motivate the Prophet's followers to practice the powerful principles they taught. To demonstrate this point, the following is a statement on faith that the Prophet made in his early ministry: *"It is the privilege of every Elder to speak of the things of God; and could we all come together with one heart and one mind in perfect faith, the veil might as well be rent today as next week, or any other time, and if we will but cleanse ourselves and covenant before God, to serve Him, it is our privilege to have an assurance that God will protect us at all times"* (*Teachings of the Prophet Joseph Smith,* Deseret Book, 1976, p. 9).

The Prophet also taught that: *"FAITH comes by hearing the word of God, through the testimony of the servants of God."* He added that such a *"testimony is always attended by the Spirit of prophecy and revelation"* (*History of the Church,* 3: 379).

In stressing the principle of faith, Joseph did not have in mind an ineffectual and unfruitful memorization of the recorded scriptures on the subject. Preferably, he intended that the Saints would use it as a principle of power and achievement. It was customary that he remind them that through faith, *"worlds were framed by the word of God"* (Hebrews 11: 3), and that the Church and kingdom of God were to be built up in the latter days by the same means. He never became tired of looking back on the great achievements of the Prophets of old which were attained through the nurturing of this basic, underlying principle. It was his objective to instill in the Elders of the Church the same fearless, confident courage and iron will demonstrated by the saints in the early days.

The School of the Elders was not simply a forum where the students were taught theological concepts. It was a place where they learned the practical application of the principles, which they then taught to others. At this time, the concept of faith had not been officially classified as the first principle of the gospel. It was not until later that the Prophet voiced in a formal way the basic doctrines of the Church. One cannot read the scriptures prayerfully or reflect upon life's purpose and meaning however without recognizing that this concept lies at the root of all spiritual development.

The significance of the power of faith that the Prophet communicated to his followers is contained in this journal entry made in the latter part of 1834: *"No month ever found me more busily engaged than November; but as my life consisted of activity and unyielding exertions,* ***I made this my rule: 'When the Lord commands, do it'****"* (*History of the Church,* 2: 170).

At this time, the Prophet and the Church were besieged with heavy financial obligations. Construction of the temple, aid to the poor, financing of the printing press, assistance to the Saints who were struggling for survival in Missouri, and an abundance of other demands for money, made him especially mindful of the vital need to be out of debt, and to have the necessary means to do his work. Having received the sum of $430 from some of the brethren in the East, which helped to ease the financial burdens minimally, the Prophet joined with Oliver Cowdery in a special prayer on November 29, 1834 *"for continuance of blessings."* After *"rejoicing before the Lord on this occasion,"* they entered into the following covenant with the Lord, which had far-reaching implications, not only for them and their families, but also for the entire membership of the Church at that day, and in the years ahead. The **covenant** reads . . . *"we agreed to enter into the following covenant with the Lord, viz.:*

That if the Lord will prosper us in our business and open the way before us that we may obtain means to pay our debts, that we be not troubled nor brought into disrepute before the world, nor His people; after that, of all that He shall give unto us, we will give a tenth to be bestowed upon the poor in His Church, or as He shall command; and that we will be faithful over that which He has entrusted to our care, that we may obtain much; and that our children after us shall remember to observe this sacred and holy covenant; and that our children, and our children's children, may know of the same, we have subscribed our names with our own hands" (*History of the Church,* 2: 174-75).

Probably, even more remarkable than this unusual covenant, was *a prayer* the Prophet later composed and included in his record, referring to this meaningful event:

A PRAYER

"And now, O Father, as Thou didst prosper our father Jacob [Old Testament], *and bless him with protection and prosperity wherever he went, from the time he made a similar covenant, before and with Thee; that Thou didst even the same night, open the heavens unto him and show great mercy and power, and give him promises, wilt Thou do so with us his sons; and as his blessings prevailed above his progenitors unto the utmost bounds of the everlasting hills, even so may our blessings prevail like his; and may Thy servants be preserved from the power and influence of wicked and unrighteous men; may every weapon formed against us fall upon the head of him who shall form it; may we be blessed with a name and a place among Thy Saints here, and Thy sanctified when they shall rest. Amen"* (*History of the Church,* 2: 175).

This wonderfully prayerful experience opens a gateway into the innermost depths of the Prophet's soul. We recognize a man with a childlike faith in the reality and power of God and with confidence that God would deal with him as He had dealt with the great prophets of the Old Testament. Whatever Joseph's motivation, determination, and intentions may have been, there can be no doubt about the meaning and importance to himself of what he did. **He made a solemn pledge that thereafter, he would pay a tenth** *"of all that He shall give unto us"* **for the benefit of *"the poor in His Church"*** or *"as He shall command."* He also pled that his children after him, would remember to observe *"this sacred and holy covenant."*

This unique covenant was actually the forerunner of a general covenant, a commandment given to all members of the Church, by revelation a few years later. There had been previous references to the ancient **Law of Tithing** in modern revelations given to Joseph, but it was not until 1838 at Far West, Missouri, that it was given to the Saints in Zion as *"a standing law unto them forever,"* and to be *"an example unto all the stakes of Zion"* (Doctrine & Covenants 119).

In both the Old and New Testaments, the Bible proclaims tithing as a law of the Lord to His people (Gen. 14: 17-20; Mal. 3; Matt. 23: 23; Luke 11: 42; Heb. 7: 4-9).

The involvement of Oliver Cowdery in this significant experience signaled his return to a position of high leadership in the Church. A revelation received in April 1830, when the Church was officially organized, had called Oliver *"the second elder"* of the Church (Doctrine & Covenants 20: 3; *History of the Church,* 2: 176). In the meantime, he had spent most of his time in Missouri, far removed from the center of power that naturally gravitated around the Prophet. Now it was like old times, finding these two young men together again, joining in solemn covenant to obey the ancient law of tithing and receiving the great blessings for obedience that God had promised to the prophets of an earlier time. Their joint participation in this event without question stirred many memories of past epic events that had bound them together with special, enduring bonds no one else could share. Nothing but their own disobedience could sever those bonds. Yet even while serving with selfless dedication amidst the severe trials of Missouri, Oliver must have wondered about his status in the Church when the Prophet selected Sidney Rigdon and Frederick G. Williams as his counselors. Any question that Oliver may have been concerned about in this respect, was answered on December 5, 1834, when, without any warning or note of preparation, the Prophet ordained him as an assistant president of the Church. The minutes of the meeting at which this event took place, make it plain that the failure of the Prophet to bring Oliver into the inner circle of the Church sooner, resulted solely from Oliver's absence (*History of the Church,* 2: 176).

If the events of the past that the Prophet and Oliver reviewed were considered inspiring and unique—the ones that they would face in the months ahead were designed to produce feelings of awe, wonder, and amazement.

QUORUM OF THE TWELVE APOSTLES

One of the most important and meaningful events in the Restoration of the Messiah's Church was the formation of the **Quorum of the Twelve Apostles**. Before the Church was organized, the members had hoped for and expected this significant step. Joseph Smith and Oliver Cowdery had received the authority of the apostleship (see Doctrine & Covenants 20: 2-3), probably as early as 1829. During that same year, a revelation directed Oliver Cowdery and David Whitmer to search out the twelve who would be *"called to go into all the world, to preach my gospel unto every creature"* (Doctrine & Covenants 18: 28). Later, Martin Harris was also called to assist in this selection. This meant that the three original witnesses to the Book of Mormon, under the direction and consent of the First Presidency of the Church, would choose the Twelve Apostles, who were to serve as special witnesses of the Savior in this dispensation. The modern-day Twelve Apostles we speak of are like the Twelve Apostles chosen by the Savior during His ministry to carry His word to all the world (see Matthew 10: 1-5).

What is an apostle and what are his duties? Jesus Christ is the great Apostle of the Church (see Heb. 3: 1). This means, not that He held the ordained office of Apostle in the Melchizedek Priesthood, but that He Himself stands as a special witness of His own divine mission. *"I am the Son of God"* is the witness He bears of Himself (Doctrine & Covenants 45: 52; also see John 10: 36). An apostle is a special witness of Christ, who is sent to teach the principles of salvation to others. He is one who knows of the divinity of the Savior by personal revelation, and who is appointed to bear testimony to the world of what the Lord has revealed to him.

Every Elder in the Church is or should be an apostle; that is, as a minister of the Lord, and as a recipient of personal revelation from the Holy Ghost, every Elder has the call to bear witness of the truth on all proper occasions. Indeed, every member of the Church should have apostolic insight and revelation, and is under obligation to raise the warning voice: *"Behold, I sent you out to testify and warn the people, and it becometh every man who hath been warned to warn his neighbor"* (Doctrine & Covenants 88: 81; Mosiah 18: 9).

In the ordained sense, an apostle is one who is ordained to the office of apostle in the Melchizedek Priesthood. Ordinarily, those so ordained are also set apart as members of the Council of the Twelve, and are given all of the keys of the kingdom of God on earth. This apostleship carries the responsibility of proclaiming the Gospel to all the world, and also of administering the affairs of the Church. **Christ *"chose twelve, whom also he named apostles"*** (Luke 6: 13), and upon their shoulders, the burden of the kingdom rested after He ascended to His Father (1 Cor. 12: 28). The original Twelve in the latter days were selected by revelation by the three Witnesses to the Book of Mormon (Doctrine & Covenants 18: 26-47).

For over five and a half years, the revelation pertaining to the calling of Twelve Apostles had lain dormant because the need did not yet exist for the special services of such a body. The Prophet was certain now, however, that the call of the Twelve was both timely and necessary, and he went forth with preparations to put it into effect. In the formation of both the Quorum of the Twelve and the Quorum of the Seventy, which occurred at about the same time, he referred not only to Section eighteen of the Doctrine and Covenants, but also to visions he had received on the subject (*History of the Church,* 2: 182, 202).

On Sunday, February 8, 1835, Joseph called both Brigham Young and Joseph Young to his house in Kirtland. The Prophet began to speak of the men who went to Missouri in Zion's Camp, and those who died in the plague of cholera. The Lord had shown to him a vision of the spirit world, and the happiness of those who had died while on that journey; and the Prophet said: *"If I get a mansion as bright as theirs, I ask no more."*

As he spoke of this, he wept. Then he began a heart-to-heart talk with Brigham Young, asking him to call all of the brethren to a special conference on the following Saturday, February 14, 1835, Valentine's Day. *"I shall then and there, appoint twelve Special Witnesses to open the door of the Gospel to foreign nations, and you,"* he said to Brigham, *" you will be one of them."*

As the time drew near for calling the Twelve, attention was focused on those who comprised Zion's Camp. Where else in the entire Church could be found men who, by their deeds, had demonstrated their willingness to serve with full purpose of heart, by laying their lives on the line? It was from this group then, that the twelve men would be selected for membership in this unique quorum.

The Three Witnesses were called upon to pray in order. Then they were blessed *"by the laying on of the hands of the Presidency,"* following which they called up, ordained, and blessed the Twelve (*History of the Church,* 2: 182). Because they were all called at the same time, the Apostles' seniority in the quorum was set according to age, the oldest being Thomas Marsh in his thirty-fifth year. Lyman E. Johnson, three of the younger brethren were twenty-three years of age. Joseph then asked the rest of the congregation if they were willing that these men be called. They voted their approval.

An insight into the enthusiasm shown on this occasion is further increased from the following excerpt of the blessing conferred upon Brigham Young: *"He shall go forth from land to land, and from sea to sea; and shall behold heavenly messengers going forth; and his life shall be prolonged; and the Holy Priesthood is conferred on him, that he may do wonders in the name of Jesus; that he may cast out devils, heal the sick, raise the dead, open the eyes of the blind; and that heathen nations shall even call him God himself, if he does not rebuke them"* (*History of the Church,* 2: 87-88).

Little did these Twelve realize the great pressures to which they would be exposed to, and the trials they would be called upon to endure. Only three of them, David W. Patten, Brigham Young, and Heber C. Kimball were to remain confidently, unwaveringly and most assuredly true to the high standards of the apostleship set for them at the time of their call. Unfortunately, David W. Patten was to suffer a martyr's death within four years, so that only the two courageous and inspired Apostles, Brigham Young and Heber C. Kimball, who later led the exodus westward, endured to the end.

One week after their selection, the Twelve received an apostolic charge from Oliver Cowdery, similar to the one the Savior gave the New Testament Apostles. "*Go ye therefore, and teach all nations, baptizing them in the name of the Father, and the Son, and the Holy Ghost; Teaching them to observe all things whatsoever I have commanded you: and, lo, I am with you always, even unto the end of the world"* (Matt. 10; 28: 19-20; Acts 1: 8). They will have to combat all the prejudices of all nations.

Oliver Cowdery then read the revelation located in Doctrine and Covenants Section eighteen saying:

"I therefore warn you to cultivate great humility; for I know the pride of the human heart. Beware, lest the flatterers of the world lift you up; beware, lest your affections be captivated by worldly objects. Let your ministry be first.

"It is necessary that you receive a testimony from heaven for yourselves; so that you can bear testimony to the truth.

"You are to bear this message to those who consider themselves wise; and such may persecute you—they may seek your life. The adversary has always sought the life of the servants of God; you are therefore to be prepared at all times to make a sacrifice of your lives, should God require them in the advancement and building up of his cause.

"He then took them separately by the hand, and said, 'Do you with full purpose of heart take part in this ministry, to proclaim the Gospel with all diligence, with these your brethren, according to the tenor and intent of the charge you have received?' Each answered in the affirmative" (*History of the Church,* 2: 195-96; 198).

The reactions of the Twelve to this impressive teaching and learning session, was as the Prophet had anticipated. His lifetime of experiences with spiritual beings and events demonstrated the passion and enthusiasm that they produce. He had learned by experience, nevertheless, that his natural high spirits had to be tempered with discipline and order to produce any lasting good. In reviewing his own experiences, he noted that he had procrastinated especially in keeping accurate records of important events. A notable example of this neglect was the fact that he had failed to record the exact date upon which the resurrected apostles Peter, James, and John had conferred the Melchizedek Priesthood upon him and Oliver Cowdery. While he retained a bright recollection of the incident itself and of the important things that transpired during the course of it, his memory was vague about the precise date it occurred. Years later, when pressed to provide the specifics, the best he could do was report that it happened sometime in the late spring or early summer of 1829. (It should be noted, that his failure to mention a specific date on which this visitation occurred, lends credit to his account. Had he been of a temperament to mislead or misrepresent, it would have been simple for him to have picked a date at random—any date—in order to satisfy his critics. But the fact still remains that he had forgotten it, and since he had failed to make a record at the time, his only recourse was to deal in generalities.) It was, therefore, with this and other similar events in mind that the Prophet Joseph felt prompted to impart some words of counsel to the newly selected members of the Twelve:

"Since the Twelve are now chosen, I wish to tell them about a course which hopefully they will pursue. If they will, every time they assemble, appoint a person to preside over them during the meeting, and one or more to keep a record of their proceedings, and on the decision of every question or item, be it what it may, let such decision be written, and such decision will forever remain upon record, and appear an item of covenant of doctrine."

Here is another important item from the Prophet: *"If you assemble from time to time, and proceed to discuss important questions, and pass decisions upon the same, and fail to note them down, soon you will be driven to difficulties and much embarrassment from which you will not be able to liberate yourselves, because you may be in a situation, not to bring your faith to bear with sufficient perfection or power, to obtain the desired information; or, perhaps, for neglecting to write these things when God had revealed them, not esteeming them of sufficient worth, the Spirit may withdraw and God may be angry."*

The Prophet then added this significant prophecy: *"Here let me prophesy. The time will come, when, if you neglect to do this thing, you will fall by the hands of unrighteous men. Were you to be brought before the authorities, and be accused of any crime or misdemeanor, and be as innocent as the angels of God, unless you can prove yourselves to have been somewhere else, your enemies will prevail against you; but if you can bring twelve men to testify, that you were in a certain place at that time, you will escape their hand"* (*History of the Church,* 2: 198-99).

THE SEVENTY QUORUM

Two weeks later at a special conference, the Prophet organized another key Priesthood quorum—**the Seventy**—from those who had been in Zion's Camp (Doctrine & Covenants 107: 93). To accommodate their unique role as **a "traveling" quorum,** with responsibility to preach the Gospel worldwide, they were presided over by seven presidents. This was according to a vision of Church organization given to the Prophet (*History of the Church,* 2: 181, 201-2).

What is a Seventy, and what are his duties? One of the ordained offices in the holy Melchizedek Priesthood (higher Priesthood) is that of a Seventy. Seventies are Elders with all the powers of Elders, plus a special call and ordination *"to preach the gospel, and to be especial witnesses unto the Gentiles and in all the world—"* (Doctrine & Covenants 107: 25). As the Lord's *"traveling ministers, unto the Gentiles first, and also unto the Jews"* (Doctrine & Covenants 107: 97).

Speaking of the First Quorum of Seventy, the Lord says: *"The Seventy are to act in the name of the Lord, under the direction of the Twelve or the traveling high council, in building up the church, and regulating all the affairs of the same in all nations, first unto the Gentiles, and then to the Jews . . . It is the duty of the traveling high council to call upon the Seventy, when they need assistance, to fill the several calls for preaching and administering the gospel, instead of any others"* (Doctrine & Covenants 107: 34, 38). It appears from the Old Testament account that at least from the days of Moses, the Elders of Israel have been ordained Seventies and given special Priesthood blessings and obligations. It was the *"seventy of the elders of Israel"* who went up with Moses, Aaron, Nadab, and Abihu—*"And they saw the God of Israel,"* thus certainly becoming especial witnesses of His name (Ex. 24: 1-11). And when the Lord gave Moses additional administrative help to aid in bearing the burdens of the multitudes of Israel, it was the seventy whom he chose. *"I will come down and talk with thee,"* the Lord said to Moses, *"and I will take of the spirit which is upon thee, and will put it upon them; and they shall bear the burden of the people with thee, that thou bear it not thyself alone"* (Num. 11: 17). Those seventy became mighty prophets in Israel.

In the Meridian of Time, our Lord *"appointed other seventy also, and sent them two and two before his face into every city and place, whither he himself would come."* He gave them pointed missionary direction, they performed their labors, the very devils were subject unto them, and they rejoiced because their names were written in heaven (Luke 10: 1-24). The indication is clear that these *"other seventy"* were in addition to previous quorums organized for like purposes (Doctrine & Covenants 107: 95).

Joseph Young, brother of Brigham Young, was ordained as senior president of the First Quorum of the Seventy at this time.

A month later, the Lord revealed additional information concerning Priesthood and Church government. The Twelve, who were preparing to depart on their missions shortly, felt they had not fully accepted the weighty responsibilities of their calling. In a spirit of repentance, they petitioned the Prophet to ask the Lord, once again, for further guidance. In response, the Lord instructed the Twelve and the Seventy on their respective responsibilities. The Twelve were to be *"special witnesses of the name of Christ,"* and serve under the direction of the First Presidency to *"build up the church, and regulate all the affairs of the same in all nations"* (Doctrine & Covenants 107: 23, 33). **The Seventy were to serve under the direction of the Twelve** and accomplish the same purpose. Together with the First Presidency, these quorums constituted the presiding councils of the Church. The revelation also outlined the duties of those who preside over the various quorums of the Priesthood, and it closed with this admonition: *"Wherefore, now let every man learn his duty, and to act in the office in which he is appointed, in all diligence. He that is slothful* [lazy], *shall not be counted worthy to stand"* (Doctrine & Covenants 107: 99-100).

In compliance with instructions given in the revelation, the first Aaronic Priesthood quorums were formed in 1835 in Kirtland. They were made up of mature men. There were no set ages for worthy candidates to advance from one office to another.

In the light of instructions in Doctrine and Covenants 107, the *"standing"* stake High Councils assumed an increasingly important role during the mid-1830s, particularly in the capacity of Church courts. Questions soon arose concerning the status and jurisdiction of the High Councils and of the Twelve, who were referred to as "a Traveling Presiding High Council" (Doctrine & Covenants 107: 33).

The Prophet responded that the authority of the standing High Councils was limited to the stakes, while the Twelve had the jurisdiction over the Church abroad (*History of the Church,* 2: 220). This raised the additional question about the jurisdiction of the Twelve in local matters. The Prophet assured them that since they stood next to the First Presidency in authority, they were not subject to any other body. Brigham Young later looked back on these months of discussion as a time of trial, when the Twelve had to prove their willingness "to be everybody's servant for Christ's sake. 'This was necessary,' according to Young, for only 'true servants' may receive the power."

* * *

Not to go too far afield from the present subject matter, just take a moment or two with me, to briefly touch on another important aspect of Joseph Smith's life. With all the reading you've done thus far, doesn't it seem ridiculous and absurd for people in general to label The Church of Jesus Christ of Latter-day Saints a cult? A cult denotes a kind of unusual worship, devotion, ritual, or dogma to a person, cause or thing, that does not have a belief in the existence of a God or Gods or belief in the existence of one God, the Father of us all, which is viewed as the creative source of man and the world in the principle. The cult is known to be somewhat faddish in practice, ie., cult of nature, cult of Satan, the worship of people in the entertainment world (music, television, motion pictures, sports, etc.), following for a time with exaggerated zeal and reverence. The cult follower is regarded as extreme, as well as one who dissents from the normal, accepted everyday religious belief. The cultural shock today is the increase in the number of different things and people that consider money to be their god. And the real God, the true and living God could likely be saying, "how about me, where do I fit into your lives-don't you want or need me?"

The Church of Jesus Christ, as you have found thus far, worships God the Eternal Father in the name of His Only Begotten Son Jesus Christ. They do not follow the same form of worship of Jesus Christ as do the majority of Christian Churches throughout the world. That may make the Church of Jesus Christ different from other churches, but certainly not wrong in its beliefs, practices and worship. The Church lives by and believes in the Holy Scriptures: Old Testament, New Testament (King James Version), and the Book of Mormon (A Second Witness that Jesus is the Christ), under the direction of God and Jesus Christ, it is guided by a Prophet of God and Twelve Apostles, as well as others called to serve. As you have read, Joseph Smith was called by God and Jesus Christ as the Prophet of the Restored Church and Gospel of Jesus Christ in this, the Seventh and Last Dispensation of the Fulness of Times.

Why would a man get caught up in a religious revival, claim to be called by God as a Prophet, and surround himself with a multitude of people that endeavored to help him spread the true Gospel of Jesus Christ, if his desire in life was fame and fortune? There are so many other ways to dupe the public than by claiming revelation from God, seeing angels and messengers from God and Jesus Christ. To claim that Joseph was a deceiver just doesn't make any sense to me. Certainly not from the facts you've read thus far . . . the Saints were constantly on the run, driven from one community to another by intense persecution because of their desire for religious freedom and their determination to build good communities in order to raise their families. And there's nothing wrong with those desires.

* * *

The program of organized proselyting had been temporarily interrupted by Zion's Camp in the summer of 1834. During the fall, however, missionary work resumed as Church leaders called more and more men to fill missions. Some of them spent only a few weeks in nearby communities. Others worked longer periods proclaiming the Gospel in distant areas. Many of the missionaries served more than one mission, often leaving home at times that were personally inconvenient and untimely. In 1836, William W. Phelps wrote: *"The Elders are constantly coming and going"* (Journal, *History of the Church,* June 2, 1835).

Formal missions were added to by the efforts of enthusiastic converts who were eager to share their newly-found treasure of spiritual wealth with family and friends. New convert, Caroline Crosby exclaimed: *"How often while listening to the voice of the Prophet have I wished, Oh that my friends, parents, brothers, and sisters, could hear the things that I have heard, and their hearts be made to rejoice in them, as mine did"* (*Caroline Crosby Journal,* SLC, Deseret Book, 1982, pp. 49-50).

Many leaders of the Church were also involved in missionary service. The Prophet Joseph Smith went to Michigan in 1834 and 1835. The most important effort was the five-month mission of the Quorum of the Twelve to the East in 1835. From May to September, they traveled hundreds of miles throughout New York, New England, and Canada. Besides doing missionary work and regulating and strengthening local congregations, their assignment included acquiring funds for temple construction, for purchase of lands in Zion, and for the printing purposes of the church. **Traveling without purse or scrip,** they experienced the usual problems of persecution, rejection, fatigue and hunger; nevertheless, at one large meeting, they counted about 144 carriages, and estimated that from 2-3,000 people attended.

This mission is significant in Church history, since it is the only time that all twelve members of the Quorum undertook a mission together. Upon their return to Kirtland, Heber C. Kimball reported that they had felt God's power, and were able to heal the sick and cast out devils (*History of the*

Church, 2: 222-26). In this same period, the Quorum of the Seventy also filled missions, primarily in the Eastern States.

During the mid-1830s, many Church leaders served numerous individual missions. Elder Parley P. Pratt's Canadian mission is a notable example. In April 1836, fellow Apostle Heber C. Kimball blessed Parley, and prophesied that he would go to Toronto, and there "find a people prepared for the fulness of the Gospel, and they shall receive thee, and it shall spread thence into the regions round about; and from the things growing out of this mission, shall the fulness of the Gospel spread into England, and cause a great work to be done in that land" (Pratt, *Autobiography Parley P. Pratt,* p. 110). While Parley was in Hamilton en route to Toronto, a stranger gave him a letter of introduction to John Taylor, a Methodist lay preacher in Toronto. Taylor was affiliated with a group who believed existing churches did not correspond with New Testament Christianity. For two years, this group had met several times a week for the "purpose of seeking truth, independent of any sectarian organization." In Toronto, Elder Pratt was courteously received by the Taylors, but they were not at first enthusiastic about his message (Pratt, *Autobiography Parley P. Pratt,* pp. 113-19).

Discouraged at being unable to find a place to preach, Parley decided to leave Toronto. Before going, he dropped in at the Taylors to get some of his luggage, and say good-bye. While he was there, Leonora Taylor told her friend, Mrs. Isabella Walton about Parley's problem and said she was sorry he was leaving. "He may be a man of God," she said. Mrs. Walton replied that she had been inspired by the Spirit to visit the Taylors that morning because she was willing to let Elder Pratt stay at her home and preach. He did so, and was eventually invited to attend a meeting of John Taylor's group, in which John read the New Testament account of Philip's preaching in Samaria. "'Now,' said he, 'where is our Philip? Where is our receiving the Word with joy, and being baptized when we believed? Where is our Peter and John? Our Apostles? Where is our Holy Ghost by the laying on of hands?'" (Pratt, *Autobiography Parley P. Pratt,* p. 119). When Parley was invited to speak, he declared that he had answers to John Taylor's questions.

For the better part of three weeks, John Taylor attended Elder Pratt's meetings making detailed notes of his sermons, and carefully comparing them with the scriptures. Gradually he became convinced that the true Gospel of Jesus Christ had been restored. He and his wife, Leonora, were baptized on May 9, 1836. Soon thereafter, John Taylor was ordained an Elder, and became an active missionary. The work spread so rapidly that Orson Hyde was sent from Kirtland to assist Parley, while Orson Pratt and Freeman Nickerson, who were already in Canada, joined Parley in Toronto. When the missionaries left Toronto, John Taylor was set apart to preside over the congregations these Elders had established.

The Fielding family, who also became important in the history of the Church, was part of this Canadian harvest. Mary Fielding later married Hyrum Smith, brother of the Prophet Joseph, and became the mother of the sixth and grandmother of the tenth Presidents of the Church—Joseph F. Smith and Joseph Fielding Smith, respectively. A year after his baptism, Mary's brother Joseph joined the first missionaries to Britain, and played a key role in establishing the work there.

Missionaries in other areas also enjoyed rich spiritual experiences. Wilford Woodruff, for example, went to Missouri in 1834 at the age of twenty-seven. That fall, he was ordained a priest and sent to Arkansas and Tennessee as one of the earliest missionaries to carry the Gospel to those regions. In later years, he testified often that: "in all his life, he never had enjoyed more of the Spirit and power of God than when he was a priest doing missionary work in the Southern States."

Gradually, congregations sprang up throughout the Northeast, the Midwest, and Eastern Canada, and eventually the Gospel spread into West Virginia, Kentucky, and Tennessee. At first, local groups were called churches, but by 1835, the term branch was common. Usually, several branches joined together for periodic conferences, and in 1835, the Twelve organized them into districts, called conferences, each having definite boundaries like modern stakes.

As Joseph Smith turned from the challenges of organization and administration, he began focusing on doctrinal matters and gospel truths. Foremost in his thinking was the publication of a compilation of revelations he had received over the years, which was called at the time the Book of Commandments. The Missouri persecutions had disrupted the publication of this book in 1833. Steps were taken in Ohio to publish an expanded compilation of the revelations. In September 1834, the First Presidency was appointed to select the revelations to be published, and the Prophet revised some of them to correct printing errors and to add information revealed since 1833. The following summer the committee's work was completed. In 1835, another standard work of the Church was published. On August 17, 1835, a general assembly was convened in Kirtland, when the volume now called the **Doctrine and Covenants,** was accepted to "become a law and a rule of faith and practice to the Church" (*History of the Church,* 2: 243).

Not only was there a general acceptance of the book by the assembly, but by every branch of the Church leadership who bore witness of the divine origin of the revelations it contained. Characteristic of these testimonies were manifest in the one given by the Quorum of the Twelve:

"We therefore feel willing to bear our testimony [witness] to all the world of mankind, to every creature upon the face of all the earth, that the Lord has borne record to our souls, through the Holy Ghost shed forth upon us, that these Commandments were given by inspiration of God, and are profitable for all men, and are verily true. We give this testimony unto the world, the Lord being our helper; and it is through the grace of God, the Father, and His Son Jesus Christ, that we are permitted to have this privilege of bearing this testimony unto the world, in the which we rejoice exceedingly, praying the Lord always that the children of men may be profited thereby" (*History of the Church,* 2: 245).

Included in the book were the lectures on faith, which the Prophet had delivered to the Elders, a statement on the Church's attitude toward marriage, and a statement of government and laws.

With the publication of the Doctrine and Covenants and its distribution throughout the Church, Joseph now had a powerful tool for bringing about a uniformity of understanding and order with respect to doctrine and policies among the Saints. Most of the revelations had already been heretofore published, but only a small percentage of the members subscribed to the periodicals in which they appeared, and a still smaller percentage took the trouble to cut out and preserve them for future reference.

Now, the revelations, conveniently bound together in book form, could be purchased and retained by the Saints for recurrent use in the years ahead. They had become an essential tool in the hands of the missionaries. Here was objective evidence to support their insistence that a modern-day prophet had been raised up, who in the tradition of Israel's ancient prophets, spoke with power, influence, and authority in the name of God.

The Doctrine and Covenants' title referred to its two major divisions. The first part, designated ***"Doctrine,"*** included five Lectures on Faith, and a series of lectures on important doctrine of salvation which were delivered in the School of the Elders the previous winter. The second part, entitled ***"Covenants"*** included forty-five revelations in addition to those found in the "Book of Commandments" (Doctrine & Covenants, 1835 edition, pp. 5, 75). The book's Preface pointed out the differences between the theological lectures and the Lord's revelations (*History of the Church,* 2: 250-51). The distinction became the basis for a decision, in 1921, to publish the revelations without the Lectures on Faith, to avoid confusing readers about the status of the lectures.

Even though the Book of Mormon and the Doctrine and Covenants were accepted and designated as scripture, events began falling into place to usher in the third volume of scripture that Joseph Smith was to contribute to the body of religious literature and enlightenment.

It all began in a tomb on the west bank of the Nile River, across from the ancient Egyptian city of Thebes (now called Luxor). Antonio Lebolo, a French-speaking explorer from the Piedmont (a region of Northwestern Italy), discovered several mummies and along with them, some papyrus scrolls. Following the death of Lebolo in 1830, the mummies and papyri were shipped to the United States, where Michael H. Chandler, who identified himself as Lebolo's nephew, came into possession of them in 1833. In 1835, Chandler displayed his artifacts in several Eastern cities.

When he arrived in Kirtland at the end of June, the Saints showed great interest in the mummies and papyri. Chandler had heard that Joseph Smith claimed he could translate ancient records. He asked Joseph if he could translate the papyri. Orson Pratt recalled: "The Prophet took them and retired to his room, and inquired of the Lord concerning them. The Lord told him they were sacred records," and revealed the translation of some of the characters. Chandler had previously submitted a few characters from the records to some Eastern scholars in order to determine their probable meaning. Upon receiving the Prophet's translation, he provided a signed testimonial that it corresponded in the most minute matters with those of the scholars (*History of the Church,* 2: 235).

Greatly interested in their content, a group of Saints in Kirtland purchased the mummies and the scrolls, and presented them to Joseph. He immediately began translating the writings, using Oliver Cowdery and W. W. Phelps as scribes. The Prophet soon discovered to his surprise that the scrolls included accounts of the lives and ministries of Abraham, and of Joseph who was sold into Egypt. He continued translating the account of Abraham, which was later included in the third volume of latter-day scripture, the Pearl of Great Price. With the translation of this writing, he included a copy of some of the hieroglyphics found in the scrolls along with his English translation or interpretation, thereby intentionally providing the means by which scholars of his day or of some future time could appraise his abilities as a translator. (In November 1967, some of the scrolls acquired by the Prophet in 1835, came into the possession of the Church. Parts of these scrolls have since been translated by a noted scholar, who has uncovered evidence verifying Joseph's prophetic and linguistic claims.)

The writings of Abraham enlarge upon the concept of a pre-existent state. One especially striking passage, points to the "intelligences" that existed before the world was formed, and confirms that Abraham was one of a select group from among these, and was chosen for a leadership role before he was born (Pearl of Great Price, Abr. 3: 22-23). The writing also tells about Abraham's personal life, including the circumstances under which he obtained Priesthood authority from God. Finally, it touches on the subject of Celestial astronomy and makes reference to the realm in which God dwells.

During the remainder of his time in Kirtland, Joseph maintained an active interest in working with these ancient writings. The fruit of his efforts, the Book of Abraham, was not printed however, until 1842, after more translating was completed in Nauvoo. In February 1843, the Prophet promised to provide more of the translation of the Book of Abraham, but his demanding schedule did not allow him the time to complete the work before he was assassinated.

During the mid-1830s, Kirtland developed into a sizable Latter-day Saint community. While the number of nonmembers in the community remained relatively unchanged at about twelve to thirteen hundred, the number of Saints almost tripled, growing from nearly 500 to about 1,500 between 1834 and 1837. As time progressed, the Church and its activities were having a greater influence on community life. At times this led to tensions between the two different lifestyles and ideologies.

While most of the Saints were grateful and pleased for such remarkable and memorable events as the calling of the Twelve Apostles and the publication of the Doctrine and Covenants, their day-to-day lives were centered on earning a living on the farm or in town. Despite long hours of hard physical work, the Saints found time for some recreation, education, and worship.

Although leisure time was limited, the Kirtland Saints enjoy hunted, fishing, swimming, and horseback riding. Wintertime favorites included ice skating and sleigh riding. Family relationships were especially important to the Saints. After a long day's work, parents and children often enjoyed the evening together, singing, playing, studying, and discussing topics of common interest.

The Saints considered education essential, and the home was the setting for most of the learning. Private tutors, such as Eliza R. Snow, who lived with Joseph Smith's family while tutoring his children, were common. Occasionally, teachers offered their services for private classes in a home or community building.

Following the early efforts of the School of the Prophets in 1833, the School of the Elders met during the next two winters, when the men were not so busy with their farming or missionary assignments. The meetings took place in a 30 x 38 foot room on the main floor of the printing building, just west of the temple. Its purpose was to prepare the men, who were about to go forth as missionaries, or to serve in other Church callings. The curriculum included English grammar, writing, philosophy, government, literature, geography, and ancient—as well as modern—history. Theology, nevertheless, received the major emphasis.

An important outgrowth of the School of the Elders was a Hebrew school conducted from January to April of 1836, under the direction of a young Hebrew instructor named Joshua Seixas. He was contracted for $320 to teach about forty students for seven weeks. Interest was greater than expected, and so two additional classes were organized. After Seixas left, interest in Hebrew continued. W. W. Phelps, for example, often shared his translations from the Hebrew Bible with his friends (*History of the Church,* 2: 355-56).

The Prophet Joseph Smith was particularly enthusiastic about his study of Hebrew. He declared: *"My soul delights in reading the word of the Lord in the original"* (*History of the Church,* 2: 396).

One young nonmember, Lorenzo Snow, from nearby Mantua, Ohio, attended the Hebrew school. One day, while on his way to Oberlin College, Lorenzo met Elder David W. Patten. Their conversation turned to religion, and Elder Patten's sincerity and testimony made a lasting impression on Lorenzo. He was therefore receptive when his sister Eliza, a recent convert, invited him to attend the school. While there, Lorenzo became acquainted with the Prophet Joseph and other Church leaders, and was baptized in June 1836. He subsequently became the fifth Prophet and President of The Church of Jesus Christ of Latter-day Saints.

It must be noted that Sabbath worship was central in the lives of the early Latter-day Saints. Many people gathered enough firewood and completed other chores on Saturday, so they could devote Sunday to spiritual matters. They met in homes, and later in schools for their services, but during warm weather, they gathered outdoors. Sunday meetings were simple. The morning meeting normally began at 10:00 a.m. with a hymn and prayer, followed by one or two sermons. The afternoon service was similar, but usually included the administration of the Sacrament. Occasionally, confirmations and marriages were performed during these gatherings.

The first Thursday of each month was a fast day. In meetings that often lasted six hours, the Saints, sang, prayed, bore their testimonies describing divine personal revelations in their lives, and urged and counseled each other to live the Gospel. Eliza R. Snow fondly remembered these gatherings as: "Hallowed and interesting beyond the power of language to describe." Week nights were also filled with Priesthood quorum meetings, preaching services, or meetings where patriarchal blessings were given.

Music has always been an important part in the Saints worship. The July 1830, revelation that directed Emma Smith, Joseph's wife, to compile a hymnbook for the Church resulted in a small book that finally appeared in 1835. It included the words for ninety hymns (thirty-four that were written by Church members), and bore testimony of the Restoration. The remainder of the hymns were collected from popular contemporary hymnals. No music was printed in the hymnbook. The Saints sang the hymns to popular tunes, and many times, branches and choirs used a variety of melodies for the same hymns. Several of the hymns selected by Emma Smith, with the assistance of W. W. Phelps, are still in the present hymnbook.

The Church of Jesus Christ, the

Prophet Joseph Smith, and the Latter-day Saint Church were the topics of conversation throughout the country due to its unique approach to religious belief. There was an almost endless stream of people making their way to Kirtland to see the Mormon Prophet in person. Among them were believers and non-believers, scoffers and adulators, the righteous and the wicked. Their appraisals of the Prophet were as diverse as their own personalities, but upon one point they were all in agreement: they had been in the presence of an unusual man who did not fit into the common, everyday mold.

There were many revealing insights into Joseph's character and his unwavering knowledge of the existence of God and of the fact that God hears and answers the fervent prayers of His children on earth. The Prophet knew how to use prayer as a tool in attaining righteous objectives and in learning the mind and will of the Lord. Nothing was too insignificant for him to make a matter of prayer. In fact, as his understanding matured and his experiences multiplied, he became even more reliant upon the Lord through prayer. This had two significant results. First, the longer Joseph served in the ministry, the clearer it became to him that he was an agent, not a principal. Therefore, it became incumbent upon him to ascertain in each instance what his principal, the Lord, would have him do. And second, through long experience, and from a study of the scriptures, he became absolutely convinced of the essential partnership that must exist between God and man. On the one hand, he recognized that God is all-knowing, and all powerful, the Creator of the earth and the Father of our spirits. Yet he knew also that earth life is a testing or proving ground for man, and that out of God's great respect for the integrity and independence of His children, He does not or will not intervene in their lives without invitation. It was intended from the beginning that men would have their **"free agency"** and that the condition upon which God would enter their lives was that they would invite Him in. Joseph understood this principle well, and he applied it frequently and effectively. He recognized that God, through His Omniscience (all-knowing), and His infinite love for men, was better able than he to chart a safe course through any difficulty. And knowing that God would not upbraid or criticize him for asking, Joseph continued to the end of his life the practice of imploring Him for guidance or comfort. It is significant that his last reported words, uttered just before he fell from the second-story window of the Carthage jail, where he was fatally shot, were *"O Lord, my God!"* (*History of the Church,* 6: 618).

For about three years, the time and energies of the Kirtland Saints were devoted to the building of the first temple of this dispensation. This endeavor began in December 1832 when the Lord commanded them to: *"establish a house, even a house of prayer, a house of fasting, a house of faith, a house of learning, a house of glory, a house of order, a house of God"* (Doctrine & Covenants 88: 119). Five months later, the Lord chastised the Church for their delay and admonished them to move forward with the building of the temple (Doctrine & Covenants 95). The Saints then faithfully devoted themselves to the task at hand.

In addition to their great personal efforts, the Saints received several thousand dollars in contributions to help complete the temple. Because they were so willing to sacrifice their all in building the temple, the Lord poured out great blessings upon them. From

January 21 to May 1, 1836, "probably more Latter-day Saints witnessed visions and other unusual spiritual revelations, than during any other era in the history of the Church." Members of the Church saw heavenly messengers in at least ten different meetings, and at five of these gatherings, different individuals testified that they had seen the Savior Himself.

Some of the most memorable spiritual experiences occurred on the day the temple was dedicated, Sunday, March 27, 1836. Hundreds of Latter-day Saints came to Kirtland, anticipating the great blessings the Lord had promised to confer upon them. Early on the morning of the temple dedication, hundreds of people gathered outside the temple hoping to attend the dedicatory service. The doors opened at 8:00 a.m., and the First Presidency assisted in seating the congregation of nearly a 1,000 people. When the leaders of the Church were seated at the elevated pulpits and benches at each end of the hall and when all the available seats in the temple were filled, the doors were closed. This left hundreds of people still outside, including many who had sacrificed tremendously for the temple's construction and had come long distances to attend the dedication. Sensing their disappointment, the Prophet directed the overflow to the schoolhouse just to the west, and the temple windows were opened to allow those on the grounds and in the schoolhouse to hear the service. The dedicatory service was repeated a second time the following Thursday for the benefit of those who had been unable to attend the first.

After the choir's opening hymn, President Sidney Rigdon spoke for two-and-a-half hours, declaring that the temple was unique among all the buildings of the world because it was built by divine revelation. After a brief intermission, the officers of the Church were sustained. The climax of the day was the dedicatory prayer, which had previously been given to the Prophet by revelation. He expressed gratitude for God's blessings and asked the Lord to accept the temple, which was built *"through great tribulation; . . . that the Son of Man might have a place to manifest himself to his people"* (Doctrine & Covenants 109: 5). He petitioned that the blessings promised in the Lord's initial command to build the temple (Doctrine & Covenants 88: 117-21), might now be realized, and he prayed that Church leaders, members, and the leaders of nations, would be blessed, and that the promised gathering of the scattered remnants of Israel would be accomplished (Doctrine & Covenants 109: 60-67). This prayer became a pattern for other temple dedicatory prayers.

Following the prayer, the choir sang the hymn: "The Spirit of God." It had been written especially for the dedication by W. W. Phelps. The Sacrament was then administered and passed to the congregation. Joseph Smith and others testified that they saw heavenly messengers at the service. The congregation concluded the seven-hour service by standing and rendering the sacred Hosanna Shout: "Hosanna, hosanna, hosanna to God and the Lamb, amen, amen, and amen," repeated three times. Eliza R. Snow said the shout was given "with such power as seemed almost sufficient to raise the roof from the building" (Morgan, *Eliza R. Snow,* p. 62).

That evening, over 400 Priesthood bearers met in the temple. While George A. Smith was speaking, "a noise was heard like the sound of a rushing, mighty wind which filled the Temple, and all the congregation simultaneously arose, being moved upon by an invisible power . . . **I beheld the Temple was filled**

with angels, which fact I declared to the congregation." We find in the journals of many who were in attendance at the services that night, that angels appeared in the congregations, and that heavenly choirs were heard. David Whitmer bore testimony that he saw three angels passing up the south aisle. "The people of the neighborhood came running together (hearing an unusual sound within, and seeing a bright light like a pillar of fire, resting upon the Temple), they were astonished at what was taking place." Others saw angels hovering over the temple and heard heavenly singing (*History of the Church,* 2: 428).

The most glorious spiritual manifestation of all occurred a week after the dedication. After the afternoon worship service, Joseph Smith and Oliver Cowdery hastened to the Melchizedek Priesthood pulpits in the west end of the lower room of the temple. The canvas partition, called a veil, was lowered so that they could pray in private. As they prayed— *"THE veil was taken from their minds, and the eyes of their understanding were opened"* (Doctrine & Covenants 110: 1). They saw a series of remarkable visions. The Lord Jesus Christ appeared, accepted the temple, and promised to appear Himself therein *"if my people will keep my commandments, and do not pollute this holy house"* (Doctrine & Covenants 110: 8).

Moses next appeared and restored *"the keys of the gathering of Israel from the four parts of the earth, and the leading of the ten tribes from the land of the north"* (v. 11). Elias then conferred *"the dispensation of the gospel of Abraham"* (v. 12). Finally, in fulfillment of Malachi's prophecy (Mal. 4: 5-6) and Moroni's promise (Doctrine & Covenants 2)— *"To turn the hearts of the fathers to the children, and the children to the fathers"* (Doctrine & Covenants 110: 15), Elijah appeared to the Prophet and Oliver, testifying that *"the keys of this dispensation are committed into your hands"* in preparation for *"the great and dreadful day of the Lord"* (v. 16). Through the sealing (confirmation) keys that were restored by Elijah, Latter-day Saints could now perform saving Priesthood ordinances in behalf of their kindred dead, as well as for the living. These sacred ordinances for the dead were not introduced to the members of the Church until the Nauvoo Era.

This great day of visions and revelations occurred on Easter Sunday, April 3, 1836. What better day in the Dispensation of the Fulness of Times to reconfirm the reality of the Resurrection? That weekend was also the Jewish Passover. For centuries, Jewish families have left an empty chair at their Passover feasts, anticipating Elijah's return. Elijah *has* returned—not to a Passover Feast, but to the Lord's temple in Kirtland.

The authority for doing temple work in the Church, which has grown to tremendous proportions today, is based upon this restoration of the keys of the Priesthood necessary to those functions, and especially upon the restoration of the keys held by Elijah.

The Kirtland Temple was not constructed for the ordinances referred to by Elijah. It contained no baptismal font for the work of the dead. Nor was it designed for other work now performed in Latter-day Saint temples. It was a holy meeting place. A place for instruction under the Spirit of God, a place of preparation for the great temple-building era which is now in full swing.

The period from the fall of 1834, through the summer of 1836, was one of glorious progress for the Church and it looked as if the momentum would continue. Nevertheless, dark and dreary days were still ahead for the Kirtland Saints, as forces from both within and without threatened the Church's growth and advancement.

For anyone with an open heart and mind, it is not difficult to believe and accept the truth, when it comes from God through His Prophets, and through personal revelation when one prays about it in the name of Jesus Christ, the Messiah and Savior of the world. God does live; Jesus Christ lives; and the Holy Ghost lives also as our Comforter and Friend.

This Bible scripture offers a simple set of rules: ***"Ask, and it shall be given you; seek, and ye shall find; knock, and it shall be opened unto you: For every one that asketh receiveth; and he that seeketh findeth; and to him that knocketh it shall be opened"*** (Matthew 7: 7-8).

Chapter 9

1836 -1838
The Declining Kirtland Years

The Prophet Joseph and his Unique Team

Poverty in Kirtland
The Kirtland Safety Society
Financial Panic of 1837 hits Ohio
Economic Conditions Worsen

Apostasy in Kirtland

First Mission to Great Britain
Missionaries Preach the Gospel

Kirtland Camp
General Exodus from Kirtland
The Saints Journey to Missouri

The Search Continues

It doesn't seem possible to read and comprehend, with an open, fertile mind, the journals of such men as Heber C. Kimball, Brigham Young, Orson Pratt, Parley P. Pratt and Wilford Woodruff, who were intimately acquainted with Joseph Smith, without being impressed and excited by two meaningful and significant points. First, that these men were instilled with the same spiritual qualities held and enjoyed by the Prophet. They prophesied, they healed the sick and cast out devils, they had dreams and visions, and they followed without question, accepted without hesitation, and with obedience, "the whisperings of the Spirit." Although they were men of intellect, understanding, and wisdom, who were forceful and independent by nature, they were without exception, willing to yield their will to the inner promptings, sentiments, or impressions they received from the highest sources of power **God the Father, the Messiah Jesus Christ, and the Holy Ghost.**

The second aspect in their lives that deserves special attention is their persistence, endurance, steadfastness of purpose, and loyalty to the Prophet Joseph Smith. These men would routinely leave their families and friends, cross mountains, plains, and oceans, and endure hunger, thirst, and fatigue. They suffered every hardship and privation imaginable in order to fulfill their ministry—all without monetary reward, and at great personal risk and sacrifice. This was not a one-time effort, but rather a continuing, lifelong occupation in which they engaged with enthusiasm, eagerness, and passion.

Aside from the frequent prompting they received through the Spirit, the chief motivating force that inspired these men was the personal influence of the Prophet Joseph Smith. They emulated him, they followed in his footsteps, and did constantly strive to perform well enough to receive his approval. Nothing he asked of them was ever turned down or considered drastic, excessive, or unreasonable. Their loyalty to him was absolute and without question.

Against this setting and background, the remarkable and phenomenal growth, life, spirit, and vitality of the Church and the monumental influence of the Prophet Joseph among his followers, certainly becomes understandable. Nevertheless, even while the Church was enjoying and rejoicing in their extraordinary growth, the seeds of turmoil, violence, and persecution were being sown among the Saints by destructive forces. These forces were in large partly beyond their control; however, some were brought about by their own follies—which were in their control.

The gathering of new converts to the Kirtland area continued without restriction and in great numbers following the dedication of the temple in March of 1836. The majority of these Saints were hard-working, committed people, but most of them were of the poorer class. Too often the few well-to-do members would stay back and withhold their money, while the poor went ahead. Some of them arrived without advance planning, hoping to be cared for by the funds of the Church or through the generosity of the members, but the Church was in poor financial condition and most of the members were living from hand-to-mouth. The increasing number of Mormons living in poverty aroused and frightened the old-time residents of Kirtland, who banded together as early as 1835, and warned the poor to leave the city. Recognizing this major upheaval, the Prophet Joseph Smith advised the branches not to send penniless families to Kirtland.

With all the existing problems, a spirit of optimism began to fill Kirtland after the temple dedication, as ambitious Church members attempted to improve and revive the impoverished conditions. The rapid movement of incoming Saints into Kirtland, nevertheless, hastened the demand for property, homes, and goods. As commented by Warren Cowdery in *The Latter-day Saints Messenger and Advocate* newspaper, "the noise, the hustle and bustle of teams with lumber, brick, stone, lime or merchandise, were heard from early dawn till the grey twilight of the evening. The starting up, as if by magic, of buildings in every direction around us, was proof to us of encouraging hope, lively anticipation, and a firm confidence that our days of pinching adversity had passed by, that the set time of the Lord to favor Zion had come."

Even though the Saints' prospects began to increase, the Church was still basically in debt. Capital, such as gold and silver, remained in short supply. In addition, funds were needed to purchase property for settling the Saints in Kirtland and in Northern Missouri. Church leaders anxiously searched for ways to relieve the debt and increase the amount of usable money.

The number of banks in the United States had nearly doubled during the 1830s, as the demand for credit and money increased. Banks provided loans, paper currency, a medium of exchange, and a safe depository for money. Also, during this period of time, the entire country was caught up in a wave of false prosperity brought about in large part by widespread speculations in land and the absence of a sound, controlled banking system. The banking laws of Ohio and other states were extremely loose, allowing the formation of banks without adequate precautions and protections. Once the banks were formed, they issued what seemed to be unlimited quantities of notes. More often than not, the notes were secured by the land with values that had been inflated all out of proportion.

In an effort to provide a convenient instrument of exchange among the Saints and to permit them to share to a greater extent in what eventually proved to be an entirely false prosperity, the Prophet Joseph and other **Church leaders pursued the idea of establishing a bank.** With legal assistance, an article of agreement was drafted to incorporate a bank in Kirtland to be called the Kirtland Safety Society. On the supposition that the Ohio legislature would grant them a charter as it had done in numerous other cases, the organizers of the bank proceeded to have its banknotes engraved, and to take other preliminary steps to prepare for business.

Orson Hyde went to the capital of Ohio with a petition to the legislature, requesting that they approve the proposal to incorporate the bank. At the same time, Oliver Cowdery went to Philadelphia to purchase plates for printing currency. Cowdery succeeded, but Orson returned from Columbus, Ohio with discouraging news. A powerful, anti-Mormon sentiment had taken over the government of Ohio, which resulted in a rejection of the application.

The Prophet noted that: *"because we were Mormons, the legislature raised some superficial, trivial excuse on which they refused to grant us those banking privileges they so freely granted to many others."* Responding to this narrow-minded bias and prejudicial treatment, Joseph and his associates took what later proved to be an unwise and impulsive step that showed their disregard for the officials who had unfairly ruled against them. Greatly disappointed and concerned for the best interests and economic status of the Saints, the day after they had received word of the legislature's decision, **Joseph and his associates decided to create a private joint-stock company to be called the Kirtland Safety Society Anti-Banking Company.** Since other unchartered or unauthorized banks were organized in Ohio, they assumed that individuals had a legal right to organize a private company that engaged in banking activities. Many people in the Western Reserve, both members of the Church and nonmembers alike, initially supported the formation of the society with Joseph Smith as its treasurer and Sidney Rigdon as secretary. The Kirtland Safety Society opened for business on January 2, 1837.

Serious problems soon appeared to undermine the success of the bank. A number of other banks refused to accept the Safety

Society's notes as legal tender, and the anti-Mormon newspapers branded the currency as worthless. In addition, the society's capital was primarily in the form of land; it did not hold or own much specie (hard currency, such as gold and silver) for satisfying any large demands for redeeming its paper currency. Enemies of the Church acquired enough notes to initiate a run on the bank, forcing the society to suspend payment in specie to its customers just a few weeks after the first notes were issued.

The project was doomed to failure from the start. The lack of a sound banking system, coupled with an uncontrolled spirit of speculation that gripped the entire country, created a disastrous situation. Bank failures and panic became a frequent and familiar tune when banks were unable to convert their principal asset, land, into cash in order to redeem the notes and bonds presented for payment. Unfortunately, the number of failures in May, 1837 totaled approximately 800 banks with over $120 million in deposits.

The failure of the Kirtland Safety Society was a devastating blow to the Prophet and to those who had invested in it. Those of shallow belief could not understand how a man who had communed with eternal beings through the veil could have failed so badly in a business venture. These critics did not understand that a prophet is not immune from economic or other difficulties that beset all of us at one time or another in our lives. They also drew the wrong implication and conclusion from the incident, being ignorant of the broad scope of the economic ills that were affecting the entire country.

When God the Father and Jesus Christ called upon Joseph Smith to become the Prophet of God for the Restoration of the true Gospel and Church of Jesus Christ, he was also called to be the Prophet of the Seventh and Last Dispensation of the Fulness of Times. **God did not hire Joseph Smith to become a Chief Executive Officer (CEO) of a business, nor as a (CEO) for the kingdom of God.** He was not chosen as a prophet for his business skills. When Joseph was acting in his calling as a Prophet of God, he worked as a Prophet of God. When he was acting in his role as a man, husband, and father, he was carrying out his role as a man, husband, and father. A prophet is a prophet twenty-four hours a day, but many of his mundane decisions are made as a man. There has never been a prophet on the face of the earth that was a perfect prophet or a perfect man. Again, a prophet is chosen to be the person on earth that God communicates with for His children on the earth. In Old Testament times (unlike now) there were many prophets on the earth at the same time. The Prophet is God's line of communication to all mankind.

THE PAIN OF ECONOMIC DESPAIR

The Saints were in dire financial straits in both Kirtland and throughout Zion a condition, which precipitated the formation of the Kirtland Safety Society. It was hoped that this could be the way to earn the funds to assist the Saints in purchasing property, building homes and farms, schools and churches, and building a better community where the Saints could practice their religion in peace.

Almost overnight, the attitude in Kirtland had changed from one of hope and love to one of hatred and despair. How things can change overnight! It had only been two years since the Kirtland Temple was dedicated, and the Saints had been enjoying a great spiritual exhilaration and looking forward to a bright future. What happened to shatter their hopes and dreams and force the Saints to leave Kirtland? Even though the pain that came into their lives was not caused by the Prophet Joseph Smith nor many of his dedicated disciples, but there were some who wanted revenge and tried to cause "big" trouble for Joseph Smith and the Church. The Prophet wrote concerning the radical change that took place at this time: *"As the fruits of this spirit, evil surmisings* [thoughts and judgments], *fault finding, disunion, dissension, and apostasy followed in quick succession, and it seemed as though all the powers of earth and hell were combining their influence in an especial manner to overthrow the Church at once, and make a final end"* (*History of the Church,* 2: 487).

Caught up in the turmoil and unrest created by the financial panic of 1837, many members and some leaders lost their spiritual anchor and became disaffected from the Prophet and the Church. There were others who were aroused, having an apostate spirit which caused them to ridicule, scorn, and make fun of Joseph in a most cruel and vicious manner. Heber C. Kimball wrote: "This order of things increased during the winter to such an extent that a man's life was in danger the moment he spoke in defense of the Prophet of God."

The Kirtland church newspaper, *The Latter-day Saints Messenger and Advocate*, reported that some unscrupulous brethren were taking advantage of newcomers to the community by describing unusual investment opportunities to them, taking their money, and then deserting them.

Conditions had deteriorated to the point that on one Sunday afternoon in early June, a group of disgruntled, rebellious, and defiant members met in the Kirtland Temple and bitterly attacked Joseph. The protesters were led by one of the Prophet's scribes and close associates who was ultimately excommunicated from the Church. Others close to the Prophet, including some of the Twelve, similarly became disloyal, unfaithful, alienated and embittered—and why? Was Joseph dishonest? No! Was he involved in the Safety Society for personal gain? Absolutely not! In fact, his concern was for the best interests of the Saints. Nevertheless, numbers of Saints spoke out against the Prophet and accused him of being responsible for all their financial problems.

Many members of the Church apostatized during this dark period of economic hardships. Eliza R. Snow commented that, following the temple dedication in 1836, a number of members of the Church felt that "prosperity was dawning upon them, and many who had been humble and faithful, were getting haughty in their spirits, and lifted up in the pride of their hearts. As the Saints drank in the love and spirit of the world, the Spirit of the Lord withdrew from their hearts, and they were filled with pride and hatred toward those who maintained their integrity."

Wilford Woodruff also remembered that the members were warned by their leaders that unless they humbled themselves and repented of their pride, a scourge awaited them as in the days of the ancient Nephites. It is easy to observe that even great spiritual experiences—signs and wonders—can be easily forgotten unless we maintain our efforts to stay close to the Lord. As was earlier explained—slander and mudslinging against Joseph Smith was common practice during the spring and summer of 1837 in Kirtland, particularly when he was away on business or on missions. Some men who held positions of trust in the Church, rejected his leadership and declared that he was no longer a true prophet. When Elder Parley P. Pratt returned from a Canadian mission, the apostasy was well under way. He was temporarily caught up in these difficulties, and left a candid account of his involvement.

"There were also envyings, lyings, strifes, and divisions, which caused much trouble and sorrow. By such spirits I was also accused, misrepresented, and abused. And at one time, I also was overcome by the same spirit in a great measure, and it seemed as if the very powers of darkness, which was against the Saints, were let loose upon me. But the Lord knew my faith, my zeal, my integrity of purpose, and He gave me the victory.

"I went to brother Joseph Smith in tears, and, with a broken heart and contrite spirit, confessed wherein I had erred in spirit, murmured, or done or said amiss. He frankly forgave me, prayed for me and blessed me. Thus, by experience, I learned more fully to discern and to contrast the two spirits, and to resist the one and cleave to the other" (Pratt, *Autobiography Parley P. Pratt,* Deseret Book, 1985, p. 144).

On several occasions, the valiant, bold, and courageous men such as Brigham Young and Heber C. Kimball, defended the Prophet at various meetings, even though their lives were exposed to danger. In February 1837, several Elders called a meeting in the temple for all those who considered Joseph Smith to be a fallen prophet. They intended to appoint David Whitmer as the new Church leader. Brigham Young, Heber C. Kimball, and other faithful members attended the meeting. After listening to the arguments against the Prophet, it was Brigham who arose and testified in his behalf. He later wrote: "Joseph was a Prophet, and I knew it, and that they might rail and slander him as much as they pleased, they could not destroy the appointment of the Prophet of God, they could only destroy their own authority, cut the thread that bound them to the Prophet of God, and sink themselves to hell." On February nineteenth, in the Kirtland Temple, the Prophet spoke for several hours with the power of God. The complainers were silenced, and the Saints were strengthened in their support of the Lord's chosen servant" (Dean C. Jessee, *"The Kirtland Diary of Wilford Woodruff,"* BYU studies, summer 1972, p. 385).

In late June or early July, the Prophet formerly and totally discontinued his connection with the Kirtland Safety Society. Still, the failure of the Kirtland Safety Society and the ongoing turmoil and dissensions, made it evident to the Prophet that he was be facing one of the greatest challenges to his leadership ever. His economic trials and tribulations were further added upon, expanded, and intensified by numerous alienations, disputations, disloyalty, and unfaithfulness among the brethren, including some in the highest positions of leadership in the Church. This was the real test for the Church which only a short year before, seemed unquestionably secure.

The Prophet Joseph, through the power of prayer, was struggling to find something that would reverse the backward trend and put him and the Church on the offensive. The answer came in the early part of June 1837: *"God revealed to me that something new must be done for the salvation of His Church,"* the Prophet wrote: *"And on or about the first of June 1837,* ***Heber C. Kimball, one of the Twelve was set apart*** *by the spirit of prophecy and revelation, praying and laying of hands, of the First Presidency,* ***to preside over a mission to England,***

to be the first foreign mission of the Church of Jesus Christ in the last days" (*History of the Church,* 2: 489). On Sunday, June 4, 1837, the Prophet approached Heber C. Kimball in the temple and whispered to him: *"Brother Heber, the Spirit of the Lord has whispered to me:* ***'Let my servant Heber go to England and proclaim my Gospel,*** *and open the door of salvation to that nation' . . . I felt that the cause of truth, the Gospel of Jesus Christ, outweighed every other consideration"* (*History of the Church,* 2: 490).

Heber C. Kimball wanted his close friend and fellow Apostle Brigham Young to be his companion, but the Prophet needed Brigham to help with matters in troubled Kirtland. While Heber was being set apart (receiving a blessing and the keys for his mission), Orson Hyde walked into the room. Upon hearing what was happening, Orson was prompted to repent, for he had been among the leaders of the Church who had been caught up in the spirit of speculation and criticism of Joseph Smith. He acknowledged his faults, asked forgiveness, and offered to accompany Heber on his mission. The Prophet accepted his repentance, and also set him apart to go to England (*History of the Church,* 2: 489-90).

This was the initial step in a long journey that was to end in the conversion of thousands in the British Isles and Northern Europe. And it was these new converts, who were motivated, stimulated, and driven by the spirit of gathering, who immigrated to the United States in a continuous flow, and provided the support for the westward exodus of the Saints, in their endless drive for religious freedom.

Those who do not believe in God's existence and the power of spiritual influences, are prompted to explain away this happening and the nearly unbelievable consequences that resulted from it on the basis of Joseph's genius or his shrewdness. Nevertheless, Joseph straightforwardly acknowledged that his course of action had been revealed to him by God, and that Heber had been set apart *"by the spirit of prophecy and revelation, prayer, and the laying on of hands."*

Although somewhat surprising in its effect, the missionary call received by Elder Kimball was not totally unexpected. Several months earlier, in a conversation with Willard Richards, he had, in a spirit of prophecy, predicted for himself a mission to the shores of Europe. "'Shall I go with thee,' enquired Willard. 'Yea, in the name of the Lord, thou shalt go with me when I go,' Heber replied.'" And it became a reality (Whitney, *Life of Heber C. Kimball,* pp. 106-07).

This was an ongoing occurrence with Joseph and his followers. It was happening regularly, as if they were all anchored to a central communication system, receiving and relaying messages other than through the physical senses. This explanation is found in the theology revealed and taught by the Prophet Joseph Smith:

First: All who have lived or who will live are influenced from birth by the Light of Christ, which proceeds forth from the presence of God to fill "the immensity of space." Anyone may avail himself or herself of the vast benefits of this light by living the principles taught in the scriptures, and everyone who is attuned to this light will have similar perceptions, regardless of their locality, even as persons separated by distance have similar perceptions of the sun.

Second: Those who comply with the basic teachings of faith in Christ, repentance from sin, and baptism by immersion by one authorized of God, may receive the **Gift of the Holy Ghost**, which furnishes them with extraordinary spiritual powers and perception. The Prophet is reported to have said that the possession of the Holy Ghost by the Latter-day Saints was the chief element that distinguished them from all other religions.

It is unmistakable from the lives led by Heber C. Kimball and other disciples of the Prophet, that this teaching about the Holy Ghost was not an idle piece of oratory or elevated rhetoric. Instead, it was something that entered into every facet of their lives.

THE MISSION OF THE CHURCH CONTINUES

To understand the religious reasons behind the overseas missionary effort originated by the Prophet in 1837, it is important to concentrate on an event that was in company with the dedication of the Kirtland Temple the year before. This was the appearance to Joseph Smith of the biblical prophet Moses, who conferred the keys of the gathering. It was understood by Joseph and his followers from the beginning, that by the authority that accompanied these keys, the Prophet, acting in the role of Moses, would lead modern Israel out of the world to a promised land, even as the ancient Moses led the children of Israel out of captivity in Egypt.

It was now time for Elder Kimball and his six missionary associates to move on to their mission. Along with Orson Hyde, five others were set apart to assist the two apostles: Willard Richards, a Church member of only six months; Joseph Fielding, a native of Bedfordshire, England who had emigrated to Canada in 1832; and three other Canadians, John Goodson, Isaac Russell, and John Snider, who all had relatives and friends in England with whom they corresponded. These last four had been converted to the Gospel at the same time as John Taylor—during Parley P. Pratt's mission to Canada the year before.

Joseph Fielding's brother James, an Independent (formerly Methodist) minister in Preston, England, wrote to his brother in Canada and invited him to come and preach his new religion in his chapel. Upon their arrival in Britain, the missionaries went to Preston, about thirty miles north of the port city of Liverpool, to preach to James's congregation. Some of the people in that congregation had exerted such great faith and prayer that they had seen these American missionaries in dreams before their arrival in England. Beginning on July twenty-third, the brethren preached before three overflow crowds in Reverend Fielding's church, the Vauxhall Chapel. Just as soon as several parishioners requested baptism, however, Reverend Fielding denied the brethren the use of his chapel any longer. He later agonized: "Kimball bored the holes, Goodson drove the nails, and Hyde clinched them" (Whitney, *Life of Heber C. Kimball,* p. 125).

The Elders were persistent and enduring, and were able to reach audiences on the street corners and in private homes that had been licensed for preaching. Being perceptive and sensitive of the poverty and illiteracy of most of their listeners, the missionaries spoke on the intellectual level of their audiences, acted as simple, common men, wore no distinguishing apparel, and did not teach for hire. They immediately extended the hand of fellowship and brotherhood, making all people feel equal before God. The unmistakable sincerity of the missionaries was a dramatic contrast to the lordly attitude of the English religious leaders of the day. Shortly thereafter, many people in the area desired and applied for baptism.

On the morning of July thirtieth, the day that the first baptisms were to be performed, Satan and his hosts launched a potent attack on the missionaries. Elder Russell came to Elder Kimball, seeking relief from the torment of evil spirits. As Elders Hyde and Kimball laid their hands on him to bless him, Elder Kimball was knocked senseless to the floor by an invisible power. As he regained consciousness, he saw his brethren praying for him.

"I then arose, said Elder Kimball, and sat up on the bed, when a vision was opened to our minds, and we could distinctly see the evil spirits. I shall never forget the vindictive evilness pictured on their countenances as they looked me in the eye; and any attempt to paint the scene which then presented itself, or portray their malice and enmity (hatred), would be in vain.

"Years later, recounting the experience of that awful morning to the Prophet Joseph, Heber asked him whether there was anything wrong with him [Heber] that he should have such a manifestation.

"*'No, Brother Heber,'* he replied, *'at that time, you were nigh* [near] *unto the Lord; there was only a veil between you and Him, but you could not see Him. When I heard of it, it gave me great joy, for I then knew* ***that the work of God had taken root in that land****. It was this that caused the devil to make a struggle to kill you.'*

"The nearer a person approaches the Lord, a greater power will be manifested by the adversary to prevent the accomplishment of His purposes.'"

Heber's experience reminded the Prophet of his own terrible exposure to the power of evil as he knelt in the grove seventeen years earlier. On that occasion, the most powerful manifestation of Satanic influence occurred just before the appearance of the Father and the Son. Similarly, the incredible experience of Heber C. Kimball and his brethren in Preston, England, occurred just a few hours before the first converts were baptized.

Despite the hatred, fear, and terror presented by Satan and his host, the baptisms in the River Ribble went on as scheduled. This group of nine converts was the beginning of an army numbered in the tens of thousands who embraced the Gospel, immigrated to America, and helped to establish the Latter-day Saints in the Rocky Mountains West. George D. Watt won a foot race to the river, which determined the honor of being the first to be baptized in England. These baptisms began a flood of English converts. The missionaries went on to the villages of Chatburn and Downham, approximately twenty miles northeast of Preston in the Ribble Valley. In Chatburn, Heber baptized twenty-five people the first night he preached there. During the next five days, with the assistance of his companion, Joseph Fielding, Heber baptized 110 people, and organized branches in Downham, Chatburn, Waddington, and Clithero.

As Heber walked the streets of Chatburn one day, children went before him "singing the songs of Zion, while their parents gazed upon the scene with delight, and poured their blessings upon our heads, and praised the God of heaven for sending us to unfold the principles of truth and the plan of salvation to them" (Whitney, *Life of Heber C. Kimball,* p. 172).

Heber explained: "I went through the streets of that town feeling as I never before felt in my life. My hair would rise on my head as I walked through the streets, and I did not then know what was the matter with me. I pulled off my hat, and felt that I wanted to pull off my shoes, and I did not know what to think of it.

"When I returned to the United States and home, I mentioned the circumstance to brother Joseph, who said: *'some of the old prophets traveled and dedicated that land* [England], *and their blessing fell upon you.'"*

Within eight months of the beginning of the English mission, about 2,000 individuals had joined the Church, and twenty-six branches had been organized. Heber C. Kimball remembered that when he was set apart to head this special mission, he was promised: "that God would make him mighty in that nation in winning souls unto him; angels should accompany him and bear him up, that his feet should never slip; that he should be mightily blessed, and prove a source of salvation to thousands, not only in England but America as well." This first mission to England set the stage for an even greater effort between the years of 1839 and 1841 by the Quorum of Twelve, and for a continuous missionary gathering in the British Isles throughout most of the nineteenth century.

The missionaries, under the direction of Heber C. Kimball, worked in England for nearly a year. After making a great many converts to the Church, they organized them well, taught them to be self-sufficient so that they could be left, and yet continue to follow the teachings of the Church and its Prophet, Joseph Smith. Then, in April 1838, the brethren started on their return journey to Kirtland. They took the same ship, the Garrick, on the return trip, and arrived safely, receiving a warm welcome home.

While the Prophet's main center of attention during the late 1830s was the progress of the missionary efforts in England, many other activities, pressures, and problems were competing for his attention as well. In early August 1837, plans were laid for construction of a temple in Far West, Missouri. The August issue of *The Latter-day Saints Messenger and Advocate* contained a prospectus for a new Church-sponsored paper to be published in Kirtland to be called *The Elder's Journal*.

Also in August 1837, while Joseph Smith and most of the Quorum of the Twelve were away on missions, Warren Parrish, a former scribe for the Prophet and an officer of the Kirtland Safety Society; and John Boynton, a member of the Twelve Apostles, led a group, armed with pistols and bowie knives in an attempted takeover of the temple. In a state of panic and terror, several people jumped out of the temple windows. The police managed to suppress the disturbance and remove the men. When the Prophet returned, these men were disfellowshipped for their actions. Those who showed sincere remorse and sorrow were later reinstated.

As the Church struggled to understand the great crisis which engulfed them, many despaired, losing hope and courage in their testimonies. Since the Kirtland Safety Society had been instituted under the direction of the Prophet Joseph, some believed (one was John F. Boynton) this automatically meant that "the bank was instituted by the will of God" (*History of the Church,* 2: 509-10), and that "it should never fail, let men do what they would" (*History of the Church,* 2: 510). In a council held in September 1837, the Prophet rejected these ideas and *"stated that if this had been declared, no one had authority from him for so doing, for he had always said that unless the institution was conducted on righteous principles, it would not stand"* (*History of the Church,* 2: 510).

Is every action—every word—of a man holding the prophetic office to be considered the will and word of God? Does The Church of Jesus Christ of Latter-day Saints hold to the doctrine of infallibility taught by some other denominations? Does it believe that its prophet can speak no error—that his every word is the expression of God's revealed will? The Prophet Joseph later answered this important doctrinal question when he wrote: "[Joseph] *visited with a brother and sister from Michigan who thought that 'a prophet is always a prophet;' but I told them that a prophet was a prophet only when he was acting as such'*" (*History of the Church,* 5: 265).

There is always a danger in a blind, unknowing faith which fails to make this distinction. To a great extent, the apostasy which stunned the Saints in Kirtland and soon spread to Missouri, took place because the Saints failed to recognize that the Kirtland Safety Society was a secular (worldly) activity in which Joseph was just another participant instead of a God-given cure-all for their temporal problems. **The spirit of contention and malice grew day by day in the closing months of 1837. It shows once again, *"the natural man* [all mankind] *is an enemy of God* . . . *unless*** *he yields to the enticings of the Holy Spirit and putteth off the natural man and becometh a saint through the atonement of Christ the Lord"* (Mosiah 3: 19).

In the fall, however, when Joseph Smith and Sidney Rigdon left for Missouri, troubles flared up once again. The same Warren Parrish and John F. Boynton with the addition of Luke Johnson and thirty other leading citizens, organized a group called the: "Old Standard," or the "Church of Christ." They considered themselves reformers, insisting that Joseph Smith was a fallen prophet who, with other Church authorities, had departed from the true faith. The group sought to overthrow the Church, take over the temple, and still teach most of the Church's doctrines, while rejecting the Book of Mormon and discrediting Joseph Smith and the Priesthood (the power and authority to act in the name of God). They encountered opposition from Martin Harris, who, though in a state of apostasy himself, bore witness that the Book of Mormon was true, and that those who rejected it would be damned.

As a result of the apostasy, fifty leading members of the Church were excommunicated, under the direction of Joseph Smith, but the problems continued to multiply and provoke. Several apostates tormented the faithful members with lawsuits and threatened loss of property. Anti-Mormons added their part by boycotting, ostracizing, and denying employment to those who were true to the Prophet and the Church. Hepzibah Richards, sister to Willard Richards, wrote the following:

"For the last three months, we as a people have been tempest tossed, and at times, the waves have well nigh overwhelmed us. A dreadful spirit reigns in the breasts of those who are opposed to this Church. They are above the law and beneath whatever is laudable. Their leading objective seems to be to get all the property of the Church for little or nothing, and drive them [the Saints] out of the place.

Between November 1837 and June 1838, possibly two or three hundred Kirtland Saints withdrew from the Church, representing from 10 to 15 percent of the membership there."

The "great apostasy" also carried over somewhat to Missouri. In a nine month period, the Three Witnesses, a member of the First Presidency (Frederick G. Williams), four members of the Twelve Apostles, and several members of the First Quorum of the Seventy left the Church. Because he continued to boldly defend the Prophet, Brigham Young was threatened and forced to flee on horseback to Missouri.

In January 1838, Luke Johnson, an apostate himself, but still sympathetic to Joseph Smith, warned the Prophet of an assassination plot. While the mob was nearby, Joseph was placed inside a box and taken out of town on an ox cart. When he was safely out of the reach of the mob, he mounted his horse and rode westward with Sidney Rigdon. Nevertheless, their enemies followed them for 200 miles, and were sometimes so near that the brethren could hear cursing and threats. Emma Smith and their children joined Joseph en route, and after a severely trying journey, they were heartily welcomed by the Missouri Saints in March 1838. Sidney Rigdon arrived a few days later, having separated from the Prophet at Dublin, Ohio.

On the same date that Joseph Smith fled from Kirtland (January 12, 1838), the lives of the members of the High Council were also threatened, and most of the faithful decided to follow their leader to Missouri. Hepzibah Richards wrote of this drastic situation: "All our friends plan on leaving this place as soon as possible. The feeling seems to be that Kirtland must be trodden down by the wicked for a season. Probably several hundred families will leave within a few weeks." But before most of the faithful could leave Kirtland, enemies began ransacking homes of the Saints and starting fires in basements.

Early in March, the Seventies began planning ways to help the poorest Saints move to Missouri. One of the presidents of the quorum, James Foster, had a vision of an orderly company of about 500 Saints traveling to Missouri and camping by the way. Directed by vision and prophecy, the Seventies drew up a constitution, formed a camp of those willing to abide by it, and designated leaders to preside over companies. Captains were to encourage their companies to keep the commandments and observe the Word of Wisdom.

The journey was delayed for several weeks as the Saints struggled to settle their debts, sell their property, and purchase wagons, teams, and equipment. They finally left Kirtland on July 6, 1838 with over 500 Saints, twenty-seven tents, fifty-nine wagons, ninety-seven horses, twenty-two oxen, sixty-nine cows, and one bull. Benjamin Johnson wrote: "All means for defraying expenses were put together, and so all were to fare alike, and did so as long as they remained in camp together. Even so, the travelers had to pause occasionally to earn money for supplies and equipment."

The Kirtland Camp was also met with persistent persecution along the trail. Many people were suspicious of the disheveled travelers who passed through their towns and cities. *"As we passed along the road in the morning, molesting no one, some of the company were saluted in modern style by having eggs thrown at them by some ruffians"* (*History of the Church,* 3: 112). Ridicule was sometimes combined with threats of violence. In Missouri, the citizens of one community placed artillery in the street to prevent the camp from passing through. They were only allowed to proceed when one of the Seventies soothed the citizens' anxious feelings, and even then, several of the camp's leaders were jailed overnight. Many forces contributed to the suffering in the Kirtland Camp.

"Accidents and illness constantly afflicted the pioneers. Some persons were crushed under wagon wheels; others succumbed to disease. They perspired by day and slept on cold and sometimes damp terrain by night. They crossed streams, climbed up and down inclines, and followed rutted roads and trails, continually weakened by fatigue, a meager and changing diet, and polluted drinking water.

"In the midst of their suffering and afflictions, they turned to their Heavenly Father [God] for help. Throughout the journey, Elders administered to the sick and the injured; and diarists reported that through the power of the Priesthood, many of the sick and afflicted were instantly healed" (Milton V.Backman Jr., *The Heavens Resound,* LDS, Deseret Book, 1983, pp. 359-60).

When the camp arrived at the Mississippi River in September, they were informed that war had broken out in Western Missouri between the Mormons and their enemies, that all Mormons would soon be driven from the state, and that if they continued on with their journey, they would be attacked and would suffer a similar fate. Several members of the camp refused to enter Missouri as a result of these threats. But most of the Saints pressed on, finally joining the Prophet in Far West, Missouri, on October 2, 1838. Two days later, they arrived at Adam-ondi-Ahman, where they were to settle. They would soon discover that their problems had not been left behind in Ohio. Within a few short weeks, they would be facing even worse persecutions in Missouri.

Aside from a very few non-Mormon sympathizers, there were no friendly communities who would open their doors and hearts to the Mormons or show any compassion or kindness towards these Mormon strangers who were in dire need of a helping hand. Although the United States is a land of freedom, liberty ,and religious freedom, the Mormons experienced something quite different during the early days of this country.

It was one complication after another one upheaval after another, for Joseph Smith and his followers—all because they desired to have the opportunity and purpose of practicing their religion with freedom granted by the United States Constitution.

* * *

Why can't people live in simple peace and harmony, respecting one another's religious beliefs especially if the belief is not infringing upon another? Why can't people then and now, be kind, friendly and helpful to one another? Why does there have to be pain and suffering, anger and hatred? Once again, the scriptures tell us that *"the natural man is an enemy of God"* (Mosiah 3: 19).

I bear testimony that the counsel we received in our pre-earth life, as spirit children of God, is that our Heavenly Father is a God of love and peace. I know we are on this earth to be tested—to do all we can to perfect our lives—so that one day we can return to the presence of God the Father to live with Him, Jesus Christ, and our families. Yes, now *is* the time to learn from the mistakes of our forefathers. We shouldn't have to wait until disaster strikes before we humans help one another. We must build friendly, loving relationships now. I know it is the time, for us to stop, think, and pray, so we may grow closer to each other and to our God, the one God for all mankind, and to His Son, Jesus Christ, who is the God of this earth.

Chapter 10

1836-1838

The Church moves on to Northern Missouri

Mormons Requested to Leave Clay County

Establishing Two New Counties in Northern Missouri—Caldwell and Daviess

A New Community Called Far West

The Founding of Adam-ondi-Ahman

Sidney Rigdon's Provoking Salt Sermon and Independence Day Message

Law of Tithing

The Prophet and other leaders of the Church left Kirtland, in January 1838. Most of the members followed later in the year. There was no decision to desert Kirtland, regardless of the internal and external pressures at the time, but the concentration of Church members was clearly to Northern Missouri. It is likely that a few members recalled the revelation given in 1831: *"I, the Lord, will to retain a strong hold in the land of Kirtland, for the space of five years"* (Doctrine & Covenants 64: 21). By early 1838, the years of Kirtland's prominence and glory had passed. The members in Northern Missouri were already establishing new headquarters in Far West. Other scattered Saints in the United States and Canada were preparing to assemble there. Latter-day Saints were enthusiastic, anxious and eager to find an interval of peace after the disastrous year of apostasy in 1837. Following their ejection from Jackson County in late 1833, the Missouri Saints lived in relative peace with the original local residents of Clay County. Nevertheless, the leaders of the Church never intended that arrangement to be permanent. **They consistently petitioned government authorities for assistance to re-enter Jackson County** and regain their property, but all their efforts went for naught. Meanwhile, Latter-day Saints continued to arrive, magnifying the fear among the Clay County residents that the Mormon settlements would become permanent.

Recognizing these concerns and anxieties, Bishop Edward Partridge and William W. Phelps began two exploring expeditions in the spring of 1836, hoping to find potential areas for Mormon settlements in Northern Missouri, a region commonly referred to as the "Far West." Most of the territory was prairie, covered by tall grass, with timber only along the streams and rivers. At that time, only forested land was considered good for settlement. W. W. Phelps reported: "Nearly every skirt of timber to the state line on the north . . . has some one in it." Fortunately, the brethren found an uninhabited area in Northern Ray County along the Shoal Creek, although they feared there was not enough timber available to support a large population (*History of the Church,* 2: 445). Nevertheless, the brethren began purchasing land in the Shoal Creek area on May third.

A mass meeting of the Clay County residents was held on June 29, 1836, in the Clay County courthouse in Liberty, to discuss objections to the Mormons remaining in the area. Some were concerned that the "crisis" would erupt into a civil war. Opponents gave five reasons for their objection to the Saints: (1) They were poor. (2) Their religious differences stirred up prejudice. (3) Their Eastern customs and dialect were alien to the Missourians. (4) They opposed slavery. (5) They believed the Indians were God's chosen people, who were destined to inherit the land of Missouri with them. The citizens also reminded the Mormons of their pledge to leave the county, and suggested that they consider moving to Wisconsin in the slave-free north where there were many areas suitable for settlement. These Clay County leaders promised to control any violence toward the Mormons if they would agree to leave the area.

Church leaders were hopeful that they would soon be moving to Shoal Creek, and found no objection to the petition for a covenant of peace, and called a public meeting on July first, to outline their response. Unhesitatingly, the Saints expressed by resolution their gratitude to the citizens of Clay County for the kindness they had been extended to the Saints and for their desire for a peaceful end to the crisis. Church leaders promised to lead the Saints out of the county and stop the flow of immigration. The following day, Clay County leaders accepted the reply, and began forming a committee to help the Saints in their move.

The First Presidency, while yet in Ohio, having learned of these developments, wrote separate letters to leaders of the Church and to the Clay County committee. They urged members of the Church to preserve the peace, but not to settle in Wisconsin. The Brethren informed the Clay County committee that they had advised the Saints to avoid any bloodshed, and to move from the county.

On July seventh, the Church leaders in Missouri wrote Governor Daniel Dunklin of their intentions to move to the 1,600 acres they had purchased in Northern Ray County, and requested his assistance in breaking up potential mobs. In 1836, the "Mormon problem" was not as prominent in Missouri politics as it had been in 1833-34; and since it was an election year, the governor was less inclined to help the Saints. In addition, many voters in Ray County opposed the move of the Saints into their county, even the uninhabited Northern prairies. Governor Dunklin replied on July eighteenth that, although he sympathized with the plight of the Saints, "public sentiment may become dominant law; and when one man or society of men become so bitter and repulsive to that sentiment as to determine the people to be rid of him or them, it is useless to run counter to it.

"The consequences will be the same . . . unless you can, by your conduct and arguments, convince them [the people of Missouri] of your innocence. If you cannot do this, all I can say to you is that in the Republic the '*vox populi* is the *vox Dei*' [the voice of the people is the voice of God], (*History of the Church,* 2: 462).

Conditions for the Saints were critical and urgent. Without any promise or assurance of protection from the governor, and with the growing hostility and conflict in both Clay and Ray Counties, the Stake Presidency and the High Council met in an emergency session on July twenty-fifth. To further complicate matters, the brethren had just learned that approximately 100 families of immigrating Saints were camped on the Crooked River in lower Ray County. Many of them were ill, and most of them were without funds to purchase either provisions or land. Citizens in Ray County threatened them with violence if they did not move on. Additionally, another 100 poverty-stricken families were en route from the Mississippi River. "To prevent mobbing, chaos and confusion, as well as pestilence and death" Church leaders advised the immigrants to scatter among the people in the settlements, and find temporary housing and work. Thomas B. Marsh and Elisha H. Groves, who was a convert from Kentucky, were sent to branches of the Church in other states to gather and collect money to benefit "Poor Bleeding Zion," while W. W. Phelps, John Whitmer, Edward Partridge, Isaac Morley, and John Corrill were assigned to locate more land for settlement.

Church leaders also promised and assured the citizens of Ray County that the Saints intended to settle only in the prairies to the north, and to apply for a new county, which the local residents readily agreed to. A proposal was offered and accepted to establish a six-mile buffer zone, three miles on each side of the dividing line between the countries, as a "no-man's land" where neither Mormon nor non-Mormon could settle.

In the meantime, early in August 1836, W. W. Phelps and John Whitmer searched out and located an area in Northern Ray County which was ideal for a city. They so designated it and named the proposed city "Far West." It was twelve miles west of Haun's Mill, a small Mormon settlement, established by Jacob Haun on Shoal Creek a year earlier. The Saints began gathering in the late summer and fall, and soon Far West and numerous smaller settlements sprang into existence.

Alexander W. Doniphan, a friend to the Saints and a state legislator, introduced a bill into the December 1836 legislative session to create two small counties out of the sparsely settled regions of Northern Ray County. Doniphan named the new counties where he was also born and raised Daviess and Caldwell, after two famous Indian fighters from Kentucky. Caldwell County, the location of the Far West and Shoal Creek settlements, was to be exclusively for Mormons, and they would be allowed to send representatives to the state legislature. The segregation of the Latter-day Saints was considered an excellent solution to the "Mormon problem." Newly elected Governor Lilburn W. Boggs signed the bill creating the two new counties on December 29, 1836.

Internal difficulties and pressures were near at hand as the Saints poured into Caldwell County, where they constructed log houses and prepared the soil for spring planting. Thomas

Marsh and Elisha Groves returned early in 1837 from their fund-raising mission in Kentucky and Tennessee, and turned $1,450 over to W. W. Phelps and John Whitmer, counselors in the Stake Presidency. His counselors handled the matter since President David Whitmer was in Ohio. The counselors used the money to purchase more land, but they purchased it in their own names, and then sold it to the Saints at a small profit which they personally retained. Several members of the Church immediately protested, and some of the High Council complained that the counselors were making decisions regarding Far West without consulting them. At a series of meetings in Far West in April, these brethren acknowledged their wrongs, and agreed to overcome their greed. It was decided that Bishop Edward Partridge, acting with the counsel of the Stake Presidency, the High Council, and two Apostles who were in Missouri—Thomas B. Marsh and David Patten—would distribute the lands.

Nevertheless, about a month later, Phelps and Whitmer again offended the High Council and the Apostles with further attempts to profit from land deals. When the Prophet learned of this conflict, he sought and obtained guidance from the Lord: *"Verily thus saith the Lord unto my servant Joseph—my servants John Whitmer and William W. Phelps, have done those things which are not pleasing in my sight, therefore, if they repent not they shall be removed out of their places. Amen"* (*History of the Church,* 2: 511). Nevertheless, this conflict and confusion continued on until November 1837.

On September 17, 1837, a conference was held in Kirtland at which time it was decided to send Joseph Smith and Sidney Rigdon to Missouri to seek other areas for stakes of Zion *"so that the poor may have a place of refuge"* (*History of the Church,* 2: 516). In addition, and in response to the conference, Bishop Newel K. Whitney sent a letter on September eighteenth, to all branches of the Church scattered throughout the United States, asking them to send their tithing in gold and silver for the relief of Kirtland and for the building of Zion in Missouri.

The Prophet and several other brethren arrived in Far West in early November and spent approximately ten days there holding meetings. It was determined that there were resources and space in Northern Missouri for the gathering of the Saints, and a committee was chosen to locate areas for new stakes. Joseph decided to postpone the building of a temple in Far West until he received further direction from the Lord, but the size of Far West was enlarged from one square mile to two. The problems associated with the activities of the Stake Presidency in Missouri were temporarily resolved, and they were sustained in their callings. On November 7, 1837, at a conference of Elders held in Far West, Frederick G. Williams was released as second counselor in the First Presidency and Hyrum Smith was sustained in his place.

During the winter months, new conflicts arose between the Stake Presidency and the High Council in Missouri. Oliver Cowdery and Frederick G. Williams, who had been out of harmony with the Prophet in Kirtland, had now moved to Far West, and together with the Stake Presidency, decided to sell some Church lands in Jackson County held in their names. Selling lands in Zion violated the Lord's direction that the Saints should continue to hold claim upon their lands in Jackson County (see Doctrine & Covenants 101: 99).

In early February 1838, the High Council tried "William W. Phelps and John Whitmer for persisting in unchristian-like conduct" and misusing Church funds, David Whitmer for willfully and intentionally breaking the Word of Wisdom (the health code of the Church). In spite of some feelings that the High Council was not authorized to try the Presidency, a majority voted to reject the two of them, and a resolution to this effect was sent to the branches and accepted by the Saints. When the Presidency claimed that the trial was illegal and that they had not been present to defend themselves, the High Council was convinced that they were "endeavoring to palm themselves off upon the Church, as her Presidents, after the Church had by a united vote, removed them from their presidential office" (*History of the Church,* 3: 6-7). Accordingly, on February tenth, the High Council, with the assistance of two Apostles, excommunicated W. W. Phelps and John Whitmer and sustained Thomas B. Marsh and David W. Patten as acting presidents until the expected arrival of Joseph Smith. Additional action against David Whitmer, Oliver Cowdery, and Lyman Johnson, who had joined the dissenters, was postponed pending the Prophet's arrival. In a letter to the Prophet Joseph Smith, Elder Marsh explained: "Had we not taken the above measures, we think that nothing could have prevented a rebellion against the whole High Council and Bishop; so great was the disaffection against the presidents, that the people began to be jealous, that the whole authorities were inclined to uphold these men in wickedness, and in a little time, the church undoubtedly, would have gone, every man to his own way, like sheep without a shepherd" (*The Elders' Journal,* July 1838, p. 45).

The Prophet Joseph was still in Ohio; news of persecution and the unsettled state of the Church in Missouri disheartened and saddened him. On January 12, 1838, he received a revelation explaining that only the First Presidency could form a stake. This revelation meant that the creation of the Far West stake was invalid. And so he went to Missouri, not only to escape his enemies, but to set the Church in Far West in order. The trip was difficult, but when Joseph arrived in Missouri in March, with Emma, who was six months pregnant, many excited Saints met them to accompany them to Far West. Eight miles from town, another eager escort gladdened their hearts. After so many difficulties in the East, the Prophet was encouraged by the support of the Missouri Saints, and they were equally glad to have him settle among them.

While in Far West, Joseph approved the removal of the Stake Presidency. By the end of March, he was optimistic about the unity in Far West, despite the arrival of several letters from Kirtland apostates which spread falsehoods among a few. Joseph wrote back to Kirtland that: *"peace and love prevail throughout; in a word, heaven smiles upon the Saints in Caldwell"* (*History of the Church,* 3: 11). Two days before April General Conference, they were heartened when Sidney Rigdon and his party arrived after a long and difficult journey.

At the conference, the Prophet called the three senior members of the Quorum of the Twelve Apostles, Thomas B. Marsh, David W. Patten, and Brigham Young—as the new Stake Presidency in Missouri. This action, however, was only a temporary solution. Nine days later, he received a revelation instructing Elder Patten to arrange his affairs so that he and others of the Twelve could leave in the spring of 1839 for a new mission abroad (Doctrine & Covenants 114). In a later session, David

Patten reviewed the status of the Quorum of the Twelve, not all of whom were in Missouri. He commended six of his brethren "as being men of God," he spoke somewhat doubtful of five others "as being men whom he could not recommend to the conference" (*History of the Church,* 3: 14). It became apparent that four of the men would have to be replaced. During the sessions on April seventh and eighth, additional action was taken to put the Church in Missouri in order.

After the conference, the new Stake Presidency dealt with the cases of former leaders who had apostatized. They wrote to John Whitmer, who had been both the Church historian and a member of the Stake Presidency in Missouri, asking him to give his historical notes and writings to the Church. He did not consent. Only recently has his history been published in its entirety.

Two men who held high positions in the Church and had been very dear to Joseph Smith, now turned against him. They were David Whitmer, who had been president of the branch of the Church in Missouri, and Oliver Cowdrey. Both had been witnesses to the Book of Mormon, and had stood by the Prophet's side from the beginning of the work. It was a source of great sorrow and pain for the Prophet to see these two special men fall away from the faith.

The High Council in Missouri excommunicated David Whitmer on April 13, 1838. He was charged with not observing the Word of Wisdom, joining with the enemies of the Prophet in Kirtland and in Missouri, writing letters filled with false accusations against the Prophet, and neglecting his duties in the Church, in addition to usurping too much authority.

David Whitmer fought against the Church for years, and never did join it again. Nevertheless, through it all, he was faithful to his testimony of the Book of Mormon, and on his deathbed, made another public statement declaring that the Book of Mormon was true.

The second serious matter was the case of Oliver Cowdery. He was charged by the High Council for persecuting Church leaders with intolerable, offensive, and irritating lawsuits, seeking to destroy the character of Joseph Smith, not sustaining religious authority in temporal affairs, selling lands in Jackson County, and leaving his calling as Assistant President of the Church. He was tried by the High Council court only after a careful investigation of the charges against him.

Oliver was a proud man. He had been raised to a high position in the Church and had been with Joseph during some of the most important events in the work of the Lord. But now, jealousy entered his heart. He was not content to be the second Elder in the Church. He no longer wished to follow the Prophet; he thought that he knew more than the Prophet because of his formal education. Nevertheless, a Prophet is not chosen for his educational skills, but only by the calling from God.

Oliver refused to appear before the council, but answered by letter. He denied the Church's right to dictate how he should conduct his life, and asked that his fellowship with the Church be ended. At last, because he was openly fighting against the leaders of the Church, Oliver was excommunicated, on April 12, 1838. Hyrum, the faithful brother of the Prophet, was chosen in Oliver's place, and all of the powers and authority which had been given to Oliver, were now given to Hyrum.

The Prophet dearly loved Hyrum. Of him, Joseph once wrote: *"I could pray in my heart that all of my brethren were like unto my beloved brother Hyrum, who possesses the mildness of a lamb, and the integrity of a Job, and in short, the meekness and humility of Christ; and I love him with that love that is stronger than death, for I never had occasion to rebuke him, nor he me, which he declared when he left me today"* (*History of the Church*, 6: xliii).

Oliver, on leaving the Church, went to the State of Michigan, where he practiced law. During the years he was separated from the Church, he, too, was always true to his testimony to the Book of Mormon.

Ten years after he had left the Church, and four years after the Prophet Joseph Smith had been martyred, Oliver became humbled in his spirit, and once again, desired to be joined with the Saints. He heard that the Saints were beginning to move West to Utah. He started to follow them. When he got to the little town of Kanesville, Iowa, he found a meeting being held there. He entered the room, and at first no one knew him. He asked permission to speak, and it was granted. He told the people who he was Oliver Cowdery and that he had assisted Joseph Smith in translating the Book of Mormon, that he was present with him during many wonderful manifestations. He confessed his wrongdoing, and asked forgiveness. Then he asked to be permitted to join the Church once again. He did not ask for any high position. "All I ask," he said, "is that you will permit me to come back and be one with you, and partake of your sorrows and pleasures."

He told the small congregation that he desired to go to the Rocky Mountains, and join the Saints. Later he hoped to go to England on a mission, there to bear his testimony to that people.

He was rebaptized into the Church in October 1848 in Kanesville, Iowa. After this baptism, he went to visit his brother-in-law, David Whitmer. While there, he became ill and died. Oliver knew the truth. Even though he stepped away from it, he found his way back to the truth.

SETTLING THE COMMUNITY OF FAR WEST

Toward the end of April 1838, the Prophet received a revelation concerning the building up of Far West. It first designated the correct name of the Church as: *"The Church of Jesus Christ of Latter-day Saints"* (Doctrine & Covenants 115: 4). This settled any confusion on the subject; the Church had been called The Church of Christ, The Church of the Latter-day Saints, and The Church of Christ of Latter-day Saints. At the time of the ministry of the Savior upon the earth, His Church too, was called after His name with members referred to as *Saints*. *"And how be it my church save it be called in my name? For if a church be called in Moses' name, then it be Moses' church; or if it be called in the name of a man, then it be the church of a man; but if it be called in my name, then it is my church, if it so be that they are built upon my gospel"* (3 Nephi 27: 8). The Lord also commanded the building of a temple: *"Let the city, Far West, be a holy and consecrated land unto me; and it shall be called most holy, for the ground upon which thou standest is holy"* (Doctrine & Covenants 115: 7). But the First Presidency was told not to incur debt for this temple as had been done in Kirtland. The Lord also directed the brethren to establish stakes in the surrounding regions. This was to be done so *"that the gathering together upon the land of Zion, and upon her stakes, may be for a defense, and for a refuge from the storm, and from wrath when it shall be poured out with-*

out mixture upon the whole earth" (Doctrine & Covenants 115: 6).

During the next three weeks, the Prophet visited the Saints in Caldwell County and taught them principles of the Gospel. Then, with the assistance of Sidney Rigdon, he took upon himself the ambitious task of writing the history of the Church from its beginning. The history written by John Whitmer, the first Church historian, had been incomplete, and in any event, was now unavailable. The history of Joseph Smith and the early events of the Restoration, now found in the Pearl of Great Price, were a product of this project begun in April 1838.

Shortly after Joseph Smith settled in the community of Far West, Missouri, in March 1838, he began preparing for an expanded missionary effort by the Twelve to Great Britain. The Lord also told the Apostles the exact day, April 26, 1839, that they were to leave Far West to depart for England.

When the revelation was received, the brethren anticipated little difficulty in fulfilling their mission, but the subsequent persecution and the expulsion of the Saints from Missouri made the mission departure in April impossible. There were no further preparations for the mission to Great Britain until the Saints had found a new gathering place which was at Commerce (Nauvoo, Illinois).

Having set the affairs of the Church in order in Caldwell County, the Prophet Joseph turned his attention to locating land, places of settlement, and housing for the oncoming Saints from Ohio and other Eastern States who would come to Missouri in the spring and summer of 1838. In 1837, a few of the Latter-day Saints had settled north of Caldwell County in the newly-created Daviess County. They did so in accordance with the gentleman's agreement that they would obtain permission from the "gentile" inhabitants to settle there. The most prominent Mormon to settle in Daviess County was Lyman Wight, who founded Wight's Settlement on a beautiful hillside overlooking the Grand River.

Joseph Smith and a large group of brethren headed northward in an exploring expedition in mid-May 1838. When they reached Wight's Ferry on the Grand River, the Prophet directed the laying out of a city at that location. **He also received a revelation that this was the location of Adam-ondi-Ahman.** In 1835, the Lord revealed that three years before Adam died, he called his righteous posterity together *"into the valley of Adam-ondi-Ahman, and there bestowed upon them his last blessing"* (Doctrine & Covenants 107: 53; and Doctrine & Covenants 78: 15-16). Orson Pratt said the name means: "Valley of God, where Adam dwelt. It is in the original language spoken by Adam" (*Journal of Discourses,* 18: 343). Adam-ondi-Ahman, shortened to Diahman by the Saints, will yet be the location of a very important meeting for selected righteous people to greet the Savior and the resurrected Adam. In the words of the revelation: *"it is the place where Adam shall come to visit his people"* (Doctrine & Covenants 116: 1). This knowledge so excited the brethren that plans were discussed to create a stake at Adam-ondi-Ahman.

These exploring brethren did search for other locations for settlement along the heavily timbered and navigable Grand River. With the explorations finished for the moment, Joseph Smith returned to Far West, realizing that Emma was soon to deliver another child. She gave birth to a son on June 2, 1838. They named him Alexander Hale Smith.

Within a short period of time, Joseph was back in Adam-ondi-Ahman surveying the new city for the building of houses. He designated the community as a gathering place for the Kirtland Saints, some still in Ohio and others en route to Missouri. When his uncle John Smith and family arrived in Far West, the Prophet counseled him to settle in Adam-ondi-Ahman. A conference was held on June twenty-eighth, in the new community affectionately nicknamed "Diahman," and John Smith was sustained as the President of the Stake, with Reynolds Cahoon and Lyman Wight as his counselors. A High Council was also organized. Vinson Knight was called as acting bishop until the arrival of Bishop Newel K. Whitney from Kirtland (Doctrine & Covenants 117: 11).

Latter-day Saint immigrants poured into Adam-ondi-Ahman throughout the summer of 1838. They considered themselves greatly blessed to live in the land where Adam dwelt. An article in the August issue of *The Elders' Journal* portrays their excitement:

"The immense immigration . . . encourages the Saints, and induces us to believe that God is about to bring to pass His unique acts, of which He has spoken by His ancient Prophets."

"The immense growth of corn and other produce, this season . . . has not to our knowledge, had a parallel in this generation; and if the Lord should continue to bless, as He has now set His hand to do, there must soon be a surplus."

Indeed, a plentiful harvest that fall helped provide for the poverty-stricken members of the Kirtland Camp when they arrived in Missouri, and settled in Diahman in early October.

About the time that Diahman was being settled, the Saints also began to establish themselves in DeWitt, located in Carroll County, near the point where the Grand River entered the Missouri River. This benefited the Church, because the members built a steamboat landing where immigrants could move around it, from the other Latter-day Saint settlements. John Murdock and George M. Hinkle, members of the Far West High Council, were authorized to purchase property in DeWitt, and begin a settlement. DeWitt grew rapidly. A housing shortage developed in the fall when a large group of Saints from Canada arrived. In consequence, the Mormon city of DeWitt became largely a tent city.

By far the most prosperous of the Latter-day Saint communities was Far West. By the summer of 1838, the population of Caldwell County approached 5,000, and over half of them lived in Far West proper. The Saints built more than 150 homes, four dry goods stores, three family grocery stores, several blacksmith shops, two hotels, a printing shop, and a large schoolhouse that doubled as a church and courthouse.

Although the Saints were busy planting crops and building log houses, they paused often to worship and study the Gospel. Twenty-four-year-old Sarah Rich was a new bride when she and her husband, Charles, settled in a "cozy and happy" log house four miles from Far West, "religion being first with us in all things," she declared. Each Sunday, they rode horseback to town to attend meeting, "often listening to the Prophet Joseph Smith preach and instruct the people, a privilege we both appreciated very much" (K.W. Godfrey, A.M. Godfrey, and J.M. Derr, *Women's Voices,* SLC, Deseret Book, 1982, p. 98).

During the summer of 1838, the Prophet began looking into the important issue of filling the vacancies in the Quorum of the Twelve Apostles. He reaffirmed their responsibilities, and counseled the Saints on the financing of the Lord's kingdom. There was great sadness and somberness in the Church over the loss of four of the original Twelve. Elizabeth Barlow reflected: "We all felt more sorrowful at seeing Apostles leave the Church, than we did over our trials and persecutions."

In spite of grief and anguish, Joseph Smith began replacing these four Apostles, and preparing the Twelve for their assignment to take the gospel to the world. In the fall of 1837, prior to his visit to Far West, he sent word to John Taylor, a bold and courageous convert from Toronto, of his future call to the apostleship (*Life of John Taylor*, SLC, Bookcraft, 1963, p. 47). At the time, Elder Taylor was not presented before the membership of the Church for a sustaining vote. The following July, the Prophet prayed: *"Show unto us thy will O Lord concerning the Twelve* (*History of the Church,* 3: 46). The revelation that followed had a deep and profound impact on the history of the Church. First, the Lord directed that: *"men be appointed to supply the place of those who are fallen"* (Doctrine & Covenants 118: 1). John Taylor, John E. Page, Wilford Woodruff, and Willard Richards were called.

As a missionary in Canada for two years, Elder John E. Page had traveled more than five thousand miles and baptized over 600 converts. When the revelation was given, he was en route to Missouri with a company of Canadian Saints. They arrived in DeWitt in October 1838. Elders Taylor and Page were ordained Apostles on December 19, 1838 in Far West by Brigham Young and Heber C. Kimball. Elder Woodruff was a missionary in Maine when he received his call in a letter. He led a group of New England converts toward Missouri, but the Saints were driven from the state before they arrived, so he settled them in Illinois. Wilford Woodruff was ordained an Apostle in Far West on April 26, 1839, when he accompanied other members of the Twelve there to fulfill the commandment that the Twelve were to take up their mission to England from Far West (Doctrine & Covenants 118: 3-5). Elder Richards, an English convert, was a missionary and Priesthood leader in Great Britain, and was not ordained until members of the Twelve arrived there in 1840.

The revelation concerning the Twelve also instructed Thomas B. Marsh to continue publishing the Lord's word (in *The Elder's Journal*) in Far West, and directed the others to preach *"in all lowliness of heart, in meekness and humility, and long-suffering"* (Doctrine & Covenants 118: 3). The Lord further charged the Twelve to prepare to depart April 26, 1839 from Far West *"to go over the great waters and there promulgate my gospel"* (Doctrine & Covenants 118: 4).

On the day the revelation to the Twelve was given, Joseph Smith also read two revelations concerning Church revenue to the Saints. With the Church deeply entangled in economic difficulties, the Prophet had sought clarification and enlightenment on how the law of consecration should be applied. The Lord modified the original law given in 1831 when he replied:

"I require all their surplus property to be put into the hands of the bishop of my church in Zion, For the building of mine house, and for the laying of the foundation of Zion, and for the priesthood, and for the debts of the Presidency of my Church. And this shall be the beginning of the tithing of my people. And after that, those who have thus been tithed, shall pay one-tenth of all their interest [income] *annually; and this shall*

be a standing law unto them forever" (Doctrine & Covenants 119: 1-4). The second revelation assigned a committee of General Authorities the responsibility of expending the tithes (Doctrine & Covenants 120).

Although the Saints in Northern Missouri were optimistic and in generally good spirits, there was reason for anxiety and uneasiness. The Saints, having endured persecution, discontent, and rebelliousness for seven years, were understandably impatient with dissenters who resided in Far West. These dissenters harassed them with lawsuits and condemned their Church leaders. In June, Sidney Rigdon erupted in a heated speech commonly referred to as the "Salt Sermon." He drew his text from the scripture: *"Ye are the salt of the earth: but if the salt have lost his savour, . . . it is thenceforth good for nothing, but to be cast out, and to be trodden under foot of men"* (Matt. 5: 13). The meaning was quite evident—the dissenters should be cast out from among the Saints.

Shortly thereafter, an unauthorized document appeared, addressed to Oliver Cowdery, David and John Whitmer, W. W. Phelps, and Lyman E. Johnson, the leading dissenters. The document was signed by eighty-four members of the Church. It pointedly ordered the apostates to leave the county or face serious consequences. The sermon and letter obviously had the desired effect. The dissenters fled in haste, and were soon followed by their families. This extreme behavior on the part of a few, horrified some people in the Church, and complaining and grumbling continued. Most unfortunately, it also intensified the growing anti-Mormon hostility and opposition in Northern Missouri.

Also contributing to the conflict with the gentiles was Sampson Avard's formation of an underground society called the Danites. This was an oath-bound group with secret identification and warning signs. Avard convinced his followers that they operated with the approval of the Presidency of the Church, and that they were authorized to avenge themselves against the Church's enemies by robbing, lying, and murder if necessary. His object was to overthrow the Church, which, according to the Prophet, *"he tried to accomplish by his smooth, flattering, and winning speeches which he frequently made to his associates."* His speeches became more and more inflammatory—even too much for the most gullible of his followers to accept. His last major speech caused a literal eruption and violent rejection of what he was pressing for. With the mask of his deception ripped away, those present, for the first time, recognized Avard for what he was: a conspiring, vicious, and unprincipled man, who in the name of religion, was attempting to use the same evil tools wielded by the ancient secret orders so much condemned in the Book of Mormon. When word of Avard's actions reached the First Presidency, he was promptly excommunicated, *"and every means proper used to destroy his influence"* (*History of the Church,* 3: 181). Avard reacted by joining the mobbers and spreading false and malicious rumors about the Prophet and his followers.

Upon reflection, it seems apparent that the apostasy of Thomas B. Marsh and Orson Hyde was brought about in large part by the lies and misrepresentations of Sampson Avard. These two inexperienced apostles lacked the discernment to see through Avard, to withstand the terrible pressures built up by the mob spirit all around them and by their own inherent weaknesses. To their credit, it must be acknowledged that they later saw their error and returned to the Church; Orson Hyde was even reinstated as a member of the Twelve. However, through this apostasy, he lost his place of seniority, and thereby failed to succeed to the presidency of the Church upon the death of Brigham Young.

One can only imagine the feelings of betrayal and frustration Joseph experienced at this time. It was obvious that the anti-Mormons were rejoicing in the heartaches and hardships the Mormons were experiencing.

Sidney Rigdon's Independence Day speech in 1838 added more fuel to the Mormon-gentile conflict. As the Saints in Far West celebrated the nation's birthday, and laid the cornerstones of the temple, Sidney Rigdon's speech whipped them into high emotion. He thundered out the Saints' own Declaration of Independence from any further mob violence or illegal activity. He warned potential mobs that the Church would no longer meekly bear persecution, but would defend itself to the death. "It shall be between us and them, a war of extermination, for we will follow them, till the last drop of their blood is spilled, or else they will have to exterminate us." Copies of this inflammatory speech were imprudently published and circulated. Some copies reached the hands of several Missouri officials, and eventually provided the basis for charges of treason and violence filed against the Saints.

The stage was set for the frightful conflict and the terrible loss of life and property that followed. The Saints would have to pass through still more of the "refiner's fire" before they could find that elusive peace and religious freedom they had so long sought.

Come, Listen to a Prophet's Voice

Joyfully ♩= 80-96
1. Come, lis - ten to a proph-et's voice, And hear the word of God,
2. The gloom of sul - len dark-ness spread Thru earth's ex-tend - ed space
3. 'Tis not in man they put their trust, Nor on his arm re - ly.
4. Then heed the words of truth and light That flow from foun-tains pure.
And in the way of truth re-joice, And sing for joy a - loud.
Is ban-ished by our liv - ing Head, And God has shown his face.
Full well as - sured, all are ac-cursed Who Je - sus Christ de - ny.
Yea, keep His law with all thy might Till thine e - lec - tion's sure,
We've found the way the proph - ets went Who lived in days of yore.
Thru err - ing schemes in days now past The world has gone a - stray;
The Sav - ior to his peo - ple saith, "Let all my words o - bey,
Till thou shalt hear the ho - ly voice As - sure e - ter - nal reign,
An - oth - er proph - et now is sent This knowl-edge to re - store.
Yet Saints of God have found at last The straight and nar - row way.
And signs shall fol - low liv - ing faith, Down to the lat - est day."
While joy and cheer at - tend thy choice, As one who shall ob - tain.

Text: Joseph S. Murdock, 1822-1899.
Verse four, Bruce R. McConkie, 1915-1985. © 1985 LDS
Music: Joseph J. Daynes, 1851-1920

Joseph Smith—History 1:14-17
Doctrine and Covenants 21:4-7

Chapter 11

1838-1839

And the Noose Gets Tighter . . .

Missouri Rejection—Persecutions—and Expulsion

Election Day Battle at Gallatin

War was Becoming a Reality

Battle of DeWitt

Guerrilla Warfare in Daviess County

Battle of Crooked River

Governor Bogg's—"Extermination Order"

Haun's Mill Massacre

Siege of Far West

Jail, Jail, Liberty Jail

Large Scale Migration of Saints from Missouri

Joseph Smith Arrives in Quincy, Illinois after Months of Imprisonment

The Beginning of Nauvoo—a New Life for the Saints

***Joseph Smith met with the President of the United States—
Martin Van Buren in Washington, D.C.***

The pot was beginning to boil over during the hot summer months of 1838, as the relationship between the Latter-day Saints and their Northern Missouri neighbors was steadily deteriorating.

The Sidney Rigdon *Independence Day* speech angered the Missourians at Far West. They had offered the Saints a temporary home after Jackson County, but they did not want the Mormons living among them. They felt that the Mormons had anti-slavery sympathies and sided with the Indians. In addition, their religious beliefs were so different that they felt the Mormons would always be a threat. The fired-up Missourians used Sidney Rigdon's statements as an excuse for continuing the persecutions. Elder Parley P. Pratt, who had arrived in Far West in May after returning from missionary service in the East, described the tense situation that existed by July 1838. He said: "War clouds began again to lower with dark and threatening aspects. Those who had combined against the laws in the adjoining countries, had long watched our increasing power and prosperity with jealousy, and with greedy and avaricious [lustful] eyes. It was a common boast that, as soon as we had completed our extensive improvements, and made a plentiful crop, they would drive us from the State, and once more, enrich themselves with the spoils." For these, and other reasons, violence erupted which eventually resulted in the expulsion of the entire Church from the State of Missouri.

In 1831, a family named Peniston had become the first white settlers in what was to become Daviess County. The next year, they built a mill on the Grand River to grind flour and meal for incoming settlers. They developed the Village of Millport. When the county was created in 1836 there were still fewer than a 100 settlers. The town of Gallatin was chartered to serve as the county seat, and as it grew, Millport, just three miles to the east, declined.

The Saints poured into Diahman, some four miles north of Gallatin, in the summer of 1838. They quickly began to outnumber the local residents in Daviess County.

The year of 1838 was an election year. The original settlers naturally wanted to elect a state legislator who was one of their own. William Peniston, a staunch foe of the Saints, was a candidate. He was afraid that with the rapid growth of the Mormon community, he would not win the election because most Church members supported John A. Williams. About two weeks before the election, a Judge, Joseph Morin of Millport, advised two Elders of the Church to go to the polls prepared for an attack by mobbers who were determined to prevent Mormons from voting. The election was to be held on Monday, August sixth, in Gallatin, which at that time was a disorganized row of "ten houses, three of which were saloons."

Hoping that the judge's prediction would be proven false, a number of Mormon men went unarmed to Gallatin to vote. As expected, some of the old Mormon enemies got together, and talked about how they would stop the Saints from voting, some of those enemies from Jackson County. In that way, they could prevent the Saints from influencing the election. Election days in the West were rarely orderly. At 11:00 a.m., **William Peniston addressed the crowd of voters, hoping to excite them against the Mormons:** "The Mormon leaders are a set of horse thieves, liars, counterfeiters, and you know they profess to heal the sick, and cast out devils, and you all know that is a lie" (*History of the Church,* 3: 57). With Peniston's inflammatory speech, and with some of the crowd filled with whiskey, a fight was inevitable. Dick Welding, the mob bully, punched one of the Saints, and knocked him down. A fight naturally ensued. Even though they were outnumbered, one of the Mormons, John L. Butler, grabbed an oak stake from a nearby woodpile, and began to fight back against the Missourians with strength that surprised even himself. The Missourians armed themselves with clapboards or anything that came to hand. During the brawl that followed, several persons on both sides were seriously hurt. Although few Mormons were able to vote that day, Peniston still lost the election.

The jealousy and hatred persisted from the Mormon enemies as they saw the industrious Latter-day Saints building fine farms and cities in a part of the state that had never been settled before. The building up of these desolate areas made these formerly useless lands, valuable. The enemies wanted to get the lands for themselves, and if they could without paying for them, so much the better.

Some of the religious leaders of other churches in Missouri, were also worried about the large number of Saints moving into the state. What would happen to their churches? Would the "Mormons" interfere with them? The Latter-day Saints had a newly-revealed religion, given them from the Lord. Their Elders did not preach for money as did ministers of other churches. These things caused the ministers to worry about their own living. All of these things raised bitterness against the Saints, and unrest began to grow once again among the Missourians. As a matter of record, it is important to report that **there is no paid ministry in The Church of Jesus Christ of Latter-day Saints.**

Distorted reports of the fight between the mob and the Saints reached Church leaders in Far West the following morning that two or three of the brethren had been killed. The First Presidency and about twenty others left immediately for Daviess County on Wednesday, August eighth. They armed themselves for their own protection, and were joined en route by Church members from different parts of Daviess County, some of whom had been attacked by the election mob. They arrived that evening at Diahman, and were relieved to learn that none of the Saints had been killed.

While in the vicinity, the Prophet determined that it would be wise to ride around the region with some of the other brethren to determine political conditions and to calm the fears that had arisen in the county. They visited several of the old settlers in the vicinity, including Adam Black, the Justice of the Peace and newly-elected judge for Daviess County. Knowing that Black had participated in the anti-Mormon activities, they asked him if he would administer the law justly and if he would sign an agreement of peace. According to Joseph Smith, after Black signed an affidavit certifying that he would disassociate himself from the mob, the brethren returned to Adam-ondi-Ahman (*History of the Church,* 3: 59-60). The next day, a council composed of prominent Mormons and non-Mormons "entered into a covenant of peace, to preserve each other's rights, and stand in each other's defense; that if men did wrong, neither party would uphold them nor endeavor to screen them from justice, but deliver up all offenders to be dealt with according to law and justice" (*History of the Church,* 3: 60).

The good will lasted less than twenty-four hours. On August tenth, William Peniston swore out an affidavit in Richmond, Ray County, before the Circuit judge, Austin A. King, stating that Joseph Smith and Lyman

Wight had organized an army of 500 men, and had threatened death to "all the old settlers and citizens of Daviess County" (*History of the Church,* 3: 61). Upon hearing this information, Joseph waited at home in Far West for further developments. The sheriff learned that Joseph was willing to submit to arrest if he could be tried in Daviess County he declined serving the writ and went to Richmond to consult with Judge King.

For about two weeks, the tensions increased in Daviess and Carroll Counties. Adam Black falsely claimed the 154 Mormons had threatened him with death unless he signed the agreement of peace. The Prophet responded that Black's statement: *"shows him in his true light—a detestable, unprincipled mobocrat and perjured man"* (*History of the Church,* 3: 65). Civil war appeared imminent as rumors and exaggerated stories circulated throughout Missouri and false reports of a Mormon uprising reached Governor Lilburn W. Boggs.

In September, the Prophet reflected upon the deteriorating circumstances, and outlined the Church's course of action. He made the following statement:

"There is great excitement at present among the Missourians, who are seeking if possible, an occasion against us. They are continually chafing [irritating] *us, and provoking us to anger if possible, one sign of threatening after another, but we do not fear them, for the Lord God, the Eternal Father is our God, and Jesus the Mediator is our strength and in the great I Am is our strength and confidence.*

"Their father the devil, is hourly calling upon them to be up and doing, and they, like willing and obedient children, need not the second admonition; but in the name of Jesus Christ the Son of the living God, we will endure it no longer, if the great God will arm us with courage, with strength and power, to resist them in their persecutions. We will not act on the offensive, but always on the defensive" (*History of the Church,* 3: 67-68).

The next day, **Joseph Smith asked Major General David Atchison and Brigadier General Alexander Doniphan of the Missouri state militia for advice on how to end the hostilities in Daviess County.** Both had been lawyers for the Saints during the Jackson County troubles in 1833-34, and continued to be friendly toward the Church. General Atchison promised he would do all he could within his power as a military officer, to disperse the mob. They advised the Prophet and Lyman Wight, who was also present, to volunteer to be tried in Daviess County. Accordingly, a trial was held on September seventh, just north of the county line, at the home of a non-Mormon farmer. Suspicious of possible mob activity, Joseph Smith stationed a company of men at the county line *"so as to be ready at a minute's warning, if there should be any difficulty at the trial."* No incriminating evidence or indictments against the two leaders was presented, but bowing to pressures, Judge King ordered them to stand trial before the circuit court and released them on 500 dollars bond (*Church History In The Fulness Of Times,* LDS, Education System, pp.195-96).

Unfortunately, this did nothing to subdue the mob spirit. Enemies of the Church, including many from other counties, prepared to attack Adam-ondi-Ahman. Lyman Wight held a colonel's commission in the fifty-ninth regiment, of the Missouri Regiment, which was directed by the state under General H.G. Parks. Lyman directed the arming of over 150 men, part of the state militia, to defend the town against the mobs. Both Mormons and mobbers sent scouts throughout the countryside, occasionally taking prisoners, and generally insulting each other. Only the cautious actions of Generals Atchison and Doniphan prevented violence. Late in September, General Atchison wrote to the governor. "Things are not so bad in that county [Daviess] as represented by rumor, and, in fact, from affidavits I have, there is no doubt that your Excellency has been deceived by the exaggerated statements of designing or half crazy men. I have found there is no cause of alarm on account of the Mormons; they are not to be feared; they are very much alarmed."

About this same time, a committee of "old citizens" in Daviess County agreed to sell their property to the Saints. Joseph Smith immediately sent messengers to the East and South to try and raise the necessary funds, but the rapidly expanding conflict made their agreement impossible to fulfill.

The harassment and intimidation caused by these false charges against Joseph Smith and Lyman Wight were insignificant in comparison to the stormy reaction they caused among the Gentiles, and even among some of the Prophet's supporters. In such a state of mind, every known or imagined shortcoming or weakness of Joseph Smith and his loyal followers, was magnified all out of proportion, and the Saints were made to appear as militant aggressors rather that as a group of citizens who had been provoked into defensive action by a mob that threatened their lives, their liberty, and their property.

When over exaggerated reports of the difficulties reached Governor Lilburn Boggs from his informants, he ordered several generals of the state militia to increase their forces. It was unfortunate for the Saints and for the reputation of the State of Missouri, that **Governor Boggs, who was also Commander-in-Chief of the Missouri militia, had an ingrained hatred toward the Latter-day Saints.** That hatred, as later events proved, blinded him to reality and caused him to misinterpret and misunderstand the goals of the Saints and to use the powerful forces at his command as an instrument of unlawful oppression and violence.

The mob, pressured by its leaders and by false reports of the size, conduct, and intentions of the Mormon forces, engaged in repeated and indiscriminate acts of violence against the Saints. Any acts of retaliation or defense on the part of the Saints were interpreted as aggressions—that endangered the peace.

During the ongoing conflicts, equally threatening and somber events were taking place between the Saints and their neighbors in DeWitt, Carroll County. A few Mormons had been welcomed earlier when they began settling in DeWitt in June 1838, but by July, it was obvious to the citizens of Carroll County that the Latter-day Saints would soon outnumber them. As in Jackson, Clay and Daviess Counties, the fear of losing political control motivated the old settlers to believe the false reports about the "deluded Mormons," and to develop a plan for driving them out. Three separate meetings were held in July to unify the citizens to eject the Mormons.

When approached with the ultimatum telling them to leave, George M. Hinkle, leader of the Saints and a colonel in the Missouri state militia, boldly declared that the Saints would defend their rights to remain in DeWitt. Conditions throughout September remained at a standoff. Violence was initially avoided partly because many Carroll militiamen were away fighting in Daviess County during September. Late in September, the Saints at DeWitt sent a letter to Governor Boggs asking for assistance in defending themselves against "a lawless mob" from Carroll and other counties, but they received no response.

In the meanwhile, the non-Mormon forces in DeWitt continued to increase, with troops from Ray, Howard, and Clay Counties, arriving almost daily. The Latter-day Saints also received reinforcements and began building barricades.

The first week of October was a fearful one for the Saints because fighting broke out between the two camps. John Murdock recorded: "We were continually employed day and night guarding [the Saints]. One night, I found myself traveling all night from one sentinel to another to keep them to their duty." The need for food and shelter became critical. **The anti-Mormon forces considered their siege "a war of extermination."**

While exploring for a new settlement, the Prophet Joseph Smith was met by an anxious and harassed messenger headed for Far West to inform the brethren of the situation in DeWitt. Disappointed, the Prophet said: *"I had hoped that the good sense of the majority of the people, and their respect for the Constitution, would have put down any spirit of persecution which might have been manifested in that neighborhood"* (*History of the Church,* 3: 152). Changing his plans, Joseph traveled secretly by unfrequented roads to avoid enemy guards, and quietly slipped into DeWitt, where he found a handful of defenders opposing the large mob. The Prophet found that the Saints were experiencing systemic starvation and deplorable destruction.

Church leaders decided to appeal once again to the governor for assistance. They obtained affidavits from sympathetic non-Mormons about the outrageous treatment of the Saints and their perilous situation. On October ninth, they received the governor's reply that: "'The quarrel was between the Mormons and the mob,' and that 'we might fight it out.'" This blasted whatever hopes the Saints may have fostered for relief.

Under these trying circumstances, the earliest Mormon settlers of DeWitt urged their brethren to leave in peace. The Saints, Joseph Smith included, gathered up seventy wagons and sadly abandoned DeWitt on October eleventh. That evening, a woman who had recently given birth, died from exposure suffered by having to travel before her strength would allow. She was buried without a coffin in a grove of trees. The mob continually harassed and threatened the traveling Saints, and several more of them died from fatigue and poverty (*History of the Church,* 3: 159-60).

The highest executive officer of the state clearly did not intend to protect the rights of his people; on the contrary, it was obvious that he was sympathetic toward the mob. This left the Prophet Joseph with only two alternatives. Either he could submit to the mob and leave Missouri, or he could follow Governor Bogg's unusual suggestion and try to enforce the rights of his people by self-help.

As he returned to Far West, the Prophet pondered these unpleasant options. If the first were adopted, where would the Saints go? At that moment, no place seemed very friendly or receptive to the Saints. They had tasted the bitter fruit of bigotry and mobocracy wherever they had lived—in New York, in Pennsylvania, in Ohio, and now in Missouri. Conceivably, the problem could be solved if the Saints were to move to a remote, uninhabited area. This consideration likely caused Joseph to eye the vast wilderness to the West as a place of temporary refuge, but the circumstances were not ripe yet. **(Later, the Prophet Joseph prophesied that his followers would ultimately be driven to the Rocky Mountains, where they would become a powerful people, prior to their return to Missouri.)**

For the moment, the better of the two questionable alternatives seemed to be for the Saints to remain in Missouri and protect their rights as best they could. It was with this intention that the Prophet arrived back in Far West to help arrange for the defense that Governor Boggs had refused to provide.

Encouraged by their success against the Saints in DeWitt and assured of the noninterference of the governor, the anti-Mormon forces marched toward Daviess County intending to remove the Mormons. News that 800 men were advancing on Adam-ondi-Ahman and that a still larger force was being raised to move against Caldwell County, alarmed Church leaders. General Doniphan, who was in Far West when the message was received, ordered Colonel Hinkle to mobilize a militia from among the local residents to protect the Saints. Since the anti-Mormons were fundamentally also members of various other militia units, a conflict of militia versus militia developed.

On the Sabbath, the Prophet spoke to the Saints, using as his text a saying from the Savior: ***"Greater love hath no man than this, that a man lay down his life for his friends"*** (John 15: 13). He concluded his message by asking for volunteers to join him in the public square the next morning. A company of about 100 men, authorized by General Doniphan as state militia from Caldwell County, left for Diahman on Monday.

In the meantime, the enemy was hard at work in Daviess County. John D. Lee reported that several settlers were "tied to trees and fearfully whipped with hickory switches, some of them being horribly mangled by the mob." A number of homes were burned, and livestock was driven off. In addition, many of the scattered families were forced to flee to Adam-ondi-Ahman for safety and shelter, in the midst of a heavy snowstorm on October seventeenth and eighteenth. Joseph Smith remembered: *"My feelings were such as I cannot describe when I saw them flock into the village, almost entirely destitute of clothes, and only escaping with their lives"* (*History of the Church,* 3: 163).

General H.G. Parks, commanding officer of the Missouri militia in Daviess County who witnessed these events, informed General David Atchison of the worsening situation. General Atchison, commander of the militia in Northern Missouri, appealed to Governor Boggs, warning him that the Missourians intended to drive out the Mormons from Daviess and Caldwell Counties, and he strongly urged the governor to visit the scene of trouble. This was Atchison's third, futile appeal to the governor; as with others to follow, it was completely ignored. Governor Boggs never appeared willing to hear the Saints' side of the story, even from trustworthy sources such as General Atchison, but instead he chose to believe the inflammatory anti-Mormon reports.

As the hostilities in Daviess County increased, General Parks authorized Lyman Wight, a colonel in the militia, to organize a force of Mormon men, and use them to disperse all mobs found in Daviess County. General Parks addressed the assembled troops: "I have visited your place frequently, and find you to be an industrious and thriving people, willing to abide the laws of the land; and I deeply regret that you could not live in peace and enjoy the privileges of freedom" (*History of the Church,* 3: 443-44).

Guerrilla warfare raged between Mormon and anti-Mormon forces for two days as both sides plundered and burned. Some members of the Church considered taking from the gentiles a necessity laid upon them because their own goods had been stolen. A young Mormon militia officer, Benjamin F. Johnson, said: "We were being hemmed in on all sides by our enemies, and were without food. All the grain, cattle, hogs, and supplies of every kind were left in the country, or so far from home that they could not be obtained except with a strong guard. So our only possible chance was to go out in searching and foraging companies, and bring in whatever we could find without regard to ownership." This matter was magnified and overstated by the non-Mormons in the court proceedings that followed the Mormon War. For their part, the anti-Mormons often set fire to their own haystacks and property, and then blamed it on the Saints. Rumors began spreading to the rest of Missouri that the Mormons were either stealing or destroying all the property of their neighbors.

In Far West, the Saints were warned that two notorious and disreputable anti-Mormons, Cornelius Gilliam and Samuel Bogart, officers in the militia, were planning assaults on the Caldwell County settlements. Meetings were held where the Saints covenanted to defend themselves and not desert the cause. Residents of the outlying settlements were instructed to gather to Far West, and the city hurried its preparations for its defense.

Unfortunately and tragically, two members of the Quorum of the Twelve Apostles, Thomas B. Marsh and Orson Hyde, (as we mentioned earlier) deserted the cause of the Church on October eighteenth, and joined with the enemy at Richmond. Marsh swore out an affidavit, which was primarily endorsed by Hyde, stating that: "the Prophet, inculcates the notion, and it is believed by every true Mormon, that Smith's prophecies are superior to the laws of the land. I have heard the Prophet say that he would yet tread down his enemies, and walk over their dead bodies; and if he was not let alone, he would be a second Mohammed to this generation" (*History of the Church,* 3: 167). This statement further justified the actions of the anti-Mormons in their own minds.

Regarding this treachery, Joseph Smith remarked: *"Thomas B. Marsh had been lifted up in pride by his exaltation of office, and the revelations of heaven concerning him, until he was ready to be overthrown by the first adverse wind that should cross his track, and now he has fallen, lied and sworn falsely, and is ready to take the lives of his best friends. Let all men take warning by him, and learn that he who exalteth himself, God will abase* [bring down]*"* (*History of the Church,* 3: 167). Thomas Marsh was excommunicated on March 17, 1839, while Orson Hyde was relieved of his duties in the Council of the Twelve. On May 4, 1839, Orson Hyde was officially suspended from exercising the functions of his office until he met with the general conference of the Church and explained his actions. On June twenty-seventh, after sufficiently repenting and confessing his error, he was restored to the Quorum of the Twelve. After years of misery, Brother Marsh returned to the Church in 1857 (*History of the Church,* 3: 345).

A turning point in the "Mormon War" in Missouri was the Battle of Crooked River, which took place at dawn on Thursday, October 25, 1838. A principal cause of this tragedy was the provocative actions of Captain

Samuel Bogart an enemy of the Saints from Jackson County. For days, Bogart ranged the line between Caldwell and Ray Counties, allegedly and supposedly trying to prevent a Mormon attack. Nevertheless, instead of simply conducting their assigned patrols, Bogart's men twice entered Caldwell County and attacked the homes of the Saints, ordered the members to leave the state, and took three Mormon men as prisoners. When word reached Far West, Elias Higbee, the Caldwell County judge and highest civil authority in the area, ordered Colonel Hinkle, the highest officer in command in Far West, to send out a company to disperse "the mob" and rescue the prisoners, whom they expected to be murdered that night.

Members of the militia had been waiting several days for a call to arms. When the drums beat at midnight, calling them to the public square, seventy-five men were mobilized into two companies commanded by David W. Patten and Charles C. Rich. As dawn approached, they arrived at a ford on the banks of the Crooked River, twenty miles from Far West. Patten's patrol approached the crossing, unaware of Bogart's concealed position along the banks of the river. Suddenly, one of Bogart's guards opened fire. Elder Patten ordered a charge, but silhouetted by the dawn, his men made good targets. In the quick, hard-fought skirmish, several men on each side were wounded. One of the wounded was Elder Patten of the Council of the Twelve. Young Gideon Carter was fatally shot through the head, and left lying on the ground, defaced so badly that the brethren did not recognize him.

The brethren freed the three prisoners, one of them also wounded. They drove the enemy across the river, and then turned to care for their wounded. Elder Patten was carried to the home of Stephen Winchester near Far West, where he died several hours later. He therefore became the first martyred Apostle in this dispensation. His faith in the Restored Gospel was such that he had once expressed to the Prophet Joseph the desire to die the death of a martyr. *"The Prophet, greatly moved, expressed extreme sorrow, for said he to David, 'when a man of your faith asks the Lord for anything, he generally gets it.'"* At his funeral in Far West, two days after the battle, Joseph Smith eulogized him: *"There lies a man that has done just as he said he would—he has laid down his life for his friends"* (*History of the Church,* 3: 175).

Patrick O'Bannion also died later from his wound. James Hendricks, another of the critically injured, was temporarily paralyzed from his waist down, and had to be carried about on a stretcher. The entire responsibility for his family fell upon his wife, Drusilla, who endured the additional dangers in Missouri and the difficult journey to Illinois with strength of character and deep faith.

Exaggerated and overstated accounts of the battle soon reached Governor Boggs in Jefferson City. One of the rumors was that Bogart's entire force was massacred or imprisoned and that the Mormons intended to plunder and burn Richmond. These reports provided Boggs, the ammunition and excuse he needed to order an all-out war against the Saints.

Northern Missouri was in an uproar the last week of October as "mobs were heard and seen in every direction." The mobs burned houses and crops, rustled cattle, detained and delayed prisoners, and threatened the Saints with death. General Atchison again urged Governor Boggs to come to the area, and see the havoc for himself. But, instead, on October twenty-seventh, he ordered his militia to war. Relying solely upon the false and misleading reports of the Mormon rebellion, Boggs claimed that the Saints had defied the laws and initiated hostilities and combat. **Therefore, Bogg's wrote: "The Mormons must be treated as enemies and *must be exterminated* or driven from the state, if necessary, for the public good. Their outrages are beyond all description"** (*History of the Church,* 3: 175). **The extermination order from Governor Boggs—sealed the doom of the Latter-day Saints in Missouri.** It was a signal to the bigots and the Mormon-haters that the law and other civilized restrictions were to be suspended until they were rid of Joseph Smith and his followers. Even more so, it put the executive power of the state, including the militia, absolutely and strictly behind the mobs.

The governor's order stirred several units of the state militia into action to build up their forces—chiefly through recruitment of the mobbers. This made it possible for the enemies of the Saints not only to fight under the representation of law, but also to receive pay for it. During this period of time, public opinion became so strong against the Saints that even those who knew the truth, would not openly side with them. Governor Bogg's "extermination order" was—a by-product, an outgrowth and expression, and demonstration of the popular desire and will of the people.

General Atchison was in charge of the state troops, but was dismissed by the governor prior to the surrender of Far West. The command was given to General John B. Clark. General Clark did not arrive at Far West until a few days after the surrender. General Samuel D. Lucas, a longtime anti-Mormon from Jackson County, was left in temporary command of the militia that was rapidly growing and gathering from all sides to encircle Far West. By October thirty-first, over 2,000 men surrounded Far West, and most of them were determined to fulfill the governor's order.

It was at Haun's Mill that the resentment, rage, and violence erupted again. This small settlement, twelve miles east of Far West, was founded by Jacob Haun, a convert from Green Bay, Wisconsin. He had moved to Shoal Creek in 1835, hoping to avoid the persecutions his fellow Saints were experiencing elsewhere in Missouri. Haun's Mill consisted of a mill, a blacksmith shop, a few houses, and a population of about twenty to thirty families at the mill itself, and 100 families in the greater neighborhood. On October thirtieth, nine wagons with immigrants from Kirtland arrived at the site. They had decided to rest a few days before traveling to Far West.

Immediately following the battle of Crooked River, the Prophet Joseph Smith advised all Saints in outlying areas to move to Far West or Adam-ondi-Ahman. Unwilling to abandon his property and withdraw from the area, Jacob Haun disregarded the Prophet's counsel, and instructed the small community to remain. This unwise decision proved to be fatal. Haun's group planned to use the blacksmith shop as a fort in the event of an enemy attack. Guards were posted to protect the mill and the settlement.

On Sunday, October 28, 1938, Colonel Thomas Jennings, of the Livingston County militia, sent one of his men to the settlement to conclude a peace treaty. Both sides pledged not to attack each other. The non-Mormons, however, did not disband as promised. On Monday, a group of Missourians in Livingston County decided to attack Haun's Mill, probably intending to carry out the governor's order. On Tuesday afternoon, October thirtieth, approximately 240 men approached Haun's Mill. Joseph Young Sr., a member of the Seven Presidents of Seventy and a recent arrival at Haun's Mill, described the late afternoon setting: "The banks of Shoal creek on either side teemed with children sporting and playing, while their mothers were engaged in domestic employments, and their fathers employed in guarding the mills and other property, while others were engaged in gathering in their crops for their winter consumption. The weather was very pleasant, the sun shone clear, all was tranquil, and no one expressed any apprehension of the awful crisis that was near us—even at our doors" (*History of the Church,* 3: 184).

At about 4:00 p.m., the mob approached Haun's Mill. The women and children fled into the woods, while the men sought protection in the blacksmith shop. David Evans, the military leader of the Saints, swung his hat and cried for peace. The sound of a 100 rifles answered him, most of them aimed at the blacksmith shop. The mobbers shot mercilessly at everyone in sight, including women, elderly men, and children. Amanda Smith seized her two little girls and ran with Mary Stedwell across the millpond on a walkway. Amanda recalled: "Yet though we were women, with tender children, in flight for our lives, the demons poured volley after volley to kill us" (Andrew Jensen, *The Historical Record,* July 1886, p. 84).

The rabble entered the blacksmith shop and found ten-year-old Sardius Smith, son of Amanda Smith, hiding under the blacksmith's bellows. One ruffian put the muzzle of his gun against the boy's skull and blew off the upper part of his head. The man later explained: "Nits will make lice, and if he had lived, he would have become a Mormon" (Jensen, *The Historical Record,* Dec. 1888, p. 673). Alma Smith, Sardius's seven-year-old brother, witnessed the murder of his father and brother and was himself shot in the hip. He was not discovered by the mob, and was later miraculously healed through prayer and faith. Thomas McBride was hacked to death with a corn knife. Although a few men along with women and children escaped across the river into the hills, **at least seventeen people were killed, and about thirteen were wounded** (*History of the Church,* 3: 326). Jacob Haun was among the wounded, but he recovered. Years later, the Prophet remarked: *"At Hauns' Mill, the brethren went contrary to my counsel; if they had not, their lives would have been spared"* (*History of the Church,* 5: 137).

The survivors hid throughout the evening and night, fearing another attack. The next day, a few able-bodied men buried the dead in a dry hole that had been dug for a well. Joseph Young had become so closely attached to young Sardius Smith during their trip from Kirtland, that he broke down and could not lower the boy's body into the common grave. Amanda and her eldest son buried Sardius the following day.

The devastated survivors left Missouri during the winter and following spring, along with other Church members. The mob continued to persecute some of the widows before they left, but the Lord helped them. Amanda Smith remembered the reassurance she received from the Lord as she crept into a cornfield to pray aloud, as she recorded: "It was as the temple of the Lord to me at that moment. I prayed aloud and most fervently. When I emerged from the cornfield, a voice spoke to me. It was a voice as plain as I ever heard one. It was no silent, strong impression of the spirit, but a voice, repeating a verse of the Saints' hymn:

The soul that on Jesus
hath leaned for repose
I will not, I cannot, desert to his foes;
That soul, though all hell
should endeavor to shake,
I'll never, no never, no never forsake!

"From that moment, I had no more fear. I felt that nothing could hurt me" (Jenson, *The Historical Record,* July 1886, p. 87).

In the meantime, the anti-Mormon militia forces continued to grow and gather in cannon and guns around Far West in preparation for an attack. The militia of Far West barricaded the city with wagons, logs, and heavy timber, but by Wednesday, October thirty-first, the anti-Mormon forces outnumbered those of the Saints by five to one. Neither side was eager to begin the battle, and the day was spent in a virtual standoff with each side trying to decide what to do.

Within hours of the Haun's Mill massacre, word had reached the Prophet Joseph. He was devastated by the news. Knowing of the governor's extermination order, and seeing in the massacre precisely what the consequences of the order would be to his beloved people, Joseph knew instinctively that the time had come to yield and comply with the demands to leave the state, in order to avoid further retaliation and bloodshed.

Unfortunately, before the Prophet could convey his feelings to those who led the troops stationed at Far West, Colonel Hinkle of the Caldwell County militia, a member of the Church, took upon himself the authority to open negotiations with General Samuel D. Lucas, who commanded several thousand troops surrounding Far West. Hinkle assumed authority over the civilian Mormon population that he never possessed. **Colonel Hinkle had been enlisted by the Saints to protect them. Nevertheless, he became secretly embittered and resentful against the Church,** but did not allow anyone to know his personal feelings. In the evening of October thirty-first, General Lucas sent a flag of truce, which was met by Colonel Hinkle. **Colonel Hinkle secretly agreed to Lucas's demands that the Prophet and other Church leaders be surrendered, tried, and punished;** that Mormon property be confiscated to pay for damages, and that the balance of the Saints surrender their arms and leave the state.

Returning to Far West, Hinkle convinced Joseph Smith, Sidney Rigdon, Lyman Wight, Parley P. Pratt and George W. Robinson that Lucas wanted to talk to them in a peace conference. The brethren were appalled when Hinkle turned them over to Lucas as prisoners. The Prophet and his associates, met Hinkle's betrayal in shocked disbelief. Under the terms of the Lucas agreement, they were to be placed in the hands of their acknowledged enemies; their property was to be confiscated without any appearance of proper legal procedure; and their families and followers were to be left leaderless and unprotected, subject to the whims of an executive who already had ordered their extermination.

In any event, under these stressful circumstances, there was little the Prophet could do since the troops committed to the defense of Far West had linked hands with the troops that surrounded it. And in view of the butchery at Haun's Mill, Joseph knew that any resistance to the demands of General Lucas would likely bring about the brutal deaths of many more of his loyal followers.

Being faced with these hard realities, the Prophet did yield to the unavoidable. And in the process, there seemed to settle upon him—a veil, a mantle of endurance, long-suffering, patience, and serenity, that was to remain with him for the rest of his days.

Parley P. Pratt described the tragic scene: "The haughty General Lucas rode up, and without speaking to us, instantly ordered his guard to surround us. They did so very abruptly, and we were marched into camp surrounded by thousands of savage looking beings, many of whom were dressed and painted like Indian warriors. These all set up a constant yell, like so many bloodhounds let loose upon their prey, as if they had achieved one of the most miraculous victories that ever graced the annals of the world" (Pratt, *Autobiography. Parley P. Pratt,* p. 160).

The shrieking continued throughout the night, terrorizing the citizens of Far West, who feared that their Prophet may have already been murdered. Most Saints spent the night in prayer. In the enemy camp, the brethren were forced to lie on the ground in a cold rain, and listen to a constant tirade of mockery and vulgarity from the guards. **"They blasphemed God; mocked Jesus Christ; swore the most dreadful oaths; taunted brother Joseph and others;** demanded miracles; wanted signs, such as: 'Come, Mr. Smith, show us an angel. Give us one of your revelations. Show us a miracle.'"

"Come, there is one of your brethren here in camp whom we took prisoner yesterday in his own house, and knocked his brains out with his own rifle, which we found hanging over his fireplace; he lays speechless and dying; speak the word and heal him, and then we will all believe. Or, if you are Apostles or men of God, deliver yourselves, and then we will be Mormons. Next would be a volley of oaths and blasphemies; then a tumultuous tirade of lewd boastings of having defiled virgins and wives by force, etc., much of which I dare not write; and, indeed, language would fail me to attempt more than a faint description."

The first night of their captivity brings to mind the mocking, blasphemous spirit of the Savior's tormentors at the crucifixion.

With the Prophet Joseph and other Church leaders in custody, the militia in Far West surrendered their arms according to the Hinkle agreement, which left the city defenseless. On the following day, General Lucas's men ransacked the city on the pretext of looking for concealed weapons. It was recorded that in the process, "the people were robbed of their most valuable property, insulted and whipped. The chastity of a number of women were defiled by force; some of them were strapped to benches and repeatedly ravished" (Francis M. Gibbons, *Joseph Smith Martyr, Prophet of God,* SLC, Deseret Book, 1977, p. 235; [Roberts, p. 244]).

In a secret and illegal court-martial held during the second night of captivity, the prisoners were sentenced to be executed the next morning on the public square in Far West, as an example to Joseph's followers. Had it not been for the bold stand of General Doniphan, these executions likely would have been carried out. General Doniphan, recognizing that the prisoners were civilians and thus not subject to the jurisdiction of a military court, bluntly told General Lucas that the executions would be cold-blooded murder, and he said: "I will not obey your order." General Doniphan also warned that if General Lucas went forward, Doniphan would remove his troops before the executions, as he did not intend to witness them nor have anything to do with them. General Doniphan said: "My brigade shall march for Liberty tomorrow morning, at 8 o'clock; and if you execute these men, I will hold you responsible before an earthly tribunal, so help me God" (*History of the Church,* 3: 190-91). Intimidated by Doniphan's courageous response, Lucas lost his nerve. The prayers of the Saints were answered. General Lucas, recognizing that this action could pave the way for later criminal charges against him, rescinded the order. Instead, he decided to take the prisoners to Independence, to exhibit them as trophies of his conquest.

The same night, word reached Far West that the enemy intended to arrest the remaining participants of the Battle of Crooked River. So before dawn, about twenty brethren slipped out of Far West and headed northeast toward Iowa territory. Hyrum Smith and Amasa Lyman were not so fortunate. They were arrested and joined the other prisoners.

Thinking they might yet be executed, Joseph Smith and his fellow prisoners begged to see their families one last time, and they returned to Far West on November second. Joseph found his wife and children in tears because they thought he had been shot. *"When I entered my house, they clung to my garments, their eyes streaming with tears, while mingled emotions of joy and sorrow were manifested in their countenances,"* he wrote. He was denied the privilege of a few private moments with them, but Emma wept and his children clung to him until *"they were thrust from me by the swords of the guards"* (*History of the Church,* 3: 193). The other prisoners suffered similarly as they bade farewell to their loved ones.

Lucy Smith, the mother of Joseph and Hyrum, hurried to the wagon where they were kept under guard, and was barely able to touch their outstretched hands before the wagon departed. After several hours of grief, she was comforted by the Spirit and blessed with personal revelation from the Lord, "that her children shall not be harmed by their enemies." In addition, the Prophet Joseph also received revelation for the comfort of his companions. The next morning, as the prisoners began their march, Joseph spoke to his companions in a low, but hopeful tone: ***"Be of good cheer, brethren; the word of the Lord came to me last night, that our lives should be given us, and that whatever we may suffer during this captivity, not one of our lives should be taken"*** (Pratt, *Autobiography Parley P. Pratt,* p. 164).

Meanwhile, General John B. Clark, the governor's designated commanding officer for the Mormon War, arrived in Far West. He ordered everyone to stay in the city, and the starving Saints were forced to live on parched corn. On November sixth, he addressed the suffering citizens and indicated that he would not force them out of the state in the depths of winter. He said: "For *this* lenity you are indebted to *my* clemency. I do not say that you shall go now, but you must not think of staying here another season, or of putting in crops. As for your leaders, do not once think—do not imagine for a moment—do not let it enter your mind that they will be delivered, or that you will see their faces again, for their *fate is fixed—their die is cast—their doom is sealed"* (*History of the Church,* 3: 203).

Another contingent of militia surrounded the Saints who had fled to Adam-ondi-Ahman for safety. After a three-day board of inquiry, all Mormons were ordered out of Daviess County, but permission was granted for them to go to Far West until spring.

While preparing for their exodus, the Saints again sought relief from the Missouri legislature. Although their grievances were clearly defined and considerable sympathy was shown by many members of the legislature and newspapers in Missouri, an official investigation was never launched. Instead, the legislature appropriated a meager 2,000 dollars for the relief of the citizens of Caldwell County.

The trip to Independence took on the aspect of a triumphal procession for the militia, whose officers proudly exhibited their prisoners at every stop along the route. False stories about the Prophet had so poisoned the minds of most nonmembers that they expected to find some kind of monster of ungodly and evil appearance and behavior. For these people, it came as quite a distinct shock to find instead, a handsome, powerfully built, mild mannered gentleman.

General Moses Wilson, who commanded the brigade that escorted the prisoners to Independence, was sympathetically and emotionally affected by his prisoners' behavior and conduct. Parley P. Pratt had written a caustic and scathing condemnation of General Wilson for his performance after the fall of Far West: "I went to General Moses Wilson in tears, and stated the circumstances of my sick, heart-broken and destitute family in terms which would have moved any heart that had a hidden spark of humanity yet remaining. But I was only answered with a boastful laugh and a scoff of denunciation by this hardened murderer." As the trip wore on, General Wilson became better acquainted with the Prophet and his brethren. His attitude toward the prisoners softened until at the end, he had feelings of harmony, and understanding toward them.

Of this radical change, Parley noted: "Indeed, it was now evident that he was proud of his prey, and felt highly enthusiastic in having the honor of returning in triumph to Independence with his prisoners, whom his superstition had magnified into something more than fellow citizens—something noble or supernatural, and worthy of public exhibition" (Pratt, *Autobiography of Parley P. Pratt,* pp. 190, 192).

One day, during the course of the trip to Independence, General Wilson, in a relaxed, expansive mood, made an almost clinical analysis of the difficulties between the Latter-day Saints and their nonmember neighbors in Missouri. Said he: "We know perfectly that from the beginning, the Mormons have not been the aggressors at all. As it began in '33 in Jackson County, so it has been ever since. You Mormons were crowded to the last extreme, and compelled to self-defense; and this has been construed into treason, murder and plunder. We mob you without law; authorities refuse to protect you according to law; you then are compelled to protect yourselves, and we act upon the prejudices of the public, who join our forces, and the whole is legalized for your destruction and our gain. Is not this a shrewd and cunning policy on our part, gentlemen?"

"When we drove you from Jackson County, we burned two hundred and three of your houses; plundered your goods; destroyed your press, type, paper, books, office and all . . .tarred and feathered old Bishop Partridge, as exemplary an old man as you can find anywhere. We shot down some of your men, and, if any of you returned the fire, we imprisoned you, on your trial for murder etc. Damn'd shrewdly done, gentlemen: and I came damn'd near kicking the bucket myself; for, on one occasion, while we were tearing down houses, driving families, and destroying and plundering goods, some of you good folks put a ball through my son's body, another through the arm of my clerk, and a third pierced my shirt collar and marked my neck. No blame, gentlemen; we deserved it. And let a set of men serve me as your community had been served, and I'll be damn'd if I would not fight till I died" (Pratt, *Autobiography of Parley P. Pratt*, p.191).

The patient and tolerant attitude of the Prophet had prepared him for either life or death, for his confidence remained absolutely unshaken whether he lived or died. He would ultimately prevail over all of his enemies, either in time or in eternity.

The prisoners and their escort arrived at Independence in a torrential rainstorm. Despite this, hundreds lined the streets to gaze with curiosity at them as they slowly passed by to the accompaniment of a drum and bugle corps. General Wilson, peacock-proud of his role as captor, introduced the prisoners, one by one, calling them by name. With this pageantry over, the prisoners were taken to a vacant house and placed under guard.

Joseph and the brethren were moderately surprised at the charitable treatment they received during their detention in Independence. By comparison with the treatment they had received at Far West, they felt comfortable and well off. The intense hatred of the Jackson County residents toward the Saints had subsided following the bloody expulsion a few years earlier. In the meantime, many new settlers had moved to the area who were unaware of the hostile feelings that previously existed. They seemed especially curious about the man they had heard about, who was accepted as a Prophet, and who had conversed with heavenly beings. Being mindful of every opportunity to proselyte, Joseph and the others took the time to preach and to explain the policies and doctrines of the Church to the great number of people who came to look them over.

Within a short period of time, the supervision over the prisoners was relaxed to the extent that they were permitted to walk the street alone without guards. In due time, they were allowed to move to a comfortable hotel, although they were required to pay for their own accommodations.

When the local residents saw the good-natured and harmless character of the prisoners, and realized that the stories being circulated about them were unfounded, the surge of public opinion turned in their favor. This was advanced by the courteous, almost bending-over-backward, respect shown by community leaders who invited the men to their homes on a social basis. It was apparent, after such exposure, that the prisoners were not dangerous, but were men of intelligence with broad interests, practical experience, and high moral and spiritual qualities.

This relatively pleasant interval was not destined to last. The enemies to the north were demanding the return of the prisoners to subject them to their own special brand of "kangaroo-court justice." Not content with conquering and crushing the Mormon community and imprisoning their leaders, the mob was determined to spill the blood of the Prophet and his chief aides, and they intended to accomplish this under the guise of law. Therefore, General Clark made repeated demands that the prisoners be sent to Richmond for trial, and tried to get volunteers to take the prisoners there. But these efforts failed because by then, the sympathies in Independence ran in favor of the prisoners. Some even disobeyed orders to take them to Richmond. "At last, a colonel and two or three officers started with us, with their swords and pistols," wrote Parley P. Pratt, "which were intended more to protect us than to keep us from escaping."

Concerning the prisoners, their arrival

into Richmond was another decline and setback into a state of turmoil and confusion, from which they had been rescued when they were moved to Independence. At the direction of General Clark, the prisoners were chained together and imprisoned in a ramshackle, vacant house, which had the windows boarded up; they were guarded by a group of illiterate, profane men.

Confident that the prisoners were secure and would not escape, General Clark turned his attention to the trial that lay ahead. Despite the unsuccessful attempt at a military trial at Far West, he chose that procedure as being much speedier, and far less cumbersome than a civil trial. In fact, he had reached his decision even before the military court was convened, and was overheard making assignments to the firing squad before the trial was brought to order.

When word of General Clark's intention became known to friends of the Prophet, they confronted the general in the same way that General Doniphan had confronted General Lucas at Far West. When it was pointed out to him that the military probably lacked jurisdiction to try the prisoners for the offenses of which they stood accused, he postponed the trial and sent to Fort Leavenworth for a military code of laws. After examining and scrutinizing these for about a week, he came to the grudging conclusion that he lacked the authority to try the prisoners. Therefore, he yielded jurisdiction to the local Civil Judge, Austin A. King, a recognized enemy of the Church, who had recently published a letter in the *Missouri Argus* newspaper accusing the Mormons of arson and murder.

The pressures continued to grow. Sidney Rigdon became very ill from exhaustion and exposure during these hardship days, but he, too, was kept in chains with the other brethren, and forced to lie on the cold floor. He was so sick that he became delirious. When this condition was discovered, the guards allowed Elder Rigdon's daughter to come into the jail and nurse him back to health.

The guards were vicious men who abused the brethren and spoke in vile language. The Prophet stood it as long as he could, and then in a powerful manner rebuked them. Parley P. Pratt, who was there, tells the story as follows:

"In one of those tedious nights, we had lain as if in sleep until the hour of midnight had passed, and our ears and hearts had been pained while we listened for hours to the obscene jests, the horrid oaths, the dreadful blasphemies and filthy language of our guards. Colonel Price as their head, they recounted to each other their deeds of rape, murder, robbery, etc., which they had committed among the Mormons while at Far West and vicinity. **They even boasted of defiling by force, wives, daughters, and virgins, and of shooting or dashing out brains of men, women and children.**

"I had listened till I became so disgusted, shocked, horrified, and so filled with the spirit of indignant justice, that I could scarcely refrain from rising upon my feet and rebuking the guards; but had said nothing to Joseph or anyone else, although I lay next to him and knew he was awake.

"Suddenly Joseph arose to his feet, and spoke in a voice of thunder, or as the roaring of a lion, uttering as nearly as I can recollect the following words:

"SILENCE, ye fiends of the infernal pit. In the name of Jesus Christ, I rebuke you, and command you to be still; I will not live another minute and bear such language.

Cease such talk, or you or I die THIS INSTANT!"

"He ceased to speak. He stood erect in terrible majesty. Chained and without a weapon; calm, unruffled and dignified as an angel, he looked upon the quailing guards, whose weapons were lowered or dropped to the ground; whose knees smote together, and who, shrinking into a corner, or crouching at his feet, begged his pardon, and remained quiet till a change of guards" (Pratt, *Autobiography of Parley P. Pratt,* pp.179-80).

"I have seen the ministers of justice, clothed in magisterial robes, and criminals arraigned before them while life was suspended on a breath in the courts of England; I have witnessed a Congress in solemn session to give laws to nations; I have tried to conceive of kings, of royal courts, of thrones and crowns, and of emperors assembled to decide the fate of kingdoms; but dignity and majesty had I seen but once, as it stood in chains, at midnight in a dungeon, in an obscure village in Missouri" (Pratt, *Autobiography of Parley P. Pratt,* p. 211).

The Missouri authorities prepared to hold a trial for the Prophet Joseph Smith and his brethren, accusing them of treason against the state, as well as murder, arson, larceny, theft and stealing. The star witness was the apostate Sampson Avard. He was joined by over forty others, including several men who had once stood close to the Prophet—William W. Phelps, John Whitmer, John Corrill, and George N. Hinkle.

Judges and lawyers were in sympathy with the mobs. Only a few were friendly to the Saints. Among them was General Doniphan. He held out against the accusers of the brethren whenever he had opportunity. At the time, when the Prophet was condemned to be shot in the public square, he said it would be the murder of an innocent man, and was instrumental in saving the Prophet's life. General Doniphan agreed, as a lawyer, to defend the Prophet and his friends at the trial.

For fifteen weary days, the prisoners listened to a seemingless endless parade of perjured and bribed witnesses. Each night, the Prophet was returned to his cell and shackled to his fellow prisoners. Questioning by the prosecutors failed to produce any authentic evidence to support a criminal charge.

Once the prosecution had ended its laborious and wearisome presentation, the defendants were asked to submit a list of potential witnesses to testify in their behalf. They complied by submitting a list of between forty and fifty men. To their alarm and bewilderment, this list was turned over to their old enemy, Captain Bogart, who himself had been a witness for the prosecution. Bogart proceeded to arrest and charge every man on the list whom he could find. This charade was repeated a second time with the same result. Almost miraculously, seven witnesses, four men and three women, succeeded in evading Captain Bogart's dragnet and the intimidations of the court, in order and to testify in behalf of the prisoners. In light of the theatrical and humorous nature of the proceedings, it came as no great surprise or shock that the Prophet, his brother Hyrum, Sidney Rigdon, and three other men were bound over for trial on the charge of treason, and sent to the jail in nearby Liberty. Parley P. Pratt and four others were bound over for trial on the charge of murder, and were left in Richmond in the filthy quarters where the Prophet and the others had been shackled during the trial. All the other prisoners were released.

Confined for several months in jail, and

facing with uncertainty the outcome of the formal trial that still lay ahead, **the Prophet was greatly concerned about the safety of his family** and about the leadership of the Church members, most of whom were perplexed and sorely disappointed by the dramatic turn of events that had put their Prophet behind bars. Many turned away from him at this time, either because of indifference or because they had been infected by the apostate spirit that had taken others out of the Church.

Nevertheless, a large number of the Saints still would, the Prophet knew, follow him to the death if necessary because they knew he represented Heavenly Father and Jesus Christ. It was upon these courageous and valiant members that he would concentrate his attention once he had settled down in the cold, dimly lighted quarters of the Liberty Jail. Rather than wasting time bemoaning his fate and feeling sorry for himself, he set about to use the resources at hand. A stream of letters began to flow from him to members of his family and the brethren. These letters lacked any hint of cynicism, depression, sadness or self-pity. On the contrary, they exhibited a spirit of resiliency, responsiveness, and lightheartedness. In a letter addressed to the Church at large in December 1838, he wrote: *"Dear brethren, do not think that our hearts faint, as though some strange thing had happened unto us, for we have seen and have been assured of all these things beforehand, and have an assurance of a better hope than that of our persecutors. Therefore, God hath made broad our shoulders for the burden.* ***We glory in our tribulation, because we know that God is with us, that He is our friend, and that He will save our souls"*** (*History of the Church,* 3: 227).

Due to the powerful impact of his writings, the Prophet's enemies found him almost as formidable, astounding and yet troublesome, while imprisoned as while he was free. In fact, his imprisonment added another dimension of authenticity to his already impressive credentials as a prophetic man of God. Words sent from the Liberty Jail were read avidly by his disciples, and told and retold through the efficient Mormon grapevine, and these served to strengthen the testimonies of many of the loyal Saints who may have wavered.

In reality, the two-story, twenty-two-foot square stone jail in Liberty was a dungeon. The small, barred windows opened into the upper level, and there was little or no heat. A hole in the floor was the only access to the lower level, where a man could not stand upright. **During the four winter months, the Prophet and his companions suffered from cold, filthy conditions, smoke inhalation, loneliness, and filthy food. One guard did boast that they had fed the prisoners human flesh. At another time, the prisoners were fed poison which caused them to vomit for several days.** The guards were also very abusive to the prisoners. Probably worst of all, they were unable to accompany the faithful Saints who were being driven from the state. Nevertheless, these were months of special significance to Joseph Smith and the Church. In the Prophet's absence, Brigham Young, Heber C. Kimball, and John Taylor demonstrated superior leadership ability and commitment. **In his despair, Joseph Smith received priceless spiritual instructions from the Lord.** Because of the things revealed there Liberty Jail could be called—a temple-prison.

So preoccupied was Joseph with the condition of his family and followers, that in a way, he seemed oblivious to the subhuman conditions under which he and his fellow prisoners lived. Except for the occurrence when he rebuked the profane guards at Richmond, Joseph appears to have taken the inconvenience of his imprisonment in stride, and to have endured it with patient silence.

In the midst of the confusion, the harassment, and the endless inconvenience of prison life, Joseph maintained a basic composure and serenity. His main concern, aside from his family and his followers, was whether his imprisonment would jeopardize his ability to lead. His feelings are reflected in a sensitive, touching letter he wrote to Emma in his own hand on March 21,1839. Disclosing the lonesome feelings of any man separated from his family, he pleaded for news from home: *"I want you to try to gain time and write to me a long letter, and tell me all you can, and even if old Major* [a favorite family pet] *is alive yet, and what those littler pratlers* [chatterboxers] *say that cling around your neck."* Toward the end of the letter, in a rare introspective subjective mood, he raised several questions about the effect of his imprisonment upon his family and his friends. *"I feel like Joseph in Egypt,"* he wrote, almost as if talking to himself in a daydream. *"Doth my friends yet live? If they live, do they remember me? Have they regard for me? If so, let me know it."* Focusing then upon his beloved wife, he asked: *"Dear Emma, do you think that my being cast into prison by the mob, renders me less worthy of your friendship?"* Answering his own question, he concluded, *"No I do not think so"* (N.B. Lundwall, *"The Fate of the Persecutors of the Prophet Joseph Smith* 1952, pp. 112-14).

From his prison cell in Liberty, the Prophet, carried on a correspondence with the Church which gives great insight and perception into the man's nature. Some of the finest pieces of Mormon literature came from his pen during that time. By his words and encouragement the Prophet kept faith and hope alive in the Church. He comforted the Saints in their suffering while counseling and warning them of *"wolves in sheep clothing,"* to be aware of those who would come amongst them to teach false doctrines in the name of the First Presidency. Joseph counseled love and tolerance to a people with every cause for bitterness and hatred: "*We ought always to be aware of those prejudices which sometimes so strangely present themselves, and are so congenial to human nature, against our friends, neighbors, and brethren of the world, who choose to differ from us in opinion and in matters of faith. Our religion is between us and our God. There is a love from God that should be exercised toward those of our faith, who walk uprightly, which is peculiar to itself, but it is prejudice; it also gives scope to the mind, which enables us to conduct ourselves with greater liberty towards all that are not of our faith, than what they exercise toward one another"* (*History of the Church*, 3: 304; "Letter from Liberty Jail" dated March 25, 1839).

It was very characteristic of the Prophet Joseph that his mind did not long dwell on the afflictions and suffering of the moment, but turned toward a bright, glorious future. This bounteous optimism was caught by the great majority of the Church members, so that historian says of them: "Their trails and sufferings instead of dampening the ardor of the Saints, increased it tenfold."

When Joseph was not busy writing letters to his family and friends, or writing documents for a redress of grievances, or conferring with the lawyers about his defense, he was devising schemes to escape. Several of these were tried but failed.

A number of people saw the exodus from Missouri as evidence that the Lord had given up on the Saints. The Prophet Joseph was in Liberty Jail with little prospect of release. Whatever hope the Saints had of regaining their political rights and property in Missouri or establishing the City of Zion in Independence (Jackson County) was bleak. Even some Church members questioned the worth of gathering the Saints again into one location.

Where were Church members to go for refuge? Where could they escape for a new beginning? The vast Indian tracts to the west were not open to settlers. Iowa to the north was sparsely settled, but offered little timber upon its enormous, rolling plains. Going south meant traveling through hostile Missouri communities. The route east was the most familiar and reassuring to Church members. Many of the Saints had traveled this road a few months before in their banishment from Kirtland. At this time though, some of them were certainly considering returning to Ohio. Crossing the Mississippi, they paused briefly in some of the small Illinois communities along the bank, providing the pause necessary for the Saints to receive new direction from Church leaders.

The months following the surrender of their Far West, Missouri, community severely tested the leadership of the Church. The entire First Presidency of the Church (Joseph Smith, Sidney Rigdon and Hyrum Smith) were in jail. The ranks of the Quorum of the Twelve Apostles had been thinned. One of the schemes that communities used to rid themselves of the Mormons, (having mentioned this before), was to file all kinds of false and demeaning charges against Joseph Smith and other Church leaders. The idea was to commit them to jail, then disrupt and destroy the latter day religion because their leader, the Prophet Joseph Smith was not available to lead them.

The responsibility of overseeing the needs of the Church during the winter of 1838-1839, and throughout the exodus from Missouri to Illinois, **fell mostly upon Brigham Young** and Heber C. Kimball. John Taylor was called to the apostleship in December 1838. Wilford Woodruff and George A. Smith were added the following April; both of these men were able to provide valuable assistance during this critical time.

Church leaders delayed the decision to leave Missouri as long as possible, hoping beyond hope that the Missouri legislature would revoke Missouri Governor Bogg's Mormon extermination order. The Church leaders sent numerous petitions to state officials and to the legislature requesting them to let the Saints remain in their own homes, but these pleas fell on deaf ears. Nevertheless, the leaders were able to buy some much needed time because of severe weather.

Meanwhile, the Missourians grew steadily impatient with the delaying tactics of the Saints. In early 1839, Church leaders became convinced that they could no longer hold out hope to remain in Missouri. On January 26, 1839, Brigham Young created a "Committee on Removal" to facilitate the exodus.

Emma Smith, the wife of the Prophet, had visited Joseph twice after his imprisonment in Liberty Jail. With the help of Stephen Markham, she left Missouri with her children, carrying the two youngest in her arms. They walked 150 miles across Missouri to the east towards Illinois. When Emma crossed the frozen Mississippi River on February 15, 1839, she had her four small children with her at her side. She carried two cotton bags full of Joseph's most sacred papers hidden under her full skirts, including his Inspired Revision of the Bible. She crossed the river and reached Quincy, Illinois, on the other shore, where she stayed until Joseph was freed from prison.

Throughout the winter and spring of 1839, Brigham Young's Committee arranged to feed, clothe, and transport the poor. By formal resolution, nearly 400 Latter-day Saints covenanted to place all of their available property at the disposal of the committee "for the purpose of providing means for the removing from this state of the poor and destitute who shall be considered worthy, till there shall not be one left who desires to remove from the state." Even Joseph Smith somehow sent 100 dollars from Liberty Jail to assist the effort.

By mid-February 1839, conditions were such that a large scale migration of the Saints had begun. Wagons and teams, although not of the best quality, had been acquired; food reserves were in place along the migration route; and fortunately, there was a temporary break in the weather. Nevertheless, leaving Missouri was not easy for the refugees. Many people sold precious possessions and lands at unreasonably low prices to obtain means to flee the state. One Missourian bought forty acres of good land from a Church member for a "blind mare and a clock." Some other tracts of land sold for only fifty cents per acre.

Until mid-spring 1839, Church leaders who were not in jail had no definite plan for where the Saints should settle. Word reached the leaders that the citizens of Illinois were sympathetic to their plight and would welcome the Saints. Many people in Illinois believed that a large influx of Mormons would help their struggling economy. The state's politicians also encouraged immigration because Illinois was nearly equally divided between the Whigs and Democrats. Each party hoped to attract the large Mormon vote.

Consequently, **the Saints were warmly received in Quincy following their expulsion from Missouri.** The citizens of Quincy, and especially a group known as the Democratic Association, had met there the previous February to consider the plight of the exiles and the ways in which they might be assisted. Out of the meeting came a resolution that stated: "Resolved: That the strangers recently arrived here from the state of Missouri, known by the name of the 'Latter-day Saints,' are entitled to our sympathy and kindest regard, and that we recommend to the citizens of Quincy to extend all the kindness in their power to bestow on the persons who are afflicted" (*History of the Church,* 3: 268).

Without demeaning the sincerity of those who extended this welcome to the Saints, it should be noted that at the time, the State of Illinois was heavily in debt; and the chief hope in avoiding public bankruptcy lay in attracting new settlers to the area, thus broadening the tax base. So, the kindness reflected in this resolution was not founded entirely upon Christian charity. There was a good deal of self-interest mixed up in it. It should be noted also that at the time, there existed in Illinois in large numbers, many of the irreligious, hard-drinking settlers of the kind whom the Saints had known, to their sorrow, in Ohio and Missouri. This element would surface in the years ahead to harass and ultimately kill the Prophet.

Benevolent residents in Quincy, a community of 1,200, were generous and sympathetic to the predicament of the Saints. Many of them opened their homes and provided jobs. They collected money, food, clothing and other necessities on more than one occasion. Throughout the late winter and spring of 1838-39, thousands of Latter-day Saints arrived at the western bank of the Mississippi across from Quincy. In late February, about twelve families at a time crossed, on the only ferryboat available. Moderating weather caused dangerous ice flows to inhibit further crossings. When another cold spell set in and the river again froze over, scores of Saints hurried to cross on the ice.

Eight to ten thousand Latter-day Saints migrated to Western Illinois that season. As Quincy filled with hundreds of refugees, the living conditions deteriorated. The Saints, most of whom were destitute, suffered from hunger in the cold, rain, and mud because the of community of Quincy could not accommodate all the new arrivals.

At this time, several of the Saints met with Isaac Galland, the large land speculator in the area. After hearing the plight of the Saints, Galland offered to sell the Church large parcels of land in Iowa and Illinois. In February, the men took this information to the Church leaders in Quincy who were meeting to decide what to do next.

Sidney Rigdon and a few others questioned the wisdom of gathering to one place again; they felt that this had been the major source of their problems in Missouri and Ohio. On the other hand, Brigham Young counseled the Saints to gather closely to better help one another. Uncertain how to proceed, the brethren wrote to the Prophet in Liberty Jail asking his advice. On March twenty-second, the Prophet advised the brethren to buy the property and not to scatter the people.

Public opinion in Missouri was turning against Governor Boggs and the mob as Joseph Smith and his colleagues continued to linger and endure in jail, waiting for state officials to determine what to do with them. Toward the end of March 1839, the Prophet wrote a long letter to the Church, parts of which now appear as Sections 121, 122, and 123 of the Doctrine and Covenants scriptures. After reviewing the wrongs perpetrated upon the Saints, the Prophet had appealed to the Lord:

"O GOD, where art thou? And where is the pavilion that covereth thy hiding place?

"How long shall thy hand be stayed, and thine eye, yea thy pure eye, behold from the eternal heavens the wrongs of thy people and of thy servants, and thine ear be penetrated with their cries?

"Yea, O Lord, how long shall they suffer these wrongs and unlawful oppressions, before thine heart shall be softened toward them, and thy bowels be moved with compassion toward them?" (Doctrine & Covenants 121: 1-3).

"Let thine anger be kindled against our enemies, and, in the fury of thine heart, with thy sword avenge us of our wrongs. Remember thy suffering saints, O our God; and thy servants will rejoice in thy name forever" (Doctrine & Covenants 121; 5-6).

The Prophet then inserted the Lord's response to his plea:

"My son, peace be unto thy soul; thine adversity and thine afflictions shall be but a small moment; And then, if thou endure it well, God shall exalt thee on high; thou shalt triumph over all thy foes. Thy friends do stand by thee, and they shall hail thee again with warm hearts and friendly hands. Thou art not yet as Job; thy friends do not contend against thee, neither charge thee with transgression, as they did Job" (Doctrine & Covenants 121: 7-10). He continued to speak comfort to the Prophet, urging him to be patient in

his suffering. At another time, He spoke to Joseph saying:

"If thou art called to pass through tribulation; if thou art in perils among false brethren; if thou art in peril among robbers; if thou art in peril by land or by sea; If thou art accused with all manner of false accusations; if thine enemies fall upon thee if they tear thee from the society of thy father and mother and brethren and sisters; and if with a drawn sword, thine enemies tear thee from the bosom of thy wife, and of thine offspring, and thine elder son, although but six years of age, shall cling to thy garments, and shall say, 'My father, my father, why can't you stay with us? O, my father, what are the men going to do with you?' and if then he shall be thrust from thee by the sword, and thou be dragged to prison, and thine enemies prowl around thee like wolves for the blood of the lamb; And if thou shouldst be cast into the pit, or into the hands of murderers, and the sentence of death passed upon thee; . . . if fierce winds become thine enemy; if the heavens gather blackness, and all the elements combine to hedge up the way; and above all, if the very jaws of hell shall gape open the mouth wide after thee, know thou, my son, that all these things shall give thee experience, and shall be for thy good.

"The Son of Man hath descended below them all. Art thou greater than he? Therefore, hold on thy way, and the priesthood shall remain with thee, for their bounds are set, they cannot pass. Thy days are known, and thy years shall not be numbered less; therefore, fear not what man can do, for God shall be with you forever and ever" (Doctrine & Covenants 122: 5-9).

The Lord loved the Prophet, and was with him in his afflictions, just as he was with other prophets who had been persecuted before him.

As the weight of public opinion shifted more and more toward the Saints, his captors seemed almost as anxious for his escape as was he, but the timing was as important as were the appearances.

Sidney Rigdon had been released on bail on February 25, 1839, because of his failing health. Sometime later, Joseph and the others petitioned the court for their release. Three weeks later, Judge Turnham responded, and came to visit them in jail. He explained that if he were to admit them to bail, too, it would cost him his life. He went on to say, however, that the governor was "heartily sick" of the affair, and that he had "arranged a plan for their escape" (Francis M. Gibbons, *Joseph Smith Martyr, Prophet of God,* SLC, Deseret Book, 1977, [Roberts, p. 271]).

After the Prophet and his friends were locked up in Liberty Jail, they were told that if any judge or jury should free them, the brethren would never get out of the state alive. The mob would kill them first.

Having heard these comments so often, the brethren felt that they would never get justice in the courts, and that the only way for them to save their lives would be to escape from the prison.

One of the judges made an investigation of the case of Sidney Rigdon, who had been ill in jail, and found he was not guilty of any crime, and told him he could go free. But at first, Sidney was afraid to leave the jail for fear of being caught by the mob.

At this time, the jailer was a man who was friendly to the brethren. Late one night, he let Sidney out of jail secretly, telling him to get out of the state as fast as he could. Sidney understood the danger of being caught by the mob, and fled for his life. Some of the mob discovered he had gone and followed him, but in the darkness he was able to get away and make his way to Illinois.

A few days later, about fifty Missourians met together and swore that they would never eat or drink until they had killed the Prophet. This made it even more important that the Prophet must escape to Illinois as soon as possible.

A plan was consummated in April 1839, but first, the prisoners were sent to Daviess County for trial. A grand jury brought in a verdict against them for "murder, treason, burglary, arson, larceny, theft, and stealing" (*History of the Church,* 3: 315).

While in Daviess County, they were placed in the hands of William Morgan, the sheriff. A new judge came to hear the case. He was sympathetic with the brethren, and felt this long persecution should be stopped. At the trial, many false charges were brought against the brethren. The brethren became discouraged, but during the night, the Lord gave the Prophet a vision in which he saw that he would soon be set free.

This whole situation became a sticky affair for Governor Boggs. Other states were watching his actions. With the Mormons driven out due to his extermination order, he now needed to get rid of: "the major fly in his ointment," the Prophet Joseph Smith. Only this he felt would resolve his Mormon headache.

It was then decided that the trial should be moved to still another county—Boone County. The prisoners started their journey under heavy guard. They had to purchase their own horses to make the journey. This they did with funds which their friends had sent them. Neither the judge nor the sheriff who was guarding them felt that they were guilty, and both were quite willing to have them freed.

When they stopped for the night, Sheriff Morgan told the brethren that he did not have to take them to Boone County if he did not wish to, and that he was going to get a big drink of liquor and go to bed. Then he said the prisoners could do anything they wanted to do.

There were three other guards. They all drank very heavily and became drunk. They too, soon went to bed, and before long were sound asleep. A fourth guard was very friendly. He helped the brethren saddle the two horses they had brought, and all five of the prisoners got away. It took them ten days to get to Quincy, Illinois. When they got there, they found their families poverty-stricken—but well.

The next morning, the sheriff and the guards returned to their homes, and when they reported that the prisoners had escaped, they were cruelly treated by the people there. The sheriff was ridden out of town on a rail, and one of the other men was dragged over the square by the hair of his head. They were accused of permitting the prisoners to escape.

During the six months of their imprisonment, Joseph and his companions had been under sentence of death three times, but the Lord preserved their lives and permitted their safe return to their families.

Of the confidence Joseph had that he would survive and of the feelings he entertained during his confinement he wrote: *"During the time I was in the hands of my enemies, I must say, that although I felt great anxiety respecting my family and friends, who were so inhumanly treated and abused, I felt perfectly calm, and resigned to the will of my Heavenly Father. From my first entrance into the camp, I felt an assurance that I, with my brethren and our families, should be deliv-*

ered. Yes, that still small voice, which has so often whispered consolation to my soul, in the depths of sorrow and distress, bade me be of good cheer, and promised deliverance, which gave me great comfort. And although the heathen raged, and the people imagined vain things, yet the Lord of Hosts, the God of Jacob was my refuge; and when I cried unto him in the day of trouble, He delivered me; for which I call upon my soul, and all that is within me, to bless and praise His Holy Name. For I was troubled on every side, yet not distressed; perplexed, but not in despair; persecuted, but not forsaken; cast down, but not destroyed." The Prophet paid special tribute to those who had stood by him and who had befriended him while he was imprisoned. Of them he wrote: *"Their attention and affection to me, while in prison, will ever be remembered by me; and when I have seen them thrust away and abused by the jailer and guard, when they came to do any kindness, and to cheer our minds while we were in the gloomy prisonhouse, gave me feelings which I cannot describe; while those who wished to insult and abuse us by their threats and blasphemous language, were applauded, and had every encouragement given them."*

Joseph and Hyrum and those who had escaped with them from Missouri in April arrived in Quincy on April 22, 1839. The Prophet felt that it was the prayers of the brethren and the Saints that had helped them escape. Joseph and the others arrived at the Quincy ferry, pale, unshaven, weary, and exhausted. Since the Prophet wanted their arrival to be unnoticed, they took the back streets of the city to the home of a friend about four miles away from town where Emma was staying. She immediately recognized her husband as he climbed down off his horse, and met him joyfully halfway to the gate.

It was with feelings of great frustration that Joseph had turned his back on Missouri. He was gratified to leave behind the stench and turmoil of the filthy jails that had been his home for many months. He was relieved to be free of the menacing and hurtful neighbors who for years had harassed, intimidated, and murdered his people. He was overjoyed with the prospect of having the love and companionship again of his family and friends, and of getting on with the urgent work of building up the Church. At the same time, he could not help but feel regret over the devastated hopes and the outward failures left behind. Gone, temporarily, was the hope of a heaven on earth fit to receive the Savior at His Second Coming. Gone, for the moment, were the plans to build the holy temple to which the Savior was to return. And the founding of the City of Zion would now have to be delayed to some indefinite time in the future.

The Prophet knew from the revelations he had received that these failures had come about in large part through the disobedience and the stiff-neckedness of the Saints. As a faithful, responsible, and conscientious leader, he could not help but wonder the degree these failures could be attributed to faulty leadership on his part. Nevertheless, these reactions were brief. It was not in keeping with the Prophet's character to brood over the past or to permit past failures to hinder his present performance. In this, Joseph was not only a great leader, but follower of the second fundamental principle of the Gospel—repentance—which is founded on the premise of man's fallibility and his power to change and improve. As Joseph has said, over and over again: ***"When I'm a Prophet of God, I'm a Prophet of God—when I'm a man and acting as a man,***

making manly decisions, I'm a man" (Refer to—*History of the Church,* 5: 265). As Joseph led his people, sometimes his personal "manly" decisions weren't the best, as we have read. Nevertheless, any message Joseph received from God was always right on target. Never did he presume to change any of God's communications. He was the communicator for God, and all that God gave him was truth for all of God's children.

While Joseph recognized the inadequacies in his conduct and the conduct of his people while in Missouri, he was determined to learn from them. Despite failure there, the revelations and teachings about Zion had implanted in the minds of his followers the idea that they, or their descendants, would one day return to Missouri to build the **New Jerusalem**.

Parley P. Pratt, King Follet, and Morris Phelps did escape from the Boone County prison on July 4, 1839, after over seven months of imprisonment. King Follett was quickly recaptured. Several days later, Pratt and Phelps arrived safely in Quincy, Illinois. In mid-October 1839, King Follett, the last prisoner in Missouri, was finally freed.

With frank realism and probably with some anxiety, Joseph recognized that the Saints had not seen an end to persecution. In fact, he held it out to his followers as a way of life. Wrote he: *"We shall therefore do well to discern the signs of the times as we pass along, that the day of the Lord may not 'overtake us as a thief in the night.' Afflictions, persecutions, imprisonments, and death we must expect, according to the scriptures, which tell us that the blood of those whose souls were under the altar, could not be avenged on them that dwell on earth, until their brethren should be slain as they were."*

The Prophet concluded this remarkable account by severely castigating those who were responsible for the abuse and persecution that had been heaped upon the Latter-day Saints: *"If these transactions had taken place among barbarians,"* he wrote, *"then there might have been some shadow of defense offered. But can we realize, that in a land which is the cradle of liberty and equal rights . . . a persecution the most unwarrantable was commenced, and a tragedy the most dreadful was enacted, by a large portion of the inhabitants of one of those free and sovereign states which comprise this vast Republic"* (*History of the Church,* 3: 327-31).

For the fifth time in less than ten years, many of the Latter-day Saints had left their homes and began anew to build a place of refuge. Though the last several months were marred by financial disaster, bitter persecution, apostasy, and expulsion from Missouri, most Church members did not lose sight of their divine destiny. As Joseph said in his letter to the Saints: *"As well might man stretch forth his puny arm to stop the Missouri River in its decreed course, or to turn it up stream, as to hinder the Almighty from pouring down knowledge from heaven upon the heads of the Latter-day Saints."*

It took 137 years before the truth of the persecutions against the Mormons was acknowledged by the State of Missouri . . .

NEWSPAPER STORY which appeared in the **DESERET NEWS,** June 25,1976 . . . Headline . . . 1838 Anti-Mormon Law Lifted-Missouri Apologizes.

Jefferson City, Mo.—The Missouri "Mormon Extermination Order" of 1838 was not rescinded until 1976, when Governor Christopher S. Bonds labeled the incident as a dark chapter in Missouri history.

The extermination order was issued on Oct. 27, 1838, by Missouri Governor L.W. Boggs, who directed General John B. Clark to drive the Mormons from his state.

The 137-year-old executive order said, "The Mormons must be treated as enemies and must be exterminated or driven from the state, if necessary for the public good."

In rescinding the order, Bond expressed "on behalf of all Missourians our deep regret for the injustice and undue suffering which was caused by this 1838 order."

The governor's assistant, Don Sipple, said the action to rescind the order was prompted by a Missouri citizen's group which brought the matter to the governor's attention.

After signing the order to rescind the earlier order, Bond said, "This is a dark chapter in Missouri history. In this, our country's 200th birthday, it is fitting to reaffirm our belief in the principles which our founding fathers recognized in our state's and nation's Constitution and Bill of Rights."

He also said Boggs' order "clearly contravened the rights of the Mormon people to life, liberty, property and religious freedom."

The extermination order was issued at a time in Missouri's history when there was friction between Mormons and non-Mormons. Boggs accused the Mormons of having "made open war upon the people of this state." The issuance of the order resulted in large-scale attacks on Mormons in Missouri by state troops and citizens. Many Mormons—men, women and children—were killed in attacks that followed Boggs' order.

Boggs' order to Clark said, "you will proceed immediately to Richmond and there operate against the Mormons. Brigadier-General Parks, of Ray, has ordered to have 400 men of this brigade in readiness to join you at Richmond. The whole force will be placed under your command."

Sipple said Bond has rescinded the Boggs' order, "Executive Order 44," now as a Bicentennial tribute to the Mormon people, and as a reaffirmation of basic American principles.

"As we reflect on our nation's heritage, the exercise of religious freedom is without question one of the basic tenets of our free democratic republic," Bond said.

The order has long since been ignored in Missouri, where The Church of Jesus Christ of Latter-day Saints, with its thousands of members residing within its borders, now have three stakes located in Columbia, Independence and Kansas City.

In 1839, the Mormons were driven completely out of Missouri and moved on to Illinois. The expulsion led to the founding of Nauvoo in Illinois, at one time, the largest city in Illinois.

Boggs moved West, where he died in California in 1861 (*History of the Church,* 3: 175).

When Joseph arrived in Quincy he expressed his gratitude in these words: *"We continued on our journey; both by night and by day; and after suffering much fatigue and hunger, I* [Joseph] *arrived in Quincy, Illinois amidst the congratulations of my friends, and the embraces of my family, whom I found as well as could be expected, considering what they had been called to endure"* (*History of the Church,* 3: 327).

Joseph hardly had time to say hello to his family and followers before he was caught up in the monumental task of finding a suitable location for the permanent settlement of the Saints. Three days after his arrival in

Quincy, he had crossed the river into Iowa to examine potential sites. Their traumatic experiences in Missouri and Ohio had convinced Joseph and the other brethren of the desirability of establishing a separate community of their own rather than moving into an existing area that had been settled previously by others. Thus, the brethren were looking for a sizeable tract that would accommodate a town site with nearby agricultural land sufficient to sustain a population of 15-20,000 people. It was not their intention to preclude nonmembers from living in their midst. Quite the contrary. It was their intention to structure a community in a way that would make life wholly compatible with their customs and ideals.

The Prophet appointed a committee consisting of Newel Knight and Alanson Ripley as his key counselors to find land for a gathering place.

As has been mentioned, one of the friends of the Church in Illinois, was a man named Isaac Galland. He had learned from reliable sources that the Saints were good people, and that they deserved to be helped. He knew they needed to find a place to build their homes, and he felt that the settlement of Commerce, about fifty miles north of Quincy, would be a suitable place. He told the Saints about it and urged them to visit the place and judge for themselves, which the Prophet did. The whole City of Commerce consisted of one stone house, three wooden ones, and two blockhouses. The place was not healthful, because it was low and swampy. The swamp was covered with underbrush and scattered trees, and the land was practically deserted. Swarms of mosquitos, the then unknown carriers of malaria fever were everywhere. After seeing this, the brethren felt they should look into Iowa as well.

After studying all available places, they came back to Commerce. Although the place was unhealthy, and was avoided by settlers and travelers, the Prophet felt that it was the place, and he was confident that if the Saints settled there, the Lord would bless them and make it free of disease. As Joseph stood on the gentle horseshoe bend, half-circled by the wide Mississippi, he liked what he saw. The land, covered with trees and bushes, rose to the level of the prairie, rich with grasses, wild flowers, and stands of timber. At this point of the land, the river makes a broad bend giving the land on its east bank the appearance of a peninsula—a beautiful sight to behold.

On May first, the initial purchase of land was completed. The committee purchased 135 acres of swampland from Hugh White on the Illinois side, and forty-seven acres of improved land from Isaac Galland. A total of $14,000 in promissory notes was paid to Galland and White for the initial tracts of land. Other purchases were subsequently made until extensive holdings were secured on both the Iowa and Illinois sides of the river. Although Commerce was chosen as the gathering place, some of the Saints decided to live in Montrose, Iowa, just across the river.

Mr. Galland continued his friendly attitude toward the Saints. He wrote articles to the Illinois newspapers praising the Prophet and his people, and showing how false the accusations against them were. He began studying the Gospel and claimed to be converted. On July 3, 1839, the Prophet baptized and confirmed him a member of the Church.

Even though the land was bought from Isaac Galland at what appeared to be very favorable terms, in reality, Galland who seemed to be a generous supporter of the Saints, turned out to be a promoter who had sold lands he didn't own and a swindler who made off with the funds of the Church and necessitated new negotiations for land.

The lands that the Saints purchased were extensive enough to enable the Prophet to project the building of a city of somewhat grand proportions. The unique ideas that had been incorporated in the Prophet's plan of the City of Zion some years before, were to find practical expression in building the new city. Sites in the center of the town were to be reserved for public buildings and for the temple. Residential lots were to be large enough to accommodate homes and associated buildings and to enable the residents to raise gardens, poultry, and barnyard animals. Industrial and business activities were to be segregated, and the surrounding farm land was near enough to make commuting easy and convenient.

This particular site also had the advantage of being adjacent to a large, navigable river, which would enhance its value as a commercial center, and would facilitate access to it by the thousands of Latter-day Saints who would flock there from the surrounding areas and from the fruitful missions abroad.

After the necessary property acquisitions, the Prophet arranged for a survey of the area and the subdivision of lots within the townsite. These lots were then sold for 500 dollars each, although those Saints who had suffered extreme losses during the Missouri persecutions were given their lots free.

As the Prophet reflected upon the plans for the city, it occurred to him that the name of Commerce was totally unsuited for the kind of city he had in mind. Relating back to his Hebrew studies several years earlier before he came up with a name for the city that more nearly coincided with the image he had conceived for it. It would be known as **Nauvoo.** This Hebrew name literally signified "a beautiful situation" and, according to the Prophet, carried with it *"the idea of rest—the beautiful location*—or—*the city beautiful."*

Once the preliminaries of property acquisitions and surveys had been completed, the Saints began to gather to Nauvoo, where they set about with characteristic vigor and enthusiasm to build a new life. **The terrible losses in property and life they had suffered in Kirtland and Missouri had in no way dampened their fervor.** On the contrary, loss seemed only to fuel the Saints' energies and their determination to show the world the fruits of their religion.

On Friday, May 10,1839, the Prophet, Emma, and their four children moved into a two-story log house on the banks of the Mississippi River in Commerce, which had served as the first Indian agency in Illinois. It was from these humble quarters that the settlement of the Prophet's last city of residence was to be directed.

In May and June, hundreds of Saints crossed the river, drained the swamps, plowed the land, and cut down trees. A city began to take shape. A scattered people suddenly had an objective again, a place of gathering, and a Prophet of God as a leader.

Joseph did not envision, nor did he contemplate, any illusions about the permanence of his stay there. He was aroused from within with vague impressions about the brief time he had left to complete his earthly mission. He was also conscious of the rough road that lay ahead for him and the Saints.

Joseph would not permit the endless responsibilities of building a new city to interfere with his basic lifestyle. Once he had defined the objective, delegated authority to his subordinates, and set the wheels of progress in motion, he turned to the spiritual and intellectual pursuits that always took precedence with him, including the monumental task of continuing to write his history. As urgent matters arose that could not be postponed, he would lay aside his literary efforts or other intellectual tasks that claimed his attention, and do what had to be done at the moment, and then pick up and continue his study or dictation where he had left off.

We see in this practice, a pattern that was evident from the very beginning of his ministry. He was rarely ever able to devote long, uninterrupted periods of time to these pursuits, but he had mastered the law of particles, and he completed his writing, translating, and editing tasks—line upon line, as he could squeeze out a moment here or there. Ever present was a scribe or secretary to assist him—Emma, his wife; Oliver Cowdrey; Sidney Rigdon; one of the Whitmer boys; a member of the Twelve, or whoever was available. When it was practical, he would employ someone who could be with him constantly during his working hours, to record or jot down whatever was important at the moment. During the early part of his ministry in Nauvoo, James Mulholland was his principal scribe. Later, the English convert William Clayton filled this role.

The Prophet used a scribe or secretary for several reasons. When freed from the mechanical necessity of recording his thoughts; he found himself thinking more clearly while he spoke, his thoughts flowed more smoothly and logically. In addition, when he was moved upon by the Holy Spirit as revelations came, he could focus all his attention upon the substance of the things being shown or told him and upon their translation or explanation. For him to have recorded them manually would have greatly impeded his work. The most obvious reason related to his limited opportunities for formal schooling. His handwriting was almost illegible, his spelling was poor, and he knew practically nothing about punctuation during this period of his life. Being keenly perceptive of his educational inadequacies, Joseph was inclined to gather around him those who possessed the mechanical skills he sorely lacked. A final reason for his use of a scribe seems to be that the Prophet, whether unconsciously or deliberately—always wanted a witness or witnesses to what he did, and a sure way to achieve this was to always have a scribe at hand.

As the Prophet found opportunities to do so, he preached to the Saints around Nauvoo to build them up in their confidence and faith, to give them instructions, and when necessary, to correct his associates in preparing them for the challenges which lay ahead. Indications of the enthusiasm with which his words were received are found in many accounts of his preaching and teaching to congregations, so crowded there was often standing room only.

During those first months in Nauvoo, the dreaded malaria took a heavy toll of the weakened people. The Prophet Joseph's home was crowded with the sick and many of the newly-arrived camped in his dooryard under tents. In his care of them, Joseph himself was stricken.

Wilford Woodruff, who was present, wrote of the events occurring at this time: "After being confined to his house several days, and while meditating upon his situation, he [Joseph] had a great desire to attend to the duties of his office. On the morning of July 22, 1839, he arose from his bed and began administering to the sick in his own house and dooryard, and he commanded them, 'in the name of Jesus Christ, to arise and be made whole;' and the sick were healed upon every side of him. Many lay sick along the bank of the river. Joseph walked along up to the lower stone house, occupied by Sidney Rigdon, and he healed all the sick that lay in his path. Among the number was Henry G. Sherwood, who was nigh unto death. Joseph stood in the door of his tent and commanded him in the name of Jesus Christ to arise and come out of his tent, and he obeyed him and was healed."

The remarkable faith of the Prophet in the destiny of his people, caused him to forget their poverty, their miserable homes and the past bitter experiences. **Faith is mightier than steel.**

"Brother Benjamin Brown and his family also lay sick, the former appearing to be in a dying condition. Joseph healed all that lay sick upon the bank of the river, as far as the stone house, he called upon Elder Kimball and some others to accompany him across the river to visit the sick in Montrose. Many of the Saints were living at the old military barracks. Among the number were several of the Twelve Apostles. On his arrival, the first house he visited was that occupied by Elder Brigham Young, the President of the Quorum of the Twelve. Joseph healed him, then he arose and accompanied the Prophet on his visit to others who were in the same condition. They visited Elders Orson Pratt, and John Taylor, all of whom were living in Montrose. They also [arose and] accompanied him."

"As they crossed the public square, and entered Brother Fordham's house. Brother Fordham had been dying for an hour, and we expected any minute would be his last. I felt the Spirit of God that was overpowering His Prophet. When we entered the house, Brother Joseph walked up to Brother Fordham and took him by his right hand, his left hand holding his hat. He saw that Brother Fordham's eyes were glazed, and that he was speechless and unconscious.

"After taking his hand, he looked down into the dying man's face and said . . . *"Do you believe that Jesus is the Christ?"* 'I do, brother Joseph,' was the response. Then the Prophet of God spoke with a loud voice, as in the majesty of Jehovah: *"Elijah, I command you, in the name of Jesus of Nazareth, to rise and be made whole"* (*History of the Church,* 4: 4).

"The words of the Prophet were not like the words of man, but like the voice of God. It seemed to me that the house shook on its foundation. Elijah Fordham leaped from his bed like a man raised from the dead. A healthy color came into his face and life was manifested in every act. His feet had been done up in Indian meal poultices; these he kicked off, scattering the contents, and then called for his clothes and put them on. He asked for a bowl of bread and milk and ate it. He then put on his hat and followed us into the street, to visit others who were sick."

Elijah Fordham lived forty-one years after that. This occasion has gone down in the history of the Church as "a day of God's power," in the latter days. And in a like manner in the Former Days in the New Testament, The Acts, chapter three verses six to eight: *"Then Peter said, Silver and gold have I none; but such as I have give I thee: In the name of Jesus Christ of Nazareth rise up and walk. And he took him by the right hand, and lifted him up: and immediately his feet and ankle bones received strength. And he leaping up stood, and walked, and entered with them into the temple, walking, and leaping, and praising God."*

Joseph's power was great, but so was the faith of the people. Joseph had physical limitations and was unable to visit everyone. One man with sick twins gladly accepted Brother Woodruff in Joseph's place. Wilford Woodruff took the Prophet's silk bandana with Joseph's instructions to wipe the children's faces with it and they would be healed. He did so, and the children were restored to health. The hearts of the weary Saints rejoiced with this outpouring of love and strength.

With the Church seeming to be at its lowest decline to the casual onlooker, the strength within was greater than ever before. The faith of these people, their loyalty to the Prophet, and their missionary zeal would carry the Gospel into many lands and increase the membership of the Church many times over, in the period of only five years. Even in the midst of the sickness and struggle, they remembered the revelation received by the Prophet in July 1838 commanding the Twelve Apostles to depart for missions "over the great waters." Although hardly able to sustain their own lives, the Twelve were willing to give their all to accomplish the work. Joseph began instructing the Twelve for their mission. He taught them about the eternal nature of the Priesthood and counseled them—even more strongly warned them—not to betray heaven, Christ, or the Brethren.

As the Latter-day Saints began settling Nauvoo, the Prophet Joseph Smith was counseled by the Lord on further overseas expansion of the Church. This expansion had begun with the call of Elder Heber C. Kimball and Orson Hyde to England in 1837. As early as 1835, the Lord had instructed members of the Quorum of the Twelve, that they were to be *"special witnesses of the name of Christ in all the world—"* and regulate all the affairs of the same in all nations. They were given the spiritual keys *"to open the door by the proclamation of the gospel of Jesus Christ"* to all the world (Doctrine & Covenants 107: 23, 33, 35). The Twelve were further promised that *"in whatsoever place ye shall proclaim my name, an effectual door shall be opened unto you, that they may receive my word"* (Doctrine & Covenants 112: 19). This promise was fulfilled the very day it was revealed, July 23, 1837, when Elder Heber C. Kimball and his companions were invited to preach in the Vauxhall Chapel in Preston, England—an invitation resulting in the first baptisms in the British Isles. As the work went forward in that land with great success, even more participation from the Apostles was anticipated.

From their organization in 1835, the Twelve Apostles had been initially called to proselyte in the Eastern United States. In 1837, two Apostles, Orson Hyde and Heber C. Kimball, opened a mission in England, where they baptized more than 1,300 people. When the full body of Apostles (led by Brigham Young) arrived there in 1840, they found a fulfillment of the Prophet's prophecy to them—a field of converts *"white already to harvest."* The depression of 1837, social oppression, political reformers schemes, disillusionment with the Church of England, and various religious agitation, had prepared the way. Mormon preachers could promise not only salvation and truth, but also the tangible reality of a prosperous Zion in the New Zion of America, a city where the common man could find employment, inexpensive land, dignity, and peace. In one year, (April 1840 to April 1841), the Twelve Apostles baptized about 4,500 people and dispatched over 800 members to America, thereby launching a major emigration effort that lasted almost fifty years. **Between 1837 and 1846, Mormon missionaries in England baptized almost 18,000 English citizens. Of these, 4,733 emigrated to Nauvoo and its environs in the early 1840s.** While the power, the energies, and abilities of these leaders who were sent abroad would have provided tremendous momentum toward the building up of Nauvoo, the Prophet had his short and long range eyes on a more distant goal.

The Twelve were to be about their task of warning the world of the approaching judgment, of calling the world to repentance, and of stimulating, invigorating and energizing Nauvoo with a steady stream of new converts from abroad. Joseph had recognized the great impact upon the Church of the first harvest of converts from England, and could foresee that while keeping the Twelve at home might be temporarily beneficial in helping to build up Nauvoo, in the long run, their labors would be vastly more productive as they increased the working capacity of the Saints through conversions.

In anticipation of the departure of the Twelve for England to continue their proselyting efforts the Prophet commenced to give them detailed and explicit instructions, including the disclosure of Church doctrines and direction on personal conduct. In a journal entry, he noted that he had *"taught the brethren at considerable length on the following subjects: faith, repentance, baptism, the gift of the Holy Ghost, tongues, and the resurrection.*"

On June 27,1839, the First Presidency and the Twelve met in a special conference. A week later in Montrose, Iowa, following additional instructions, the First Presidency blessed each Apostle and his wife individually. Concerning those who were blessed, Wilford Woodruff recorded that: "if we were faithful, we had the promise of again returning to the bosom of our families, and being blessed on our mission, and having many souls as seals of our ministry." After the blessing, Joseph Smith instructed them once again that they were *"not sent out to be taught, but to teach—let every man be sober, be vigilant, and let all his words be seasoned with grace, and keep in mind that it is a day of warning and not of many words."* On July 2, 1839, Joseph called a meeting for the Twelve to give them final instructions before they departed for their missions abroad.

His teachings on this occasion reveal the depth of the Prophet's maturity and his understanding of human nature. He summarized his remarks as being *"calculated to guard them against self-sufficiency, self-righteousness and self-importance . . . and especially teaching them to observe charity* [the pure love of Christ]*, wisdom, with love one towards another in all things, and under all circumstances"* (*History of the Church,* 3: 383).

These men were powerful missionaries. The trials through which they had passed had strengthened their convictions concerning the cause with which they were connected, and they won hundreds of converts through the powerful testimonies which they bore.

Never did missionaries begin their work under more heartrending conditions. Penniless themselves, with little extra clothing, they would be leaving their families equally destitute. The only assurance was the promise of neighbors, equally poor, that they would care for them.

On Sunday, July seventh, the Twelve spoke at a farewell meeting held in their behalf. Each one bore a powerful witness of the work they were engaged in. Clearly they were anxious to be on their way to England; unfortunately, they were not able to leave immediately. The following week, a malaria epidemic hit the Nauvoo community. The Apostles were stricken, and their mission was temporarily postponed. But after the day of God's power, on July twenty-second, "All of the Twelve were determined, 'sick or not,' to fulfill their mission."

On Sunday, August fourth, a day of fasting and prayer, the Prophet renewed this instruction to *"go forth without purse or script,"* according to the revelations of Jesus Christ.

The first to start was Wilford Woodruff. In the early part of August, he arose from a sickbed in Montrose, on the Iowa side of the Mississippi River, and was rowed across the river in a canoe by Brigham Young. On reaching the shore he was so weak, he lay down upon a side of cowhide. Joseph Smith happened to see him there and said: *"Well Brother Woodruff, you have started on your mission."* The reply was: "Yes, but I feel and look more like a subject for the dissecting room than a missionary."

"What did you say that for," asked Joseph. *"Get up and go along, all will be well with you."*

Wilford Woodruff got up and joining Elder John Taylor, started north along the riverbank. They passed Parley P. Pratt, stripped to the waist, barefooted, and bareheaded hewing logs for a cabin. He gave them a purse, but had nothing to put in it. Elder Heber C. Kimball came up and said: "As Brother Parley has given you a purse, I have a dollar I will give you to put in it."

The other of the Twelve soon followed, under similar circumstances. In the journal kept by Elder Heber C. Kimball, we find the following:

"On September fourteenth, President Brigham Young left his home at Montrose to start on his mission to England. He was so sick that he was unable to go to the Mississippi, a distance of thirty rods [one rod measures 5 1/2 yards or 16 1/2 feet] without assistance. After he crossed the river, he rode behind Israel Barlow on his horse to my house, where he continued sick until the 18th of September. He left his wife with a babe only three weeks old, and all his other children were sick and unable to wait upon each other. Not one soul of them was able to go to the well for a pail of water, and he was without a second suit to his back, for the mob in Missouri had taken nearly all he had. On September seventeenth, Sister May Ann Young got a boy to carry her up in his wagon to my house that she might nurse and comfort Brother Brigham to the hour of starting.

"September eighteenth, Charles Hubbard sent his boy with a wagon and span of horses to my house; our trunks were put into the wagon by some of the brethren; I went to my bed to hold the hands of my wife, who was then shaking with a chill, having two children lying sick by her side; I embraced her and my children and bade them farewell. My only well child was little Heber, and it was with difficulty he could carry a couple of quarts of water at a time to assist in quenching their thirst.

"It was with difficulty we got into the wagon and started down the hill about ten rods [160 feet]; it appeared to me as though my very inmost parts would melt within me at leaving my family in such a condition, as they were almost in the arms of death. I felt as though I could not endure it. I asked the teamster to stop, and said to Brother Brigham, 'This is pretty tough, isn't it; let's rise up and give them a cheer.' We arose and swinging our hats three times over our heads, shouted, 'Hurrah, hurrah for Israel.' My dear wife Vilate, hearing the noise, arose from her bed and came to the door. She had a smile on her face. Vilate and Mary Ann Young cried out to us 'Good-bye, God bless you'. We returned the compliment, and then told the driver to go ahead. After this, I felt a spirit of joy and gratitude having had the satisfaction of seeing my wife standing upon her feet, instead of leaving her in bed, knowing well that I should not see them again for two or three years" (B. H. Roberts, *Comprehensive History of the Church,* 2: 12-13).

At this time, we cannot follow these missionaries through all their trials and difficulties in reaching New York City and securing passage by ship to England. The readers of their journals become amazed at their remarkable spirit, and their ability to travel without "purse or scrip."

Seven of the Apostles arrived in New York City during the winter of 1839. There they preached the Gospel, conducted other Church business, and obtained funds for their passage to England. During the few days that they were together in New York City, they held many precious meetings in which the Saints were filled with joy, and the people became more and more convinced of the truth of their message. Wilford Woodruff, John Taylor, and Theodore Turley were the first to sail for England, leaving December 19, 1839 and arriving twenty-three days later. The others left in March and arrived in Liverpool on April 6, 1840, the Tenth Anniversary of the Church's organization.

THE TWELVE IN BRITAIN

The need of the Twelve in Britain was soon apparent. After the first mission there in 1837, many members had fallen into apostasy and had left the Church because of persecution and lack of mature local direction. Attacks on the Church in local newspapers grew in number and intensity, and ministers of various denominations aroused opposition through sermons and lectures.

Within the Church, some had challenged the authority of the mission presidency, and had led small factions of the Saints astray, slowing missionary success. Elder Heber C. Kimball had written several encouraging letters from America that buoyed up the Saints and identified those disrupting the progress of the work in England. Within a short period of time, the Church was favored with mature and experienced leaders—strong preachers and teachers—and the work of the Lord spread like wildfire and success was forthcoming. The Gospel and the Restored Church grew rapidly because it was true.

The Lord was always there to help, and the missionary success of the Twelve in England was overwhelming. Elder Wilford Woodruff's efforts were particularly successful. While preaching in Hanley in the Potteries district of England, he felt impressed to leave that area without knowing why. Obedient to personal revelation, he traveled to a rural section of Herefordshire.

At the home of a John Benbow, a substantial farmer of the district, he received a cordial welcome and the news that a large group of religionists in that area had broken away from their Church and had united themselves to study the scriptures and seek for the truth.

Elder Woodruff was given an invitation to speak to them. The organization numbered 600, including more than a score of preachers. All of these, with one exception, embraced Mormonism. Before he left the district, 1,800 members had been converted to the Church through his efforts. An attempt on the part of alarmed ministers and rectors in the south of England to get a bill through Parliament, prohibiting the Mormons from preaching in the British dominions, failed.

The great success of the British mission soon made itself felt in the Church. The converts became imbued with the spirit of gathering and desired to go to the central gathering place in America. The first shipload left Liverpool, England, on the sixth day of June 1840. This was the beginning of a migration movement of such magnitude that the Church in America became predominantly English for the next fifty years.

The rapidity of this movement, which swelled the population of Nauvoo, can be realized from a notation in the Autobiography of Parley P. Pratt of the movement for one particular month: "Between the middle of September (1840) and my own embarkation in October, I chartered three vessels for New Orleans, and filled them with migrating Saints."

Most of the English Saints needed no urging to emigrate. Letters from English Saints in America encouraged English Saints to come to America and gather with their fellow Saints. Even before the Apostles mentioned the gathering, they wanted to go to America to see the Prophet and to live among their fellow Saints. Brigham Young wrote to his brother Joseph: "They have so much of the spirit of gathering that they would go if they knew they would die as soon as they got there or if they knew that the mob would be upon them and drive them as soon as they got there." **Approximately 1,000 Saints emigrated early in 1841,** and a shipping agency was soon established to oversee travel arrangements.

The Prophet Joseph Smith wrote to the Twelve in early 1841 requesting their return to Nauvoo in the spring. As the time for their return to America drew near, the Apostles visited the regions where the Saints lived and held a series of meetings to uplift the Saints to look forward to the important days ahead. Most of the Apostles departed from England in late April 1841 and arrived in Nauvoo in July. The mission was an important time of training and maturing for the Quorum of the Twelve were united in a way that assured the Church of strong leadership in the years ahead.

The Prophet recognized both the leadership experience gained by the Apostles and the sacrifice that they and their families had made as a result of the Twelve's mission to Britain. He recorded: *"Perhaps no men ever undertook such an important mission under such incredibly distressing and adverse circumstances. However, notwithstanding their afflictions and trials, the Lord always intervened in their behalf, and did not suffer them to sink in the arms of death. One way or another, a door would open for their escape, friends would rise up when they most needed them, and helped relieve their necessities; and thus they were empowered to pursue their journey and rejoice in the Holy One of Israel. They, truly, 'went forth weeping, bearing precious seed, but have returned with rejoicing, bearing their sheaves with them.' Missionary work to other parts of the world was also furthered as a result of the work in Britain. The British Empire became the avenue through which the Gospel was spread into many parts of the world."*

ORSON HYDE'S DEDICATION OF

THE HOLY LAND

Another major mission, which was to have great significance, began during the April 1840 Conference in Nauvoo.

For eighteen centuries, the Jewish people had been a scattered people, residing in various locations throughout the world, driven from their native land of Palestine. Twelve million of them congregated chiefly in great and large cities. These were bitter in their denial and rejection of Jesus of Nazareth. They found no opportunity to reestablish their nation, and had given up all practical hopes of doing so.

Apostles Orson Hyde and John E. Page were called by revelation to carry the Gospel to these people—to converse with their leaders in . . . "London, Amsterdam, Constantinople, and Jerusalem," and to dedicate the Holy Land for their return. This mission was ridiculed and spurned by all but the little band of Saints in Nauvoo, Illinois, and considered useless by many of them. Even the repeated prophecies of the Bible and the Book of Mormon that the Jews should be gathered in the last days had lost its meaning among men. It was nevertheless a courageous and inspirational program which had to be carried out.

About the middle of April 1840, the two left Nauvoo and set out for New York, the port from which they were to embark for Palestine. They spent some time in the branches at Cincinnati, New York, and Philadelphia until January 1841. They were admonished by the First Presidency, and instructed to "hasten their journey towards their destination."

Elder Page lost his desire to fulfill the mission and left Orson Hyde to travel to Palestine alone. Nevertheless, the faith of Orson Hyde in his mission was unshakable. Even when Elder Page deserted the mission, Elder Hyde did not waver. He carried on alone one of the longest missionary pilgrimages ever undertaken, more than 20,000 miles in all.

Elder Hyde's situation was a difficult one. Left alone without sufficient funds to make the difficult journey, his determination was fortified when he was handed a bag of gold by an unidentified stranger who had learned of his plight. He was now able to undertake his mission. He crossed the ocean to England, passed over to Germany, stayed in Bavaria to learn the German language, went on to Cairo and Alexandria, and after encountering many hardships, reached the Holy City. On October 24, 1841, a Sunday morning, he went out alone to the top of the Mount of Olives and there, solemnly, in the hearing of none but God, **dedicated and consecrated the land for the gathering and return of the Jewish people.** As a memorial of his prayer, according to a vision given to him previous to leaving Nauvoo. Elder Hyde built stone altars after the fashion of the early Israelites on the Mount of Olives, and also upon Mount Moriah in Jerusalem.

Surely the dedication of Palestine was a "great work," which served to prepare the way and greatly facilitate the gathering together of that people. With his mission completed, Elder Hyde returned to Nauvoo in December 1842. (Since that time, the descendants of Judah have begun to return to their native land in increasing numbers. On May 14, 1948, the State of Israel was established.)

PROPHET GOES TO WASHINGTON D.C.

While the Quorum of the Twelve were doing their proselyting in England, back in Nauvoo, the Prophet Joseph Smith wanted to do all he could to help alleviate the financial losses suffered by the Saints when they were driven from their homes in Missouri.

In October 1839, Joseph was chosen by the High Council of the Church to travel to Washington, D.C., to present the case of the Saints to the President and the Congress. He was the natural one to represent the Saints, yet this was another burden on his shoulders. With his unusual promptness, he left nine days after the call.

Not wishing to travel alone, he took his first counselor in the First Presidency, Sidney Rigdon as well as Elias Higbee and Orrin P. Rockwell. Elder Rigdon was sick much of the trip, and so it became necessary for Orrin P. Rockwell to stay behind and care for him. Elias Higbee and Joseph continued the journey, taking a stagecoach for the East.

While traveling through the mountains, before reaching Washington, the stage stopped at an inn and the driver went in for refreshments, leaving the passengers in the coach. Besides the Prophet and Elias Higbee, others in the stagecoach included a woman with a small baby in her arms and some members of Congress.

The horses became frightened (spooked) while standing outside the inn, and ran away with no driver in the seat, and all of the passengers inside the coach. The road went downhill from the inn, and the frightened horses pulled the stage at great speed. The passengers began to fear for their lives. The mother of the baby prepared to throw it out the stage window, hoping it would land safely and be spared.

Joseph advised all the passengers to stay in their seats and told the mother to hold onto her child. He then opened the stage door, caught hold of the side of the coach as it raced down the hill, and pulled himself up into the driver's seat. Catching hold of the reins, he soon had the horses under control and stopped them in a safe place. Although the runaway horses had taken the coach about three miles off course, the Prophet's brave action prevented anyone from being hurt.

The passengers were loud in their praise of the Prophet's heroic deed. The Congressmen in the coach said they would mention this brave act in Congress, but when they found out that it was Joseph Smith, the Mormon Prophet, who had saved their lives—the subject was dropped.

On Thursday, November 28, 1839, the Prophet and Brother Higbee arrived safely in Washington D.C. and prepared a petition to Congress on behalf of the persecuted Saints. **The next morning, they went to the residence of Martin Van Buren, the President of the United States.** The Prophet described the president's home as *"a very large and splendid palace, surrounded with a splendid enclosure, decorated with all the fineries and elegancies of this world."*

They went to the door and asked to see the President. They were shown into his presence where they presented letters of identification. When he read the first letter, the President frowned and said: "What can I do? I can do nothing for you. If I do anything, I shall come in contact with the whole state of Missouri."

Nevertheless, the brethren were not to be frightened, and insisted that he give them a hearing. **They told the President that the Saints had certain rights under the Constitution of the United States, and insisted on being given those rights.**

He listened with great reluctance, and before they left, he promised to reconsider the matter, and said he felt sorry for the Saints because of their sufferings.

The President did not keep his word to the Prophet and refused to give help. He was soon to come up for re-election, and wanted and needed the votes of the Missouri people. He feared the loss of votes more than the Lord.

In writing about his visit with the President at a later time, the Prophet said: *"Van Buren had treated him very unkindly,"* and had said: **"Gentlemen, your cause is just but I can do nothing for you.** If I take up for you, I shall lose the vote of Missouri." As the Prophet left Mr. Van Buren, he felt that he wasn't fit to be President of so great a country as the United States.

The Prophet next visited John C. Calhoun and Henry Clay who also turned a deaf ear to him. Joseph also presented a very clear appeal to Congress. Many of the Senators and Representatives were polite, curious, even sympathetic, but no action was taken.

Soon after, the Prophet returned home to Nauvoo, leaving his case in the hands of the Great Jehovah. Brother Higbee remained in Washington D.C. to continue the matter with Congress, and he, too, received no help. Congress told him that the trouble happened in the State of Missouri, and therefore if any help was to be given, Missouri should give it and not the federal government.

On his way home, the Prophet told many people about the bad treatment he had received from President Van Buren. He said: *"May he never be elected again to any office of trust or power by which he may abide the innocent and let the guilty go free."*

Van Buren was **never elected** again to the Presidency, although he sought after it. In the election of 1840, he was opposed by William Henry Harrison, who received 234 electoral votes compared to only sixty for Van Buren. In 1848, Van Buren tried again. In that election, Zachary Taylor was chosen President. Van Buren did not win a single electorial vote in that election.

After the Prophet returned to Nauvoo, the governor of Missouri, angered at the Mormons appealing to Washington D.C., requested the governor of Illinois to have Joseph Smith arrested and delivered to Missouri on the charge of fugitive from justice, although two years had elapsed since Joseph and his friends had been allowed to escape. Governor Carlin of Illinois honored the request. The Prophet obtained a writ of habeas corpus, was tried before Judge Stephen A. Douglas at Monmouth, Illinois, and was set free.

Hope of Israel

Energetically ♩= 100-120
1. Hope of Is - rael, Zi - on's ar - my, Chil - dren of the prom-ised day,
2. See the foe in count-less num-bers, Mar-shaled in the ranks of sin.
3. Strike for Zi - on, down with er - ror; Flash the sword a - bove the foe!
4. Soon the bat - tle will be o - ver; Ev - 'ry foe of truth be down.
See, the Chief-tain sig - nals on-ward, And the bat - tle's in ar - ray!
Hope of Is - rael, on to bat - tle; Now the vic - t'ry we must win!
Ev - 'ry stroke dis - arms a foe-man; Ev - 'ry step we con-q'ring go.
On - ward, on-ward, youth of Zi - on; Thy re-ward the vic-tor's crown.
Hope of Is - rael, rise in might With the sword of truth and right;
Sound the war - cry, "Watch and pray!" Van - quish ev - 'ry foe to - day.

Text: Joseph L. Townsend, 1849-1942
Music: William Clayson, 1840-1887

Ephesians 6:10-18
2 Nephi 28:7-8, 20-28

Chapter 12

Development of Nauvoo, Illinois

Nauvoo City Charter Approved by the Illinois Legislature

The Growth of Nauvoo was Uniquely and Naturally Rapid

Estimated Population of Nauvoo at the Close of 1845 was 15,000

The Saints Organized a Militia* (Nauvoo Legion) *to Preserve Peace

***Death of the Prophet's Father, Joseph Smith Sr. in 1840—* (First Patriarch of the Church)**

The Doctrine of Baptsim for the Dead was Taught Anciently and Accepted

Saints Commanded to Build a Temple in Nauvoo

Joseph was Concerned about the Loyalty of some Church Leaders

Joseph Gave the Keys of the Priesthood and all the Endowments—to the Twelve Apostles

The Plot and a Story of Conspiracy

The Female Relief Society of Nauvoo—* (Women's Organization)*—began March 17, 1842

Joseph was Chosen to run for President of the United States

The story of the development of Nauvoo establishes one of the most progressive chapters in social history. A people who are inspired by a great faith, do not long remain in poverty. Swamps were soon drained, and with their disappearance went the mosquito, the dread malaria and other illnesses. Underbrush gave way to beautiful gardens. Tents and hastily-constructed shacks were replaced by attractive, substantial, desirable housing.

Nauvoo was created in the mind of its founder before a stone was paid for or a ditch was dug so did not develop in the careless and confused way most cities did. As early as 1833, the Prophet had received revelations concerning the construction of cities of Zion. In that year, he sent such a plan to Church associates for Independence, Missouri. Persecutions in that state had prevented more than a partial compliance to the plan. Nauvoo offered the first real opportunity to show what the Prophet Joseph might accomplish in solving the problems of city life.

The planning and organization of the city came under three classifications: General Physical Construction; Reigning Political Government; Educational and Religious Facilities.

GENERAL PHYSICAL CONSTRUCTION

The city was laid out with streets, eight rods (16 1/2 feet per rod) 132 feet in width, running directly north and south, and east and west, and crossing each other at regular intervals. Sections of the city were designated for the erection of public buildings and recreational centers. Building restrictions controlled the location of manufacturing plants, mercantile establishments, etc. In the residential sections, houses were erected a uniform distance from the street and were fronted with lawns and shrubs. Unsightly structures were prohibited. The plan embraced most of those features now common in the "zoning" of well laid out modern cities.

Nauvoo became the pattern for future cities to be built by the Saints in the Rocky Mountains. Salt Lake City, Utah, presents an example, and an amazing revelation in city planning, to those who visit it. The material welfare and happiness of his people was ever of great importance to the Prophet. Nauvoo, also known as the "City of Joseph," was a reflection of the man.

As the year 1841 began, happiness and excitement was prevalent in Nauvoo. Reports were arriving from England recounting the overwhelming success of the Twelve Apostles. Persecution, which the Saints had suffered since its founding in 1830, was at an all-time low. Furthermore, the Saints seemed assured of civil protection with the passage of the Nauvoo City Charter by the state legislature on the 17th of December 1840.

On January 15, 1841, the First Presidency published a Proclamation to the Saints "scattered abroad" explaining and expressing appreciation for the Nauvoo Charter. The Proclamation also expressed gratitude to the honorable citizens of Illinois, particularly those from the City of Quincy, who "like the good Samaritan, poured oil into our wounds, and contributed liberally to our necessities." The First Presidency promised that "by a concentration of action, and a unity of effort," the Saints would see both their temporal and spiritual interests increased as the blessings of heaven would flow unto God's people.

On January 19, 1841, the Prophet received a lengthy revelation outlining the development of Nauvoo as a *"cornerstone of Zion, which shall be polished with the refinement which is after the similitude of a palace"* (Doctrine & Covenants 124: 2).

The Lord commanded Joseph Smith and the Saints to do many things in Nauvoo for the advancement of His kingdom. They were to publish a Proclamation to the kings of the world, the President of the United States, and the governors of the several states; build a temple where the Lord would reveal sacred ordinances to His people; ordain Hyrum Smith as the Patriarch of the Church to replace Joseph Smith Sr., who had died; call William Law as second counselor in the First Presidency; organize the Nauvoo Stake with a Presidency and a High Council; and set in order each of the quorums of the Priesthood.

REIGNING POLITICAL GOVERNMENT

The bitter lessons of the Missouri period had an important bearing upon the organization of the political government of the new city. **To safeguard his people, Joseph Smith drew up the provisions for an unusual city charter and presented it to the legislature of Illinois for approval.** He said of it: *"I concocted it for the salvation of the Church, and on principles so broad that every honest man might dwell secure under its protecting influence, without distinction of sect or party."*

The charter provided for broad legislative powers resting in a City Council consisting of a Mayor, four Aldermen, and nine Councilors elected by the qualified voters of the city. It also provided for a Municipal Court, independent of any but the Supreme Court of the State and Federal Courts. **It provided for a city militia to be known as the Nauvoo Legion**, to be equipped by the State and officered by the citizens of Nauvoo.

The many enumerated powers which were granted, created practically a city-state. Within the limits of the city—and these borders might be extended indefinitely by the vote of the residents in the area to be added—the city was independent of all other agencies in the state. Only the repeal of the charter by the state legislature could curtail these powers. No other municipality in America, before or since, has enjoyed such complete control of its own affairs. The charter was a protection to the Church from the mobs, illegal court proceedings, and the whims of higher government agencies. Had the city been allowed by its enemies to continue, it might have well become a model for city governments in America. **Political circumstances aided the people of Nauvoo in getting the charter passed.** The Saints were a numerous people in that sparsely settled state, and both political parties sought their friendship. The Mormon vote could have easily swayed an election in the state at that time. Even political opponents such as Stephen A. Douglas and Abraham Lincoln, then members of the Illinois Legislature, joined hands to vote for the passage of the charter. In December 1840, Nauvoo began its official existence.

John C. Bennett, who joined the Church at Nauvoo, worked tirelessly to secure the passage of the Nauvoo Charter. For his work, he was rewarded by being elected the first Mayor of Nauvoo on February 1, 1841 with Joseph Smith, Hyrum Smith, Sidney Rigdon, and several other leading Church officials elected to the City Council.

The isolation of the Saints from those of other faiths, which had been attempted in Missouri, was abandoned. Indeed, people of all religious denominations were invited to dwell with the Saints in Nauvoo. In a **Proclamation by the First Presidency**, we read:

"We wish it likewise to be distinctly understood that we claim no privileges but what we feel cheerfully disposed to share with our fellow citizens of every denomination, and every sentiment of religion; and therefore say, that so far from being restricted to our own faith, let all those who desire to locate in this place [Nauvoo] or the vicinity come, and we will hail them as citizens and friends, and shall feel it not only a duty, but a privilege to reciprocate the kindness we have received from the benevolent and kind-hearted citizens of the State of Illinois." In keeping with this spirit, one of the first acts of the City Council was to pass an ordinance protecting people in the undisturbed enjoyment of their several religions.

Another early ordinance prohibited the sale of intoxicants and practically made Nauvoo a prohibition city.

EDUCATIONAL AND RELIGIOUS FACILITIES

In drawing up the proposed charter for Nauvoo, the Prophet had been careful to include a grant of power to the city to organize and control its own educational system. This included a charter for a municipal university, the first of its kind in America.

In accordance with their power, an educational system, including all grades from elementary to university classes, was organized by the City Council. University buildings and campuses were planned, but the plans were never carried out before the people were driven from Nauvoo. Instructors were hired and university classes held, however, in such buildings as the city afforded. It was the aim of the Prophet to educate his entire people, young and old. Nearly all who attended classes at the University of Nauvoo were adults. The organization for the control of the university was later adopted in Utah for the University of Utah.

One of the first thoughts of the Prophet in planning Nauvoo, was a site for a temple. A well constructed city, enjoying wise governmental powers, would not alone make for a happy people. **Even asked on one occasion how he governed his people, Joseph replied: *"I teach them correct principles and they govern themselves."*** So Nauvoo, the "City of Joseph" should be built around a Temple of God, and be provided with other suitable places of worship, where the Gospel of Jesus might be taught to His people. A city organized under such principles was not long in attracting the attention of thinking men. As early as the summer of 1841, the St. Louis *Atlas* referred to Nauvoo as follows:

"The population of Nauvoo is between 8,000 and 9,000, and of course, the largest town in the State of Illinois. How long the Latter-day Saints will hold together and exhibit their present aspect, it is not for us to say. At this moment they present the appearance of an enterprising, industrious, sober and thrifty population, such a population indeed, as in the respects just mentioned, have no rivals east and we rather guess, not even west of the Mississippi."

Since most of the Saints at this time were of British stock, Nauvoo took on the appearance of the English-inspired towns and villages found throughout New England. The solid, two-story brick or wooden colonial homes, the quiet, tree-lined streets, and the air of meaningful activity, distinguished the community as nothing else could have done. By July 1841, there were about 1,200 new homes; many other buildings had been completed, and hundreds more were in progress.

The overall impression the "peppy" community symbolized to outsiders is typified by the lyrics of a favorite Latter-day Saint hymn whose refrain inspired the spirit that imbued the building of Nauvoo and other Mormon communities: "Then wake up, and do something more; Than dream of your mansion above; Doing good is a pleasure, a joy beyond measure; A blessing of duty and love."

The growth of Nauvoo was uniquely and naturally rapid as it became the gathering place for the majority of exiles from Missouri, and was the destination of converts migrating from Eastern States and foreign lands. Many European converts arrived with skills that were needed to build a city. From 1840 to 1846, thirty-two companies of Saints sailed for Nauvoo, which included 5,000 British converts alone. Houses were built and being built, businesses established, and fertile lands set to the plow. All seemed to be happiness and progress from within, but from without, anger and hatred was raising its ugly head again. The very success of the Mormon society drew the attention of its neighbors and aroused imaginary fears.

The land speculators were perhaps the class most directly affected. These found it impossible to operate in the region of Nauvoo. The Church purchased land in tracts and sold it to the Saints at non-profit prices. While private land deals were made, the Church land policy dominated the situation and discouraged profit-taking. To see Nauvoo develop into the largest city of the State, without deriving a cent of profit for themselves, enraged the class of land speculators common to that period.

In addition, **the rapid growth of Nauvoo had a retarding effect upon the growth of surrounding cities.** Business naturally gravitated to the larger centers. This was a blow to those speculators who had invested money in the surrounding towns with a view to profiting by their expected growth. The Missouri mobbers were furious to see the rising prosperity of the people they had once beaten into the ground and they were going to do something about it. What, when, or where was not known for the moment, but it was coming.

In June 1844, Franklin D. Richards, the Church Historian, placed the population of Nauvoo at 14,000. Governor Ford in his History of Illinois, estimated the population of the city at the close of 1845 at 15,000. However, no actual census was taken.

As this growth had occurred in the short space of time following 1839, the city attracted many visitors who came largely out of curiosity to see the Mormon metropolis. Eastern newspapers sent representatives to interview the founder of the city and to make observations on the unusual features of the Mormon Center.

The wharf at Nauvoo became a busy place. All the important river steamers stopped to unload or pick up passengers and freight. The growth of the city overshadowed the neighboring towns of Warsaw, Carthage, and Quincy, which caused considerable loss of prestige to the older places. This provoked jealousy and envy, especially among the land speculators.

Nauvoo became a social center. It was easily accessible to settlements up and down the river, and great celebrations were held on the 4th of July and other holidays, which attracted people for many miles. Excursion boats from Warsaw and even from St. Louis were common. The vessels would dock in Nauvoo amidst much laughter and gaiety. Dances were held on such occasions, usually lasting until the early hours of the following morning. The beauty of the city and the hospitality of its people became known far and wide.

The parade of the Nauvoo Legion was a colorful event which seldom failed to attract an audience. At its height, the Legion contained 5,000 men, armed and in uniform. On many occasions, mock battles were held both for the better training of the soldiers, and for the entertainment of the people.

Wrestling, racing, jumping at a mark, pitching horseshoes, etc., were featured on the grounds of the Mansion House, home of Joseph Smith. The Mansion was also used to accommodate travelers stopping at Nauvoo, and to care temporarily for arriving converts. Early on, it gained a reputation for fine meals and accommodation. Men of renown visiting Nauvoo slept beneath its roof; the humblest were equally welcome. Whenever the Prophet was at home, he was accessible to all, and life in the city gravitated about the Mansion House.

To better accommodate travelers and converts who were constantly arriving in the city, a larger building, "The Nauvoo House" was begun. The cornerstone was laid October 2, 1841, in obedience to the revelation that such a house be erected. It was built with funds raised by the selling of stock to worthy Church members. Within the cornerstone, Joseph Smith deposited the original manuscript of the Book of Mormon translation. The building was never completed as originally designed, because the death of the Prophet and the contemplated exodus West caused a change in plans.

While the phenomenal growth of the Church, the rapid rise of the city, and the prosperity of the Saints was gratifying to the founders of the Church and city, these factors attracted a class of men quite undesirable, who recognized the phenomenal growth and prosperity of Nauvoo. They moved in on this city, spreading their evil ways, trying to deal the people out of their businesses, money, and lands. The community became overrun with thieves, counterfeiters, and con-men, using their prowess to seek position, power, and wealth at anyone's expense. Agitators and trouble-makers sought political influence for their own ambitious dreams, did all they could to lead the Latter-day Saints away from their spiritual goals, and on to more worldly endeavors.

In addition, there were disreputable persons who falsely professed conversion to the Mormon Church to cover up their corrupt, licentious, and irresponsible schemes. They saw the opportunity to make mischievous hay while the sun shone, stealing on the credit of the Mormons. The people of Illinois were ready and willing to believe anything and everything that savored of evil, as they became prejudiced against the Latter-day Saint people, Church, and religion. **But the Mormon Church was doing everything possible to build a solid relationship with the non-Mormon community.** Jealousy was the prime factor for unrest because the Mormons didn't allow any grass to grow under their feet. But ungodly characters who became attracted to Nauvoo by the prosperity that reigned there, hastened the evil day of the city's destruction.

Among these reckless adventurers, none was more skillful in winning his way into the confidences of the people than John C. Bennett, previously referred to as the first Mayor of the city. He is often alluded to by historians as a "moral leper." When his promiscuous sexual practices were discovered, he was excommunicated from the Church and deprived of all his civic positions. Other men of the same caliber as Bennett helped to bring discredit upon the community, especially among those who were searching for charges against the Saints.

In each of the locations the Saints had gathered, a printing press and a Church publication had been started. So, in Nauvoo, one of the first achievements was the establishment of a printing press. On this press was published the *Times and Seasons*. The Prophet wrote numerous editorials and articles which appeared in its issues, so that it is considered a great storehouse of historical material.

The Nauvoo Neighbor also embraced the cause of the Saints and was owned by the Church. It was perhaps read more widely outside of Mormon circles than was the *Times and Seasons* and was frequently quoted by other papers published in the West.

The great majority of the Saints were special people, following their Prophet Joseph, living their religion and serving their fellowman. The lazy or shiftless never felt quite at ease in Nauvoo or in any other Latter-day Saint community. The glorification, the dignity and the blessing of work, and the censorable, disapproving attitude toward loafers and idlers, tended to cause guilt in those engaging in purely recreational activities unless the activity accomplished some objective purpose or tangible good. However, **life amongst the Saints was not reclusive, unsociable, or dull.** In fact, judging by the standards of the day, the Mormons were the most forward-looking and daring of all the religious sects in the manner of their entertainments. **Unlike many contemporary churches, the Latter-day Saints did not prohibit or frown upon dancing.** On the contrary, they approved and promoted it as a means of raising the spirits of the people and improving their social graces. Concerts, lectures, debates, scientific societies, and athletic competitions thrived and were encouraged and participated in by Church leaders as well. At the same time, the city was entirely devoid of brothels and saloons and other marks of a wicked, evil, licentious society.

Underlying the unique and refreshing lifestyle of the Saints, were of course, the religious concepts taught them by the Prophet Joseph Smith. He had instructed them that *"the glory of God is intelligence,"* (Doctrine & Covenants 93: 36), and that **the chief purpose of the Creator is to bring about the *"immortality and eternal life of man"*** (Moses 1: 39). He also taught that earth life is the time allotted to men to prepare to return to God, and that their standing in the hereafter depends on the extent to which they, in this life, learn and apply eternal principles of truth. Further, they were taught that any degree of intelligence attained or any quality of character developed in earth life would rise with them in the resurrection. Therefore, the Saints were alert to avoid any conduct that tended to dissipate the mind and the spirit or to weaken the body. At the same time, they eagerly embraced those activities that were wholesome and elevating in nature.

Travelers from the Eastern States were attracted to Nauvoo, and visited the Prophet and his people. A reporter for the *New York Herald*, after such a visit, wrote in his paper: "Joseph Smith is undoubtedly one of the greatest characters of the age. He indicates, as much talent, originality, and moral courage as Mahomet, Odin, or any of the great spirits that have hitherto produced revolutions in the past. While modern philosophy is overspreading the Atlantic States, Joseph Smith is creating a spiritual system combined with morals and industry that may change the destiny of the race."

* * *

In pioneer days, it was the custom of many Western communities in the United States to organize small military groups known as the militia to protect themselves against robber bands, mob violence, and others who might disturb the peace.

As you have already read, the Saints had suffered so much from mobs in Missouri that they decided to immediately organize a militia of their own to preserve peace in their new City of Nauvoo. This they did under the direction of the Prophet. It was known as the Nauvoo Legion. The City Council of Nauvoo authorized its organization under the laws of the State of Illinois, and John C. Bennett, who was Quartermaster General for the State of Illinois at that time, assisted in its formation.

An organization meeting was held February 4, 1841. At this meeting, the Prophet was elected as Lieutenant General of the Legion, with John C. Bennett as Major General. Wilson Law was made Brigadier General, as was the Prophet's brother, Don Carlos Smith. These appointments were later confirmed by Governor Thomas Carlin of the State of Illinois.

It was necessary in those days, as it has been since, to enlist all able-bodied men in the army. A resolution was passed in Nauvoo saying that "no person whatsoever, residing within the limits of the City of Nauvoo, between the ages of 18 and 45 years, excepting such as are exempted by the laws of the United States, shall be exempt from military duty unless exempted by a special act of the court."

The legion grew rapidly. Within three months, it consisted of sixteen companies of well-drilled, uniformed troops, all armed. They had a cannon too, and they had a good band. They paraded on all important occasions, and practiced their skill in warfare as soldiers do today.

Some of the enemies of the Saints began circulating false stories that the Saints were organizing an army for evil purposes. The brethren issued a public statement denying these falsehoods, informing all that the Legion was organized in an orderly way under the laws of the state and with permission of the governor, for the preservation of law and order in their communities.

One of the friends of the Saints at this time, was an influential man named Stephen A. Douglas, who was Justice of the Supreme Court of Illinois. He visited the City of Nauvoo, attended some of the meetings of the Saints, and made a tour of the city. Of him the Prophet wrote: *"Judge Douglas has ever proved himself friendly to this people."*

Preeminent among the Prophet's followers, his father Joseph Smith Sr. never wavered in supporting his famous and controversial son. Others might abandon or turn on the Prophet, but never his constant, dependable father. Therefore, the unexpected death of Joseph Smith Sr., on September 14, 1840, brought special sorrow to the Prophet. The short journal entry that appears under the date, fails to convey the deep sense of loss Joseph felt at the time. It reads: *"My father, Joseph Smith, Sen., Patriarch of the whole Church of Jesus Christ of Latter-day Saints, died at Nauvoo"* (*History of the Church,* 4: 189). His feelings can best be gauged by an excerpt from the funeral sermon Joseph included in his record and by an obituary he prepared himself. Of the deceased, the speaker, Robert B. Thompson, declared: "If ever there was a man who had claims on the affection of the community, it was our beloved but now deceased Patriarch. If ever there was an event calculated to raise the feelings of sorrow in the human breast . . . it certainly is the present; for truly we can say with the king of Israel, 'A prince and a great man has fallen in Israel'. . . A man faithful to his God and to the Church in every situation and under all circumstances through which he was called to pass" (*History of the Church,* 4: 192). Excerpts from the obituary provide a special insight into the character of this unusual man: *"He was the first person who received my testimony after I had seen the angel,"* Joseph wrote: *"and exhorted me to be faithful and diligent to the message I had received . . . He was one of the most benevolent of men; opening his house to all who were destitute. While at Quincy, Illinois, he fed hundreds of the poor Saints who were fleeing from the Missouri persecutions, although he had arrived there penniless himself"* (*History of the Church,* 4: 190-91).

BAPTISM FOR THE DEAD

Just a few weeks before the death of his father, while preaching a funeral sermon for Colonel Seymour Brunson, **the Prophet laid before his people a new and far-reaching doctrinal concept.** Reading from **1 Corinthians 15: 29— *"Else what shall they do which are baptized***

for the dead, if the dead rise not at all? why are they then baptized for the dead?" Joseph declared that the Savior's disciples understood and practiced the ordinance of *"baptism for the dead,"* which had been lost through the apostasy. Since Joseph's followers understood that the spirit in man survives bodily death, and has intelligence and reasoning powers, it was clear that a disembodied spirit could understand and comply with the principles of the Gospel during the interval between death and the resurrection. And since baptism, an earthly ordinance, requires bodily immersion in water, **the doctrine of vicarious (substitute) baptism provides the means whereby one acting as a proxy upon the earth, can be baptized in behalf of another, who is dead,** thus complying with a requirement that is essential to salvation. Joseph emphasized that to be effective, a vicarious baptism would, of necessity, have to be accompanied by the exercise of faith in the Messiah by the spirit person for whom the vicarious baptism is performed.

The doctrine of baptism for the dead was new to the Saints, as it was to the rest of the world, and yet it was taught anciently. It had been developing in the Church from the time of the visitation of the heavenly messenger Moroni when he quoted from the Book of Malachi as follows:

"Behold I will reveal unto you the Priesthood by the the hand of ***Elijah the prophet,*** *before the coming of the great and dreadful day of the Lord . . . And he shall plant in the hearts of the children the promises made to the fathers, and the hearts of the children shall turn to their fathers. If it were not so, the whole world would be utterly wasted at his coming"* (Joseph Smith—History 1: 38-39).

Knowledge concerning this doctrine was received by the Prophet from time to time. The Lord made it known to him that the Gospel is preached in the Spirit World to those who died without a knowledge of it. He also explained that the living person, under proper authority, could be baptized for and in behalf of their dead.

It was not difficult for the members of the Church, and others of like mind, to accept this principle. **The idea of doing vicarious work for someone incapable of doing it himself, lies at the very root of Christian doctrine. Jesus Christ, the central figure of Christianity, was the great exemplar of the principle of vicarious work, since he did something for all which they could not do for themselves by suiting man to God through the Atonement.** The clear reference of vicarious baptism in first Corinthians, had until now, been a great source of speculation and uncertainty to the Saints. In expanding upon the principle, the Prophet explained that in his first letter to the Corinthian Saints, the Apostle Paul was making a clear statement for the universality of the Resurrection to convince those in Corinth who did not believe in life after death. To support the debate, Paul alluded to the practice of baptism for the dead, which apparently was commonplace at the time, and asked why, if there were no resurrection, the people were performing the otherwise meaningless ordinance of baptism for the dead?

The Prophet's introduction of this principle added a vital ingredient of soundness to the doctrines of Christianity that previously seemed to some to be overly restrictive and narrow, limiting the blessings of salvation, or even the chance of salvation, to a favored few who, because of chance, happened to be in the right place at the right time. Futhermore, the doctrines appealed to many who were repelled by the doctrine of infant baptism which followed from the mistaken belief that all who are not baptized during earth life are damned eternally. The unsound doctrines of predestination and original sin also have their roots sunk deep in the misconception that unless one is baptized during his mortal existence, all is lost.

The new doctrine of baptism for the dead touched off a wave of overwhelming enthusiasm among Joseph's followers. It was as if the weight of the world had been lifted from the shoulders of some who had become resigned to the false belief that departed loved ones who had died without baptism were consigned either to nothingness or eternal punishment. Elated by the prospect that they might be reunited with their loved ones, some of the Saints acted hastily to perform proxy baptisms for them. There followed thousands of these baptisms, with little thought being given to preparing an accurate, official record. Nor were there precise rules to govern the conditions under which a proxy baptism could be performed, or any description about the identity and the qualifications of those standing as proxy. Therefore, for a time, men and women haphazardly stood as proxy for deceased persons of the opposite sex.

This uncontrolled situation did not continue for long. On September 6, 1842, Joseph received a revelation which, among other things, required that a *"book containing the records of our dead* [be kept]*, which shall be worthy of all acception"* (Doctrine & Covenants 128: 24). Since that time, an elaborate, almost astounding system of record gathering and record keeping has been carried out. It is now computer controlled, and includes the micro-filming and systematic storage of millions of genealogical records from around the world. From these voluminous records, avid researchers gather the data which, according to strict rules of procedure, will entitle a person to have a vicarious baptism performed in behalf of a departed ancestor. It is important to know that even when the baptisms for the dead are performed under the proper procedure and authority here on earth, the individual in Paradise or the Spirit Prison, be they family or not, have their free agency to accept or reject the Lord's kingdom.

The Saints were happy about this doctrine. The Prophet sent word to the missionaries in the field, and they were instructed to preach it. The people of the Church were anxious to begin doing baptisms for the dead, now that they understood the doctrine. Nearly all of their own baptisms, up until this time, had been performed in rivers or in other streams. They now felt that they could perform baptisms for the dead in the same way. Writing down the names of their dead relatives, they began baptizing in the Mississippi River for them.

It was not the Lord's plan that baptisms for the dead be performed in the public view, nor in rivers or streams. Gospel ordinances for the dead are to be performed in temples built for that purpose. Special baptismal fonts inside temples are prepared for the work of baptism for the dead. *"For this ordinance belongeth to my house,"* says the Lord, *"and cannot be acceptable to me* [i.e. outside of the temple] *only in the days of your poverty, wherein ye are not able to build a house unto me"* (Doctrine & Covenants 124: 30). Therefore, when the Lord commanded the Saints to build a temple in Nauvoo, they were happy. They had left their temple in Kirtland, and were prevented from building temples in Missouri. Now that they were enjoying freedom from so much persecution, they felt they would be able to erect this temple and use it for the sacred work which the Lord had revealed.

NAUVOO TEMPLE—FOUR CORNERSTONES LAID

There was a hill in the city which overlooked the entire area. **It was a beautiful loca-**

tion, and would be an ideal site for the Lord's house. Preparations were made to build there, and **on April 6, 1841, the eleventh anniversary of the organization of the Church, the four cornerstones for the temple were laid.**

Early in the morning of that day, the sixteen companies of the Nauvoo Legion marched in parade. At 7:30 a. m., the firing of artillery was heard. Other military ceremonies were conducted during the morning. At noon, 10,000 people assembled at the building site. Banners were flying in the air, the band played, and there was joy and rejoicing.

The religious ceremonies began with the singing of a hymn and with prayer. Elder Rigdon addressed the people, telling of the suffering of the Saints and of the growth of the Church. The First Presidency then approached the southeast corner of the building site, and with the aid of the architect, laid the cornerstone. As it was being put into place, the Prophet said:

"This principle cornerstone in representation of the First Presidency is now duly laid in honor of the Great God; and may it remain until the whole fabric is completed, and may the same be accomplished speedily; that the Saints may have a place to worship God; and the Son of Man have where to lay His head" (*History of the Church,* 4: 329).

The cornerstone at the southwest corner was laid by the High Priests; at the northwest corner the stone was laid by the Stake High Council, and the fourth stone, at the northeast corner, was laid by Bishop Newel K. Whitney who said: "The fourth and last cornerstone, expressive of the Lesser Priesthood is now duly laid, and may the blessings before pronounced, with all others desirable rest upon the same forever. Amen."

In an attempt to promote goodwill, Church leaders invited Thomas Sharp, a former lawyer, and the editor of the *Warsaw Signal*, to this celebration and the laying of the temple cornerstone on April 6, 1841. As Thomas Sharp witnessed the day's events, including a parade and sumptuous banquet, and listened to Joseph Smith and other Church leaders speak about the prospects for the growth of Nauvoo and the kingdom of God, he became convinced that Mormonism was more than a religion. To him, it appeared to be a dangerous, un-American political movement aimed at domination of a vast empire. Returning to Warsaw, he launched a vigorous campaign against the Church in the columns of his newspapers, claiming that it was Joseph Smith's intent to unite Church and state; he insisted that the Saints possessed too much power and autonomy in their Nauvoo Charter.

In June 1841, Sharp helped form an anti-Mormon political party in Hancock County, which held conventions in Warsaw and Carthage and public meetings in other smaller communities. Consequently, individuals from both national political parties united against the Church. In the county elections in July, an anti-Mormon ticket was elected, which defeated the political influence of the Saints, even when they voted as a bloc.

But as Latter-day Saints continued to stream into Hancock County, including many British members who quickly became United States citizens, the political power of the Saints grew and further alienated their new enemies in Hancock County.

* * *

The remarkable mission of the Twelve Apostles in England, which the Prophet Joseph had watched with such fervent and eager interest, **drew to a close in the late summer of 1841.** By August, all of the Apostles had returned to Nauvoo except Willard Richards and Wilford Woodruff.

Anxious to learn details of their min-

istry abroad which correspondence had failed to provide, Joseph spent long hours with the Twelve. Of particular interest to him were the reports of the witness and evidence of God's power, and of the spirit of enthusiasm and commitment these produced among the converts. Also, of special interest, were the organizations that had been set up to transport the new converts to new places of gathering in Illinois and across the river in Iowa. **As he listened, studied, and evaluated the reports, Joseph was frankly amazed at the awesome results achieved by this small corps of dedicated men.**

Joseph wrote with pride of their accomplishments and his appreciation: *"Perhaps no men ever undertook such an important mission under such peculiarly distressing and inappropriate circumstances."*

After describing the adverse conditions under which they had departed for their mission and the stress and strains they had experienced in performing it, he offered this explanation for their phenomenal success: *"But knowing that they had been called by the God of Heaven to preach the Gospel to other nations, they conferred not with flesh and blood, but obedient to the heavenly mandate, without purse or script, they commenced a journey of five thousand miles entirely dependent on the providence of that God who had called them to such a holy calling."* In conclusion, the Prophet noted: *"They, truly, 'went forth weeping, bearing precious seed,' but have 'returned with rejoicing, bearing their sheaves with them'"* (*History of the Church,* 4: 390-91).

These comments typified the special relationship between Joseph and his associates. **He gloried in their successes as if they were his own,** never attempting to take credit for their accomplishments nor in any way upstage them. As if to reciprocate for his selfless attitude toward them, his disciples ordinarily ascribed to the Prophet much of the credit for any success they achieved.

Apart from his joy and excitement in hearing their reports, and in again having the pleasure of their daily companionship, there was another special and important reason why Joseph was happy for the return of the Twelve. He had begun feeling some uneasiness about the loyalty and intentions of some of those in the top echelons of Church leadership. Especially was this true of John C. Bennett, whose egotistical and corrupt qualities were surfacing. Doubts about the character and motivation of Sidney Rigdon had also begun to take shape in the Prophet's mind. The conduct of the Law brothers, the Higbees, William Marks, and other influential leaders had given him the feeling of being hemmed in by false or unreliable brethren. Consequently, to have about him a body of men who had proven the depth of their convictions by going abroad to labor under the most stressful conditions, inspired Joseph with new fervor, hope, and promise. With men of this calibre at his side, he could carry forward his heavy duties, confident that they would not betray or undercut him.

It was with these thoughts in mind that the Prophet scheduled a special conference to be held in Nauvoo on August 16, 1841. He was late in arriving at the conference because of the death the day before of his infant son Don Carlos. He sent word that Brigham Young was to conduct the meetings. Until that time, the ministry of the Twelve had been proselyting in the mission fields; they had not been authorized to direct the affairs of the Church in the organized stakes. Consequently, Elder Young approached this assignment with feelings of frustration. He was anxious, of course, to follow the instructions of his leader, but at the same time, he did not wish to antagonize the local brethren who had not been accustomed to the Twelve intervening in local affairs. Some sense of the unfamiliar circumstances he felt as he arose to conduct, is found in this excerpt from the minutes of the meeting: "The speaker hoped that no one would view him and his brethren as aspiring, because they had come forward to take part in the proceedings before the conference; he could assure the brethren that nothing could be further from his wishes, and those of his quorum, than to interfere with Church affairs in Zion and her stakes. He had been in the vineyard so long, he had become attached to foreign missions, and nothing could induce him to retire therefrom and attend to the affairs of the Church at home but a sense of duty, the requirements of heaven, or the revelations of God; to which he would always submit, be the consequence what it might." Echoing the sentiments of their leader, "the brethren of Brigham Young's quorum responded, Amen."

The unusual procedure of having the Twelve take charge of a conference at the headquarters of the Church created no small stir among local members and leaders. There was busy speculation between the morning and afternoon sessions regarding what to expect.

All uncertainty was removed when President Joseph Smith arrived and made an important announcement. "He proceeded to state to the conference at considerable length, the object of their present meeting, and in addition to what President Young had stated in the morning, said: *'that the time had come when the Twelve should be called upon to stand in their place next to the First Presidency, and attend to the settling of emigrants and the business of the Church at the stakes, and assist to bear off the kingdom victoriously to the nations'"* (*History of the Church,* 4: 402-03).

It is doubtful that many in attendance at this meeting grasped the far-reaching significance of what took place. They could not foresee that within less than three years, Joseph would be dead and the Twelve, who until that time, had hardly been visible on the local scene, would be in full control of the Church to the exclusion of other men whom they had come to regard as being higher than the Twelve in the scale of leadership. However, careful students of the revelations were not surprised by this change. They knew that in the formal hierarchy of the Church, the Twelve comprised a quorum equal in authority and responsibility to the First Presidency. Inherently this body had the power to act in any capacity to which it might be assigned by the Prophet, who held the ultimate authority or key. Now the key had been turned further to give the Twelve access to the broader powers of administration that until then they had possessed, but had not been permitted to exercise.

Joseph had given the keys of the Priesthood and all the endowments to the Twelve as they had returned from their missions abroad. The completion of this work filled the Prophet with joy, and he confided to this friends: ***"Now if they kill me, you have got all the keys . . .*** *the hosts of Satan will not be able to tear down the kingdom . . . because on your shoulders will be the responsibility of leading the people, for the Lord is going to let me rest for awhile."* He was able to share some of the responsibilities so that the Church would continue whether he was around or not. He also conferred on Brigham Young the keys of the sealing power which had been bestowed upon him by Elijah.

Aside from the need for moral support, and for assistance in handling the complex fast-growing administrative affairs of the Church, there was another important, urgent reason why Joseph was anxious for the return of the Twelve.

Just a few months before after years of resistance and fear to a commandment given by the Lord, Joseph knew full well that obeying this commandment would poison the public mind against him and the Church, also it would overshadow anything the Saints had previously endured. Before revealing the details of this commandment given to Joseph Smith in 1831, repeated several times over the years, especially in 1841, it is important for you to know more about how Satan was trying to destroy the Prophet and The Church of Jesus Christ of Latter-day Saints.

There was no question in anyone's mind why Joseph had formed the trained and extraordinary military force, the Nauvoo Legion, in just two short years. The Saints, needed protection while Joseph labored with the enormous charge of relocating an entire people, building a new city from the foundation up, and directing a widely spread proselyting effort.

All these accomplishments inspired awe and fear in his enemies. The prospect that his power and influence would become even more awesome as the ranks of the Church steadily enlarged by conversions caused his enemies to renew their efforts to destroy him. Therefore, in June 1841, the Missouri enemies sought to extradite the Prophet from a requisition from Governor Boggs of Missouri that had been issued several months earlier based on the charge that Joseph was a fugitive from justice. He was arrested on June fifth, while staying at Heberlin's Hotel, Bear Creek, about twenty-eight miles south of Nauvoo. The arrest was unexpected because only a few hours before, Joseph had visited with Illinois' Governor Carlin at his home in Quincy, who had said nothing about the requisition from Governor Boggs. Showing the legal knowledge had gained through long experience with various courts, Joseph obtained a writ of habeas corpus (subpoena) from the Chancery Court in Quincy, which blocked his immediate removal to Missouri. Judge Stephen A. Douglas, who happened to be in Quincy that evening, set the hearing on the writ for the following Tuesday in Monmouth.

The news of Joseph's arrest got around quickly among his followers in Nauvoo. Hosea Stout, one of the Prophet's bodyguards, and several other brethren obtained a skiff and rowed toward Quincy. Strong headwinds slowed them down, and by the time they arrived at their destination, Joseph and his party had left for Monmouth, traveling overland via Nauvoo. En route, the sheriff who had custody of the prisoner, had a recurrence of a prior illness, and Joseph nursed him as attentively as if he were one of his own. The feelings against Joseph ran very high in Monmouth. By this time, the lies and misrepresentations about him and his people, which had been so persistently publicized by his enemies in Missouri and Ohio, had begun to take root and created great bitterness in Illinois. Like a deadly disease, these unsupported ideas infected many who were exposed to them, and produced the customary symptoms of bigotry, stupidity and ignorance. As the Prophet was seeking legal counsel to represent him at the hearing, he found that threats had been made to the legal fraternity that any lawyer who accepted retainment as Joseph's attorney would be boycotted by the community. Fortunately for Joseph, the Monmouth bar included a few men of independence and courage to whom such threats meant challenge. Prodded by them, O. H. Browning, one of the most eminent of the local attorneys, agreed to handle the case. As if to demonstrate they could not be intimidated, five other lawyers joined Mr. Browning as defense counsel.

The basic issue Judge Douglas had to decide was whether the writ issued on the extradition order from Missouri should be honored and enforced. Joseph's attorneys attacked the writ on two grounds, one procedural and the other on the merits. As to the latter, they argued that the Missouri indictments, upon which the extradition order was based, were fraudulent and therefore invalid. Judge Douglas rejected this argument, but held for the Prophet on the procedural ground that the writ issued in Illinois on the Missouri extradition order was unenforceable since it had been served once before and returned and was, therefore, dead.

While he failed to convince the judge to decide the case on the merits, Mr. Browning succeeded in showing that the Prophet's conduct in Missouri had been a reasonable and necessary response to Governor Boggs' extermination order and to lawless mobbings to which Joseph and the Saints had been subjected. So eloquent was the argument that "Judge Douglas . . . and most of the officers . . . wept."

Mr. Browning's words carried conviction because he had witnessed the suffering and anguish produced by the brutal expulsion of the Saints from Missouri. He recited some of the tragic happenings he has seen at Quincy "where he tracked the persecuted women and children by their bloody footmarks in the snow" (*History of the Church,* 4: 369-70).

Although this highly emotional argument failed to determine whether the State of Missouri still had a legal hold on the embattled Mormon leader, it produced a helpful residual effect. It influenced the thinking of many important people in attendance at the trial; this in turn had a moderating effect upon the public and helped to postpone temporarily, the avalanche of hatred and ill will that ultimately was to come crashing down on Joseph's head.

There were numerous attempts made to destroy the Prophet and The Church of Jesus Christ. In May 1842, someone tried to kill ex-Governor Boggs in Missouri. He recovered from the assassin's bullet, but the assassin was never apprehended. However, on July 20, 1842, Boggs swore out an affidavit that Orrin Porter Rockwell, a resident of Illinois, had done the shooting and charged Joseph Smith as an "accessory before the fact." He asked Governor Reynolds of Missouri to demand that Governor Carlin of Illinois deliver Joseph Smith to be charged according to law. Governor Reynolds complied, and Governor Carlin issued a writ for the Prophet's arrest. On August 8, 1842, the Prophet and Orrin Porter Rockwell were taken into custody. The Prophet demanded the right of habeas corpus, and the Court of Nauvoo issued a writ requiring the prisoners to be brought before it. The sheriff was afraid either to obey or to disobey the order, and rushed away to Governor Carlin for instructions. When he returned, the prisoners were gone, and no threat against the people of Nauvoo would disclose their hiding place.

The whole proceeding on the part of Missouri was a legal farce, but probably nothing would have saved the Prophet and Rockwell from their Missouri enemies had they been taken. Every imaginable scheme was used to get Joseph to come out of hiding or to get his people to betray him. Rumors were that he had gone to Europe, or at least Washington, while all the time he was never any farther from Nauvoo than the island in the river.

The faith of the people in their Prophet was unshakable. Emma, Joseph's wife, made an appeal to Governor Carlin to rescind his order, without success. On December 8, 1842, the term of office of Governor Carlin expired and Thomas Ford took the governor's seat.

Affidavits were secured immediately to prove that Joseph Smith wasn't in Missouri at the time of the crime against Boggs, and on the basis of these, the Supreme Court of Illinois declared the writ to be illegal but decided that a trial should be held before the Governor would interfere. The Prophet submitted to arrest, and in the subsequent trial, was discharged January 5, 1843.

A NEW SCHEME ARISES

For a brief period, the Prophet was to enjoy peace. The people of Nauvoo rejoiced that their Prophet could once more walk openly among them. The breather was however, short lived. On June thirteenth of that year, **a new conspiracy arose.** John C. Bennett, one time friend of the Prophet, joined the Missouri forces against Joseph Smith. Bennett, who proved to be an unscrupulous and immoral individual, had been previously excommunicated from the Church. His bitterness toward the Prophet for exposing him knew no bounds. Both Governors Reynolds of Missouri and Ford of Illinois joined with him in his new scheme against the Mormon leader.

On June 13, 1843, a secret requisition was made to Governor Ford on the old charges. A writ was issued, and **two Missouri officers, disguised as Mormon Elders,** were appointed to serve it. An incidental remark of Governor Ford to Judge James Adams caused that highly-regarded friend of the Prophet to send him a warning. Joseph was not in Nauvoo when the warning came. William Clayton and Stephen Markham mounted fast horses and rode 212 miles in sixty-four hours to the house of Mrs. Wasson, sister of Emma Smith, near Dixon in Lee County, Illinois. The Prophet was surprised at their appearance, but felt secure and refused to leave. Somehow, the disguised officers had learned where Joseph was, and proceeded there. Still representing themselves as missionaries, they came into the Prophet's presence, and immediately took him prisoner. Without permitting him to say good-by to his wife Emma, who was in the house, they rushed him away.

The object was to get him into the hands of the waiting Missourians before Joseph's friends could rise to protect him. In this, they underrated the loyalty of his friends and the magnetism of Joseph Smith's personality. Stephen Markham, who was present at the time of the arrest, rode rapidly to Dixon to procure a writ of habeas corpus. When Joseph arrived in Dixon, he was imprisoned in a tavern and denied the privilege of consulting a lawyer. Joseph saw a man pass by the window, and shouted a request for an attorney. Two of them came but were refused admittance by the sheriffs. This aroused the neighborhood. Led by the proprietor, Mr. Dixon, they threatened violence to the sheriffs if they didn't give their prisoner his civil rights. Word was sent to a Mr. Chamberlain of the court to come to Dixon. Cyrus Walker, a great criminal attorney, was engaged to defend the Prophet.

During this time, Stephen Markham had not been idle. He had obtained a warrant for the arrest of sheriffs Reynolds and Wilson, for having made a threat upon his life, and another warrant for threatening the life of Joseph Smith, and falsely imprisoning him. Ten thousand dollars damage was claimed on the ground that the writ under which Joseph was arrested, was void in law. These men were not among friends, so could not obtain bondsmen. All things being equal, they were arrested and placed in custody by Sheriff Campbell of Lee County. It was a strange picture, Joseph Smith in the custody of Reynolds and Wilson, while they in turn were in custody of Campbell.

Meanwhile, William Clayton speedily rode over 200 miles to Nauvoo, acquainted Hyrum Smith with the circumstances, and requested his aid. It was well-known that large groups of Missourians had crossed over the river into Illinois and now were waiting to get possession of the Prophet and whisk him into Missouri. Hyrum Smith hastily called the Nauvoo Legion. Of this group, 175 marched out of Nauvoo, determined to prevent any force from taking Joseph Smith out of Illinois. Convinced as these men were that such extradition would result in their beloved leader's death, they were ready to shed their own blood in his defense. After leaving Nauvoo, the force divided to watch, those avenues through which the Missouri officers might attempt to carry-off the Prophet at a better advantage. One detachment boarded the river vessel, *Maid of Iowa.* Passing for a distance down the Mississippi, the vessel was turned up the Illinois. River to shut off any party attempting to carry off the Prophet by the water route. The remainder separated to patrol the various roads.

The officers, Reynolds and Wilson, had by this time, become so involved in legal writs that they could not carry out their assignment. Sheriff Campbell was convinced by the Prophet that Nauvoo was the closest place a court of competent jurisdiction might be found to handle the case. The group was proceeding to that place when the first detachment of troops from Nauvoo encountered it. Joseph Smith remarked: *"Well, I guess I won't go to Missouri this time. These are my boys."* As far as the Prophet was concerned, it was a triumphal procession from there to Nauvoo. At Nauvoo, Joseph Smith entertained his captors at his home, and treated them with all courtesy.

The Municipal Court, upon convening, discharged the Prophet on the grounds that the writ against him was illegal. A general rejoicing swept over Nauvoo. Reynolds and Wilson traveled to Carthage, and circulated petitions urging the governor to activate the militia to march on Nauvoo and retake the Prophet. They claimed that the Municipal Court had usurped authority, and that they had been coerced to take their prisoner into Nauvoo by Stephen Markham, and a group of Nauvoo men under arms. Tension ran high. Petitions were sent from Nauvoo to Governor Ford to dispel the falsehoods and calm the troubled waters. Governor Ford recognized the jurisdiction of the Municipal Court of Nauvoo and upheld its decision to discharge Joseph Smith. The Prophet was a free man but soon found the net of his enemies tightening about him. Even this was not so disturbing nor so dangerous as when members of his own people began to turn against him and lay plots for taking his life. It was sad to think that among those who came into prominence during the Nauvoo period were some who lost their faith in the Prophet and did seek his destruction. A study of the lives of those who were unfaithful and disloyal shows immorality, selfishness or ambition as the cause for loss of the Spirit.

One of the early ones to fall from his station was John C. Bennett. On the eve of his intended marriage to a young woman of Nauvoo, it was learned that he had deserted a wife and children in the East. Other discoveries of immoral conduct followed, and he was excommunicated in June 1842. He had previously resigned from the office of Mayor. In June, he left Nauvoo and set about to undermine the Prophet. He later wrote a book, *The History of the Saints.* It was full of misrepresentations and groundless charges, and proved to be of little interest to thinking people.

A number who had been influenced by Bennett's false teachings on sex, were also cut off from the Church. The majority of these apostates remained in Nauvoo. It was not until 1844 that their simmering hatred of the Prophet was fanned into an open flame. In January of that year the Prophet addressed some newly-appointed officers of the peace. In the course of his remarks he said: *"I am exposed to far greater danger from traitors among ourselves than from enemies without, although my life has been sought for many years by the civil and military authorities, priests, and people of Missouri . . . I have had pretended friends betray me. All the enemies upon the face of the earth may roar and exert all their power to bring about my death, but they can accomplish nothing, unless some who are among us and enjoy our society, have been with us in our councils, participated in our confidence, taken us by the hand, called us brother, saluted us with a kiss, join with our enemies, turn our virtues into faults, and by falsehood and deceit, stir up their wrath and indignation against us, and bring their united vengeance upon our heads . . .we have a Judas in our midst"* (*History of the Church,* 6: 152).

William and Wilson Law, William Marks, Leonard Soby, Dr. Charles D. Foster, and some others took offense at the Prophet's remarks. It soon was shown that these were in a secret league to assassinate the Prophet and destroy the Church.

THE PLOT AND A STORY OF CONSPIRACY

Two young and extraordinary men, Denison L. Harris and Robert Scott, exposed one conspiracy within the Church against the Prophet. These two young men, about seventeen years of age, were invited to attend a secret meeting of the conspirators. In a spirit of brotherhood, they confided in each other, wondering what course to pursue. They decided to speak to Denison's father, Emer Harris, brother of Martin Harris. He advised them to lay the whole matter before Joseph Smith. The Prophet requested that the two boys attend the meeting and report back to him about its proceedings. The meeting was held on the Sabbath Day at the house of William Law, counselor to the Prophet. A multitude of charges were laid against Joseph and Hyrum Smith.

"It seems that the immediate cause of these wicked proceedings was the fact that Joseph Smith had recently presented the Revelation of Celestial Marriage to the High Council for their approval, and certain members were most bitterly opposed to it, and denounced Joseph as a fallen Prophet, and were determined to overthrow him" (Horace Cummings, Historical Account, *Contributor,* Vol. 5: 252).

The two boys were silent observers, and after the meeting concluded, they met the Prophet secretly and reported to him. Following the Prophet's advice, they attended similar meetings the two following Sundays and received an invitation to attend a fourth meeting. In each meeting, the spirit of bitterness against the Prophet increased. Before they attended the last meeting, Joseph Smith counseled them:

"This will be your last meeting; this will be the last time that they will admit you into their councils! They will come to some determination. But be sure that you make no covenants, nor enter into any obligations, whatever, with them." After a pause he added, *"Boys, this will be their last meeting, and they may shed your blood, but I hardly think they will, as you are so young. If they do, I will be a lion in their path! Don't flinch. If you have to die; die like men. You will be martyrs to the cause and your crown can be no greater. But I hardly think they will shed your blood*" (*Millennial Star,* Vol. 5: 253, 1884).

When Denison and Robert approached the house of William Law on the Sabbath afternoon, they were stopped at the door by armed guards. After some severe questioning and cross-examination, they were admitted.

The house was filled with men, recounting many charges against the Prophet. Bitterness was everywhere. It was evident that a decision was forthcoming. The two boys took no part in the discussions, but remained by themselves. William Law and Austin Cowles spent some time explaining to them how the Prophet had fallen, and why they should join the group in ridding the Church of him. As the meeting progressed, each member present was requested to take an oath. The person being sworn would then say: "I do," after which he signed his name in the presence of the Justice of the Peace (Horace Cummings Account, *Contributor*, Vol. 5: 255).

About 200 took the oath. Among them were three heavily veiled women, who testified to attempts by Joseph and Hyrum to seduce them. When all but the two boys had complied, the attention of the group was turned to them. The boys refused to take the oath and started to leave the room. One of those present stepped in their way, raising his voice: "No, not by a d—n sight. You know all our plans and arrangements, and we don't propose that you should leave in that style. You've got to take the oath or you'll never leave here alive" (Ibid., Vol. 5: 255).

The boys were in a dangerous position. Threats were coming from all directions. One voice shouted, "Dead men tell no tales" (Ibid., Vol. 5: 255). Violent hands were laid on them. Swords and bowie knives were drawn. One of the leading men said, "If you do not take that oath, we will cut your throats" (Ibid., Vol. 5: 256).

Only the wisdom of the leader prevented their murder then and there. The house of William Law stood close to the streets, and there was a danger that the disturbance would be heard by passers-by. Better to execute them in the cellar.

Accordingly, a guard with drawn swords and bowie knives was placed on either side of the boys while two others armed with cocked muskets and bayonets at their backs brought up the rear as they were marched off in the direction of the cellar. William and Wilson Law, Austin Cowles, and others accompanied them to that place. Before committing the murderous deed, however, they gave the boys one last chance for their lives. One of them said: "Boys, if you will take that oath, your lives will be spared; but if you are determined to refuse, we will have to shed your blood" (Ibid., Vol. 5: 256).

With their death as the immediate alternative, the two boys grimly refused to turn against their Prophet. Trembling and white with fear, they awaited the sword. As the sword was raised by an angry member of the group, a sharp voice from the crowd halted it in midair.

"Hold on! Hold on there! Let's talk this matter over before their blood is shed" (Ibid., Vol. 5: 256). A hurried consultation followed, during which the young men were relieved to hear a strong voice say, "and if they do not return home, strong suspicion will be aroused, and they may institute a search that would be very dangerous to us" (Ibid., Vol. 5: 256). That counsel prevailed. The boys were threatened with death if they revealed a word of what had transpired, and sent away. A guard accompanied them for a distance to prevent some of the more bloodthirsty individuals following to kill them. The parting words of the guards were: "Boys, if you ever open your mouths concerning anything you have seen or heard in any of our meetings, we will kill you by night or by day, wherever we find you, and consider it our duty" (Ibid., Vol. 5: 256).

The boys continued on to the riverbank, where they met the Prophet, who had become anxious and had gone in search of them. Withdrawing to a secluded spot below the Prophet's home, they told the entire story. The bravery and loyalty of the two young men melted the Prophet to tears. For fear that harm might come to them, he urged them to promise never to reveal their story for twenty years. This promise was faithfully kept.

The heroism of the two boys saved the life of the Prophet for a time from the net closing about him. Subsequently, the conspirators were excommunicated from the Church, after which they openly allied themselves with all those forces seeking its overthrow.

THE GREAT NAUVOO TEMPLE GOES FORTH

During this same period of time, the Saints were making great progress on the most important building on the face of the earth. **It was a Temple to the Living God.** A people of great faith were obeying the commandment of the Lord to build this Nauvoo Temple as rapidly as possible—***"let this house be built unto my name,*** *that I may reveal mine ordinances therein unto my people; For I deign to reveal unto my church things which have been kept hid from before the foundation of the world, things which pertain to the dispensation of the fulness of time. And I will show unto my servant Joseph, all things pertaining to this house, and the priesthood thereof . . . And ye shall build it on the place where you have contemplated building it, for that is the spot which I have chosen"* (Doctrine & Covenants 124: 40-43).

The Nauvoo Temple construction was begun in January 1841. A great undertaking had commenced. The faith so timely and favorably shown when the cornerstones were laid and the spot dedicated was never renounced. The labor on the building was donated by the Saints, who also donated money to buy the materials. They hurried with the work. Men, women, and even children contributed in any way they could.

The temple was built of beautiful white stone, and by the time it was finished it cost a million dollars—a vast sum of money in those days. Stone quarries were opened a short distance down the river, and the grey sandstone blocks were transported to the temple site. When the year ended, the foundations had become visible from the surrounding countryside.

Beneath the walls of the rising symbol of faith, the very essence of the city's life passed by in a fascinating, significant, notable review. Near the walls of the temple, the Saints erected a bowery, which was called, "The Grove." There, in the open air, the people met in solemn worship. There they listened to the words of the Prophet or his associates. Men of national renown sat at times, beneath its shade. Minister of a dozen creeds, upon invitation, had the opportunity to express their views. That old bowery or "grove" so near the temple was an historic spot. The sermons delivered there would fill volumes, and the faith expressed there in worship was powerful enough to move mountains.

In its day, the temple was one of the most beautiful structures in the entire Western part of the United States. This magnificent edifice stood on the highest elevation of the city and commanded a view of the entire countryside on both sides of the river. It became the crown of Nauvoo, which in itself was remarkable in contrast to most of the frontier towns of America. Nauvoo, prior to the martyrdom, was the largest city in Illinois.

The Nauvoo Temple was finished in May of 1844, but many ordinances were performed there even before its completion. Exclusive of its impressive exterior, the ordinances being performed on the inside of the temple were truly the crown of its beauty. Within six months of the time the temple was started, the Lord made it known that baptisms for the dead were to be performed only in the temple. The Saints were so anxious to perform such baptisms that they did not wish to wait until the entire temple was complete, so a temporary font was built. (It was later replaced by a finer one, a great bowl filled with water and resting upon the backs of twelve bronze oxen like the font in the ancient Temple of Solomon.) Many baptisms were performed in the temporary font, some by the Prophet himself.

Within the walls of the temple, built through the sacrifice of a unique people, were performed some of the finest acts of love for which the human race is capable. The Saints, though burdened with the tasks of daily life and the completion of the temple, were willing to sacrifice much of their time to perform ordinances for their dead ancestors. The Prophet explained that the living and the dead are dependent upon each other for salvation, *"they* [the dead] *without us cannot be made perfect—neither can we without our dead be made perfect"* (Doctrine & Covenants 128: 15).

The ordinances to help accomplish this mutual perfection, he later explained: *"include not only, baptism for the dead, but also the endowment of the Holy Priesthood and marriage for time and all eternity."* The doctrine that marriage may be eternal, when the ordinance is performed by the power of the Priesthood of God is one of the unique contributions to religious thought, and gives definite meaning to Mormon philosophy. (It must be constantly upheld, however, that he doctrine of marriage for time and eternity, contained in Section 132 of the Doctrine and Covenants, with all the blessings promised therein, does not necessarily involve plural marriage.)

On April 2, 1836, Elijah had appeared to Joseph Smith in the Kirtland Temple, and conferred upon him "The keys of the sealing power." These keys included the authority necessary for temple ordinances for both the living and the dead. Not only baptisms, but endowments and sealing together as families were performed for both the living and the dead.

The temple represented the purity of thought which actuated its people—the love of all mankind. Joseph taught that all of God's children would have equal opportunity to hear and embrace the laws of God whether in this life for in the life to come. *"All who have died without a knowledge of this gospel, who would have received it if they had been permitted to tarry, shall be heirs of the celestial kingdom of God; Also, all that shall die henceforth, without a knowledge of it, who would have received it with all their hearts, shall be heirs of the kingdom; For I, the Lord will judge all men according to their works according to the desire of their hearts"* (Doctrine and Covenants 137: 7-9). The Saints believed that their loved ones who had not been taught the fulness of the Gospel while on the earth, would have the opportunity to accept it in Heaven, but would still need the earthly ordinances performed, such as baptism. In performing ordinance work for their departed loved ones, they were doing something for others which those others could not do for themselves. It is not strange to find that God has so chosen to bind together in love all the members of His kingdom. Joseph taught that he who will not accept the sacrifice of another in his behalf or he who is not willing to sacrifice on behalf of another, has not attained those qualities worthy of the kingdom.

* * *

It took five years to erect the Nauvoo Temple. When the capstone was laid, the Prophet and his brother Hyrum were dead, the city lay practically deserted, and its inhabitants spread out over the Iowa plains—banished once again and seeking another home. However, before the people were driven from Nauvoo, most of the adults had received their endowments, and had their husbands, wives, and children sealed to them by the Power of God in the nearly-finished temple.

The story of those grey temple walls, once the glory of Western Illinois, parallels that of the "City Beautiful." The rise, the glory and the fall of the temple was symbolic of the city upon which it looked. When the Saints were gone, the great structure seemed to invite the lightning of heaven to split it apart and let out its life's blood. On October 9, 1848, the interior of the temple was burned by an arsonist. Then on May 27, 1850, tornadoes demolished three of the exterior walls. Finally, in 1856, the last remaining wall was leveled for safety reasons.

* * *

THE RECORDS OF ABRAHAM

In early 1842, Joseph was busily engaged in *"translating from the Records of Abraham."* These records had been acquired in 1835 when the Church purchased several rolls of ancient Egyptian papyrus from Michael Chandler. Joseph and his scribes did some preliminary investigation of them, but labor on the Kirtland Temple and the subsequent apostasy and persecution precluded any opportunity for him to continue this work in Ohio or Missouri. Finally, in the spring of 1842, he was able to dedicate himself to the task for several weeks with few interruptions.

Elder Wilford Woodruff, who learned in leadership councils of the Prophet's translation and some of its contents, recorded in his journal his feelings about the Prophet's work: "Truly the Lord has raised up Joseph the Seer . . . and is now clothing him with mighty power and wisdom and knowledge . . . The Lord is blessing Joseph with power to reveal the mysteries of the kingdom of God; to translate through the Urim and Thummim ancient records and Hieroglyphics as old as Abraham or Adam, which causes our hearts to burn within us while we behold their glorious truths opened unto us."

Extracts from the Book of Abraham appeared first in the *Times and Seasons* and in the *Millennial Star* in the summer of 1842. Joseph Smith indicated that more would be forthcoming, but he was unable to continue the translation after 1842. What the Church received—five chapters of the Book of Abraham in the Pearl of Great Price—is only a portion of the original record.

The Book of Abraham excited much attention in the East. The *Boston Daily Ledger* called Joseph Smith "the greatest original of the present age," and several notable papers ran accounts and facsimiles of the Book of Abraham. The Prophet rejoiced. They *"are beginning to exhibit 'Mormonism' in its true light,"* he said.

Many of the early records of the Prophet and the Church has been stolen or destroyed by mobs. Joseph was more careful now and had several clerks. At least one was with him at all times to carefully record his actions and words. Chief among the scribes was Willard Richards, who was seldom away from the Prophet's side. Of him Joseph wrote: *"I have been searching all my life to find a man after my own heart whom I can trust with my business in all things, and I have found him—Dr. Willard Richards is the man."*

As the Prophet would call men to serve in the Church, he would select those who would have the ability and direction to advance the cause of the Church. This always seemed to be the criterion that the Prophet applied in extending or withholding calls to service. The age, the relationship, or the seniority in service of a person being considered for a position seemed to carry little weight with the Prophet if it was apparent that someone else could do a better job. The hard question he seemed always to put in himself as he juggled administrative assignments was: Can this person do the work more effectively than anyone else? If the answer to that inquiry was yes, the person ordinarily was selected.

It was this sound principle of management, as much as almost anything else, that accounted for the unusually high degree of enthusiasm and initiative among Joseph's co-workers. They came to realize that recognition, in terms of appointment to office, was based largely upon the merit of their past work or upon special qualifications to perform a certain task. Yet underlying all this was a conviction that because of Joseph's unusual, prophetic role, the special qualities of an individual, as yet unrevealed by objective performance, would be taken into account.

There was little doubt that Joseph's tendency to ignore personal relationships and length of service in making administrative appointments, alienated some of his followers. We have already seen how the Whitmers, Oliver Cowdery, Martin Harris, and others became estranged when the Prophet failed to accord them recognition to which they felt entitled by their years of service. However, the advantages that accrued from this wise policy far outweighed the disadvantages, particularly by avoiding the dulling effect of favoritism, by emphasizing performance over personal influence, and by fueling the energies of members who came to realize that superior performance would not go unrewarded or unrecognized. Furthermore, most of those who were alienated from the Prophet through false feelings of neglect or of having been passed over later, became reconciled as they gained maturity and experience.

It is important to note that the Prophet prayed about those he selected to serve in the Church. When they were chosen, they were obviously in tune with the Prophet and the Lord. As time progressed, however many allowed themselves to be taken over by the adversary (Satan) in their desire for personal power and wealth, and bitterly turned against the Prophet.

It is important to mention at this time, about the emergence of John C. Bennett because of the key role he played in obtaining the Nauvoo Charter. But, he was only one of a number of comparative newcomers—including Wilson and William Law and Chauncey Higbee—to the inner circle of leadership who were to play important roles in the unfolding drama of Nauvoo, and especially in the final tragic act that was to see the brutal assassination of the Prophet and his loyal brother, Hyrum. These men played key roles, along with others, in building up Nauvoo and subsequently in its destruction. The Prophet did have serious reservations about their loyalty from time to time, but he continued to use them as long as their affirmative contributions continued to outweigh the negative. He was truly a loving, believing Prophet of God.

On January 5, 1842, Joseph opened a General Store on Water Street, with "a tolerably good" assortment of wares. It pleased him to think of the sugar, molasses, raisins and flour which would delight the poor families who had gone without them that Christmas. He stood behind the counter himself, serving customers with a joy and sparkle of pleasure in his eyes. *"For I love to wait upon the Saints,"* he said, *"and be a servant to all."* Sometimes called the "Red Brick Store," this was a meeting place for many religious and city affairs in Nauvoo. The store was run on the first floor, and other activities were held on the second.

While the temple was being constructed, some ordinances were performed in the upper story of Joseph Smith's store in Nauvoo. Baptisms for the dead were performed during this time in the Mississippi River. As has been stated, as soon as a portion of the temple was completed, the Lord, by revelation, commanded the Saints to cease performing those ordinances outside the proper house.

The Prophet Joseph, assisted by his Brother Hyrum, introduced the holy temple endowment to Brigham Young, Heber C. Kimball, Willard Richards and others in the upper room of his store on May 4, 1842. After administering the ordinances of the endowment, the Prophet stated: *"There was nothing made known to these men but what will be made known to all the Saints of the last days, so soon as they are prepared to receive"* (*History of the Church,* 5: 1-2).

THE FEMALE RELIEF SOCIETY

The Female Relief Society of Nauvoo was organized on March 17, 1842 on the upper floor of Joseph's Red Brick General Store and completed on March 24, 1842. Emma Smith was selected as its first President, thus according to Joseph, fulfilling an earlier revelation identifying her as an *"elect lady"* (Doctrine & Covenants 25: 3). The organization's objective was *"the relief of the poor, the destitute, the widow and the orphan, and for the exercise of all benevolent purposes"* (*History of the Church,* 4: 567).

In April, the Prophet gave the sisters additional counsel and promises. He advised the women to treat their husbands *"with mildness and affection"* and to meet them with a *"smile instead of an argument or a murmur, reminding them that when a mind is in despair, it needs the solace of affection and kindness."* After promising that they would receive appropriate instruction through the order of the Priesthood, he said: *"I now turn the key in your behalf in the name of the Lord, and this Society shall rejoice, and knowledge and intelligence shall flow down from this time henceforth; this is the beginning of better days to the poor and the needy, who shall be made to rejoice and pour forth blessings on your heads"* (*History of the Church,* 4: 606-07).

Joseph Smith stated: ***"The Church was never perfectly organized until the women were thus organized."*** Although at that time, Latter-day Saint women had to apply to become members, the Relief Society was very popular and grew rapidly. Membership had grown to over 1,300 women at the time of Joseph's death. Due to the crisis created by the martyrdom, and the exodus to, and settlement in the West, there were few Relief Society meetings held until the organization was revived in 1867.

"This is an organization that was established by the Prophet Joseph Smith, and therefore, it is the oldest auxiliary organization in the Church, and it is of the first importance. It has not only to deal with the necessities of the poor, the sick and the needy, but a part of its duty—and the larger part, too—is to look after the spiritual, mental, moral, welfare and salvation of the mothers and the daughters of Zion; to see that none is neglected, but that all are guarded against misfortune, calamity, the powers of darkness, and the evils that threaten them in the world. **It is the duty of the Relief Society to "look after the spiritual welfare of themselves and of all the female members of the Church."**

Today, the Relief Society of The Church of Jesus Christ of Latter-day Saints is the largest women**'s organization in the world with approximately 3.9 million members in 160 countries. It is the second largest and oldest organization in the United States.**

In the Church of Jesus Christ of Latter-day Saints, the men hold the Priesthood and the women participate in the Relief Society, and both work hand in hand, with all organizations in the Church under the direction and power of the Holy Melchizedek Priesthood. **The Motto of the**

Relief Society's, *"Charity never faileth"* (1 Cor. 13: 8).

* * *

Many brethren in the early Church, including the Prophet Joseph Smith became members of the Masons. Free Masonry is an international society preaching brotherliness, charity and mutual aid. This affiliation was a good one for the Church, and in harmony with Joseph's teachings. In March 1842, the Grand Master Mason of Illinois granted authority for the Mormons to establish a Masonic Lodge. Several thousand people attended the celebration. "The Rising Sun Lodge of the Ancient York Masons" soon became the largest in the state. When the brick building was dedicated in April 1844, over 550 members attended. Although the Prophet was true to his Masonic pledges, this commitment did not succeed in overcoming persecution or in establishing good will toward his people. If anything, it seemed to increase nonmembers jealousies and fears.

Soon Masons were further angered by the Prophet's alleged use of the Masonic ceremony in Mormon temple ordinances. (While recognizing that there were similarities as well as differences, the Mormons insisted that their own ceremonies were divinely revealed.) God does not have to steal anything from anyone. He is God Almighty and all truth comes from Him only. Man established the Mason organization to help those less fortunate, and they do an outstanding work within their community. Nevertheless, God has restored His Church to this earth—The Church of Jesus Christ of Latter-day Saints—through His Chosen Prophet Joseph Smith—to help mankind to find their way back to God's presence one day—if they obey and live the commandments of God. This is God's hope. This is His plan.

* * *

One of the best recognized and famous prophecies of the Prophet Joseph Smith is that in which he announced that the Saints would at some time be driven from their homes in Nauvoo, and would go to the Rocky Mountains, where they would become a mighty people.

In the summer of 1843, the Prophet joined a number of the brethren at a meeting in Montrose, Iowa, just across the river from Nauvoo.

The Prophet wrote of this event: *"I had a conversation with a number of the brethren on the subject of our persecutions in Missouri, and the constant annoyance which has followed us since we were driven from the state."*

"I prophesied that the Saints would continue to suffer much affliction and would be driven to the Rocky Mountains; many would apostatize, others would be put to death by our persecutors or lose their lives in consequence of exposure or disease, and some of you will live to go and assist in making settlements and build cities, and see the Saints become a mighty people in the midst of the Rocky Mountains" (*History of the Church,* 5: 85-86).

Anson Call was one of the brethren present who heard this prophecy. He gave an account of what took place, and his writing was also included in the official *Documentary History of the Church,* volume four.

According to his account, the brethren were very warm from the heat of the summer day. As they stood in the shade of the building, the Prophet drank a glass of cool, clear water. While holding the glass in his hand, he said that, *"the Saints would be driven to the Rocky Mountains, where there were clear, crystal streams of water. This water,"* he said, *"tastes much like that of the crystal streams that are running from the snow-capped mountains"* (*History of the Church,* 5: 86).

Brother Call said that then the Prophet's face became luminous and bright with a very white but heavenly light. Others have described this appearance in the Prophet's face when at various times, he was under the influence of the Holy Spirit, and when he was talking, his countenance would change to white; not the deadly white of a bloodless face, but a living, brilliant white. He seemed absorbed in gazing at something at a great distance.

According to Anson Call, the Prophet then said that: *"he was looking at the Rocky Mountains, and could see their snow-capped peaks."* The Prophet spoke, saying: *"Oh the beauty of those snow-capped mountains! The cool refreshing streams that are running down through those mountain gorges.!"*

After describing those beautiful scenes, the Prophet said: *"There are some men here who shall do a great work in that land."* Pointing to Brother Call, he said: *"There is Anson; he shall go and shall assist in building up cities from one end of the country to the other."* He told the brethren that: *"the Saints would perform in the Rockies as great a work as has ever been done by men, so that the nations of the earth will be astonished, and many will be gathered into that land and will assist in building cities and temples, and Israel shall be made to rejoice"* (*History of the Church,* 5: 86).

Brother Call said that the Prophet then looked in another direction, and cried out: *"Oh, the scenes that this people will pass through; the dead that will lie between here and there. Oh, the apostasy that will take place before my brethren reach that land! But the priesthood will prevail over its enemies, triumph over the devil and be established upon the earth, never more to be thrown down"* (*History of the Church,* 5: 86).

The Prophet then appealed to the brethren to be true to the faith, avoid apostasy, and live the Gospel. *"Remember these things,"* he said, *"and treasure them up"* (*History of the Church,* 5: 86).

Joseph recorded many prophecies, all of which saw fulfillment. One interesting prophecy was made in May of 1843 when Joseph dined with Judge Stephen A. Douglas at Carthage, Illinois. The judge offered sympathetic words to the many injustices the Mormons had suffered. Unexpectedly, Joseph said with a solemn warning: *"Judge, you will aspire to the Presidency of the United States, and if you ever turn your hand against me or the Latter-day Saints, you will feel the weight of the hand of the Almighty upon you; and you will live to see and know that I have testified the truth to you, for the conversation of this day will stick to you through life."*

In June of 1857, when the Mormons had settled in Utah, Douglas betrayed the Saints, uniting with their enemies in an untrue assault upon them. In 1860, Douglas was nominated for the Presidency of the United States. He was the favored candidate, yet he was badly beaten. Abraham Lincoln, a most unpromising opponent, received 180 electoral votes to Douglas' twelve! Douglas died six weeks later, a demoralized, heartbroken man.

* * *

As opposition against the Saints grew, their oneness at the polls became a thorn in the flesh of some candidates who hoped to gain the Mormon's vote, while retaining the vote of the non-Mormons. This midway position of the politicians became more and more impossible as the opposition to the Saints increased. By 1843, the politicians of the state and nation had sided with the majority against the Saints in order to save their own political careers.

It soon became impossible for the Saints to support the candidates of either political party, a condition which meant the end of political protection for them in Illinois, and eventually the repeal of those rights and privileges which they had obtained. In fact, a repeal of the Nauvoo Charter was attempted in 1843, and the bill for repeal succeeded in passing the House of Representatives which had most readily responded to feelings within the state against the Mormons.

* * *

During the latter part of the year 1843, Joseph Smith communicated with the prospective political candidates for the United States Presidency. Clay, Calhoun, Cass, and Van Buren were asked for their views toward the Mormon people. The answers were evasive. It was evident that the Saints could expect little help, whichever candidate was elected. Anxious to exercise their right of the ballot, and especially anxious to place their cause and views before the nation, the Mormon leaders made a surprising move. In a council meeting, it was decided to place their own candidates in the field. **A state convention of a "Reform Party" was called and met at Nauvoo, May 17, 1844.**

From that convention, Joseph Smith emerged a candidate for the office of President of the United States. None expected Joseph to be elected, least of all himself. Nevertheless, it offered a real opportunity to lay before the nation the Mormon cause. The press would eagerly publish the views of a candidate to the office of the President of the United States while rejecting those same views as the expressions of a Prophet. Sidney Rigdon accepted the nomination for Vice President.

Missionaries of the Church began to campaign in behalf of the Prophet, and in this way, had the opportunity to explain "Mormonism" to many people who might not have listened otherwise.

The Prophet had some very sound and constructive ideas on government. The Lord had made it known in revelation, that the Constitution of the United States was an inspired document, and that the Lord himself had raised up the men who wrote it. Another revelation taught that to have peace and order, the law of the land must be upheld. There was no need to break the laws of the land if mankind kept the laws of God.

Slavery was an important issue in the United States at this time. The Prophet urged that slavery be abolished, and that every slave holder be paid a fair price for his slaves by the Congress. This would be cheaper than a war, and the whole country could help bear the cost of it.

Prisons in those days were places of severe punishment. The Prophet had felt it while he was in Liberty Jail for six months. He now urged that the prisons be turned into places where criminals would be well-treated, taught useful trades and reformed.

He urged economy in government, and lower taxes. He believed in a greater equality among the people, and advised the establishment of a national bank, with branches in all states and territories of the United States. He also urged a law to allow the President to send troops into any part of the nation to put down uprisings.

Neither Oregon, Texas, nor Mexico (which at that time included what is now Utah) belonged to the Union. The Prophet recommended that steps be taken to include them in the Union of States.

He believed that Congress was too large, and urged that it be reduced in number by two-thirds. He urged that the government be based on honesty and truth, making honor the standard of all men.

He had several other teachings on government which were spread throughout the nation by the missionaries.

There was very little hope that the

Prophet would actually become President, because the Saints knew that many people hated him and the Church. But they used this candidacy as a means of spreading their views, that the Saints were a people of high ideals, and that they had been unjustly treated by their enemies . . . that The Church of Jesus Christ had been restored to the earth and that an invitation was extended to all mankind to participate in the blessings offered by living the Gospel.

Chapter 13

Coming Down to the Wire . . .

Who Said the Mormons Invented Polygamy and Plural Marriage?

Emma Smith Refused to Accept the Principle of Plural Marriage

Good Friends became Great Enemies

The Expositor Incident—Printed only one Edition

Unmerciful personal attacks against Joseph Smith

Expositor Declared a Nuisance and Destroyed

The Carthage Period—a City in a Riotous State

The Assassination—Martyrdom—(Joseph and Hyrum Smith)

The End and a New Beginning

In the Introduction of this book—we began the Joseph Smith story in Nauvoo, Illinois, during the last few years of Joseph's life. From Nauvoo, we traced his steps back in time to his earlier years in New York, Pennsylvania, Ohio, and through the Missouri persecutions and expulsion. **We now return to Joseph's story and pick up the threads of his life,** and examine the devastating events which took place in Nauvoo and Carthage, Illinois, leading up to the assassination and martyrdom of Joseph Smith and his brother, Hyrum.

Even when he began his ministry, the Prophet Joseph Smith knew that he might have to die for his religion. While Joseph was translating the Book of Mormon, the Lord promised him eternal life if he was *"firm in keeping the commandments . . . even if you should be slain"* (Doctrine & Covenants 5: 22). A month later, the Lord again spoke of possible violent death. *"And even if they do unto you, even as they have done unto me, blessed are ye, for you shall dwell with me in glory"* (Doctrine & Covenants 6: 30). The Prophet received some promises and assurances, in any case, regarding his earthly mission several years later in Liberty Jail. The Lord promised him: *"Thy days are known, and thy years shall not be numbered less; therefore, fear not what man can do, for God shall be with you forever and ever"* (Doctrine & Covenants 122: 9).

In 1840, his father's dying blessing promised him, "'You shall even live to finish your work.' At this, Joseph cried out, weeping: *'Oh! My father, shall I?'* 'Yes,' said his father, 'you shall live to lay out the plan of all the work which God has given you to do.'" Joseph Smith, heeding the Spirit's promptings, valiantly completed his mission, suffered martyrdom, and qualified for a divine, glorious, and magnificent reward; thus these prophecies were fulfilled.

As the Prophet Joseph continued his ministry during the Nauvoo period, he increasingly felt the promptings of the Spirit that his ministry on earth was nearing its end. He revealed these feelings to those closest to him, and on occasion, would speak of them to the Saints in general. To a large congregation in the uncompleted Nauvoo Temple on January 22, 1843, Joseph spoke of the power of the Priesthood being used to establish the kingdom of God in the latter days. He explained that the temple endowment would *"prepare the disciples for their mission into the world."* Referring to his own role, Joseph declared: *"I understand my mission and business. God Almighty is my shield, and what can man do if God is my friend. I shall not be sacrificed until my time comes. Then I shall be offered freely"* (*Wilford Woodruff Journal,* 22 January 1843, LDS Historical Department, SLC).

It seems obvious that the Prophet was sometimes weighed down with an impression that death was near. It wasn't that he feared death because his understanding of eternity led him to expect both a continuation and a growth of life beyond the grave. The source of anxiety was his uncertainty as to whether the Church was fit to withstand the storms he foresaw, and whether his disciples had been sufficiently taught to pilot a true course. It was this concern that would take the center stage of his thoughts during his remaining year of life. Of course, **polygamy and politics were to play major roles as well,** but were the side issues. Joseph's major focus was on perpetuating the system of religion created through his agency and inspiration. He was very aware of the lesson history had taught him: that the growth of a religion or a philosophy is due as much to the passion of its disciples as to the work of its founder. He had observed this principle at work in the life of Jesus Christ. He also knew, in spite of the reality of his own experience, that the work organized through him would falter unless vigorous disciples succeeded him . . . unless men imbued with the dedication of a Paul would pick up the torch he had lit. And so, during the last year of his life, he never missed an opportunity to train his disciples in the operation of the Church. Like a master technician, he took pains and delight in explaining the complexities of Church government.

The Twelve were the chief recipients of the Prophet's frequent briefings. He saw in them the qualities necessary to spread the faith and build securely on the foundation he had laid. **The revelations clearly stated that the Twelve stood next to the President and Prophet of the Church, Joseph Smith,** in authority and responsibility. These, then, were the heirs apparent, the men upon whom the burden of leadership would fall once Joseph was gone, and he spared no effort in making certain that they learned their lessons well.

One of the most deeply-felt, keenly sensitive, and remarkable points of Joseph Smith's martyrdom prophecies was made to the Quorum of the Twelve Apostles in the spring of 1844. Orson Hyde remembered the account: "We were in council with Brother Joseph almost every day for weeks. Said Brother Joseph in one of those councils, there is something going to happen; I don't know what it is, but the Lord bids me to hasten and give you your endowment before the temple is finished. He conducted us through every ordinance of the Holy Priesthood, and when he had gone through with all the ordinances, he rejoiced very much, and said, now if they kill me, you have got all the keys, and all the ordinances, and you can confer them upon others, and the hosts of Satan will not be able to tear down the kingdom as fast as you will be able to build it up."

Like everyone, the Prophet wanted to live. He wanted to enjoy the company of his wife, play with his children, speak to the Saints, and enjoy the friendship and fellowship of good people. In spite of knowing that he would probably die soon, he was a man who loved life. He met very often with the Saints, and some of his greatest sermons were given within weeks of his martyrdom.

The Saints in Nauvoo frequently listened to the Prophet Joseph Smith preach, and many of them wrote of how moved they were by the experience. They thrilled to his words and were strengthened in their testimonies. Brigham Young said: "Such moments were more precious to me than all the wealth of the world. No matter how great my poverty, I never let an opportunity pass of learning what the Prophet had to impart" (*Journal of Discourse,* 12: 270).

Wandle Mace, a new convert, said that listening to the Prophet in public or private, in sunshine of shower, he became convinced that Joseph Smith had been taught by God. He never missed a chance to hear Joseph preach because, he said, Joseph "had been feeding us deliciously with spiritual food" (*Biography of Wandle Mace,* Brigham Young University).

James Palmer, a British Convert, said the Prophet "looked and had, the appearance of one that was heaven born while preaching, or as tho he had been sent from the heavenly worlds on a divine mission" (*James Palmer Reminiscences,* LDS Historical Department, SLC).

There was no meetinghouse in Nauvoo large enough for all the Saints to gather to hear their Prophet, so in good weather, they met outdoors under the trees. A typical place was in a grove that formed an amphitheater, such as the area on the hillside west of the temple. This was one of Joseph's favorite places to speak to the Saints. During the Nauvoo period, he became accustomed to giving public discourses. In the early days of the Restoration, he had left most of the preaching to others whom he felt were better orators. Now, however, he preached with great power and authority in Nauvoo and surrounding communities. His nearly 200 discourses during these years shaped Latter-day Saints understanding of Gospel doctrines and immeasurably influenced the Church.

On Sunday, March 20, 1842, at the funeral of the deceased child of Windsor P. Lyon, Joseph chose to speak in the grove about the salvation of little children. He said that he had: *"asked the question, why it is that infants, innocent children, are taken away from us, especially those that seem to be the most intelligent and interesting."* He said: *"that they were taken to be spared the wickedness that was increasing in the world."* He then stated one of the most comforting doctrines revealed in the latter days: *"All children are redeemed by the blood of Jesus Christ, and the moment that children leave this world, they are taken to the bosom of Abraham. The only difference between the old and young dying is, one lives longer in heaven and eternal light and glory than the other, and is freed a little sooner from this miserable, wicked world"* (*History of the Church,* 4: 553-554).

In the spring of 1843, **Joseph frequently visited the outlying settlements of the Saints to teach and guide them.** When in Ramus, he stayed at the home of his friend Benjamin F. Johnson. The teachings of the Prophet in Ramus, Illinois, on Sunday, April 2, 1843 were so important that they were incorporated into the official history of the Church and later into the Doctrine and Covenants scriptures as Section 130. In a morning meeting, Elder Orson Hyde had spoken about the Father and the Son dwelling in the hearts of the Saints and said that the Savior at His Second Coming would "appear on a white horse as a warrior." At lunch, Joseph Smith told Orson that he was going to offer some corrections to his sermon in the afternoon meeting. Elder Hyde replied: "They shall be thankfully received" (*History of the Church,* 5: 323).

The Prophet explained to the Saints: *"WHEN the Savior shall appear, we shall see him as he is. We shall see that he is a man like ourselves"* (Doctrine and Covenants 130: 1). In further correction he added that: *"the idea that the Father and the Son dwell in a man's heart is an old sectarian notion, and is false"* (v. 3). Later in his sermon, he boldly declared that: *"The Father has a body of flesh and bones as tangible as man's, the Son also; but the Holy Ghost has not a body of flesh and bones, but is a personage of Spirit"* (v. 22). In that monumental discourse, Joseph Smith also taught other eternal truths that have since inspired Latter-day Saints to diligently search for truth and seek good works. He explained that: ***"Whatever principle of intelligence we attain unto in this life, it will rise with us in the resurrection.*** *And if a person gains more knowledge and intelligence in this life through his diligence and obedience than another, he will have so much the advantage in the world to come"* (vv. 18-19).

A month and a half later, the Prophet visited Ramus again. In an evening meeting, a Methodist Preacher, Samuel Prior, who was visiting the town to find out more about the Church, was asked to speak to the congregation. Following his remarks, Joseph Smith arose and differed with Reverend Prior's remarks. Prior wrote: "This he did mildly, politely, and affectingly; like one who was more desirous to disseminate truth and expose error, than to love the malicious triumph of debate over me. I was truly edified with his remarks, and felt less prejudiced against the Mormons than ever" (Samuel A. Prior, The *Times and Seasons,* 15 May 1843). Joseph Smith's teachings on this occasion reflect his prophetic calling and are now recorded as scripture.

THE ENDOWMENT AND MARRIAGE COVENANTS

For those who were already members of the Church, temple ordinances consisted in receiving **Endowments**—a promise of blessings based upon obedience to God's laws, and the **Sealing of Families Together Forever.** Within the temple walls was taught the beautiful doctrine of eternal marriage given by revelation from the Lord: *"Behold, mine house is a house of order, saith the Lord God, and not a house of confusion"* (Doctrine & Covenants 132: 8).

Among Latter-day Saints, the term civil marriage means a marriage performed solely by civil authorities as distinguished from an Eternal or Celestial marriage, which is performed both by civil authority and by that power which binds on earth and seals eternally in the heavens. Marriages—until death do us part—which represent most marriages on the earth, have an automatic written bill of divorcement when life on earth ends. **These civil marriages are performed by man's authority,** regardless of the facility where they are held, and last until death or divorce separates the parties.

Celestial marriages are by God's authority, and the unions endure for time and eternity. For those who are not qualified and worthy to enter into the Lord's order of matrimony, civil marriages are proper and honorable, and there is *no* sin attached to the relationship that results from them. But for a true Latter-day Saint, one who loves the Lord and has in his heart the hope of eternal life, no marriage will prove satisfactory but one that is eternal, as performed in a Temple, in the House of the Lord. Marriages performed in the temples—**"for time and all eternity"**—by virtue of the sealing keys restored by Elijah, are called Celestial Marriages. The participating parties become husband and wife in this mortal life, and if after their marriage, they keep all the terms and conditions of this order of the Priesthood, they continue on as husband and wife in the Celestial Kingdom of God.

Those ordinances performed in the temples whereby husbands and wives are sealed together in the marriage union for time and all eternity, and whereby children are sealed eternally to parents, are commonly referred to as sealings. In the infinite mercy and justice of an Omnipotent God, these ordinances are available for righteous living persons and on a proxy basis for the dead also. Therefore, the expressions *"sealings for the living and sealings for the dead"* are in common usage in the Church.

If the family unit is sealed and continues, then by virtue of that fact, the members of the family have gained eternal life (Exaltation), "the greatest of all the gifts of God," for by definition: Exaltation consists in the continuation of the family unit eternally!

* * *

As construction on the Nauvoo Temple progressed, the Prophet Joseph gave some of his greatest sermons to special gatherings in the unfinished building. One such occasion was the April 1843 General Conference. At that period of time, William Miller's widely publicized prophecies that Christ would come on April 3, 1843 had caused quite a stir throughout America and among the Latter-day Saints. (Miller was a religious zealot who founded Millerism.) In the conference session on April sixth, Joseph said that as the Lord's Prophet, he had been praying and learned that *"the coming of the Son of Man never will be—never can be till the judgements spoken of for this hour are poured out which judgements are commenced."* The Prophet also listed some events that had not occurred yet, but which would take place prior to the Second Coming: *"Judah must return, Jerusalem must be rebuilt, and the temple, and water come out from under the temple, and the waters of the Dead Sea be healed. It will take some time to rebuild the walls of the city and the temple"* (*History of the Church,* 5: 336-37).

One of his most profound messages concerned God and man's destiny in relationship to him. **He declared: *"God himself was once as we are now, and is an exalted man, and sits enthroned in yonder heavens!"*** (*History of the Church,* 6: 305).

While the Saints were residing in Nauvoo, they witnessed a blossoming of theology. They listened to their Prophet leader elaborate upon doctrinal themes that had been only touched upon earlier. As they read the *Times and Seasons* newspaper, they savored a more fully developed theology than they had known in Ohio or Missouri. As they built the temple and participated in its sacred ordinances, they received power, knowledge, and blessings unknown in earlier years. The doctrinal developments in Nauvoo created an **enduring legacy** for the Church in the future.

In spite of the public relations efforts of the Church, opposition intensified in the early months of 1844. Thomas Sharp, editor of the *Warsaw Signal* newspaper repeatedly attacked the Church and accused its leaders of every crime imaginable. He also promoted the anti-Mormon party's day of fasting and prayer on Saturday, March ninth, in an effort to speedily bring down the "false prophet" Joseph Smith. The anti-Mormon party in Carthage appointed a grand—wolf hunt—in Hancock County for the same day. These hunts were a common sport in the area, but in this and future cases, the wolf hunt was merely a pretext for a mob to gather to harass, pillage, and burn the farms of the Saints in outlying areas.

In contrast to the lawless actions of the anti-Mormon party and the *Warsaw Signal*, Joseph Smith joined with Governor Ford that spring in an effort to establish more cordial relations among the citizens of Western Illinois. An editorial in the *Nauvoo Neighbor* called upon all honest men to join with the governor "in his laudable endeavors to cultivate peace and honor the laws." The editorial urged the Saints to treat kindly those who did them wrong and reminded them of the wise man's proverb: *"A SOFT answer turneth away wrath"* (Proverbs 15: 1). The *Neighbor* editorial declared that their motto was "Peace with all" (B.H. Roberts, *Comprehensive History of the Church,* 2: 218). In spite of these overtures, Thomas Sharp continued his attack through the *Warsaw Signal* and hinted that trouble was brewing between Joseph Smith and some Church members and that a breach was imminent (*Warsaw Signal,* 8 May 1844).

By May 1844, the Latter-day Saints were once again embroiled in an apparently irreconcilable conflict with their neighbors. There were many reasons for this: politically the Saints were alienated from nearly everyone else in Illinois, other communities were jealous of Nauvoo's economic growth and political autonomy, many people in Illinois feared the power of the Nauvoo Legion, the Masons were disturbed by alleged irregularities of the order in Nauvoo, and there was a general distaste among the people for peculiar Mormon doctrines and practices which had been misrepresented by John C. Bennett and others.

Before revealing the details of the commandment on plural marriage, given to Joseph Smith by the Lord in 1831, and repeated several times over the years, especially in 1841 and 1843, (as I have said before in the Introduction) it is vitally important that you know that I have prayed mightily, researched thoroughly, and prayed as if my life depended upon how I treated this subject due to all the lies and misinformation bandied about to influence people more for the negative than the positive.

WHO SAID THE MORMONS INVENTED—"POLYGAMY" AND "PLURAL MARRIAGE?

What better place to begin this section—than at the very beginning with the scriptures. The first book of the Bible is Genesis, which means "Beginnings." What do we know about the beginning of the world? *"IN the beginning, God created the heaven and the earth"* (Genesis 1: 1).

To create is to "organize." It is an absolutely false and unrealistic supposition to believe that the world or any other thing was created out of nothing, or that any created thing can be destroyed in the sense of extinction. *"The elements are eternal"* (Doctrine & Covenants 93: 33).

Joseph Smith said in the King Follett sermon: *"You ask the learned doctors why they say the world was made out of nothing; and they will answer, 'Doesn't the Bible say He created the world?' And they suggest, from the word create, that it must have been made out of nothing."* Now, the word create came from the word **baurau**, which does not mean to create out of nothing; it means to **organize**; the same as a man would organize any materials to accomplish a project. Therefore, we imply that God has had materials to organize the world out of matter, which is element—in which dwells all glory. Element has had an existence from the time—time began. The pure principles of element are principles which can never be destroyed; they may be organized and reorganized, but not destroyed. They had **no** beginning, and can have **no** end.

By what power did God create the world? By His Word (Hebrews 1: 3: 2 Peter 3:5). And who is called the Word of God? *Jesus Christ* (John 1: 14). How do we know that Jesus Christ was with God in the creation? *"IN the beginning was the Word, and the Word was with God . . . All things were made by him; and without him was not anything made that was made"* (John 1: 1, 3). What was the last thing God created? *"And God said, Let us make man in our image, after our likeness . . . So God created man in his own image, in the image of God created he him; male and female created he them. And God blessed them, and God said unto them. Be fruitful, and multiply, and replenish the earth, and subdue it"* (Genesis 1: 26-28).

So God created Adam, the male, Eve, the female, and God married Adam and Eve in the Garden of Eden. And God gave Adam and Eve the commandment to: *"Be fruitful, and multiply, and replenish the earth,"* (Genesis 1: 28), which means simply—people the earth. We have no significant information about how the earth was peopled, but what we do know is: that it was through the male, Adam, the female, Eve, their children, and their children's children. Consequently, polygamy and plural marriage began—I believe—with Adam and Eve which as I see it, is indisputable, with the understanding of the formation of the earth by God the Father, Jesus Christ and others, this was how the earth became replenish.

God, not man, issued the commandment of polygamy as an earthly principle—plural marriage as an eternal principle, and it all began at the beginning.

Adam and Eve went on living a long time after losing two of their children, Cain and Abel, as spoken of in Genesis four. People lived many hundreds of years when the world was new. In time, Adam and Eve had many more children, the first child mentioned, was a boy, very much like Abel. They called him Seth. When Seth grew to manhood he too married, and established a branch of the family. When Adam and Eve died, 800 years after the birth of Seth, their family had grown into a vast tribe of people. The earth on which they had lived and labored was no longer a lonely wilderness but a productive land jam-packed with their children, their children's children, and great grandchildren who themselves were grown, had children of their own, then the seeds of life were raised up unto the Lord. It should have been a good and wonderful world, but it seemed that the more the population grew, the more wickedness there was upon the earth. The Lord showed the way to build families, and people the earth, but the people generally turned away from righteousness.

Among them all there were only a few who found favor in the eyes of the Lord, because of their love for what was good and right. These few were descended from Seth. Men multiplied on the face of the earth, working, playing, and having families, peopling the earth, but soon forgetting all about the Lord who made it all possible.

Nevertheless, even in those bad days there was one man who found grace in the eyes of the Lord, his name was Noah. Noah was commanded by God to build an Ark, since the Lord was about to destroy the people on earth who had turned evil. There was forty days and nights of torrential rains which did put and end to the land as we knew it. The rain did stop, the land did dry out, and Noah gave God a great thanksgiving, gratitude and praise for their safety. The Lord told Noah and his family that the earth was now cleaned, and they were to be fruitful, having many children and replenish it. **This was a commandment of God.**

The three sons of Noah were to be the founders of a new human race, one that would start anew and refreshed in the world, washed clean by the flood. Then after leaving the Ark and receiving God's blessings, they made new homes for themselves, it was not long before sons were born to their wives. The family of Noah increased greatly—generation after generation, so that in the course of time, the world was indeed replenished through Japeth, Shem, and Ham. **This was a commandment of God.** Noah died at the age of 950 years, knowing that his sons were the fathers of the nations of the world.

From Japeth's seven sons came the Gentiles or the non-Jewish nations. Shem's five sons were to be fathers of the Shemites, or Hebrews; and from his line would spring two upright men called Abram and Lot. Ham's four sons would go forth and people Africa and would also be the fathers of the non-Hebrew inhabitants of Canaan. Eventually, the descendants of Shem, later to be called the Israelites, would be in constant battle against the Canaanite descendants of Ham, which would come about many years after the death of Noah.

And in the beginning, we now enter the time and life of Abram (Abraham) at age seventy-five years. He heard the voice of the Lord say to him: "Abram leave your country and you father's house, and go to a new land that I will show you. I will make you a great nation, and I will bless you and make your name great. Through you shall all the families of the earth be blessed." And Abram, even though he was no longer young and still without a son to help him, listened to the voice of the Lord and gathered his people together. His wife Sarai, of course, would go with him at his side. **This was a commandment of God.**

The Lord spoke unto Abram and said, "Lift up your eyes Abram. Look northward from where you stand, southward, eastward and westward. All the land that you see I will give to you, your children and your children's children forever. I will give you many descendants, as many as there are grains of dust upon the earth. Arise, walk through the land, across the length of it and the breadth of it, for I will give it all to you." Abram and his wife Sarai thought about the children they did not have and wanted. Sarai thought about it for a long time, for she wanted children very badly. Even though she knew of God's promise to her husband, time was passing by and she could no longer believe that she would ever have a baby of her own. One day she said to Abram: "The Lord has not let me have a child. Go to my handmaid Hagar. Take her to yourself; in that way I may have a child through her." Now Hagar was an Egyptian maidservant who had become attached to Abram's household during his journey to Egypt at the time of the famine in Canaan. In those days, it was not unusual for a man to have more than one wife, or for a wife to give her handmaid to her husband. Sometimes childless women like Sarai would ask their husbands to produce children through a trusted handmaid, then the wife would be thought of as the mother of the handmaid's children. **This was a commandment of God.** Abram agreed to Sarai's request, Sarai gave the handmaid Hagar to him so that she might bear a child. It was not long before Hagar knew that she was going to have a baby. She was proud of it, she began to mock her mistress because Sarai had not been able to have a child of her own. This was not at all what Abram's wife had hoped for, she was most unhappy. Instead of feeling like a mother herself she felt she was a failure as a wife. And Hagar let her feel it; Hagar despised her openly. "I was wrong to do what I did," Sarai said sadly to Abram. "It was a mistake, for now I am despised in Hagar's eyes. Tell me, what should I do?" Abram replied: "She is your maid, do with her what you will."

Sarai was hard on the mocking Hagar; she treated her so severely that Hagar could no longer bear it, Hagar ran away into the wilderness. It was not long before she tired and was obliged to rest. She stopped by a fountain of water on the way to Shur, it was here that the angel of the Lord found her in the wilderness. "Hagar, Sarai's maid!" he said: "What are you doing here, and where are you going?" She replied: "I am running from my mistress Sarai." The angel of the Lord said unto her: "Return to your mistress, and obey her. God has seen your suffering. You will have a child, and he will grow up to be a strong and mighty man who will dwell in the wilderness. Through him, you will have a great family of your own. But now you must go back, Hagar. The Lord sees you, and is with you."

Hagar returned to the tents of Abram and Sarai. When her time came she bore a son to Abram, they called him Ishmael. Abram was eighty-six years old, proud to have a son even though it was not Sarai's; but Sarai could never bring herself to forgive Hagar or to accept Ishmael as her own beloved son. It was true the Ishmael was not the child that God had promised Abram. He grew into a strong, wild lad, loved by Abram but disliked by Sarai; as Abram and Sarai kept on growing older.

When Abram was ninety-nine years old Sarai herself though younger, was past the age when she might have a child, the Lord appeared again to Abram and said: "I am the Almighty God, I shall make a covenant with you. You have been faithful and have served me well; you will be the father of many nations, the Lord told him that his name would change. Instead of being Abram, which meant "exalted father," he would be become Abraham, which meant "father of a multitude." Sarai too, must change her name. Her new name would be Sarah, meaning "queen," for she would be the mother of nations and from her would come men who would be kings.

Then Abraham who had believed the Lord all the years of his life, hardly dared to believe what he was hearing now. That the would still have his own child was so incredible to him that he laughed, in his heart he said: "Shall a child be born to a man who is nearly a 100 years old? And to a women who is ninety? He thought of the one son he did have, whom he loved even though the boy was not Sarah's child. Abraham wanted good things for him too. "O Lord what of Ishmael?" he asked. God said: "I have blessed Ishmael. He too will have many children. Twelve princes will descent from him, I will make of him a great nation. But my covenant is not with him but with the son of Sarah. For Sarah shall indeed bear a child, you will call him Isaac. I say to you now that Sarah shall have a son at this same time next year." Yet it was still hard for Abraham to believe, and harder still for Sarah!

One day the Lord appeared to Abraham as he sat in the shaded doorway of his tent in the heat of the day. The old man looked up and saw three strangers walking towards him. He knew at once that they were from a very far country. In his heart he was sure that the Lord had come to him in the form of three angels from heaven. "The Lord shall bless her," said one, the one whom Abraham thought must be the Lord Himself. "Sarah you will have a son at the appointed time, as I did promise." Now Sarah stood hidden within the doorway of the tent, when she heard this, she laughed. Many times before she had heard about this promise, now it was much too late for it to come true. Both she and Abraham being very old were well past the age when she could have a child. Therefore that's why—Sarah laughed silently.

And the Lord, who was indeed among the strangers, said: "Why did Sarah laugh, and think to herself that she is too old to bear a child? Is anything too hard for the Lord? At the time appointed, I will return to you and Sarah and she will surely have her son" . . . The three messengers departed in peace. As they had promised, the aged couple were blessed with a son, the only one they were to have. Since both of them had laughed at the absurdity of a baby ever being born to them, Abraham decided to name him Isaac, which is a word meaning "laughter." **This was a commandment of God.**

Isaac grew, Sarah saw the son of Hagar, the Egyptian woman making fun of little Isaac. Ishmael was a lad of fourteen by this time, and Sarah did not like the way he treated her small boy. Angrily, she said to Abraham: "Send away this Egyptian women and her son!" Abraham did not want to be unfair to Hagar and Ishmael, he would miss his firstborn son. God saw his sorrow and told him not to grieve. That it is with Isaac that I have My covenant, it is through Isaac said God, that your name shall be forever known and your family shall all be blessed. As for the son of the Egyptian women, I will also make a nation of him, because he is your child. Therefore, have no fear for Ishmael and Hagar." The boy Ishmael grew tall and strong, becoming a man skilled in hunting with the bow and arrow. His mother took him a wife out of the land of Egypt, soon Ishmael had children of his own. His sons were strong, rough men of the outdoors even as he. Thus, out of Ishmael there came a nation.

As the years passed Isaac grew into a fine young man who loved his father as much as Abraham loved him. Just as Abraham obeyed the Lord, so did Isaac trust and obey his father Abraham in every way. God watched over them both, never forgetting His promise that Abraham would become the father of a multitude through his son Isaac. **This was a commandment of God.**

Abraham was wise when he arranged for Isaac to marry Rebekah whose cultural and racial background was the same as his, and whose moral and spiritual ideas were also the same. Isaac was a man who preferred peace. Instead of returning evil for evil, he actually fed his enemies, showered them with kindness, understanding and love. It is obvious that God approved of him, and that faith in God and living His commandments gave him great peace of mind, for so it has been written.

Abraham himself took another wife, whose name was Keturah, she bore him six fine sons. The old man was fond of them and gave them many gifts, but he still remembered that God's promise would come true through Isaac, he was determined that Isaac should be his only heir. He sent his young sons away to live in the east country, while he and Isaac, remained in the southland, apart from the gifts that he had given the six boys, he gave all he had to Isaac. It was then that Abraham died at the ripe old age of 175 years. Ishmael, the son of Hagar, came from the wilderness to say farewell, he and Isaac buried Abraham in the cave of Machpelah near Mamre, where Abraham's wife Sarah had been laid to rest more than forty years earlier.

Isaac and his wife Rebekah, loved each other deeply, and were married for quite some time before they had any children. Then their first-born were twins. The first to be born was named Esau the second they called Jacob. Prior to the birth of the twins, Rebekah was troubled, she inquired of the Lord why she felt as she did. The Lord said to Rebekah: "Two nations are within you, and two kinds of people. The one shall be stronger than the other, the elder shall be the strongest, and the elder shall serve the younger."

Isaac loved both his sons, but he loved Esau the more because he was so very strong and manly. But Rebekah loved Jacob, the quiet man of dignity and felt more tenderly toward Jacob. The Hebrews in their family order, awarded a special privilege to their firstborn. His was the privilege of the "birthright," which made him head of the family when his own father died, and put in his possession a double portion of his father's inheritance property. The firstborn who possessed the birthright, also received a spiritual blessing from his father which was a great inspiration to him in helping him discharge his duties as the head of the clan. There was a time when Esau came from the field, very tired and faint, he found Jacob had prepared a very delicious dish which the Hebrews called pottage. The sight and smell of the food was tantalizing to Esau who was faint with exhaustion, it was all he could do to keep from pouncing on the delicious food. "Feed me, I pray you," he begged his brother Jacob: "give me some of that pottage, for I am faint with hunger." Jacob turned and looked at him thoughtfully: "I will if you will sell me your birthright this day." Esau said in his rough way: "I am starving to death! What good will a birthright do me if I die of hunger?"

"Swear it to me!" said Jacob: "Swear that you will sell it to me if I give you food this day." Esau replied: "I swear, I swear! The birthright is yours. Only give me the food before I drop." And he sold his birthright to Jacob, then Jacob gave his brother Esau bread and lentil soup in exchange for all the rights of an elder son. Esau ate, drank, and went upon his way, satisfied with his meal; not until long after did he give any thought to the bargain he had made. Thus did Esau throw away his birthright, for a mess of pottage.

As the years passed the boys' father grew old. Isaac became quite feeble and his eyesight began to fail. When he realized he might not live many more years, he wanted to give his firstborn the blessing due him. And so the deception took place that Isaac thought that he was giving Esau his blessing when in essence, he was blessing Jacob!

Jacob received a remarkably fine blessing, which told him his posterity would be very great in numbers, that they would be a blessing to all mankind. In the blessing, Isaac said to him: *"Therefore God give thee of the dew of heaven, and the fatness of the earth, and plenty of corn and wine: . . . be lord over thy brethren, and let thy mother's sons bow down to thee: cursed be everyone that curseth thee, and blessed be he that blesseth thee"* (Genesis 27: 28, 29).

There has been much misunderstanding about Jacob, even well-meaning students of the Bible criticize some of Jacob's dealings. The supposed deception of his father in obtaining the blessing (Genesis 27), cannot be taken at face value. The Lord is not obligated to bless an unworthy person simply because gracious words were pronounced upon him by mistake. The key to the matter is expressed in Genesis twenty-seven verse thirty-three wherein Isaac, after learning Jacob's true identity, said: *"yea, and he shall be blessed."* Isaac could have revoked the blessing at that time, but he seemed to affirm that it had been rightly delivered. Jacob's subsequent life demonstrates that he deserved the blessing he received, while Esau's life shows disobedience and some displeasing choices of wives (Genesis 26: 34, 35; 28: 8, 9). The so-called purchase of the birthright from Esau may very well be equally justified by items of Esau's errant behavior that disqualified him, but which are not recorded in our Bible. We learn from latter day revelation that Jacob *"did none other things than that which* [he was] *commanded"* (Doctrine & Covenants 132: 37), and is today exalted upon a throne in heaven, in company with Abraham and Isaac.

Jacob married four special women over a twenty year period, Leah, Rachel, Bilhah and Zilpah, who gave Jacob twelve sons. From Leah came Reuben, Simeon, Levi, Judah, Issachar and .Zebulon. From Rachel came Joseph and Benjamin. From Bilhah came Dan and Naphtali. From Zilpah came Gad and Asher. Leah and Rachel were the wives of Jacob, Bilhah and Zilpah were the handmaidens of Leah and Rachel, as it was the custom of the times. **This was a commandment of God.**

Being the sensitive person that he was, Jacob was concerned about his relationship with his brother Esau ever since the deceptions of Jacob in their earlier lives. It was about the birthright and the special blessing from his father Isaac. Although somewhat hesitant about reaching out to Esau, who threatened his life earlier, Jacob made a sincere attempt to make things to work out. Time had been a great healer. People are more inclined to be forgiving, more willing to settle their differences in peace, and they are less apt to commit offenses if they live close to God, if they pray and worship Him and live His holy laws. The way Jacob and Esau settled their differences and made peace with each other was a thing of beauty. They did forgive, they did forget, and they lived in harmony the rest of their days.

Great and mighty are the promises of the Lord unto the seed of Abraham, Isaac and Jacob: *"For thou are an holy people unto the Lord thy God: the Lord thy God hath chosen thee to be a special people unto himself, above all people that are upon the face of the earth"* (Deuteronomy 7: 6).

Since the Lord has chosen the seed of Abraham *"to be a special people unto himself, above all people that are upon the face of the earth,"* it is of the utmost importance that they fully understand why the Lord had chosen them, and to learn of their great mission in the earth.

The Lord has planned His work from the beginning, just as the architect plans a building before it is built. The Lord's plan will never fail. The Prophet Amos declared: ***"Surely the Lord God will do nothing, but he revealeth his secret unto his servants the prophets"*** (Amos 3: 7). **This was a commandment of God.**

Since the Lord has declared: *"the end from the beginning;"* (Isaiah 46: 10), and since *"the word of the Lord endureth for ever;"* (1 Peter 1: 25), it is important that the seed of Abraham, through the loins of Isaac and Jacob, familiarize themselves with the word of God spoken through the mouths of His Prophets. It is important that they understand the promises of the Lord unto them, what He expects of them, that He may fulfill His promises to their fathers that *"in thy seed shall all the nations of the earth be blessed* (Genesis 22: 18).

The covenant made with Abraham is renewed with Isaac: *"And I will make thy seed to multiply as the stars of heaven, and will give unto thy seed all these countries; and in thy seed shall all of the nations of the earth be blessed; Because that Abraham obeyed my voice, and kept my charge, my commandments, my statutes, and my laws"* (Genesis 26: 4-5). How did we seed? How did we people? How did we establish the family unit in the world?... The way I believe, was that of polygamy and plural marriage when needed—as required by God. **This was a commandment of God.**

The Lord made the same covenant with Jacob, the son of Isaac: *"And thy seed shall be as the dust of the earth, and thou shalt spread abroad to the west, and to the east, and to the north, and to the south: and in thy seed shall all families of the earth be blessed"* (Genesis 28 10-14).

The promises made to Abraham, Isaac and Jacob were:

1. "Seeing that Abraham shall surely become a great and mighty nation."
2. "I will give unto thee all these countries."
3. "I will multiply thy seed as the stars of the heavens, and as the sand which is upon the seashore."
4. "And in thy seed shall all the nations of the earth be blessed."

In keeping with the wonderful promises of the Lord to the posterity of Abraham and Isaac, through Jacob—He gave them a special name by which they would be known among all people, even the name of "Israel or Israelites," which name or designation has continued with them to this day. Their God is referred to as the "God of Israel."

"And he said, Thy name shall be called no more Jacob, but Israel: for as a prince hast thou power with God and with men, and hast prevailed" (Genesis 32: 26-28). Jacob's new name—Israel, became the family name. The posterity of Abraham, Isaac, through Jacob came to be known variously as "Israel; Children of Israel; House of Israel; and Tribes of Israel."

The seeding and peopling of the earth was accomplished, as has been mentioned—by means of polygamy and plural marriage, as I see it. **God gave a commandment to all of His prophets, ancient and present day, that the use of polygamy and plural marriage was the way to seed and people the earth—to raise a righteous seed unto the Lord. However it was *only* to be used when commanded and approved by God. This was a commandment of God, not man.**

It is significant that the Law of Moses most empathically teaches polygamy or the marriage of one male to more than one female. Of course, this is considered shocking to those who have been taught that a man is to be married to only one women. Nevertheless, the Jews are descendants of polygamists.

Remembering again that—Abraham had two wives simultaneously, namely Sarah and Hagar—Jacob had his four wives whose names are Leah, Rachel, Bilhah, Zilpah. Also we know that—David was empowered by God to take upon himself several wives, for the building up of the kingdom of God. David was a man of deep faith and love, he acknowledged God in everything. In addition, it is important to remember that the Twelve Tribes of Israel are a result of a polygamous marriages as well. In the Jewish tradition the purpose of marriage was not to satisfy carnal desires, but to raise up a family. Unmistakably, the Jewish scholars realized that God had sanctioned multiple marriage.

Unfortunately, Solomon David's son, although he was able to build the temple, did not live the Law of Moses. He took upon himself without approval from God, over 700 wives and

300 concubines. Solomon involved himself with many foreign women, their religions, their idols, and they influenced him to adopt their pagan ways and beliefs. In this situation the taking of many wives by Solomon in his era was an abomination. **He had no right because he was *not* commanded by God to do so.** *"Behold, David and Solomon truly had many wives and concubines, which thing was abominable before me, saith the Lord"* (Book of Mormon, Jacob 2: 24; in the preface of Jacob, Chapter two, it is written: "Jacob condemns the unauthorized practice of plural marriage.")

The Lord's basic law of marriage is that no man shall have more than one wife at a time—under normal circumstances, (Jacob 2: 27-30; Doctrine & Covenants 49: 15-17), ***unless* by revelation from the Lord** and He commands plurality of wives in the new and everlasting covenant of marriage (Doctrine & Covenants 131: 2; 132: 4).

From such piecemeal scriptural records as are now available, we learn that the Lord did command some of His ancient Saints to practice plural marriage. Abraham, Isaac, and Jacob—among others, (Doctrine & Covenants 132), confirmed to this ennobling, exalting principle; the whole history of ancient Israel was one in which plurality of wives was a divinely accepted and approved order of matrimony. Those who entered this order at the Lord's command, and who kept the laws and conditions appertaining to it, have gained for themselves eternal exaltation in the highest degree of the Celestial kingdom.

All truth comes from God—man is of error, much error, much ignorance, much close mindedness, and certainly much misunderstanding, but that is the nature of man who is the natural enemy of God.

God is the one who commanded man to practice polygamy and plural marriage under certain conditions, and yet Joseph Smith fought the revelation for years before accepting and practicing the commandment with a small percentage of Latter-day Saint Priesthood Brethren.

THE NEW AND EVERLASTING COVENANT OF MARRIAGE

Even when the principle of plural marriage was first revealed to Joseph in 1831 he felt strongly that its practice would cost him his life. He had no desire to circumvent the Lord's commands, but knowing the problems that were inherent and inevitable, he was in no hurry to begin the practice. During the summer of 1840, an angel from God visited the Prophet and told him the time had come and commanded him to obey the law or perish. Thus, after nearly ten years of painful reflection and anguish, Joseph took his first plural wife—a fateful step that he knew would lead inescapably to his death. He was intelligent enough to know that while a large segment of the public might tolerate adultery and fornication, they would be incensed at the thought of a man having more than one wife.

In addition, **Joseph was mindful of his wife Emma's refusal to accept the principle of the plurality of wives.** It was not that she doubted her husband's prophetic calling. She did not. She, above all others, had been in a position to observe his emergence as a man of God whose spiritual qualities had opened the heavens to him. She had been a witness of his struggling as he had translated the Book of Mormon. She had been present on many occasions when the influence of God had rested upon him as he had uttered prophecies, rebuked evil, or healed the sick. Often she had seen Joseph serve as a channel through whom God's power was evidenced. The assembling effect of these experiences as well as her knowledge of Joseph's forthright character convinced her that the commandment was true. Nevertheless, she rejected it and fought bitterly against it. In her moments of anguish, she was greatly influenced by prominent but weak men who had rejected the doctrine. Torn between her knowledge and better instincts and the basic jealousy of her nature, Emma fluctuated between joy and despair, outgoing love and suspicion, depending upon whose company she was in. Thus was revealed in her character an instability reminiscent of her agnostic father and prophetic of the wavering course she would follow once her husband was gone.

Surely, Joseph must have spent hours attempting to reason with her, reassure her, show her from the scriptures that the basic law of marriage (that no man shall have more than one wife) has been and can be altered by revelation, the Lord may command plurality of wives in the *"new and everlasting covenant"* (Doctrine & Covenants 49: 15-17; 132: 4; and Bruce R. McConkie, *Mormon Doctrine*, SLC, Bookcraft, 1966, p. 577).

Speaking of the Doctrine of Plurality of Wives, the Prophet said: *"I hold the keys of the power in the last days; for there is never but one on earth at a time on whom the power and its keys are conferred; and I have constantly said that no man shall have but one wife at a time, unless the Lord directs otherwise"* (*Teachings of the Prophet Joseph Smith*, p. 324).

In the Book of Mormon, the Lord, by the mouth of his Prophet Jacob, gave similar direction to the Nephites: *"For there shall not any man among you have save it be one wife; and concubines he shall have none; For I, the Lord God, delight in the chastity of women. And whoredoms are an abomination before me; thus saith the Lord of Hosts. Wherefore, this people shall keep my commandments, saith the Lord of Hosts, or cursed be the land for their sakes. For if I will, saith the Lord of Hosts, raise up seed unto me, I will command my people; otherwise they shall hearken unto these things"* (Jacob 2: 27-30).

* * *

Again to review these truths, we know from scriptural records available in the Old Testament that the Lord did command some of His ancient Saints to practice plural marriage. The whole history of ancient Israel was one in which plurality of wives was a divinely accepted and approved order of matrimony. It is significant to remember that the Law of Moses most emphatically teaches polygamy—the marriage of one male to more than one female. Yet we rarely consider the fact, that the Jews are descendants of polygamists. **We should remember that the Twelve Tribes of Israel are also a result of polygamous marriages.** Remembering again, that David was commanded by God to take upon himself several wives for the building up of the kingdom of God, that he was a man of deep faith who acknowledged God in everything—*until* with the incident concerning Bethsheba—where he defied the word of the Lord and proceeded on his own, he was punished.

* * *

Emma knew that the Prophet Joseph had first become concerned with the polygamy question when working on the revision of the Old Testament dealing with the times of the ancient patriarchs. Joseph had been impressed with the respect and esteem the Lord held for many of the Bible Patriarchs of that period, notwithstanding—they had a plurality of wives. His mind was full of earnest questions. Logic convinced Joseph that if an unchangeable God commanded Abraham, Isaac, and Jacob and other ancients to practice this principle for righteous purposes, there should be no reason that the Lord could not command modern Prophets and Saints to adopt it—especially since the Restoration was to be a fulness of doctrine and practice.

Never being content with surface reasoning and explanations, Joseph inquired of the Lord concerning the eternity of the marriage covenant and the principle of plurality of wives at that time—though not then committed to writing (*History of the Church* 5: xxix). This revelation he received was kept in his mind and heart as he reflected upon it often over the years. He withdrew from announcing it or from putting it into practice as long as possible because it ran against the grain of his own strict Christian upbringing. It also threatened to weigh heavily upon the new, struggling Church and impose an extra burden of criticism, judgement, and abuse that could curtail, if not destroy its growth. Because of prejudice and misunderstanding, it might permanently close the minds of many honest, searching people who otherwise would be receptive to its message. **So, with few exceptions, he kept this explosive revelation to himself** throughout those many growing years. On occasion he would discuss portions of the revelation with some of his close confidants, emphasizing that the time was not right, either to publish the revelation or to put into the practice the principles it imposed.

To his alarm, the Prophet found that either through carelessness or through a desire to show a closeness to the Prophet, some of these confidants had broken their word and spoken about the revelation to persons outside Joseph's inner circle. Once this disquieting information was released, it spread like wildfire by word of mouth.

Corroborative evidences of the fact that the revelation had been given early in the Prophet's career, are to be found in the early charges against the Church about its belief in polygamy. For example: When the Doctrine and Covenants scriptures were presented to the several quorums of the Priesthood of the Church for acceptance in the general assembly of that body, on August 17, 1835, an article on marriage was presented by William W. Phelps, which for many years was published in the Doctrine and Covenants. It was not a revelation, nor was it presented as such to the general assembly of the Priesthood. It was an article, however, that represented the views of the assembly on the subject of marriage at that time, unenlightened as they were about the revelation already given to the Prophet on the subject. What the Prophet Joseph's connection was with this article cannot be known. Whether he approved of it or not is uncertain, since he was absent from Kirtland at the time of the general assembly of the Priesthood which accepted it (*History of the Church,* 2: 243-53). In this article on marriage, the following sentence occurs: "Inasmuch as the Church of Christ has been reproached with the crime of fornication and polygamy, we declare that we believe that one man should have one wife, and one woman but one husband, except in case of death, when either is at liberty to marry again" (*History of the Church,* 2: 247).

While this statement accurately reflected the official policy of the Church at the time, Joseph knew that it would have to be changed when the time was right. However, it placed him in a vulnerable position, requiring him to support a policy adopted by the conference that was at variance with the revelation he had received.

It is evident that as early as 1835, a charge of polygamy was made against the Church. Why was that the case unless the subject of polygamy had been discussed within the Church? Is it not plain why—someone to whom the Prophet had confided the knowledge of the revelation, concerning the righteousness of plural marriage under certain circumstances, had unwisely made some statement concerning the matter?

Again, in May 1836, in Missouri, in a series of questions asked and answered through the *Elder's Journal,* the following occurs: "Do the Mormons believe in having more wives than one?" To which the answer is given: "No, not at the same time." This again represents the belief of the Saints at that time, unenlightened as they then were about the revelation received by their Prophet. But again, why was this question asked unless there had been some agitation on the subject? Had someone before the time had come for making known the doctrine to the Church—unwisely referred to the knowledge which had been revealed to the Prophet some seven years earlier? All these incidents blend together and make it clearly evident that the revelation on marriage was given long before July 12, 1843—doubtless, as early as 1831 (*History of the Church,* 5: xxix-xxxii). The revelation wasn't written down until: July 12, 1843, almost twelve years later. The circumstances under which it was recorded on that date, are described by William Clayton, who took it in shorthand as the Prophet dictated: "On the morning of the 12th of July, 1843, Joseph and Hyrum Smith came into the office in the upper story of the brick store, on the bank of the Mississippi River. They were talking on the subject of plural marriage."

In the discussion that followed, Hyrum persuaded Joseph to reduce the revelation to writing. Continuing with his narrative, William Clayton said: "He then requested me to get paper and prepare to write. Hyrum very urgently requested Joseph to write the revelation by means of the Urim and Thummim, but Joseph in reply, said: *"I do not need to, for I know the revelation perfectly from beginning to end."* Joseph and Hyrum then sat down and Joseph commenced to dictate the revelation on Celestial Marriage, and I wrote it, sentence by sentence, as he dictated. After the revelation was written, Joseph asked me to read it through slowly and carefully, which I did, and he pronounced it correct. He then remarked that there was much more that he could write on the subject, but what was written was sufficient for the present" (*History of the Church,* 4: xxxii-xxxiii).

During the long years since 1831, Joseph had tried to keep this revelation under lock and key. But now the time had arrived for polygamy to be instituted in the Dispensation of the Fulness of Times—Joseph Smith's dispensation. It was for him here and now. And this was a commandment from God.

Once instituted many inside the Church were able to see the Lord's wisdom, since the number of faithful convert women so far outnumbered the men and marrying outside the faith was strongly discouraged. Suffering for want of protection and support and deprived of the opportunities for growth that comes only with marriage and having children, many of these women were now taken into well-established homes and cared for as polygamous wives. Since only the most righteous men and women were called to live this law, (never more than **two to three percent** of the Priesthood holders) it became apparent that the purpose of raising up a righteous seed unto the Lord—would also be fulfilled.

But while **The Principle of Plural Marriage** solved some problems, it escalated many others. Even though the men and women who entered into plural marriage were among the most moral people this world has ever known, the initial concealment which surrounded the introduction of the practice led to outrageous misrepresentations and charges of adultery—a potent factor in creating great resentment against the Prophet. None of the other teachings of the

Church clashed so directly with the social order of the day or aroused such bitterness. If the doctrine caused such a struggle on the part of the most devoted and dependable men and women inside the Church, (see Introduction), **it is little wonder that announcing the doctrine publicly aroused greater opposition to the Church and increased mob violence.**

Aside from the need for moral support and for assistance in handling the complex, fast-growing administrative affairs of the Church, the doctrine of polygamy was the urgent reason Joseph was anxious for the return of the Twelve from England. Joseph knew full-well that his obedience to the commandment he had received from the Lord to practice plural marriage **would poison the public mind against him and the Church** and would lead to scenes of violent persecution that would overshadow anything the Saints had previously enjoyed.

Increasing feelings of opposition over the rapid growth of Nauvoo and other Mormon communities now blazed hot over the polygamy issue. It was in Warsaw and Carthage, the Hancock County seat, that the anti-Mormon feelings began to unite in Illinois.

Joseph found himself troubled by the mounting demands of his enemies that the Nauvoo Charter be revoked. The legal safeguards this document provided had been both a practical and a psychological shelter for him. Time and time again he had relied upon it as a shield from unfounded legal attacks. The Nauvoo period was really **the first time the scales of justice had been tipped in favor of the Saints,** and Joseph was anxious to retain this advantage. But the chances of doing so were waning. In spite of other problems, the Saints still might have been able to maintain peace if it had not been for the apostasy developing within the Church. Polygamy was a primary factor in the apostasy of several of the most influential leaders in the Church, which resulted in a conspiracy against the Prophet Joseph Smith. Unhappily, all signs pointed toward eventual violence. On May 29, 1844, Thomas Sharp told his readers he "would not be surprised to hear of his [Joseph Smith's] death by violent means in a short time" (*Warsaw Signal* 29 May 1844).

Your having read this earlier—it now bears repeating—so that the facts cannot be disputed or twisted, here once again are those facts: With the ongoing feelings of hate, prejudice and persecution, thrust on the Latter-day Saints at the time, primarily caused by the practice of harassment from the U.S. Government to discontinue the practice of plural marriage, the Prophet Wilford Woodruff, having received revelation from the Lord—which was not a revelation of convenience—issued an official declaration known as the ***Manifesto*** dated October 6, 1890, which reads as follows:

"Inasmuch as laws have been enacted by Congress forbidding plural marriages, which laws have been pronounced constitutional by the court of last resort, I hereby declare my intention to submit to those laws, and to use my influence with the members of the Church over which I preside to have them do likewise" (following Doctrine & Covenants—OFFICIAL DECLARATION—1, pp. 291-292).

TRAITORS, TRIALS, AND MORE TRAITORS

The most notable contrast to the righteousness of most of the Saints, who lived in prospering and affluent Nauvoo, was the spreading apostasy in their midst. Some of the truly great trials, which brought the **Prophet Joseph enormous suffering and struggles,** came about because of some of his closest, personal friends who turned on him as bitter traitors and became his very worst enemies.

Of course, there were various causes for this—some thought they knew more than Joseph or were better educated—some turned against him because they were really seeking power and authority for themselves. Still others were more interested in money and the things of this world than they were in their religion. And then there were some who sinned deeply and had to be cut off from the Church for their transgressions. A few of the brethren pretended to receive revelations from the Lord and did all they could to make the Saints believe in these false revelations; a few were deceived by them. Nevertheless, Joseph was able to show that these so-called revelations were not of God. Then, the pretenders would declare that Joseph was a fallen prophet. All of these situations brought bitterness among men and women who had been friends of the Prophet.

As you have already read—one of these men who turned against the Prophet after he had been a close friend, was John C. Bennett. This man had joined the Church after careful study. He was a doctor, a college professor, and after joining the Church, became a General in the Nauvoo Legion. Later, becoming Mayor of the City of Nauvoo, and was highly respected by the people.

It seemed that Joseph always knew more than people realized. Sometimes this knowledge saved his life. In May 1842, the Nauvoo Legion gathered for exercises and a practice battle. John C. Bennett urged Joseph to lead the charge—when Joseph refused, Bennett asked Joseph to take a position in the rear without his guard—Joseph refused again. Even at this early date, Joseph knew that Bennett's heart had turned against him. He knew that Bennett might make an attempt on his life during the mock battle.

It was a lust for women in Nauvoo that first prompted John C. Bennett toward apostasy. Because of his actions, he lost the spirit of the Gospel. He was criticized, denounced, and cut off from the Church. This made him so bitter against the Prophet that he began to make offensive, unsavory, and repulsive speeches filled with lies about Joseph Smith. He joined with the enemies of the Church, pressuring them to persecute the Saints. He also helped the men who finally took the life of the Prophet. In John C. Bennett's later life, he suffered from violent seizures. He lost the use of his limbs and tongue, and died in misery, completely friendless.

Another man at one time, a member of the First Presidency in the early Church, who also took the wrong road, was Lyman Wight. He was with Joseph in Liberty Jail, and suffered with him there for many weeks. But he too, fell into temptation, sinned, and lost the spirit of the work. Lyman began to fight against the Church, then went to Texas where he tried to set up a church of his own, which soon failed.

There were also two brothers named Law, one was William and the other Wilson. Both had been outstanding workers for the Church. William was also a member of the First Presidency at one time. Nevertheless, it was the Law brothers, William who was second to Joseph Smith and his brother Wilson who led the conspiracy against the Prophet, both being excommunicated from the Church. Throughout the early months of 1844, their followers gradually grew to approximately 200 people. Other leaders including the brothers Robert and Charles Foster, Chauncey and Francis Higbee, joined by two influential non-Mormons—Sylvester Emmons, a member of the Nauvoo City Council, and Joseph H. Jackson, a notorious criminal were also part of this ongoing conspiracy. They openly boasted that they would help kill the Prophet, and it is believed they were with the mob at the time Joseph and Hyrum were assassinated. Joseph H. Jackson at one time loaded his gun and told his friends that he would have vengeance on the Prophet. But Joseph never did learn why Jackson was angry with him.

It was now Sidney Rigdon's turn to be heard. Sidney Rigdon wanted to become the leader of the Church. He went through much persecution, and for a time, was a loyal supporter of the Prophet. Nevertheless, he began to tire of the troubles that came to the Saints in those early days, and he also became jealous of the Prophet. Joseph was greatly grieved by the actions of Sidney Rigdon, because Sidney had been with him on several glorious occasions such as the time these two men were given a vision of the Savior and they gave us a wonderful testimony of what they had seen (Doctrine & Covenants 76).

Sidney was the postmaster of Nauvoo for a brief period of time. Due to his jealousy of the Prophet, he did everything he could to acquire information about the Prophet that might hurt him. As postmaster, he opened nearly all of Joseph's mail before, it was delivered. Upon learning of this, Joseph condemned Sidney for his actions. Sidney wanted to live in the country, and not in the main part of Nauvoo. It was the Lord's desire that he live in the city, and this was mentioned in one of the revelations. But Sidney, would not take this advice. It wasn't long before he desired to move totally away from the Saints, and moved to Pittsburgh, many miles from Nauvoo and the Saints. He felt safe from persecution there, and no doubt he was glad of that. Actually, he ran away from his people and the Prophet, and refused to do his duty in the Church. He did not return to Nauvoo until after the Prophet was dead, when he tried to become the head of the Church.

Knowing of these brethren, who had turned against him the Prophet said one day: *"This generation is as corrupt as the generations that crucified Christ, and if he were here today, and should preach the same doctrine he did to them, they would put him to death.* **The Prophet also said: *"I am exposed to far greater danger from traitors among ourselves than from the enemies without.*** *I defy all the world to destroy the work of God, and I prophesy that they never will have the power to kill me until my work is accomplished, and I am ready to die.*

My life has been sought after for many years, but there were many friends who also betrayed me."

On Sunday, March 24, 1844, Joseph Smith spoke at the temple about the conspiracy, having just learned of it from an informant. He revealed who some of his enemies were and added that: *"The lies that Higbee had hatched up as a foundation to work upon, was that I had men's heads cut off in Missouri, and that I had a sword run through the hearts of the people that I wanted to kill. I wouldn't and didn't swear out a warrant against them, because I didn't fear any of them. They would not scare off an old setting hen."*

While Joseph struggled to overcome the external forces that threatened his destruction, the fatal disease of apostasy continued to weaken the hearts of some of the Church's leadership. At the core of this destructive force, as we said, was the Prophet's second counselor, William Law. It seemed almost inconceivable that within a span of less than five years, the Prophet would witness the rise and fall of two counselors, and then see them link hands to bring about his destruction.

The key to William Law's heart was the inducement and fascination of wealth and power, although he, too, was an admitted adulterer.

The first rift in the Prophet's relationship with William Law happened when Joseph commenced to instruct his inner circle in the doctrine of plural wives. This occurred in 1841, a few months after Law was called as second counselor in the First Presidency. From then until the final breakdown and split in their relationship, Law knew, either directly or indirectly of the doctrine.

While he resisted it from the beginning, he did so from a purely selfish point of view, and not from any moralistic or idealistic voice of conscience. For him, it was simply a matter of dollars and cents. His clever and shrewd business judgement convinced him that once the doctrine of plural wives surfaced, Nauvoo was doomed, and with it, his wealth. So he argued and pressured Joseph behind the scenes to abandon and reject the doctrine, but to no avail. Knowing of Emma's aversion and opposition to the doctrine, he played upon her sympathies, thinking to influence her to change her husband's views, again to no avail.

He opened negotiations with the Prophet's Missouri enemies, to betray him into their hands. This failing, Law plotted and schemed unsuccessfully with a group of men and women in Nauvoo to kill Joseph. The later efforts of these conspirators to destroy the reputation of the Prophet through the pages of the *Nauvoo Expositor*, opened the curtain on the act of his martyrdom.

The chain of events that transformed William Law from a counselor to a conspirator, presents an interesting study of the changing Law personality. He emigrated from Canada to Nauvoo as a new convert, with high hopes and some capital which mostly was invested in real estate. He became associated with Robert D. Foster, a real estate promoter and financier. His business sharpness and skills soon brought him to the attention of the Prophet Joseph and other leaders, who saw in him qualities vital to building a new city. He soon became trusted with positions of importance, serving as an officer in the Nauvoo Legion, as a trustee of the Agricultural and Manufacturing Association, and as the registrar of the Nauvoo University. In addition to real estate, his broad, diverse business interests included ownership of steam, grain, and saw mills. So absorbed and involved did he become in the intricacies and objectives of his business ventures, that he began to lose sight of the original spiritual motives and excitement that had led him to join the Church and emigrate to Nauvoo. This change in direction was also accompanied by a new appraisal and re-evaluation of the man Joseph. While he originally had accepted Joseph as a Prophet of God, after expanding upon their personal association, he decided that the Prophet was his inferior in business judgement. And where is it written that a Prophet of God had to be a business professional or have a college education? William Law was a businessman, and quite proficient in his field, but he measured everything, including the running of the Church, by business standards, which is not God's way. From this point, it was an easy step for Law to begin to question and criticize Joseph's policies, using his own business expertise as the measuring rod.

He was negative about the construction of the Nauvoo House. He thought the area on the hill near the temple, instead of the bottom lands should be built up commercially. He doubted the wisdom of speeding the construction of the temple, believing that other construction in the city should be given priority, including the many buildings he and his partner, Robert Foster were building. These attitudes brought him into direct conflict with the Prophet, who was aggressively pushing for the prompt completion of both the temple and the Nauvoo House, and who absolutely needed the materials and labor that Law wanted to be diverted to the Law-Foster enterprises.

As his relationship with Joseph deteriorated, the pressures upon William Law became increasingly intense. To alienate the Prophet meant to alienate most of his followers, who were Law's potential customers and employees. Beside the distress and anguish that Law felt, he was faced with the threat of bankruptcy, because his wealth was frozen in assets that he could not readily dispose of. Caught up in this retentive grip, he began to search desperately and furiously for options and a new direction to protect his investments. He knew it was impossible, for him to remain with Joseph, whose policies he felt were questionable and unpredictable, (particularly the plural wife doctrine and the possibility of migrating to the West) . . . once again Law was out of touch, and certainly not in tune with God and His Prophet Joseph Smith. Under these circumstances, it seemed to him that there were only three directions he could go. He could try to coerce Joseph into accepting his views, dispose of him, or try to humiliate, embarrass, and disgrace him by attacks upon his character and morals.

When Law realized that the Prophet Joseph could not be prevented from teaching and practicing the doctrine of plural wives, he decided to join forces with Joseph's enemies in Missouri, who had been thirsting for his blood. Although he took painstaking precautions to disguise his identity and the extent of his implication and involvement, he learned subsequently, as all conspirators do, that no scheme or plot to kill another is foolproof, and that the word always gets out, one way or another.

Not long after Law opened negotiations with his co-conspirators in Missouri, the efficient scandalmongers picked up and broadcasted the news that one of Joseph Smith's most intimate associates—had deceived him, and was plotting his death. This information was intercepted and passed on by Joseph's bodyguard, Orrin Porter Rockwell, whose frequent exposure to Missourian anger, had made him especially alert to these underground messages.

Being alerted to this new danger, and being concerned about the mounting threats from enemies in nearby Warsaw and Carthage, Joseph and the Nauvoo City Council increased the city police force in late December 1843, and established a system of night patrols. During a speech delivered to the expanded police force on December twenty-ninth, the Prophet made a statement that frightened William Law and others who were in league with him. Said Joseph: *"I am exposed to far greater danger from traitors among ourselves, than from enemies without."* Later, he observed that he could live as Caesar might have lived *"were it not for a right-hand Brutus"* (*History of the Church,* 6: 152).

No sooner were these comments out of Joseph's mouth than all of Nauvoo began buzzing with speculation about his meaning. The gossipers concentrated their attention on William Law and William Marks as the most likely candidates for the Prophet's comments. The rumors and insinuations carried around the city, which intensified the pressure on these two men, and they became obsessed, envisioning imaginary dangers in the most innocent of conditions and surroundings. William Marks, for example, inferred some dark meaning into the fact that several policemen built a fire across the street from his house one cold winter night, in order to keep themselves warm. Marks was so disturbed by the incident that he insisted a session of inquiry be called by the City Council, at which the policemen were sworn and interrogated. At about the same time, William Law demanded a hearing before the council to voice complaint about the buildup of the police force.

After witnessing these proceedings, Joseph reflected in his journal: *"What can the matter be with these men? Is it that the wicked flee when no man pursueth, that hit pigeons always flutter, that drowning men catch at straws, or that Presidents Law and Marks are absolutely traitors to the Church, that my remarks should produce such an excitement in their minds? Can it be possible that the traitor whom Porter Rockwell reports to me, as being in correspondence with my Missouri enemies, is one of my quorum?"* (*History of the Church,* 6: 170).

* * *

It's a sign of the times as we must candidly admit, that the language of the early 1800s was somewhat different and difficult to understand. Nevertheless, I muddled through it, and gained a great deal of insight and color of the times, and especially that of the Joseph Smith's period.

* * *

Although these investigations and discussions disclosed nothing that William Law did not already know, they further heightened his anxieties, since he was the one that had set in motion the betrayal of the Prophet. As a result, he moved further underground and began plotting against the Prophet with some of the local people, while still maintaining his ties with his co-conspirators in Missouri. The group in Nauvoo, with which he became allied, included his brother Wilson Law, Chauncey L. Higbee, Joseph H. Jackson, his own wife, Jane Law, and Mr. and Mrs. Robert D. Foster.

The personal attack that the Nauvoo conspirators made upon Joseph, began when he was accused of trying to seduce the wives of William law and Robert D. Foster. The impact of this accusation was defused when Joseph published the affidavits of two men, A. B. Williams and M. G. Eaton, who had heard Foster speak of the supposed attempted seduction of his wife. Foster's wife later denied that the alleged incident ever occurred. One of these informants also revealed that the conspirators were actually plotting Joseph Smith's death. Mounting the stand near the temple on Sunday, March 24, 1844, Joseph laid the whole affair before the public, specifically naming the Laws and Foster as being among those who were conspiring to kill him (*History of the Church,* 6: 272). Nauvoo was electrified by this announcement. No longer was there a need to speculate about the identity of the Brutus to whom the Prophet had made reference to earlier. It was none other than his second counselor, William Law.

With these facts out in the open, the final break, the final falling-out in the official relationship between William Law and the Prophet occurred on April 18, 1844. On that date, Law, his wife, his brother Wilson, and Robert D. Foster were excommunicated from the Church for *"unchristianlike conduct"* (*History of the Church,* 6: 341). Foster's wife escaped this fate because she had ultimately denied the false rumors that Joseph had tried to seduce her.

Once the disguise, the false front, the deception had been ripped away, Law had to abandon any plans for an insidious, clandestine, deceptive killing. He and his co-conspirators then turned to the last weapon available to them in the death struggle with their former leader—character assassination by libel, slander, and gossip. To make certain that their vociferous voice of scandal, defamation, and dissent, would clearly be heard, they invested some of their dwindling funds in a press, and announced plans to begin the publication of a newspaper in Nauvoo, under the provocative name of the *Nauvoo Expositor.*

While waiting for their press to arrive, the apostates intensified their campaign of slander and vilification by appealing and petitioning to the power of the courts. William Law persuaded a grand jury in Carthage to indict Joseph for polygamy and adultery; Jackson and Foster were able to get an indictment for false swearing; and Francis Higbee pressed an earlier suit against him for alleged slander. The anti-Mormon press loudly proclaimed the news of these suits abroad as if the allegations upon which they were based were true, further inflaming the public mind against the Mormon leader, Joseph Smith.

In an effort to hide his vicious intentions under a cloak of respectability, William Law organized a church at this time, patterned after the Church from which he had just been excommunicated. Announcing this own appointment as the president of the newly formed church, he called it a "reformed" church, adopting the basic beliefs of Mormonism, while rejecting the doctrine of plural wives and Joseph's prophetic status. The selective acceptance of some of Joseph's teachings was explained on the premise that he was a fallen prophet.

The apostates and protesters in Nauvoo, rushed to this new representative symbol, bringing with them the pent-up hatreds, disputations, and bitterness they had nurtured over the years. Feeding on each others' poison and animosity, these dissenters generated the fatal, deadly, and poisonous toxin that was to bring death to the Prophet. The corrupt foundations upon which William Law's church was built, caused it to crumble and fall soon after it was formed, leaving hardly any trace that it had ever existed.

The enduring fame of the *Nauvoo Expositor* newspaper was guaranteed by the publication of only one issue. This **journalistic bomb** exploded in Nauvoo on June 7, 1844. **Twenty days later, shock waves from that bomb produced the martyrdom of Joseph and his brother Hyrum in Carthage jail.**

Reading the unfolding drama of the *Nauvoo Expositor* incident, Joseph's diary imparts the sense of observing the evidence that this explosion was coming. On May seventh, the Prophet commented: *"An opposition printing press arrives at Dr. Foster's."* Three days later, he recorded: *"A prospectus of the* Nauvoo Expositor *was distributed among the people by the apostates."* And on the day that the paper hit the streets, he wrote with prophetic finality: *"The first and only number of the* Nauvoo Expositor *was published, edited by Sylvester Emmons"* (*History of the Church,* 6: 357, 363, 430).

The sum, substance and tone of the *Nauvoo Expositor* was even more offensive than Joseph had expected. He was portrayed as a fallen prophet, ambitious and power hungry. A trumped-up, fabricated story suggested that the missionary effort abroad was simply a lure to trap unsuspecting women into polygamy. Joseph was condemned for his political activity, accused of being corruptible and arrogant, and labeled as a blasphemer. The language in which these charges were presented was vulgar, excessive, and unrestrained. Joseph, for example, was characterized as "one of the blackest and basest scoundrels that has appeared upon the stage of human existence since the days of Nero, and Caligula." The specific remedy proposed was the forerunner to the bloody killings, which were to take place in less than three weeks. "Let us arise in the majesty of our strength," the writer intoned, "and sweep the influence of tyrants and miscreants [reprobates] from the face of the land, as with the breath of heaven" (*Nauvoo Expositor,* June 7, 1844, p. 3).

Joseph's attention became totally focused on the *Nauvoo Expositor's* discernibly obvious lies, harsh, and grating tone. At a meeting of the Nauvoo Council the next day, he contended that the *Nauvoo Expositor* would in effect, produce an unruly mob temperament in the city if they were permitted to continue publishing it.. He argued, therefore, that the *Nauvoo Expositor* should be declared a nuisance and as such, should be nullified, meaning in simple terms—done away with.

So enormous were the possible consequences that depended upon this decision, that the City Council debated this issue all that day, Saturday, June eighth, and were unable to reach any decision, adjourned until the following Monday, when the debate continued. The feeling was strong from the beginning that the paper should be declared a nuisance. Respectable and ethical common law authority existed to support this conclusion. Therefore, the issue in dispute was the compensations to be requested for the damage inflicted or to be inflicted by the paper.

A moderate view was urged by Councilman Warrington, a non-Mormon, that in lieu of doing away with the paper, that a $3,000 fine be imposed for each libel. Joseph insisted that this would be a foolhardy solution, since to enforce it would require repeated trips to the county seat at Carthage, that would endanger the lives of the Church leaders. In the meantime, the publishers would be free to enlarge, expand, and spew their poisonous lies into the public mind. The Prophet genuinely feared that this would produce the kind of opposing extremes that had taken place in Ohio and Missouri, with his enemies enraged and urging people to violence, and his loyal followers militantly prepared to stand in self-defense.

At this time, the council suspended one of their members, the non-Mormon Sylvester Emmons, who was the editor of the *Nauvoo Expositor,* and discussed the identity of the publishers and their intent. Using the famous English jurist, William Blackstone, as their legal authority, and having examined various municipal codes, the council ruled that the newspaper was a public nuisance in that it slandered individuals in the city. In addition, they reasoned that if nothing were done to stop the libelous paper, the anti-Mormons would be aroused to mob action.

Disregarding the legal niceties in favor of a decision that they felt was in the best interest of the city, the council accepted Joseph's views and adopted an ordinance that declared the *Nauvoo Expositor* a nuisance and ordered the Mayor to eliminate it. Acting without delay, the Prophet, in his role as Mayor, ordered the City Marshal, John M. Greene to destroy the press with the assistance of members of the Nauvoo Legion.

This order was executed immediately, and by Monday evening, June tenth, only an hour and a half after the council meeting ended, the *Nauvoo Expositor* press had been destroyed, the type scattered and the remaining newspapers burned.

The City Council acted legally to remove a public nuisance, although the legal opinion of the time allowed only the destruction of the published issues of the offending paper. The demolition of the press was a violation of property rights (Dallin H. Oaks, "The Suppression of the *Nauvoo Expositor*," Utah Law Review, Winter 1965, pp. 890-891).

The destruction of the *Nauvoo Expositor*, which took place on June 10, 1844, proved to be the major spark which ignited all the smoldering fires of opposition into one great flame. It offered the occasion for which the apostates from the Church and other anti-Mormons were waiting for, a legal excuse to get the Prophet Joseph and other leaders into their hands. The cry that the "freedom of the press" was being violated, united the factions seeking the overthrow of the Saints as probably nothing else would have done. It was the perfect excuse to get rid of Mormon leaders.

Protest meetings were held throughout Hancock and neighboring counties. Bitter enemies of the Prophet aroused these meetings into threats of open violence. The fury that this bold act unleashed must have made Joseph feel as if he had quieted one obscene voice while unstopping a thousand others. Newspapers in nearby Quincy, LaHarpe, and Warsaw, Illinois, displayed the matter in bold type, as they exploded with self-righteous indignation at what they considered to be the ultimate affront by the hated Mormons. Thomas C. Sharp, the detestable and worldly-wide editor of the neighboring *Warsaw Signal,* was the most explicit and deadly of all in his violent discourse, and in the remedy he proposed. Wrote he: "We hold ourselves at all times, in readiness to cooperate with our fellow citizens . . . to exterminate, utterly exterminate the wicked and abominable Mormon leaders."

After the destruction of the press, the publishers rushed to Carthage and obtained a warrant against the Nauvoo City Council on charge of riot, for the action. On June thirteenth and fourteenth, however, Joseph Smith and the other council members were released following a habeas corpus hearing before the Nauvoo Municipal Court. This, of course, further aroused the public. In addition, even though Illinois had experienced twenty similar destructions of printing presses over the previous two decades with hardly a notice, the enemies of the Church proclaimed the *Nauvoo Expositor* action as a flagrant violation of the freedom of the press. These actions prompted citizens' groups in Hancock County to call for the removal of the Saints from Illinois.

* * *

And here we go again, anything relating to the Mormons becomes a blight on a community, and why? All the Mormons ever worked for, ever wanted, ever needed, and ever hoped for to fulfill their lives was religious freedom as promised in the United States Constitution. Is that so outrageous; is that so wrong?

* * *

Thomas Sharp vehemently expressed the feelings of many of the enemies of the Church when he editorialized in the *Warsaw Signal*: "War and extermination is inevitable? **Citizens Arise, One and All!!!** Can you stand by, and suffer such **Infernal Devil's!** To rob men of their property and rights, without avenging them. We have no time for comment, every man will make his own, Let it be made with **Powder and Ball!!!"** (*Warsaw Signal,* 12 June 1844, p. 2).

It seemed ironic to the Latter-day Saints that the event which provoked the fatal storm in Illinois, had an almost exact precedent in Missouri. However, the destruction of the Mormon press in Jackson County had no resemblance of legality about it, and the event went almost unnoticed in the public media. Yet in Nauvoo, an action taken under the guise of law, following two days of debate by a proper government body having jurisdiction, was made to appear a hideous, offensive thing.

While the hostile press stirred the anger of Joseph's enemies with a steady flow of denunciation and abuse, the apostates, led by William Law, were busy agitating and pressing for legal action against him. Urgent calls for arms and money to capture Joseph circulated among anti-Mormon cliques within a wide radius of Carthage. A delegation waited on Governor Ford, who was urged to direct the state militia to take the Mormon leader into custody. And the Prophet's most deep-rooted enemies, sensing a golden opportunity to crush him once and for all, stirred up substantial support among the Mormon-haters in Missouri and across the river in Iowa.

Alarmed at the threatening and menacing tone of his enemies and at reports of the size and increase of the mobs being raised and enlarged on a daily basis, **the Prophet declared martial law in Nauvoo on June eighteenth,**

to protect his people. He called out the Nauvoo Legion to defend it against what he anticipated was a forthcoming—imminent attack. In a last address to his soldiers and people he said:

"I call God and angels to witness that I have unsheathed my sword with a firm and unalterable determination, that this people shall have their legal rights, and to be protected from mob violence, or my blood shall be spilt upon the ground like water, and my body be consigned to the silent tomb. While I live, I will never tamely submit to the dominion of cursed mobocracy" (*History of the Church,* 6: 499).

The militia of the Saints at Ramus and Montrose came into Nauvoo and joined forces with the defender of the City. Governor Ford, who feared that a full-scale civil war would be accelerated, and responding to pleas from both sides, intervened to try to mediate the dispute. The situation was so dangerous that Joseph Smith wrote Governor Ford, apprising him of the circumstances, and including many affidavits to explain the threats against the Saints. On June twenty-first, Governor Ford arrived at Carthage and requested of the Nauvoo City Council by letter that representative men be sent to present their case before him. Dr. Willard Richards, Dr. John M. Bernhisel, and John Taylor were elected by the City Council for that mission. In the meantime, Hyrum Smith wrote Brigham Young that the Twelve and all other Elders on political missions should return at once to Nauvoo. Hyrum stated: "You know we are not frightened, but think it best to be well prepared and be ready for the onset" (*History of the Church,* 6: 487). Joseph mobilized his guards and the Nauvoo Legion in preparation for any possible attack. The Hancock County citizens recommended to Governor Ford that he mobilize the state militia and bring the Nauvoo offenders to justice.

The emotions and turbulence became so intense that Ford published an open letter urging calmness, and then tried to neutralize a situation that threatened civil war. In the meantime, Dr. Willard Richards was detained by Joseph Smith for other duties, and Lucien Woodworth was sent in his place, representing the Nauvoo City Council. Governor Ford made his headquarters at the Hamilton Hotel in Carthage. His natural hostility toward the Latter-day Saints was well-established as he listened to the damning accusations against Joseph Smith, which were made primarily by the clique of apostates, headed by William Law. So intense was the hatred and bitterness against the Prophet in Carthage, and so glib, talkative, and uncompromising were his enemies, that any positive voice raised in Joseph's defense was either not heard or was promptly shouted down. In this heated provocative setting—given his anti-Mormon bias, it came as no surprise that the governor conceded completely to the demands of Joseph's deadly enemies. Their object was to pry him loose from the security of the Nauvoo Legion and the Nauvoo courts, to get him under their control on their own ground.

Lucien Woodworth, a member of the Nauvoo City Council, carried a letter to Governor Ford, inviting him to come to Nauvoo and carry out his own complete investigation. It appears that Governor Ford was strongly influenced by the feeling which prevailed at Carthage. In his reply letter, later in the day, he charged the Nauvoo City Council with an abuse of power, ordered the Nauvoo Legion to disband, and discontinued martial law. **He requested that Joseph Smith submit to arrest and be tried at Carthage.** His letter ended with a promise and a threat: "If it should become necessary to have witnesses on the trials, I will see that such persons are duly summoned, **and I will also guarantee the safety of all such persons as may**

be thus brought to this place from Nauvoo, either for trial or as witnesses for the accused. If the individuals accused cannot be found, when required by the constable, it will be considered by me as an equivalent to a refusal to be arrested, and the militia will be ordered accordingly" (*History of the Church,* 6: 533-537).

In answer, Joseph dispatched a second letter, a brilliant and inspiring defense of the action of the City Council to the Governor. He added: *"we would not hesitate to stand another trial according to your Excellency's wish, were it not that we are confident that our lives would be in danger. We dare not come. Writs, we are assured, are issued against us in various parts of the country. For what? To drag us from place to place, from court to court, across the creeks and prairies, till some bloodthirsty villain could find his opportunity to shoot us. We dare not come, though your Excellency promises protection . . . you have expressed your fears that you could not control the mob, in which case, we are left to the mercy of the merciless"* (*History of the Church,* 6: 538-541).

A meeting of the leading brethren who were in Nauvoo, was held in the evening of June twenty-second, at the Mansion House. After reading the letter from Governor Ford to the Council, the Prophet remarked: *"There is no mercy—no mercy here."* Hyrum added: "No, just as sure as we fall into their hands, we are dead men." A little later, the Prophet's countenance lighted up and he said: *"The way is open. It is clear to my mind what to do. All they want is Hyrum and myself; then tell everybody to go about their business, and not to collect in groups, but to scatter about. There is no doubt they will come here and search for us. Let them search; they will not harm you in person or property, and not even a hair of your head. We will cross the river tonight and go away to the West"* (*History of the Church,* 6: 545-56).

The personal journal of the Prophet closes with these words uttered on that occasion: *"I told Stephen Markham that if I and Hyrum were ever taken again, we would be massacred, or I was not a prophet of God. I want Hyrum to live to avenge my blood, but he is determined not to leave me"* (*History of the Church,* 6: 545-46). Stephen, a close personal friend of the Prophet Joseph who had been present in the all-night council, heard Joseph Smith say that: *"it was the voice of the Spirit for him to go to the West among the Natives and take Hyrum and several others along with him, and look out for a place for the Church"* (*Church History In The Fulness Of Times*, LDS, Church Education System, p. 276). In order to provide leadership and personal moral strength, the Prophet had ordered the Twelve, who were away campaigning in support of his presidential candidacy, to return to Nauvoo immediately. **As Joseph once again reviewed his options, there were only three practical courses of action remaining open to him.** He could stand and fight, backed by the arms and discipline of the Nauvoo Legion and supported by the loyalty of his followers. Reason convinced him, however, that this was the least acceptable of the three since it held the real prospect of injury or death to many of his followers. Behind the furious mobs that surrounded Nauvoo, Joseph could see the ranks of the Illinois militia, which Governor Ford had threatened to order into the encounter; beyond them loomed the appearance of federal troops, backed by the unlimited resources of the American government. The possibility of intervention by federal troops was a very real threat. If Governor Ford was to commit the state militia, and if an impasse became a reality, the federal government could ill afford to remain on the sidelines; with the general indifference, bitterness, and hostility toward the Saints that existed in all branches of the government, there was little doubt as to the side it would defend and support.

Joseph retreated from the second option of submitting to arrest and trial in Carthage. He knew that this would mean the end of him. Several times he commented that if he were to go to Carthage, he would be killed. On one occasion, he used the word **butchered**. On another, he emphatically predicted his death in Carthage, stressing that if it did not happen, he was not a Prophet of God.

Faced with impending death if he were to remain or if he were to submit to arrest, it was inevitable that this charismatic leader, not yet thirty-nine years of age, who possessed a personal magic of leadership, through the power of the Holy Ghost, would choose the third alternative, which would take him and his people into the vast wilderness beyond the Mississippi. His plans for an organized mass exodus had not yet unfolded. Nevertheless, he had so often been forced to improvise and to adjust to radical changes without adequate preparation, that the thought and willingness to venture forth into unchartered plains and mountains to the West, did not give him a moment's hesitation. The decision to go West was made on Saturday, June twenty-second. Plans were immediately made to take the first step when Joseph and Hyrum arranged to cross the river into Iowa.

Late in the evening of June 22, 1844, Joseph and Hyrum did tearfully bid their families farewell. Together with Willard Richards and Orrin Porter Rockwell, they crossed the Mississippi River in a skiff. The boat was so leaky and the river so high, that it took most of the night to get to the other side. Early in the morning of June twenty-third, a posse arrived in Nauvoo to arrest Joseph and Hyrum, but were unable to find them. The posse returned to Carthage after threatening the citizens with an invasion of troops if Joseph and Hyrum did not give themselves up. That same morning, some of the brethren, who went to see Joseph, and argued that mobs would drive the Saints from their homes despite his departure. Joseph replied: ***"If my life is of no value to my friends it is of none to myself"*** (*History of the Church,* 6: 549).

On June 23, 1844, three men were busily engaged in the home of William Jordan in Montrose, Iowa packing supplies for a journey on horseback to the Great Basin in the Rocky Mountains. The Prophet spoke often to the Brethren about the Great Basin, which is the area in which Utah is located. He was counseled by the Lord that the Saints would be going there in the not-too-distant future. That he and some of his associates would be opening up the area for the Mormons to have and enjoy their religious freedom away from the persecution, and away from the ways of the world perpetuated by unruly mobs, anti-Mormons and apostates.

The journey that Joseph and his followers were about to embark upon meant freedom for them and eventually for their people. Subsequently, when the Saints finally came to the Great Basin, under the leadership of Brigham Young, much of the credit for what was done was given to Joseph Smith by the Pioneers, who said they were but following the plans made by the Prophet Joseph before his death.

In the meantime, they were awaiting the arrival of Orrin Porter Rockwell with horses for the journey. Rockwell came, but without horses. Instead, he was accompanied by Reynolds Cahoon, with a letter from the Prophet's wife, Emma. His people, at least some of them in Nauvoo, were calling him a coward. **Those who**

should have been his greatest friends, admirers, and supporters were denouncing his running as an act of cowardice, but was he running away? Absolutely not.

* * *

Would a Prophet of God ever run away from his divine calling, even when the pressures become unbearable? Joseph Smith was and is a true Prophet of God, and he continually proved that, over and over again, during his short life-span on earth. He remained strong in the faith, obedient to his Heavenly Father and Jesus Christ, and always on target in being ever thoughtful about the best interests of his people.

* * *

Even his loving and devoted wife, Emma, in her letter pleaded for him to return and submit to arrest and trial. In Emma's eyes, Joseph having been through so much antagonism over the years, having been arrested approximately **forty-seven** times, but never convicted, only meant that his presence would remove the anxiety of everyone, and that he would be able to straighten out their current situation, relating to the *Nauvoo Expositor* incident, and he being vindicated. It was one thing to destroy the first and only copies of the *Nauvoo Expositor* newspaper, which printed the hateful and bitter lies about Joseph and the Mormons, but the destruction of the *Nauvoo Expositor* press, although approved by the Nauvoo City Council, further opened the floodgates of hatred. It was the clarion call of the anti-Mormons and apostates to bring down the Prophet Joseph Smith. The *Nauvoo Expositor* people wanted Joseph's head. **Joseph knew that his life was hanging by a thread, but Emma didn't realize that her letter to Joseph, and her plea for his return, would be his undoing.** Emma had great faith in Joseph and his relationship with Heavenly Father and Jesus Christ, but Joseph knew that his time on earth was almost up. Reynolds Cahoon likened Joseph to the shepherd who left his flock to the wolves.

Shocked by the insults, the ridicule and criticism of being labeled a coward, Joseph once again, repeated: *"If my life is of no value to my friends, it is of none to myself"* (*History of the Church,* 6: 549). Joseph and Hyrum then made plans to return to Nauvoo, and submit to arrest the next day. They also notified Governor Ford of their action. Joseph was certain that arrest would mean his death.

Safety did lie within his grasp. The open West had called to him, and for the many reasons mentioned previously, the most important was religious freedom. The Spirit had whispered to him the wisdom of flight. Nevertheless, safety without the faith and devotion of his beloved people would be an empty shell.

For some time, Joseph had felt that a continuation of his teachings would result in his death; death was no longer an improbability to him. As early as April 9, 1842, he had declared: *"Some have supposed that Brother Joseph could not die; but this is a mistake; it is true that there have been times when I have had the promise of my life to accomplish such and such things; but, having accomplished those things, I have not at present any lease of my life; I am as liable to die as other men"* (*History of the Church,* 4: 587).

Joseph sadly returned to Nauvoo. He wanted to speak to the Saints once more, but there was not enough time. He went home to his family, fully aware that it would probably be his last evening with them.

The Prophet requested of Governor Ford by letter that a posse conduct him into Carthage. Because of the influence of apostates with the Governor, the request was denied and Joseph was ordered to appear in Carthage by 10 o'clock the next morning without a posse. If the Mayor and City Council did not come, "Nauvoo would be destroyed, and all the men, women, and children that were in it" (*History of the Church,* 6: 552).

On Monday, June twenty-fourth, at 6:30 a.m., Joseph, Hyrum, John Taylor, and fifteen other members of the Nauvoo City Council, set out on horseback for Carthage, accompanied by Willard Richards and a number of other friends. It had rained for about two weeks, but that morning was sunny and beautiful. Pausing at the temple site, the Prophet looked upon the sacred edifice, then on the city, and remarked: *"This is the loveliest place, and the best people under the heavens, but little do they know the trials that await them"* (*History of the Church,* 6: 554). To the assembled Saints, he said: *"If I do not go there* [to Carthage] *the result will be the destruction of this city and its inhabitants; and I cannot think of my dear brothers and sisters and their children, suffering the same kind of hate, bitterness, devastation and sacrifice, the same scenes of Missouri repeated again in Nauvoo; no, it is far better for your brother Joseph to die for his brothers and sisters, for I am willing to die for them. My work is finished."*

On the outskirts of the city, the party stopped again, this time at the home of a non-Mormon, Daniel H. Wells, who had been ailing. After visiting with the man, who always had been a staunch friend of the Saints, and who was later to join the Church and play a key role in the development of the empire in the Rocky Mountains, the Prophet said, in parting: *"Squire Wells, I wish you to cherish my memory, and not to think me the worst man in the world either"* (*History of the Church,* 6: 554).

About four miles west of Carthage, shortly before 10 o'clock, as the group approached the farm of Albert G. Fellows, they were startled to see a large company of mounted militia riding toward them. Uncertain about the intentions of these armed riders, and sensing an undercurrent of anxiety among his companions, Joseph commented: *"Do not be alarmed, brethren for they cannot do more to you than the enemies of the truth did to the ancient Saints—they can only kill the body"* (*History of the Church,* 6: 554-55).

Much to their relief, Joseph and the brethren found no combative attitude in this company of Illinois militia. They were led by a courteous, mild-mannered man, Captain Dunn, who presented an order from Governor Ford to surrender all the state arms in the possession of the Nauvoo Legion. While he may have had some mental reservations in doing so, Joseph promptly countersigned this order as Commander-in-Chief of the Legion. He also agreed to accompany Captain Dunn to Nauvoo to help organize and supervise the surrender of the arms.

Before returning though, Joseph dictated and dispatched two letters, one to Governor Ford, explaining his delay in reaching Carthage, and the other to an officer of the Legion, giving directions about gathering the arms.

While relaxing briefly at the Fellows farm before returning to Nauvoo, the Prophet wandered off into one of his thoughtful, meditative moods. Reflecting upon his perilous condition and the ordeal that still lay ahead, he verbalized a statement, simple yet eloquent and majestic, that has ever been associated with his name, and that gave voice to his deepest feelings: ***"I am going like a lamb to the slaughter; but I am calm as a summer's morning; I have a conscience void of offense toward God, and toward all men. I SHALL DIE INNOCENT, AND IT SHALL YET BE SAID OF ME—'HE WAS MURDERED IN COLD BLOOD!'"*** (*History of the Church,* 6: 555; Doctrine & Covenants 135: 4).

Upon returning to Nauvoo, Joseph directed that three small cannons and about 200 firearms be turned over to the militia. His action called to mind the agonizing memories of the Mormon disarmament that had preceded the Missouri massacre. The Prophet had another opportunity to briefly visit with his family at the Mansion House, and to further comfort them. As he was saying his loving farewell to them, it would be the last time that Emma and the children would ever see him alive.

It was near midnight on June twenty-fourth, when Captain Dunn and his company of sixty mounted men of the Augusta militia rode into Carthage with Joseph and Hyrum Smith and the members of the Nauvoo City Council as voluntary captives. Joseph and Hyrum were weary from travel, from hiding out, and from threats of assassination. Nevertheless, the brothers were imposing figures as they rode into town—the Prophet, age thirty-eight, and Hyrum, forty-four—both tall men who towered over most of the others.

Carthage was in a riotous state. Mobs of irate townsmen and farmers from throughout Western Illinois had been clamoring for the arrest of the Mormon Prophet. They were now eager to see the captives. Among the mob were more than 1,400 unruly militia, including the local Carthage Greys. During the earlier part of the day, the crowds were roaming the town, drinking and brawling They wanted to get their hands on the Smith brothers. As the day wore on, the excitement and anticipation intensified in the quiet little country town, inflated with hundreds of strangers who had come to witness the spectacle. The militia and several of the local volunteer units were quartered in tents pitched on or near the public square, as were some of the mobocrats who had been drawn to Carthage by the lure of an assassination that had been openly discussed for weeks. Carthage was awake and boisterous as if it were midday.

The Hamilton Hotel was filled to capacity. It's guest list included Governor Ford and his party from the state capitol, and all the principle apostates from Nauvoo including William and Wilson Law, the Higbees, the Fosters and Augustine Spencer.

Throughout the day, prior to the Joseph Smith arrival, the apostates worked over a scheme to detain Joseph and Hyrum in Carthage as long as it would be necessary to accomplish their purpose. What they had in mind was evident from a statement attributed to them that "the law could not reach Joseph and Hyrum, but powder and ball would." Aware of the weak, flimsy nature of the devised and contrived charge of riot, and the excellent chance that the defendants would win the contest quickly or would be freed on bail, they invented eighteen other false charges against Joseph so that "as one failed, they would try another, and another and so on to detain him there." They freely acknowledged "that they had had so much trouble and hazard, and worked so hard in getting him [Joseph] to Carthage, that they would not let him out of it alive" (*History of the Church,* 6: 566, 569).

By midnight, when Joseph and his party arrived, many of the militia and mobocrats were wildly intoxicated. Through Captain Dunn's efforts, arrangements were made to lodge the prisoners safely in the Hamilton House Hotel. As Joseph and his followers passed through the public square, on their way to the hotel, they were insulted and threatened by the drunken militiamen, who were supposed to be there to protect them. Some protection! The Carthage Greys were especially vulgar and abusive. "Where is the damned prophet?" they shouted, "Stand away you McDonough boys, and let us shoot the damned Mormons. G—d—you, old Joe, we've got you now. Clear the way and let us have a view of Joe Smith, the prophet of God. He has seen the last of Nauvoo. We'll use him up now, and kill all the damned Mormons" (*History of the Church,* 6: 559).

By the time the weary travelers arrived in front of the Hamilton Hotel, hundreds of curious spectators had assembled, alerted by the news that the Mormons had reached town. The shouting and cursing, mingled with the general commotion of the large crowd, brought Governor Ford to the window of his room. Instead of condemning the drunken troops, he simply soothed their ruffled feathers by promising them a parade, to be organized the next day to enable them to see the prisoners clearly. With this, and a few scattered hurrahs for the governor, the crowd began to disperse, and Joseph and his companions disappeared into the hotel.

Early the next morning, Tuesday, Joseph arose for a meeting with H. T. Reid and James W. Woods, who had been retained as legal counsel. He and the other defendants voluntarily surrendered to Constable Bettisworth on the writ issued under the charge of riot. A bit later, the apostates did spring their first legal surprise that they had plotted and devised. Shortly after 8:00 a.m., the Prophet was interrupted in a conversation and arrested again by Constable Bettisworth under a writ for treason, based upon an affidavit sworn to by the apostate Augustine Spencer. The alleged treasonable act was the Prophet's declaration of martial law at Nauvoo. With this extra hold on him, to add to their own list of false charges Joseph's enemies felt confident of their ability to retain custody, despite the outcome of the hearing that afternoon on the riot charge.

It was midmorning when Joseph and Hyrum joined the governor to review the militia and volunteers, who had been assembled in formation on the town square. Several times, during the course of the review, Governor Ford would stop before the troop units to introduce the Smiths as "General Joseph Smith, and General Hyrum Smith." With the soberness that a good night's sleep had brought them, most of the troops maintained silence. The striking exception, once again, was the Carthage Greys. When the Prophet and Hyrum were introduced to them, some of the officers threw their hats in the air and drew swords, declaring that they would introduce themselves to the "damned Mormons" in their own way (*History of the Church,* 6: 564). After that demonstration, it was difficult for the governor to restore order, although later he censured them, if he did not have them arrested. Under the circumstances, it was both a dilemma and embarrassment that the governor would have assigned these same Carthage Greys, the most violent and insubordinate of all, to guard the prisoners when they were later confined to jail—obviously a disturbing and dangerous situation unless the governor harbored a secret, deadly intent toward Joseph and Hyrum.

Even with the forthcoming threat of his death, the Prophet did not alter his work habits. Between the morning review of the troops and his arraignment in late afternoon, he counseled with the governor about a report that the apostates were planning to ravage and plunder Nauvoo; dictated several letters, including one to Emma and one to Orrin Porter Rockwell; and received a large group of militia officers, who came out of curiosity to converse with him in his room. These men left with a healthy respect for his serenity and composure under extreme pressure, and not a little shaken by the chilling prediction he made about them, delivered with his accustomed stability, steadiness, and impartiality. Answering a humorous statement by one of the officers, that Joseph's mild appearance was no indication to his thoughts or intentions, he startled them by saying that while his aims were shielded from them, he could read theirs with clarity. *"I can see that you thirst for blood,"* he told them, and then he prophesied: *"in the name of the Lord:"* that they would *"witness scenes of blood and sorrow to their entire satisfaction,"* and that their souls would be *"perfectly satiated* [gratify with more than enough] *with blood"* (*History of the Church,* 6: 566).

No one who heard Joseph Smith prophesy in this manner ever forgot the occasion, nor failed to be impressed by the solemnity of his manner or the substance of what he said. As the officers filed out from Joseph's room, they were more subdued and thoughtful than when they had entered. Had they been willing to share their deepest impressions with each other, they would have likely acknowledged that this man, who then stood on the threshold of death, was one of the most truly remarkable and extraordinary persons they had ever been exposed to.

Joseph and his fellow defendants thought it somewhat strange at the late afternoon hearing in the riot case, that they were arraigned before Justice Robert F. Smith. Governor Ford had *"turned supreme court,"* as Joseph put it, and had rejected the decision of Justice Daniel H. Wells in Nauvoo expressly because the writ had not been returned to the justice who issued it, Thomas Morrison. What was even more confusing and bewildering was the fact that this same Robert Smith, who now had legal jurisdiction over them, was also a commander of a company of Carthage Greys and active in the anti-Mormon party. In addition, there was great concern that the apostate Chauncey L. Higbee was one of the prosecutors.

Following the arraignment, the prisoners were bound over for trial to be held at the next term of the Circuit Court and bail was set at $500 for each defendant, an amount that was considered high under the circumstances. To the surprise of the court and the apostates, the full amount of the bail was posted immediately. According to prearrangement, however, the justice adjourned the court without calling up the treason case, which had the effect of leaving Joseph and Hyrum in the custody of the constable, while setting free the other defendants, who were not charged with treason. Most of the men accused on the riot charge, whose bond was posted, returned to Nauvoo.

Thus far, the tactics of the conspirators had been working. The first legal hurdle had been passed safely, and Joseph and Hyrum were still in custody in Carthage. It was really of little concern to the conspirators that the other defendants were freed on bail, since their prime interest was centered on the Smiths. Nevertheless, there were still some loose ends that troubled them. They were uncertain, for example, of the effect of the day's events on Governor Ford. Although they knew of his sympathy toward their position and of his disposition, temperament, and negative leaning toward the Smith brothers, they also recognized that he was an elected politician, easily influenced by public opinion and vain enough to be concerned about the record he would leave behind. Based upon this presumption, they began speculating and theorizing whether he might begin shifting his position because the Mormon Leaders had not been taken before Justice Morrison, as the governor had originally ordered. It also concerned them that Joseph and Hyrum were now being held in custody on a false charge. They also knew that the Prophet had been trying unsuccessfully to obtain an interview with Governor Ford since Monday night, and they were uncertain about the possible effect on the governor of the Prophet's persuasive eloquence, especially since his side of the controversy had not yet been presented. Finally, they were afraid that Joseph and Hyrum, in evaluating the new developments, might decide that they had complied with the spirit, if not the letter of Governor Ford's demands. If so, they might elude Constable Bettisworth at the hotel and take off for the homey, peaceable confines of Nauvoo. There a friendly court, and the right of a citizen to obtain a writ of habeas corpus as a protection against illegal imprisonment awaited them.

Considering all of these factors, the conspirators decided to put into effect a course of action that was clearly illegal, oppressive, and dictatorial, but was deliberately designed to put Joseph and Hyrum behind bars, where they could be securely held until the assassination plans had matured and been accomplished. By some devious means, never revealed, they induced Justice Smith to issue an order—a mittimus (a commitment to prison)—committing Joseph and Hyrum to jail under the treason suit, even though a preliminary hearing to determine the probability of guilt had never been held. Constable Bettisworth served this writ on them in their hotel rooms after dinner, Tuesday evening. In actuality, the constable did not produce the mittimus until Joseph and Hyrum demanded to know by what authority he proposed to lock them up. Once they had seen the order, which falsely stated that a hearing had been postponed for lack of a material witness, they immediately sent for their legal counsel.

Pleas were made to Governor Ford to intervene, especially in view of the pledges of protection and impartial handling he had made to persuade the Mormon leaders to come to Carthage. Although he felt no qualms about intervening earlier to demands that Joseph and Hyrum would ignore the judgement of the Nauvoo Court on threat of habeas corpus, nevertheless, he was now unwilling to interfere. He knew the order he had was false, and would violate the promises he made to the prisoners. Joseph and his lawyers protested that the mittimus was illegal, since there had been no mention of that charge at their hearing. Their complaints were taken to the governor, but he said he could not interrupt a civil officer in the discharge of his duty.

After more than an hour of fruitless, ineffectual, and unsuccessful arguing and protesting, the brothers realized that without force of arms or the power of an impartial judiciary, neither of which was available to them, there was no way to avoid being imprisoned. As a consequence, they submitted to the constable, who prepared to escort them across the square to the jail.

During the debate over the commitment order, word got out that the Smith brothers were about to be moved, and a large, unruly crowd quickly assembled to witness the dramatic happening. Elder John Taylor, who had been arguing valiantly, but unsuccessfully, with Governor Ford, was fearful for the safety of the Church leaders, if they were taken unescorted through the fast-growing crowd, so he arranged for Captain Dunn and about twenty other members of the militia to escort the prisoners to jail. Eight of their friends accompanied them including John Taylor and Willard Richards. Dan Jones with his walking stick, and Stephen Markham with his hickory cane, which he called the "rascal beater," walked on either side of the Prophet and his brother, holding off the drunken crowd. As it turned out, the stone jail was the safest place in town. Several of Joseph's and Hyrum's friends were permitted to stay with them. Ahead of them were Constable Bettisworth and members of Captain Dunn's escort. These formed a literal military troop that plunged quickly into and through the uneasy, angry crowd.

The jailer, George W. Stigall, checking in his prisoners, at first lodged them in the criminal's cell, a small rectangular, iron-barred room upstairs at the rear of the building. Since they requested it, the jailer permitted the prisoners' friends to be locked up with them. Late in the evening, he moved the entire party to the larger debtors' quarters in the front of the upstairs floor, at the head of a steep stairway. The door to this room was a conventional wooden door, and the glassed windows in the room had no bars. Here is where the Prophet, Hyrum, and their friends spent the night, sleeping either on the double bed in the southeast corner or on the floor.

From the moment he entered the Carthage Jail, Joseph seemed to be under the influence of a depressing, discouraging, and threatening spirit. On Wednesday, June twenty-sixth, following an unproductive meeting with Governor Ford, he revealed the depths of these feelings: *"I have had a good deal of anxiety about my safety since I left Nauvoo," he said, "which I never had before when I was under arrest. I could not help those feelings, and they have depressed me"* (J. C. Conkling, *A Joseph Smith Chronology,* p. 240).

This day of imprisonment seemed endless for the Prophet. Never idle, he managed to keep occupied in dictating, reading, counseling with the brethren, and sending and receiving messages through the visitors who came and went. Nevertheless, nothing he did seemed to make difference, nor to be directed toward any meaningful end. There was movement and activity, but no progress. Unlike the days he spent in Missouri jails, when he was confidently undertaking plans for the future and actively giving direction and instruction to the Church from his cell, he now seemed to be in a state of suspension and uncertainty. He knew in his heart what the future held for him—after all, he was God's Prophet on earth in the Dispensation of the Fulness of Times.

In any case, he continued to demonstrate through his actions and speech, the sense of calmness and self-confidence that had made his life so unique, so uncommon and extraordinary. But the essential ingredient of forward-looking action was missing.

It was not necessary to search for an explanation concerning the fundamental change in the Prophet's manner. He knew that whatever time was left for him, would be spent playing a protective and defensive waiting game. The effect of this was to increase the intensity of his concentration upon any subject that claimed his attention for the moment. Since his work for God had been completed and he foresaw no earthly future, all that remained to be done was to live out the moment, the hour, the day—however long God would permit him to remain in mortality—in a manner consistent with his prophetic calling.

In the late afternoon, the prisoners were aroused from their make-work activities by loud, argumentative voices from the jailer's quarters downstairs. The hotly contested debate centered around whether the conscientious jailer, Stigall, would relinquish custody of the prisoners to Constable Bettisworth, who carried another order from Justice Robert Smith for Joseph and Hyrum to appear before him for a hearing on the charge of treason. The order stated that the prisoners were committed to jail without the benefit of a hearing "for safe keeping until the trial could be had" (*History of the Church,* 6: 596).

The jailer refused to surrender custody because he held the prisoners under a direct order from the court, while the present order was directed only to Constable Bettisworth. In addition, an angry crowd had gathered in front of the jail, and in view of the loose talk about assassination that had been circulated around town for days, he feared that to give up the prisoners would be to commit them to their graves. Nevertheless, his loud emphasis on legal principle was to no avail. When the constable saw that he could not win the argument with words, he did so by force and intimidation.

Calling upon the assistance of several willing Carthage Greys in the crowd, he pushed aside the jailer, took his keys, gained access to the debtors' room, and ordered the prisoners to follow him. Reflecting on the ugly mood of the crowd and being aware of the many threats that had been made against their lives, Joseph and Hyrum suspected that their hour had arrived, that this was simply a trick to get them out in the open where their enemies could make good on their threats. The strong, vigorous protest of the jailer was a signal to them that the constable's action was legally doubtful. In any case, with Bettisworth standing at the door and some of the Carthage Greys there to back him up, there was little else to do but to go along. Sizing up the situation in a glance, Joseph decided that the best thing to do was to act positively with assurance and faith. Putting on his hat, he walked energetically outside, with Hyrum close behind. With no sense of hesitation or fear, he plunged into the crowd, politely linking arms with the most vicious mobocrat in sight, and linking the other arm with Hyrum's, striding as quickly as possible to the court.

The so-called court hearing before Justice Robert Smith was a sham, incomprehensible; it just didn't make sense. Since the prisoners had no witnesses with which to contest the treason charge, the court ordered that witnesses be subpoenaed, and a hearing be set for the next day at noon. Since treason was a non-bailable charge, they were required to remain in custody until another hearing could be held on June 29, 1844. The Judge entered another Order of Commitment, and the prisoners were returned to jail, again being required to face the challenge and defiance of a boisterous, profane crowd.

That day, some of the brethren met with Governor Ford and told him that if he went to Nauvoo, Joseph and Hyrum would not be safe in Carthage. Ford promised that he would take Joseph and Hyrum with him when he left Carthage.

Safely back in jail, the prisoners and their friends had a light supper and then retired to the debtors' room where they were to spend the night—the last one for the Prophet and his brother. Sensing that his life had about run its course, Joseph spent several hours affirming, confirming, validating and testifying to his brethren the truthfulness of the things he had taught during his ministry. With the guards listening in, he bore powerful testimony of the divine authenticity of the Book of Mormon. Joseph testified of the reality of the Spirit World, and of the communications through the veil by resurrected beings. He also affirmed that the kingdom of God had been established upon the earth, and that it was for this cause and reason, and not because of any violation of law that he was and ever had been in prison.

It was late when Joseph and Hyrum retired to the only bed in the room. The others lay on the floor to rest, except Willard Richards, who stayed up to finish some of the many letters Joseph had dictated to him during the day. He remained at this task until the last dim candle flickered out; then he joined the others on the floor.

During the night, a loud gunshot was heard nearby and awakened the sleepers. Joseph arose to look around, and instead of returning to the bed, he stretched out on the floor between John Fullmer and Dan Jones. Not being able to get back to sleep, he visited in quiet tones with these loyal followers. Believing that Brother Fullmer was uncomfortable on the hard floor, he whispered: *"Lay your head on my arm for a pillow, Brother John."* He then confided in these brethren the sense, the impression and feeling that death for him was near. This reminded him of the two things that were most dear, prompting him to express the wish that he could see his family and preach to the Saints once again. After a long pause, he made his last night-time comments. To Dan Jones, the riverboat captain, he whispered, *"Are you afraid to die?"* Dan said: "Has that time come, think you? Engaged in such a cause, I do not think that death would have many terrors." Joseph replied: *"You will yet see Wales* [Jones's native land], *and fulfill the mission appointed you before you die"* (*History of the Church,* 6: 601). Elder Jones later fulfilled the prophecy, serving a great mission in Wales.

About midnight, several men surrounded the jail, and started up the stairs to the prisoners' room. One of the brethren grabbed a weapon that had been smuggled into their room during the day. Members of the mob, standing near the door, heard them moving and hesitated. "The Prophet with a 'Prophet's voice' called out: *'Come on ye assassins, we are ready for you, and would as willingly die now as at daylight.'"* The mob retreated.

The brethren were awakened from a short, uneasy sleep at 5:00 a.m. by John P. Greene and William W. Phelps, who were on their way to Nauvoo. After giving them messages for the family and the leaders there, Joseph asked Dan Jones to inquire about the reason for the shot during the night. It was the next morning of Thursday June 27, 1844, when Jones confronted Frank Worrell, an officer of the Carthage Greys who was on guard duty, he got more than he bargained for. Instead of responding to the question, Worrell warned that unless Jones left town before sundown, he would be killed along with the Smiths, and anyone else who was with them. He said that they had waited too long to get "Old Joe" in their power to let him slip away . . . and Worrell, with his bitter spirit said, 'you'll see that I can prophesy better than "Old Joe"' (*History of the Church*, 6: 602).

When the report of this conversation was communicated to the Prophet, he immediately sent Brother Jones to advise Governor Ford of what he had heard. The governor, who was preparing to leave for Nauvoo with the militia, brushed aside the report with the observation that Joseph and his friends were just excessively alarmed, and that "the people were not that cruel" (*History of the Church,* 6: 603). To dramatize his nonacceptance of any thought that the prisoners were in danger, he took all of the militia with him, including Captain Dunn and his company, assigned the Carthage Greys to guard the jail, and dismissed all the other volunteer troops.

Despite several unsuccessful attempts to do so, Dan Jones was never allowed to get back into the jail to be with the Prophet and Hyrum. From every direction, he continued to hear reports of plans for an assassination discussed openly and freely. The apostate Chauncey Higbee frankly told him that " We are determined to kill Joe and Hyrum, and you had better go away to save himself" (*History of the Church*, 6: 604).

In the meantime, inside the jail, Joseph carried on with untiring, unwavering persistence with the limited things available for him to do. That Thursday morning, June 27, 1844, the **Fateful Day,** he continued to dictate to Willard Richards, including a last letter to Emma. Showing no sign of self-pity, shame, or disgrace, the letter was designed to calm his wife's fears. He took pains to assure her that there was *"no danger of any extermination order."* Then, in a very touching postscript, he said: *"I am very much resigned to my lot, knowing I am justified, and have done the best that could be done. Give my love to the children and all my friends . . . May God bless you all"* (*History of the Church,* 6: 605).

There were many others outside the jail

besides Dan Jones who were concerned by the widespread reports of plans for an assassination. Among these was Cyrus H. Wheelock. He too, went to Governor Ford for help, and he, too, was rejected.

The role played by Governor Ford on that fateful day of June 27, 1844, would have to be considered dishonorable. A man of high position, he was nevertheless weak and vacillating, anxious to please all parties and factions. Whether by design or ignorance, his actions on that day set the stage for the perpetration of the tragic injustice. Early on the morning of the twenty-seventh, he marched the militia toward Nauvoo, his promise to Joseph was totally disregarded. Fifty men of the Carthage Greys were left to guard the prisoners at the jail. Since these men were the recognized enemies of the Prophet, it caused much alarm to his friends. Cyrus H. Wheelock overtook and appealed to the Governor on behalf of the Prophet. Once again Ford replied: "I was never in such a dilemma in my life; but your friends shall be protected, and have a fair trial by law; in this pledge, I am not alone; I have secured the pledge of the whole of the army to sustain me" (*History of the Church,* 6: 607).

Governor Ford had planned to display his military force in Nauvoo to overwhelm the inhabitants; in addition, he ordered the militia from Warsaw to join his forces at Golden Point. Then they were to disband and return to their homes. Some of them did so. Nevertheless, about 150, being disappointed at not having carried out their intention and objective to sack Nauvoo, became aroused by radical officers to a hasty and careless spirit of vengeance. These men started for Carthage, declaring death to Joseph and Hyrum. About seventy-five, disguised by blackened faces, arrived in time to join in the terrible deed of that day.

Meanwhile, back at the jail, Wheelock, feeling powerless and ineffective to the deadly forces that had been set in motion, decided to do what he could to provide at least a limited although insufficient—defense for the prisoners.

Having acquired a pass from the governor to visit the prisoners in jail, Wheelock carried a six-shooter with him, concealed in the overcoat he wore as protection against a light rain that fell in the morning. While visiting with the Prophet, he passed this gun to him, which added to a small pistol which John Fullmer had left for the brethren, which gave them two guns. It was insignificant fire-power of protection but better than nothing.

Shortly after lunch, Willard Richards became ill, and Stephen Markham was sent out to get some medication for his relief. As he was returning to the jail, he was surrounded by several members of the Carthage Greys, and forced to leave town without getting a message to the brethren. Now the number of occupants in the debtors' room of the jail was reduced to four the Prophet, Hyrum, John Taylor, and Willard Richards.

Late in the afternoon, the Prophet asked John Taylor to sing a popular hymn entitled: **"A Poor Wayfaring Man of Grief,"** about a suffering stranger who revealed himself at last as the Savior. Joseph asked John to sing the song again, which he did. This seemed to touch a melancholy chord in the Prophet's feelings.

About 4:00 p.m., the guard at the jail was changed. Only eight men were left to protect the prisoners from violence. The jailer, Stigall, noticing this, suggested to the prisoners that they *would* be safer in the cell on the lower floor. It was decided this transfer back to the criminal cells would afford them better protection and would take place following supper. Joseph said to Dr Richards: *"If we go into the cell, will you go with us?"* The doctor answered: "Brother J seph, you did not ask me to cross the river with you—you did not ask me to come to jail with you—and do you think I would forsake you now? But I will tell you what I will do; if you are condemned to be hung for treason, I will be hung in your stead, and you shall go free" (*History of the Church,* 6: 616).

A few minutes after 5:00 p.m., a mob of about 100 men with disguised and blackened faces arrived in town and headed for the jail. Soon after, as one of the guards was leaving after having brought supper to the prisoners, a loud commotion was heard outside the jail, followed by three or four shots. Glancing out the window, Elder Richards saw a sizable group of armed men circling the building, while **others forced their way through the back door and ran upstairs, firing as they came. Instantly and instinctively, the four men took possession of the weapons at hand. Joseph took the six-shooter, Hyrum the single-barrel gun, John Taylor, a cane which Elder Markham had left behind, and Elder Richards took Elder Taylor's cane.**

The Prophet and Elders Taylor and Richards leaped to the left of the door, where the two cane bearers pounded away at the guns of the attackers that were being pushed through the door. Hyrum, who had been unable to maneuver out of the way, was standing in the line of fire when the first volley of shots was discharged through the door. He was hit first by a ball on the left side of his nose, which snapped his head back violently, and sent him crashing to the floor. As he fell, he cried out in anguish: "I am a dead man." In quick succession, he was hit by three other balls, one entering his left side, the second his head, via his throat, as he lay prostrate on the floor, and the other lodging in his left leg.

When Joseph saw his brother fall, and the blood gushing from his ugly wounds, he cried out: *"Oh dear, brother Hyrum!"* Joseph then stepped to the door, reached around the door casing, and discharged his six-shooter into the crowded hall. Only three of the six chambers fired, wounding three attackers.

In the meantime, John Taylor, seeing that Elder Markham's cane was no match for the determined killers and their guns, ran to a window and attempted to jump out, but was hit by gunfire. A shot through the window from below, hit the watch in his vest pocket, stopping it at 5:16 p.m., and knocking him back into the room. He fell to the floor, and was shot again in his left wrist and below his left knee. Rolling to get under the bed, he was hit again from the stairway, the bullet tearing away his flesh at the left hip. His blood was splattered on the floor and the wall.

Joseph recognized the futility of trying to avoid and dodge the guns of the killers as did Elder Taylor. There was no safety in the room, and so he dropped his pistol to the floor and tried to jump out of the window. Instantly, the mob fired on him. He was hit by four bullet—two came from inside the room, and two from without. *"O Lord, my God!"* he cried. His body fell out of the window, landing near a well on the southeast corner of the jail. Eyewitnesses claimed that he pulled himself up against the well curb, then died. The mob on the stairs rushed outside to assure themselves that Joseph Smith was dead (*History of the Church,* 6: 617-18).

Willard Richards, a large, overweight man, alone remained virtually unharmed, having only had a bullet graze his ear. Indeed, it was a miracle. This was a literal fulfillment of a prophecy Joseph had made a year earlier. He had told his dear friend that one day he would stand while bullets whizzed around him, and would escape unharmed. Only then did Willard fully understand what Joseph had meant. Willard dragged the terribly wounded John Taylor into the next room, laid him out on the straw, and covered him with an old mattress. Elder Taylor believed that the straw saved his life by helping stop the bleeding.

Meanwhile, Willard, expecting to be killed at any moment, was awaiting his fate. And then a loud cry from somewhere, "The Mormons are coming!" saved the lives of Dr. Richards and John Taylor. Who voiced that statement is unknown, but it was entirely without foundation. **The air was charged with fear and confusion and the assassins, seemed to melt away, dispersing and scattering in every direction.** It was a great surprise and blessing when the mob took off, suddenly disappeared, leaving Elder Richards alone with his dead and wounded comrades. It was nearly midnight before he could find any help. That help became a reality when Samuel Smith, younger brother of the Prophet, heard about the death threats to his brothers, and hurried to Carthage. He arrived in Carthage that evening, physically exhausted, having been chased by the mobbers. Samuel did lend a helping hand in getting John Taylor to the Hamilton House, where his wounds were attended to, and in addition, helped to move the bodies of his martyred brothers to the Hamilton House. After a coroner's inquiry, Willard Richards wrote to the Saints in Nauvoo: **"Joseph and Hyrum are dead."**

Many mobbers headed back to their own communities, and then, fearing vengeance and retaliation from the Mormons, continued to cross the river into Missouri. Governor Ford heard about the assassinations shortly after he left Nauvoo to return to Carthage. When he arrived, he urged the few remaining citizens to evacuate the town, and had the county records moved to Quincy for safety. None of this was necessary. When the Saints heard of the deaths of their beloved leaders, they were overwhelmed with grief, rather than desire for revenge.

On the morning of June 28, 1844, the bodies of the murdered leaders were gently placed on two different wagons, covered with branches to shade them from the hot summer sun, and driven to Nauvoo by Willard Richards and Samuel Smith, with the assistance of eight other men. The wagons left Carthage about 8:00 a.m., and arrived in Nauvoo about 3:00 p.m.; about a mile east of the temple, they were met by a solemn procession of Joseph's people. **It would be impossible to describe the feelings of sorrow and indignation that struggled in their hearts . . .** the wagons were met by a large gathering of Saints a sense of great loss and solemnity prevailed. The bodies were taken to the Mansion House to be prepared for burial. At this time, Willard Richards spoke to some 8-10,000 people outside. He tried to calm their shock and sense of outraged justice. He also challenged them to the limit, when he asked **that they trust to the law to deal with murderers and assassins, and if the law failed, to "call upon God to avenge them of their rights."**

Although they had the means and the reasons to take swift vengeance, every person there voted to follow Brother Richard's counsel. This stands as a magnificent testimony of the devotion of the Latter-day Saints to abide by law and order.

When the families of the Prophet and Patriarch were allowed to view the bodies, Lucy, the mother of Joseph and Hyrum, recorded the scene that took place: "When I entered the room, and saw my murdered sons extended both at once before my eyes, and I heard the sobs and groans of my family, and the cries from the lips of their wives, children, brothers and sisters, it was too much; I sank back, crying to the Lord in the agony of my soul, 'My God, my God, why has thou forsaken this family?' A voice replied: 'I have taken them to myself, that they might have rest.'

Oh, at that moment, how my mind flew through every scene of sorrow and distress which we had passed together, in which they had shown the innocence and sympathy which filled their guileless [plain, simple and trusting] hearts. As I looked upon their peaceful, smiling countenances, I seemed almost to hear them say: 'Mother, weep not for us, for we have overcome the world by love; they slew us for our testimony, and thus placed us beyond their power; their ascendancy [influence] is for a moment; ours is an eternal triumph.'"

The bodies lay in state in open coffins in the Mansion House the following day from eight in the morning until five in the afternoon. **Thousands of people filed past the coffins to look for the last time upon the features of the men they had loved, the men who had served them so well.** The family had a last moment alone before the coffins were removed from their outer pine boxes, and taken to a locked room. The pine boxes were then filled with sandbags, and carried to the cemetery, east of the city.

William Phelps, one who had left the Church, and then returned in full fellowship, preached the funeral sermon—with "the Spirit of God like a fire" within him. Later he expressed his devotion to Joseph in poetic beauty: "Great is His glory, and endless His Priesthood, ever and ever the keys He will hold; Faithful and true He will enter His kingdom, crowned in the midst of the prophets of old."

Near the hour of midnight, the coffins containing the bodies were secretly buried in the basement of the Nauvoo House. This precaution was prompted by reports that a 1,000 dollars was being offered for the dead Prophet's head.

The night was dark, dismal, and gloomy, and the air moist and heavy. The spirit of death and desolation (despair), which the Saints had felt the night before still lingered. Many of the people who were in Nauvoo on the night of the martyrdom, observed a strange eerie spirit, which spread over the city.

"There was such a barking and howling of dogs and bellowing of cattle all over the city of Nauvoo, that I never heard before or since," Bathsheba Smith recorded: "I knelt down and tried to pray for the Prophet, but I was struck speechless, and knew not the cause till morning."

"There was an unspeakable something, an ominous significancy in the firmament," said Orson Hyde: "O, the repulsive chill! The melancholy vibrations of the very air, as the prince of darkness receded in hopeful triumph from the scene of slaughter! That night, could not the Saints sleep, though uniformed by man of what had passed with the Seer and the Patriarch; yet in them, sleep refused a visitation—the eyelids refused to close—the hearts of many sighed deeply in secret, and inquired, 'Why am I thus?'"

Chapter 14

"Vengeance is mine . . . saith the Lord"

"Joseph Lived Great, and He Died Great in the Eyes of God and his People"

Joseph Smith lived only thirty-eight and one half years

Brigham Young was Miraculously Transfigured—by the Power of the Holy Spirit , before the eyes of the people

Although it was President Young who was speaking—it was truly the voice of Joseph Smith

The Spirit and Mantle of Joseph was upon Brigham

Brigham Young was Chosen Unanimously as The President of the Quorum of the Twelve Apostles

Brigham Young renamed Nauvoo "The City of Joseph"—a name approved by the Saints

Leaving Nauvoo was an "Act of Faith" for the Saints

The first of the Saints left Nauvoo in early 1846

Brigham Young was called by God the Father to be the Prophet, Seer and Revelator in 1847

Brigham Young lead the Saints West to a New, Fulfilling Life and Religious Freedom

The Twelve Apostles were scattered across the country, but all experienced premonitions and overwhelming sadness which they could not explain. Some shed tears, not knowing the reason. Parley Pratt was on board a canal boat near Utica, New York, traveling with his brother. He recorded the experience he had in the afternoon of June 27, 1844. This happened to be very near to "the same hour that the Carthage mob were shedding the blood of Joseph and Hyrum Smith."

"As we conversed on the deck, a strange and solemn awe came over me, as if the powers of hell were let loose. I was so overwhelmed with sorrow, I could hardly speak; and after pacing the deck for some time in silence, I turned to William and exclaimed: 'Brother William, this is a dark hour; the powers of darkness seem in triumph, and the spirit of murder is abroad in the land. Let us observe an entire and solemn silence, for this is a dark day, and an hour of triumph for the powers of darkness.'"

Elders Heber C. Kimball and Lyman Wight were traveling between Philadelphia and New York City when Elder Kimball felt mournful, as if he had just lost a close friend. In Boston, Orson Hyde was examining maps in the hall rented by the Church, when he felt a heavy and sorrowful spirit come upon him. Tears ran down his cheeks, as he turned from the maps, and paced the floor. In Michigan, George A. Smith was tormented with a depressed spirit and discouraging thoughts all day long. When he retired to bed, he could not sleep. He said that: "Once it seemed to him that some fiend whispered in his ear, `Joseph and Hyrum are dead; ain't you glad of it?'" (*History of the Church,* 7: 133).

Back in Nauvoo, a warm, steady rain began to fall, sighing over the river, soaking the land and erasing all traces of the secret burial. The bodies of Joseph and Hyrum were safe and at rest. The men themselves, were now forever beyond the powers of darkness.

"I could do so much more for my friends, if I were on the other side of the veil," the Prophet had confided to friends near the end of his life. He had told Benjamin Johnson: *"I would not be far from you, and if on the other side, I would still be working with you, and with a power greatly increased to roll on this kingdom."*

Where was the rage, the hate, and the storm? Where was the violence and vengeance? There was none because Mormons don't live by the worldly law of, "an eye for an eye, and a tooth for a tooth." No vengeance was the counsel from Church leaders. The whole city of Nauvoo, on hearing of the tragedy, were like sheep without a shepherd. They were stunned at that which had befallen them. Their beloved Prophet and Patriarch were dead . . . **A Prophet of God had fulfilled his mission here on the earth. Was the loss of Joseph the end of the Mormons? Was this the end of The Church of Jesus Christ of Latter-day Saints?**

Elder John Taylor, who miraculously survived the Carthage murders, wrote an account of the event, and a eulogy to the Prophet, now found in the Doctrine and Covenants scriptures 135: ***"Joseph Smith, the Prophet and Seer of the Lord, has done more, save Jesus only, for the salvation of men in this world, than any other man that ever lived in it."*** He added that the names of Joseph and Hyrum Smith ***"will be classed among the martyrs of religion; and the reader in every nation, will be reminded that the Book of Mormon, and this book of Doctrine and Covenants of the church, cost the best blood of the nineteenth century, to bring forth for the salvation of a ruined world"*** (Doctrine & Covenants 135: 3, 6).

"The martyrdom," he said, fulfilled

an important spiritual purpose: Joseph *"lived great, and he died great in the eyes of God and his people; and like most of the Lord's anointed in ancient times, has sealed his mission and his works with his own blood; and so has his brother Hyrum. In life, they were not divided, and in death, they were not separated!"* (*History of the Church,* 6: 630).

While Joseph Smith lived only thirty-eight and a half years, his accomplishments in the service of mankind are incalculable. In addition to translating the Book of Mormon, he received hundreds of revelations, many of which are published in the Doctrine and Covenants and the Pearl of Great Price. He unfolded eternal principles in a legacy of letters, sermons, poetry, and other inspired writings that fill volumes. He established the Restored Church of Jesus Christ on the earth, founded a city, and superintended the building of two temples. He introduced vicarious ordinance work for the dead and restored temple ordinances by which worthy families could be sealed (united) by the Holy Priesthood for eternity. He ran for the Presidency of the United States, served as a Judge, Mayor of Nauvoo, and Lieutenant General of the Nauvoo Legion. He was called by God as a Prophet in the Seventh and Last Dispensation of the Fulness of Times, and fulfilled his assignment with great zeal, passion, fervor, and devoutness.

Josiah Quincy, a prominent New England citizen who later became the Mayor of Boston, visited Joseph Smith two months before the martyrdom. Many years later, he wrote about the people who had most impressed him during his life. Regarding Joseph Smith, he wrote, "It is by no means improbable that some future textbook, for the use of generations yet unborn, will contain a question something like this: What historical American of the nineteenth century has exerted the most powerful influence upon the destinies of his countrymen? And it is by no means impossible that the answer to that interrogatory may be thus written Joseph Smith, the Mormon Prophet."

From the lips of the Prophet Joseph Smith just two months before his death . . .

"I love you all. I am your best friend, and if persons miss their mark, it is their own fault. You never knew my heart; no man knows my history; I cannot tell it. I shall never undertake it. If I had not experienced what I have, I should not have believed it myself. I never did harm to any man since I have been born into the world. My voice is always for peace; I cannot lie down until my work is finished; I never think any evil nor do anything to the harm of my fellow man. When I am called at the trump of the archangel and weighed in the balance, you will all know me then" (Joseph Smith, in a talk—two months before his death, June 27,1844).

And now, with the death of the Prophet Joseph Smith, the First Presidency of the Church was dissolved. While lamenting and grieving for their slain leader, the Saints were wondering who would now lead the Church. Sidney Rigdon, who had left Nauvoo earlier in 1844, reappeared in the city on August third, and asserted that he should be appointed guardian of the Church. In the absence of most of the Twelve Apostles, who were still en route back to Nauvoo from their Eastern missions, Sidney made some inroads with his claim. A meeting was called for August eighth, to consider his guardianship.

When Joseph Smith was assassinated, a deep gloom had covered the City of Nauvoo. As the Saints in other branches of the Church learned of the martyrdom, they felt great anguish and grieved also. Only the arrival of the Quorum of the Twelve and the firm direction they gave the Church, turned away this depressive spirit.

The Twelve, except for John Taylor and Willard Richards, were in the East serving missions at the time of the martyrdom. Within three weeks, however, everyone had learned about the tragic and deplorable news and had hurried back to Nauvoo.

One of the greatest achievements in Nauvoo between the assassinations and the return of the apostles, was the maintenance of peace. Although the citizens in Western Illinois feared reprisals, the Saints obeyed John Taylor and Willard Richards, who instructed them to remain calm and allow the government officials to find the murderers. Three days after the Carthage disaster, Elder Richards wrote to Brigham Young: "The Saints have borne this trial with great fortitude and forbearance. They must keep cool at present. We have pledged our faith not to prosecute the murderers at present, but leave it to Governor Ford; . . . vengeance is in the heavens" (*History of the Church,* 7: 148). The City Council also instructed the residents: "Be peaceable, quiet citizens, doing the works of righteousness, and as soon as the Twelve and other authorities can assemble, or a majority of them, the onward course to the great gathering of Israel, and the final consummation of the dispensation of the fulness of times will be pointed out" (*History of the Church,* 7: 152).

Elder John Taylor, who had been seriously wounded in the Carthage Jail, returned to Nauvoo on July second. Throughout the month, he steadily improved, but remained confined to his bed. In spite of his disability, he helped Elder Richards direct the Church until the return of the Twelve. Together, Elder Richards and Elder Taylor wrote to the many Saints in Great Britain and explained:

"The action of the Saints has been of the most pacific kind, remembering that God has said: 'Vengeance is mine, I will repay'. . . These servants of God have gone to heaven by fire—the fire of an ungodly mob. Like the Prophets of ancient days, they lived as long as the world would receive them; and this is one furnace in which the saints were to be tried, to have their leaders cut off from their midst, and not be permitted to avenge their blood" (*History of the Church,* 7: 173).

Church publisher, City Councilman, and scribe to the Prophet, William W. Phelps helped immeasurably in keeping order in the city. Since his return to the Church in 1842, Elder Phelps had persistently sought to build up the kingdom and had helped the Prophet with a number of important projects, such as the publishing of the Book of Abraham, and the campaign for the presidency. Now, he helped Elders Taylor and Richards during this critical interim period. As a poet, he memorialized the Prophet in the lines which later became a favorite Church hymn:

Praise to the man who
communed with Jehovah!
Jesus anointed that Prophet and Seer.
Blessed to open the last dispensation,
Kings shall extol him, and nations revere.
Hail to the Prophet, ascended to heaven!
Traitors and tyrants now fight him in vain.
Mingling with Gods, he can plan
for his brethren;
Death cannot conquer the hero again.
("Praise to the Man," Hymns, 1985, p. 27).

Within a month, as previously mentioned, the Saints suffered another great tragedy: the death of Samuel H. Smith, younger brother to Joseph and Hyrum. Samuel was one of the first Saints on the scene at Carthage following the martyrdom. He had fled from the enemies of the Church to reach his brothers in Carthage only to find them already dead. The stress weakened him physically. Shortly thereafter, he contracted a serious fever; his health gradually failed, and he died on July 30, 1844. He was praised and glorified in the *Times and Seasons* as one of the great men of this dispensation. His grief-stricken mother, Lucy Mack Smith, had seen within four years, the death of her husband and four of her sons: Don Carlos, Hyrum, Joseph and Samuel.

Parley P. Pratt was the first Apostle outside of Nauvoo to learn of the assassinations. He was on a steamboat headed across the Great Lakes toward Chicago. At a landing in Wisconsin, boarding passengers brought news of the Carthage murders. There was great commotion and excitement on board, and many passengers taunted him, asking what the Mormons would do now. His answer was simple and to the point, "they would continue their mission and spread the work that he [Joseph Smith] had restored in all the world. Observing and remarking that nearly all the churches and apostles, who were before him had been killed, and also the Savior of the world, yet their deaths did not alter the truth nor hinder its final triumph" (Pratt, *Autobiography of Parley P. Pratt,* p. 292).

In sorrow, Elder Pratt walked 105 miles across the plains of Illinois, hardly able to eat or sleep, wondering how he should meet the entire community controlled by grief and inexpressible sorrow. He prayed for assistance, and the Spirit of God came upon him, filling his heart with joy and gladness without description, and the Spirit of Revelation glowed in his heart with as visible a warmth and gladness as if it were fire. The Spirit said unto him: "Go and say unto your people in Nauvoo, that they should continue to pursue their daily duties, and take care of themselves, and make no movement in Church government to reorganize or alter anything until the return of the remainder of the Quorum of the Twelve. They were instructed to continue to build the House of the Lord, which they are commanded to build in Nauvoo."

Arriving in Nauvoo on July eighth, Parley helped Elders Richards and Taylor keep order in the unnerved, shaken, and stricken community.

George A. Smith learned of the martyrdom from a newspaper account in Michigan on July thirteenth. At first he thought it was a hoax, but when the report was confirmed, he hurried home with his three missionary companions. Worn out with anxiety and loss of sleep, he came down with hives. His whole body was swollen and he was unable to eat, but he continued his journey, arriving in Nauvoo on July twenty-seventh. Soon he was meeting in council with the three Apostles already there.

In Boston, rumors of Joseph Smith's death began on July ninth. During the week, before confirmation came from family letters and more complete newspaper accounts, Brigham Young, Wilford Woodruff, and Orson Pratt struggled within themselves about what the terrible news meant. Brigham recorded in his journal: *"The first thing which I thought of was, whether Joseph had taken the keys of the kingdom with him from the earth; brother Orson Pratt sat on my left; we were both leaning back on our chairs. Bringing my hand down on my knee, I said the keys of the kingdom are right here with the Church."*

Brigham Young, Heber C. Kimball, Orson Pratt, Wilford Woodruff, and Lyman Wight contacted each other, joined together, and hurried home by railway, stagecoach, boat, and buggy. Subsequent events proved the wisdom of their haste. They arrived in Nauvoo the evening of August sixth. Wilford Woodruff recorded his feelings: "When we landed in the city, there was a deep gloom that seemed to rest over the City of Nauvoo, which we never experienced before. We were received with gladness by the Saints throughout the city. They felt like sheep without a shepherd, as being without a father, as their head had been taken away."

The arrival of most of the Apostles on August 6, 1844, was none too soon. A crisis had arisen as to who should lead the Church, and Willard Richards had nearly worn himself out trying to keep the Saints united. On Saturday, August 3, 1844, Sidney Rigdon had returned from his self-imposed exile in Pittsburgh, Pennsylvania, where he had moved contrary to revelation (Doctrine & Covenants 124: 108-9). Sidney returned with the expectation of taking over the Church. Not all of the Saints in Nauvoo realized that the Prophet had lost confidence in his first counselor quite a while before the martyrdom.

Sidney avoided meeting with the four Apostles who were already in Nauvoo, choosing instead to speak to the assembled Saints at the grove on Sunday, August fourth. He claimed that he had received a vision: "He related a vision which he said the Lord had shown him concerning the situation of the church, and said there must be a guardian appointed to build the church up to Joseph, as he had begun it." He said: "he was the identical man that the ancient prophets had sung about, wrote and rejoiced over, and that he was sent to do the identical work that had been the theme of all the prophets in every preceding generation" (*History of the Church,* 7: 224).

Elder Parley P. Pratt later remarked that Sidney Rigdon was "the identical man the prophets *never* sang nor wrote a word about" (*History of the Church,* 7: 225). At the meeting, Sidney asked William Marks, Nauvoo Stake President, who sympathized with Sidney's claims, to call a meeting of the Church on August sixth, to sustain a new leader. President Marks changed the meeting to Thursday, August eighth, which proved to be providential since the remainder of the Twelve did not arrive until the evening of August sixth.

Sidney also met with William Marks and Emma Smith in Joseph Smith's home, in order to appoint a trustee-in-trust for the Church. Emma wanted this done quickly to prevent loss of personal and Church property that was in Joseph Smith's name. Parley P. Pratt came into the meeting and immediately protested the move. He explained that appointing a trustee-in-trust was the business of the entire Church through its General Authorities, not the business of the local authorities of any one stake. Parley insisted that: "dollars and cents were no consideration with me, when principle was at stake, and if thousands or even millions were lost, let them go. We could not and would not permit the Authorities and principles of the Church to be trampled under foot, for the sake of any monetary interest." The meeting broke up without any decision being made.

On Monday, August fifth, Sidney Rigdon finally met with the Apostles who were in Nauvoo. He declared: "Gentlemen, you're used up; gentlemen, you are all divided; the anti-Mormons have got you; the brethren are voting every way . . . everything is in confusion, you can do nothing, you lack a great leader, you want a head, and unless you unite upon that head, you are blown to the four winds, the anti-Mormons will carry the election—a guardian must be appointed."

Elder George A. Smith said: "Brethren, Elder Rigdon is entirely mistaken, there is no division; the brethren are united; the election will be unanimous, and the friends of law and order will be elected by a thousand majority. There is no occasion to be alarmed. President Rigdon is inspiring fears there are no grounds for" (*History of the Church,* 7: 226).

Under such circumstances, the arrival of the Twelve from the East on the evening of August sixth, was timely. They met the next morning in the home of John Taylor, and rejoiced to be together again "and to be welcomed by the Saints who considered it very fortunate and opportune for the Twelve to arrive at this particular moment, when their minds were distressed, their hearts sorrowful, and darkness seemed to cloud their path." Brigham Young took firm control of the meeting. After a discussion of all that had transpired, he announced that there would be another meeting at 4:00 p.m., to be attended by the Apostles, the Nauvoo High Council, and High Priests, to discuss Sidney's claims made to the Saints the previous Sunday.

At the meeting, Sidney Rigdon was invited to make a statement about his vision and revelations. He said: "The object of my mission is to visit the saints and offer myself to them as a guardian. I had a vision at Pittsburgh, June 27th [the day of the martyrdom]. This was presented to my mind, not as an open vision, but rather a continuation of the vision mentioned in the *Book of Doctrine and Covenants,*" which was referring to the vision he and Joseph Smith had experienced, that is recorded in Doctrine and Covenants seventy-six (*History of the Church,* 7: 229). He went on to say that no one could take the place of Joseph as the head of the Church, and that he, as the designated spokesman for the Prophet, should assume the role of guardian of the Church. Wilford Woodruff recorded in his journal, that Sidney's statement was a "long story—it was a kind of second class vision."

Following Sidney's remarks: **Brigham Young spoke: *"I do not care who leads the church . . . but one thing I must know, and that is what God says about it. I have the keys, and the means of obtaining the mind of God on the subject . . .*** *Joseph conferred upon our heads, all the keys and powers belonging to the Apostleship which he himself held before he was taken away, and no man or set of men can get between Joseph and the Twelve in this world, or in the world to come. How often has Joseph said to the Twelve, 'I have laid the foundation, and you must build thereon, for upon your shoulders the kingdom rests'"* (*History of the Church,* 7: 230).

President Young then designated Tuesday, August thirteenth as a special conference day, in which the people would be organized in a Solemn Assembly, to vote on the matter. The next morning, however, the Twelve Apostles met privately and, "in consequence of some excitement among the people, and a disposition by some spirits to try to divide the Church," decided to hold the Solemn Assembly that afternoon rather than wait until the following Tuesday.

One of the most important days in the history of the Restoration was Thursday, August 8, 1844. On that memorable day, a miracle occurred before the body of the Church—Brigham Young was magnified (glorified, acclaimed by the Spirit) before the people, and the succession crisis of the Church was determined and resolved. A prayer meeting was held that morning at ten o'clock in the grove, according to the arrangements of William Marks. Sidney Rigdon spoke for an hour and a half about his desires to be the *guardian* of the Church, but he did not awaken any emotion, and said nothing that would mark him as a true leader. Brigham Young, who arrived after the meeting had started, also spoke; his remarks were short and to the point. He told the audience that he would rather had spent a month mourning the dead Prophet, than so quickly attend to the business of appointing a new shepherd. While he was speaking, he was miraculously transfigured (changed, transformed) by the power of the Holy Spirit before the eyes of the people.

People of all ages were present, and they later recorded their experiences. Ben-

jamin F. Johnson, twenty-six years of age, remembered: "As soon as he [Brigham Young] spoke, I jumped upon my feet, for in every possible degree, it was Joseph's voice, and his person, in look, attitude, dress and appearance was Joseph himself, personified; and **I knew in a moment, that the spirit and mantle of Joseph was upon him." Zina Huntington,** who was a young woman, twenty-one years old at that time, said, "that although **it was President Young who was speaking, it was truly the voice of Joseph Smith**—not that of Brigham Young. His very person was changed. I closed my eyes, and I could have cried out, I know that it was Joseph Smith's voice! Yet, I know he was gone. Nevertheless, the same spirit was with the people."

George Q. Cannon, then a boy of fifteen, declared that: "it was the voice of Joseph himself; and **not only was it the voice of Joseph which we heard; but it seemed in the eyes of the people as though it was the very person of Joseph which stood before them.** They saw and heard with their natural eyes and ears, and then the words which were uttered came, accompanied by the convincing power of God to their hearts, and they were filled with the Spirit and with great joy" ("Joseph Smith the Prophet," *Juvenile Instructor,* 29 Oct. 1870, pp. 174-75).

Wilford Woodruff testified: "If I had not seen him with my own eyes, there is no one that could have convinced me that it was not Joseph Smith speaking."

Reflecting upon these statements, **Brigham Young's own record of the events** that day is especially meaningful: *"My heart was swollen with compassion towards them, and by the power of the Holy Ghost, even the spirit of the Prophets, I was enabled to comfort the hearts of the Saints."* The meeting was then dismissed until 2 o'clock in the afternoon.

At 2:00 p.m., thousands of Saints gathered for what they knew would be a significant meeting. With the Quorums of Priesthood seated in order, Brigham Young spoke frankly about the proposed guardianship of Sidney Rigdon and his alienation from Joseph Smith during the previous two years. He boldly prophesied: *"All that want to draw away a party from the church after them, let them do it if they can, but they will not prosper"* (*History of the Church,* 7: 232).

President Young continued, and then turning to his main point declared: *"If the people want President Rigdon to lead them, they may have him; but* ***I say unto you that the Quorum of the Twelve have the keys of the kingdom of God in all the world.***

"The Twelve are appointed by the finger of God. Here is Brigham, have his knees ever faltered? Have his lips ever quivered? Here is Heber and the rest of the Twelve, an independent body who have the keys of the priesthood—the keys of the kingdom of God, to deliver to all the world: this is true, so help me God. They stand next to Joseph, and are as the First Presidency of the Church" (*History of the Church,* 7: 233).

He pointed out that Sidney could not be above the Twelve because they would have to ordain him to be President of the Church. Brigham urged everybody to see Brother Rigdon as a friend and stated that if he were to sit in cooperation and counsel with the Twelve, they would be able to act as one. Following President Young's two hour speech, talks were delivered by Amasa Lyman, William W. Phelps, and Parley P. Pratt; each eloquently contending for the authority of the Twelve.

Brigham Young then arose, and asked the basic question: *"Do you want Brother Rigdon to stand forward as your leader, your guide, your spokesman. President Rigdon wants me to bring up the other question first, and that is, Does the church want, and is it their only desire to sustain the Twelve as the First Presidency of this people?"* Brigham then asked: *"If there are any of the contrary mind, every man and every woman who does not want the Twelve to preside, lift up your hands in like manner."* No hands went up (*History of the Church,* 7: 240).

Convinced and assured by the heavenly manifestation, the evidence in which the Lord had transfigured Brigham Young, the Saints voted unanimously to accept him and the Twelve as their leaders. **The Apostles, who were chosen of the Lord to lead the Saints, were now accepted by the vote of the people.** As the Saints returned to their homes that day, their minds were at ease and rest.

Before concluding the conference, President Young called for the members' approval on the following issues: tithing the members to complete the temple, allowing the Twelve to preach to all the world, financing of the Church, teaching Bishops in handling the business affairs of the Church, appointing a patriarch to the Church to replace Hyrum Smith, and sustaining Sidney Rigdon with faith and prayers. The conference was then adjourned. Once more, the Church had a Presidency—the Church had brought together their combined leadership—the Quorum of the Twelve Apostles—with Brigham Young as their President.

As in the times of the **Lord Jesus Christ, the Twelve Apostles were chosen by the Lord** from among the people, with the approval of Heavenly Father, to teach, preach and advise through the Gospel of Jesus Christ, to every nation, kindred, tongue and people, Jesus Christ being the Messiah, Savior, Redeemer, and God of this earth.

* * *

I have a firm testimony that The Church of Jesus Christ of Latter-day Saints is the Restored Church of Jesus Christ on the earth in these latter days, beginning with Joseph Smith, called by God and Jesus Christ to be the Prophet of the Seventh and Last Dispensation of the Fulness of Times. Did the death of Joseph Smith destroy the Restored Church? Was the Restored Church really the church of Joseph Smith? A gigantic **absolutely not**. The Restored Gospel, The Church of Jesus Christ of Latter-day Saints, the **true** Restored Gospel, is not, nor will it ever be, controlled by one person, acting individually and personally as a worldly titled or religious leader. The Lord's Church on earth is under the direction of a Prophet of God, a Prophet chosen for all the world, chosen by God and Jesus Christ, along with Twelve Apostles, to help spread the **true** Gospel of Jesus Christ throughout the world.

* * *

In the case of the martyrdom of Joseph Smith, Joseph had been chosen as a Prophet of God, and with his death, the responsibility for the running of the Church clearly did abide in the hands of the President and Quorum of the Twelve Apostles, all of whom held the Holy Melchizedek Priesthood.

Brigham Young was chosen unanimously by the membership of the Church as the President of the Quorum of the Twelve Apostles. When the Lord requires a new Prophet He will choose one, and more than likely, Brigham Young will become the next Prophet.

For several years, the Lord had carefully prepared the Quorum of the Twelve to assume the leadership of the Church. When the Twelve were first called in 1835, their duties were restricted to areas outside the organized stakes. But in time, their responsibilities were expanded and increased to include authority over the members of the Church. Thomas B. Marsh, David W. Patten, and Brigham Young were called to lead the Stake in Far West in 1838. And while Joseph and Hyrum were being held in Liberty Jail in Missouri, Brigham Young, Heber C. Kimball, and John Taylor of the Twelve, directed the exodus of the Saints from Missouri to Illinois.

The mission of the Twelve to Great Britain, was brought together by the Spirit as a united Quorum, under the direction of Brigham Young. When they returned to America, the Prophet Joseph increased the responsibilities of the Twelve in both temporal and ecclesiastical affairs. They were involved in raising funds for the Nauvoo House and the temple, as well as constructing them, helping the poor, managing land, and directing the settlement of new immigrants into Illinois. They participated in decisions affecting Nauvoo business and economic development. The Twelve were among the first to receive instruction from the Prophet Joseph Smith on plural marriage and the temple ordinances. Members of the Twelve were given the responsibility over Church publishing, directed the calling, assigning, and instructing of missionaries, presiding over conferences both in the field and in Nauvoo, and they regulating the branches abroad.

Most importantly, Joseph Smith, feeling that he might soon die, took great care during the last seven months of his life to carefully prepare the Twelve. He met with the Quorum almost every day they were in Nauvoo to instruct them, and give them additional responsibilities. In an extraordinary council meeting in late March 1844, he solemnly told the Twelve that he could now leave them because his work was done, and the foundation was laid so that the kingdom of God could be uplifted and nurtured.

Wilford Woodruff later recalled those days of 1844: "I am a living witness to the testimony that he [Joseph Smith] gave to the Twelve Apostles, when all of us received our endowments from under his hands. I remember the last speech that he ever gave us before his death. It was before we started upon our mission to the East. He stood upon his feet some three hours. The room was filled as with consuming fire, his face was as clear as amber, and he was clothed upon by the power of God. He laid before us our duty. He laid before us the fulness of this great work of God; and in his remarks to us he said: *'I have had sealed upon my head, every key, every power, every principle of life and salvation that God has ever given to any man who ever lived upon the face of the earth. And these principles and this Priesthood and power, belong to this great and last dispensation, which the God of Heaven has set His hand to establish in the earth. 'Now,'* said he, addressing the Twelve, *'I have sealed upon your heads, every key, every power, and every principle which the Lord has sealed upon my head.'*

"After addressing us in this manner he said: *'I tell you, the burden of this kingdom now rests upon your shoulders; you have got to bear it off in all the world, and if you don't, you will be damned.'"* On this same occasion, Joseph conferred the keys of the sealing power on Brigham Young, President of the Twelve. Brigham later explained that: *"this last key of the Priesthood is the most sacred of all, and pertains exclusively to the First Presidency of the Church"* ("Parley P. Pratt's Proclamation," *Millenial Star*, Mar. 1845, p. 151).

* * *

The adversary, (Satan) will do anything and everything to destroy the Lord's Church, and he continues trying, never letting up, always pushing his evil agenda, then and now!

* * *

Even as the Twelve began to firmly exercise their authority, Sidney Rigdon and James J. Strang, a new convert to the Church, worked behind the scenes trying to seize and assume the leadership of the Church. Rigdon, an embittered man, claimed his authority was superior to that of the Twelve, and being unwilling to submit to their counsel, was excommunicated on September 8, 1844. He returned to Pittsburgh, and the following spring organized a "Church of Christ" with apostles, prophets, priests and kings. This attracted a few people, those who opposed the Twelve and felt that Joseph Smith had been a fallen prophet. He published a small newspaper there proclaiming his personal views against the Lord's Church. By 1847, this small organization completely fell apart, disintegrated. Rigdon nevertheless, hung on to a handful of followers for another thirty years as the self-appointed "president of the kingdom and the church." He finally died in obscurity in the State of New York in 1876. He, like others who had been close to the Prophet Joseph Smith, was jealous because he did not get the authority he desired, and allowed these feelings to drive him out of the Church.

James J. Strang seemed to be a more creative and imaginative leader. Following his baptism by Joseph Smith four months before the martyrdom, he returned to his home in Wisconsin. In August 1844, he presented a letter that he claimed had been written by Joseph Smith, appointing himself as the Prophet's successor and designating Voree, Wisconsin, as the new gathering place. Brigham Young and the Twelve correctly branded the letter a forgery and excommunicated Strang. He nevertheless convinced some to follow him to Voree, eventually winning over three former members of the Twelve, who had lost their standing in the Church—William E. McLellin, John E. Page, and William Smith. For a time, he also had the support of William Marks and Martin Harris. His church had some missionary success in the East. In 1848, he located his colony on Beaver Island in Lake Michigan, and had himself crowned "king of the kingdom." The group eventually ran into numerous economic difficulties, and in 1856, Strang was murdered by disaffected followers, and the movement virtually collapsed.

Some of Joseph Smith's own family did not follow the Twelve. The Prophet's widow, Emma, did not become submissive or resign herself to the Twelve on economic and theological matters. Regardless of the calling of Brigham Young and the Twelve by the Lord, and with the approval of the members by vote, Emma stayed in Nauvoo and influenced her children against following the direction of the Twelve to go West with the body of the Saints.

Yet Lucy Mack Smith, the Prophet's mother said of Emma: "I have never seen a woman in my life, who could endure every species of fatigue and hardship, from month to month, and from year to year, with that unflinching courage, zeal, and patience, which she has ever done; for I know that which she has had to endure; she has been tossed upon the ocean of uncertainty; she has breasted the storms of persecution, and buffeted the rage of men and devils, which would have borne down almost any other woman. Only five of Emma's eleven [two adopted] lived beyond childhood."

Although Emma had a pretty fair size testimony, considering all that she had endured in her life with Joseph as Prophet of God, the loss by death of several of her children, and other theological matters in which she did not always agree with Joseph or the Lord, she had a great love and devotion for her husband, her children and her family. She stood at Joseph's side, being the *elect lady* of the Church, although the Church was an important part of her life, it was not until after Joseph's assassination that her testimony began to wane especially with the changing of the guard, certainly there was a good deal of confusion in everyone's life during this spiritual and emotional period of time.

Emma's testimony seemed to be totally centered around a Smith running the Church. Of course, this was not the Lord's way. **This was not the Church of Joseph Smith.** Since The Church of Jesus Christ of Latter-day Saints is the Lord's true Church, the leader of the Church is chosen by the Lord, not by any person or group, nor the passing on down by heritage or heir. Emma decided to remain in Nauvoo, deciding not to travel West under the direction of Brigham Young, and the Twelve—as chosen by the Lord.

When William Smith belatedly returned to Nauvoo from the East, he was ordained Church Patriarch to replace Hyrum. After a few months, he advanced his own claims and personal agenda to be the Church leader. He was consequently excommunicated. Following a short association with Strang, William taught that Joseph Smith's eldest son should, by right of lineage, inherit the presidency, and that he, William, was to be guardian and president pro tem until Joseph III was of age.

Of course, there were some others who refused to follow the leadership of Brigham Young and the Twelve. A few members were alienated over the concept of plural marriage; some isolated branches did not go West, and became confused as to what course they should take.

* * *

During the 1850s, a new organization gradually emerged. In 1860, leaders of the new organization (among them William Marks) formed the Reorganized Church of Jesus Christ of Latter-day Saints, and succeeded in naming Joseph Smith III to be its president. And from then on until 1996, a Smith descendant has been president of the Reorganized Church. Independence, Missouri has been the headquarters of the Reorganized Church for many years.

Aside from the changes in the teachings of the Gospel, the Book of Mormon, Joseph Smith and other theological changes made by the Reorganized Church there is "no longer any Smith heritage or lineage," coming from the Reorganized Church since the last Smith resigned from the that church in 1996, and a new president was chosen by the hierarchy of that church. I might add to the following at this time, that the Reorganized Church is allowing women to become ministers in their new approach to a living church in modern times. This too, is not in keeping with the Lord's true Church.

* * *

The apostolic succession in 1844 established the principles and set the pattern for future reorganizations of the Presidency of the Church. Following the death of each: President, the keys of the kingdom, which have been conferred upon each Apostle at his ordination, reside with the Quorum of the Twelve as a body (Doctrine & Covenants 107: 23-24, 112: 15).

Elder Spencer W. Kimball, in a general conference address in 1970, explained the process: "The moment life passes from a President of the Church, a body of men become the composite leader—these men already seasoned with experience and training. The appointments, have long been made, the authority given, the keys delivered . . . the kingdom moves forward under this already authorized council. No 'running' for position, no electioneering, no stump speeches. What a divine plan! How wise our Lord, to organize so perfectly beyond the weakness of frail, grasping humans" (Conference Report, April 1970, p. 118).

The Lord controls succession in His Church. President Ezra Taft Benson explained, "God knows all things, the end from the beginning, and no man becomes President of The Church of Jesus Christ by accident, nor remains there by chance, nor is called by happenstance" (*Ezra Taft Benson,* in Korean Area Conference, 1975, p.52).

The State of Illinois was shocked and appalled over the tragedy at Carthage. Governor Ford expressed his determination to bring the murderers of Joseph and Hyrum to trial. The honest, respectable citizens of the State felt that some steps should be taken to punish the men who killed the brothers. This sentiment grew until about four months after the shootings, when a grand jury was organized to study the crime.

The nine men accused of the murders had fled to Missouri, but finally returned. A trial was ordered in October, but it was postponed until May of the following year because state officials did not have the heart to carry on. Governor Ford himself was partly responsible for what had happened. He had broken his word to the Prophet Joseph, and had withheld protection from the brethren. When the murders were committed, he ran into hiding like a frightened animal, to save his own neck.

The trial turned out to be little more than a farce. The attitude of the people in that part of the state was so bitter that there was no sincere attempt to obtain justice. The evidence presented at the trial was not relevant, and though the men themselves were guilty, and many more like them, the judge gave instructions to the jury to declare the accused men "not guilty." This was done, and the men were set free. No action was taken after that to punish the murderers. The mob was pleased with the verdict, and this trial encouraged them. They felt that they could persecute the Saints still further and not be punished. Soon, it became open season on the Saints once again.

When the verdict reached Nauvoo, the City Council voted to refer the case to God for a righteous judgement, and leave the matter in His hands.

With the question and subject of succession settled, the Quorum of the Twelve Apostles began immediately to exercise its authority in leading the Church. In the *Times and Seasons* of August 15, 1844, they unhesitatingly assured the Saints that as a body and a team for the Lord, they were prepared to preside and administer over the Church, and to advance and promote its growth. They also reaffirmed and reiterated the importance of gathering to Nauvoo and finishing the temple. They were equally eager and desirous to continue in the footsteps of the Prophet Joseph Smith in sending the Gospel "forth through every neighborhood of this wide-spread country, and to all the world" ("An Epistle of the Twelve," *Times and Seasons,* 15 Aug. 1844, p. 619). Despite their optimism, new challenges, pressures, and difficulties lay ahead, which would threaten the existence of Nauvoo and would test their ability and courage as religious leaders.

The Twelve met in council the day after they were sustained as the Presiding Authority of the Church. In that meeting, and in several others in succeeding weeks, they began to set in order the organization and affairs of the Church. The Church organization in the United States and Canada was expanded.

The Twelve also continued to weed out and excommunicate apostate elements of the Church. Brigham Young recalled a dream where he saw a fruit tree with dead branches at the top, which had to be pruned away so that the tree could flourish. He urged: *"Let us cut off the dead branches of the church that good fruit may grow, and a voice will soon be heard, go and build up Zion and the Temple of the Lord"* (*History of the Church,* 7: 260).

In 1844, Nauvoo was one of the most flourishing cities in Illinois. By perseverance, industry, and unity, the Saints had replaced the swamps with a thriving community in only five years. It was remarkable program, and what an accomplishment! Here was a people who had been stripped of all their earthly possessions—money, homes, factories, and lands—who, in five short years, built and peopled a city-state which was the envy of many long-settled communities.

Two thousand years ago, Jesus of Nazareth said: *"seek ye first the kingdom of God, and his righteousness; and all these things shall be added unto you"* (Matthew 6: 33). These people proved it.

Advantageously and conveniently situated on the Mississippi River, Nauvoo promised to become a great commercial center. Nevertheless many citizens in the surrounding communities, feared the Latter-day Saints and their religion, and were determined to frustrate and hinder the growth and development of Nauvoo.

Some Illinois residents were particularly unhappy with what they considered to be special privileges given Nauvoo by its charter, and they called for its repeal and for the disbandment of the Nauvoo Legion. When the legislature convened in January 1845, these demands were accepted, and the Nauvoo Charter was revoked. The damage to the reputation of the Mormons, however, was already done, and with the repeal of the Nauvoo Charter, the Saints were without a legal government or the protection of their own militia. The brethren decided to continue the Legion on an extralegal basis as an instrument of internal control, and as a means of defense.

Brigham Young renamed Nauvoo: *The City of Joseph,* a name approved by the Saints at the April General Conference. Although part of Nauvoo was reincorporated as an official town by the legislature, there was still a need for additional protective measures. The city was kept relatively free of unwanted characters by an organized group of young men and boys known as the "whistling and whittling brigade." They followed unwanted visitors, whistling and whittling until the irritated and frightened persons left town.

In spite of the challenges, Nauvoo continued to grow. The building industry particularly flourished and outdistanced all other trades in Nauvoo. New frame and brick homes, gardens, and farms were established. Many earlier settlers to Nauvoo built new homes, since their original shelters were often hastily constructed log or frame huts. Heber C. Kimball and Willard Richards replaced their log homes with handsome two-story brick houses in 1845. The Church also constructed a home for Lucy Mack Smith during this period. Public construction projects, such as the Seventies Hall and Concert Hall, complemented the residential building boom. A stone dike, or wing dam in the Mississippi River, intended as a source of water power for workshops and machinery, was also begun. The largest project, however, continued to be the completion of the Nauvoo Temple.

In June of 1845, Brigham Young sent a letter to Wilford Woodruff, then serving as President of the British Mission, about the growth of Nauvoo. He wrote that the city *"looks like a paradise. All of the lots and land, which had been vacant and unoccupied, were fenced in the spring, and planted with grain and vegetables, which made it look more like a garden of gardens than a city . . . Hundreds of acres of prairie land had also been enclosed, and were now under good cultivation, blooming with corn, wheat, potatoes, and other necessities of life. Many strangers from different areas were pouring in, to view the Temple and the city. They expressed their astonishment, surprise, and wonderment to see the rapid progress."*

Indeed, the city was prospering. **By the**

end of 1845, Nauvoo had a population of about 15,000 residents. It was a showcase, and numerous visitors from the East and England, wrote complimentary articles about the Mormon center of attraction.

Nauvoo's phenomenal and remarkable growth certainly increased the antagonism, opposition, and bitterness of the Church's enemies. Those enemies of the Church felt certain that the Church would definitely fall apart, that it would not endure without its charismatic leader with his unique personable magnetism of leadership as a Prophet of God. Yet it quickly became evident that the death of Joseph Smith had not diminished or lessened the strength, power, or vigor of the Saints.

As early as September 1844, Colonel Levi Williams of Warsaw, who was involved in the Joseph and Hyrum Smith murders at Carthage, organized a major military campaign to drive the Latter-day Saints from Illinois. It was advertised as "a great wolf hunt in Hancock County." When word of this action reached Governor Ford, he ordered General John Hardin of the state militia to Hancock County to neutralize and disrupt the effort. General Hardin remained in Hancock County throughout the winter to keep peace.

One of the nine men who was brought to trial in Carthage for the murder of Joseph Smith and was acquitted, was Thomas Sharp. He unleashed a new anti-Mormon attack in his *Warsaw Signal* newspaper in the summer of 1845. He opposed Latter-day Saint officeholders in the county, and reopened the debate over Mormon political activity. These actions provided a smoke screen for a barrage of vandalism against the Saints. **Early in September, a mob of 300 men led by Levi Williams systematically burned outlying Mormon farms and homes.** They first raided Morley's settlement and torched many unprotected farm buildings, mills, and grain stacks. In mid-September, Brigham Young asked for volunteers to rescue the besieged Saints. One hundred thirty-four teams were secured and immediately sent to bring the families of the outlying settlements in South Hancock County and North Adams County safely to Nauvoo.

The sheriff of Hancock Country, Jacob Backenstos, a friend of the Latter-day Saints, endeavored to preserve order, but citizens in Warsaw refused to join a posse he tried to organize. After he drove off the mob with a posse made up of ex-members of the Nauvoo Legion, his life was threatened by the non-Mormons of Hancock County, and he fled. Frank Worrell, who had supervised the guard at Carthage the day of the martyrdom, led the chase after Backenstos. Near the railroad shanties north of Warsaw, Backenstos overtook several members of the Church and immediately deputized them. When Worrell raised his gun to fire at the sheriff, deputy Orrin Porter Rockwell took aim with his rifle and shot Worrell dead. This further intensified the hostilities in Hancock County and with civil war becoming imminent, citizens in Quincy, Illinois, and Lee County, Iowa, asked Church members to move from Illinois. On September 24, 1845, the Quorum of the Twelve Apostles promised that the Church would leave the following spring.

Governor Ford ordered 400 militia troops under the direction of General Hardin, and three other prominent citizens, including Congressman Stephen A. Douglas, to act as an independent police force during this period of civil unrest. **The plundering, the pillaging and the destruction ended, and peace was restored temporarily.** Acting as the governor's on-the-spot advisory committee, the four leaders investigated the circumstances, and learned that the anti-Mormons had initiated the conflict with their aggressive raids and onslaught. They also recognized that there would be no peace in Hancock County until the Mormons left Illinois.

Congressman Douglas was an advocate of manifest destiny—a philosophy supporting the growth of the United States completely across the continent. He counseled Church leaders to find a place to settle in the West, and promised to use his influence in assisting their move. For some time, **Church leaders had planned a move to the Rocky Mountains, and so these negotiations proceeded smoothly.** Finally, the Saints agreed to leave Nauvoo the following spring as soon as the grass on the prairies was high enough to sustain their livestock. Trustees of the Church would remain in Nauvoo to sell the property of those who could not dispose of it by springtime.

During this time period, and in spite of the continued persecutions from their enemies, Brigham Young and members of the Twelve kept the work on the temple moving forward, which Joseph had begun. They met frequently with the architect and temple committee, and repeatedly invited the members to *"gather to Nauvoo with their means"* to help build the House of the Lord (*History of the Church,* 7: 267). In the October 1844 General Conference, Brigham Young said: *"I believe this people is the best people of their age that ever lived on the earth, the church of Enoch not excepted. We want you to come on with your tithes and offerings to build this Temple"* (*History of the Church,* 7: 302). In response, the Relief Society sisters each pledged to contribute a penny per week for glass and nails, while those of means contributed large sums without which the project would not have progressed. Joseph Toronto handed Brigham Young 2,500 dollars in gold saying "he wanted to give himself and all he had" to build the kingdom of God (*History of the Church,* 7: 433). Numerous craftsmen were also called to help with the project. **Now, after four years of painful endeavor, with constant interruptions due to mob action, they were finally bringing the temple to its completion.** By the spring of 1845, the capstone was in position. The workers then assembled the roof and finished the interior. When the capstone was laid in place, the Saints were grateful and thankful. On that day, under the leadership of the Twelve, a large crowd of the Saints gathered at the temple. Their band was stationed on top of the walls playing the Saints' favorite selections. As the stone was placed in position, there was a great shout of: "Hosanna to God and the Lamb, Amen, Amen, Amen." Hymns were sung and there was great rejoicing. Plans were set for a formal dedication in April 1846.

Rooms in the temple were dedicated as they were completed so that ordinance work could begin as early as possible. General Conference convened in the partially finished edifice in October 1845. Brigham Young opened the services for the day by a dedicatory prayer, presenting the Temple, thus far completed, *"as a monument of the saints' liberality* [responsiveness, unselfishness, generosity], *fidelity* [truthfulness, exactness, honesty], *and faith,* concluding: *'Lord, we dedicate this house and ourselves, to thee.'* The day was occupied most agreeably in hearing instructions and teachings, and offering up the gratitude of honest hearts, for so great a privilege, as worshiping God within, instead of without an edifice, whose beauty and workmanship will compare with any house of worship in America, and whose motto is: 'HOLINESS TO THE LORD'" (*History of the Church,* 7: 456-57).

The attic story of the temple was dedicated for ordinance work on November 30, 1845. President Young prayed that the Lord would sustain and deliver His servants until they accomplished His will in the temple. The rooms were soon prepared for ordinances, and Brigham Young and Heber C. Kimball began giving endowments to faithful Latter-day Saints on the evening of December tenth. On December eleventh, endowment sessions were continued until 3:00 a.m..

When enemies of the Church observed this increased temple activity, they renewed their harassment and persecution. A new threat against the Church leadership soon came in the form of an indictment issued by the United States District Court in Springfield against Brigham Young and eight other Apostles on charges of instigating and harboring a counterfeiting operation in Nauvoo . . . more lies, more fabrication, more trumped-up charges to destroy the Church. On December twenty-third, government officials approached the temple, hoping to find and arrest Brigham Young. Knowing that they were there, Brigham Young knelt down and asked the Lord for guidance and protection so that he could *"live to prove advantageous to the Saints"* (*Journal of Discourses,* 14: 218). He noticed William Miller in the hall, who agreed to act as a decoy. Brother Miller, who was the same height as Brigham, left the temple dressed as Brigham Young, and stepped into the president's carriage. Waiting marshals arrested him and took him to the Mansion House where friends and relatives of Brigham joined in on the charade. Miller was then taken to Carthage. Only after someone there identified him, did his captors learn that they had a "bogus Brigham." Meanwhile, Brigham Young and his brethren had gone into safe hiding.

The Brethren redoubled their efforts to endow as many Saints as possible before the evacuation of Nauvoo began. By the end of 1845, over a 1,000 members had received these ordinances. In January, Brigham Young recorded: *"Such has been the anxiety manifested by the saints to receive the ordinances* [of the Temple], *and such the anxiety on our part to administer to them, that I have given myself up entirely to the work of the Lord in the Temple, night and day, not taking more than four hours sleep, upon an average, per day, and going home but once a week"* (*History of the Church,* 7: 567). There were many others among the brethren and sisters who gave freely of their time by washing the temple clothing each night so that the work could continue unimpeded the next morning.

On February third, the Brethren planned to stop the ordinance work, and Brigham Young left the temple to make final preparations to leave the following day for the West. But seeing a large crowd gathered to receive their endowments, he compassionately returned to serve them. This delayed his departure for an additional two weeks. According to temple records, 5,615 Saints were endowed before going West, thus fulfilling one of Joseph Smith's fondest desires.

There is an importance and urgency of building temples, **thus saith the Lord**, which has to do with both the living and the dead, which has to do with marriages, that can only be solemnized in a temple, along with the sealing of children and families, and only through temple endowments for the living and the dead can these sacred ordinances be accomplished. This special work can only be achieved in a temple, the sacred House of the Lord.

Shortly after the martyrdom, several important events took place in other areas of the Church, specifically in Britain and the Eastern United States. Wilford Woodruff had arrived in England in early 1845, traveling throughout Britain and holding conferences, transacting mission affairs, and opening new areas for missionary activities. At the end of 1845, Elder Woodruff was released from his short but effective mission. Even

THORNTON 04

"Nauvoo Temple, Nauvoo, Illinois, Mid 1840s"
Artist, Dan Thornton
Used by Permission

though there was some emigration from England to Nauvoo in 1845, **the Church continued to prosper and grow rapidly in England, reaching a membership of over 11,000.** By the end of 1845, the faithful Saints in England had contributed over 300 pounds worth of sterling for the Nauvoo Temple. As he again left this land where he had performed so many great works during his two missions, Elder Woodruff noted how peaceful and happy the British Saints were.

Elder Parley P. Pratt's mission to the Eastern States, was not unlike Wilford Woodruff's to Britain. He was to put in order the affairs of the Church in the East before the Saints began their long-awaited exodus to the West. Unfortunately, Elder Pratt had found more serious problems in the East than Wilford Woodruff had in England.

As he was examining the situation, Parley and his two companions discovered that William Smith and a few others were teaching "all manner of false doctrine and immoral practices, by which many of them stumbled, and had been lured away from virtue and truth, while many others, seeing their iniquity, turned away from the Church and joined various dissenting parties." In accordance with instructions previously received from Brigham Young, the Brethren sent the guilty parties to Nauvoo for discipline by the Twelve. Parley also assumed editorship of *The Prophet,* the Church's newspaper in New York. His writings instructed and inspired many. One important item he published was a Proclamation to the heads of governments worldwide, thus fulfilling an assignment given by revelation to the Church in 1841 (Doctrine & Covenants 124: 2-7). Elder Jedediah M. Grant was one of those who ably assisted Elder Pratt "in setting the churches in order and re-establishing pure Gospel principles." For several years, Elder Grant had made significant contributions as a missionary, and in December 1845, he was called as one of the seven presidents of the First Quorum of Seventy.

Elder Pratt returned to Nauvoo in August 1845. There he stood with his brethren as the Church faced the anti-Mormon outrages in Hancock County. He also contributed to the building of the temple, and labored in it night and day during December and January, administering the endowment to faithful Latter-day Saints.

Long before he died, the Prophet Joseph had discussed moving the Church to the West. In 1842, Joseph Smith had prophesied that the Saints would continue to suffer much affliction and *"some of you will live to go and assist in making settlements and build cities, and see the Saints become a mighty people in the midst of the Rocky Mountains"* (*History of the Church,* 5: 85). **In the spring of 1844, plans for colonizing in the West were initiated.** An exploring party was organized to "investigate the locations of California and Oregon, and hunt out a good location, where we can remove to after the temple is completed, and where we can build a city in a day, and have a government of our own, get up into the mountains, where the devil cannot dig us out, and live in a healthful climate, where we can live as old as we have in mind to" (*History of the Church,* 6: 222). After the Prophet's death, further preparations for such an exodus were made.

The planned move West gave some people an excuse to lead away groups from the Church. Joseph Smith had authorized Lyman Wight and Bishop George Miller to establish a colony in Texas; President Young encouraged this effort until it became obvious that Wight and Miller wanted the whole Church to settle there. In late August 1844, Elder Wight was counseled to limit his company to those working with him at the Wisconsin pineries. These he led to Texas. Rather than exploring for a colony, however, he established a permanent settlement. In November 1845, the Saints in Texas were asked to return to Nauvoo, but the independent-minded leader and his followers refused. In 1848, after more reconciliation attempts, Elder Wight was excommunicated from the Church.

Brigham Young and his associates wanted to remain in Illinois until the temple was completed and sufficient preparations were made for the departure. During the winter of 1844-45, they read the journals of fur trappers, the reports of government exploring parties, and newspaper articles by Western travelers, to accumulate as much information about the region as possible. Resettlement committees considered three great Western territories as potential sites: Texas, an independent nation; Upper California, a large ill-defined and loosely governed Mexican province (of which the later State of Utah was a part), and Oregon, encompassing the entire Northwest, and jointly claimed and administered by the United States and England. Gradually, their focus centered on the eastern rim of the great Basin, because this area provided the desired isolation and thousands of acres of fertile land.

Leaders of the Church assured the Saints, some of whom were surprised at the announcement, that the exodus was a well-planned transplantation necessary to give the Church the essential room it needed to grow. The main thrust of the October General Conference was largely devoted to preparing for an orderly and unified withdrawal. After the conference, the Twelve issued a general epistle, explaining that: "a crisis of extraordinary and thrilling interests has arrived. The exodus . . . to a far distant region of the west, where bigotry, intolerance, and insatiable oppression lose their power over them—forms a new epoch [a new era, a new period of time]." It went on to counsel the Saints everywhere to sell their property, and prepare for the gathering (*History of the Church,* 7: 478-80). Despite the onset of winter, Nauvoo was a beehive of activity as the Saints began to prepare for the exodus.

The departure from Western Illinois was originally planned for April 1846, but two new threats prompted an early, hasty exit. The first was the indictment against Brigham Young and eight other Apostles, accusing them of counterfeiting. The second was a warning by Governor Ford and others that federal troops in St. Louis planned to intercept the Mormons and destroy them. Years later, it was learned that this was only a rumor, started to induce the Saints to leave sooner than they had planned.

In January 1846, the Brethren decided to prepare several companies to leave at a moment's notice. A committee was appointed to dispose of all property and effects left behind, including the temple and the Nauvoo House. **The decision to leave was made on** February second, and the first group, led by Charles Shumway, crossed the **Mississippi River on February fourth.** Soon there were several hundred Saints assembled in temporary camps in Iowa. Brigham Young and others who remained behind briefly to administer endowments to the Saints, did not leave Nauvoo until mid-February. Unfortunately, there were too many who left who were inadequately outfitted, but chose to depart earlier than was wise.

If the Saints had left Nauvoo beginning in April, as originally planned, unquestionably there would have been a more orderly exodus. The original blueprint called for twenty-five companies of 100 families each, with adequate provisions, and presided over by a company captain. The companies were to have left at prearranged intervals to ensure order. But these plans were shattered by the Saints who panicked and did not want to be left behind after the Twelve had left. Many of the previously appointed captains abandoned their assignments to align themselves with the advanced vanguard companies and be with the Twelve. But in spite of the temporary confusion, there was optimism and cheerfulness among the Saints as they entered Eastern Iowa. One of the most remarkable migrations in the history of Western civilization had begun.

Under the energetic, spirited, and influential leadership of Brigham Young and the Quorum of the Twelve Apostles, the Saints crossed the Mississippi River into Iowa. They had begun their new quest for a home where they could build the kingdom of God without oppression and persecution. The way to this new refuge (haven) would certainly not be easy; it would take its toll through toil, struggle, sacrifice, and death. **The first leg of the journey—the trek across Iowa territory—proved to be the hardest. From the start, the main body of Saints was known as the "Camp of Israel,"** and Brigham Young was its president. As with ancient Israel, there were companies and captains of hundreds, fifties, and tens. In the next two years, more Old Testament similarities were made, as illustrated by terms such as—Zion being in the tops of the mountains—chosen people—exodus—Mount Pisgah—Jordan River—Dead Sea—making the desert blossom as a rose—and a modern Moses in the person of Brigham Young. The main "Camp of Israel" took 131 days to cover the 300 miles they initially traveled across Iowa. The Pioneer Company, a year later, took only 111 days to cover 1,050 miles from Winter Quarters to the Great Salt Lake Valley. Inadequate preparation, lack of knowledgeable guides, delays, miserable weather, and difficult terrain, made the Iowa journey one of the most trying in the Church's history. Nevertheless, **these vigorous and hearty people knew no such word as failure.** The Iowa journey simply hardened their resolve and provided valuable experience for the future.

* * *

And again, why should any people have to suffer and be persecuted because they believe in and love God and Jesus Christ?

And so, the last days of a flourishing Nauvoo was history. In any case, their last days in Nauvoo deserves repeating as a lesson for all time. The enemies of the Church believed that with the death of Joseph and Hyrum Smith, Mormonism would pass out of existence quickly. They thought that it was by the strength and uniqueness of Joseph's personality that the people were kept together, and that with him out of the way, the entire cause and crusade would soon come to an end. They did not know that the work of The Church of Jesus Christ of Latter-day Saints was God's work, and that the Gospel was restored to remain on the earth until **the Second Coming of the Savior**. They did not know that the Church was divine, and that it was built upon the work of God, and not of man.

When they learned that Brigham Young had become the leader of the Church after the death of the Prophet, and saw the Saints once again rise above their grief and work hard together, they were surprised. And when they saw the temple being hurried to completion, they began to realize that **the death of Joseph did not stop the Church after all.**

They began to scheme and plot in the same way the Missourians had done. They saw the beautiful homes in Nauvoo, the fine streets, the beautiful temple, and coveted them for themselves. Nauvoo was the largest and most beautiful city in the State. If the Mormons were driven out, their enemies believed that they could take possession of their property for themselves, and become affluent and well-to-do. The trouble-makers and the agitators renewed their efforts to stir up the hatred and bitterness against the Saints.

The apostates who had helped to martyr the Prophet started a new campaign of lies and untruths about the Mormons. Many people believed these false and misleading reports and became angered and infuriated. They demanded that the Saints leave the state entirely, give up their homes in Nauvoo, and move elsewhere. Brigham Young and other leaders appealed to the governor once more, demanding help and protection. But the governor, who had failed miserably to prevent the martyrdom at Carthage, backed away from helping them.

The persecutions grew more intense by the fall of 1845, and by Christmas, the Saints were quite sure they would have to leave. They remembered the prophecy of the Prophet Joseph Smith regarding their removal to the Rockies, and felt that the time was near at hand.

Nevertheless, they loved their homes and their lifestyle and did not want to leave them. If they left, they knew for a surety they would have to face the reality of a desert, hostile Indians, and wild animals. In the Rockies, there were no cities or farms, not even log cabins. They would have to build these for themselves, and conquer a desert as well.

Realizing that time was running out—but still trying to hang on to their hopes, their dreams, and their homes by further appeals to the governor, the Saints began to prepare for their long journey. Every vacant building in the city was converted into a workshop. Wood was brought in, boiled in salt water, and then thoroughly dried to make it tough and hard to withstand the long trek. Then the wood was made into wagon wheels, frames, and boxes. Leather was made into harnesses. Men were sent to all nearby areas to buy iron for the wagon wheels and other parts. Blacksmiths, carpenters, and other skilled men worked day and night, rushing their preparations so that when spring came, the Saints could start West.

Shortly after Christmas, the enemies of the Saints continued their brutal treatment, and it soon became clear to the brethren that they could not wait for spring. If they were to preserve the lives of the Saints from enemy attack, they would have to start while it was still winter.

On Wednesday, February 4, 1846, the first of the Saints left Nauvoo. They loaded their wagons with all that they could carry, including "bed warmers," to keep them warm as they sat in the wagons. They went down to the riverbank, and loaded their wagons on ferries; men, women, and children rode in rowboats. All the way across, they had to dodge drifting ice which seemed to almost fill the river.

Only six wagons were able to cross the first day, but each day thereafter, more would cross. When they arrived on the Iowa side of the Mississippi, the Saints were instructed to travel nine miles to Sugar Creek, which would be the first stopping place where they could organize for the longer trip. There at Sugar Creek, they awaited the arrival of Brigham Young.

A few days after the first of the Saints had arrived at Sugar Creek, the weather became extremely cold, dropping down to twelve degrees below zero. The Saints were camping out in wagons and small tents, some of which were opened at both ends. The wind blew through these, causing great suffering among the people.

The extreme cold spell lasted for several days, and during it, nine babies were born to mothers in these open camps. The weather was so cold that it froze the ice a foot thick on the Mississippi River. All the ferries and small boats were frozen solid in ice, so thick it would bear up a wagon and a team of horses. Learning of this miracle, many of the Saints drove their wagons across the ice to the Iowa side. During February, over 3,000 people crossed the river and gath-

"Exodus from Nauvoo," by Edward T. Grigware, ©The Church of Jesus Christ of Latter-day Saints, Used by Permission

"Martin Handcart Company, Bitter Creek," by Clark Kelley Price, © The Church of Jesus Christ of Latter-day Saints, Used by Permission

"Three Young Men Rescue The Martin Handcart Company," by Clark Kelley Price, © The Church of Jesus Christ of Latter-day Saints Used by Permission

ered at Sugar Creek under the direction of Hosea Stout, captain of the Nauvoo police.

The Prophet Joseph Smith had taught the Saints that the word **Zion** had two meanings: *"the pure in heart,"* and *"the place where the pure in heart live together in righteousness."* He referred them to the Saints in Enoch's day. The scriptures say of them: *"And the Lord called his people ZION, because the were of one heart and one mind"* (Moses 7: 18). He declared that a successful **Zion Community is impossible—without a Zion people.**

Those people on the banks of the Mississippi, who like Jesus of Nazareth, had nowhere to lay their heads, were nearer to Zion than they had ever been before. Their heartbreaking troubles had swept them clean of greed. Those who were not pure in heart had most likely remained behind. For the first time, it began to dawn upon the Saints that a Zion People was far more important than a Zion Place, for without a Zion People, no spot in all the world could remain holy.

Leaving Nauvoo was an act of faith for the Saints. They left without knowing exactly where they were going or when they would arrive at a place to settle. They only knew that they were being driven out of Illinois by their enemies, and that their leaders had received revelation to locate a refuge somewhere in the Rocky Mountains. Before leaving Nauvoo, Brigham Young had appointed agents to sell the property of the Saints in Nauvoo, but the mobs openly threatened the persons who planned to buy, and drove them away.

By the time that most of the Saints had crossed the river, the mobs found out what was going on. The anti-Mormons organized an armed group, and attacked the city, firing on many of the Saints. The Church members still there defended themselves as well as they could, but they were unable to keep them from taking over the city. Their enemies went from house to house, stealing everything of value they could find. Then they rushed to the temple, which they severely damaged, breaking down pulpits and other furnishings.

The beautiful Nauvoo Temple fell into the hands of the enemies of the Church, and was occupied briefly by a sectarian church. Before long, the temple caught fire and burned down. Only the walls remained. A tornado next struck it, and leveled the walls. The beautiful white stones of which it had been built, were taken by curiosity seekers, and put in other building for miles around.

During the time the Saints occupied Nauvoo, no other city of the Mississippi Valley could triumph over such rapid growth. Few could match its civic dignity or economic prosperity. Yet the unseen faith of its inhabitants was mightier than its masonry. This **faith** had been responsible for the building of a city where a swamp had been, and when the people who possessed that faith were gone, Nauvoo quickly sank to the common level of its neighbors.

Nauvoo the Beautiful, the City of Joseph, was no more the beautiful city of the Saints It was now a deserted town, taken over by mob violence and wicked men, who sought to profit by the losses of the persecuted Mormons.

As spring 1846 came to Iowa, the Saints moved away from Sugar Creek. They had been organized into companies under the direction of Brigham Young. They knew that they were going to face many hardships, but they were willing to endure them. They loved their religion above all else, and they were prepared to make any sacrifice for it. They also loved the **United States and the Constitution**, which gave to them the explicit right of freedom of religion. Their enemies had always tried to take this right away from them. Now, the Saints would go to a place where they could **worship Heavenly Father and Jesus Christ** as they pleased.

On Sunday, December 5, 1847, **Brigham Young was called by God the Father to be the Prophet, Seer and Revelator, and Second President of The Church of Jesus Christ of Latter-day Saints.**

On Monday, December 27, 1847, **Brigham Young was sustained as Prophet, Seer, and Revelator and Second President of The Church of Jesus Christ of Latter-day Saints.**

And it all began in the year 1820, in a grove of trees, just outside the small town of Palmyra, in Upstate New York. With all the religious confusion going on at that time in his community, Joseph Smith Jr. wanted to know which of all the churches was true, and which should he join.

He remembered reading in the epistle of James, first chapter and fifth and sixth verses plus: ***"If any of you lack wisdom, let him ask of God, that giveth to all men liberally and upbraideth not; and it shall be given him. But let him ask in faith nothing wavering."*** With this passage of scripture in mind, and wanting to know which of the churches was true, he decided to spend some time on his knees praying, in a grove of trees near his home. He needed to communicate his feelings to God and seek guidance and direction. As he knelt in prayer, a force of blackness and evil overcame him, and he felt that he was about to be destroyed. At that very moment, he thought he was a goner—these are his own words: *"just at that moment of great alarm I saw a pillar of light, exactly over his head, above the brightness of the sun, descended gradually until it fell upon me. It no sooner appeared than I found myself delivered from the enemy which had me bound. When the light rested upon me, I saw two Personages, whose brightness and glory defy all description, standing above me in the air. One of them spake unto me, calling me by name, and said, pointing to the other—**"This is My Beloved Son. Hear Him!"*** (Joseph Smith—History 1: 16-17).

Joseph's purpose in going to the grove was to inquire of the Lord as to which of the various religions he should join. He was counseled to join none of them, that *"they draw near to me with their lips, but their hearts are far from me; they teach for doctrines the commandments of men, having a form of godliness, but they deny the power thereof"* (Joseph Smith—History 1: 19).

I humbly testify, that the greatest message of our time, is this account given by Joseph Smith, which is the absolute truth.

The God of Abraham, Isaac, and Jacob raised up Joseph Smith Jr. to be a true Prophet in the Seventh and Last Dispensation of the Fulness of Times, to restore the true Gospel and the Church of Jesus Christ in these, the latter days.

JOSEPH SMITH—was he an Imposter? That's Ridiculous, and Preposterous.
JOSEPH SMITH—was he a Pretender? That's Nonsense, and Unbelievable.
JOSEPH SMITH—was he a Deceiver? That's Outrageous, and Absurd.
JOSEPH SMITH—***was, is, and will always be without question . . .***

A TRUE PROPHET OF GOD.

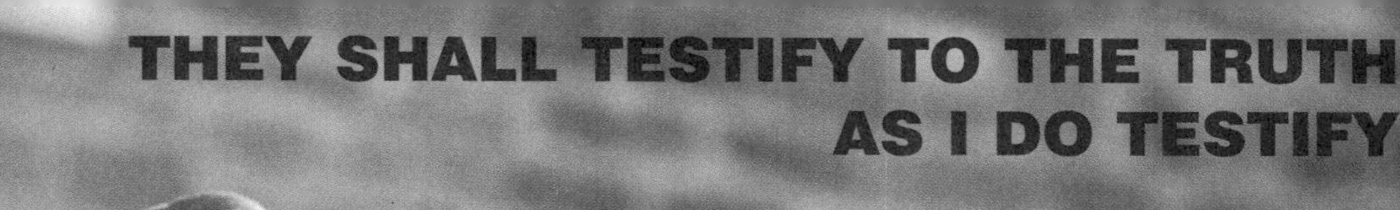
THEY SHALL TESTIFY TO THE TRUTH
AS I DO TESTIFY

Norman Rothman was born in the Bronx, New York, January 2, 1927, of goodly Jewish parents, Louis and Ida Sarah Rothman. He graduated from Morris High School in the Bronx, January 1944.

He enlisted in the U.S. Navy in 1944, spending the last half of World War II in the Pacific Theater of War, attached to the Naval Construction Battalions [Seabees], and was Honorably Discharged in June 1946.

He attended New York University and Pace College in New York City. His business activities took him worldwide in the field of marketing, management and public relations.

Although having very close ties to his Conservative Jewish background, after his return from World War II, he felt something missing in Judaism—not wrong, just missing—and so he began to search out other religions for an answer.

Norman Rothman authored another book titled—*"So How Come A Nice Jewish Boy Became A Mormon?"* He and his dear wife, Sadie Annette, traveled extensively for 3½ years; their tour taking them into 212 cities throughout the United States. He was interviewed on over 256 radio and television shows, 139 newspapers and had speaking engagements in over 135 cities as well.